W9-BKC-250

# America Is
## Teacher's Manual

Frank Freidel
Henry N. Drewry

Charles E. Merrill Publishing Co.
A Bell & Howell Company
Columbus, Ohio

Toronto London Sydney

# Contents

ISBN 0-675-01899-4

Published by

**CHARLES E. MERRILL PUBLISHING CO.**
**A Bell & Howell Company**

Columbus, Ohio 43216
Copyright © 1978 by Bell & Howell

All rights reserved. No part of this book may be reproduced in any form, electronic or mechanical, including photocopy, recording, or any information storage or retrieval system, without permission in writing from the publisher.

Printed in the United States of America

# Introduction

**AMERICA IS** materials have been designed for you *and* your students and can be covered effectively and comfortably within a single school year. While learning and using significant facts of America's history, your students can also gain insight into the relationships among people, their ideas, and corresponding events.

The **Student Edition** is concise and thorough and has a balanced narrative style. Its twenty-five chapters are organized chronologically to help students use the elements of time and place in developing historical perspective. The chapters are grouped into eight units for easy management. Each unit title can be used to describe what the United States has meant to its people at different times in history. America was and is Opportunity, Independence, Democracy, Expansion, Division, Growth, Conflict, and Challenge.

Besides the chapter narratives, there are fourteen American city profiles that give special focus to the social, cultural, economic, and geographic aspects of American life in particular eras. These studies, which are five to eight pages long, follow related chapters in the text. In them, students are given a chance to relive history through the firsthand accounts of the people who made it.

Special features within the chapters help students understand how history has been recorded and develop their abilities to study it effectively. These features include biographies of famous and not-so-famous Americans; colorful illustrations, maps, and charts which support general content with specific data; and topic close-ups of particular events and ideas. The features also stimulate student interest.

Helping students gain a sense of accomplishment is vital to maintaining their interest and motivation. To achieve this, AMERICA IS has a controlled reading level, appropriate concept development, short chapters, and explanation of terms within the narrative. Every student will be able to provide some answers to, and achieve some success in, the comprehensive chapter reviews where questions are arranged in sequence of difficulty. Answers build from simple recall of knowledge to more thoughtful analysis.

Additional Study Aids are found at the end of the student text. They include a glossary, an index, an annotated Declaration of Independence, an annotated Constitution, a chart of pertinent facts about Presidents and Vice-Presidents, and a list of important events in American history.

The complete AMERICA IS program offers other important supplementary materials.

> The **Discovery Book** has twenty-five sections of skills-building student activities corresponding to and reinforcing the content of the twenty-five chapters of the student text.

> The **Evaluation Program** consists of chapter and unit tests patterned after the chapter reviews. These spirit master tests are keyed with nonreproducible answers for easy grading.

> The **Media Program** is comprised of six sound filmstrips, thirty copies of a student study guide, and a teacher's guide. Designed to extend and reinforce ideas presented in the student text, the media program may also be used independently.

The **Teacher's Annotated Edition** of AMERICA IS contains a complete Student Edition with annotations which are overprinted on the student text pages. These suggest aims for the units and chapters, provide additional details, and give references to coordinate concept development. The Teacher's Manual section provides suggestions for general teaching procedures and references to additional resources. It particularly offers, chapter by chapter, suggested teaching strategies, main ideas and aims, and answers to the chapter review questions. The Teacher's Annotated Edition has been organized to reduce your preparation time and to allow for easy adaptation to your individual teaching style and to your students' needs.

# Effective Program Use

## Prologue

In today's classrooms, *history* is broadly viewed both as a body of information and as a process through which we attempt to understand the human experience. The AMERICA IS program employs this broad viewpoint and brings the experiences of the people of the United States into sharper focus. In dealing with this specific subject matter, the program has three main goals:

- to help students gain insight into the relationships among people, ideas, and corresponding events as they learn and use significant facts of America's history,
- to help students sharpen their social studies skills while developing an appreciation of the study of history, and
- to help students develop wholesome values concerning the democratic process.

A variety of elements have been included in the program to ensure the achievement of these goals. This section of the **Teacher's Manual** offers some procedures for using these elements to best advantage. The procedures apply generally to classroom situations throughout the year, and they fit easily with other suggestions found in this **Teacher's Annotated Edition.**

## Student Expectations

### Introducing the Text

Students usually have a better spirit of cooperation when they know what is expected of them and what aids are available to help them meet those expectations. Following you, the teacher, the students' next most important classroom aid in the study of history is the textbook. They should become very familiar with the layout of the text so that they can make the best possible use of its contents. A class reading and discussion of the Preface is one way to introduce the students to text design. The order of information in the Preface carries students from a consideration of why we study history through an explanation of the various parts of the

Preface

text to a concluding challenge that they learn more about American history by taking advantage of sources outside the textbook.

As the sections of the Preface are read in class, cite examples of each item mentioned and have the students turn to them in their texts. Reading through the Table of Contents at this time may also be helpful to them.

**Table of Contents**

If a more thorough examination of a rationale for the study of history seems appropriate, you might use the quote from President Kennedy to lead the students into such discussion:

> After reading aloud the quote from President Kennedy, ask students to cite examples from their own past actions and experiences which influence their decisions today. An important point to make is that no two situations have taken place under *exactly* the same circumstances. The discussion might take any of several directions. Aim at helping students realize that the study of America's history provides us with valuable clues on why we live as we do today.

## Setting the Scene

The chapters of the text are grouped into eight units to help you divide the course content into manageable parts. Each unit is organized around a theme which reflects an important concept appropriate to the period under study. Set the scene for each unit to prepare students for the information to be gained in their chapter studies. You might use the two-page unit openings to introduce students to the *who, what, where,* and *when* facts of the period. Each unit opening contains pictures taken from the chapters to represent major social, cultural, economic, and political concerns. The artist's rendering which flows across the pages depicts either a major event of the time or a principal way of life for Americans in that era.

**Unit Openings**

You might use the title of each unit to set the conceptual scene for students' consideration of the *why* and *how* of the period. The theme of Unit 2, for example, could be presented to the class in this way:

> Discuss the word *independence*. Ask first for a show of hands from those students who think independence is a good thing and then from those who do not think so. Ask those who responded positively why they believe that independence is good. As discussion develops, elicit a proper definition of independence from the class and write it on the board. If some students indicated that they did not think independence to be good, ask them to explain. If no students supported that position, which is likely, ask the class if anyone can think of a situation in which independence is not good. At this point, student comments have probably touched on personal independence from rules and regulations and perhaps on the independence of nations from control by other nations.

Guide the discussion through the following questions: "Should babies be independent from their parents? Should adults be independent from their parents? Should fourteen-year-olds be independent from their parents?" Bring out the group's concern with the degree and timing of independence. Carry out the discussion on these points with questions such as: "What is the opposite of independence? Would parents want a son or daughter to be dependent on them at the age of six months? At the age of thirty years?" Help the students arrive at the generalization that most parents think independence is a good thing for their children although they may disagree with them about the timing (age) or about the degree of it.

Transfer the discussion from the viewpoint of the family unit to the viewpoint of nations by asking students the following questions: "Do you think independence for the colonies was a good thing? Do you think it was a good thing from the American point of view? From the British point of view? What action did the colonists take to secure their independence from England? Do 'revolutions' ever occur when children seek to establish their independence? Are such revolutions necessary for a child to become independent? Was the revolution necessary for the colonies to become independent?" The aim of the discussion at this point is not to produce specific answers but to foster an attitude of inquiry. The students have probably commented on the differences between independence for a child and independence for a nation. Summarize the main points of the discussion.

## Clarifying the Learning Requirements

Consider at least three main points before you make actual assignments of chapter material. First, examine the type of reading involved and determine the quantity most appropriate for the reading abilities of your students. Second, decide the order in which you want them to read such features as the biographies, topic close-ups, and city profiles. Also instruct students to study, as they read, any illustrations within the assigned material.

Third, determine what you want students to learn from the assignments. For the features, ideas are offered for this in the margin annotations and the Suggestions by Chapter found in other sections of this **Teacher's Annotated Edition.** For the chapter content, review questions under the title Chapter in Perspective are given. These four review sections ask students to be able to (1) "Identify" key people and places; (2) "Explain" key terms, pieces of legislation, treaties, and organizations; (3) "Check Your Memory of the Facts" by recalling important factual information; and (4) "Check Your Understanding of the Ideas" by explaining the how

annotations

Suggestions by Chapter

Chapters in Perspective

and why relationships behind specific events as given in the text. You might want students to check the review questions *before* they begin assignments to give sharper focus and direction to their readings. The items within each section appear in sequence so they can be easily separated to match assignments of partial chapter content.

As well as knowing what questions are to be answered, it is important for the students to understand how you want them answered. Do you want oral or written answers? Do you want a phrase, a sentence, or a paragraph? Do you want them to be general or specific? A further aid in making appropriate assignments for individual students is the style in which the Chapter in Perspective answers are provided. Two levels of answers are given for many of the individual items: minimum answers appear in boldface type; extended answers in regular type. This section begins on page 63 of this Manual.

**Chapter in Perspective Answers**

The Expand Your Knowledge section of the Chapter in Perspective is intended to enrich the learning that results from reading and studying chapter content. These activities can be used when they fit the resources available and should be structured to conform to the needs of your students. Even with enrichment activities, students should know what is expected of them. Some of the activities suggested will require more direction than others, including instruction on where to find the required information. Some sources which will be useful for these and other assignments are included in the Bibliography of the Manual, beginning on page 139. Students may need to refresh their library skills to know how to find the sources. You might want to work with the librarian to set up a class period for this.

**Expand Your Knowledge**

**Bibliography**

# *Developing Effective Study Habits*

## Reading With Understanding

The reading level of the AMERICA IS student text has been carefully controlled not to exceed the abilities of the average student. Key terms are defined at their first appearance within the narrative, and the Declaration of Independence and the Constitution are fully annotated in today's language. Students should also realize that terms defined in the text are repeated in the Glossary with extended definitions when appropriate. The Glossary is their most convenient reference when terms appear throughout the text and their memories need refreshing. Some students will need even more reading aids than these, however, and the value of their having and using dictionaries cannot be overstated.

**Annotated Declaration of Independence**

**Annotated Constitution**

**Glossary**

**[dictionary]**

Your students may need preparation in addition to the remarks of the Preface regarding quoted material before it is assigned for reading. They should know how to recognize its quotation marks, indented blocks of type, or blocks of italic type, and how to read it. You should help them understand that when the ellipses are followed by a period indicating material deleted and the end of a sentence and when brackets contain a definition for the preceding word, there generally should be a pause in reading. When the ellipses are not followed by a period and the brackets contain substitute words or corrected spellings, there is no hesitation in reading.

Students may need some practice reading quoted materials, and hearing you read some of it could help them grasp the proper techniques. Most often, there is no hesitation needed when brackets or ellipses are encountered in the AMERICA IS selections. And, not all words with old spellings or misspellings have been changed, only those which might be very difficult to interpret. Rather than emphasizing the mechanics of the material, you might encourage students to concentrate on reading "for the sense of it." Your abler students might be assigned larger portions of the quoted materials from the original sources. Reference information for the sources begins on page 591 of the student text.

Acknowledgments

## Studying for Accuracy and Retention

Keeping a course notebook is usually a valuable activity for students of history. The notebook can be used for class notes, answers to the chapter review sections and the chapter and unit evaluations, information gathered from Expand Your Knowledge activities, city profile notes, and any other activities you suggest. Note taking will enable students to retain the material studied more easily and to practice a skill that will be even more important to them as they advance in their educations. The notebooks should be examined occasionally at the beginning of the course so that students who need to improve their work can be helped. The value of the notebooks rests on the ability of the students to take good notes. One approach to help students develop this ability can be used with almost any class discussion or class report, but it would be most helpful very early in the school year:

[notebook]

As information is brought out in the discussion or report, write the important points students should include in their notes on the board. When the discussion is completed, take the time to explain the reasons for your selections and the reasons you did not include other discussion points. Also call attention to the way you have organized the notes. Stress that there is no single correct way to take notes, but that key points which serve as reminders of important information should be included, and that the organization of the notes can assist students in clarifying important relationships and the sequence of events.

One technique that can help students learn to recognize key points of chapters is to have the students write a sentence summary of one of the paragraphs. To clarify the process of writing summaries, have them contrast that by writing an elaboration of the paragraph. When the assignments are completed, check to see that each student has done the assignment properly. A common problem to correct is that the single sentence reflects one aspect of a paragraph but does not summarize it. The single sentence assignment is usually much more difficult to do; the elaboration is fairly easy. Discuss with the class the concepts of moving from generalities to specifics and from specifics to generalities. They should realize that the more they write the more specific they can be, and the less they write on the same subject the more general they can be.

Now ask students to write a single paragraph summary of the *chapter*. These should also be read and evaluated. If you wish to give good outside examples of how a great deal can be summarized in a few sentences, draw on book reviews or catalog descriptions. The Chapter in Brief exercises of the **Discovery Book** will be of further help in developing summarizing skills.

*Discovery Book*

Those students who feel uncomfortable with note taking because of the audiovisual nature of communication today and those students with unusually good memories who see no reason for taking notes may need your special attention at the introduction of this continuing activity. You should point out to *all* students that as they advance in their educations it will not be possible for them to recall all they learn when they need it without the aid of notes.

You might want to use note-taking activities as an approach to help students appreciate the work of historians who interpret many pieces of written and visual evidence in the appraisal of a given event. Several topic close-ups support this approach. For example, the topic close-up on pages 96-97 suggests some problems faced by historians in considering sources. A later feature on page 116 introduces students to the distinction between primary and secondary sources. Examples on pages 313 and 418-419 illustrate visual evidence, and statistical data are discussed on pages 404-405.

*topic close-ups*

## Reviewing

While the notebooks should be valuable for review, students should also be encouraged to skim the chapter material and use the Study Aids at the end of their texts. The charts of Important Dates and of Presidents and

*Study Aids*
*Important Dates chart*

Vice-Presidents will help them put order to the facts and details of a given time period. The Glossary will provide an overview of main terms, and the Index will help them locate topics or people of continuing concern through different time periods.

**Presidents and Vice-Presidents chart**

**Glossary**
**Index**

# *Sharpening Social Studies Skills*

## Skills Coverage

The AMERICA IS program offers both skill development and content reinforcement exercises. In some instances, students will be considering different forms of historical evidence such as artifacts, oral tradition, and recorded accounts — written and visual. They will also be studying various influences on the interpretation of historical events such as:

- time sequence
- distinctions between first and second hand information
- considerations of frame of reference, purpose, opinion and fact, and underlying assumptions
- the relationships among pieces of evidence
- place relationships

The exercises may incorporate one or more of the preceding elements. In them, students will use any or all of the following levels of thought:

- Remembering Facts — being able to recall important facts.
- Understanding Ideas — being able to interpret factual information and being able to identify and remember an idea, principle, or value.
- Using Ideas — being able to correlate a general rule, value, or set of principles to an action or an expressed idea.
- Analyzing Ideas — being able to separate ideas and concepts into basic parts and being able to determine the relationships among them.
- Applying Ideas — being able to organize or reorganize data or acquired knowledge into a new form and being able to relate it to a new situation.
- Evaluating Ideas — being able to appraise acquired knowledge and decide one's own point of view.

## Using Text Features and Supplements

Various features of AMERICA IS provide opportunities for students to build their social studies skills. Topic close-ups and charts encourage

**topic close-ups**

**charts**

students to examine the recording and the study of history as well as to critically read and interpret data. Biographies help students remember that people make history and encourage their discovery of the continuity of human experience.

**biographies**

**illustrations**

Illustrations throughout the text should be studied not only for evidence of time and place, but also to appreciate the interpretation of the artist. Students should recognize that art forms like paintings and drawings involve a degree of interpretation by the artist which is generally greater than that found in a photographer's work. Discussions on artistic interpretation, however, should not be carried too far. To ask students what they think an artist was feeling will almost certainly result in a discussion so open-ended that it loses usefulness.

**maps**

The maps of AMERICA IS provide visual support for the historical element of place, and students should be encouraged to "read" them as an integral part of the text. Perhaps the most obvious example of maps as useful study guides is found on page 202. That map summarizes in a very concise manner the periods of continental expansion in the United States. Other maps in the book provide similar information. Those on pages 304 and 371 could be used for examination of geographic features, while the maps on pages 38, 375, and 434-435 might be used to discuss political features. Economic subjects are handled in the maps on pages 74, 157, 218, and 298. The map on page 74 could be used to discuss the purpose of historical maps, those indicating change over time. If necessary, review the elements of map-reading skills such as directions, scales, and legends with your students before assigning them study material which includes maps.

**Media Study Guide**

**Discovery Book**

The **Media Program Study Guide** and the **Discovery Book** provide additional analytical practice for the students. The **Discovery Book** particularly reinforces chapter content of the text and offers skill development exercises under such titles as "The Chapter in Brief," "Working With Maps," "Elements of History," and "You and History." These exercises should be assigned according to their best use by your particular students. Teaching aids are provided in accompanying supplements, the

**Media Teacher's Guide**

**Teacher's Discovery Book**

**Media Program Teacher's Guide** and the **Teacher's Edition** of the **Discovery Book.**

# Maintaining Student Interest

## Striving for Focus and Continuity

Whether you prefer to emphasize cognitive or affective responses from your students, it is important for you to encourage a classroom climate of participation and the sharing of ideas since one purpose for the study of American history is to prepare students as thinking-acting-feeling citizens of tomorrow. While most students respond to such a climate, they also appreciate the fact that there is a point to their efforts. Chapter aims and program goals as well as the annotations on the student text pages will help you maintain focus for class discussions and questioning processes.

chapter aims
program goals
annotations

Suggestions for teaching AMERICA IS are provided in the Suggestions by Chapter sections of this Manual and the annotated student text pages. These are varied to meet a range of individual teaching and learning needs. It is vital that you plan ahead so that you establish a pace that will allow a complete survey of American history and yet will not be so fast as to hinder learning. While it should be possible for most average students to read and study the text within a given school year, it will not be possible to use all of the teaching examples appearing in this Manual. Choose and adapt those which are most appropriate for your situation and set up a tentative teaching plan.

Suggestions by Chapter
annotations

## Varying Teaching Techniques

In addition to the variety found in Suggestions by Chapter, you may sometimes wish to use other general techniques to elicit affective responses, or just to keep students alert. A familiar game as a base for a questioning or study exercise is one example. The following strategy is similar to the game "Twenty Questions."

Draw up a list of important people, organizations, laws, and activities covered in the chapter and place each on a 3" × 5" or a 5" × 8" card. Consider items one at a time. The class should be told the nature of the item — a person, a law, an organization, or an action. Each student in turn will have a chance to ask the teacher a question — phrased in a way to receive a *yes* answer — which will elicit information to lead to the identification of the item. If a student asks a question for which he or she receives a *yes* answer, three "plus" points are earned. If a *no* answer is received, three "minus" points are earned. (Each student will keep his or her own score.) When a student attempts to name the person, law, action, or organization, a *yes* answer earns 10 plus points, but a *no* answer will put the student out of the game. Repeating a question previously asked earns one minus point. The idea is to stay in the game and to get as many plus points as possible. The final score for each student still involved at the end of the game is determined by finding the difference between the total number of plus points and the total number of minus points.

## Varying Content Presentation

Varying the presentation of the content will also help maintain student interest. Special features such as topic close-ups and biographies can

topic close-ups
biographies

city profiles be used as "breaks" within the chapter study. The city profiles are planned breaks between chapters even as they support and extend chapter content. They are designed to help students place themselves in history. Your teaching plans regarding the city profiles should be flexible enough to encourage maximum student enjoyment while firm enough to relate them to the aims and goals of the whole program.

Another way to vary the day-to-day presentation of content is to provide audiovisual experiences for the students. The AMERICA IS **Media Program** presents a series of episodes in which an individual or a particular social group faces a difficult problem or decision. These episodes include the concerns and struggles of a variety of people from different geographical areas over a wide span of time.

Media Program

- "The Boston Massacre" — a lead-up to the Revolution
- "What Is Our Crime?" — an examination of the Cherokee removal
- "How Can I Draw My Sword?" — a study of Lee's decision to join the Confederacy
- "Land of Opportunity" — a contrast of life on the frontier and that of the city
- "Old Dusty Road" — a study of the Dust Bowl and the migration of the 1930's
- "Walking for My Children" — an examination of the Montgomery bus boycott

Suggestions by Chapter    Refer to the Suggestions by Chapter section for appropriate scheduling of these within the unit studies and the **Media Program Teacher's**
Media Teacher's Guide    **Guide** for suggested usage.

# Evaluating Student Progress

## Chapter Reviews

An important point to consider in maintaining interest is the fostering of each student's sense of accomplishment. The developmental aspects of
Chapters in Perspective    the chapter review sections will make the job of monitoring individual progress somewhat easier. To help students appreciate their own progress, they should have an opportunity to discuss these sections after they have completed them. Such discussions will also allow for misconceptions to be cleared up before additional assignments are made. While minimum and extended answers are provided for many review items, there should be other allowances made for individual student frame of reference and for lesser amounts of time given for assignments or in-class help.

# Quizzes

Another technique for determining how well individual students are grasping the material or adapting to your style of delivering information is the occasional use of impromptu quizzes.

Draw up a list of questions on important factual information covered in a portion of the text, making the questions comparable in difficulty. For example: "What three groups of Americans were unable to vote or hold office in the early nineteenth century? What two political parties developed from the split in the Republican party after the election of 1828?" On the day following the reading assignment and before any discussion has taken place, announce that there will be a quiz. Instruct students to number a blank sheet of paper with the number of questions you have and to write the answers to the questions as you read. In presenting the first half of the questions, repeat each one. If students ask for another reading, do so. When the last of the first half of the questions has been presented, ask students if they want any questions repeated and read those again, using any different wording that might clarify what is being asked. Proceed to the second half of the questions but announce to the class that you will read these questions only once. Read them clearly and distinctly at your normal rate of speed, just as you usually present material to your classes.

When the papers have been corrected, compare the responses on the first half with those on the second half. The comparisons can help you identify those students who do not assimilate information quickly but who do well when given extra time. It is also possible to get some idea of the ability of students to grasp information and act on it when the information is delivered in your usual manner. Needless to say, students who did not do the assignment or did not complete it will present problems in your analysis; and one such activity will not provide definitive information about individual students or about your presentation. However, if the activity is repeated from time to time, you can gain some valuable information about your teaching style, and your students can discover what facts in the reading you consider important and can find out how well they recall facts from their reading.

# Formal Tests

The AMERICA IS **Evaluation Program** provides tests that parallel the developmental nature of Chapter in Perspective reviews. The unit tests review the most important points from the chapter tests.

Evaluation Program

The material tested is grouped under three main headings and incorporates several levels of learning. "Remembering Facts" requires students to recall important people, places, or events; "Understanding Ideas" requires students to interpret factual information and to identify and remember an idea, principle, or value; "Working With Ideas" requires students to use, analyze, and apply ideas.

Nonreproducible answers appear on the spirit master tests for easy grading. Whether a test is given as an open book or a closed book test, the answers should be discussed so that misconceptions and misunderstandings can be discovered and corrected before proceeding to new material. These chapter and unit tests may provide the entire basis for evaluating student progress or may be combined with your own more subjective methods of evaluation.

# *Epilogue*

survey form

Perhaps one of the best ways to ensure that effective learning-teaching materials are produced is to let authors and publishers know how you feel about the ones you have been using. Please help us in our planning of revisions and new programs by completing and returning the form found on the last two pages of the Manual. After removing the AMERICA IS survey from the book, fold and staple it so that the Charles E. Merrill address label shows. We will appreciate hearing from you.

# Suggestions by Chapter

## *Unit 1 – Opportunity*

**Unit aim:**  to show the combination of elements from the New and Old Worlds which led to the development of a unique "American" society.

## *Chapter 1*

**Aim:**  to develop students' appreciation of the natural and cultural resources present in the Americas before European immigration.

## Important Points

1. All people who live in North and South America can properly be called Americans.
2. People who make up the United States today have a variety of origins including American Indian, Eskimo, African, Asian, and European.
3. The New World's many natural riches offered great opportunities for those who wanted to make use of them.
4. Europeans and Indians differed over how to make use of the land and other resources in the Americas.
5. Contact between people from the Old and New Worlds resulted in each learning from the other.
6. Indians in the Western Hemisphere had various forms of culture, and some had highly developed civilizations before the arrival of Europeans.

## Teaching Ideas

● Introduce the course and this chapter by asking students to find definitions for the following words: *history, culture, environment, element, opportunity,* and *introduction.* Identify these as words which will be useful in understanding this first chapter and unit. Begin discussion of the meanings without reference to specific material in the text. As good definitions for each term are secured, have students write them in their notebooks.

Use the definition of "opportunity" as a bridge from the discussion of definitions to the introduction of the first chapter. Use the definition of "introduction" to alert students to what they should expect from this chapter. After their expectations have been discussed, the first chapter should be assigned for student reading.

- To help students identify the elements of the events of history as time, people, and place, present the following questions: "When did this event take place? Who was involved? Where did it happen?" Discuss the meaning of history in terms of these elements, citing these as points to be considered throughout the study of history in this course or elsewhere. Later in the year, you may wish to raise more sophisticated questions having to do with the ways we categorize people and their ideas within a setting of time and place.

- Have students make lists of the things in our life today which they consider better than things in the life of pre-Columbian Indians and lists of the things that seem better in the lives of the Indians. If necessary, guide students toward consideration of the environment. This could lead to a discussion of the conflicts possible between taking advantage of opportunities and maintaining a desirable environment because of the different values acted upon by people.

- In working with the feature "Views of History," ask students which of the descriptions of Indians fits best with their own ideas. Explore how students' ideas about Indians and their history came to be formed through books, movies, television, personal experience, or travel, and why they hold the ideas they do. Direct the discussion to the idea that the featured descriptions tell us something about the historians as well as about the Indians. Raise such questions as: "Can one historian be more correct than another? Can all three be correct? Can all be wrong? How would a student of history decide which description is likely to be more correct than another?" Help students realize the need for careful examination of specific information when making generalizations.

# Secota

- Before assigning this first city profile, you might remind the students of the use of ellipses and brackets in quoted material as mentioned in the Preface. Call their attention to the different kinds of type used in these features so that they quickly recognize the italic type as the quoted material. Use the map detail found at the beginning of each city profile as a map reading skill exercise. Map scales vary among the profiles. As each city is studied, have the students locate each area on a larger map in the classroom or on the text map on page 507 as a constant.

- After the students have read the material on Secota, divide them into groups to see what answers they can work out to such questions as "What do the pictures and information on Secota tell us about the climate in which the village is located? What do they tell us about the plants and animals of the area?" Have the students examine the pictures carefully and hold a general discussion following their work in groups. Use the discussion of their answers as an opportunity to demonstrate how much can be learned from pictures if they are examined carefully.

- Have the students begin a chart for comparing features of Secota and the thirteen other towns and cities which appear in profile later in the text. They could compare such topics as the dress of the people, types of homes and other buildings, ways people make their livings, and geography of the areas. This material can be used from time to time to provide examples of changes taking place over periods in the country's history.

# Chapter 2

**Aim:** to develop students' understanding that Europeans competed for dominance of New World opportunities at the expense of the Indians who occupied the land and of the Africans who were brought in as forced labor.

## Important Points

1. Many events in the Old World combined to cause Europeans to seek new trade routes to the East in the fifteenth century.
2. Columbus, an Italian navigator sailing for Spain, reached the Americas while trying to find a route to India and China by sailing westward from Europe.
3. Spain established the first European empire in the Americas.
4. Following Spain, other European countries joined in exploring and building empires in the New World.
5. Europeans conquered and oppressed the Indian populations in the Americas and brought Africans to the New World to work as slaves.

## Teaching Ideas

- Have each student make a list of the difficulties people might encounter when exploring an area which is unknown to them such as weather, land formations, forms of life, and sources of food. Ask one student to put his or her list on the chalkboard, and let other students add their ideas to it. Use the composite list to introduce the chapter.

- Have students prepare a time line using the explorers listed in the chapter. They might be asked to find information about other explorers and place them on the time line as a homework assignment. Students should pay particular attention to the reasons for these explorations.

- In working with the feature "Letter From Columbus," recall for the students the feature in Chapter 1 which dealt with point of view. Ask them to consider whether or not point of view applies to this feature. Does Columbus' description of the new lands reflect his aim of finding a trade route to the East? Help students understand the descriptions of navigable rivers and good harbors, cultivatable lands, and sources of metals as important aspects of trade.

# Chapter 3

**Aim:** to develop students' understanding of British colonial policies and attitudes which led to the British dominance of North America.

## Important Points

1. The English colonies became the most successful ones in North America although they were established later than those of Spain or France; large numbers of colonists came to them, which was not true in the Spanish or French colonies.
2. Some English colonies were established by merchants expecting to make large profits for themselves.
3. Some English colonies were established by people who could not practice their religions as they wished in Europe.
4. Some English colonies were established by the rulers of England to benefit the homeland.
5. Merchant groups sometimes raised the large amount of money needed to start a colony by pooling their funds and forming joint stock companies.
6. The first successful English settlement in North America was Jamestown, established in 1607.
7. Twelve of the original colonies were established in the seventeenth century. Georgia, the thirteenth, was established in the eighteenth century.
8. The colonists thought of themselves as part of England. They developed many different ways of life in North America because of its different environment.

## Teaching Ideas

- Introduce the chapter by telling the class that they have been chosen to start a colony on another planet. Lead them in discussion of the things which they would take with them like languages, religions, customs, and tools. You might want to put this in the form of asking each student to list five items which they would take, or simply to list how life would be the same at the colony. A variation would be to introduce changes into the colony such as telling the students that the soil of the planet is different from the earth's, which would affect agriculture and therefore diet. It is important that the students see that certain things, like some customs, will be the same in the colony but that other things may be different in response to a different environment.

- Bring to class some examples or replicas of colonial tools and household items. Allow students to inspect them carefully. See if students can identify the items, what each is made of, and its use. Ask what tools or items are used today for the same purpose.

- If your school provides a kitchen for use by the students, you can have an enjoyable learning experience cooking colonial foods. Dividing the class into groups, let each group identify a colonial recipe and prepare the item. The food can be enjoyed in a class meal followed by a discussion of the food eaten, how it was prepared in colonial times, and how it compares with the daily diet of the class members. Work with the home economics teacher on this project if necessary.

- In working with the feature "Time," you might have the students prepare a time line with their family members on it. They may wish to see if they can go further back in time than their grandparents and great-grandparents. If a family time line might be a problem for some students, they could interview an elderly neighbor and report on that person's family in time line form. A variation of this activity would be for the students to develop some significant dates in the country's history and put them on the time line to correspond to or compare with the dates in the family history.

# *Plymouth*

- The profile of Plymouth could be used to emphasize the element of place in history by asking the students to pay particular attention to the reasons given for the Pilgrims' selection of this site. What aspects of geography did they consider important to their survival? How does the site chosen for Plymouth compare to the location of Secota?

- Some musically talented students might like to create a tune for the Pilgrim ballad on page 60 and teach it to the class. The ballad can also be sung to the tunes of "On Top of Old Smokey" and "The Gypsy Rover," with a little modification. Such an activity could lead to a discussion of songs as a part of oral tradition in history.

- Have the students add material on Plymouth to the chart begun with Secota. They might also begin recording population figures. When a significant amount of information has been entered on this chart, it will provide a basis for discussing why some cities grow faster than others.

# Unit 2 – Independence

**Unit aim:**   to clarify the factors contributing to the emergence of a separate, new nation and government.

# Chapter 4

**Aim:**   to increase understanding of the conditions of colonial life which led to the maturing of a separate American culture.

## Important Points

1. An American culture which was different from those of the Old World developed in the English colonies in North America. This culture was British for the most part, but it was changed and enriched by the cultures of American Indians, Africans, and other Europeans.
2. Most Europeans came to the New World to improve their ways of life or to practice their religions as they wished.
3. Many people were brought to the New World against their wills. These people included Africans brought as slaves and Europeans who were criminals or debtors and sold as indentured servants.
4. The population of the English colonies was a mixture of people from many different geographic, social, and economic backgrounds.
5. The vast supply of land was the base for the economic life of the English colonies.
6. To European immigrants, labor was more difficult to secure than land.

7. Most of the colonists practiced farming, but fishing, lumbering, shipbuilding, and some home manufacturing were also important.
8. Colonial cities, though small, were the centers of trade and cultural life.
9. Social class distinctions were stronger in the colonial period than in later years, but they were not so rigid as in Europe.
10. The development of slavery placed most Africans at the bottom of the social scale. As slaves, they came to be considered property rather than people.

## Teaching Ideas

● As an introduction to this chapter, have the students recall the introduction to Chapter 3 and its conclusion that people establish a colony while maintaining much of the culture of their homeland although environment may alter some ways of life. Guide the class into discussing some generalizations which might apply to them as a group such as mode of living (suburban homes or urban apartments) or types of work their parents do. In reading Chapter 4, the students will be learning some of the generalizations which apply to the ways of life in the English colonies. After the students have been alerted to that, assign the chapter for reading.

● Organize the class into a newspaper staff whose job will be to produce one or more editions of a colonial newspaper. Set the time around 1750 or 1760, and assign the staff its responsibility of producing an edition which is concerned with, and reflects, the life of people in the colonies. Topics can include trade, slavery, government, Indian affairs, land and the frontier, fashion, theater, poetry, advertisements, or any other topic relevant to the time. Let the group select a managing editor who will make the assignments of topics and needed art work. Work with that editor to assure a wide selection of topics. Assistant editors can check each article, and the editorial staff can meet to decide on lead stories, headlines, and features. Working with the Language Arts or English teacher on this project may be beneficial. Stories and artwork can be put on stencils so that multiple copies can be made.

● Have each student write a brief story while imagining that he or she is a person living in colonial society. They may want to imagine that they are young or old. Their stories should give some hint of occupation, place of residence, and time without mentioning these specifically. All or some of the stories might be read to the class, and they should be evaluated on how well they reflect the person, place, and time the student has chosen.

- In working with the chart "Population of Colonial Cities," you might have the students find population figures for American cities at another time period for comparison. An alternative would be to compare the population figures listed on page 77 with figures for European cities of the same period. A valuable comparison would be to have the students with the necessary math skills figure the percentage of growth for each of the cities during the years shown on the chart.

# Philadelphia

- Duplicate and distribute to the students one or two pages of sayings from *Poor Richard's Almanac*. Discuss each to determine if the students understand the sayings. You might ask which of the sayings seem applicable today, leading the students to discuss what conclusions can be drawn from the fact that statements made more than two hundred years ago are still applicable. This should lead to some elementary discussion and understanding of the similarities of some of the human concerns and problems throughout history.

- Have the students discuss the reasons that Philadelphia became the largest city in colonial America, listing those which are valid on the board. When the matter of location is discussed, use a large detailed wall map or a map of the area on a transparency to help the students understand specific features of the topography which were important. When the board list is complete, engage the class in discussing other colonial cities which had all or most of the same favorable features as Philadelphia. Ask them to consider possible reasons that Philadelphia did not remain the largest city in the United States.

# Chapter 5

**Aim:** to increase understanding of economic and political factors which led to war between Britain and the British American colonies.

## Important Points

1. The colonists had experience in self-government before the American Revolution.
2. Colonial governments were modeled after the government of England. Each had a governor and a legislative body.

3. Quarrels between the colonies and England centered around economic matters and foreign wars.
4. Laws passed by England after the French and Indian War were considered by the colonists as harmful to their economic interests.
5. The thirteen colonies declared their independence in 1776.
6. The colonies won their independence in a long war with the help of both black and white Americans.
7. The colonies produced many outstanding leaders during the Revolution including George Washington, Thomas Jefferson, Benjamin Franklin, John Adams, and others.
8. The Revolution ended with the Treaty of Paris in 1783.

## Teaching Ideas

● Review with the class the discussion about independence which introduced this unit. Use it as a bridge to discussion of possible ways in which countries gain independence. Work with the students in developing their understanding of revolution. Have available copies of current newspaper articles which deal with conflicts in other parts of the world involving colonial rule or revolutionary movements available for the class. Discuss with the students the possible reasons behind those movements and alert them to the need for retaining this information for comparison after reading Chapter 5 about the American Revolution. Encourage the students to continue to bring in any news items which deal with this subject.

● Present the AMERICA IS sound filmstrip entitled "The Boston Massacre."

● Read to the students, or have one of them read, several poems written about the American Revolution. Assign the writing of an original poem about the same subject.

# *Chapter 6*

**Aim:**  to help students understand the evolution of ideas over time which resulted in ratification of the Constitution and Bill of Rights.

## Important Points

1. The future of the United States was uncertain at the time immediately following the winning of independence from England.
2. The new state governments organized in each of the former colonies were given limited power.

3. The government organized under the Articles of Confederation was a weak union of states headed by a President who had little power.

4. The most important legislation passed by Congress under the Articles of Confederation was that which provided for the organization of the Northwest Territory and set provisions for the addition of new states on an equal basis with the original thirteen states.

5. The Articles of Confederation proved to be too weak to provide effective government for the new nation.

6. The Constitutional Convention met during 1787 and drew up a new Constitution of the United States.

7. The Constitution provided for representative government in a legislative branch made up of two houses and for a strong executive branch.

8. After much debate, the Constitution was ratified by June, 1788, and became the basis for the government of the United States.

9. Soon after ratification, a Bill of Rights was added to the Constitution.

## Teaching Ideas

● Engage the class in discussion of the term *assumption* as an idea on which other ideas or actions are based. Develop some examples from the lives of the students to clarify the meaning of the term. They come to school in the morning, for instance, assuming that the teachers will be there and that other students will attend that day. Emphasize that assumptions may be spoken or unspoken, that assumptions do not always turn out to be correct, and that ideas or actions change if they are not. Use that discussion as a bridge to a discussion of the assumptions held by the leaders of the United States when they drew up the Articles of Confederation. List some of those important assumptions on the board such as the following:

Monarchies are bad.

Strong central government threatens the rights of citizens.

State governments are the units to which citizens owe their major allegiance.

Tell the students that, as they read Chapter 6, they will find out more about the Articles of Confederation and about the assumptions on which they were based. Students will also find out that the government of the country was changed. Have them compare the new plan of government with the assumptions made for the Articles of Confederation after they have read the chapter.

● Assign the reading of the Bill of Rights as homework. Later discuss each of the first ten amendments in terms of what they meant at the time they were written and what they mean today. Have the students consider changes in today's society, such as the development of long-range listening devices for surveillance, in terms of the guarantees in the Bill of Rights.

● In working with the chart "Powers of the Government," make up a chart of the powers as shown on page 117 with individual cards for each of the powers listed, or simply write them under the proper headings on the chalkboard. Move one of the powers listed into a different column. Ask the students to consider some possible consequences of this.

# Unit 3 – Democracy

**Unit aim:** to help students understand that the establishment and maintenance of United States democracy is a developing process.

# Chapter 7

**Aim:** to clarify the main structures and interrelationships of the United States federal government.

## Important Points

1. George Washington was elected the first President of the United States, and John Adams was elected first Vice-President.
2. Washington set examples for the operation of the presidency which were followed by later Presidents.
3. Congress created the federal court system by the Judiciary Act of 1789.
4. Alexander Hamilton, the first Secretary of the Treasury, drew up an economic program that was intended to help the nation prosper and which was particularly favorable to the wealthy business people of the country.
5. Disagreement over the creation of the Bank of the United States marked the beginning of two interpretations of the Constitution, the narrow interpretation of Thomas Jefferson and the broad interpretation of Alexander Hamilton.
6. The President assumed more power in foreign affairs than the framers of the Constitution had intended.
7. Two political parties, the Federalists and the Republicans, developed as a result of disagreements over the Jay Treaty and other matters.

8. The Alien and Sedition Acts were passed by the Federalists to maintain their control of the federal government.

9. The Republicans gained control of the federal government with the election of Thomas Jefferson in 1800. It marked the first changeover of power from one party to another in the nation's history.

10. The Louisiana Purchase in 1803 doubled the size of the United States.

11. The Supreme Court established its right of judicial review in the case of *Marbury v. Madison*.

## Teaching Ideas

● To introduce Chapter 7, you might engage the class in a discussion of problems common to all new organizations or to new groups working under a new plan for the first time. An example of that could be the difficulties faced by a sports team at the opening of each new season. It is important for the students to understand that success was not guaranteed to the country under the Constitution any more than it was under the Articles of Confederation.

● Divide the class into groups of six or eight students. Have each group work with the text to make a list of the major problems faced by the new government in order of their importance for the success of the new nation. Instruct each group to have a recorder who will report on the group's work to the whole class. After the reports have been made, discuss the major problems and the steps taken by the United States to deal with them. When this discussion is completed, tell the class that you want them to analyze the way they worked in their groups. Pass out a previously prepared sheet containing the following questions:

Did you take part in the discussion in your group?

Were there people in your group who did not take part? (No names, please.)

What effort was made by you or other group members to involve those who were not taking part?

Did any person act as leader in your group?

If a leader developed, was the person accepted by all of the group's members?

Did you do all that you could to see that your group was successful in its assignment? If not, what else might you have done?

What are the characteristics of a good leader?

Review the student responses to the questions on group activity and leadership. Report the results of the responses to the class. Place on the board those characteristics which students cited for a good leader, adding any which you consider important. When there is general agreement about the list, tell the class that they are to apply the list of characteristics to George Washington to evaluate the authors' claim that he was a good leader. Allow the students a day or two for gathering information from other sources about Washington. Then discuss each of the characteristics as it applies to the first President.

# Washington, D. C.

- Assign each student a library study project on Washington, D. C. Some of the subjects might include the various buildings, the government of the District of Columbia, the system of naming streets in the District, biographical sketches of Pierre L'Enfant, Andrew Ellicott, and Benjamin Banneker. Each student should make a brief report to the class.

- Collect information, or have students collect information, on any city recently built, being built, or being planned in this or other countries. Compare the planning and building with that of Washington, D. C. You might have students who would enjoy developing a plan of their own for a capital city.

# Chapter 8

**Aim:** to improve students' understanding of sectionalism and nationalism as both uniting and dividing forces.

## Important Points

1. A long war between Britain and France in the early 1800's brought both prosperity and problems to the United States.
2. Under the leadership of Tecumseh, the Indians along the frontier formed a confederation to stop white settlers from taking more of their lands. A United States army defeated this confederation at the Battle of Tippecanoe.
3. The United States declared war on Britain in 1812 as a result of conflicts over shipping rights, the impressment of United States citizens, and British activities along the western American frontier.
4. The Treaty of Ghent ended the war in 1814 and returned all boundaries to what they had been before the war. Nothing was settled about American rights on the sea.

5. The American victory in the Battle of New Orleans, fought after the treaty was signed, made many Americans feel that they had won the war.

6. In the years following the war, the forces of nationalism and sectionalism worked to both unite and divide the country.

7. The spirit of nationalism was expressed in the creation of a new Bank of the United States, the passage of a protective tariff, and federal grants to build roads and canals.

8. Sectional interests in the North, South, and West created divisive problems for the country. The most serious sectional differences involved slavery.

9. The Missouri Compromise was an attempt to solve the problem of sectional conflict involving slavery and to establish the steps for the admission of new states.

10. The Monroe Doctrine was an expression of American nationalism warning the European nations away from further colonization in the Western Hemisphere.

## Teaching Ideas

- Locate your particular state for the class on a large map of the United States. Introduce students to the term *section* as it applies to a collection of states like the Northeast or Southwest. Have the class determine in which particular section of the United States they live. Discuss with them some things like climate, topography, ways of earning a living, and so on which might distinguish their section of the country from others. Have available a list of topics to read to the class, asking after each if the subject could be one of major importance to their section. Such topics might include the following:

  an oil pipeline

  nuclear power plants

  a law to prevent killing mountain lions

  money for education

  money for building a new subway

  Try to include topics of interest to your section as well as things of interest to the entire nation.

- Engage the class in providing information for two lists to be placed on the board. The first list will include the causes of the War of 1812. The second will include the results of the war. Discuss each cause and each result as it is given. When both lists are completed, ask each student to write two or three generalizations which can be made about the War of 1812. These generalizations should also be listed on the board. When this is completed, introduce the term *evaluation* and explain its meaning. Ask students how they would evaluate the War of 1812 from the point of view of the interests of the United States as reflected by the material on the board.

# New Orleans

● After students have read the New Orleans profile, begin discussion by asking how the city was different from the other cities studied so far. Discussion should bring out that New Orleans was not on or near the eastern coast, that it was under the control of France and Spain for much of its early history, that its culture had a heavy mixture of French and Spanish influence, and that a majority of its people were of the Catholic religion.

● Ask the students to read carefully the material in the feature from the book by Eliza Ripley. Discuss each paragraph separately for what it tells about the life of people, especially children, in the mid-nineteenth century.

# Chapter 9

**Aim:** to help students understand that in the midst of great diversity and argument, an "American" national character was being formed.

## Important Points

1. America was a democracy in form of government but not in practice since all women, Indians, and slaves, as well as most other blacks and poor whites, could not vote or hold public office.
2. The new states formed from the territories led the way in allowing all white males to vote and hold public office. However, other groups remained excluded from participating in government even in the new states.
3. Disagreement over the election of 1824 and the tariff led to a split in the Republican party resulting in two groups, the Democratic Republicans and the National Republicans.
4. The election of Andrew Jackson in 1828 marked an expansion in the involvement of Americans in presidential elections.
5. Those people who supported Jackson dropped the word Republicans from their party name and have since been called the Democrats. Those who were against Jackson called themselves Whigs.
6. Under President Jackson, most Indians living east of the Mississippi River were forced to move to the Great Plains.

7. The expansion of participation in the political process was accompanied by an expansion in educational opportunities for many Americans.
8. American writers, artists, and musicians turned away from European styles and produced many more works with American themes.
9. The period was marked by a number of reforms aimed at improving American life.

## Teaching Ideas

● Introduce Chapter 9 by asking the students to recall from previous chapters those groups of Americans who had been excluded from voting and holding public office. Alert them to the fact that in this chapter they will read about a period in which participation in voting and holding office grows considerably. Along with this political growth, the students will read about growth in other areas like education which contributed to an overall growth in democracy.

● Present the AMERICA IS sound filmstrip entitled "What Is Our Crime?"

● Prepare a multimedia presentation of the Jacksonian period. Use films, slides, pictures, records, and tapes as available. Architecture, fashion, and literature are three of the many subjects which might be pursued with interest. Comparisons with these subjects in the colonial period would also be useful. The aim of the presentation should be to give students some feeling of the spirit of the times.

● Divide the class into groups for the purpose of gathering additional information about the Indian removals during the Jacksonian period. Focus their attention upon the adjustments which the people had to make in such moves, both physical and psychological.

# Unit 4 – Expansion

**Unit aim:** to show the advantages and disadvantages resulting from rapid physical and economic growth in the United States.

# Chapter 10

**Aim:** to clarify the means of physical expansion during a period of tremendous growth for the United States.

# Important Points

1. Many Americans claimed that it was the Manifest Destiny of the United States to expand its borders from the Atlantic to the Pacific Oceans.
2. Expansion was partly the result of strong political motives, some of which reflected sectionalism while others reflected nationalism.
3. Large numbers of white settlers again moved into lands occupied by Indian peoples who were forced to move.
4. The area of Texas won its independence from Mexico, governed itself for a time as the Lone Star Republic, and later became a state.
5. When Texas became a state, it further strained relations between the United States and Mexico, and war was fought in 1846.
6. The United States invaded Mexico and captured Mexico City.
7. In the Treaty of Guadalupe Hidalgo, Mexico recognized the independence of Texas and turned over to the United States all of its lands north of the Rio Grande and the Gila River.
8. American settlers, in spite of resistance from many Mexicans, declared California independent from Mexico and established the Bear Flag Republic. California was added to the United States by the Treaty of Guadalupe Hidalgo.
9. The United States and Britain worked out an agreement over the Oregon territory which gave the United States the southern half of the area.
10. The discovery of gold led many Americans and others from around the world to California in the late 1840's.
11. By the end of the 1840's, the continental boundaries of the United States had been established except for Alaska and a small area in the Southwest.

# Teaching Ideas

- Introduce Chapter 10 by asking the students to define and discuss the words *fate* and *destiny*. Ask if any of them believe that their lives, or certain parts of them, hold certain fates. Guide the discussion to the realization that people sometimes claim those things they want to happen as "fate." Assign the chapter reading and alert students to look for the ways the idea of Manifest Destiny influenced the growth of the nation and affected different groups of people.

- Use the writings of people who lived during this period to acquaint students with the spirit, hardships, and joys of the westward movement. Assign readings of selected parts of long books or all of short articles and poems. Have the students write a brief review of their reading which includes when the piece was written, a brief biographical sketch of the author, what the author was saying, and how well the author presented the ideas. Additional titles can be found in the bibliography section, but a beginning list of main sources for the assignments is given below.

Richard Henry Dana, Jr., *Two Years Before the Mast*

Ralph Waldo Emerson, "The Young American"

Mark Twain, *Life on the Mississippi*

Walt Whitman, "A Passage to India"

- Organize the class into groups for studying the geography of the different sections of the United States. Each group should be assigned a section which became a part of the Union as shown on the map on page 202. The students themselves can help to establish the exact divisions of the territories to be researched. Have them develop generalizations about the climate, terrain, and types of vegetation as well as specific details on land area, major rivers, and so on.

# San Francisco

- Read to the class some of the material in *Three Years in California* by Walter Colton which covers the period of May through July, 1848. Discuss the influence of gold on the people of San Francisco as described in the selections. Identify other situations in other places and times where large numbers of people have been excited to immediate and often irrational action — the Chicago fire, the stories of the earth's invasion by Martians brought on by the radio program "War of the Worlds," and so on. Discuss with the class some of the things about people in general that these events may reveal, guiding them to the understanding that information can be distorted when spread quickly among large groups of people.

# Chapter 11

**Aim:**   to help students understand the continuing development of different regional economies through presentation of contributing factors.

## Important Points

1. Most Americans were optimistic that they could improve their lives by working hard.
2. There was considerable growth in manufacturing during the 1840's and 1850's.

3. The factory system developed mainly in New England and to a lesser extent in other areas of the country.

4. Transportation was greatly improved with the building of canals, roads, and railroad systems.

5. The invention of the telegraph made immediate communication across long distances possible.

6. New ways of farming and new farm machinery led to great increases in food production.

7. Farming was still the main factor in the United States' economy in the 1840's and 1850's.

8. The development of the factory system and improvements in transportation spurred the growth of cities.

9. Large numbers of immigrants from Europe and smaller numbers from Asia came to the United States.

10. Sectional differences between North and South increased during this period.

## Teaching Ideas

● As an introduction to Chapter 11, have the class review in generalizations the physical, or territorial, expansion discussed in Chapter 10. Explain to them that Chapter 11 deals with expansion, too, but that it focuses on the economic expansion of the United States in the 1840's and 1850's. You may want the students to look up the word *economy* in the glossary at the back of the text. Follow that with a brief discussion of the term because it is so central to the study of history. Discuss with the students some factors influencing the economy of a country such as population growth or decline or the depletion of oil resources. Guide the students' discussion toward a consideration of the effects of such things on the different ways people earn their livings. Focus on how people make their livings now and some of the ways that the future might offer like jobs related to computers, space exploration, or solar heating. Assign the writing of a short in-class paper on "A Career in the Twenty-first Century." Accept any plausible stories so long as the student establishes some link in the paper between the career described and possible technology and available resources.

● Explore changes in transportation and communication during this period. You might begin with a question like, "What was the fastest way to travel or to send a message several hundred miles overland in the early nineteenth century?" The answer should be "by horse." Asking the same question about the early eighteenth century, the early fifteenth century, and ancient times should bring the same response. Students will soon realize that there was little change in the speed of overland transportation until the middle of the nineteenth century. Have information available on the relative speeds of horses and steam locomotives in the mid-nineteenth century. Introduce other changes in transportation and communication into the discussion, especially the telegraph. It is important for students to realize that the telegraph was valuable both for its usefulness in sending messages and for its effect on methods of transportation like the railroad.

# Unit 5 – Division

**Unit aim:** to help students understand the economic, political, and social factors which contributed to the Civil War and to the difficulties of Reconstruction.

# Chapter 12

**Aim:** to improve student understanding of the sectional forces which led to civil war in the United States.

## Important Points

1. The abolitionist movement supported by free blacks and by whites opposed to slavery kept the issue of slavery before the American people in the 1840's and 1850's.
2. The idea of popular sovereignty added to the dispute over the extension of slavery into new territories.
3. Efforts to settle the dispute over slavery in the Compromise of 1850 eased tensions for a while but did not settle the issue.
4. The Fugitive Slave Act of 1850 did much to anger abolitionists, and it led to resistance of the law by people in some areas of the North.
5. *Uncle Tom's Cabin,* a novel written by Harriet Beecher Stowe, did much to increase popular support for the abolitionist movement.
6. The Kansas-Nebraska Act split the leaders of the North and South even more over the issue of the spread of slavery. As a result of the decision — that the people of the two territories could decide for themselves about slavery — Kansas became a battleground for antislavery and proslavery forces.
7. The Republican party was formed in 1854 as a result of the arguments over the Kansas-Nebraska Act.
8. The Supreme Court's Dred Scott decision stated that Congress had no right to prohibit slavery in the territories.
9. John Brown's raid on Harpers Ferry further divided Americans on the issue of slavery.

10. Abraham Lincoln was considered by Southern leaders to be opposed to their interests in maintaining slavery. When Lincoln was elected President in 1860, several states withdrew from the United States and formed the Confederate States of America.

## Teaching Ideas

● To introduce Chapter 12, ask the class to consider the following question: "Does the American concept of democracy give each individual and every group the right to decide whether or not they wish to remain a part of the country?" In guiding the discussion, you may want to have the students first consider these questions: "If democratic systems provide for majority rule, what happens when the majority refuses to respect the rights of the minority of a population? What happens if the majority takes a position that is morally sound but the minority refuses to go along with it?" After you are satisfied that the students grasp some of the problems in the main issue, assign Chapter 12.

● Compare the free states in the United States with the slave states on the eve of the Civil War. This comparison will help the students get a better understanding of some of the issues and ideas included in Unit 5. It will also provide information to which they can refer as they study the unit. This material should be made a part of the student's notebook and referred to as necessary. Display a large map of the United States in 1850 showing free and slave states or make use of the text map on page 239. Assign students the task of collecting the following information concerning the free and slave states:

> number of states in each section
> total population
> black population
> representation in Congress
> railroad mileage
> major cities in order of their sizes

# Chapter 13

**Aim:** to present students with military and nonmilitary factors involved in the Civil War and the eventual success of the Union forces.

## Important Points

1. The Civil War caused more death, suffering, and damage for the people of the United States than any war in the nation's history.

2. Most people in the North believed that secession should not be allowed.

3. The Confederate government was modeled after the Constitution of the United States with two major exceptions: it gave more power to the states, and it stated that its congress could not pass laws against slavery.

4. The Civil War military fighting began with the Confederate attack on Fort Sumter near Charleston, South Carolina, in 1861.

5. After the attack on Fort Sumter, President Lincoln asked for army volunteers. Several Southern states considered that action a declaration of war against them. Four additional states joined the Confederacy.

6. The military plan of the South was to defend the Confederacy until the North gave in and to obtain help from Britain or France.

7. The military plan of the North was to blockade the South's coast with Union ships, to divide and conquer the South with the Union army, and to prevent other countries from helping the South.

8. Lincoln believed that the war was being fought to preserve the Union, not to abolish slavery. He issued the Emancipation Proclamation to improve the Union's chances of victory.

9. After some setbacks and four years of fighting, the North was able to carry out its plan, and the South was defeated.

10. President Lincoln moved to restore the former Confederate states to the Union as quickly as possible.

11. President Lincoln was assassinated only five days after the surrender of Confederate General Lee's forces to Union General Grant.

## Teaching Ideas

● It is important that students have the opportunity to develop the skill of asking questions. Because Chapter 13 deals with a clearly defined topic in terms of both subject and time period, work with the class before they begin the chapter to draw up a list of questions to be answered. Have each student write down at least one question whose answer they consider important to the study of the Civil War. After they have had time to do so, discuss their questions and decide with the class which ones to list on the board as most important. You could have the students keep their question lists, or you might collect them so that additional questions about the Civil War can be answered by their own outside research. Have the students then read the chapter to answer the questions which they helped develop.

● Present the AMERICA IS sound filmstrip entitled "How Can I Draw My Sword?"

● Since Chapter 11 dealt with the development of industry and the factory system, it might be valuable to have the students consider the applications of technology to the waging of the Civil War. Give them an opportunity to locate additional sources of information about earlier wars including the text. Ask them why the Civil War has often been called the first modern war. Do not limit the discussion to technology applied to weapons, but try to guide the students to considering the effects of improved transportation and communication as well.

- Divide the class into three groups and have each group discuss and report to the class on a different question. To the first group, assign the question, "Why did the South think it could win the Civil War?" To the second group, assign the question, "Why did the North win the Civil War?" To the third group, assign the question, "Was there a chance that the South could have won the Civil War?" Circulate among the groups to give any help needed to develop their line of reasoning. Emphasize that each group must give reasons for their answers to the question assigned to them. You might also allow for minority opinions within the groups.

# New York and Atlanta

- After the students have read the New York and Atlanta city profiles, have them compare the lives of the people as they were affected by the Civil War. Develop a list of effects and then ask the students to what degree they apply to the people of each city.

- Have the students identify by name or occupation each of the people who provided information on the cities profiled. Stress the point that it is not enough to find something that is written by a person who lived at a particular time, but that it is necessary to evaluate that person's writings. Such information as the following is needed about each writer:

    Was the person writing about something he or she saw, took part in, heard, or read?

    Was the person old enough to understand fully what was seen, heard, or experienced?

    Was the material written so long after the event that errors of memory could be important?

    How objective was the person? Alert the students to be on the lookout for opinions not backed by evidence.

    How skillful was the person as an observer and writer?

# Chapter 14

**Aim:** to help students understand the complex political, social, and economic problems facing Americans after the Civil War.

## Important Points

1. The Northern victory in the Civil War had preserved the Union and settled the issue of legal slavery, but the task of rebuilding the nation was a long and difficult one.

2. Both North and South had suffered as a result of the war, but because the fighting had taken place mostly in the South, the destruction there was far greater.

3. President Johnson attempted to continue Lincoln's plan for the return of the seceded states to the Union, but he was opposed by Congress.

4. Radical Republicans who controlled Congress were concerned with protecting the rights of the former slaves and with maintaining their control of the government through the Republican party.

5. Support for the Radical Republicans increased as a result of Southern states sending former Confederate officials to Congress and enacting local Black Codes.

6. Radicals blocked the admission of former Confederates to Congress and passed a series of laws to provide civil rights and to protect the freedom of the former slaves.

7. Conflict between President Johnson and Congress led to the President's impeachment, but the Senate voted against conviction.

8. Governments set up in the South during Reconstruction included both black and white citizens. Black people were elected to offices in several states.

9. Terrorist groups developed in the South as some whites used violence against blacks and their white allies to force them out of politics. Groups like the Ku Klux Klan wanted to prevent blacks from voting as well as to destroy the control of the Republican party.

10. Southern Democrats were able to regain control of the Southern states within a decade of the war's end.

11. The last federal troops were removed from the South as part of a political deal between the two major parties which decided the presidential election of 1876.

12. Reconstruction provided the basis for legal freedom and civil rights for black people, but it provided little or no economic aid to the former slaves. Most of them were forced to depend on former slave owners for work.

## Teaching Ideas

● To introduce Chapter 14, ask the class to think of some things suggested by the title of the chapter which might have to be rebuilt after the war. The students will probably concentrate on physical rebuilding in their answers. It might be necessary for you to introduce them to the idea that local governments and other institutions, as well as people's feelings, had to be repaired or healed. As the students read the chapter, have them be on the lookout for examples of rebuilding as well as examples of continued divisions during the Reconstruction period.

● Give the following questions as a problem for students to work out: "How and why were Southern states stronger in Congress after the passage of the Fourteenth Amendment than they had been before the start of the Civil War?" If it is necessary to give them a clue, only suggest that the students compare the provisions of the Amendment with the provisions of the original section in the Constitution on slavery and representation. They should arrive at the answer that following the Amendment, representation was based on all blacks, not three fifths of the slave count, which entitled the Southern states to more members in the House of Representatives.

# Unit 6 – Growth

**Unit aim:**   to increase student understanding of how the United States grew to be one of the most powerful industrial nations in the world.

# Chapter 15

**Aim:**   to help students recognize the many factors which influenced growth in agriculture, business, and industry in the United States' economy after the Civil War.

## Important Points

1. Women worked for the national right to vote without success, but they did win that right in a few states.
2. A system of sharecropping developed in the South as a means of providing labor for agricultural production.

3. Population increases, the growth of the factory system, and improvements in transportation influenced the production of goods and services in the 1870's and 1880's.

4. Many new inventions contributed to a growing economy and made many people's lives easier.

5. The corporation developed as the major form of business organization. Combinations of several corporations developed into trusts.

6. Some industrial leaders developed huge businesses which have continued in existence today.

7. Transcontinental railroads were completed to greatly improve transportation which contributed to the settlement of the Great Plains and to the growth of the cattle industry.

8. New discoveries of gold in the West and the increasing settlement of the Great Plains renewed conflicts between the government and the Indians who occupied the land.

## Teaching Ideas

● To introduce Chapter 15, you might write the words *growth* and *change* on the board, asking the class if they can see any relationship between the words. Hopefully, they will come up with the answer that where there is growth, there is change. Have the students imagine some of the changes that people go through as they grow from childhood to being adults. Recall for them the unit's title of "Growth," and ask if they can think of any situation they have studied so far in which the country was not changing. They will probably feel that the United States has changed continuously. Explain to them that the material of Chapter 15 deals with a period in the nation's history in which the rate and amount of change was unusually great. Have the students read the chapter while looking for examples of growth which brought about changes.

● Railroads are a favorite subject of both children and adults. Some of the activities you might plan involving that subject would be to (1) prepare an exhibit with photos, maps, and models; (2) contact resource people within the community to talk to the class about railroads; and (3) have the students do research on individual railroad companies including their present condition. Using the map on page 298 of the text, you might have students find out the history of the western lines shown and report on their existence today.

● Read to the class sections from the chapter entitled "The Advantages of Poverty" from Andrew Carnegie's book, *The Gospel of Wealth*. Engage the class in a discussion of Carnegie's point of view and its implications.

# *Abilene*

- Have the students read the city profile with the idea of comparing the reasons for its importance to those of the cities studied earlier. Discuss location as a factor of growth. Have the class also consider the reasons why Abilene did not continue to grow into a major city.

- Check local television listings to see if there is a particular western film available which the students might view for the purposes of discussion. Describe the life of cowhands as viewed in American films, television shows, and literature, comparing it with that described in the feature. Discuss with the class the possible reasons why we have perpetuated such a different picture from the reality of the cowhand's life.

# *Chapter 16*

**Aim:** to help students understand the economic, political, and social changes which accompanied economic growth in the United States.

## Important Points

1. Some of the changes in the United States as a result of economic growth were beneficial, others were harmful.
2. The idea of laissez-faire came increasingly under attack as some people called for government regulation of corporate monopolies and trusts.
3. Important changes developed in the way goods were bought and sold, including the development of chain and department stores and mail order businesses.
4. Increasing food production and falling prices created serious problems for American farmers.
5. Several groups like the Grange and the Farmers' Alliance were organized to help farmers deal with their problems.
6. While the Interstate Commerce Act was passed in an attempt to regulate railroads, it had little immediate effect because of the interpretation of the law by the courts.
7. The development of large companies created new problems for workers, and some of them attempted to solve their job problems by forming labor unions.
8. The National Labor Union and the Knights of Labor were attempts to organize all workers. Public opinion, the actions of the government, and actions by employers reduced their effectiveness.

9. The American Federation of Labor was created as a union of skilled workers.
10. A Civil Service Commission was created by the Pendleton Act in an effort to reform the spoils system.
11. Congress passed legislation to exclude Chinese people from immigration to the United States. It was part of a widespread prejudice against Asians.
12. Laws were passed to improve the conditions of American Indians, but they resulted in as much harm as good.

## Teaching Ideas

● To introduce Chapter 16, call attention to its title, "New Ideas, New Roles." Ask if anyone can define the word *role*, aiming at the definition of it as the way a person lives and acts, or is expected to live and act, as defined by his or her job or social status. Remind the class of the main points of Chapter 15 which were growth and change. Ask the students if they can think of any relationship between "growth and change" and "new ideas and new roles." Allow the students to come to some conclusions on these relationships before assigning Chapter 16. In it, they will learn how the people of the United States reacted to the growth and change discussed in Chapter 15.

● Have two or three students do research and report to the class on a department or chain store in the community. Some of the facts they should determine could include (1) when the store was built, (2) what merchandise is offered, and (3) how many other stores are owned by the same company.

● Present the AMERICA IS sound filmstrip entitled "Land of Opportunity."

● In working with the feature "Visual Evidence," you might want to expand upon the text presentation by gathering a collection of pictures, paintings, and photographs of the same or similar subjects to show to the class. Discuss the evidence given as well as the limitations inherent in each type. Before the development of photography, for example, artists had to rely upon memory to reconstruct scenes unless the subjects were still. In any kind of visual evidence, the influence of the person who chose the subject is important.

# Chapter 17

**Aim:**  to help students relate factors of increasing industrial power in the United States to government policy of overseas expansion at the turn of the century.

## Important Points

1. In the 1890's, the United States became the world's leading industrial nation.
2. Dissatisfaction with the policies of the federal government led some people to create the National People's party in 1892.
3. The members of the National People's party, or Populists, were successful in electing people to Congress and in controlling the legislatures in several states in the early 1890's.
4. Many of the ideas of the Populists were adopted by the other major political parties.
5. Most of the civil rights gained by black Americans at the end of the Civil War were lost to them by the 1890's. Reasons for this included local laws which disenfranchised black voters, the *Plessy v. Ferguson* decision of the Supreme Court, and the establishment of segregation by law in most southern states.
6. Black leaders held differing views on the best ways to protect and promote the interests of black citizens in the United States. Booker T. Washington and W. E. B. DuBois were leading advocates of differing main views.
7. The United States gained control of overseas territories including Puerto Rico, the Philippines, and Guam as a result of the Spanish-American War.
8. In some of these territories, the people were opposed to rule by the United States.

## Teaching Ideas

● You might introduce Chapter 17 by holding a brief oral review of Chapters 15 and 16, bringing out those points on America's internal growth which underlie the country's ability to assume a world position. Assign Chapter 17, pointing out that in reading it students will learn about some events outside the country as well as more about conditions and events within the United States.

● Hold a class discussion comparing the laws disenfranchising black voters and the *Plessy v. Ferguson* decision with the Fourteenth and Fifteenth Amendments. It is important that students have some understanding of the difference between the spirit of the law and the word, or letter, of the law. Have them consider the idea that a court might find such laws as the grandfather clauses not in violation of the Fifteenth Amendment since the wording of the law was not based on color, although its practical effect was to exclude blacks from voting. You might read through the *Plessy v. Ferguson* decision and Justice Harlan's dissenting opinion and share appropriate sections with the class in the course of their discussion.

- In working with the feature "Imperialism," have the students read carefully the reasons McKinley gave for taking over the Philippines. Help them to examine the assumptions behind McKinley's reasoning. For further study, assign investigations of the views of Americans like Jane Addams or Andrew Carnegie who were opposed to the Philippine takeover.

# Chapter 18

**Aim:** to help students understand the American people's response to the increasing industrialization and urbanization of American life in the early 1900's.

## Important Points

1. Increased industrialization brought more conveniences and greater opportunities to many Americans in the early twentieth century.
2. Increased industrialization was the result of the growing use of machinery to do work which had previously been done by hand or animal power.
3. A number of leisure time activities developed in American culture as a result of increased free time.
4. A major reform movement took place in the United States early in the twentieth century which is called the Progressive Era.
5. Progressive Era reformers worked at local, state, and federal levels of government.
6. Political reforms of the period included new types of city government, changes in the election of senators to Congress, and an increased voice for citizens in the operation of government.
7. Economic changes in the Progressive Era included regulation of railroads and trusts, trustbusting, banking reform, and the introduction of the income tax. All of these represented the federal government's increasing involvement in the country's economy.
8. Several groups of people in the United States did not benefit from the Progressive movement, including blacks, Mexican Americans, and the rural poor.

## Teaching Ideas

- Introduce the chapter with a brief class discussion of the term *era* as a period of time set off or typified by some important person, event, or movement. Using the chapter's title as a reference point, have the class consider their ideas of "progress." Ask them if other events, attitudes, or movements studied in American history so far also suggest progress in some areas. It is important for students to understand that the period of history studied in Chapter 18 is called the Progressive Era because of common agreement among historians and that other periods in our history could also use that title.

- Use the study of the Progressive Era to have students reconsider the general issue of reform in United States history. Have them identify each of the reform periods studied prior to the Progressive movement. Identify the major problems which concerned the reformers. Ask students what areas of American life might concern them as reformers today.

- If available, bring some recordings of Sousa, Joplin, and Herbert music to class. The class could listen to the music and then hold a discussion on the various types of music which can be popular during the same time period.

# Chicago

- Read Carl Sandburg's poem "Chicago" to the class. After they have read the city profile, ask them to decide if Sandburg's poem is an accurate description of their own feelings about the city. You might have them locate other poems or songs about different American cities for general class discussion.

# Unit 7 – Conflict

**Unit aim:**  to help students gain insight into the contributing factors which led to the major role played by the United States today in world affairs.

# Chapter 19

**Aim:**  to help students understand how the United States became involved in World War I and how the nation's economy was altered to meet its military needs.

## Important Points

1. United States trade interests in China led to the government's Open Door Policy in an effort to prevent colonial powers from excluding the United States from participation in China's trade.

2. The United States and other countries sent troops to China to put down the Boxer Rebellion which was an attempt by some Chinese to rid their country of outsiders.

3. United States influence in the peace treaty concluding the war between Japan and Russia and discrimination against people of Japanese ancestry in the United States resulted in poor relations between America and Japan.

4. The United States aided the overthrow of Colombian control in Panama and signed an agreement with the newly independent country for building a canal through the isthmus.

5. The Panama Canal, a major engineering achievement, was opened to the ships of all nations.

6. Under the Roosevelt Corollary to the Monroe Doctrine, the United States acted as a police power in the Western Hemisphere.

7. When war broke out in Europe, the United States acted to protect the rights it claimed as a neutral nation.

8. Germany's submarine warfare against all ships bound for Allied nations and Germany's efforts to get the support of Mexico against the United States led the United States to declare war on Germany on April 2, 1917. From the outbreak of war in Europe, most Americans had shown sympathy for the Allied nations.

9. The United States mobilized its economic resources on the home front to support its military forces and to supply the Allies.

10. Opportunities for women and minority groups expanded as a result of the wartime economy. These people played a significant role in the war effort, including maintaining war supplies production.

11. President Wilson's plan for peace, called the Fourteen Points, was accepted by the defeated Germans but only partly accepted by the victorious Allies.

12. The Senate of the United States refused to ratify the Treaty of Versailles mostly because it included the establishment of the League of Nations.


## Teaching Ideas

● Work with the class to develop a short list of the events which led to increased involvement of the United States in foreign affairs. The list should include general items such as trade, missionary activity, and the desire for national defense. It may include more specific items such as the Spanish-American War and the possession of overseas territories. Ask the class to evaluate the list according to which items on it suggest that the United States acted out of national self-interest (to provide for defense and promote independence) and which suggest individual or group ideals. Students should realize that a combination of motives determine the actions of most nations.

- The Panama Canal was one of the technological wonders of its day. An exercise on the Canal can be used to show students how technology is used to solve some problems. After students have read the material in the text, ask them to draw up a list of the problems which had to be solved before the Canal could be built. The teacher may need to suggest some problems so that the list will include at least the following:

    planning a canal in which ships need to be raised over a mountain range and lowered on the other side

    digging a canal through mountains and jungle

    maintaining water in a canal higher than sea level

    dealing with problems of sanitation and disease control for the work crews

Divide the class into teams to study each of the problems and report to the class. Diagrams, models, or other pictorial aids will help students gain fuller understanding of the technology involved in building the Canal.

# Detroit

- Use the city profile on Detroit as a means of exploring the influence of the automobile on American life-styles. Have mimeographed sheets of paper ready with three subject headings: Work, City Planning, and Recreation. Leave space under each heading for the students to make lists of as many aspects of automobile influence on the subject as they can. You may want to add more headings and use this as a homework assignment. Make it clear that the students can list problems as well as benefits.

- If possible, take the class on a field trip to visit an assembly line in operation. An automobile assembly line would be most relevant to the chapter and city profile studies, but visiting any assembly line will enhance the students' understanding of the benefits and problems in this type of production.

# Chapter 20

**Aim:** to help students understand the social, political, and economic changes in American life following World War I.

## Important Points

1. New forms of entertainment developed in the years after the war including radio, jazz music, and movies.
2. With the Eighteenth Amendment, prohibition became the law of the land. Because of widespread opposition to prohibition, the government was largely unsuccessful in enforcing the law.
3. Significant advances were made in health care and education during the 1920's.
4. Women won the right to vote in national elections with the ratification of the Nineteenth Amendment in 1920.
5. Legislation was passed making all Indians citizens who were not already citizens. Some Indian groups opposed the law without success.
6. Mexican Americans and blacks who had served in the armed forces during World War I made strong efforts to improve their lives and the lives of their families after the end of the war.
7. Marcus Garvey's Universal Negro Improvement Association encouraged black people to have pride and dignity in being black and to look to Africa to strengthen their pride in their background.
8. Conflicts over strikes, fear of communism, and the active opposition of business leaders weakened labor unions.
9. Fear of communism after the Russian Revolution of 1917 led to the Red Scare in which people known or suspected of being Communists were arrested or deported.
10. New immigration laws were passed aimed at limiting immigration from southern and eastern Europe and favoring immigration from northern and western Europe.
11. There was a revival of the Ku Klux Klan which declared itself against Catholics, Jews, blacks, Asians, Asian Americans, and immigrants.
12. The economy of the United States expanded rapidly in the 1920's although there was difficulty in some industries and in farming.

## Teaching Ideas

- Collect pictures and recordings of the music of the 1920's. Put them together into an audiovisual presentation which clearly shows different life-styles of the 1920's. Include jazz, flappers, fast automobiles, advertisements for new products, flagpole sitting, pictures of Americans at work in everyday life, religious music and other popular songs, the Women's Christian Temperance Union, the Ku Klux Klan, and so on. Use the presentation as an introduction to the chapter and a discussion of "the real 1920's." The students should realize that all views are part of the reality of the twenties.

● There are many recordings of radio programs from the 1920's available. Play some of these for the class and have students compare them with the radio programs of today. Have a group of students find out how early radio programs were technically produced, especially sound effects, and work with them to develop a program for the class. They can either do a program as if the classroom were the studio or record their program elsewhere and play it for the class. Their program should reflect life, news, sports, and music of the 1920's.

● Write the topics Red Scare, Immigration Laws, and Ku Klux Klan on the board. Ask the class to discuss what the three have in common, what their existence tells us about this era, why people supported them, and the aim of each. Have the students evaluate the degree to which each fits in with the national ideals of liberty, equality, and democracy.

● Have the students interview grandparents, great grandparents, and other relatives or friends of the family who remember the 1920's. The entire class can work together to develop questions to be covered in the interviews. A tape recording of a good interview from a television or radio program can be played for the class to serve as a model for their own project. Their interviews could also be recorded. The interviewers should make a report to the class which can be used to compare information from these firsthand accounts to the text or other written material.

# Chapter 21

**Aim:** to help students relate the economic effects of the depression of the 1930's to the changed relationship between government and business.

## Important Points

1. The economic growth of the 1920's ended with a severe depression that began in 1929.
2. The stock market crash in 1929 was the result of over-speculation and contributed to the start of the depression.

3. The causes of the depression were the result of troubles with both the national and international economies and had been building for some time.

4. President Hoover believed that business and state governments should help themselves during the depression. He did not favor major federal involvement in the economy to end the depression.

5. President Roosevelt believed that the federal government should take a major role in ending the depression. His plan, the New Deal, involved federal assistance to agriculture, business, and industry, and to individuals through relief programs.

6. Roosevelt's Good Neighbor Policy toward Latin America represented a new approach to foreign affairs in the Western Hemisphere.

7. The New Deal included reform measures as well as measures for recovery and relief.

8. The Indian Reorganization Act of 1934 attempted to offset some of the negative influence of the Dawes Act and the Indian Citizenship Act.

9. Conflict developed between the executive and judicial branches of the federal government over the constitutionality of some New Deal legislation.

10. The depression seriously affected countries all over the world and aided the rise of military dictatorships in some of them.

## Teaching Ideas

● Devote some time to a discussion of the word *depression* and the conditions which exist when there is a depression before the students read the chapter. Have them recall previous depressions mentioned in the text, checking the index if necessary. The students should realize that the causes of depressions are not always the same but that certain results like severe unemployment characterize periods of economic depression.

● Some historians have called the New Deal an extension of the Progressive Movement. Make a chart on the board, with the students supplying the information to complete it, that compares the two periods. Label one column *Progressive Movement* and the other *New Deal*. Have students provide the following information:

> political party in control of the presidency
> condition of the economy at the start of the movement
> laws passed concerning business
> laws passed concerning banks
> laws passed concerning farmers
> foreign affairs

- There are many songs, poems, and books about the lives of the people during the depression. Gather a collection of these materials for the use of the class. Hopefully, this will give students a better understanding of the psychological impact of the depression upon the American people. Have them compare the material with that of other periods which they have studied.

- Present the AMERICA IS sound filmstrip entitled "Old Dusty Road."

- In working with the feature "Political Cartoons," have the students bring in current political cartoons. Discuss with them the concerns of the artist as reflected in the work. Have them notice, also, how often the artist uses everyday happenings to have a common reference to make a point. Have the students develop political cartoons of their own which reflect current issues. You might also ask them to make a political cartoon reflecting concern about some historical issue which they have studied.

# Muncie

- After the class has read and discussed the city profile, organize the students for a project to study their community during the same period. Students should be divided into teams with each responsible for gathering material on some aspect of life in the community. This can be a valuable exercise to acquaint students with what sources are available for information on the history of the community. One group of students can be given the responsibility of organizing the material into an orderly form for study and discussion. Compare the material with the Muncie profile. If the students have success in gathering and presenting a great deal of community information, it might be of interest to a local newspaper or radio station.

# Chapter 22

**Aim:**  to help students understand the factors which contributed to the involvement of the United States in a second world war.

## Important Points

1. During the worldwide depression of the 1930's, military dictatorships were established in Italy, Japan, and Germany.

2. Japan, Italy, and Germany sought to recover from the depression and to increase the prestige and power of their countries by taking over the lands of other nations.

3. Because of the people's preoccupation with the depression and feelings about World War I, the United States government attempted to avoid international conflicts.

4. Americans began to shift their positions about European involvement as the Axis countries took over more and more territory from others.

5. When World War II began, President Roosevelt proposed the Lend-Lease Act as a way to avoid breaking United States laws against involvement in the European conflict.

6. As a result of the Japanese attack on Pearl Harbor on December 7, 1941, the United States entered the war against the Axis powers.

7. The Atlantic Charter set forth the war aims of the United States and Britain.

8. Americans mobilized to increase the size of the armed forces and to gear the economy toward the production of war materials. Women and minorities were again important to both the armed forces and to war production at home.

9. Because of prejudice and fear, persons of Japanese ancestry living on the West Coast were taken from their homes and placed in inland relocation camps during the later part of the war. Many of them were American citizens.

10. Along with the Soviet Union and Britain, and to a lesser extent France, the United States played a major part in the war in Africa and Europe. In the Pacific, the United States provided the majority of the forces and supplies.

11. After atomic bombs were dropped by the United States on two Japanese cities, Japan surrendered in September, 1945, and the war ended.

## Teaching Ideas

- Have the students compare several things about the United States at the start of World War I and the start of World War II including the following:

    population

    condition of the economy

    foreign affairs

    size of the armed forces

    positions held economically and socially by women and minority groups

After the comparisons have been developed, ask students to write down several generalizations about the material. This should help the students realize that while the United States was involved in two world wars within a relatively short period of time, the conditions within the country and its relations with other nations were often quite different from one period to the next.

- There was great controversy over the war crimes trials held by the Allies after the war. One of the concerns was that, in the future, leaders of any defeated country could be tried for war crimes by the victorious country. Have the class debate the issue after further researching the trials of German and Japanese leaders and the charges made against them.

# *Los Angeles*

- Use the pictures which appear in the text and other pictures of Los Angeles with comparable pictures of New York and Philadelphia to give students another example of the value and use of visuals as historical evidence. Have the students study the pictures and identify those which clearly depict Los Angeles. Ask them which city is the youngest in terms of metropolitan growth and what clues they found in the pictures leading them to choose Los Angeles. The development of the automobile before the major growth of Los Angeles will be reflected in wider streets, the number of houses with garages, freeways, and so on.

- Use the pictures mentioned above to guide the class in a discussion of the differences between Los Angeles and other United States cities because of location. Among the things to be identified are the availability of space in Los Angeles compared to the eastern cities, the structure of houses, vegetation, and the more outdoor character of the life reflected in the pictures.

- By this time, your students may want to write a city profile for themselves. If your community has a good volume of local history reference material available, the students might select some particular period of five or ten years in their own city's history to profile. If not, they could select a city they have studied and write a current profile for it, from 1970 or 1975 to the present. Sources of current information would include the city's historical society, City Clerk's office, Chamber of Commerce, travel agency brochures, airline magazines, weekly or monthly news magazines, and so on. The class should be divided into groups for working on the profile either by subject area to be researched, such as jobs and industry, or by sources to be investigated or contacted. The final profile should be duplicated so that each member of the class has a take-home copy.

# Unit 8 – Challenge

**Unit aim:** to present students with the various challenges facing the people of a complex, free society in a rapidly changing world.

# Chapter 23

**Aim:** to show the changes in domestic and foreign policies resulting from the United States' position as a world power following the war.

## Important Points

1. After World War II, the United States became a charter member of the United Nations, believing a return to isolationism was not possible.
2. Competition developed between the United States and the Soviet Union after the war as each attempted to influence governments of many newly independent countries around the world. This competition became known as the cold war.
3. Inflation became a major problem for Americans in the peacetime economy following World War II.
4. With the Fair Deal, President Truman attempted to continue and improve the programs of the New Deal. Only a few of his plans were enacted by law.
5. The Marshall Plan, or European Recovery Act, was established to help countries in Europe recover from the destruction of the war.
6. The United States joined other western countries in a North Atlantic Treaty Organization for collective security against possible attack from the Soviet Union.
7. The success of the Communists in winning control of China changed America's attitude toward the defeated Japanese.
8. The United States became involved in war in Asia when North Korea attacked South Korea in 1950.
9. United States military involvement in Asia continued as military aid was given to South Vietnam to fight against Communist influence.

10. Senator Joseph McCarthy's claims of Communist influence in the making of America's foreign policy and in many parts of government and the military heightened the fear of communism, affecting domestic politics.

11. The Supreme Court reversed the position on segregation it had established in *Plessy v. Ferguson* in 1896. In the case of *Brown v. Board of Education of Topeka* in 1954, the Court held that segregation based on race was unconstitutional.

12. The rapid development of large numbers of atomic weapons by the Soviet Union and the United States created a serious problem for world peace.

13. The United States was a prosperous country in 1960, but millions of Americans did not share in that prosperity.

## Teaching Ideas

● In preparation for studying the cold war, assign groups of students to make the following reports:

a brief history of Russia before 1917

a brief report on the Communist revolution in Russia

a brief history of the Soviet Union to 1960

comparison in terms of size, population, resources, and production, between the United States and the Soviet Union

After the reports have been given, hold a discussion on the reasons for each nation distrusting the other. Have the class evaluate each reason for its validity. If possible, conclude this activity by reading to the class the excerpt from Alexis de Tocqueville's writings in the nineteenth century in which he predicts competition between the United States and Russia.

● Provide students with two outline maps of the world. Instruct them to complete one showing the major political divisions in the world in 1930 and the other showing the major divisions in 1960. Have the students indicate in some way the alignments of nations with the Soviet Union, the United States, or as neutrals on the 1960 map.

● The text of the Supreme Court decision in *Brown v. Board of Education of Topeka* is relatively straightforward and easy to understand. Read to the class those parts of it which deal directly with the decision of the Court about separate but equal facilities. Help them discuss various points in the decision to make sure that they understand the reasoning of the Court.

● In working with the feature "Television," secure copies of the local newspaper TV guide. Give a copy to each student after the class has read the feature. Ask students to use the material and their knowledge of TV programing to answer the following questions:

> During what hours do you generally watch television?

> How many programs are shown during those hours?

> How many programs do you watch among those listed in the guide?

> Which of the programs do you consider educational?

> Would you watch more TV if allowed to do so?

> How, if at all, do you think TV influences people's ideas, habits, or life-styles?

Use the students' answers as a basis for discussion on the influence of television. In the process, evaluate TV as an educational device and as a form of entertainment.

# Chapter 24

**Aim:** to help students recognize Americans' increased social awareness in the 1960's which altered the patterns of American life.

## Important Points

1. President Kennedy's administration was active in pressing for civil rights of minority groups, but Congress did not pass much of the New Frontier program as legislation.
2. President Kennedy continued the efforts of other Presidents in foreign affairs aimed at stopping the growth of communism.
3. The Cuban missile crisis posed the most serious threat of nuclear war since the development of the atomic bomb. It was resolved when Russia withdrew its missiles from Cuba.
4. There were many civil rights demonstrations in the 1960's with the largest civil rights demonstration in American history taking place in 1963 when more than 200,000 people marched on Washington.
5. Violence grew out of the civil rights movements as people opposed to civil rights for blacks attempted to halt demonstrations through intimidation and murder.
6. President Kennedy was assassinated in 1963, and Lyndon Johnson became the President of the United States.
7. President Johnson was successful in having Congress pass laws for civil rights and a war on poverty.

8. The Civil Rights Act of 1964 was an important piece of legislation forbidding discrimination against anyone using public services or involved in a program using federal funds.

9. Mexican Americans continued to press for full civil rights and for improved economic conditions.

10. The war in Vietnam seriously divided the American people and caused considerable opposition to the Johnson administration.

11. The methods used by many young people to express their opposition to discrimination, war, pollution, and other aspects of American life led to a social situation called by some a "generation gap."

12. Efforts of blacks to gain full rights led to a change in focus from ending segregation to full equality in education, jobs, and civil rights. The "black power" movement represented the efforts of blacks to have a greater voice in making decisions about their communities.

13. Martin Luther King, Jr., leader of many black civil rights movements, was assassinated in 1968.

## Teaching Ideas

● To introduce Chapter 24, give to, or get from, the students a definition of the word *discontent* which appears in the chapter title. Ask the students about the changes people might try to make when they are discontented or dissatisfied with something. Make sure that the class understands that not all Americans were discontented in the period studied, nor were those who advocated changes necessarily dissatisfied all of the time. Chapter 24 deals with some of the major issues that Americans faced in the 1960's.

● Have the class develop a chart for display listing all of the laws mentioned in the text which were passed in the 1950's and 1960's to end discrimination. Next to the title of each law, list the specific subject with which the law dealt, such as voting or housing, and which group or groups were directly benefited. This should help students deal more effectively with the many laws passed during this period.

● Write the word *riot* on the board and ask for a definition. When a clear definition has been secured which you feel the students understand, ask why riots take place. List the reasons given by students and add any you think necessary. Then list the major riots in American history including the tarring and feathering of loyalist tax officials, draft riots of the Civil War period, bank failures of the late 1920's, and so on. When these have been discussed, add the riots of the

1960's. Lead the class in an exploration of the ways in which all the riots were similar and the ways in which they differed from one another.

- In working with the feature "I Have a Dream," secure recordings of some of King's speeches if possible. Play them for the class and have the students analyze King as a speaker and the effectiveness of his speeches.

- Present the AMERICA IS sound filmstrip entitled "Walking for My Children."

# Houston

- Provide students with information on the growth of Houston, Chicago, New York, and Washington, D. C., since World War II. Houston grew much faster than the other cities during this period. If possible, show slides or pictures of scenes in present-day Houston, asking the students to identify features which reflect this growth.

- There are ten large cities profiled in the text. Make lists of the cities on the board under the appropriate headings of North, East, South, and West. Discuss the growth of each of the cities and when that growth took place. Lead the class in a discussion of the reasons for the later growth of southern cities which are continuing to grow at a greater pace today.

# Chapter 25

**Aim:** to help students recognize that American attitudes, policies, and institutions change and that this is the challenge facing all Americans.

## Important Points

1. In 1969, American astronauts became the first humans to land on the moon.
2. Under President Nixon's policy of Vietnamization, American soldiers began returning from the war in Vietnam. In 1973, an armistice was signed in which the United States agreed to withdraw all of its troops.
3. The conflict between Arabs and Israelis in the Middle East increased world tensions and the possibility of general war.

4. The Nixon administration sought to improve relations with China and the Soviet Union. Relations with Communist China were established for the first time.

5. President Nixon's New Federalism sought to reduce the role of the federal government in the economy and in decisions about the use of tax revenues.

6. Busing students from one neighborhood to another to end segregation in schools became an issue of strong disagreement among Americans as more and more school districts were ordered to comply with the ruling of the Supreme Court in *Brown v. Board of Education of Topeka*.

7. During the 1960's and 1970's, women's groups became more active in working for better economic conditions and legal equality.

8. The Twenty-sixth Amendment was added to the Constitution in 1971, lowering the voting age in federal elections to eighteen years.

9. President Nixon was reelected in 1972 by a wide margin. Soon after the election, the American people began to learn of a political scandal, known as Watergate, involving members of the President's staff.

10. During the investigation of Watergate, Vice-President Agnew resigned from office while being investigated on income tax violation charges.

11. The Judicial Committee of the House of Representatives approved three articles of impeachment against President Nixon because of Watergate charges. As a result of public displeasure and loss of support, President Nixon resigned before impeachment proceedings were concluded.

12. Gerald Ford, picked to replace Spiro Agnew as the Vice-President, became the new President. He pardoned Nixon for any crimes the President might have committed while in office.

13. President Ford, the first President not elected to either the vice-presidency or the presidency, attempted to continue the programs of the Nixon administration.

14. In 1976, the United States celebrated the two hundredth birthday of the signing of the Declaration of Independence.

## Teaching Ideas

● Engage the class in a discussion of the relative difficulty of studying the history of the recent past because of the difficulty of identifying trends that have, or will have, long-range influences. You might help to clarify the discussion with a question like, "Would the long-range effects of slavery have been clearer to the history student of 1870 or 1970?" They should see that a student in 1870 would not be able to see the effects of a Reconstruction policy which left blacks without land or the political power to protect their freedom. When you think that the class clearly understands the problems of studying the recent past, assign the reading of Chapter 25. The class should understand that Chapter 25 deals with the recent past and that long-range results of the period cannot be clearly known, part of the challenge facing all Americans.

- After the students have read the chapter, help them develop a list of the challenges they consider most important in American life today. Use this as a base for considering some possible long-range effects of recent government actions and events.

- Assign different groups of students the task of locating and reporting on the United States' supply of various raw materials such as iron ore, coal, oil, and copper. Have the students find out from atlases and other sources how much of each material is produced in this country, how much is imported, and the estimated future supply of each material within the United States. After each group has reported its findings, hold a discussion encouraging the students to make generalizations about the possible long-range trends in our economy and in trade with other countries based on the information acquired.

# Chapter in Perspective Answers

## Chapter 1

### Identify

Minimum answers in boldface type; extended answers in regular type.

*Americans*   **term correctly used to refer to all people living in North and South America,** frequently used by citizens of the United States to refer only to themselves.

*Incas*   **a South American Indian people who had developed a high level of civilization prior to the arrival of Europeans in America.** Their large empire in the Andes Mountains was conquered and destroyed by the Spanish in the sixteenth century.

*Aztecs*   **a North American Indian people whose highly developed empire in the valley of Mexico** was also conquered and destroyed by the Spanish.

### Explain

*culture*   **the ways of life of a group of people.** Culture includes a group's art, religion, agriculture, language, and customs.

*environment*   **the surrounding conditions of a time and place** which include physical, such as the land and climate, as well as social conditions.

*domesticated*   **tamed, or brought into use by humans.** Both animals and plants are domesticated for use by humans. The Indians of America, for example, domesticated more than eighty different plants.

### Check Your Memory of the Facts

1. *When did the first people arrive in the American continents?*   **more than twelve to fifteen thousand years ago.**
2. *From what continent did the first people come who entered the Americas?*   **probably from Asia,** crossing the Bering Straits and spreading throughout North and South America.
3. *When did Europeans and Africans first arrive in the Americas?*   **as settlers, in the sixteenth century.**
4. *What foods grown by the early inhabitants of America are still cultivated today?*   corn, potatoes, beans, pumpkins, tomatoes, squash, peanuts, peppers, avocados, pineapples, chocolate, vanilla.

5. *Other than foods, what developments of these early inhabitants are still in use?* Other developments of the Indians still in use include cotton, rubber, chicle, tobacco, many medicines, hammocks, canoes, toboggans, ponchos, designs for jewelry, pottery, baskets, and cloth, and names for places, foods, animals, and trees.

6. *Where were the empires of the Incas and the Aztecs located?* **The Inca empire was located in the Andes Mountains area of South America** in present-day Peru. **The Aztec empire was located in what is now Mexico;** Tenochtitlán, its capital, was built where Mexico City is today.

7. *In general, what were relations like between the Indians and the settlers?* **Generally, relations between the Indians and the settlers were poor.** Early settlers had found the Indians to be friendly toward them. As more settlers arrived, conflicts and wars, especially over land, were more common.

## Check Your Understanding of the Ideas

1. *Is it correct to use the term American to refer only to citizens of the United States? Explain.* No. All the people living in North and South America are correctly called Americans. However, by custom, the term is used to refer to citizens of the United States. People from the United States frequently refer to those living in Central and South America as Latin Americans or South Americans. South Americans often refer to people living in North America as North Americans.

2. *How did the Indians and the Europeans differ in the way they felt about the land?* Indians believed that the land was there for everyone to use. Europeans felt that individuals should own the land. According to the Europeans, other persons could not use the land owned by another without permission.

3. *What was the long-range influence of the English on the Indians of North America?* Answers will vary but should indicate an understanding of loss of land and lives and disruption of culture.

4. *Why were various Indian groups different in their ways of living?* Different groups of Indians adapted to widely different environments throughout the Americas.

# Chapter 2

## Identify

*New World*   **a term referring to the Western Hemisphere.**
*Crusades*   **a series of religious wars fought between Christians and Muslims** in the Middle East from 1100 to about 1250.

*Columbus*   **an Italian navigator and mapmaker who led, for Spain, an expedition to the New World in 1492.** He landed on an island in the Bahamas, and because he thought he was in India, he called the people there Indians.

*Old World*   **a term referring to the Eastern Hemisphere,** especially Europe.

*Reformation*   **a time of religious changes and conflicts in Europe.**

*Española*   **the island where the Spanish established their first settlement in the New World.** The island today is made up of the countries of Haiti and the Dominican Republic.

## Explain

*monopoly*   **the exclusive control of trade.** For example, the merchants of Venice, Italy, had a monopoly of trade with the Muslims, and King Henry of France granted fur monopolies to traders in the lands claimed by France in the New World.

*colonies*   **settlements started by a country in another land.**

*armada*   **a fleet of warships.**

## Check Your Memory of the Facts

1.  *Who were the first Europeans to visit North America?*   **The Vikings** visited the New World five hundred years before Columbus.

2.  *Why did Europeans want to travel to Asia?*   **Europeans wanted to trade directly with the peoples of India, China, and Southeast Asia** to avoid the Venetian monopoly.

3.  *What country supported Christopher Columbus in his search for a water route to the Far East?*   **Spain.**

4.  *What happened to Indians as a result of the Spanish conquests in Peru and Mexico?*   **The great Indian empires were destroyed,** and the people were forced to work in mines and fields. They were also converted to the Catholic religion. Most died from overwork and disease.

5.  *Why did people leave their homes to come to the New World?*   **People came to the New World because of a desire to improve their ways of life, to practice their religion freely, to escape from the rule of kings and nobles, or from a spirit of adventure and ambition.**

6.  *What areas in the New World came under the control of the Spanish? Of the French? Of the English?*   **The Spanish controlled the West Indies, much of South and Central America, the southwestern part of North America, and Florida. The French controlled the land around the Great Lakes, Nova Scotia, and the Mississippi**

Valley. The English controlled the land of the Atlantic Coast of North America north of Spanish Florida.

## Check Your Understanding of the Ideas

1. *What developments in Europe and the East led to Columbus' voyage to the New World?* Better sailing ships and instruments were developed, making it possible to sail out of sight of land.
2. *How did Columbus' plan for reaching the East differ from that of the Portuguese?* The Portuguese wanted to reach India and the East by sailing around Africa. Columbus believed that he could reach India by sailing directly west from Europe.
3. *How did the French and Spanish differ in their treatment of the Indians?* The French made friends with many groups of Indians for the purpose of trading in furs and other goods and sometimes joined them as allies in war against English settlers and Iroquois Indians. The Spaniards ruled the Indians, directing their work, teaching them religion, and preventing their revolt.
4. *Would it be correct to say that the arrival of Columbus in America was a mistake? Why?* Yes. Columbus did not know that there was any land between Europe and Asia and thought that China was only 2400 miles to the west of Europe.
5. *What does the European treatment of Indians and the enslavement of Africans tell us about the attitudes Europeans had toward people of different races and religions?* Answers will vary. Europeans believed that they, their religions, and their cultures were superior.

# Chapter 3

## Identify

*London Company* **the Virginia Company of London, a joint stock company organized to set up a colony** in the southern part of the land in America claimed by England. It was made up mostly of nobles and wealthy merchants who hoped to make large profits in the New World.

*Captain John Smith* **leader of the Jamestown colony.**

*Powhatan* **powerful chief of the Algonquin Indians of Virginia at the time of the founding of the Jamestown colony.** Because Powhatan was willing to trade food for other items with settlers, the colony was able to survive.

*House of Burgesses* **the legislature elected by the people of the Virginia colony. Established in 1619, it was a representative form of government.**

*Pilgrims*  **settlers who established the colony of Plymouth.** They had been badly treated in England because of their religious beliefs.

*Separatists*  **the Pilgrims who desired to separate themselves from the Church of England.**

*Mayflower Compact*  **a written agreement made among the Pilgrims themselves to set up a government in the new land.**

*Puritans*  **people who wanted to improve or purify the Church of England. Some of them settled the Massachusetts Bay Colony.** They wished to establish a model community, an example of the type of religious and civil society in which they believed.

# Explain

*joint stock company*  **an organization set up to provide money for starting colonies.** The people who bought shares of stock in the company were then to receive a part of any profits made by the colonies.

*charter*  **an official paper allowing people to settle in a certain region and giving them the right to establish a government there.**

*legislature*  **the body of people who make laws in a government.** The House of Burgesses, for instance, was the legislature for the Virginia colony.

*compact*  **an agreement.**

*proprietors*  **rich nobles who owned colonies in America.**

# Check Your Memory of the Facts

1. *Why did the English settle the Atlantic Coast of North America instead of farther south?*  **It was the only land left for the English to settle.** Spain controlled lands in the Caribbean, Central and South America, and southwestern North America. The French controlled the land around the Great Lakes and the Mississippi Valley.

2. *When did the English settlements along the coast of North America begin?*  **The first English attempts to start colonies in North America in the 1580's failed. The first successful English colony was Jamestown, 1607.** Many successful colonies were later founded.

3. *What advantages did England expect to gain from its colonies?*  **England expected the colonies to send raw materials like tobacco and tall pine trees for ships' masts to England. In return, the colonists would buy manufactured goods made in England.** The colonies would also be a place for people seeking new opportunities outside of England like freedom of worship, land, and work.

4. *What part did John Smith play in the success of the settlement at Jamestown?*  **Smith played the part of a firm leader whose skill at trading helped the colonists survive the first winter.**

5. *How did the Indians help in the successful start of the colonies of Jamestown and Plymouth?* **The Algonquin Indians of Virginia traded food and land with Jamestown settlers. Squanto, a Pawtucket Indian, showed the people of Plymouth how to live in the wilderness.**

6. *What religious groups played a part in the establishment of the English colonies?* **Pilgrims (Separatists), Puritans and other members of the Church of England, Quakers, other Protestant groups, Jews, and Catholics** all played a part in establishing the English colonies.

## Check Your Understanding of the Ideas

1. *In what ways did the English and Spanish colonies differ?* The Spanish controlled their colonies using few of their own people. Their colonies were mainly trading posts and missions. The English colonies were considered overseas extensions of England settled by large numbers of people who brought their animals, seeds, household goods, ways of life, and laws with them.

2. *What is the importance of the Mayflower Compact? Why did the Pilgrims agree to obey it?* The Mayflower Compact was important because it established a government agreed to by the Pilgrims and became the basis of government in the Plymouth colony. The people agreed to the compact to avoid trouble among themselves when they began their colony.

3. *What was the Puritan attitude toward religious freedom?* The Puritans forced new settlers to practice Puritanism. They hoped to keep the Massachusetts government in the hands of a small group of Puritan leaders. The people were to worship and live according to the ideas of these leaders.

4. *How did royal colonies and proprietory colonies differ?* Royal colonies were set up by people representing the king. Control of the colony was in the hands of the king. Proprietory colonies were set up by people who had been given land grants by the king. Control of the colony was in the hands of the proprietor.

# Chapter 4

## Identify

*New England Colonies*   **Connecticut, New Hampshire, Massachusetts, and Rhode Island.**

*Middle Colonies*   **New York, Pennsylvania, New Jersey, and Delaware.**

*Southern Colonies* **Maryland, Virginia, North Carolina, South Carolina, and Georgia.**

*Paul Revere* **famous silversmith who rode to warn colonists of approaching British troops.** Revere was also a dentist and made false teeth, and he later started a foundry and invented a process for rolling sheet copper.

*Daniel Dulany* **founder of a powerful Maryland Colony family.** Dulany had come to America as an indentured servant and worked in a law office. After his term of indenture, he became a rich lawyer and planter and made more money buying and selling land.

*Oloudah Equiano* **also known as Gustavus Vassa, active in the British antislavery movement, his autobiography was widely read in England and America.** Equiano was an African kidnapped and taken to the West Indies as a slave. Sold to a Philadelphia merchant, he was able to earn enough money to buy his freedom and move to England.

# Explain

*indentured servant* **a person who agreed to work for a person for a limited number of years, usually in payment for the cost of the trip to America.** Both whites and blacks came to America as indentured servants.

*export* **the sending of goods out of a country for sale.** The Middle Colonies, for example, produced more goods than they needed so they could export the extra products.

*import* **the bringing of goods into a country to sell.** The Southern Colonies, for example, produced tobacco for sale overseas and imported British manufactured goods to meet their own needs.

# Check Your Memory of the Facts

1. *From what countries in Europe did people come to settle in the English colonies?* **The majority came from England, Scotland, and Ireland.** Others came from Germany, Poland, Denmark, Italy, Portugal, Spain, Norway, and Finland, as well as what is now Czechoslovakia and Belgium and nearly every other European country.

2. *For what reasons did people come to the New World?* **Most came to improve their ways of life and to escape religious oppression.** Others such as criminals, debtors, and slaves were forced to come to the New World.

3. *Why was the demand for blacks to be slaves so great? Why was it greater than for Indians or Europeans?* **Black people were preferred as slaves because their skin colors made it difficult for them to**

**successfully escape;** they stood out in a country where the majority of people were white-skinned. **They also proved to be less likely to die from some diseases than did American Indians.** Slaves were wanted because it cost less to provide food and housing for them than it did to pay wages to hired workers.

4.  *Which was more difficult to get in the colonies, land or labor?* **Labor** was more difficult to get since there were very large areas of cheap or free land available. Workers were always needed.

5.  *Where in North America were most Africans located? Why?* **Most Africans were located in the Southern Colonies where they were forced to work under the plantation system of farming.**

6.  *What different kinds of work were done by people living in the English colonies?* **Most of the people in the colonies were farmers. A much smaller number also worked at fishing, hunting, lumbering, ship-building, home manufacturing, and running small businesses.**

## Check Your Understanding of the Ideas

1.  *Why did people living in the colonies develop characteristics different from those of people remaining in Europe?* The colonists developed their own ways of living in an environment which was different from that of Europe. They were a mixture of people from many different countries and backgrounds. Social classes became less important in the colonies than in Europe, and most whites could improve their lives.

2.  *Why was the trip to the New World difficult? For what group was it most difficult? Why?* The trip was long, and the ships were small with poor sanitary conditions. Epidemics aboard ship were common because of poor diet and lack of fresh air. Slaves had the most difficult trip because of overcrowding with little freedom of movement, terrible sanitary conditions, and a very poor diet of unfamiliar food. It was sometimes common for the death rate to be as high as one fourth of the people on the ship.

3.  *Why did the colonists treat African and European servants differently?* Since most Africans were forced to come to America, the way they were treated did not affect the number who came. Europeans might have chosen not to come if they knew that they would be poorly treated. Many European colonists also viewed people of other races and religions as inferior to themselves, and they came to regard African slaves as property rather than as people.

4.  *What was the effect of the abundance of land on methods of farming used in the colonies?* Most of the colonists wasted the soil, seldom using fertilizer or rotating crops. As the land wore out, colonial farmers often felt that it was easy to move farther west to new land.

5. *How is the life of a teenager different today from what it was in colonial America?* Teenagers today attend school much more and longer than did teenagers in colonial America. They have more free time for social activities and interests which are different from those of adults. They usually are not expected to work full time and contribute to the family income. Teenagers in colonial America were expected to work with their parents at farming or were apprenticed to learn a trade. In most ways they were considered small adults who worked and dressed as did older people.

6. *How did farming differ in New England, the Middle Colonies, and the Southern Colonies?* Much of the soil in New England was rocky and poor, and farms were generally small. Land was very rich in the Middle Colonies, and crops were plentiful enough for use at home and for export. In the Southern Colonies, the land was also rich. Most people there worked small farms, but a small number of planters controlled large areas of land which produced such crops as tobacco and rice for export through the use of slave labor.

7. *What were the major colonial cities? What features did they have in common?* The major colonial cities were Philadelphia, New York, Boston, and Charleston. Except for Philadelphia, they were small compared to most European cities. All were located on the seacoast, and trade with England and the West Indies was important to their economies. They served as the centers of trade and cultural life, and all were growing very quickly.

# Chapter 5

## Identify

*Navigation Acts* **laws passed by Parliament in the 1660's to control colonial trade.** The laws listed such items as tobacco, cotton, indigo, and turpentine and stated that the colonists could export these only to Britain. These laws also ruled that the colonies could import only British goods. All goods traded between the colonies and England had to be carried on British, Irish, or colonial ships.

*George III* **King of Great Britain at the time of the American Revolution.** During his reign, the British government tried to tighten its control of the colonies in order to make them more profitable to Britain.

*Sugar Act* **a law passed by Parliament in 1764 which lowered the tax on sugar imported from outside British territory, but it also provided for strict enforcement to stop smuggling.**

*Stamp Act* **a law passed by Parliament to put a tax on certain kinds of printed papers used in the colonies.** Each paper had to bear a stamp to prove that the tax had been paid. Passed in 1765, the law was designed to raise money to help pay the costs of keeping British soldiers in the colonies.

*Patrick Henry* **Virginia colonist who spoke out against the Sugar and Stamp Acts.**

*Charles Townshend* **British official who ordered a new set of taxes to be passed for the colonies in 1767.** These taxes were placed on imported items like paper, glass, lead, paint, and tea.

*Intolerable Acts* **a series of laws passed by the British to punish the people of Boston for the "tea party."** One of the acts closed the port of Boston to shipping until the people paid for the tea they had destroyed. Another put Massachusetts under the control of the royal governor and the British troops. The Quebec Act stated that lands west of the Appalachian Mountains belonged to Canada, not to the American colonies, and so could not be settled by Americans.

*George Washington* **Virginia colonist chosen by the Second Continental Congress to lead the Continental Army.** His ability and determination kept the small and poorly equipped army together and enabled them to survive and eventually defeat the British.

*Benjamin Franklin* **Pennsylvania colonist who helped to write the Declaration of Independence and who later served as colonial representative to France,** persuading the French to enter the Revolutionary War on the side of the colonies.

## Explain

*mercantilism* **economic policy of Britain and other countries through which they tried, with tight controls of trade, to make their colonies profitable to the home countries.** The British colonies in America were to produce raw materials not found in England and sell these only to England. The colonies were not to manufacture anything that could be bought from England. Mercantilistic laws were made to keep the colonies and home country from competing against each other. The colonies benefited from a monopoly on the sale of several major crops, and their merchants took part in trade which was closed to other nations and was protected by the powerful British navy.

*French and Indian War* **the American part of the Seven Years' War between Britain and France in Europe.** In North America, the Indians usually sided with the French to resist further loss of land to the English colonists. The war began in 1754, and the English colonists joined with England to fight against the French and Indians for control of the Ohio Valley and the fur trade. The colonists saw the war as an opportunity also to end the threat of the Indians living along the colonial frontier. As a result of the British victory in the war, England gained most of the French lands in North America.

*"new colonial policy"* **the plan of the British government to enforce old economic laws and to make new ones in order to strengthen their policy of mercantilism with the American colonies.** According to this plan, the colonies were to be kept from becoming too independent of British rule. They were not to join in the fur trade and could not settle in the lands west of the Appalachian Mountains. Colonists were also supposed to pay a large part of what the war had cost and bear some of the expense of keeping British troops in the colonies.

*Sons of Liberty* **secret protest groups formed in many colonial towns.** These groups rioted against tax officials and got merchants to stop importing goods from Great Britain.

*boycott* **refusal to buy or use certain goods.**

*patriots* **colonists who supported a break with Britain.** They boycotted British goods and sometimes tarred and feathered tax officials.

*loyalists* **colonists who remained loyal to England and wanted to keep their ties to England.** They were sometimes tarred and feathered by the patriots.

*minutemen* **patriot soldiers who could be ready to fight at a moment's notice.** The minutemen took part in the opening battles of the Revolution at Lexington and Concord.

*Treaty of Paris of 1783* **agreement between the United States and Great Britain, ending the Revolutionary War.**

## Check Your Memory of the Facts

1. *What actions by the English led to the end of good relations with the colonies?* **Sugar Act, Stamp Act, tax laws set up by Townshend, and the Intolerable Acts.**

2. *Why did the colonies oppose the Sugar Act and the Stamp Act?* **These British laws hurt the economic interests of the colonists, and if they obeyed them, the colonists could no longer say that they had all the rights of English people including the right of self-government.**

3. *What was Patrick Henry's position on taxation?* **He believed that the colonies should not be taxed by Parliament since they had no representatives there.** He attacked the Stamp and Sugar Acts as "taxation without representation."

4. *What was the cause and the result of the Boston "tea party"?* **The Parliament passed a new tea act in 1773 which allowed the British East India Company to sell tea at a price lower than the prices of**

**other companies. Some colonial merchants who smuggled tea from Holland faced ruin from this competition.** Riots broke out in several areas, and Sons of Liberty dumped cargoes of British East India tea into Boston Harbor. The Parliament responded with the Intolerable Acts. The colonists responded to those with the First Continental Congress.

5. *Which colonies sent representatives to the First Continental Congress? Which did not?* **All except Georgia sent representatives.**

6. *Who were the leading colonists opposed to the British policy toward the colonies?* **Patrick Henry, Samuel Adams, and John Adams were among the leaders** as were Paul Revere, Thomas Paine, Thomas Jefferson, George Washington, Benjamin Franklin, George Rogers Clark, and others.

7. *What country aided the colonists in the war against England?* **France.**

## Check Your Understanding of the Ideas

1. *What were the immediate and long-range causes of the Revolution?* The immediate causes of the Revolution included the Intolerable Acts passed as a result of the Boston "tea party" and the attempt by the British to arrest patriot leaders and capture stored arms which led to the battles of Lexington and Concord. Long-range causes were the laws passed as part of the "new colonial policy." The disallowance of a colonial share in the benefits of victory in the French and Indian War, the stationing of British troops in the colonies, various tax laws and the Intolerable Acts increased discontent and protest in the colonies and brought about revolt.

2. *What different view of English policy existed among colonists before the start of the war?* One group of people called loyalists supported English policies and wanted to maintain colonial ties to England. Patriots, those who favored a break with England, had other views. Some favored asking the king to help solve the problems of the colonists caused by Parliament's policies, and others took the view that Parliament had no power to make laws for the colonies. Most patriots came to support a complete break with England.

3. *Why did France come to the aid of the colonies?* to hurt Britain who was a long-time enemy. France had lost much of its North American lands to Britain less than twenty years earlier.

4. *How were the thirteen English colonies able to win independence from a much stronger England?* Colonial advantages included fighting a defensive war on known territory with close supply points, the leadership and determination of Washington and the dedication of the patriots, and the very important factor of French aid.

5. *What were the major provisions of the Treaty of Paris of 1783?*  Britain recognized the independence of the United States, gave it the lands west of the Appalachian Mountains as far as the Mississippi River, and gave it navigation rights on the Mississippi.

# Chapter 6

## Identify

*Articles of Confederation*   **the plan for a federal, or central, government of the new United States.** It was drawn up by the Second Continental Congress and went into effect in 1781.

*Northwest Territory*   **the lands west of the Appalachian Mountains to the Mississippi River and north of the Ohio River** which the United States won from England in the Revolution and for which the Second Continental Congress drew up a plan of governmental organization.

*Shays' Rebellion*   **a revolt by some farmers of western Massachusetts, led by Daniel Shays, against high taxes.** It was put down by the state militia.

*Federalists*   **those people who favored the adoption of the Constitution and a strong federal government for the United States.** James Madison, Alexander Hamilton, and John Jay were three important Federalists who wrote and spoke in favor of ratification.

*Anti-Federalists*   **those people who were against adopting the new Constitution. Concerned about how strong the federal government should be,** some of them favored keeping the Confederation government.

## Explain

*democracy*   **a system of government that is run by the people who live under it.**

*federal government*   **central government.** The federal government in the United States was given stronger powers under the Constitution than under the Articles of Confederation.

*Northwest Ordinance*   **the plan passed by Congress in 1787 to outline the steps through which areas in the Northwest Territory could become states.** The plan became the model for other territories later admitted to the Union.

*"Great Compromise"*   **that part of the Constitution which settled the question of representation in Congress.** It provided for a Senate in which each state had the same number of representatives, so that

smaller states would have power equal to the larger states, and for a House in which the number of representatives would be based on the number of people in each state, so that the states with more people would have more power. An act would have to pass both houses before it could become law. Within this compromise was another. It settled the arguments between southern leaders who wanted all slaves counted as population and northern leaders who wanted none of the slaves counted. The compromise stated that three fifths of the number of slaves would be counted in determining the population for representation.

*ratify*   **to approve.** The Constitution of the United States had to be ratified by the states before it went into operation.

*Bill of Rights*   **the first ten amendments to the Constitution** listing those personal rights of citizens with which the government may not interfere.

## Check Your Memory of the Facts

1.  *What did the Revolution achieve for the American people?*   **The people of the United States won the right of self-government** when they won their political independence from Great Britain.

2.  *What things did the new state governments established after the Revolution have in common?*   **Most of them were based on English laws and political ideas and had a governor and two legislative houses.** In most states, the governor and upper house had very little power.

3.  *What were the powers of Congress under the Articles of Confederation?*   **Congress could declare war, make peace, maintain an army and navy, coin money, borrow money, and run a mail service.**

4.  *What were the chief weaknesses of the Articles of Confederation?*   **The Articles did not give Congress power to raise money, did not provide strong protection for Americans at home or overseas, and could not stop each state from taxing goods which crossed its borders which was harmful to trade within the country.**

5.  *What provisions for new states were made in the Northwest Ordinance?*   **The Northwest Territory would be divided into not less than three nor more than five territories. When there were sixty thousand free settlers in a territory, they could write a constitution and apply to Congress for admission as a state.**

6.  *What powers were given to the federal government under the Constitution?*   **All of the powers it had under the Articles as well as the power to tax and to look after trade among the states and with other countries.**

# Check Your Understanding of the Ideas

1. *How did the American experience with the British government influence the kind of state and federal governments created after the Revolution?* The colonists had feared the power of the British government, so they created weak governments at state and federal levels. Taxes were one of the main concerns of the colonists under British rule. As a result, the federal government under the Articles of Confederation was not given the power to tax but could only ask the states for money. In most states, little power was given to the governor, and most of the power was given to the lower house of the legislature. That enabled the people to keep more control of the government through their representatives.

2. *What groups in America did not secure full citizenship rights after the Revolution?* Black men and women did not gain full citizenship rights; most of them were slaves and had no rights at all. Women, black and white, could not vote or hold office and, in most states, had no legal control of their property or children. In many states, there were restrictions on voting and holding office for white men who did not own property.

3. *Were the Articles of Confederation able to provide the government needed by Americans? Why or why not?* In general, the Articles did not provide the government needed — the flow of trade between the states was hampered by state taxes, and Congress had no power to raise money to pay for the army, navy, or other services to protect or promote American rights at home or overseas. The Articles did state that there was a national citizenship so citizens of any state were free to travel and trade throughout all the states. They also stated that courts in one state must respect the findings of courts in other states.

4. *Was the federal government under the Constitution more like the colonial government under Britain than it was like the government under the Articles of Confederation? Why or why not?* Yes, because it had the right to tax and to regulate trade which the Confederation government did not. The Constitution government was not so strong as British colonial government, however, because certain individual rights were protected by the first ten amendments and rights not specifically given to the federal government were reserved to the states.

5. *What caused some people to oppose the Constitution?* Some opposed the Constitution because, at first, it did not spell out the personal rights of individuals. Many of those people were satisfied after the Bill of Rights was added to the Constitution. Others continued to oppose the Constitution because they felt that it gave the federal government too much power.

6. *What was the purpose of the Bill of Rights?* to clearly spell out those rights of individual citizens which the government could not take away. The Bill of Rights set limits on the power of the federal and state governments.

# Chapter 7

## Identify

*Judiciary Act of 1789* **the law which set up the federal court system.**

*Alexander Hamilton* **secretary of the treasury under President George Washington.** He drew up an economic program for the new nation to bring money into the federal government and to help business people prosper.

*Thomas Jefferson* **secretary of state under President George Washington.** He opposed Hamilton's plan for a Bank of the United States as unconstitutional. Jefferson became the third President of the United States.

*Jay Treaty* **an agreement between the United States and Great Britain to settle problems in the western American territories and questions of trading rights in the West Indies.** Under it, Britain agreed to remove its trading posts from United States lands, and the United States agreed to send only small ships to trade in the West Indies.

*Pinckney Treaty* **an agreement between the United States and Spain made in 1795 which allowed Americans to send goods down the Mississippi River and through New Orleans and fixed the border of Florida where the United States claimed it should be.**

*Whiskey Rebellion* **a revolt in 1794 by Pennsylvania farmers against a federal tax placed on the whiskey they made.** The federal government sent troops to put down the revolt and capture the leaders of the rebellion.

*John Adams* **Vice-President under President George Washington and second President of the United States.**

*Alien and Sedition Acts* **laws passed in 1798 which allowed the federal government to send foreigners out of the country and to punish anyone who wrote or spoke against the government.**

*Louisiana Purchase* **the land bought by the United States from France in 1803.** It stretched from the Mississippi River west to the Rocky Mountains, and its purchase doubled the size of the United States.

*John Marshall* **Chief Justice of the United States Supreme Court from 1801 to 1835.** He helped to increase the power of the Court by establishing the Court's right to judge acts of Congress unconstitutional.

# Explain

*Cabinet*  **the body of advisers to the President.** It is made up of the people who serve as executive department heads. President Washington started the tradition of meeting with these people to ask their advice, and the practice has been continued by later Presidents.

*negotiate*  **to work disagreements out through discussion.** President Washington began the practice of Presidents negotiating treaties with other countries as they see fit and then presenting them to the Senate for approval.

*judicial review*  **the power of the courts to judge an act of Congress unconstitutional when the question arises in an actual court case.** The Supreme Court established the right of judicial review in the case of *Marbury v. Madison* in 1803.

*neutrality*  **not taking sides in conflicts or disagreements.** President Washington favored a policy of neutrality for the United States concerning the quarrels of European countries.

*Federalists*  **members of the political party which developed in support of strong central government.** Alexander Hamilton was an important leader of the party and claimed that the Constitution meant much more than it actually said.

*Republicans*  **members of the political party which developed in support of limited government.** Thomas Jefferson was an important leader of the party and claimed that the Constitution meant only what it specifically said.

*Twelfth Amendment*  **an amendment stating that electors will vote for President and Vice-President separately.**

*states' rights*  **the idea that the states have the right to judge the acts of the national government and decide whether to follow them or not.** The Kentucky and Virginia Resolutions, which said that the Alien and Sedition Acts were unconstitutional and so could not be upheld by the states, are early examples of the states' rights view.

# Check Your Memory of the Facts

1. *What were the major concerns of the new government as the United States began operating under the Constitution?* **The first major concern was that no one could be sure that the new Constitution would work. Other concerns included developing an economic program to help the nation prosper, establishing a strong court system, and avoiding trouble with the stronger European countries.**

2. *What three levels of federal courts were formed by the Judiciary Act of 1789?* **federal district courts, federal circuit courts, and the Supreme Court.**

3. *What were the main parts of Hamilton's economic policy?* **Hamilton wanted to bring money into the Treasury through taxation, pay back the money owed to foreign countries from the Revolution, have the federal government take over the debts of the states from the Revolution, and set up a Bank of the United States.**

4. *Where was the first capital of the United States? What other city served as capital before Washington, D.C.?* **New York, Philadelphia.**

5. *What were the first two national political parties started in the United States?* **Federalists and Republicans.**

6. *Why were the Alien and Sedition Acts passed?* **to hurt the interests of the people who supported the Republican party.**

7. *How did the United States buy Louisiana?* **President Jefferson learned that Napoleon of France was taking Louisiana back from Spain.** He sent representatives to find out about buying it for the United States. **Because Napoleon needed money to go to war, he agreed to sell it to the United States.**

## Check Your Understanding of the Ideas

1. *Why did George Washington become the first President?* He was unanimously elected because of the great respect others held for him. No one else seemed to have as much experience as an executive, and Washington had shown his abilities by running a large plantation and by commanding the Continental Army successfully.

2. *Why is a strong court system important for a nation?* to protect the rights of its citizens from harm by the government or other people.

3. *What were the economic advantages of the Bank of the United States?* The Bank kept the money supply of the United States in one place and issued secure paper money based on that supply. It was able to loan money to business people who developed the nation's industry and trade. These business people then looked to the federal government for help and gave it their support.

4. *Why did the United States decide not to support France in its war with Britain?* President Washington felt that it would be better for the United States to remain neutral because the nation was young and not very strong militarily. He also did not want to encourage the disagreements among Americans who favored opposite sides in the war.

5. *In what way did the Pinckney Treaty help the United States?* The treaty settled the Florida boundary dispute as the United States wanted and improved American trade by giving the United States the right to use the port of New Orleans which cut the costs of transporting goods.

6. *Why did political parties form in the United States?* The immediate reason for the formation of the parties was the disagreement over the Jay Treaty. However, the parties represented two different views on many issues. The Federalists favored more power for the federal government and a broad view of the Constitution. The Republicans favored limited federal government power and a strict view of the Constitution.

7. *In what ways were the supporters of the Virginia and Kentucky Resolutions like those who opposed the ratification of the Constitution?* They favored less power for the federal government and more power for the states.

8. *What was the significance of Thomas Jefferson's election in 1800?* It proved that control of the government could change from one group to an opposing group without violence, and that people in the United States had a right to openly oppose the ideas and policies of the people in office.

# *Chapter 8*

## Identify

*Tecumseh* **Shawnee chief who organized a confederation of Indian groups** to oppose expansion of the United States. He was killed at the Battle of the Thames in 1813.

*James Madison* **fourth President of the United States,** in office during the War of 1812.

*Battle of New Orleans* **battle fought between American and British troops in 1814,** after the peace treaty had been signed ending the War of 1812. It caused many Americans to feel that the United States had won the war. Andrew Jackson became a hero for leading the Americans to victory.

*John C. Calhoun* **member of Congress from South Carolina.** He was a strong nationalist in the early 1800's and a leader of the "War Hawks."

*Erie Canal* **a waterway built from New York City to the Great Lakes.** It was part of President Madison's program to build roads and canals to improve transportation and trade among the different parts of the United States.

*National Road* **also called the Cumberland Road, a road planned in 1806 to connect the eastern United States with the new western lands.** It was still being built in the 1840's, connecting the Potomac River to the Ohio River and stretching west to Vandalia, Illinois.

*James Monroe*   **fifth President of the United States.** His term was called the "era of good feelings," and he developed the Monroe Doctrine as part of American foreign policy.

*Henry Clay*   **member of Congress from Kentucky who worked out the Missouri Compromise of 1820;** also a "War Hawk."

*Seminole War*   **a war fought between the United States and the Seminole Indians of Florida in 1816.** It was caused by claims of settlers that the Indians, with the help of blacks who had escaped from slavery, were crossing the border from Spanish Florida to attack them. Andrew Jackson led the United States troops to a semi-victory. In 1819, Spain ceded Florida to the United States.

# Explain

*War Hawks*   **United States leaders who favored war as a means of protecting neutrality.** In 1812, they especially called for war against Britain. They were proud of the growth of the United States and strongly nationalistic.

*impressment*   **the act of removing sailors by force from American ships to serve in the British navy.** The impressment of sailors greatly angered many Americans and increased demands for war.

*embargo*   **an order of the government which forbids a country's ships from leaving for foreign ports.** President Jefferson convinced Congress to place an embargo on American ships in 1807, hoping to force England and France to respect American neutrality by not selling them American goods.

*nationalism*   **a feeling of pride in the nation as a whole and loyalty to its goals.**

*sectionalism*   **a feeling of pride in a particular section of the country and loyalty to its goals.**

*protective tariff*   **a tax on imported goods** which protects a country's industries from some competition by raising the price of goods made outside the country so that people will buy the less expensive local goods.

*Panic of 1819*   **financial scare caused by the closing of many banks in the West.** When the Bank of the United States called for the money which it had loaned to western banks, many were unable to pay. They had loaned too much money to too many people buying land who could not pay back their loans, either.

*Missouri Compromise*   **a plan worked out by Henry Clay to decide the issue of slavery in the West.** Under it, Missouri was admitted to the Union as a slave state, and Maine was admitted as a free state, maintaining for a while the balance of power in the Senate. A line was drawn west from the southern border of Missouri to divide future slave from future free states. The compromise did not satisfy some southerners, and many Americans believed that it was only the beginning of more serious conflicts over slavery.

*Monroe Doctrine* **a statement of foreign policy made by President Monroe in 1823,** warning European nations not to attempt to take any more land in the Western Hemisphere or to interfere with the affairs of any countries there. At the time it was made, the statement was respected by European countries only because England and its strong navy backed the policy.

## Check Your Memory of the Facts

1. *Who were the leaders who urged the United States to go to war to solve the problem of neutrality rights?* **The "War Hawks,"** including John C. Calhoun and Henry Clay.

2. *What actions by the British and the French angered Americans?* **Each country tried to keep the United States from trading with the other by capturing American ships. In addition, the British angered the United States because of its impressment of sailors from American ships.**

3. *What happened to the U.S.S.* Chesapeake? *How did Americans react?* **In 1807, the British fired on the Chesapeake and forced some of its sailors into the British navy. Americans were greatly angered and many called for war.** Instead, Congress passed the Embargo Act of 1807 to stop trade with Britain and France.

4. *Why did the United States go to war against Britain in 1812?* **British interference with American trade, impressment of American sailors, and the desire of some American settlers to take over British lands in Canada.**

5. *Who were the American military leaders in the War of 1812?* **General William Henry Harrison, Captain Oliver Perry, and General Andrew Jackson** were three of the main leaders in the war.

6. *Why was a new Bank of the United States needed?* **The charter for the first bank had run out.** Leaders felt that without a new bank, the federal government had no safe place to deposit its money, and there would be no sure way to see that the state banks issued secure paper money. These banks did not always have enough gold or silver to back up their paper money.

7. *What were the major routes taken by travelers to the West?* **National Road, Ohio River, and Erie Canal.** (See map, page 157, for Wilderness Road, Natchez Trace, Zane's Trace, Main Line Canal, Wabash and Erie Canal, Ohio and Erie Canal, and others.)

8. *What was the main point of the Monroe Doctrine?* **European countries were to keep hands off the nations in Latin America.** European

nations were thinking of helping Spain reconquer Latin-American countries which had recently won their independence.

## Check Your Understanding of the Ideas

1.  *How successful was President Jefferson's plan to force the British and French to respect American neutrality rights?* The embargo of 1807 actually harmed American farmers and merchants even more than it did other countries. It was such a failure that Congress lifted it before Jefferson left office and passed new laws to allow Americans to trade with any nations except England and France.

2.  *What did the United States gain in the peace treaty ending the War of 1812?* Nothing material because all land boundaries were returned to what they had been before the war. Many Americans, however, felt that much had been gained because the power of the Indian groups east of the Mississippi River had been broken. The war also increased the spirit of nationalism in the country and that contributed to the country's growth in the peaceful years that followed.

3.  *How did the War of 1812 affect the two major political parties, the Federalists and the Republicans?* The Federalist party was considered disloyal to the country because some members had opposed the war. The party lost its influence and soon disappeared. The Republicans had supported the war and gained strength as the party of nationalism and growth.

4.  *What were the reactions of the sections of the United States to the issues of the Bank, the protective tariff, and federal grants to build roads and canals?* Different sections of the country often changed their support of these issues at different times, according to their sections' needs. Many state banks all over the country were opposed to the Bank of the United States, but it was most seriously an issue between East and West. Many westerners blamed the Panic of 1819 on the Bank which they believed was controlled by eastern business people. The country was also split over the protective tariff. Owners of New England cotton and woolen mills, iron manufacturers from Pennsylvania, and western suppliers of these new factories demanded a protective tariff. Most southerners who traded their crops directly for English goods were opposed to the tariff. People in the South and West favored the federal aid plan for canals and roads, while the people of New England generally did not, since they already had better roads than the rest of the country. Later, the people of New England changed their view and favored aid because better roads in the West would improve trade. The South then, in competition with New England for the western trade, opposed federal aid.

5. *What changes were made in the boundaries of the United States in the years following the War of 1812?* There were no boundary changes as a direct result of the war, but a few years later, the United States and Great Britain signed an agreement that set the northern boundary of the United States at the forty-ninth parallel from Lake of the Woods in Minnesota to the top of the Rocky Mountains. In 1819, Spain ceded Florida to the United States.

6. *What actions by Americans during the period reflect strong feelings of nationalism? What actions reflect strong sectionalism?* Nationalistic actions were the establishment of a new United States Bank, the War of 1812, the protective tariff, the plan for federal aid to build roads and canals, and the Monroe Doctrine. Sectionalistic actions included opposition to the Bank, the protective tariff, and federal aid for road and canal building. The debates over slavery were also a reflection of strong sectional feelings.

# *Chapter 9*

## Identify

*Andrew Jackson* **seventh President of the United States elected in 1828.** Many people saw Jackson as an example of the western or frontier spirit and as a hero from the Battle of New Orleans.

*Democrats* **members of the Republican party who supported Jackson** and called themselves Democratic-Republicans. They dropped the word Republican to further distinguish themselves from his opponents who called themselves National-Republicans.

*Whigs* **those who were against Jackson,** including the National-Republicans, **because of the way he used his power as President.** They thought of themselves as being like the Whig party in England which was against the royal power of the king.

*Osceola* **leader of the Seminole Indians** who resisted removal by United States troops from their home in Florida for seven years.

*Martin Van Buren* **President of the United States elected in 1836.** Van Buren had agreed with Jackson's economic plans and continued them which made the depression in the country worse.

*William Henry Harrison* **President elected in 1840, but died within a month after taking office.** His death also ended Whig plans of building a program to help the nation out of the depression.

*John Tyler* **Vice-President under Harrison who became President upon Harrison's death.** Tyler had been a Democrat but had broken his ties with Jackson before running with Harrison on a Whig ticket. As

President, Tyler still held Democratic views and often vetoed Whig bills.

*Horace Mann*  **leader in education from Massachusetts.** Mann believed that a basic education for all children should be paid for by taxing all the people of the town, and that all students should be offered the same beginning subjects.

*Mary Lyon*  **founder of the Mount Holyoke Female Seminary in 1836** which was a school for women that average families could afford.

*Margaret Fuller*  **writer for a New York newspaper** who stressed the ideas of individual independence and self-responsibility. Fuller also wrote a book titled *Women in the Nineteenth Century.*

*Hudson Valley School*  **a group of American artists who were famous for their paintings of forests, mountains, and streams.** They were part of the movement by Americans to write about and paint American subjects for the enjoyment of the many people, rather than the few.

*Dorothea Dix*  **an American reformer who visited jails and hospitals and reported to lawmakers about the horrible conditions she found there.** Her reports helped to get laws passed for better conditions.

## Explain

*average American*  **a term used to describe the ordinary people,** from farmer to city worker, who were neither rich nor poor.

*spoils system*  **the practice of replacing government jobholders with members of the winning party after an election.**

*caucus*  **a private meeting.** In national politics at this time, Congress picked the candidates for President and Vice-President through party caucuses. By the early 1820's, the Republican party was the only party in Congress, so its caucus choices were usually the people elected.

*Indian Removal Act*  **a law passed by Congress in 1830 giving the President the power to negotiate land exchanges with the Indian peoples living east of the Mississippi River in order to move them west of the river.** It did not say that the army could be used to carry out the plans, but Jackson used federal troops to crush resistance by the Indians who did not want to move to the Great Plains.

*nullification*  **the idea that each state had the right to cancel, or nullify, a federal law if the people there thought it was unconstitutional.** A plan for nullification was proposed by John C. Calhoun of South Carolina in 1828. Like the Virginia and Kentucky Resolutions of 1798, it said that final power in the country was found in the states, not in the federal government.

*Webster-Hayne debates*  **a series of debates in the Senate in 1830 over western lands and issues** during which Robert Hayne of South Carolina suggested that western states could nullify a law they did not like. Daniel Webster of Massachusetts argued against the idea of nullification.

*pet banks*  **state banks which received the federal government money that Jackson ordered removed from the Bank of the United States.** These banks used the money to start a credit boom by loaning much of it to business people who wanted to buy western lands from the governmental land offices. The land offices then deposited the money back into the pet banks. More money and credit became available to more people, and by 1836, there was a heavy increase in the buying of land on credit.

*depression*  **a time of very slow business activity and high unemployment.** In the Panic of 1837, many banks did not have enough gold or silver to cover the paper money they had issued, and the amount of credit they had given to people was larger than the amount of available hard money. When banks called in their loans, people could not pay all that they owed. The Panic turned into a depression as prices dropped and business slowed because people were buying fewer products. Many people lost their jobs since fewer products could be sold, and many businesses and banks failed.

*reform*  **to improve or change for the better.** In the mid-1800's, many people worked to reform various parts of American society.

## Check Your Memory of the Facts

1. *How were President Jackson's reasons for vetoing bills different from those of earlier Presidents?*  Earlier Presidents had vetoed bills only when they thought the bills were unconstitutional. Jackson did this, but **he also vetoed bills for political reasons or to control Congress.**

2. *When did President Jackson act as a nationalist?  As a supporter of states' rights?*  **Jackson acted as a nationalist in supporting federal aid for interstate programs to improve transportation and in opposing the idea of nullification. He acted as a supporter of states' rights on the issues of the Indian Removal and the Bank of the United States.**

3. *Over what issue was the idea of nullification tested?  What was the result?*  **The test of nullification came when Jackson signed a new high tariff into law in 1832. A special convention in South Carolina nullified the tariff in that state. Jackson said the idea of nullification could not be accepted and prepared to send troops against South Carolina to enforce the law. Henry Clay set up a compromise to**

**lower the tariff which was accepted by the other southern states. South Carolina could not stand alone against federal power, and the idea of nullification died.**

4. *What political party supported John Tyler for President?* **The Whig party had nominated Tyler for Vice-President, but as President, Tyler vetoed many Whig bills and did not get along with Whig leaders or Congress.**

5. *What kinds of things did the reformers of this time period help change?* **treatment of people in jails and hospitals, drinking of liquor, laws about putting people in jail for owing money, religions, education for blind and deaf, slavery, and women's rights.**

## Check Your Understanding of the Ideas

1. *How did voting become more democratic by 1830?* More white men were allowed to vote because the old requirements of property, religion, or education were generally dropped. The states also changed their laws so that citizens voted directly for the electors who voted for President and Vice-President instead of having the electors chosen by the state legislatures.

2. *Why did Henry Clay support John Quincy Adams for President?* Both Clay and Adams wanted a new protective tariff. The money from it would be used for canals and roads to join the different sections of the country.

3. *How was the President of the United States elected in 1824?* None of the four candidates won a majority of votes in the election, so the House of Representatives had to choose the President from the top three, according to the Constitution. Clay, who had come in fourth, encouraged his friends in the House to vote for Adams. With Clay's support, Adams was named President.

4. *How could the Southeast Indians lose their lands if treaties protected their rights of ownership?* The treaties were ignored. President Jackson decided that the states' power over the Indians and their lands was stronger than the federal government's. He refused to enforce the Supreme Court ruling in favor of the Indians, and few white Americans spoke out against the use of force to remove the Indians from their lands.

5. *Why did Jackson want to destroy the Bank of the United States?* Jackson viewed the Bank as a monopoly that made a few rich people richer, and like many other westerners, he blamed the Bank for the Panic of 1819 in which he had lost money.

6. *What connection was there among the works of American authors, artists, and musicians of this period?* All were beginning to reject

English styles in favor of American ones which reflected their pride in the country and which could be appreciated by all the people.

7. *What ideas did Horace Mann want people to accept?* Mann believed that all children should receive a basic education, paid for by taxing all the people of the town, and that all students should be offered the same beginning subjects in order to give them an even start at success. His ideas were part of a general movement to make the schools more democratic by opening them to rich and poor alike.

8. *What connection was there between American religions and American reform movements? Between the reform movements and the spirit of democracy?* Most reform leaders were average Americans with strong religious beliefs, among which was the belief that people and society could become perfect with enough hard work. One of the main ideas behind the reforms was to make American society more democratic by helping all Americans make the best possible use of the many opportunities available in the United States.

# *Chapter 10*

## Identify

*Stephen Austin* **an American who started a settlement in Texas on the Brazos River in the 1820's.** He brought three hundred families to Texas, and they received over thirteen thousand acres of land because of an agreement Austin's father had made with the Mexican government.

*John Sutter* **Swiss settler who owned a fort,** on the Sacramento River **in California,** where James Marshall discovered gold in 1848, starting the California gold rush.

*John McLoughlin* **agent for the British Hudson's Bay Company on the Columbia River who helped others settle in the Willamette Valley of Oregon.**

*James K. Polk* **President of the United States elected in 1844.** During Polk's term, Texas became a state, and the U.S. fought a war with Mexico, concluded the Treaty of Guadalupe Hidalgo, and agreed upon dividing the Oregon Territory with Britain.

*Zachary Taylor* **an American general in the war with Mexico** known to his troops as "Old Rough and Ready" because he fought with little planning but great courage.

*Joseph Smith* **founder of the Church of Jesus Christ of Latter-Day Saints, the Mormons,** in New York in 1830. Smith was killed by a mob in Illinois in 1844.

# Explain

*Manifest Destiny* **the belief held by many Americans that it was the certain fate of the United States to stretch its boundaries from the Atlantic Ocean to the Pacific Ocean.** The term was first used by a newspaper editor in 1845 and became popular with other Americans who wanted the United States to expand into other areas.

*the Alamo* **an abandoned mission in San Antonio, Texas, where a small force of Texans held out against nearly four thousand Mexican soldiers for several days before being killed.**

*annexed* **added.** In 1837, Texas asked to be annexed to the United States.

*reservations* **areas of land set aside by the government for the use of Indian groups.**

*Oregon Trail* **a route used by many American settlers moving west to the Oregon Territory in the 1840's.** The route was along the Platte River through a break in the Rocky Mountains at South Pass and along the Snake River to the Columbia River.

*Gadsden Purchase* **a strip of land which was purchased by the United States from Mexico in 1853 to provide a southern railroad route to the Pacific Ocean.** The land now forms the southern portions of the states of New Mexico and Arizona.

*Mormons* **members of the Church of Jesus Christ of Latter-Day Saints,** founded by Joseph Smith in New York in 1830. They were persecuted by their neighbors and moved farther west several times, finally establishing Salt Lake City in the Utah territory in 1847.

*forty-niners* **those people from all over the world who went to California in search of gold in 1849.** Only a few of the many thousands of them became rich from gold strikes, but many stayed on in the West to farm its fertile lands or to establish businesses.

# Check Your Memory of the Facts

1. *What reasons did people give to support the idea of Manifest Destiny?* **Merchants wanted ports on the Pacific coast where American ships could stop on their way to trade with Asia. Settlers wanted to live on the northwest lands of Oregon and California. Some southerners wanted the land in the Southwest for growing cotton. Political reasons included more states desired by northerners and southerners which would favor their own ideas on slavery. Most Americans also wanted to prevent any European nations from taking over these areas.**

2. *What were some of the Indian groups originally living west of the Mississippi River?* Shoshone, Paiute, Pueblo, Navaho, Apache,

about 105 different groups in California, Kiowa, Cheyenne, Arapaho, Comanche, and Nez Percé. (See also map on p. 197.)

3. *What did the Mexican government ask of Americans who wanted to settle in the territory of Texas?* **to swear loyalty to Mexico and to practice the Catholic religion.**

4. *What happened to the Spanish missions in California after Mexico gained its independence from Spain?* **The lands of the missions were turned over to the government.**

5. *Why were the Mormons persecuted? Where did they finally settle?* **for their religious beliefs; Salt Lake City in Utah in 1847.**

## Check Your Understanding of the Ideas

1. *Why did the Spanish explorers come to western North America?* Spanish explorers had come to search, in vain, for gold in the sixteenth century. In the seventeenth and eighteenth centuries, a small number of Spanish missionaries built missions from Texas to California, hoping to convert the many Indian groups to the Catholic faith. Soldiers and settlers established small outposts like the one at Santa Fe, New Mexico, to serve as a border to protect the lands of central Mexico.

2. *What changes did horses make in the lives of some of the Indians?* Hunting was made easier because larger areas could be searched for food; power in warfare increased; and some groups increased their wealth by trading in horses.

3. *Why was Mexico's independence from Spain in 1821 important to people in the United States?* The Spanish government had greatly restricted trade with, and settlement by, people of the United States. The Mexican government opened these lands to trade and allowed many more settlers from the United States.

4. *Why did the Texans want to be independent from Mexico?* By 1830, most of the eight thousand settlers in Texas were from the southern United States and were slave owners. The Mexicans ended slavery in their country, but the Texan slave owners did not want to give up their slaves. This issue and other problems led to quarrels between the Americans in Texas and the Mexican government which began to doubt the loyalty of these settlers. When Santa Anna became Mexican president in 1835, he ordered new laws which limited the freedom of American Texans even more, and they rebelled.

5. *Why did the candidates for President in the 1844 election agree or disagree with annexing Texas?* In general, political leaders had avoided the issue of adding new lands because they feared that disagreements over slavery would split their parties. In the case of

Texas, there was the additional concern that annexation might lead to war with Mexico. By the time of the election, party leaders felt that public opinion favored annexation more than it was split over slavery. The Democrats chose Polk as their candidate, and he promised to annex Texas and secure Oregon for the United States. Whig candidate Clay, fearing the loss of southern votes if he stood against it, also promised to annex Texas if it could be done without war. Polk won the election by a narrow margin.

6. *In what ways did the westward movement affect the government? The Indians? The settlers?* The westward movement of United States citizens caused serious problems in the government's relations with Mexico and England because of the demands of these settlers to make the new lands part of the United States. Once the lands were brought into the United States, the problem of balancing the slavery interests of North and South grew worse. As the territory of the country grew in size, so did the responsibility of the government to protect its citizens and promote their welfare.

The Indian peoples who lived on the western lands suffered greatly as white settlement increased. All Indians' landholdings and cultures were permanently changed by the advance of whites, and some Indian groups died out completely. Those who survived lost most of their land and were pushed onto reservations.

Some settlers died on the long, hard journey west or in battles against the Indians. Those who settled there found rich lands for farming and ranching. Some acquired wealth in mining, trade, or other businesses.

# Chapter 11

## Identify

*Samuel Slater* **builder of the first textile mill in the United States** at Pawtucket, Rhode Island, in 1790. He had come to the United States from England and had memorized the plans for the machines he had used there.

*Elias Howe* **inventor of a machine which could sew cloth faster than a person could sew it by hand.**

*Eli Whitney* **inventor of the cotton gin** in 1793 which made the task of separating the cotton seeds from the fiber much faster and easier.

*Cyrus McCormick* **developer of a mechanical reaper** which enabled farmers to harvest five times more wheat in one day than they had done before.

*Nat Turner*   **a slave who led a revolt against slave owners in Virginia in 1831.** Turner and his followers killed sixty whites before state and federal troops put down the revolt. Turner was captured and put to death; more than two hundred blacks were killed, some of whom were not part of the revolt.

## Explain

*industry*   **the making and selling of goods.** The development of machinery greatly helped the growth of industry in the United States.

*textile machines*   **machines for making cloth.**

*factory system*   **a method of production in which the making of a product is divided into separate tasks and machines are used to produce standard parts for an item.** The factory system enabled business owners to use workers with less training because they would perform the same task over and over. Using machinery to make parts ensured that the parts would be so alike that they could be used to replace each other in an item. The factory system greatly increased the speed of production, lowered the price of many items, and led to the loss of jobs for many skilled artisans.

*interchangeable parts*   **those parts of a manufactured item that are standard, or made so alike they can be used to replace each other.** Their development and use made repairing a damaged item much easier and less costly. Interchangeable parts were also very important in making machines.

*cotton gin*   **a machine which made the separation of cotton seeds from cotton fiber much easier and faster,** greatly reducing the amount of time needed to prepare the cotton for market. The use of the cotton gin made large crops more profitable, so many growers wanted more land and slaves.

*labor unions*   **organizations of workers who attempt to improve working conditions by bargaining with employers.**

*strike*   **a refusal by workers to do their jobs until their employers agree to certain demands,** usually such things as higher pay, shorter working hours, or safer working conditions.

*immigrants*   **people who come from one country to live and work in another country.**

*discrimination*   **unfair treatment because of a person's race, religion, nationality, or sex.**

## Check Your Memory of the Facts

1. *Who started the first textile mill in the United States?   Where was it located?*   **Samuel Slater, Pawtucket, Rhode Island.**

2. *Which section of the United States developed more factories in the years before 1860?* **the North,** especially New England.
3. *What methods of transportation and communication developed?* **hard-surfaced roads, canals, steamboats, and railroads; telegraph.**
4. *What new farm machines were invented?* **cotton gin, steel plow, mechanical reaper.**
5. *From what countries did most of the immigrants come in the 1840's and 1850's?* **Ireland and Germany,** mostly because of crop failures and political troubles there.
6. *How many slaves were there in the South in 1860? How many of them worked on large plantations?* **about four million; over half.**

## Check Your Understanding of the Ideas

1. *What two ideas were important to the factory system? Why?* Dividing the manufacture of an item into separate tasks and the use of interchangeable parts in an item enabled employers to hire less-skilled workers, increased speed, and lowered costs of production.
2. *What things contributed to the growth of cities?* development and growth of factories, population increase, development of better means of transportation and communication.
3. *Why were labor unions formed?* Most factory workers earned barely enough money to cover living costs in spite of working very long hours, generally under poor conditions.
4. *How did some people feel about the immigrants?* Some people feared change like the growing number of immigrants. There was often resentment of immigrants among workers because the immigrants would accept work for lower wages at a time when American-born workers were beginning to demand higher pay. Religious differences added to this resentment. Most Americans were Protestants and feared that the Catholic immigrants might become a strong political group, endangering freedom of religion in the United States.
5. *What were some of the attitudes of slave owners toward slaves? Of slaves toward slavery?* Slave owners generally considered slaves as property to be bought or sold and used as workers under any conditions the owners wished. Most owners feared slave revolts and kept tight control over the activities of their slaves. Some owners defended slavery as a secure way of life for blacks and whites to live together. Most slaves did not agree with a way of life in which another person could make any demands and give any punishment they wished to a person "owned." Many tried to escape by running away or joined in slave revolts.

# Chapter 12

## Identify

*William Lloyd Garrison*  **an abolitionist who published a newspaper** called the *Liberator* in which he called for freedom for all slaves.

*Frederick Douglass*  **a former slave who worked for abolition.** Publisher of the *North Star* newspaper, he wrote and spoke against slavery and religious and racial discrimination.

*Sojourner Truth*  **a former slave who traveled around the country to speak for the rights of women and blacks.** She had been set free by a New York law ending slavery in 1827.

*Stephen A. Douglas*  **a senator from Illinois who wrote the Kansas-Nebraska Act of 1854.** He fought in Congress to pass Clay's plan known later as the Compromise of 1850. He participated in a series of debates against Lincoln on slavery issues.

*Harriet Tubman*  **a former slave who became one of the most famous and successful conductors on the Underground Railroad.**

*Harriet Beecher Stowe*  **author of *Uncle Tom's Cabin,*** a novel describing the severe and cruel conditions of the slave system.

*Abraham Lincoln*  **President of the United States elected in 1860.** His election resulted in the secession of several states from the Union.

*John Brown*  **abolitionist who led a raid on the federal arsenal at Harpers Ferry, Virginia.** He hoped to operate a fort in the Allegheny Mountains and start a war to free the slaves. Brown was captured after a fight and later hanged.

*Jefferson Davis*  **former United States senator chosen to be president of the Confederate States of America.**

## Explain

*abolition*  **the movement to end slavery.** It was an issue between people in the North and South from the beginning of the United States.

*prejudice*  **an attitude or opinion about a person, group, or race that is not based on sound reasoning.** Prejudice against black people was widespread.

*Wilmot Proviso*  **a proposed law stating that any land the United States gained as a result of the Mexican War would be free from slavery.** Because of opposition from members of Congress from the South, it was voted down each time it came up.

*popular sovereignty*  **a term used for the idea of letting settlers in new territories decide for themselves whether or not to allow slavery.**

*Fugitive Slave Act*  **a part of the Compromise of 1850 which made the return of blacks to slavery easier. Federal officers were used to capture and return the slaves, and any citizen could be required to help.** Blacks were not allowed jury trials if accused of being runaway slaves and could not speak in court to defend themselves.

*Underground Railroad*  **the name for secret groups who helped slaves escape to the North or to Canada.** The groups hid slaves in their homes during the day and helped them along to the next station at night to avoid being caught.

*Kansas-Nebraska Act*  **a law passed to divide the land of the Great Plains into two territories called Kansas and Nebraska.** The law also repealed the Missouri Compromise and allowed the question of slavery there to be decided by popular sovereignty.

*Dred Scott decision*  **a ruling by the Supreme Court which denied freedom to a slave, Dred Scott, and also stated that Congress had no right to prohibit slavery in the territories.**

*secession*  **the act of withdrawing.** Secession from the Union was the answer of some states in the South to the election of Abraham Lincoln.

## Check Your Memory of the Facts

1. *What position did Zachary Taylor take on the issues of the 1848 election?*  **Taylor did not defend slavery and was strongly opposed to sectionalism.** As a candidate, he did not make his stand on slavery in the territories known. As President, Taylor favored the idea of popular sovereignty.

2. *What were the main parts of the Compromise of 1850?*  **California was admitted to the Union as a free state; New Mexico and Utah were to decide for themselves about slavery; the slave trade was stopped in the District of Columbia; the Fugitive Slave Act was passed; and land claimed by both New Mexico and Texas became part of New Mexico.**

3. *What events led to "Bleeding Kansas"?*  **The Kansas-Nebraska Act divided the land into two territories and repealed the Compromise of 1850** which had not allowed slavery in the area. The people were to decide for themselves about slavery. Kansas then became the battleground between proslavery and antislavery forces.

4. *What issues did Stephen Douglas and Abraham Lincoln debate in the race for senator from Illinois?*  **the spread of slavery, popular sovereignty, and the Dred Scott case.**

5. *What helped the Republicans win the presidential election of 1860?*  **Northern and Southern Democrats could not agree on a person who would represent both sections. They chose two differ-**

ent candidates and that split the Democrat votes, allowing Lincoln to win the election.

6. *Which states joined to form the Confederate States of America?* **South Carolina, Mississippi, Florida, Alabama, Georgia, Louisiana, and Texas.**

## Check Your Understanding of the Ideas

1. *What were the main issues in the conflict over slavery at this time?* The main issues included the spread of slavery into new territories, the activities of abolitionists, the return of runaway slaves, and the representation of free and slave states in Congress.

2. *What was the purpose of the Compromise of 1850? Did it succeed?* to remove the issue of the spread of slavery from national politics by allowing the people in new territories to decide for themselves about slavery. The acts eased tensions for a time but did not succeed in ending the disagreements over slavery.

3. *What was the significance of* Uncle Tom's Cabin? The book introduced thousands of readers to the view of slavery as a cruel system and led many to begin to work for abolition. Over 300,000 copies of the book were sold in the first year of publication.

4. *Why was the Kansas-Nebraska Act written? What effect did it have on the nation?* to organize the land of the Great Plains into territories. It further split the North and South over the issue of slavery and led to the formation of the Republican party which was opposed to the spread of slavery.

5. *What effect did the Dred Scott decision have?* further weakened the legal position of black Americans by stating that slaves were property. The decision also increased sectional conflict by stating that the federal government had no right to prohibit slavery in the territories.

6. *Why did the Republican victory in the 1860 election lead to the secession of several Southern states?* Many Southern leaders believed that Abraham Lincoln would try to destroy slavery and the Southern way of life it supported. They felt that the Republicans would soon control all of the federal government and that Northern policies would harm the South.

# *Chapter 13*

## Identify

*Robert E. Lee* **commander of the main Confederate army in the Civil War.** He surrendered to United States General Ulysses Grant at Appomattox Court House, Virginia, in 1865.

*Clara Barton*   **nurse during the Civil War who later founded the American Red Cross in 1882.**

*Gettysburg*   **a small town in Pennsylvania and the site of one of the most important battles of the Civil War** which took place in July, 1863, ending the Confederate invasion of the North.

*Ulysses S. Grant*   **commander of all Union forces in the Civil War** after his forces won the Battle of Vicksburg, Mississippi, in 1863.

*William T. Sherman*   **general in charge of Union troops in the West,** who marched through Georgia, captured Atlanta, and continued to the Atlantic Ocean. His success again divided the Confederacy.

*John Wilkes Booth*   **the person who shot and killed Abraham Lincoln.**

## Explain

*blockade*   **to close off.** The North established a navy block of the Southern coast, especially the chief ports, during the Civil War.

*Emancipation Proclamation*   **an official announcement made by President Lincoln in 1863 that all slaves within lands under Confederate control were free.**

*drafts*   **the selection of people who must serve in the army.** Both the North and South had to draft soldiers during the Civil War.

## Check Your Memory of the Facts

1.  *Why did the South want to leave the Union?*   **Southern leaders thought that their constitutional rights were being threatened** and that their culture and economy were different from and better than those of the North.

2.  *Why was the North unwilling to let the South leave the Union?*   **Northern leaders felt that the American people had been one nation since before the Constitution was written, that Northern and Southern people shared the same language and culture, that trade flowed back and forth between the two sections, and that the long border between them could lead to disputes if they were separated.**

3.  *How did the constitutions of the Confederate States and the United States differ?*   **The Confederate constitution said that its congress could not pass laws against slavery and that it could not enact tariffs to protect industry.**

4.  *Which slave states did not leave the Union?*   **Missouri, Kentucky, Maryland, and Delaware.**

5.  *Where did the first military action of the Civil War take place?*   **Fort Sumter, South Carolina.**

6. *How did the South and the North compare in population and railroads?* **The North had over twice the population of the South, and it had twenty-one thousand miles of railroad compared to nine thousand miles for the Confederate States.**

7. *Which slaves were freed by the Emancipation Proclamation?* **Although the announcement said that slaves in land under Confederate control were freed, they were not actually freed until those lands were taken over by Union forces.**

## Check Your Understanding of the Ideas

1. *Why did the South claim it had a right to withdraw from the Union?* Southern leaders argued that states' rights were more important than the power of the federal government. They thought that the United States was a joining of the states through an agreement which could be ended at any time.

2. *How did Southerners try to use cotton to influence Great Britain to support them in the war? Why were they unsuccessful?* They withheld their cotton from the British market because they believed that Great Britain's textile mills depended so much on the cotton grown in the South that the British would come to the aid of the Confederacy to keep that trade open. Britain, however, was able to find other sources of cotton after the Union blockade cut off trade between Britain and the Confederate States.

3. *What were the Confederate military plans for the war? The Union plans?* The Confederate plans were to defend the South from invasion and to try to get help from Europe. Southern leaders believed that fighting in the South would give their army an advantage because of its knowledge of the land and resources. The Union plans were to invade and conquer the South, to blockade it against trade with other nations, and to prevent other countries from entering the war to help the Confederacy.

4. *How did Lincoln's actions to end slavery relate to his goal of preserving the Union?* At first, Lincoln feared that ending slavery would cause some Union slave states to join the Confederacy. He later came to feel, as abolition became more popular, that ending slavery would unite the North, hurt the Confederacy, and bring an end to the war. He decided to issue the Emancipation Proclamation.

5. *What attitude toward the South was expressed by Lincoln in his second inaugural address?* Lincoln wished to heal the differences between the North and South as quickly as possible without punishing the people in the seceded states.

# Chapter 14

## Identify

*Andrew Johnson*   **Vice-President of the United States under Lincoln. He became President when Lincoln was assassinated.**

*Hiram Revels*   **the first black senator in the nation's history,** elected from Mississippi in 1870.

*Blanche K. Bruce*   **a former slave who was elected to the United States Senate from Mississippi in 1874.**

*Rutherford B. Hayes*   **President of the United States, elected in 1876.**

## Explain

*reconstruction*   **the process of rebuilding the nation after the Civil War.** It included physical, legal, political, and economic aspects of life.

*freedmen*   **men, women, and children who had been slaves but had received their legal freedom after the Civil War.**

*Black Codes*   **laws passed by many Southern state governments after the Civil War to limit the rights and opportunities of blacks.** The codes often kept black people from testifying against whites or from serving on juries. Some codes described the kinds of jobs which blacks could hold or forced jobless freedmen to work for their former owners.

*impeach*   **to charge an official with crimes while in office.** Under the Constitution, a President who is impeached by the House of Representatives has a trial in the Senate. A President who is found guilty is removed from office.

*scalawags*   **a name applied, by their enemies, to Southern whites who supported the Republican party aims during Reconstruction.** Many had owned plantations or businesses and wanted to control black voters as they had controlled black slaves.

*carpetbaggers*   **a name applied, by their enemies, to Northern whites who moved to the South after the Civil War.** They were also supporters of the Republican party. Many Southerners considered these people as adventurers carrying all they owned in a bag made from pieces of carpet.

*Ku Klux Klan*   **organization begun in 1866 by former Confederate soldiers to keep blacks from voting.** The KKK waged a campaign of terror against blacks and anyone who helped them.

*Crédit Mobilier*   **a construction company set up by the directors of the Union Pacific Railroad.** The directors gave contracts to their own company to build the railroad at very high prices. They took the profits for themselves and their friends in the federal government, cheating the stockholders of the railroad. The scandal that followed was one of several that turned people's attention away from reconstruction.

## Check Your Memory of the Facts

1. *What years were known as the Reconstruction period?* **1865 to 1876.**
2. *What were two views about returning the seceded states to the Union?* **One view was that certain individuals had led a rebellion but that the states themselves were still part of the Union. Another view was that the seceded states were no longer part of the United States and that they would have to apply for admission as new territories did.**
3. *What did the Radical Republicans want to do?* **They wanted to protect the rights of the freed slaves and to increase the power of the Republican party in the North and the South.**
4. *Which states responded to Lincoln's plan for reconstruction?* **Louisiana, Arkansas, Tennessee, and Virginia.**
5. *Which states responded to Johnson's plan for reconstruction?* **South Carolina, North Carolina, Alabama, Mississippi, Florida, Georgia, and Texas.**
6. *What was the Freedmen's Bureau?* *What did it do?* **The Bureau of Refugees, Freedmen, and Abandoned Lands was a government agency established by Congress in 1865. It was to provide food, clothing, fuel, and land to poor or homeless blacks and whites in the South after the Civil War.** Agents of the Bureau traveled throughout the South helping people in need.
7. *Which was the first state to return to the Union with the approval of Congress?* *What did Congress ask of the seceded states at that time?* **Tennessee was the first state to return to the Union with the approval of Congress. States were asked to approve the Fourteenth Amendment before being returned to the Union.**
8. *What did Congress ask of the seceded states applying to return to the Union after 1869?* **States had to approve the Fifteenth Amendment before being returned to the Union.**

## Check Your Understanding of the Ideas

1. *What were the important differences between the plans for reconstruction of Lincoln, Johnson, and the Radical Republicans?* According to Lincoln's plan, 10 percent of the voters in each state had to take an oath of loyalty, and states had to accept the Emancipation

Proclamation. Under Johnson's plan, a majority of voters had to take an oath of loyalty. Under the plan of Congress, each state had to hold constitutional conventions to create new state governments. All men who took an oath of loyalty, except certain Confederate officials, could vote for delegates to the state conventions. The states had to allow black men to vote. The new state governments then had to approve the Fourteenth Amendment to be returned to the Union.

2. *What actions by Southern governments showed that their attitudes toward blacks were the same as before the Civil War?*   The passage of Black Codes returned many Southern blacks to conditions much like slavery. They could not testify at trials against whites, could not serve on juries, and were limited in job opportunities. After 1876, many states kept blacks from voting and taking part in government.

3. *What was an important result of the election of 1868?*   Republican candidate Ulysses Grant was elected President. As a result of support for their party shown by black voters, Republicans in Congress proposed the Fifteenth Amendment to guarantee that blacks would be able to vote in the future. Some Northern states also had been keeping blacks from voting before passage of the amendment. The amendment said that no state could keep a person from voting because of color.

4. *What events caused Northern voters to lose their concern for protecting the rights of blacks?*   The scandals in the federal government under President Grant helped to turn the attention of voters away from Reconstruction. Many people in the Northern states were opposed to the Fifteenth Amendment because they did not want blacks there to vote. When all of the Southern states were returned to the Union, many Northerners may have felt that it was no longer necessary to press for the rights of blacks.

5. *How was the presidential election of 1876 finally decided?*   The leaders of the two parties made a deal among themselves. In exchange for Democratic support for Rutherford B. Hayes as President, the Republicans agreed to remove federal troops from the South and to support a bill for building a transcontinental railroad through the South. A special commission was set up which gave all disputed votes to the Republican candidate Hayes.

6. *How did the Civil War affect blacks?*   The Civil War ended the issue of legal slavery in the United States, and black people gained legal freedom and the rights of citizenship. While the outcome of the war promised black people a better future, Black Codes and groups organized to oppose blacks, such as the Ku Klux Klan, created conditions which left most blacks poor and without power.

# Chapter 15

## Identify

*Elizabeth Cady Stanton*   **a leader in the women's rights movement** who helped organize the first women's rights convention at Seneca Falls, New York, in 1848. She was also an abolitionist before the Civil War and later worked especially for women's suffrage.

*Virginia Louisa Minor*   **woman who tried to register to vote in Missouri in 1872, claiming that the Fourteenth Amendment gave women that right.** Her claim was denied, and the Supreme Court later ruled that the Constitution gave no one the right to vote but only said who could not be denied that right by the states.

*Thomas A. Edison*   **an inventor who developed many things** including an electric light and an improved telegraph system. He established a laboratory at Menlo Park, New Jersey, where groups of inventors came to work.

*Edwin Drake*   **driller of the first successful oil well** near Titusville, Pennsylvania, in 1859.

*Andrew Carnegie*   **an important leader in the American steel industry** whose company bought its own supplies of iron ore and coal and also the boats and trains to ship these resources.

*John D. Rockefeller*   **head of the Standard Oil Company** which controlled over 90 percent of the oil refining business in the United States.

*Chief Sitting Bull*   **one of the leaders of the Sioux Indians at the Battle of the Little Bighorn.**

*Colonel George Custer*   **commander of a group of United States Army soldiers who were killed at the Battle of the Little Bighorn.**

*Chief Joseph*   **leader of a group of Nez Percé Indians who resisted attempts by the federal government to force them onto a small reservation** in 1877.

## Explain

*suffrage*   **the right to vote.**

*sharecropping*   **a system of farming in which a landowner supplies farmers with cabins, mules, other supplies, and a section of land in return for part of the crop grown by the farmer.** The system developed in the South after the Civil War.

*consumers*   **people who buy goods.**

*rebate*   **part of an amount charged for something which is given back to the customer.**

*corporations* **groups of investors who buy shares of stock.**

*trusts* **companies which own enough stock in other companies to control the making and selling of a product.**

## Check Your Memory of the Facts

1. *What economic changes took place in the South after the Civil War?* **Sharecropping developed, many plantations were sold or taken over by merchants or bankers, and many mills and factories were built in the South after the Civil War.**

2. *How did the organization of some businesses change in the 1870's?* **More corporations were formed** to meet the need for larger amounts of money to start or run businesses competitively. **Some corporations were organized into trusts** to control the making and selling of a product.

3. *What steps did Carnegie and Rockefeller take to gain control of the steel and oil industries?* **Both Carnegie and Rockefeller took steps to reduce competition and to lower their costs.** Carnegie bought sources of iron ore and coal and also boats and railroads to ship these resources. Rockefeller bought out smaller companies, got railroad rebates, and used other ways to reduce costs. Smaller companies could not compete, and many either sold out or were forced out of business.

4. *What is an advantage of a corporation?* **Corporations allow people to get large amounts of money from many investors to start into business.** An advantage for stockholders is that, if the business fails, they lose only what they paid for shares.

5. *What effects did the transcontinental railroad have?* **The railroad attracted thousands of immigrants to settle in the area served by the railroad; millions of acres were settled and farmed for the first time; people could ship livestock and goods more easily; and the lands and lives of many Indian groups on the Great Plains were permanently changed.**

6. *What problems did the farmers and ranchers face on the Great Plains?* **Farmers faced a shortage of rainfall, blizzards in winter, swarms of grasshoppers, and wild animals. Cattle ranchers found it difficult to take their cattle to market before the building of the railroads through the Great Plains.** Farmers and ranchers also fought over the use of the land.

7. *What events led to renewed conflict between the Indians and the settlers?* **The movement of farmers, miners, ranchers, and railroad workers onto Indian lands renewed the conflict.** The railroads crossed Indian lands and led to the destruction of most of the buffalo herds. Miners invading Sioux territory in the Dakotas and Montana led to a long series of wars.

# Check Your Understanding of the Ideas

1. *What things led to the rapid growth of production in the 1870's?* Governments at all levels helped businesses by keeping taxes low and by passing protective tariffs for industry. Population growth added more people to make goods and also more consumers to buy them. New inventions allowed work to be done faster and goods to be made quicker and easier. New sources of raw materials or new uses for them led to new industries or better ways of producing things.

2. *Why did women organize to gain the right to vote?* Many women felt that during the Civil War they had again shown that they were capable citizens who were entitled to vote. They felt that laws such as the Fourteenth and Fifteenth amendments passed to protect voting rights of black men should be applied to all women as well.

3. *What does the Constitution say about suffrage?* The Constitution does not say who can vote but only which people cannot be denied the right to vote. The Fourteenth, Fifteenth, and other later amendments state who cannot be denied the right to vote. The power to decide voter qualifications is left to the states.

4. *What were the advantages and disadvantages of sharecropping for the landowner? For the farmer?* The system of sharecropping allowed landowners to put their fields into production at very low labor costs. By signing contracts with mill owners for cotton, the landowners were assured of selling the crops when harvested. Over the years, the emphasis on growing cotton led to worn-out soil, poor harvests, and low profits. The major advantage of the system for the farmer was that it provided a living for people with no money or land. The disadvantages were that farmers were constantly in debt and often had to borrow against the next year's crop to get supplies. This meant that the farmers would have to continue to work for the landowners with little hope of getting out of debt.

5. *What things about a monopoly helped or hurt the consumer? The monopoly itself? The smaller competitors?* Most monopolies were able to offer lower prices for their products than could smaller companies. However, once the monopoly became established, the consumer had little choice of where to buy a product. Without fear of competition, a monopoly can raise prices at any time. The ability to control costs helps monopolies to lower prices which increases sales and company growth. The ability of monopolies to lower prices is a factor most harmful to possible competitors.

6. *How did the railroad companies help settle the Great Plains?* The railroads were given large grants of land by the federal and state governments which they advertised for sale and settlement in many countries. Thousands of immigrants and people from other parts of

the United States settled on this land. The railroads made it possible for ranchers and farmers to ship their products to market and to receive goods from the East and Midwest.

# Chapter 16

## Identify

*the Grange*   **an organization for farmers founded in 1867.** Its full name is the National Grange of the Patrons of Husbandry.

*Aaron Montgomery Ward*   **founder of a mail order business.** He sent a catalog to farm people offering store goods at lower prices than those charged by general stores in most farm areas. His business was very successful, and his catalog became a very important book to many American farm families.

*Knights of Labor*   **a national labor union organized in 1869.** Its full name was the Noble Order of the Knights of Labor, and it invited all workers to join, including blacks and women.

*Mother Mary Jones*   **a woman who joined the Knights of Labor.**

*Haymarket Square*   **a place in Chicago where police and protesting workers became involved in a riot in 1886.**

*Samuel Gompers*   **founder of the American Federation of Labor.**

*James Garfield*   **President of the United States elected in 1880.** He was shot and killed by an angry job seeker in 1881.

*Chester Arthur*   **President of the United States following the death of James Garfield.** He supported the law for national civil service reform.

*Helen Hunt Jackson*   **author of *A Century of Dishonor*.** Her book told of the many times that the American government had broken lawful treaties with the American Indians.

## Explain

*laissez-faire*   **a French term which means to let people do as they please.** Applied to American business, it means that government should make as few rules as possible so that there is a lot of competition which produces lower prices for the public.

*regulation*   **making rules.** Some Americans called for government regulation of the size and power of trusts as a way to restore competition in the 1870's.

*Interstate Commerce Act*   **a law to regulate railroads.** Passed in 1887, it set up the Interstate Commerce Commission to check into railroad business and to take lawbreaking companies to court.

*anarchists*   **people who believe in doing away with governments.**

*merit system*   **a method of filling government jobs through competitive examinations.** The merit system was used in place of the spoils system for some jobs after the Pendleton Act was passed.

*Pendleton Act*   **a law which established the Civil Service Commission** to give tests for government jobs. The law was passed in 1883 to partly replace the spoils system.

*Chinese Exclusion Act*   **a law which stated that Chinese workers could not come to the United States for ten years and that courts in the United States could not give citizenship to Chinese persons already in the country.** The law was passed in 1882 as a result of widespread prejudice against Chinese immigrants.

*Dawes Act*   **a law passed to make Indians become individual landowning farmers.** After twenty-five years, Indians would become citizens of the United States. The law divided lands held by Indians as a group into individual family lots, contrary to Indian customs and beliefs. Land left over was given or sold to whites. After the Dawes Act, the Indians had 60 percent less land than before.

*lobbies*   **efforts to influence legislation or government policy.** Lobbies were not always successful, and the local and national governments were slow to answer the demands of citizens in the 1880's and 1890's.

## Check Your Memory of the Facts

1.  *What did farmers want the government to do about railroads?*   **to regulate fair and standard railroad rates.**

2.  *What changes took place in the way goods were sold or marketed?*   **the development of chain stores, the development of department stores, and the beginning of mail order sales.**

3.  *Terence Powderly wanted the members of the Knights of Labor to do what kinds of things?*   **to establish their own mines, factories, and railroads by working together as a community.**

4.  *How did some party bosses gain power?*   **by use of the spoils system and through control of contracts for city work.**

5.  *From what new areas did many immigrants come in the 1880's?*   **eastern and southern Europe.**

## Check Your Understanding of the Ideas

1.  *Why would there be lower prices under laissez-faire?*   According to the ideas of laissez-faire, lack of government regulation results in a greater number of companies competing against each other to sell their goods. One of the ways they would compete is in lowering prices so that more people can afford to buy their products.

2. *Why did some people want the government to regulate trusts?* Trusts did not fit the ideas of laissez-faire and free competition. They controlled entire industries and eliminated competition, thereby having the power to set prices as high as people would pay.

3. *Why did the changes in the way goods were sold and marketed come about?* Manufacturers and store owners looked for new ways to market and sell goods in greater volume which had been made possible by increased demand from population growth and increased supply from industrial growth.

4. *Why did the Interstate Commerce Act fail to help farmers immediately?* Courts continued to rule for some years in favor of the railroads, partly because the law did not say what a reasonable rate was although it was written to force the railroad companies to charge "reasonable rates."

5. *Why did the Supreme Court say that only Congress had the power to make laws for interstate commerce?* Congress is the lawmaking body of the national government, the only level of government with authority to make laws that bind the people of more than one state. A state's authority is binding only within its own borders.

6. *What conditions caused labor unions to grow? What actions caused unions to lose members?* The increased use of machines and the growth of large, less personal companies led more workers to turn to labor groups for help with their work problems. Unsuccessful strikes, lack of effective leadership, and the violence accompanying many strikes led to the loss of union membership.

7. *How did population growth affect cities and their governments?* Population in the cities grew twice as fast as that in rural areas, and many city governments could not provide all the services needed because of lack of money and workers.

8. *What was the effect of the Dawes Act?* Under it, the Indian population lost more than 60 percent of its total lands. Reservation lands which had been returned to Indian groups were divided into lots and given to individual Indian families with "leftover" land given or sold to white settlers and business people. By forcing the policy of individual farm life upon all Indian families, the Dawes Act placed further restrictions and strains upon the separate and distinct Indian cultures.

9. *What were the reforms people asked of the government? For each reform, why was it demanded? Which group of people were to be helped? Which group or groups were hurt?* Reforms demanded by Americans included government regulation of trusts, railroad rates, and immigration, as well as reform of the Indian policy and of civil service. Many Americans supported the call for regulation of trusts as a way of restoring competition within industries and to prevent trusts from controlling prices. Those who expected to be

helped were people in small businesses and general consumers; those who expected to be hurt were the stockholders and controllers of the trusts. Regulation of railroad rates was called for because railroad companies often charged higher rates along routes where they had a monopoly on service. Those who expected to be helped were shippers in general and farmers in particular because they believed that their financial problems were a result of high costs, especially high shipping costs. Those who expected to be hurt were the investors and controllers of the railroad companies. Because of corruption and inefficiency, many people supported government reform and particularly reform of the spoils system. The merit system of filling government jobs was expected to provide all citizens with better government. Those who opposed the reform of the spoils system were the party bosses who controlled it, often members of Congress, and those people who received jobs under the spoils system but did not expect to be able to compete with others for the jobs through testing. Pressure for regulation of immigration came from prejudiced Americans as well as workers who were concerned about their jobs and wages. Regulation was expected to benefit American workers. Those who were hurt by the immigration laws passed were some of the people who wanted to come to the United States from southern and eastern Europe and from Asia, especially the Chinese people who were specifically excluded from immigration. The families and friends of those people, who already lived in the country, were also hurt. The demand for a change in the government's Indian policy was supposed to help the Indians and correct the injustices of the past. The policy change was harmful to most Indians.

# Chapter 17

## Identify

*Benjamin Harrison* **President of the United States elected in 1888.** He lost the election of 1892 to Democratic candidate Grover Cleveland.

*William Jennings Bryan* **candidate of both Populist and Democratic parties in the presidential election of 1896.**

*William McKinley* **President elected in 1896.** He served in office during the Spanish-American War.

*Booker T. Washington* **an important black leader in the United States during the 1890's and 1900's** whose views were accepted by many whites. Washington favored educating black people for jobs in trade or farming before concern over their political or social rights.

*William E. B. DuBois*  **an important black leader who wrote *The Souls of Black Folk*** in 1903. In it, he spoke against Washington's views on education for blacks and wrote of justice.

*Theodore Roosevelt*  **Assistant Secretary of the Navy who ordered American ships to take over the Philippines in case of war with Spain.**

*Emilio Aguinaldo*  **Filipino leader who led the rebellion against American rule in the Philippines** after the Spanish-American War.

## Explain

*National People's party*  **a political party formed in 1892 by people who were dissatisfied with government policies.**

*Populists*  **members of the National People's party** who included farmers, miners, industry workers, and owners of small businesses.

*platform*  **the program of a political party.** The Populist platform of 1892 called for many reforms.

*initiative*  **a way that the voters of a state can propose laws without the legislature by having a certain number of voters sign a petition to bring the proposed law before the people for a vote.**

*referendum*  **a way, through petition, to place an existing law before the voters for their approval or disapproval.**

*grandfather clause*  **a part of the new constitutional laws passed by several southern states to limit voting rights of black people.** According to it, people could vote if their fathers or grandfathers had been allowed to vote on January 1, 1867. Most blacks at that time had been slaves.

*Plessy v. Ferguson*  **a case in which the Supreme Court ruled that states could maintain separate but equal facilities for black and white people.** The ruling made the segregation of black people legal in the United States.

*segregation*  **the practice of separating black people from white people in many areas of everyday life.** Segregation was enforced by law in much of the South and was practiced in fact in much of the North.

## Check Your Memory of the Facts

1. *What were three main changes the Populists demanded in their platform?*  **coinage of silver dollars, an income tax, and the election of United States senators by popular vote.**

2. *How successful were the Populists in the elections of 1892?*  **Their presidential candidate lost, but they succeeded in electing three governors, five United States senators, and ten members of the House of Representatives.**

3. *How did some states keep black people from voting?*  **by passing voting laws like the poll tax, literacy test, and grandfather clause.**

4. *How did Alaska and Hawaii become American territories?* **The United States bought Alaska from Russia in 1867. Hawaii was annexed to the United States in 1898** after a revolution against the Hawaiian monarchy.

5. *What events led to the Spanish-American War?* **American newspaper reports on the Cuban revolt of 1895, publication of Spanish official's letter "insulting" President McKinley, explosion aboard the American battleship *Maine* killing more than 250 crew members, and Congressional recognition of Cuba's independence with the demand that the Spanish leave the island.**

6. *What were the peace settlements of the Spanish-American War?* **According to the treaty signed by Spain and the United States, Cuba received its independence. Puerto Rico and the island of Guam in the Pacific were given to the United States. The Philippines were sold to the United States for the sum of twenty million dollars.**

## Check Your Understanding of the Ideas

1. *What reasons did the Populists give for their platform demands?* Populists wanted a return to the coinage of silver in addition to gold to increase the country's supply of money. They believed that it would raise farm crop prices and would make their debts easier to pay. The Populists wanted an income tax so that the federal government could receive money to operate in some way other than by tariffs which the party believed to be an unfair burden on the poor since they raised the price of imported goods. The kind of income tax they wanted would make people with more money pay a higher tax than those with less money. Because the Populists believed that many state legislatures were controlled by business people, they wanted senators to be elected by the people's votes and not by the state legislatures.

2. *How did black leaders differ in their ideas about how to gain rights for black people?* Booker T. Washington promoted the idea that blacks should concentrate on learning trade or farming skills to make a living and should not press openly for equality with whites. Others, like Trotter and DuBois, believed that blacks should aim at full equality with whites in education, citizenship, and other areas of everyday life.

3. *Why did the Populists lose their importance as a separate party?* The Populist view of many issues was taken over by the Democratic party, and some issues became less important because of changes. The discovery of gold in Alaska, for example, increased the supply of money.

4. *Why did some people favor overseas expansion? Why did others oppose it?* Many business people favored overseas expansion as a

way to increase the nation's supply of raw materials and the number of markets for their goods. Military leaders favored the idea of overseas bases, especially for the navy, as a way to improve the defense of the United States. Other Americans felt that they had a duty to convert the people in these lands to Christianity. Some of those who opposed expansion felt that new territories would increase the cost of defending the nation against attack. Some Americans were prejudiced against people living in other countries and did not want them to be part of the United States. Still others were opposed to expansion on the grounds that gaining new lands overseas meant taking it away from others and that a democratic nation like the United States should allow other people to decide their own forms of government.

5. *Why was the Spanish-American War a short one?* Spain's control of its overseas empire had been weakened by many revolts over the years before the war began. It did not take long for the more powerful and modern United States navy to break Spain's control.

6. *How did the people in the territories gained by the United States react to the peace settlements of the war?* Some, like the Puerto Ricans, had mixed feelings. Many of their business people favored American control while other leaders did not. Many Filipinos were violently opposed to American control and wanted independence for the Philippines.

7. *How did the United States govern its new territories?* through a system of appointed governors and two-house legislatures. In Puerto Rico, the members of the legislature were elected by the people. The governor was appointed by the President of the United States, however, and had complete veto power over the legislature. In the Philippines, the people elected only the members of the lower house. The governor and a group of commissioners who served as the upper house of the legislature were appointed by the President of the United States.

# Chapter 18

## Identify

*Victor Herbert* **one of the first important American composers** in musical theater.

*Louisa May Alcott* **a popular American author** of the late 1800's who wrote stories of young people in New England.

*Mark Twain*  **the pen name of a popular American author of the late 1800's, Samuel Clemens,** who traveled widely and wrote humorous and witty stories of life as he saw it.

*Jacob Riis*  **a Danish immigrant to the United States who published a book called *How the Other Half Lives*.** It contained his photographs of overcrowded apartment houses and writings about the lack of food and poor health conditions for many people living in cities.

*Jane Addams*  **founder of a settlement house in Chicago in 1887.** She also felt that children should not be treated like adults when they got into trouble with the law. Her influence helped pass the first state law that set up juvenile courts.

*J. P. Morgan*  **a New York banker who gained a strong voice in the control of many large companies by lending them money.** He also helped organize the first billion dollar corporation, United States Steel, in 1901.

*Woodrow Wilson*  **President of the United States elected in 1912.** He continued Roosevelt's policy of "trustbusting" but also supported the Clayton Antitrust Act which stated that labor unions should not be treated as trusts.

## Explain

*Progressives*  **reformers who believed that their ideas would lead to progress and a better way of life for all Americans.**

*Morrill Act*  **a law passed by Congress in 1862 which gave land to the states for the establishment of colleges.** This law helped to increase the number of colleges in the United States.

*settlement house*  **a place in many large cities where people could go for help** in finding jobs, learning the English language, or receiving medical care. They were founded as part of the social justice movement to improve the lives of poor people.

*National Urban League*  **an organization whose members trained black people as social workers and who helped blacks find housing in large cities.**

*recall*  **a way for voting citizens to remove an elected official from office** if they feel that the person is not doing a good job.

*Federal Reserve Act*  **a law passed by Congress in 1913 to set up the Federal Reserve banking system.**

*Bureau of Corporations*  **a government agency set up under President Theodore Roosevelt to check into the operations of large corporations.** If it was believed that a corporation was breaking antitrust laws, the Bureau took its case to court.

*injunction*  **a special court order.** In the early 1900's, judges often issued injunctions to stop strikes. If striking workers ignored the injunction, they could be arrested and put in jail.

*Clayton Antitrust Act* **a law passed under President Wilson which stated that labor unions were not organizations whose actions could keep trade from taking place in the same way that trusts limited trade.**

## Check Your Memory of the Facts

1. *What were some of the reasons for increased spare-time activities? What were some of the activities?* **The growing use of many different kinds of machines,** at work and at home, gave people more spare time. They used it to attend **sporting events and the theater, for bicycle riding, reading, traveling, and in trying to improve their lives and the lives of other Americans.**

2. *Who were the reformers? What did they start out to do?* **Reformers included teachers, social workers, lawyers, church leaders, business people, and politicians. They started out to help the poor people living in large cities.**

3. *What were some of the reforms tried in the area of social justice?* **Social justice reforms included creating better opportunities for education and jobs and improving health and living conditions.**

4. *How were children affected by reforms?* **At the federal level of government, a Children's Bureau was established to investigate conditions of health, education, and work involving children.** It made recommendations to Congress for laws to protect them. **At state and local levels, a juvenile court system was established and governments were pressed to build parks and playgrounds.** Most states passed laws requiring that some amount of children's time be spent in school.

5. *What new forms of city government were introduced? What was important about them?* **The commission and the city manager forms of government were introduced. The commission form allowed each member to work on one area of government instead of having a mayor try to cover all areas. The city manager form allowed the city to hire a person trained in city planning whose job was to administer the laws made by the city council in a businesslike way.**

6. *What reform ideas of the Populists were realized in the Progressive Era?* **initiative, referendum, direct election of senators, and the income tax.**

7. *What groups of people were not affected by the reforms of the Progressive Era?* **most people living in rural areas, most black people, and most Mexican Americans.**

8. *What was the purpose of the NAACP?* **to bring cases to court against laws that kept black people from voting or receiving equal treatment.**

## Check Your Understanding of the Ideas

1. *How did increased opportunities for education affect reform movements?* As Americans read and studied more, they became increasingly aware of the needs of others and of possible new ways to solve problems.

2. *What was important about the conservation policies of the Progressives?* Their policies established the idea of the national government's concern over saving the country's natural resources like forest lands and those with important minerals or sources of power.

3. *Why was there a change in attitude toward trusts after 1911?* By that time, more leaders began to believe that there were "good" and "bad" trusts. The "bad" ones were those which charged too much or went too far in putting others out of business. The "good" ones produced goods or services cheaper than any smaller companies could. The Supreme Court decided that the large size of some companies was not always against the antitrust laws. It began to consider whether breaking up a large company would do more harm to the general public than good.

4. *What was important about the Federal Reserve Act?* It established the Federal Reserve banking system which gave the national government a way to regulate some of the country's banking methods. Each member bank had to put a certain amount of its money into the federal banks as a reserve. Members seldom faced ruin if a large number of people wanted to withdraw their savings because the banks had this reserve. The system also gave the government a way to control the general amount of money available for loans.

5. *How do the reforms of the Progressive Era show that the actions of individuals are sometimes regulated for the good of others? Give some examples. Are the reforms of the Progressive Era different from those in the 1870's and 1880's?* Some examples of Progressive reforms which regulated individuals' actions for the good of others are the laws passed to limit working hours of children and women, laws requiring property owners to repair buildings or install sanitary facilities, and laws limiting the size and power of companies and corporations. While the reforms of the Progressive Era included many of the demands of Populists and other groups from the 1870's and 1880's, the Progressives covered a much wider range of interests, as in the social justice movement, than did earlier reformers.

# Chapter 19

## Identify

*Boxers*   the name given by Europeans and Americans to those Chinese people who started a revolt in 1900 to rid their country of all outsiders.

*Manchuria*   an area of rich resources in northern China. Japan and Russia fought a war for control of Manchuria in 1904.

*Isthmus of Panama*   a narrow strip of land in Central America through which a canal connecting the Atlantic and Pacific Oceans was completed in 1914.

*Allied Powers*   those nations belonging to the alliance formed mainly by Great Britain, France, and Russia in the early 1900's.

*Central Powers*   those nations belonging to the alliance formed mainly by Germany, Italy, and Austria-Hungary in the early 1900's.

*Lusitania*   a British passenger ship sunk by a German submarine in 1915. There were 128 American citizens among the more than 1,000 people killed in the attack.

*Herbert Hoover*   director of the Food Administration during World War I.

*General Pershing*   commander of all American troops in Europe during World War I.

*Warren Harding*   President of the United States elected in 1920. He promised to return the country to the ways of life enjoyed before the war.

## Explain

*Open Door Policy*   the American government plan to have all nations with interests in China respect each other's trading rights in that country.

*Gentlemen's Agreement*   an agreement between President Roosevelt and the Japanese government leaders in which the Japanese promised to stop letting workers leave their country for the United States and the President promised that the Japanese people already in the United States would be treated fairly.

*Roosevelt Corollary*   President Theodore Roosevelt's view of the Monroe Doctrine in which he announced that the United States would act as a police power in the Western Hemisphere to protect its interests.

*dictator*   a leader who rules with total power.

*moving assembly line*  **a manufacturing method in which parts of a product are carried from worker to worker until the final product is complete.**

*Selective Service Act*  **a draft law passed by Congress in 1917** under which all male citizens between the ages of twenty-one and thirty had to register with their local draft boards. They were then selected by chance from the register lists to serve in the army.

*convoy system*  **a plan developed by American navy leaders to protect supply ships from attack by sending warships along with them.**

*armistice*  **an agreement to end fighting.** The armistice ending World War I was signed on November 11, 1918.

*Fourteen Points*  **the name given to President Wilson's plan for peace following World War I.**

*Versailles Treaty*  **the peace agreement ending World War I.** The United States did not join the nations signing the treaty but declared an end to the war between the United States and Germany by resolution of Congress in 1921.

## Check Your Memory of the Facts

1. *Why were other nations interested in China?*  **China was rich in natural resources, and its large population made it a good market for manufactured products.**

2. *What two issues made the Japanese government unhappy with the United States?*  **dissatisfaction with the treaty arranged by President Roosevelt to end Japan's war with Russia and the poor treatment given Japanese people living in the United States.**

3. *What United States military actions came from the policy of the Roosevelt Corollary?*  **The United States sent its soldiers to the Dominican Republic in 1905, to Nicaragua in 1912, and to Haiti in 1915** where they took over the collection of tariff and tax money to pay back European countries. In Haiti and the Dominican Republic, the American army actually ran the government.

4. *What German actions led the United States to enter World War I?*  **The sinking of ships by German submarines was a major reason for the United States' entry, as well as the publication of the note from the German government to the government of Mexico asking for their help in case of war against the United States.**

5. *How did the United States prepare for war? What were some of the changes that came from this preparation?*  **The United States changed over to, or increased, its manufacturing of war materials and supplies, set up government agencies to regulate the country's economy to meet new military needs, and started a draft to increase the number of people in the military. These preparations**

**caused thousands of jobs to become available, and many people moved to different areas of the country to fill them.** A large number of black Americans moved from the South to take jobs in the industries of the North. Many Mexican Americans moved from the Southwest to the Midwest for new jobs. Women filled many of the jobs in industries as more men joined the military services.

## Check Your Understanding of the Ideas

1. *What did the United States government try to do through the Open Door Policy?* to protect a share of Chinese trade for its own citizens and to maintain a balance among the foreign powers in China.

2. *Why was a canal through Central America important to people in the United States?* A canal would shorten the route between the Atlantic and Pacific Oceans considerably, which would benefit both United States trade and defense. The route around the continent of South America was long and hard.

3. *What events made poor relations between the United States and Mexico? How did they influence the United States' decision to declare war on Germany?* United States naval interference at Veracruz in 1914, Pancho Villa's attacks on United States citizens around 1916, and the German note suggesting that Mexico join Germany in case of war with the United States. Because relations were not good by the time of the German note, it greatly angered the American public and increased support for the decision to declare war on Germany.

4. *How was Wilson's plan for peace accepted by the Germans? By the Allies? By the United States Senate?* The German government and many of the German people accepted Wilson's plan and expected it to be the basis for the peace treaty ending the war. The Allies ignored many points of Wilson's plan and made plans to punish Germany and to divide its overseas territories among themselves. The League of Nations point was used by the Allies in the final peace treaty. Some members of the United States Senate resented the fact that Wilson had not asked their advice in making compromises with the Allies over peace plans, and some senators were against the idea of a League of Nations. The Senate rejected Wilson's plan by refusing to ratify the Versailles Treaty.

5. *What did the election of 1920 seem to say about the general attitudes of the people of the United States toward other countries?* Candidate James Cox spoke out in favor of joining the League of Nations while candidate Warren Harding did not. Since Harding won the election by a large number of votes, it would seem that the people supported his promise to return the United States to

ways of life enjoyed before the war and did not want to be further involved with other countries.

# Chapter 20

## Identify

*F. Scott Fitzgerald* **a popular American author** of novels about rich young people.

*Ernest Hemingway* **a popular American author** who wrote stories about people in times of war and praised those who faced death and danger.

*Langston Hughes* **a famous black writer** of the Harlem Renaissance of the 1920's who wrote about the lives of American black people.

*John Dewey* **a person who strongly influenced ideas for "progressive education."** Dewey believed that students should try different ideas and learn by doing rather than by drilling on memorized facts.

*Helen Keller* **a person who worked hard to improve conditions for handicapped people.** Keller herself had been blind and deaf from the age of two.

*Marcus Garvey* **founder of the Universal Negro Improvement Association** who believed that black people should be independent from whites. He encouraged blacks to look to Africa to find out about their backgrounds.

*Dr. O. H. Sweet* **a black dentist whose home in a white neighborhood was attacked by a mob of white people.** One of the attackers was killed, and a court later ruled that Dr. Sweet had the right to defend himself when threatened with harm.

*A. Mitchell Palmer* **attorney general of the United States following World War I** who arrested people known or suspected to be Communists during the Red Scare.

*Charles Lindbergh* **pilot who made the first solo flight across the Atlantic Ocean,** flying from New York to Paris without stopping in 1927.

## Explain

*prohibition* **common name given to the Eighteenth Amendment which was a law forbidding people to make, sell, or ship drinking alcohol.**

*yellow-dog contract* **an agreement not to join a labor union** which many employers forced workers to sign before being hired.

*open shop* **a business where there were no labor unions.**

*Red Scare* **name given to the general fear of the American people that "red" communism was spreading throughout the United States after World War I.**

*deport* **to send a person out of the country,** by legal force.

*quota system* **a method of using numbers to set limits.** The quota system was used to limit the number of immigrants allowed to enter the United States from other countries.

## Check Your Memory of the Facts

1. *What were some new forms of entertainment in the 1920's?* **radio, jazz music, movies,** and huge musical productions like the Ziegfield Follies.

2. *What does the Nineteenth Amendment cover?* **voting rights.** It states that people cannot be kept from voting because of their sex.

3. *In what ways did Indians become citizens? What reasons did some Indian groups give for not wishing to be citizens?* **through treaties, marrying white citizens, the Dawes Act of 1887, or by joining the armed services during World War I. Those who did not wish to become citizens feared property taxes on their land, local laws, and the loss of their own religions, languages, and ways of educating their children.**

4. *What was the purpose of the Order of the Sons of America?* **It worked, through political action, for greater educational opportunities for people of Spanish and Mexican background.**

5. *What were some important cases won by the NAACP in the 1920's?* **One ruling meant that black people, as well as white people, had the right to defend themselves when threatened with harm. Another ruling was that black voters could not be kept from voting in primary elections.**

6. *What kinds of things did business leaders do to stop unions from forming? How did these things affect unions?* **Some business leaders hired spies to discover union plans and brought in strikebreakers to work. Some joined the National Association of Manufacturers which set up a plan to keep open shops, kept lists of workers known to be union organizers, and used the yellow-dog contract. These activities greatly reduced the number of union members from what it had been at the end of World War I.**

7. *What new group of immigrants came to the United States in the 1920's? What were their reasons for coming?* **Filipinos came to the United States to work on farms or in the canning and fishing industries, to attend schools in the United States, or from service with the United States Navy.**

8. *How was prejudice against some groups of Americans expressed?* **Local laws were passed which discriminated against certain groups.** In some areas, for example, Asians were not allowed to marry white Americans or to own land. **In 1915, another**

**Ku Klux Klan was organized** which used threats and violence against blacks, Catholics, Jews, and people from foreign countries. The KKK members wanted to keep these people from owning land, voting, or competing against white-owned businesses.

## Check Your Understanding of the Ideas

1. *How was prohibition accepted by American citizens?* A large number of citizens broke the law by making their own liquor and beer at home or by smuggling it into the United States from other countries.

2. *What does the average life expectancy tell about living conditions?* A rising average life expectancy shows that general health and living conditions are improving. If it falls, these conditions are getting worse.

3. *Why did certain groups of Americans feel they deserved better treatment after World War I?* Women, black Americans, and Mexican Americans felt that they deserved all the rights and opportunities of full citizenship in the United States because they had contributed fully to America's successful war efforts.

4. *What ideas about black people were made popular by Marcus Garvey?* Garvey's ideas of pride and dignity for black people have lasted. He encouraged black Americans to learn about the history and achievements of the people of Africa to discover their own backgrounds.

5. *Why was the quota system for immigrants created?* Many Americans feared that there would be a great rush of people from war-torn countries to the United States. The quota system would prevent this and also satisfy the prejudice some Americans had against immigrants from eastern and southern European countries and from Asia.

6. *What kinds of information show the huge growth of the economy during the 1920's?* information on the amount of goods produced in the country, the wages of workers, how people spend their money.

# *Chapter 21*

## Identify

*Calvin Coolidge* **Vice-President of the United States who became President when Warren Harding died in 1923.** Coolidge was elected President in 1924.

*Franklin Roosevelt*   **President of the United States elected in 1932.**
Roosevelt called his program to recover from the depression the New
Deal. He was the first President to be elected to a third term.

*Frances Perkins*   **first woman to hold office in a President's Cabinet**
when she became secretary of labor for Roosevelt.

*John L. Lewis*   **leader of the United Mine Workers** who organized the
Committee for Industrial Organization (the CIO).

## Explain

*speculation*   **purchasing something with the hope of selling it again at a
high profit.**

*stock market crash*   **the term used to describe the drastic fall of stock
prices in October of 1929.** The crash was the first major sign of the
coming depression.

*Good Neighbor Policy*   **name given to the foreign policy of President
Roosevelt's administration** which tried to improve United States relations with Latin-American countries.

*New Deal*   **name given to President Roosevelt's program to help the
country recover from the depression of the 1930's.**

*Wagner Act*   **a law passed by Congress in 1935 which gave government
protection to workers who wanted to form unions.** It also set up the
National Labor Relations Board which could take cases to court to
enforce the law.

*Social Security Act*   **a law passed by Congress in 1935 which gave federal money to states to help people without jobs, retired workers,
handicapped people, and mothers and children without support.**

*Indian Reorganization Act*   **a law passed by Congress in 1934 which
allowed Indians to form corporations for the purposes of holding
land and governing their people as a group.** This law returned some
control over their lives to American Indians, but it gave final power
to overrule council governments to the secretary of the interior.

## Check Your Memory of the Facts

1. *What kinds of government action did President Hoover support to
   ease the depression?*   **Hoover supported the establishment of the
   Reconstruction Finance Corporation** to loan money to banks, businesses, and railroads in danger of going out of business. **He also
   encouraged states to create jobs through public works projects** like
   building roads. He met with business leaders to encourage them not
   to cut wages and to keep people working. Hoover did not believe
   that the federal government had to become too involved in ending
   the depression.

2. *What did the Tydings-McDuffie Bill of 1934 do?*   **This act called
   for the independence of the Philippines in ten years. It also set a**

**quota on Filipino immigration to the United States of fifty people a year.**

3. *What American government actions followed President Roosevelt's "Good Neighbor" speech?* **United States troops were removed from Haiti; Roosevelt gave up the claimed right to send United States forces to Cuba to prevent disorder there; yearly payments to Panama for the Canal were raised; new trade treaties were signed with a number of Latin-American countries.**

4. *What was a major difference between the AFL and the CIO?* **The AFL organized workers according to their craft or skill. The CIO wanted to organize all skilled and unskilled workers in the same industry into the same union.**

5. *How did the Supreme Court rule on cases involving New Deal legislation?* **The Supreme Court ruled that parts of the NRA and AAA were unconstitutional. It ruled the Wagner Act and the Social Security Act were constitutional.**

## Check Your Understanding of the Ideas

1. *Why did people have great faith in American business in the 1920's?* American industries had met the great challenge of World War I production and had increased production and prosperity in America following the war. Many Americans believed that the economy would continue to grow.

2. *What happened to cause the crash of the stock market?* Some people began to sell their stock because they believed that the economy would not continue to grow so quickly and they wanted to get rid of it before prices stopped rising. As more people decided to sell stocks, the prices dropped lower and lower.

3. *What problems in the economy led to the depression?* Farm prices were low, and farmers had little money to buy factory-made goods. Factory workers' pay had not risen as fast as the profits of business. Like farmers, these workers were not able to buy as many goods as were being made. Trade with Europe had begun to decline because those countries in debt to the United States from World War I began to buy less. Investors with large amounts of stock assumed that many businesses would soon have to cut back on their production of goods. So, to avoid lower stock prices from lower sales and profits, these investors began to sell their stocks.

4. *How were people affected by the depression?* Millions of people lost their jobs, and others worked only a few hours each week. Thousands of people began to wander around the country in search of work and food. Local governments and private citizen groups tried to raise money to feed and clothe these people and to help others who needed relief. More than 250,000 Mexican people,

some with their American-born children, were sent back to Mexico. Congress passed the Tydings-McDuffie Bill to restrict immigration to help American workers without jobs.

5. *What were some of the programs in the New Deal?  How did they work?  How were they different from President Hoover's plans?* New Deal programs included the Agricultural Adjustment Administration (AAA), the National Recovery Administration (NRA), the Civilian Conservation Corps (CCC), the Works Progress Administration (WPA), and the Federal Emergency Relief Administration (FERA). The AAA tried to reduce farm production so that what was left for sale by the farmers would bring better prices. Under it, the government paid farmers to plant fewer acres of basic crops like cotton, wheat, and corn, and to raise fewer pigs. It also bought and stored farm products, giving much of this food and cotton to people on relief. The NRA's task was to settle disputes and enforce codes among businesses to hold down prices. It also established a minimum wage for workers in industry and did away with child labor by stating that only persons at least sixteen years of age could be hired to work in industry. The CCC gave jobs mostly to young people in order to put more people back to work. The jobs included planting trees in forests, building small dams to stop soil erosion, fighting forest fires, and stocking lakes and rivers with fish. The WPA paid unemployed people to work on such projects as building roads, airports, bridges, and hospitals. It also provided work for artists and writers. The FERA gave money to states and cities to buy food and clothing for poor people and in some cases gave money directly to people in need. These programs were different from President Hoover's ideas because they involved the federal government in assuming the direct responsibility of providing assistance to local governments, businesses, and individuals.

6. *Why did President Roosevelt want to add members to the Supreme Court?*  Since decisions of the Court are decided by majority opinion, President Roosevelt wanted to make sure that a majority number of justices would favor his viewpoint, especially on New Deal programs.

# Chapter 22

## Identify

*Benito Mussolini*  **Fascist party leader who controlled Italy before and during World War II.**

*Adolf Hitler*  **Nazi party dictator of Germany before and during World War II.**

*Joseph Stalin*  **Communist leader of the Soviet Union government before and during World War II.**

*Winston Churchill*  **prime minister of Great Britain before and during World War II.**

*Dwight Eisenhower*  **United States general and commander of all Allied troops in western Europe** who directed the invasion of Normandy in 1944.

*Pearl Harbor*  **in Hawaii, largest American navy base in the Pacific Ocean.** It was attacked by the Japanese on December 7, 1941, and Congress declared war on Japan the next day.

*Douglas MacArthur*  **United States general in charge of the American forces in the Pacific during World War II.**

*Harry Truman*  **Vice-President of the United States who became President when Franklin Roosevelt died in 1945.** Truman was elected President in 1948.

*Hiroshima*  **Japanese city where the first atomic bomb used in warfare was dropped by Americans** on August 6, 1945.

## Explain

*isolationists*  **people who want to isolate, or close off, their country from outside problems.** There was strong support for isolationism in the United States in the early 1930's, and many Americans wanted to avoid becoming a part of Europe's conflicts.

*Lend-Lease*  **act of Congress passed in 1941 which allowed the President to loan arms and other war supplies to any country believed important to the defense of the United States.** It was a successful effort to get around the Neutrality Act of 1935 and the Johnson Act of 1934 which kept the United States from helping Britain fight the Germans.

*Axis alliance*  **alliance formed by Japan, Germany, and Italy during World War II.**

*Atlantic Charter*  **set of war aims agreed to by Allied countries.** It was drawn up by President Roosevelt and Prime Minister Churchill and stated that the United States and Great Britain were not seeking additional lands and that they were against any land changes that were not agreed to freely by the people concerned.

*rationing*  **the setting of limits.** During the war, the government rationed goods, or set the amounts that any one person could buy, in order to be sure that war goods could be made available for the United States and its allies.

## Check Your Memory of the Facts

1.  *What was the United States' policy toward other nations in the 1930's?*  **Throughout the 1930's, the policy of the American government was to avoid trouble with other countries.**

2. *What action did the United States take in 1935 to avoid conflict with European nations?* **Congress passed the Neutrality Act in 1935** which made it illegal for Americans to sell arms to any country at war.

3. *How did the United States prepare for war?* **After the declarations of war, more Americans were drafted into the armed services. American industries cut down the production of goods for the public so that they could make more war goods. Congress set up agencies to make sure that the right materials were sent to these industries at the right times, and it made rules for many other industries. The government also rationed many of the goods bought by the public. To help pay the costs of the war, Congress passed new tax laws, and the government raised more money through the sale of war bonds.**

4. *What roles did women have in the armed services?* **They served in nonfighting roles in all service groups.** Women made maps, operated radios, worked in offices and medical laboratories, and were teachers.

5. *How did the government raise money to help pay for the war?* **Congress passed new tax laws.** It raised the income tax rates and placed taxes on such things as telephone service, telegraph messages, movie tickets, travel fares, and some alcoholic drinks. **Congress also raised money through the sale of war bonds and savings stamps.**

6. *What was the major effort of the Allies in Europe?* **the Normandy invasion.**

7. *What were the military plans of the United States for the Pacific area?* **American forces in the Pacific planned to keep the Japanese from taking more islands. They also intended to take back many of the islands that the Japanese armies held. In their final plans, Americans intended to use the Pacific islands as air bases from which they would attack Japan with bombs.**

8. *What was the last action taken against Japan?* **the dropping of an atomic bomb on Nagasaki** on August 9, 1945.

## Check Your Understanding of the Ideas

1. *Why did Japan take land from China?* to gain complete control of raw materials needed for Japanese industry. Japan had been dealing in the area of Chinese Manchuria for raw materials for some time. They were no longer willing to share power there.

2. *Why did Italy invade Africa?* The Fascists under Mussolini promised to end the depression in Italy and to make the country a great power by building an empire in Africa and the Mediterranean area.

3. *What reasons did Hitler give for Germany's plans for Europe?* He announced that he wanted to unite all the German-speaking people of Europe into one country and to regain for the German people the lands taken from them at the end of World War I.

4. *What events or situations made many Americans change their minds about the policy of isolationism?* The President and many other Americans became increasingly alarmed by the German victories over Poland, Denmark, Norway, Holland, Belgium, and France, and the growing power of Italy and Japan. They felt that such power threatened the security of the Western Hemisphere and of the United States.

5. *Why were people in America of Japanese backgrounds placed in relocation centers?* Prejudice was strong against Asian peoples in the United States. Some Americans claimed that people of Japanese backgrounds would give aid to Japan if there were an attack against the western coast of America.

6. *What was an important aim of the Allies regarding the Axis powers?* to destroy those industries in Axis countries which were important in the making of weapons and war supplies. The Allies did not want Axis countries to be able to start another war after World War II.

7. *Why was there an Allied meeting at Yalta?* Roosevelt, Churchill, and Stalin held the meeting to discuss postwar control in Central Europe and the war with Japan.

8. *How much cooperation was there between the United States and the Soviet Union after the war?* very little. The United States had expected to follow the aims of the Atlantic Charter in Central Europe after the Yalta conference, but even before the end of the war in Europe, the Russians failed to keep some of the Yalta agreements. The United States and the Soviet Union began to compete against each other to spread their ideas of democracy and communism in Central Europe and the rest of the world.

# Chapter 23

## Identify

*NATO* **North Atlantic Treaty Organization.** Members included the United States, Canada, Great Britain, France, the Netherlands, Luxembourg, Denmark, Norway, Iceland, Italy, Portugal, Greece, Turkey, and West Germany.

*Matthew Ridgeway* **United States general who replaced General MacArthur as commander of the UN forces in Korea.**

*Joseph McCarthy*   **senator from Wisconsin who charged that the United States government,** especially the Department of State, **was full of Communists.** In 1954, he charged that there were Communists in the army. McCarthy did not provide evidence for any of his charges but for several years caused some people to lose their jobs.

*Earl Warren*   **Chief Justice of the United States Supreme Court in 1954** when the Court ruled that "separate but equal" facilities for whites and blacks were unconstitutional because they would always result in black people getting unequal treatment.

*Rosa Parks*   **black woman who refused to give up her seat near the front of a bus in Montgomery, Alabama.** Her arrest led to a boycott of the bus service by blacks in 1955.

*Martin Luther King, Jr.*   **black civil rights leader.** He organized the bus service boycott in Montgomery in 1955.


## Explain

*cold war*   **a conflict of ideas and actions without military battles.** A cold war developed between the United States and the Soviet Union after World War II as both countries tried to influence other nations to set up governments that were friendly to them.

*Security Council*   **the group within the United Nations whose major task is to prevent war.** The United States, the Soviet Union, France, Great Britain, and China are permanent members, and six other nations are elected for two-year terms. Each member has the right to veto any plan offered. The Security Council can use force to see that accepted plans are carried out.

*inflation*   **a continuing rise in general prices.**

*Taft-Hartley Act*   **a law** also called the Labor Management Act **which made it possible for companies to sue unions for broken contracts. Companies were also to be given sixty-days notice before a strike could be held in industries with interstate trade.** Congress passed the act in 1947 over the veto of President Truman.

*Marshall Plan*   **a plan in which the United States could give long-range help to countries badly damaged during World War II.** Offered by Secretary of State George Marshall, the plan enabled the United States to loan money to those countries whose plans for its use had been approved.

*domino theory*   **an idea accepted by many American leaders that if one country fell to communism, the countries touching its borders would soon fall also.** This idea was based on the domino game with the countries representing the lined up and touching pieces.

*McCarran-Walter Act*   **an immigration law which gave the attorney general the power to deport people whose actions were not in the**

**country's interests.** This law also ended the exclusion of Asian immigrants but gave the Asian countries much lower quotas than those for Europe. Congress passed the bill in 1952 over Truman's veto.

*Displaced Persons Act* **the law under which more than 400,000 Europeans from war-torn countries were welcomed into the United States.** It was passed in 1948.

*Refugee Relief Act* **a law allowing people escaping from Communist governments to enter the United States.** It was passed in 1953.

*sit-in* **an act of refusing to leave a racially segregated place as a method of protest.** In 1960, young black citizens refused to leave lunch counters in Greensboro, North Carolina. Blacks and some whites staged other sit-ins all over the South to end different kinds of segregation.

*Warsaw Pact* **an organization similar to NATO set up by the Soviet Union in eastern Europe.** Members included the Soviet Union, Poland, Czechoslovakia, Hungary, Rumania, Bulgaria, Albania, and East Germany.

*gross national product* **the value of all the goods and services produced in the country.**

## Check Your Memory of the Facts

1. *What conditions brought about inflation after World War II?* **large amounts of money to spend on a limited number of consumer products, manufacturing's inability to change over to peacetime products fast enough to meet demands.**

2. *What parts of Truman's Fair Deal program were passed into law?* **increased Social Security payments, minimum wage raised to 75 cents an hour from 40 cents, National Housing Act.**

3. *What events created the need for the Berlin airlift?* **disagreements between western powers and Russia over the kind of new German government which should be set up after the war;** Germans in western zone elected representative government; **Russian blockade of ground and water routes to West Berlin,** June, 1948.

4. *What led to the Korean War?* **Communist victory in China; Russian occupation of northern half of Korea and American occupation of southern part after World War II; Communist government in North Korea sent invading troops to South Korea, June, 1950; UN Security Council voted to send troops to stop the invasion.**

5. *What was an outcome of the Senate hearings regarding McCarthy's actions?* **The Senate voted to condemn McCarthy's actions, and public opinion also turned against him.** McCarthy lost much of his influence, but not before thousands of Americans came to feel that the government had taken away or ignored many of the civil rights belonging to American citizens.

6. *How did Puerto Rico's position change in 1952?* **Puerto Rico became a commonwealth of the United States in 1952.** As a commonwealth, it had self-government and was joined to the United
States, but it had no vote in Congress.

7. *What information shows the general economic standing of the
United States in 1960?* **Weekly paychecks of factory workers
were 15 percent higher than in 1947; more than 65 percent of
American families were buying their own homes; the gross national product had doubled from twenty years before.**

## Check Your Understanding of the Ideas

1. *Why were Americans more interested in joining the UN than they
had been in the League of Nations?* Many Americans felt that the
UN did not threaten the power and rights of the United States as
they believed the League had done. As a permanent member of the
Security Council, the United States could veto any plan it disliked.
The UN charter allowed each member to make any other treaties
for defense that it wished.

2. *Why did American leaders support the Marshall Plan?* They believed that the plan would not only help the economies of European
countries to grow, but it would also improve the economy of the
United States by increasing world trade. Leaders believed, too, that
stronger economies in those countries would help stop the spread of
communism. Communism seemed to be most popular in areas
where people felt that they had no hope of earning a good living.

3. *Why did the United States, in the late 1940's, change its policy
toward Japan? What resulted from the change?* American leaders began to see Japan as a possible friend against Communist
China. Japan had a new government based on democracy. The
United States helped to rebuild Japanese industries and signed a
treaty in 1951 that ended the American military occupation but
allowed American bases in Japan.

4. *How was the Korean War settled?* An armistice was signed in
1953 that ended the fighting. North and South Korea remained
separated at the thirty-eighth parallel. Many Americans were not
satisfied by the war or its ending because the United States had not
won a clear military victory after three years of fighting.

5. *How did the United States become involved in the fighting in Vietnam?* American leaders had favored the French against the Vietnamese people fighting for their independence in Vietnam because
they feared a Communist victory. A meeting in Geneva in 1952
settled the fighting. Vietnam was divided into North and South at
the seventeenth parallel with North Vietnam controlled by a Com-

munist government and South Vietnam by a non-Communist government. The French army left. After that, the United States began to give economic and military aid to the South Vietnamese government.

6. *Why did President Truman veto the McCarran-Walter Act?* The law favored European immigration over Asian immigration, and it gave the attorney general power to deport people whose actions he felt were not in the country's interest without defining the country's interest.

7. *Why did President Eisenhower feel the country was ready for an "Era of Good Feelings"?* He felt that the American people had suffered enough tension from the depression, World War II, and the cold war.

8. *What is important about the Supreme Court ruling in the case of Brown v. Board of Education of Topeka?* The Court ruling struck down the "separate but equal" idea that had been law since 1896 and stated that such separation would always result in black people getting unequal treatment. In 1955, the Court ordered an end to segregated schools in the United States.

9. *How did the American people react to Sputnik?* The American people were shocked by Sputnik because they had been certain that United States scientists were years ahead of the Russians in knowledge of missiles to carry satellites. People in and out of government demanded that American schools teach more science and mathematics so that future American scientists would be the best trained in the world. In 1958, Congress passed the National Defense Education Act to give funds directly to colleges around the country to be used mostly for science and research buildings and projects.

# *Chapter 24*

## Identify

*John Kennedy* **President of the United States elected in 1960;** assassinated in 1963; former Democratic senator from Massachusetts.

*John Glenn* **United States astronaut,** first American to orbit the earth in a space satellite, February 20, 1962.

*Fidel Castro* **the person who established a Communist government in Cuba** after a successful revolution in 1959.

*Nikita Khrushchev* **Soviet premier** during the Cuban missile crisis.

*James Meredith* **a black student admitted to classes at the University of Mississippi** under federal troop protection.

*Lyndon Johnson* **President following the assassination of President Kennedy** in 1963. In 1964, he was elected by the largest popular vote in the history of the United States.

*César Chávez* **a worker for civil rights, especially those of Mexican-American farm workers.** He was an early leader of the Community Service Organization and helped organize the National Farm Worker's Association.

*Robert Kennedy* **senator assassinated during his campaign to become the Democratic presidential nominee** in 1968. He had served as attorney general under his brother, President John Kennedy.

*Richard Nixon* **President elected in 1968** when running against Democratic nominee Hubert Humphrey. He had served as Vice-President under President Eisenhower.

## Explain

*New Frontier* **name given by President Kennedy to his program for government action.** He said it was a challenge to the people of the United States to honor the civil rights of all Americans, to work toward prosperity for all, and to remain strong in the face of communism.

*Peace Corps* **government program through which Americans went overseas to train people in other countries** to work in teaching, farming, medicine, and other areas.

*Head Start* **government program to help the young children of low-income families** prepare for school.

*Medicare* **government program to give aid to older people to help pay their medical bills.**

*guerrillas* **small, independent bands of soldiers who make surprise attacks, then return to their hideouts.**

*Gulf of Tonkin Resolution* **resolution passed by Congress giving the President power to use whatever force necessary to prevent attacks against American warships in Southeast Asia.**

*black power* **term used by some black leaders urging black people to control their own communities, businesses, and schools** based on the idea of separating whites and blacks.

## Check Your Memory of the Facts

1. *What type of legislation was passed from President Kennedy's New Frontier program?* **Congress passed an amendment making it illegal to charge poll taxes in federal elections; raised the minimum**

wage to $1.25 an hour; included more people in the Social Security program; passed a bill for federal aid to build more houses and apartments; lengthened the time workers could receive unemployment payments from the federal government; created a program to train unemployed workers so they could get other kinds of jobs.

2. *What problems did the United States have with Russia over Cuba?* **The Russians tried to build and supply guided missile bases in Cuba.** Such missiles could hit targets in the United States much more quickly than those launched from the Soviet Union.

3. *Near the end of Kennedy's administration, what are some examples of easing of tensions between the United States and Russia?* **an agreement in 1963 to stop testing nuclear weapons in the atmosphere, in outer space, and under water; a "hotline" set up between Washington, D. C., and Moscow.**

4. *What legislation did Congress pass from the New Frontier and Great Society programs under President Johnson?* **Congress passed a bill giving over one billion dollars for new college buildings** around the country; **made a cut in taxes; set up government agencies** like the Job Corps, VISTA, and Head Start **by passing the Economic Opportunity Act; set up the Office of Economic Opportunity** to run these programs; **set aside more than 300 million dollars for local community improvements; passed the Medicaid and Medicare bills; granted federal aid to schools through the Elementary and Secondary Education Act of 1965; passed the Civil Rights Act of 1964** making discrimination in public services or any program receiving federal money illegal; **set up the Equal Employment Opportunity Commission** to help women and minorities fight job hiring discrimination; **passed the Voting Rights Act of 1965** which outlawed the literacy test and gave federal officials the power to register voters in local areas; **passed an immigration law** to end quotas favorable to western Europeans.

5. *What immigration laws were passed in the 1960's?* **the immigration law of 1965.** Under it, no more than 20,000 immigrants a year could come from any country, and immigration was limited to 120,000 people a year from the Western Hemisphere and to 170,000 a year from the Eastern Hemisphere.

6. *How were some Americans reacting toward the Vietnam War by 1968?* **The war lost some of its support from the public.** Many young people were refusing to be drafted to fight. People who opposed the war wanted Congress to stop allowing money to be used for it. They said that the war was not legal, that it had not been declared by Congress. Both candidates for President in the election of 1968 said they would end the war.

7. *What agreements were signed by the United States, Russia, and other nations in the 1960's?* **an agreement to stop testing nuclear weapons in the atmosphere, in outer space, and under water in 1963 and a treaty to stop the spread of nuclear weapons in 1968.** The countries who had nuclear weapons agreed not to sell or give them to others; countries without them agreed not to buy or try to make them.

## Check Your Understanding of the Ideas

1. *How did President Kennedy deal with the Cuban missile crisis?* He ordered the United States Navy to Cuban waters to search approaching Soviet ships for missiles, and he threatened to invade Cuba if the Russians did not remove their bases. The United States asked for a meeting of the UN Security Council to discuss the problem.

2. *What progress did the civil rights movement make in the 1960's? Make a list showing advances and setbacks.* There was great progress made in gaining civil rights for many citizens. Advances included: the Twenty-fourth Amendment outlawing the poll tax; Meredith's admission to the University of Mississippi; the Economic Opportunity Act of 1964; the Civil Rights Act of 1964 outlawing discrimination in public services and programs receiving federal money; the Equal Employment Opportunity Act and Commission to fight discrimination in job hiring; the Voting Rights Act of 1965 outlawing the literacy test as a voting requirement and giving federal officials the right to register voters in local areas; the Civil Rights Act of 1968 outlawing discrimination in housing; Mexican-American organizations formed like Alianza and Crusade for Justice, as well as Chávez's work to unionize farm workers and improve living and working conditions for them.

   Setbacks included: the murder of Medgar Evers in June of 1963; the bombing of a Birmingham church which killed four children; the assassination of President Kennedy in November of 1963; the riots of 1964 and 1965 in many major cities; the murder of Martin Luther King, Jr., in April of 1968; the murder of Robert Kennedy in June of 1968.

3. *How did Americans become more involved in the Vietnam War?* Under President Kennedy, ten thousand American military advisers and much equipment had been sent to South Vietnam. Shortly after Lyndon Johnson became President in 1963, United States troops became directly involved in the fighting. In 1964, Congress passed the Gulf of Tonkin Resolution which approved the limited use of power in Southeast Asia but did not declare war. By

1968, more than 500,000 American soldiers were fighting in Vietnam.

4. *What were some differences in ideas that created a "generation gap"?* disagreements over the Vietnam War, technical and scientific progress, pollution, emphasis on ownership of goods, ways of living, use of drugs, adherence to the laws.

5. *What were some of the causes of the riots in black neighborhoods in the 1960's?* The Kerner Commission reported that the riots were the result of frustration over bad housing, overcrowding, high unemployment rates, and the general lack of opportunity.

# *Chapter 25*

## Identify

*Neil Armstrong* **United States astronaut** who became the first human to set foot on the moon, July 20, 1969.

*Henry Kissinger* **secretary of state under President Nixon.** He helped arrange a cease fire in the 1973 Arab-Israeli war and, with Nixon, worked out a policy of detente with the Soviet Union.

*Katharine Graham* **chairperson of the board of directors of the Washington Post Company.** She is an example of one of the few women highly successful in the top levels of business.

*Chien-Shiung Wu* **professor of physics at Columbia University.** She is an example of one of the few women highly successful in the top levels of science.

*Gerald Ford* **President in 1974 following Richard Nixon's resignation.** Ford had been the first person to become Vice-President under the Twenty-fifth Amendment when appointed by Nixon and approved by Congress to replace Spiro Agnew who resigned in 1973.

*Leonid Brezhnev* **leader of the Soviet Union.** He signed a nuclear arms limitation agreement with the United States at Vladivostok in 1974.

*Jimmy Carter* **President of the United States elected in 1976** over Republican President Ford. He is a former Democratic governor of Georgia.

## Explain

*Vietnamization* **President Nixon's announced policy to slowly withdraw American soldiers from the Vietnam War** while continuing to give aid to the South Vietnamese government. The first United States troops were withdrawn in 1969, the last in 1973.

*Middle East* **an area of northeastern Africa and western Asia** which has long been important to trade and has rich oil lands.

*detente* **a French word that means to relax tensions,** used to describe the Nixon-Kissinger policy toward the Soviet Union.

*revenue sharing* **a plan suggested by President Nixon in 1969 in which the federal government would give back part of its collected tax money to the states, counties, and cities** with few rules about how it should be spent. Congress passed an act to begin the plan in 1972.

*Equal Rights Amendment* **proposed constitutional amendment which states that equality of rights under the law cannot be denied any citizen on account of sex.** It was passed by Congress in 1972.

*Indian Claims Commission* **a group established in 1947 to deal with American Indian land rights cases.**

## Check Your Memory of the Facts

1. *How did relations of the United States with China and Russia improve under President Nixon?* **The federal government worked out a policy of detente with Russia and signed an agreement to lower the number of nuclear weapons that each country would make. The United States policy against Communist China's admission to the United Nations was changed.** President Nixon made official visits to Peking and Moscow in 1972.

2. *What legislation was passed by Congress to support the rights of women?* **the Civil Rights Act of 1964, the Equal Employment Opportunity Act of 1972, the Equal Rights Amendment to the Constitution, 1972.**

3. *What events and questions were part of the Watergate scandal?* **Events included a break-in at the Democratic party headquarters in June, 1972; the discovery that the people arrested worked for the committee to reelect the President; newspapers' articles charging presidential staff members with planning the break-in and other illegal activities; the Senate hearings to investigate those charges televised in July, 1973; John Dean's testimony to the Senate committee that President Nixon knew of the break-in shortly after it happened; other testimony revealing a tape recording system used in the White House; the President's denial of any break-in knowledge, his refusal to turn over tapes, his firing of Special Prosecutor Cox; Jaworski appointed new special prosecutor; Haldeman, Ehrlichman, Mitchell, and others charged in March, 1974, with a cover-up and lying to investigators; the Judiciary Committee of the House held televised hearings in July and approved three articles of a bill of impeachment against the President; Nixon announced his resignation on August 8, 1974; Ford**

became the President on August 9; Ford pardoned Nixon. The main question of the scandal was whether or not President Nixon had been involved in the cover-up.

4. *What agreement did President Ford make with the Russians at Vladivostok?* **to limit the making of nuclear weapons in both countries.**

5. *What information shows a contrast in American life from 1770 to 1970?* **changes from mostly rural to mostly city living, from mostly farming to mostly business and factory work, from small businesses to large corporations.**

6. *What demands did Americans make about the environment? What were some results of these demands?* **People demanded protection for the environment which resulted in regulations and laws** like mining companies having to put soil back when they had stripped it away and factories having to clean up chemical wastes before returning water to rivers and lakes. The cost to businesses for cleaning up or preventing damage was passed on to customers in higher prices for products.

7. *What laws have been passed to protect the rights of handicapped people?* **In 1973, Congress passed the Rehabilitation Act** which makes it illegal to discriminate against people because they are handicapped. **Local governments in some areas have passed laws requiring all public buildings and pathways to be accessible to people using wheelchairs** by providing ramps near stairs where needed.

## Check Your Understanding of the Ideas

1. *Why is it important to keep good relations with Middle East countries?* Both the United States and the Soviet Union trade with the Middle East countries, especially in oil and military weapons. Some people fear that a war in the Middle East would not only disrupt the trade but might also involve the United States and Russia in war.

2. *What actions did the government take under President Nixon to control inflation?* Nixon and his advisers tried to lower prices by having the government spend less money in some areas and by raising the cost of borrowing money to make less money available for others to spend. Congress gave the President the authority to use wage, price, and rent controls in 1971.

3. *What was a major change in civil rights action in the 1970's?* More people began to call for an end to segregation of schools in the North as well as in the South. By the middle of the 1970's, federal courts had increased their orders to use busing for the desegregation of schools.

4. *What was the outcome of the Watergate scandal?* Most Americans seemed to lose faith in federal government leaders. The Republican party lost support because of the scandal and President Ford's pardon of President Nixon. Democratic candidates won many seats from the Republicans in the Congressional elections of 1974 which made it very difficult for President Ford to develop his own program for the nation.

5. *What kinds of problems faced the Carter administration when he took office?* continuing energy crisis; unemployment and inflation; civil rights in the United States and human rights in the world; increasing scarcity of natural resources.

# Bibliography

## *For Teachers*

Bartlett, Richard A. *The New Country: A Social History of the American Frontier, 1776-1890.* New York: Oxford University Press, 1974.

Beck, Warren A., and Clowers, Myles L. *Understanding American History Through Fiction.* New York: McGraw-Hill Book Co., 1975.

Billington, Ray A. *Westward Expansion.* New York: Macmillan Publishing Co., 1974.

Brown, Richard M. *Strain of Violence: Historical Studies of American Violence and Vigilantism.* New York: Oxford University Press, 1975.

Brownlee, W. Elliot. *American Economic History: The Dynamics of Ascent.* New York: Alfred A. Knopf, Inc., 1974.

Callow, Jr., Alexander B. (ed.). *The City Boss in America.* New York: Oxford University Press, 1976.

Chafe, William H. *Women and Equality.* New York: Oxford University Press, 1977.

Chudacoff, Howard P. *The Evolution of American Urban Society.* Englewood Cliffs, New Jersey: Prentice-Hall, Inc., 1975.

Cochran, Thomas C. *Business in American Life.* New York: McGraw-Hill Book Co., 1972.

Corwin, Edward S. *The Constitution and What It Means Today.* Princeton, New Jersey: Princeton University Press, 1974.

DeConde, Alexander. *A History of American Foreign Policy.* New York: Charles Scribner's Sons, 1978.

Degler, Carl N. *Out of Our Past.* New York: Harper & Row Publishers, Inc., 1970.

Ferrell, Robert H. *American Diplomacy.* New York: W. W. Norton & Co., 1975.

Franklin, John Hope. *From Slavery to Freedom.* New York: Alfred A. Knopf, Inc., 1974.

Freidel, Frank, and Showman, Richard K. (eds.). *The Harvard Guide to American History.* Vol. 1-2. Cambridge, Mass.: Harvard University Press, 1974.

Goodrich, Lloyd. *Three Centuries of American Art.* New York: Praeger Publishers, 1967.

Gutman, Herbert G. *The Black Family in Slavery and Freedom, 1750-1925.* New York: Random House, Inc., 1977.

Haley, Alex. *Roots.* New York: Doubleday & Co., Inc., 1976.

Handlin, Oscar. *The Uprooted.* Boston: Little, Brown & Co., 1973.

Howard, John T. *Our American Music.* New York: Thomas Y. Crowell Co., 1965.

Hughes, Thomas P. (ed.). *Science and Technology in American History.* New York: Harper & Row Publishers, Inc., 1975.

Hundley, Jr., Norris (ed.). *The Chicano.* Santa Barbara, California: American Bibliographical Center-Clio Press, 1975.

Jones, Maldwyn A. *American Immigration.* Chicago: University of Chicago Press, 1960.

Josephy, Jr., Alvin M. *The Indian Heritage of America.* New York: Alfred A. Knopf, Inc., 1968.

Keller, Morton. *Affairs of State: Public Life in Late Nineteenth Century America.* Cambridge, Mass.: Harvard University Press, 1977.

Kutler, Stanley I. *The Supreme Court and the Constitution.* New York: W. W. Norton & Co., 1976.

May, Henry F. *The Enlightenment in America.* New York: Oxford University Press, 1976.

Meier, August, and Rudwick, Elliott. *From Plantation to Ghetto.* New York: Hill & Wang, Inc., 1976.

Meier, Matt S. *The Chicanos: A History of Mexican Americans.* New York: Hill & Wang, Inc., 1972.

Miller, Zane L. *The Urbanization of Modern America.* New York: Harcourt Brace Jovanovich, Inc., 1973.

Nash, Roderick (ed.). *The American Environment: Readings in the History of Conservation.* Reading, Mass.: Addison-Wesley Publishing Co., Inc., 1976.

Pelling, Henry. *American Labor.* Chicago: University of Chicago Press, 1960.

Randall, James G., and Donald, David. *The Civil War and Reconstruction.* Boston: D. C. Heath & Co., 1969.

Rose, Willie L. *A Documentary History of Slavery in North America.* New York: Oxford University Press, 1976.

Scheiber, Harry N., et al. *American Economic History.* New York: Harper & Row Publishers, Inc., 1976.

Schwartz, Bernard. *The Great Rights of Mankind: A History of the American Bill of Rights.* New York: Oxford University Press, 1977.

Stout, Joseph A., and Faulk, Odie B. *A Short History of the American West.* New York: Harper & Row Publishers, Inc., 1974.

Superka, Douglas P., et al. *Values Education Sourcebook.* Boulder, Colorado: Social Science Education Consortium and ERIC Clearinghouse for Social Studies and Social Science, 1976.

Trattner, Walter I. *From Poor Law to Welfare State: A History of Social Welfare in America.* Riverside, New Jersey: Free Press, 1974.

Washburn, Wilcomb E. *The Indian in America.* New York: Harper & Row Publishers, Inc., 1975.

Wertheimer, Barbara M. *We Were There: The Story of Working Women in America.* New York: Pantheon Books, 1977.

## Series

Boorstin, Daniel J. (ed.). *The Chicago History of American Civilization.* Chicago: University of Chicago Press.

Commager, Henry S., and Morris, Richard B. (eds.). *The New American Nation Series.* New York: Harper & Row Publishers, Inc.

David, Henry, *et al.* (eds.). *Economic History of the United States.* New York: Holt, Rinehart & Winston, Inc.

Handlin, Oscar (ed.). *Library of American Biography Series.* Boston: Little, Brown & Co.

Schlesinger, A. M., and Fox, D. R. (eds.). *A History of American Life Series.* New York: Macmillan Publishing Co.

# For Students

Berger, Josef, and Berger, Dorothy (eds.). *Diary of America.* New York: Simon & Schuster, Inc., 1957.

Botkin, Benjamin A. (ed.). *Lay My Burden Down: A Folk History of Slavery.* Chicago: University of Chicago Press, 1945.

Brown, Richard C. *The Human Side of American History.* Boston: Ginn & Company, 1962.

Collier, John. *Indians of the Americas.* New York: W. W. Norton & Co., 1947.

Davidson, Marshall. *Life in America.* Vol. 1-2. Boston: Houghton Mifflin Co., 1974.

Fenton, Edwin. *The Humanities in Three Cities.* New York: Holt, Rinehart & Winston, Inc., 1969.

Freidel, Frank. *Our Country's Presidents.* Washington, D. C.: National Geographic Society, 1977.

Hagen, William T. *American Indians.* Chicago: University of Chicago Press, 1961.

Huggins, Nathan I. *Black Odyssey: The Afro-American Ordeal in Slavery.* New York: Pantheon Books, 1977.

Meltzer, Milton (ed.). *In Their Own Words: A History of the American Negro.* Vol. 1-3. New York: Thomas Y. Crowell Co., 1964.

Riegel, R. E., and Athearn, R. G. *America Moves West.* New York: Holt, Rinehart & Winston, Inc., 1970.

Samora, Julian, and Simon, Patricia V. *A History of the Mexican-American People.* Notre Dame: University of Notre Dame Press, 1977.

Weitzman, David. *My Backyard History Book.* Boston: Little, Brown & Co., 1975.

## Series

Adams, J. T. (ed.). *Album of American History*. Vol. 1-4. New York: Charles Scribner's Sons.

Burns, Alan (ed.). *Urban America Series*. Westport, Conn.: Pendulum Press.

Harvard Social Studies Project. *Public Issues Series*. Middleton, Conn.: American Education Publications.

Scott, John A. (ed.). *The Living History Library*. New York: Alfred A. Knopf, Inc.

# *Reference*

*American Heritage Pictorial Atlas of United States History*. New York: McGraw-Hill Book Co., 1966.

Boorstin, Daniel J. (ed.). *An American Primer*. Vol. 1-2. Chicago: University of Chicago Press, 1969.

Commager, Henry Steele (ed.). *Documents of American History*. Vol. 1-2. Englewood Cliffs, New Jersey: Prentice-Hall, Inc., 1973.

*Concise Dictionary of American Biography*. New York: Charles Scribner's Sons, 1964.

*Concise Dictionary of American History*. New York: Charles Scribner's Sons, 1962.

Hofstadter, Richard (ed.). *Great Issues in American History*. Vol. 1-2. New York: Random House, Inc., 1969.

James, Edward T., and James, Janet W. (eds.). *Notable American Women*. Vol. 1-3. Cambridge, Mass.: Harvard University Press, 1971.

Morris, Richard B., and Morris, Jeffrey B. (eds.). *Encyclopedia of American History*. New York: Harper & Row Publishers, Inc., 1976.

Ploski, Harry A., and Marr, Warren. *The Negro Almanac*. New York: Bellwether Publishing Co., 1976.

United States Bureau of the Census. *Historical Statistics of the United States: Colonial Times to 1970*. Vol. 1-2. United States Government Printing Office, 1975.

Wesley, Edgar B. *Our United States: Its History in Maps*. Chicago: Denoyer-Geppert Co., 1965.

# AMERICA IS

Circle the number which corresponds most nearly to your opinion of each of the following items of the AMERICA IS program. Please also star (*) three factors which most influence your evaluation or choice of text.

| Student Text | Excel-lent | Very Good | Satis-factory | Fair | Poor | Comments |
|---|---|---|---|---|---|---|
| 1. Readability | 1 | 2 | 3 | 4 | 5 | _____ |
| 2. Factual accuracy | 1 | 2 | 3 | 4 | 5 | _____ |
| 3. Coverage of people & events | 1 | 2 | 3 | 4 | 5 | _____ |
| 4. Concept development | 1 | 2 | 3 | 4 | 5 | _____ |
| 5. Approach | 1 | 2 | 3 | 4 | 5 | _____ |
| 6. Organization | 1 | 2 | 3 | 4 | 5 | _____ |
| 7. Visual impact | 1 | 2 | 3 | 4 | 5 | _____ |
| 8. Chapter reviews | 1 | 2 | 3 | 4 | 5 | _____ |
| 9. Maps & charts | 1 | 2 | 3 | 4 | 5 | _____ |
| 10. Illustrations | 1 | 2 | 3 | 4 | 5 | _____ |
| 11. Topic close-ups | 1 | 2 | 3 | 4 | 5 | _____ |
| 12. Biographies | 1 | 2 | 3 | 4 | 5 | _____ |
| 13. City profiles | 1 | 2 | 3 | 4 | 5 | _____ |
| 14. Annotated Declaration of Independence and Constitution | 1 | 2 | 3 | 4 | 5 | _____ |
| 15. Glossary | 1 | 2 | 3 | 4 | 5 | _____ |
| 16. Important Dates | 1 | 2 | 3 | 4 | 5 | _____ |

## Teacher's Annotated Edition

| | Excel-lent | Very Good | Satis-factory | Fair | Poor | Comments |
|---|---|---|---|---|---|---|
| 1. Teachability | 1 | 2 | 3 | 4 | 5 | _____ |
| 2. Effective Program Use | 1 | 2 | 3 | 4 | 5 | _____ |
| 3. Suggestions by Chapter | 1 | 2 | 3 | 4 | 5 | _____ |
| 4. Chapter in Perspective Answers | 1 | 2 | 3 | 4 | 5 | _____ |
| 5. Bibliography | 1 | 2 | 3 | 4 | 5 | _____ |
| 6. Annotations | 1 | 2 | 3 | 4 | 5 | _____ |

## Supplements

| | Excel-lent | Very Good | Satis-factory | Fair | Poor | Comments |
|---|---|---|---|---|---|---|
| 1. Discovery Book | 1 | 2 | 3 | 4 | 5 | _____ |
| 2. Discovery Book Answer Key | 1 | 2 | 3 | 4 | 5 | _____ |
| 3. Evaluation Program | 1 | 2 | 3 | 4 | 5 | _____ |
| 4. Media sound filmstrips | 1 | 2 | 3 | 4 | 5 | _____ |
| 5. Media Teacher's Guide | 1 | 2 | 3 | 4 | 5 | _____ |
| 6. Media Study Guide | 1 | 2 | 3 | 4 | 5 | _____ |

Circle the appropriate information.

| | | | | | | |
|---|---|---|---|---|---|---|
| 1. Grade level of students | 7 | 8 | 9 | 10 | 11 | 12 |
| 2. Enrollment of that grade | 1-50 | 51-100 | | 101-200 | | 200+ |
| 3. Total school enrollment | 1-200 | 201-500 | | 501-1000 | | 1000+ |
| 4. Locale of school | rural | small town | | suburban | | large city |
| 5. Ability level of class | below avg | | average | | | above avg |
| 6. Appropriateness of text for your class | easy | | about right | | | difficult |
| 7. Number of years text used | 1 | 2 | 3 | 4 | | 5 |
| 8. May we quote you? | yes | no | | | | |

Name _____ Date _____

School _____ City _____ State _____ Zip _____

- - - - - - - - - - - - - - - - - - - - - - - - - - - - - - - - - - - - - - - - - - - - - - - - - - - - - - -

Fold

- - - - - - - - - - - - - - - - - - - - - - - - - - - - - - - - - - - - - - - - - - - - - - - - - - - - - - -

Fold

First Class
Permit
No. 284
Columbus, OH

Postage will be paid by:

# CHARLES E. MERRILL PUBLISHING CO.

A BELL & HOWELL COMPANY

Managing Editor, Elhi Social Studies
1300 Alum Creek Drive
Columbus, Ohio 43216

 BELL & HOWELL

# America
# Is

# America Is

Frank Freidel
Henry N. Drewry

Charles E. Merrill Publishing Co.
A Bell & Howell Company
Columbus, Ohio

Toronto London Sydney

On the cover of *America Is* are a few of the famous and not-so-famous people representing the millions who have influenced the history of the United States. Shown are, from left to right, Daniel Inouye, Martin Luther King, Jr., Benjamin Franklin, Ines Mexia, Maria Martinez, Chien-Shiung Wu, Helen Keller, Mariano Guadalupe Vallejo, Chief Joseph, and Sojourner Truth.

ISBN 0–675–01898–6

Published by

**CHARLES E. MERRILL PUBLISHING CO.**
**A Bell & Howell Company**

Columbus, Ohio 43216

Copyright © 1978 by Bell & Howell

All rights reserved. No part of this book may be reproduced in any form, electronic or mechanical, including photocopy, recording, or any information storage or retrieval system, without permission in writing from the publisher.

Printed in the United States of America

# Authors

**Frank Freidel** is Charles Warren Professor of American History at Harvard University and has written more than twenty history books. He is the author of *The Presidents of the United States*, published by the White House Historical Association. Freidel is a fellow of the American Academy of Arts and Sciences and is past president of the Organization of American Historians. He is a member of the New England History Teacher's Association and is chairman of the Advisory Board of the Schlesinger Library on the History of Women in America. Freidel is past chairman of the American Historical Association Committee on Teaching in Schools.

**Henry N. Drewry** is Lecturer with the rank of Professor of History at Princeton University. He taught for fourteen years in secondary schools before joining the university. Drewry has coauthored several books and articles and has received the Harvard University Prize for Distinguished Secondary School Teaching. He is Director of the Princeton University Teacher Preparation Program and spends Sabbaticals in secondary schools teaching social studies. Drewry is a member of the Association for the Study of Afro American Life and History, the Organization of American Historians, and National Council for the Social Studies.

# Editorial Staff

**Editors:** Cheryl Dean Currutt, E. M. Clifford,
John Lawyer, Deborah Wade,
and Ann Weiland

**Project Artists:** Shirley Beltz and Katie White
**Text Design:** Lester Shumaker
**Cover Design:** Larry Koons
**Cover and Unit Opening Illustrations:** David M. Mankins
**Text Maps:** June Barnes
**Photo Editor:** Wendy S. Rector

## Reviewers

**Dorothea B. Chandler**
Curriculum Consultant, Retired
Torrance Unified School District
Torrance, California

**Dona McSwain**
Social Studies Department Chairman
West Stanley High School
Oakboro, North Carolina

**Dorothy Bachmann**
Social Studies Consultant
Educational Development Center
Paramus, New Jersey

**William J. Burkhardt**
Curriculum Coordinator
Northeast Junior High School
Bethlehem, Pennsylvania

**Richard Ross**
Social Studies Teacher
Ada Middle School
Ada, Oklahoma

# Preface

*Before we can set out on the road to success,*
*we have to know where we are going,*
*and before we can know that we must determine*
*where we have been in the past.*

John F. Kennedy
President of the United States

The actions that people took or did not take in the past have made your present and influence your future just as you are the makers of American history for tomorrow's citizens. So this study of America is mostly a study of its people—their needs, wants, hopes, and choices. It was written to help you see more clearly the connections among people, places, events, and ideas. *America Is* has twenty-five chapters grouped into eight units. Each unit title can be used to describe what the United States has meant to its people at different times in its history. America was and is Opportunity, Independence, Democracy, Expansion, Division, Growth, Conflict, and Challenge.

The information in this book is presented in the order of time so that you can put the many parts of American history that you already know, and some facts and ideas that are new to you, into useful order. This pattern is also used in the review sections that appear at the end of each chapter. These reviews range from the simple recall of facts to a more thoughtful examination of ideas. To help you understand and to keep you interested, the chapters include photographs, drawings, maps, charts, quotations, close-up views of particular ideas or events, and biographies of famous and not-so-famous Americans.

There are also fourteen special features on American towns and cities to help you relive history from the Algonquin village of Secota to the "Space City, U.S.A." of Houston. Firsthand accounts of the social, cultural, economic, and geographic sides of American life are shown in them. Because language changes over time, aids are used to make these quotes easier to read. Words sometimes appear in brackets [like this] to replace or to explain words that are very hard to read or whose meanings have changed. Ellipses [which are sets of periods . . .] are used in place of some words, phrases, or sentences to make the quotes shorter.

At the back of the book, you will find a glossary to help you remember definitions and an index to help you find the page numbers for particular people and topics. There is a time chart of important events and a fact chart of the Presidents and Vice-Presidents for reviewing and keeping information in order. There are also copies of the Declaration of Independence and the Constitution with notes so that you can understand them better.

*America Is* briefly tells the story of our country and its people. As a student of American history, you will also find more of the story outside the pages of this book. Many of the best firsthand accounts of the recent past are told by the oldest members of your families and neighborhoods.

> *The oldest people in this country today, those who provide us with our legacy and heritage, will be gone in ten years. If we let them get away without knowing what is in their heads, we will have lost more than we could ever know. They are a resource as important to us as energy. . . .*

Alex Haley
Author of *Roots*

# Contents

# Unit Three

## America is... Democracy

# Unit Four

## America is... Expansion

# Unit Five
## America is... Division

# Unit Six
## America is... Growth

# Unit Seven

## America is... Conflict

# Unit Eight

## America is... Challenge

# Study Aids

# Maps and Charts

# Photo Credits

**Unit 1**
Page 2, Museum of the City of New York; 5, Joslyn Art Museum, Omaha, Nebraska; 9, Jim Elliott; 11, American Museum of Natural History; 14, Smithsonian Institution National Anthropological Archives; 17, 18, 19, 20, The British Museum; 22, The Bettmann Archive, Inc.; 25, The Newark Museum, Newark, N.J.; 27, Institute Nacional de Bellas Artes, Mexico City; 29, Schoenfeld Collection from Three Lions; 31, Arizona Department of Administration; 33, Public Archives of Administration; 33, Public Archives of Canada, Ottowa; 36, New York Public Library; 40, The Bettmann Archive, Inc.; 43, Thomas L. Williams; 44, The Bettmann Archive, Inc.; 48, National Park Service Photo by Richard Frear; 49, Historical Pictures Service, Inc.; 53, Pennsylvania Academy of the Fine Arts, Joseph and Sarah Harrison Collection; 58, New England Mutual Life Insurance Company; 59, 63, Plimoth Plantation, Plymouth, Massachusetts.

**Unit 2**
Page 66, The New-York Historical Society; 68, The Maryland Historical Society; 72, Courtesy Carolina Art Association, Gibbes Art Gallery; 73 left, Culver Pictures, Inc.; 73 right, The Brooklyn Museum, The Dick S. Ramsey Fund; 76, 78, The New-York Historical Society; 81, The Library of Congress; 82, The Library Company of Philadelphia; 84, New York Public Library; 86, Colonial Williamsburg Photograph; 89, The New York Public Library, Arents Tobacco Collection; 90, Glen Falls Insurance Company, The Continental Insurance Companies; 93, The Library of Congress; 98, Charles Phelps Cushing; 100, John Trumbull, *Declaration of Independence* © Yale University Art Gallery; 105, The Bettmann Archive, Inc.; 107, Editorial Photocolor Archives, Inc.; 109, The Cincinnati Historical Society; 112, Independence National Historical Collection; 115, The New-York Historical Society; 118, Independence National Historical Collection.

**Unit 3**
Page 123, Courtesy, The Henry Francis du Pont Winterthur Museum; 124, The American Museum of Natural History; 128, Independence National Historical Park Collection; 130, Photo Research International; 133, Historical Pictures Service, Inc.; 135, Thomas Jefferson Memorial Foundation, Inc.; 137, Culver Pictures, Inc.; 144, The Bettmann Archive, Inc.; 146, 147, The Library of Congress; 148, The St. Louis Art Museum; 151, The Smithsonian Institution; 152, Chicago Historical Society; 157, Ohio Historical Society; 158, Collection of the Maryland Historical Society; 165, The Bettmann Archive, Inc.; 167, The Smithsonian Institution; 169, Phelps Stokes Collection, New York Public Library; 170, State Historical Society of Pennsylvania; 173, The Library of Congress; 176, From the Original Oil Painting at Woolaroc Museum, Bartlesville, Oklahoma; 180, New-York Historical Society; 183, The Bettmann Archive, Inc.; 186, Chicago Historical Society.

**Unit 4**
Page 190, Thomas Gilcrease Institute of American History and Art; 193, National Gallery of Art; 194, Works Project Administration; 195, The Library of Congress; 204, California State Library; 207, California Historical Society; 209, 211, Courtesy, The Bancroft Library; 212, The Library of Congress; 214, Yale University Art Gallery; 217, The Bettmann Archive, Inc.; 219, State Historical Society of Wisconsin.

**Unit 5**
Page 221, 222, 225, 230, The Library of Congress; 234, The Brooklyn Museum, Gift of Gwendolyn O. L. Corkling; 237, The Cincinnati Art Museum; 238, The Library of Congress; 241, Illinois State Historical Society; 242, 244, The Library of Congress; 246, The New-York Historical Society; 250, Association of American Railroads; 253, The Library of Congress; 255, The Metropolitan Museum of Arts, the Harris Brisbane Dick Foundation; 259, The Bettmann Archive, Inc.; 262, The Edward W. C. Arnold Collection, courtesy of the Museum of the City of New York; 263, U.S. Signal Corps/The National Archives; 265, The Museum of the City of New York; 267, Atlanta Historical Society; 268, The Bettmann Archive, Inc.; 269, Atlanta Historical Society; 271, U.S. Signal Corps Photo; 275, The Library of Congress; 278, Schoenfeld Collection, Three Lions; 281, 282, The Library of Congress.

**Unit 6**
Page 288, The Nebraska State Historical Society; 290, The Library of Congress; 293, Drake Museum; 294, Metropolitan Museum of Art, Gift of Lyman G. Bloomingdale; 300, Office of the Chief of Engineers; 301, Minnesota Historical Society; 305, Kansas State Historical Society; 306, The Bettmann Archive, Inc.; 307, 309, Kansas State Historical Society; 310, F. W. Woolworth and Company; 313, permission of Chelsea House Publishers; 314, Brown Brothers; 316, 318, 319, The Library of Congress; 321, The Bettmann Archive, Inc.; 327, Museum of the City of New York; 330, Ohio Historical Society; 333 top, Culver Pictures, Inc.; 333 bottom, NAACP; 335, Brown Brothers; 338, The Library of Congress; 343, The Bettmann Archive, Inc.; 349, 350, 352, The Library of Congress; 355, Brown Brothers; 361, The Bettmann Archive, Inc.; 362, The Library of Congress; 365, Chicago Historical Society.

**Unit 7**
Page 368 left, The National Archives; 368 right, 371, 373, 376, 378, The Library of Congress; 381, The National Archives; 387, The Library of Congress; 388, 390, The Ford Motor Company; 391, Brown Brothers; 392, Kansas State Historical Society; 393, 395, 408, 410, Brown Brothers; 411, The Library of Congress; 414, The Franklin D. Roosevelt Library; 416, Brown Brothers; 418 left, cartoon by Batchelor from the New York Daily News; 418 right, cartoon by John McCutcheon from the Chicago Tribune; 419, 421, The Library of Congress; 425, The Bettmann Archive, Inc.; 427, Brown Brothers; 428, Culver Pictures, Inc.; 429, Ball Corporation; 430, Cheryl Dean Currutt; 432, 436, 438, The Library of Congress; 443, U.S. Army Photograph; 446, Franklin D. Roosevelt Library; 449, Elliot Erwit for Magnum Photos, Inc.; 451, Brown Brothers; 453, J. R. Ezerman for Black Star Publishing Company.

**Unit 8**
Page 456, 459, 461, 466, United Press International/Compix Division; 470, U.S. Army Photo; 473, Standard Oil Company; 476, Wide World Photos; 480, 482, 486, 489, United Press International/Compix Division; 491, Washington Evening Star; 495, Houston Department of Development; 496, NASA; 498, United Press International/Compix Division; 499, Gerald D. Hines Interest, Inc.; 500, NASA; 504, Magnum Photos, Inc.; 508, 512, Wide World Photos; 515, Burt Glinn for Magnum Photos, Inc.; 519, Wide World Photos.

# America Is... Opportunity

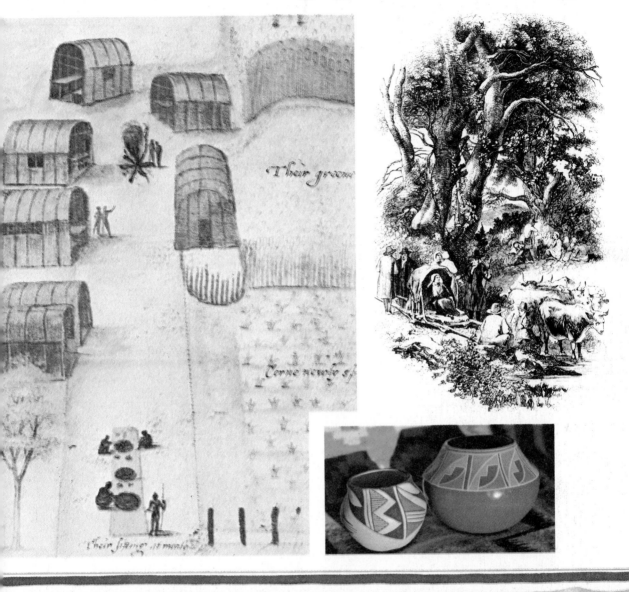

# Before Columbus: An Introduction

# 1

Aim: to develop appreciation of natural and cultural resources present in the Americas before European immigration.

All people who live in North and South America are properly called Americans, but U.S. habit limits the term to people of the U.S.

People of the U.S. have varied backgrounds including Eskimo, Indian, Asian, African, and European.

The people of the United States proudly call themselves Americans. They are not the only people who do so. In its broadest sense, the term American can be applied to all those who live on the two huge continents in the Western Hemisphere. So, the people of Chile and Argentina think of themselves as Americans. They call the people of the United States North Americans—a term which actually includes Canadians as well.

The first people to come and stay in what became the United States were ancestors of Eskimos and Indians, probably coming from Asia thousands of years ago. Beginning in the sixteenth century, Europeans and Africans began to arrive. They brought with them many languages and cultures, or ways of life. Since most of these settlers were

*People from all over the world came to America. Many of them were looking for a place to live where they could be free and equal citizens. Others were brought as servants or as slaves.*

from England, English came to be the common language of all these peoples. Not so with the culture. The peoples arriving in America contributed their ways of life to help form a new and distinct American culture. A nineteenth-century poem says:

> America, thou half-brother of the world;
> With something good and bad of every land.

Americans had many ties with Old World peoples and cultures, but it took weeks to cross the great oceans in the age of the sailing vessel. So Americans began to form their own ways of living, and at the same time, they kept some of the old. Thomas Paine wrote at the time of the American Revolution, "Not a place upon earth might be so happy as America. Her situation is remote from all the wrangling world, and she has nothing to do but to trade with them."

# Land of Wonders

In this huge land full of natural riches, Americans flourished. Changes took place more rapidly than in the Old World. A French visitor, Alexis de Tocqueville, wrote, "America is a land of wonders, in which everything is in constant motion and every change seems an improvement. . . . No natural boundary seems to be set to the efforts of man; and in his eyes what is not yet done is only what he has not yet attempted to do."

—a French noble who visited in 1831; his *Democracy in America* is considered a classic study. According to custom of his day, uses "man" generically. Clarify with students.

Many Americans who did not enjoy fully the freedom and rights of their country shared this faith in America. In 1831, some New York City blacks protested a plan to return them to Africa. They stated:

We are content to abide where we are. We do not believe that things will always continue the same. The time must come when the Declaration of Independence will be felt in the heart, as well as uttered from the mouth, and when the rights of all shall be properly acknowledged and appreciated. God hasten that time. This is our home, and this is our country. Beneath its sod lie the bones of our fathers: for it, some of them fought, bled, and died. Here we were born, and here we will die.

Love of country has always been an American characteristic. Daniel Webster, at the dedication of a monument to some of the soldiers who fought in the Revolution, exclaimed, "Thank God! I—I also

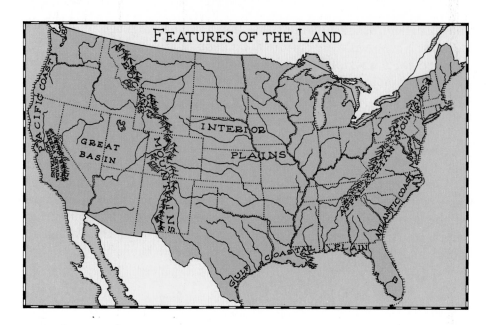

FEATURES OF THE LAND

—am an American!" This country has been praised in many poems. Walt Whitman wrote, "The United States themselves are essentially the greatest poem."

Wendell L. Willkie, a 1940 presidential candidate, described what being an American meant to him. It is now on a marker beside his grave in Indiana:

> I believe in America because in it we are free—
> free to choose our government, to speak our minds,
> to observe our different religions.
> Because we are generous with our freedom, we share
> our rights with those who disagree with us.
> Because we hate no people and covet no people's lands.
> Because we are blessed with a natural and varied abundance.
> Because we have great dreams and because we have the
> opportunity to make those dreams come true.

# The Land

Americans have always loved their land for its beauty, its size, and its wealth. In different degrees, according to their experiences upon it, their lives were shaped by the land. Before the end of the colonial period, there were not only farmers from Georgia to Maine but also people who fished off New England's rocky coasts. There were lumberjacks, ironmasters, cowhands, and fur traders. All were affected by their environment, or surrounding conditions.

In turn, Americans shaped the land. They cleared fields, developed farms, and built roads, canals, and dams. They removed blocks from streams, made harbors, and built towns and cities. Resources seemed limitless. Their rapid development could transform America from a thinly populated wilderness into a rich urban industrial nation.

Americans gained in wealth as they changed the land. However, they sometimes had to give up natural beauty and clean air and streams and learn to tolerate noise and dirt. Daniel Webster hailed the building of a railroad past his New Hampshire farm in 1847 as a sign of progress. The railroad, he said, "towers above all other inventions of this or the preceding age." Webster also expressed a feeling of regret for some of the changes the railroad had brought.

*Europeans saw great opportunities for profit in New World resources.*

*Americans have long been fascinated by their land. The earliest Americans as well as the newest immigrants loved the country for its beauty and wealth. As people settled on the land, they changed it. Sometimes, they were changed as they adapted their way of life to the place where they lived.*

*Before Columbus*

[The trains were] coming so near my farm-house, that the thunder of their engines and the screams of their steam-whistles . . . not a little disturbed the peace and the repose of its occupants. . . . It injures the looks of the fields.

Webster, like so many Americans before and since, was pleased by the improvements—for instance to be able to eat as good a fish dinner in the mountains as he could beside the ocean. However, like others before and since, he missed the earlier look of the land. Americans have always looked for a better future and yet, in their love of the land, they looked back to the unspoiled beauty of the past.

As newcomers shaped the land, they insisted that they should not only use it, but own it as well. This attitude helped set the early settlers apart from the original inhabitants, the Indians. A Pennsylvania missionary in 1777 complained to a group of Indians because they had pastured their horses overnight in *his* meadow. He had hoped to mow it in a day or two. One of the Indians replied:

Note basic conflict between Indian and European views on use of land and resources. Most Indian groups had defined territories but believed in communal use; most Europeans believed in private ownership and competition.

"My friend, it seems you lay claim to the grass my horses have eaten, because you had enclosed it with a fence: now tell me, who caused the grass to grow? Can *you* make the grass grow? I think not, and no body can except the great Mannitto. He it is who causes it to grow both for my horses and for yours! See, friend! the grass which grows out of the earth is common to all; the game in the woods is common to all. Say, did you never eat venison and bear's meat?—"Yes, very often."—Well, and did you ever hear me or any other Indian complain about that? No; then be not disturbed at my horses having eaten only once, of what you call *your* grass, though the grass my horses did eat, in like manner as the meat you did eat, was given to the Indians by the Great Spirit. Besides, if you will but consider, you will find that my horses did not eat *all* your grass. For friendship's sake, however, I shall never put my horses in your meadow again."

# The First Americans

The first people arrived in North America from Asia at least twelve to fifteen thousand years ago. They probably crossed the Bering Straits which formed a land bridge in that glacial age when oceans were

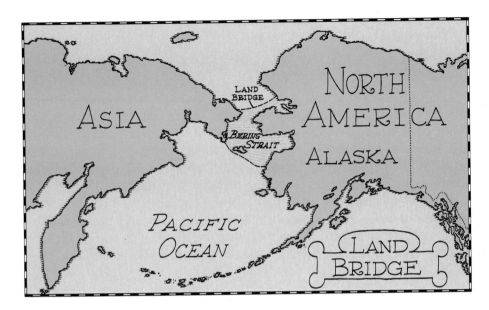

lower than they are now. For thousands of years, these early people spread through the Americas, developing very different appearances, several languages, and many cultures. They came so early that few of their descendants look today like the people of East Asia. They hunted great hairy elephants called mastodons, giant ground sloths, and primitive three-toed horses. All of these animals later became extinct.

Through the centuries in the New World, these people slowly invented many of the same things that were being invented in the Old World. Five thousand years ago, potters on the coast of Ecuador began using designs that resembled those of the potters of Japan at that time. In most tropical areas of the world, people cultivated cotton, sweet potatoes, and coconuts long before the days of Columbus. The early civilization in the New World owed little to the outside, even though many things were similar.

In the New World, there were only a few domesticated, or tamed, animals—the dog, llama, and turkey. However, agriculture was highly advanced. The Indians were very successful in growing food. One of their greatest achievements was the development of corn so long ago that its wild ancestor does not seem to exist. Tiny cobs of corn grown by Indians more than four thousand years ago have been discovered at Bat Cave in New Mexico. Altogether, the Indians domesticated eighty or ninety different plants. These account for almost half of what is grown on the farms of the world today. From the Indians, other people obtained these things:

New discoveries and advanced technology in archeology lead to continuing increase of knowledge of early peoples.

*Before Columbus*

| | | |
|---|---|---|
| corn | tomatoes | avocados |
| potatoes | squash | pineapples |
| beans | peanuts | chocolate |
| pumpkins | peppers | vanilla |

People today have adopted many things from the Indian cultures. All the cotton grown in the present-day United States (and much in other parts of the world) came from types Indians grew in Peru. From the Indians came rubber, chicle (chewing gum), tobacco, and many kinds of medicines. Hammocks, canoes, toboggans, and ponchos also are from Indian cultures. The designs they used in their jewelry, pottery, baskets, and cloth have been copied to this day. The names for some foods and some animals, such as the raccoon and the skunk, are Indian. From Indian words came names for trees, such as the hickory, and for many places, from Miami Beach to the Aleutian Islands.

See Teacher's Manual, page 18T.

Historian viewpoint is influenced by perspective of time and individual experience.

# Views of History

The American Indian has been seen by historians from many points of view. Here are three selections written by historians at different times throughout American history. What does each seem to be saying about these "first Americans"?

Michel Guillaume Jean de Crèvecoeur in 1775 described something that happened in the colonies after the French and Indian War. During the war, many of the colonists' children had been captured by the Indians.

*Many an anxious parent I have seen last war, who at the return of the peace, went to the Indian villages where they knew their children had been carried . . . ; when to their [great] sorrow, they found*

*them so perfectly Indianised, that many knew them no longer, and those [who remembered] their fathers and mothers, absolutely refused to follow them. . . . They chose to remain; and the reasons they gave me would greatly surprise you: the most perfect freedom, the ease of living, the absence of those cares . . . which so often [are with] us . . . made them prefer that life, of which we entertain such dreadful opinions. . . .*

George Bancroft wrote the following words about the American Indians in the 1800's.

*The Indian young man is educated in the school of nature. . . . he travels the war-path in search of . . . an enemy, that he too, at the great war-dance and feast*

Crèvecoeur (1735-1813) French-American who wrote *Letters From an American Farmer* while living in England after the American Revolution.

Bancroft (1800-1891) Massachusetts politician and diplomat considered leading historian in America in 1850. First to plan full study of U.S. history.

*Before Columbus*

The first Americans developed a unique and varied way of life. It survives today in their customs, language, and art.

of his band, may boast of his [adventures]; may [show off] his gallant deeds by the envied feathers of the war eagle that decorate his hair. . . . The [Indian men] are proud [that they do not work]. Woman is the laborer. The food that is raised from the earth is the fruit of her industry. . . . she plants the maize and the beans . . . and, in due season, gathers the harvest. . . . If the men prepare the poles for the wigwam, it is woman who builds it, and, in times of journeyings, [carries] it on her shoulders.

Allan Nevins had yet another way of looking at the Indians in 1927:

Certain main characteristics stamped the life of these plains Indians. They were physically of fine [build], strong and active. . . . Their chief [kind] of wealth consisted of their herds of ponies and of their weapons. . . . they

were quite unable to understand the desire of the white man to [take over] any part of the earth. Their government was simple and, in a sense, democratic, [made up of] a leadership of chiefs who [gained] their [offices] by skill and courage and whose [power] was most [strictly] exercised in time of war or other emergency.

These proud, stern, and really [frightening] peoples . . . had many faults but . . . [their] courage and [bravery] touched even their enemies to [admire them]. . . .

Does each historian have the same point of view about the Indians? What would make them each have a different point of view? What can you say about historians in general after reading these descriptions? Can you say anything in general about Indians?

Nevins (1890-1971) historian, biographer, educator born and schooled in Midwest who worked in New York.

# The Incas

At the beginning of the sixteenth century, several highly developed Indian civilizations in South and Central America became the targets of Spanish conquerors. One of these belonged to the Inca people of Peru. The Incas had risen to power over an area stretching along the Andes Mountains in South America. For centuries, this area had contained cities with paved streets, plazas, temples, and cemeteries. The skilled Inca weavers, potters, and metalworkers produced excellent cloth, pottery, jewelry, and weapons. The farmers were able to grow a surplus of food. Through a great army, good roads, and excellent communications, the Incas were able to keep their empire in control.

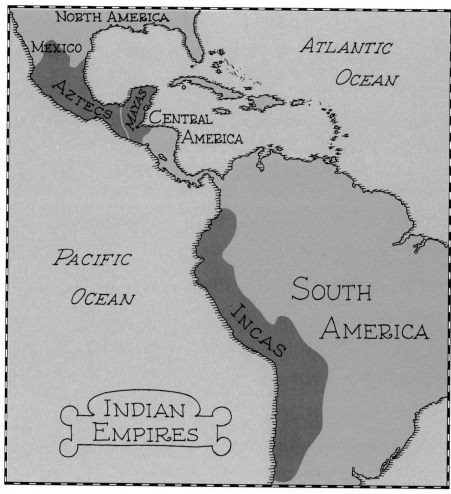

Compare to current map for identification of modern countries.

The leaders made the people work hard and kept them to a strict routine. Their government was tightly controlled by the ruler who had a great deal of power.

# The Mayas and the Aztecs

The Indian civilizations of Mexico have influenced Indians in what is now the United States. The Mayas and the Aztecs in Mexico were among the ancestors of present-day Mexican Americans. When the Spaniards arrived in Central America, there were still remains of the Mayan cities, with great temples, courts, and marketplaces. The Mayan priests were skilled in astronomy. Their calendar was more accurate than the one the Spaniards used at that time. The Mayan civilization was in decline, however, and was not as powerful as that of the strong, warlike Aztecs, who had come to rule the valley of Mexico.

*Descriptions by Spanish conquerors were used by an artist to draw this view of Tenochtitlán, the Aztec capital. It shows the city as it may have looked at the height of the Aztec's power.*

The Aztec capital, built where Mexico City is today, was a wonderful sight to the Spaniards with its palaces, busy streets and markets, and even a zoo. The Aztec culture also shocked the Spaniards. The main temple was devoted to human sacrifice, and near it were many human skulls. The need for sacrifices to their gods helped undo the Aztecs. They captured some of their victims from other powerful groups. These, in turn, joined the Spaniards to overthrow the Aztecs.

# Other Indian Cultures

Among North American Indians, there were more than 300 distinct languages and 500 separate, often complex, cultures. Many groups had well-developed systems of trade.

Many people overlook the remarkable and early achievements of Indians in North America. As early as four thousand years ago, Indians lived near the copper deposits around the Great Lakes. These people of the Old Copper Culture may have been the first metalworkers in the world. They shaped copper into spear points, tools, and jewelry. By three thousand years ago, Indians in much of the Northeast were growing crops to add to the wild food they gathered or hunted.

A "golden age" of North American Indian culture centered in the Ohio Valley from about 100 B.C. to 500 A.D. These Indians were noted for the great burial mounds they built and for their widespread trade. In their mounds have been found beautiful ornaments made from shells from the Atlantic coast, obsidian (a black volcanic glass) and bear teeth from the Rocky Mountains, and metals from other faraway places.

As this culture declined, another culture began to spread in the Southeast, along the Mississippi River, the lower Ohio, and other rivers. This has sometimes been called the Mississippian Culture. By 1200, the Mississippian Culture was flourishing through much of the Southeast. It owed much to earlier cultures and to Mexican influences. These Indians grew better corn, made excellent tools and decorative objects, and built fortified villages centering around great mounds. On top of the mounds, they built wooden temples. The greatest of these centers was at what is now Cahokia, Illinois.

Indians farther north were not so advanced in their way of life. They were in an earlier level of culture, making little or no use of metal. They cleared land to plant crops near their villages. They hunted, fished, and gathered berries, storing enough food to last through the winter. They were highly skilled in crafts.

General locations of Indian groups prior to invasion of European settlers.

13

NORTH AMERICAN INDIANS

Different groups of Indians acted in different ways toward strangers. They sometimes tortured prisoners of war to test their bravery. However, the first explorers and settlers from Europe found the Indians to be friendly toward them. An English explorer wrote of an Algonquin group along the North Carolina coast in 1584. "We found these people gentle, loving, and faithful, lacking all guile and trickery. It was as if they lived in a golden age of their own."

At first, the Indians agreed to let the settlers use their lands in exchange for goods and weapons. Sometimes, as in New England, the Indians gave up living on the land but kept hunting rights. Small groups adopted part of the newcomers' customs and religious beliefs. Most Indians chose to keep their own ways of life. As the number of settlers grew, they wanted more land. Some Indian groups moved away from the newcomers, but others stayed to fight for their lands.

Although most Indians did not accept European civilization in total, they did get many things from the settlers. They traded for metal hatchets and beads, guns and powder, as well as rum and whiskey. The use of the horse changed the life of Plains Indians. Indians in the Southwest captured herds of horses from Spanish settlements around the end of the seventeenth century. Using these horses, the Indians of the Great Plains and the Rocky Mountains were able to range farther and hunt more successfully than before.

On the whole, relations between Indians and colonists were poor. Generations of settlers lived in fear of Indian massacres. Generations of

Personal bravery was highly valued among many Indian groups.

Contact between peoples of Old and New Worlds resulted in each learning from the other. Europeans adopted much Indian technology and knowledge for their own survival.

*Before Columbus*

*The Indian groups of North America developed many different languages, customs, and styles of dress. The clothes of these Hopi women protect them from the climate of the Southwest.*

Indians suffered from massacres by settlers or were pushed westward onto the lands of other Indians. As the colonial settlements grew, they touched off serious wars among the Indians themselves.

It was difficult for the Indians to live for long on friendly terms with the new settlers. The Indians loved the land and their country. The newcomers came to love the country, too, and wanted to own it. The Indians were the "first Americans." Other cultures would mix with theirs to make up the way of life of "Americans" today.

# Chapter 1 in Perspective See Teacher's Manual, page 63T.

## Identify

Americans                    Incas                    Aztecs

# Explain

culture                          environment                          domesticated

## Check Your Memory of the Facts

1. When did the first people arrive in the American continents?
2. From what continent did the first people come who entered the Americas?
3. When did Europeans and Africans first arrive in the Americas?
4. What foods grown by the early inhabitants of America are still culti- vated today?
5. Other than foods, what developments of these early inhabitants are still in use?
6. Where were the empires of the Incas and the Aztecs located?
7. In general, what were relations like between the Indians and the settlers?

## Check Your Understanding of the Ideas

1. Is it correct to use the term American to refer only to citizens of the United States? Explain.
2. How did the Indians and the Europeans differ in the way they felt about the land?
3. What was the long-range influence of the English on the Indians of North America?
4. Why were various Indian groups different in their ways of living?

## Expand Your Knowledge

1. What different views of Indians are being taken by present-day his- torians? Look into the works of Alvin Josephy, Paul Prucha, Wilcomb Washburn, and Vine Deloria, Jr.
2. Prepare a map of North and Central America showing the locations of the major groups of Indians at the time Europeans began to ar- rive in the Americas.
3. Examine pictures of various groups of Indians and their belongings. What can you tell about the ways they lived and the differences be- tween them by these sources?

# Secota 1584-1587

Secota was an Algonquin Indian town near Roanoke Island in what is now the eastern part of North Carolina. In 1584, it was part of the land which Queen Elizabeth had given to Sir Walter Raleigh to colonize for England.

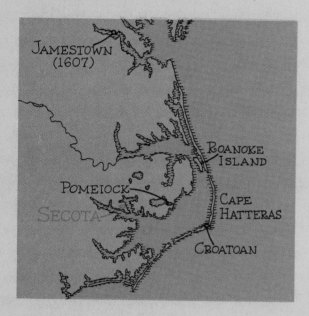

Arthur Barlowe led the first group of English explorers to the area. At different times, several groups were sent to explore and settle the land. John White drew pictures of the people, their towns, and the plants, fish, and birds which he saw on his trips. Barlowe, White, and a third explorer, Thomas Hariot, wrote down their descriptions of the new land for the people back in England. By reading the descriptions and looking at the pictures, Americans today can get an idea of how some earlier Americans, the Indians, lived in the 1580's.

## Early Towns

*Their towns are small and few, . . . a village may contain but ten or twelve houses—some perhaps as many as twenty. . . .*

*The houses are built of small poles . . . covered from top to bottom either with bark or with mats woven of long rushes. . . .*

*In one part of the country a . . . chief . . . may govern a single town, but in other parts the number of towns under one chief may vary to two, three, six, and even to eight or more. The greatest [chief] we met governed eighteen towns, and he could [get together] seven or eight hundred warriors. The language of each chief's territory differs from that of the others, and the farther apart they are, the greater the differences.*

## Secota

*Those of their towns which are not fenced in are usually more beautiful [like] Secota. The houses are farther apart and have gardens. . . . They also have groves of trees where they hunt deer, and fields where they sow their corn. In the cornfields they set up a little hut on a [platform], where a watchman is stationed. . . . He makes a continual noise to keep off birds and beasts. . . .*

*They also have a large plot . . . where they meet with neighbors to celebrate solemn feasts. . . . In the [smaller gardens] they sow pumpkins . . . and just outside the town is the river . . . from which they get their water.*

## The People

*The chieftains of Virginia wear their hair long, tied in a knot close to the ears. . . . One long bird's feather is stuck into the*

The town of Secota

[top] *and a short one above each ear. They hang large pearls in their ears. . . . Their [faces and bodies] are painted. . . . Around their necks they have a chain of pearls . . . and upon their arms they wear bracelets. . . .*

*They are dressed in cloaks made of finely cured skins. . . .*

*When the chiefs go to battle they paint their bodies in the most [scary] ways they can think of. . . .*

*The women of Secota [dress in] deerskins. . . . Their hair is cut short in front, somewhat longer at the back, and falls softly to their shoulders. . . . Their foreheads,* cheeks, chins, arms, and legs are chalked, and the pattern of a chain is pricked or painted around their necks. . . . In their ears they wear chains of long pearls or polished bones. They do not allow their nails to grow long. . . .

The priests of the town . . . are [very old] and have greater experience than the ordinary [people]. Their hair [also] is cut in a crest on the top of their heads; the rest of it is short and falls over their foreheads like a

*A woman and a priest*

*A sorcerer and a chief*

fringe. Earrings adorn their ears. They wear a short cloak made of fine rabbit skins. . . .

They have sorcerers . . . whose [spells] often go against the laws of nature. For they are very familiar with devils, from whom they [get] knowledge about their enemies' movements.

[These men] shave their heads entirely, except for the crest, which they wear as the others do. A small black bird is [tied] above one of their ears as a badge of office. . . .

The [people] pay great attention to the sorcerer's words, which they often find to be true.

## Friendly Visits

When the English first came to Virginia, they were treated well by the Indians. Arthur Barlowe wrote that:

We found these people gentle, loving, and faithful. . . . Their only care is how to protect themselves from the cold of their short winter and to obtain their food.

Barlowe's group visited the home of Granganimeo, the brother of a chief in that part of the country.

Granganimeo was not at home, but his wife came running toward us in a cheerful and friendly fashion. She ordered some of her men to draw our boat up onto the shore . . .

*to carry us on their backs to dry ground, and she saw to it that our oars were brought into her house in order that they should not be stolen. When we came into her lodging, a house of five rooms, she asked us to take our seats by a huge fire, made in one of the rooms. . . .*

*When we were warm and dry, Granganimeo's wife led us into an inner room, where she placed some food on a huge board standing along the wall. There we found boiled wheat pudding, venison, both boiled and roasted, fish, boiled and roasted, raw and boiled melons, and several kinds of root vegetables and fruits. Although ordinarily the [Indians] drink water, they have wine when the grapes are ripe. Only they have no [barrels] to keep it in; therefore when the season for grapes is over, they must drink water for the rest of the year. Their water is boiled with ginger, black cinnamon, sassafras, and other [good] herbs.*

Cooking in an earthen pot

## Secota Cooking

*Their women have the greatest skill in making large earthen pots, which are so fine that not even [the English] can make any better. These are carried around from place to place just as easily as our own brass kettles. They set them up on a pile of earth and then put wood underneath and [light] it, taking great care that the fire burns evenly on all sides. They fill the pot with water, then put fruit, meat, and fish into it, and let it boil together as in a [stew]. . . . When it is cooled, they serve it in small dishes. . . .*

## Planting Crops

The soil in the fields around Secota was very rich. Because of the long warm seasons, the Indians were able to bring in three crops of corn a year. To prepare the land for planting:

*They simply break the upper part of the ground to raise up the weeds, grass, and old stubs of cornstalks with their roots. . . . After the weeds have dried in the sun for a day or two, [they are] scraped up into many small heaps and burned. . . .*

*Then they sow the seed. For corn they begin in one corner of the plot and make a hole with a [stick]. They put four grains into each hole . . . and cover them with soil. The seeds are planted in rows. . . . between the holes . . . the [Indians] sometimes set beans and peas. . . .*

## Catching Fish

*They have a [special] way of fishing in their rivers. As they have neither steel nor iron, they [tie] the sharp, hollow tail of a certain fish . . . to reeds or to the end of a long rod, and with this point they spear fish*

*Catching fish with spears and traps*

both by day and by night. . . . And they make traps with reeds or sticks set in the water. . . .

It is a pleasing picture to see these people wading and sailing in their shallow rivers. They are untroubled by the desire to pile up riches for their children, and live . . . in friendship with each other, sharing all those things. . . .

## Building Boats

They build their boats in the following manner: first, they burn down a large tree, or take one blown down by the wind. Then they put [tar] on one side of this tree and set fire to it; when it is burnt hollow, they scrape away the burnt part with shells. . . . Thus they make very fine boats, large enough to carry twenty [people]. Their oars are like scoops, but when the water is shallow they use long poles.

## Religion and Law

The people of Secota had many gods. Some were more important to them than others. They believed that their chief god had always lived. He had created the world and then had made other gods to help him create and rule everything else.

*Then he made the sun, the moon, and the stars. . . . The [Indians] say that the waters of the world were made first and that out of these all creatures . . . were formed.*

*As to the creation of [people], they think that the woman came first. She [had] children fathered by one of the gods, and in this way the [Indians] had their beginning. But how many ages or years have passed since then, they do not know, for they have no writing or any means of keeping records of past time. . . .*

Temples were set up where the Indians worshipped their gods. They made human shapes of the gods, or idols, and prayed and sang to them.

Their religion taught them that humans have souls which do not die. After the body died, the soul of a good person would go to heaven. The soul of a bad person would go to a pit called Popogusso, at the farthest end of the world. There it would burn forever. Most of the bodies were buried, but for the chiefs:

*. . . they build a [platform] nine or ten feet high. . . . They cover this with mats and upon them they lay the dead bodies of their chiefs [after the bodies are specially treated]. . . . Near the bodies they place their idol, for they are [sure] that it keeps the bodies of their chiefs from all harm.*

*Under the [platform] lives one of their priests, who is in charge of the dead and [says] his prayers night and day. He sleeps on*

*A burial platform*

deerskins spread on the ground, and if it is cold, he lights a fire.

. . . the belief in heaven and the fiery pit makes the [people obey] their governors and behave with great care, so that they may avoid [pain] after death and enjoy bliss. Evil-doers have to pay for their crimes in this world, nevertheless. [Stealing] . . . and other wicked acts are punished with fines, beatings, or even with death. . . .

## War and Celebration

The people of Secota were often at war with the people of the nearby town of Pomeiock.

*Their manner of making war against each other is by a surprise attack. . . . Set battles are very rare. When they do take* place, it is always in the forests, where [they] may defend themselves by leaping behind a tree after they have shot their arrows. . . .

*When they have escaped some great danger on sea or land, or have returned safely from the wars, they light a great fire to celebrate. Men and women sit around it, each of them holding a rattle made of a certain kind of gourd, from which the fruit and seeds have been removed and replaced with small stones or kernels. These gourds they [tie] to sticks and shake as they sing. . . .*

## A Strange Sickness

As the English people stayed on in Virginia, the Indians of Secota and some of the other towns began to turn against them. At the same time, strange things began to happen in the towns which were visited by the English. Hariot wrote that:

*. . . within a few days [after we left a town] the people began to die very fast. In some towns twenty people died, in some forty, in some sixty. . . . And the strange thing was that this occurred only in towns where we had been. . . . The disease . . . was so strange a one that they did not know anything about it or how to cure it. . . .*

*[The Indians believed] that more of our [people] would yet come to this country to kill them and to take away their homes.*

Hariot ended his account by telling his readers that the Indians would learn to "honor, obey, fear, and love" the English. He did admit that, toward the end of their visit, some English people "were too harsh with them and killed a few of their number for [things] which might easily have been forgiven. . . ." Yet he believed that the Indians still liked the English, and he was certain that they were not to be feared.

# New World–
# New Opportunities 2

Christopher Columbus and his crew have been given credit for the discovery of America in 1492. They were not the first Europeans to set foot in the New World. The Vikings had come five hundred years earlier. But it was not until Columbus' time that many Europeans began

Aim: to develop understanding that Europeans competed for dominance of New World opportunities at expense of the Indians occupying the land and Africans brought in as forced labor.

*In the fifteenth century, the Portuguese sent many ships out of the harbor at Lisbon searching for new trade routes to the Far East.*

to expand into Africa, Asia, and the new continents across the Atlantic Ocean. What led them overseas was the desire to gain riches and to carry their religion to far-off peoples.

Some evidence suggests that Africans and Chinese reached Central and South America long before Columbus.

# Exploration and Discovery

Among the first people to search for adventure far away from Europe were those who fought in a series of wars called the Crusades. The Crusades lasted from about 1100 to 1250. During these years, Christian nobles and soldiers tried in vain to drive the Muslims from Jerusalem and Bethlehem. While fighting in the Middle East, the Europeans learned to like the spices, silks, fine cotton goods, rugs, and porcelains that Muslim traders got by caravan from India, China, and Southeast Asia. In the years that followed the Crusades, merchants from Venice, Italy, grew rich by trading with the Muslims. They had a monopoly, or exclusive control of this trade, and sold these luxuries at high prices in Europe. Because ships were small and captains did not dare sail far out of sight of land, there was no way to break the Venetian monopoly.

By the last half of the fifteenth century, things had changed, and West Europeans sought to trade directly with India and East Asia. Ships and instruments had so improved that people were sailing boldly into the unknown waters of the world. The Portuguese were the first to promote exploration, sending ship after ship down the coast of Africa in search of a water route to India. By 1498, Vasco da Gama sailed around the Cape of Good Hope and returned with precious goods from India.

An Italian navigator and mapmaker, Christopher Columbus, had a bold, new idea, but the Portuguese rejected it. He wanted them to finance an expedition to reach India by sailing directly west. Many people at that time believed that the world was round and that such a voyage was possible. However, some thought that the earth's size was far larger than Columbus believed. He expected to find China about 2,400 miles to the west, a perfectly reasonable voyage. Actually, it was over 10,000 miles, with the unknown landmass of North and South America in the way.

Finally in 1492, Columbus obtained financing from Queen Isabella of Spain and began his famous voyages. After ten weeks at sea, he landed on an island in the Bahamas. He thought he had landed on islands off the coast of India and called the inhabitants Indians. After a

# Letter From Columbus

A group of Spanish sailors under the leadership of Christopher Columbus arrived in what is now called America in 1492. This landing was one of the major events of modern history. The world was greatly changed because of the action of these people at that time and place.

In 1493, Columbus wrote about the historic event in a letter.

*Sir, —Believing that you will take pleasure in hearing of the great success which our Lord has granted me in my voyage, I write you this letter, whereby you will learn how . . . I reached the Indies . . . where I found very many islands thickly peopled. . . . To the first island that I found I gave the name of San Salvador. . . . I saw another island to the eastward . . . to which I gave the name of La Española. Thither I went, and followed its northern coast. . . . This island, like all the others, is extraordinarily large. . . . In the interior there are many mines of metals and a population innumerable. Española is a wonder. Its mountains and plains, and meadows, and fields, are so beautiful and rich for planting and sowing, and rearing cattle of all kinds, and for building towns and villages. The harbours on the coast, and the number and size and wholesomeness of the rivers, most of them bearing gold, surpass anything that would be believed by one who had not seen them.*

Note British spelling of harbor. Could discuss the responsibilities of translating and encourage an appreciation of foreign language study.

second voyage, it became clear that Columbus had found something different. "When treating of this country," wrote Peter Martyr, an Italian historian, in 1494, "one must speak of a new world, so distant is it

Only three return trips are shown because Columbus was sent back once as a prisoner, charged with failing to keep order on Española.

*New World—New Opportunities*

and so devoid of civilization and religion." It was not until 1507 that the name America was given to these lands. This came as a result of published accounts of voyages made to this new world by Amerigo Vespucci, an Italian explorer, sailing for Portugal.

Ambitious explorers and conquerors quickly made a huge empire for Spain out of the area Columbus explored. They came upon two large and rich Indian civilizations, that of the Aztecs in Mexico and the Incas in Peru. The Spaniards overthrew both empires and put these people to work in fields and mines. The Catholic Church converted the Indians and tried to protect them from the conquerors. However, its efforts were not successful. The Indians became victims of overwork and diseases brought by the Spanish. In a few years, almost all the Indians in the Caribbean were dead, and only a small part of the population of Mexico remained. To replace them, the Spaniards brought in black slaves from Africa to work on the plantations. By 1560, there may have been 100,000 of these Africans in the New World.

With great speed, other explorers sailed toward the shores of America. In 1520, a Spanish expedition headed by Ferdinand Magellan

American Indians had no natural immunities to European diseases like measles and smallpox. Such epidemic diseases were a main factor in eventual European dominance over Indian cultures. Could discuss lack of medical knowledge and compare to isolation periods for astronauts of today.

*This is an artist's view of the scene as Columbus and his crew landed in what became known as the New World.*

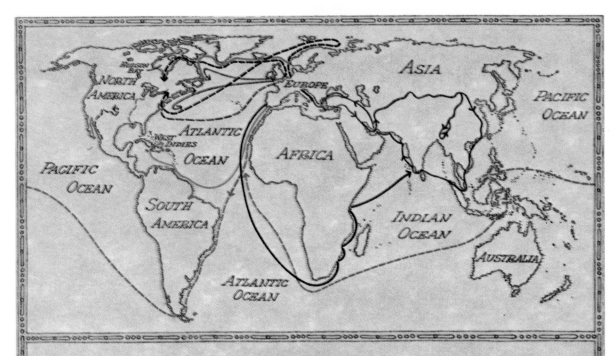

## Explorations

| Explorer | Date | Country | Achievements |
|---|---|---|---|
| Leif Ericson | 1000 | Norway | First European to reach North America |
| Marco Polo | 1271–1295 | Italy | Traveled by land from Europe to China |
| John Cabot | 1497–1498 | England | Explored the Atlantic coast of North America |
| Vasco da Gama | 1497–1503 | Portugal | First European to sail to India |
| Amerigo Vespucci | 1497–1503 | Spain and Portugal | Explored the Atlantic coast of South America |
| Ferdinand Magellan | 1519–1522 | Spain | Led the first voyage to sail around the world |
| Giovanni da Verrazano | 1524 | France | Explored the Atlantic coast of North America |
| Francisco de Coronado | 1540–1542 | Spain | Explored the southwest part of North America |
| Henry Hudson | 1609–1611 | Holland and England | Explored the Hudson Bay and Hudson River areas |
| La Salle | 1682 | France | Explored the Great Lakes region and the Mississippi River |

discovered the straits that now bear his name, sailed into the Pacific Ocean, and on to India and around the world. Only fifteen of the crew survived the voyage, but they brought back a profitable cargo. The success of this trip stimulated European sailors for years to search the bays of North America for a northwest passage to the Orient. They failed to find such a route. However, they gained an understanding of the land that led to French and British claims of ownership and, in the seventeenth century, to settlements.

# The Legacy From the Old World

The first European settlers in America brought with them the cultural heritage of the Old World. They came with habits and ideas about earning a living and the nature of government. Later, Americans developed these into ways of life that were different from those in the Old World.

*When Columbus returned from his voyage to the New World, he brought several Indians to the Spanish court of Ferdinand and Isabella.*

America became known as a nation of many peoples and cultures. The early settlers in the New World were descendants of many different peoples. Since prehistoric times, large groups of people had moved into and across Europe. The last such movement was in the early Middle Ages when the Arabs moved north to conquer what is now Sicily and much of Portugal and Spain. People from Western Asia pushed westward into Hungary, and the Norse came south into parts of England, France, and Russia.

All of this mixture was represented in the early settlers in America who made their new homes in a land already peopled by many different kinds of Indians. Others came to join them. Descendants of the Aztecs and other peoples came from Mexico. Blacks came from Africa to North America, South America, and the West Indies. In later years, people also came from the Middle East and East Asia.

Use a world map to show locations of these areas. Students could research own family histories to demonstrate this material. Encourage appreciation of diversity.

So it was that the ancestors of the present-day Americans were the builders of Stonehenge, the pyramids in both Egypt and Mexico, Solomon's Temple, the Acropolis, the Roman Forum, the palace of the King of Benin in Africa, the shrines of Japan, and the medieval cathedrals of Europe. Their arts included the earliest cave paintings in Spain and the Sahara Desert, Indian and African designs, and Greek sculpture. They read the ideas of Confucius, Homer, and Shakespeare. They knew the philosophic views of Moses, Aristotle, and the Christian leaders. Much of the knowledge of the ancient world came to them during the Middle Ages through Christians and Jews and from the Muslim centers of learning.

# A Time of Change

The people of Western Europe improved on what they had learned from others. By the end of the fifteenth century, they had developed mathematics, science, and technology better than any which had been known before in Europe. This helped them sail into unknown seas. They knew that the earth was round, made better sailing instruments, and built faster and stronger ships. In 1400, only a few ships could have sailed back and forth across the Atlantic Ocean. By 1500, many ships were sailing all over the world.

Strong national states were developed which could finance exploration and establish colonies. The people were also moving toward other ideas unknown to most of their ancestors. One of these was the idea of a government run by people who are elected to represent everyone, instead of a government ruled by one person. It was still a new

*Many people hoped to find great riches in the New World. But conditions for the early settlers were usually very harsh.*

idea, and it did not work very well yet. But it was a start toward the kind of government the United States has today.

Europe at the end of the fifteenth century was growing richer and changing. But to an American today, it must seem to have been poor and dull. Even though many new inventions had been made, most of the tools and weapons were not very different from those of ancient times. Society and culture kept people within narrow bounds. It was difficult for the child of a peasant to become other than a peasant. The child of an artisan was likely to be apprenticed to learn a trade. It was almost impossible to become a noble except by birth.

Poverty marked this society at this time. All but the very rich and the nobles often lacked adequate food, shelter, and clothing. War, starvation, and disease swept through these countries. Life was short and hard. The birthrate was high, but the death rate almost matched it. Few people lived into old age.

*New World—New Opportunities*

There were other causes for discontent among the people of the Old World. People were not always able to worship in the way they wished. This had been an important cause of the religious conflicts in Europe which are known as the Reformation. Those people who did not want to follow the official religion of their country were either punished or driven out of the country. Many English and some French and Germans were ready to go to America in order to follow their own minds rather than the rule of their governments.

The desire to improve their way of life, to practice their religion freely, to escape from the rule of kings and nobles, and often simply a spirit of adventure and ambition—these reasons drove men, women, and children to leave the Old World for the New.

# Colonial Empires

The great colonial empires in the New World began out of chance rather than out of careful planning. If Columbus had reached East Asia as he had expected, he would have started trading posts to send goods back to Europe. The Indians in America produced few such goods for trade, so it was more profitable there to set up plantations using the labor of Indians (and soon of black slaves). Colonies were started immediately; the first settlements were made by the Spanish on the island of Española, which is now the Dominican Republic and Haiti. The Indians were ruled by a small number of Spaniards who were administrators, missionaries, and soldiers. They directed the Indians' work, taught them their religion, and prevented their revolt. This kind of settlement was repeated throughout the West Indies, South America, Central America, and the southwestern part of North America. Spain gained a huge empire, and its powerful army and navy maintained tight control over it.

Spain established the first large empire claims by Europeans in the Americas.

Most of the Spanish population lived in the rich heart of the empire. On Española, there were only a thousand Spaniards as late as 1574. These soldiers and administrators controlled twelve thousand slaves engaged in growing sugar and raising cattle. In all eight settlements in Cuba, there were only 240 Spaniards. Puerto Rico was just as sparsely populated. Spanish land claims ran far up into North America —as far as Oregon in the West and the Carolinas in the East. In spite of this, Spain had only established settlements as far north as the Rio Grande in New Mexico (founded in 1598) and a fort at St. Augustine,

*Spain's huge empire in the New World was first settled by soldiers and missionaries. Estevanico, a black guide, and others led explorers and settlers through the unknown country.*

Florida (established in 1565). The army and navy of Spain were able to maintain tight control within this vast empire for centuries. Along its fringes, however, it was only weakly guarded, and its treasure ships were tempting prizes. One or more of the twenty to sixty vessels returning to Spain were lost each year.

The Spanish had to be strong to defend their American empire. The English, the Dutch, and the French were also anxious to grow rich from the wealth of the New World. Conflicts between Spain and these countries grew over the years.

The English were very eager to capture part of Spain's wealth. They attacked Spanish ships bearing silver bullion and carried on illegal trade with the Spanish colonies. Sir John Hawkins sold three shiploads of slaves to the people of Española in 1562. Five years later, he was defeated by a Spanish fleet. For the next thirty years, English sea captains, under orders from Queen Elizabeth I, pirated Spanish ships. One of the most famous English captains was Sir John Hawkins' cousin, Sir Francis Drake. In 1577, he sailed boldly into the Pacific Ocean, captured silver from Peru, and continued on around the world to England.

England drifted into a general war with Spain. In 1588, Spain sent a great armada, or fleet of warships, against England. With the aid of a storm, the English ships commanded by Drake destroyed the Spanish Armada. Spain was never again strong enough to challenge England's efforts for a colonial empire. England and Spain made peace in 1604. As part of the treaty, King James I of England agreed that Spain had a right to all areas of the New World which it occupied. King James felt free to colonize lands in North America north of Spanish Florida. In 1609, the Netherlands became independent from Spain and began establishing colonies. France was also ready at this time to begin colonizing. The English, the Dutch, and the French began looking for their own empires, and Spain was no longer strong enough to stop them.

# La Salle

Robert Cavelier, Sieur de la Salle, was born in France in 1643, the son of a wealthy merchant family. At the age of twenty-three, he came to New France and became a farmer and fur trader near Montreal. La Salle learned several Indian languages and heard stories of the great rivers and lakes to the west.

In 1669, La Salle sold his land to finance a trip to explore the Ohio River. For the next eighteen years, he also traveled through the Great Lakes region and down the Mississippi River. In 1682, La Salle reached the mouth of this great river and claimed the entire Mississippi Valley for France. He named it Louisiana in honor of King Louis XIV of France.

La Salle wanted to establish a colony at the mouth of the Mississippi River. So, in 1684, he sailed from France with two hundred colonists. The ships went too far west and landed on the Texas coast. When La Salle tried to lead the settlers overland back to the Mississippi River, they kept losing their way. Finally after many difficulties, some of the settlers rebelled and shot him.

La Salle's death ended his own dream of a settlement at the mouth of the Mississippi River. But because of his explorations, France ruled a great empire in the heart of the New World, and eventually, settlements were established. La Salle had opened the way for other explorers and settlers to move into the unknown western lands of America.

*Quebec was the first French settlement in North America to grow into a large city. Located on the St. Lawrence River in what is now Canada, it was the start of a fur trading empire for France.*

At the close of the sixteenth century, King Henry IV of France began thinking of ways to make his country a richer, more powerful nation. One way, he decided, was to create a colonial empire. Soon after Columbus' voyage, France made claims to parts of North America. Some French people were already visiting its shores to fish when plans for colonizing began. King Henry granted fur monopolies to many business people. One colony in Nova Scotia called Acadia was settled in 1605.

Samuel de Champlain started a French settlement called Quebec on the St. Lawrence River in 1608. The St. Lawrence proved to be a very good water route to the Great Lakes, the Mississippi River, and the West. Champlain followed its course inland, made friends with the Hurons and other northern Indians, and started a fur trading empire for France.

Could discuss importance of water routes at this time in history.

A few Indian groups were traditional enemies before Europeans arrived. They sometimes used Europeans as allies in limited objective wars.

For a long time, New France remained a chain of forts and fur trading posts. The French joined the Indians in the wars that were fought for more than a century against the Iroquois Indians and the English settlers. By the end of the seventeenth century, the French controlled the Great Lakes and the Mississippi Valley. They started a settlement at Biloxi on the Gulf of Mexico and, in 1718, founded New Orleans which became the capital of French Louisiana.

Both France and Spain claimed large areas in North America. They did not send many settlers. They did send soldiers and began to build forts to try to keep out intruders. In spite of their efforts, they were not able to keep England from founding colonies along the Atlantic coast. Today much of the land over which the French or Spanish flags once flew is part of the United States.

# Chapter 2 in Perspective See Teacher's Manual, page 64T.

## Identify

New World            Columbus            Reformation
Crusades             Old World           Española

## Explain

monopoly             colonies            armada

## Check Your Memory of the Facts

1. Who were the first Europeans to visit North America?
2. Why did Europeans want to travel to Asia?
3. What country supported Christopher Columbus in his search for a water route to the Far East?
4. What happened to Indians as a result of the Spanish conquests in Peru and Mexico?
5. Why did people leave their homes to come to the New World?
6. What areas in the New World came under the control of the Spanish? Of the French? Of the English?

1. What developments in Europe and the East led to Columbus' voyage to the New World?
2. How did Columbus' plan for reaching the East differ from that of the Portuguese?
3. How did the French and Spanish differ in their treatment of the Indians?
4. Would it be correct to say that the arrival of Columbus in America was a mistake? Why?
5. What does the European treatment of Indians and the enslavement of Africans tell us about the attitudes Europeans had toward people of different races and religions?

## Expand Your Knowledge

1. Using the map of North America which you prepared on the Indians, show the areas which came under control of each of the European governments in the seventeenth century. Use different colored pencils for each country. The completed map should show which Europeans had contact with which Indian groups.
2. Compare the reports of the first space explorers with those of the early explorers of the New World. How are they alike, and how are they different?

# Colonizing the New World

Aim: to develop understanding of British colonial policies and attitudes which led to British dominance of North America.

In the seventeenth century, the English began establishing colonies along the coast of North America. Compared with the Spanish who founded colonies a hundred years earlier, they were latecomers.

*Juan de la Cosa was a navigator on one of Columbus' ships during their first voyage in 1492. He was also a mapmaker, and in 1500, he drew this earliest known map of the New World.*

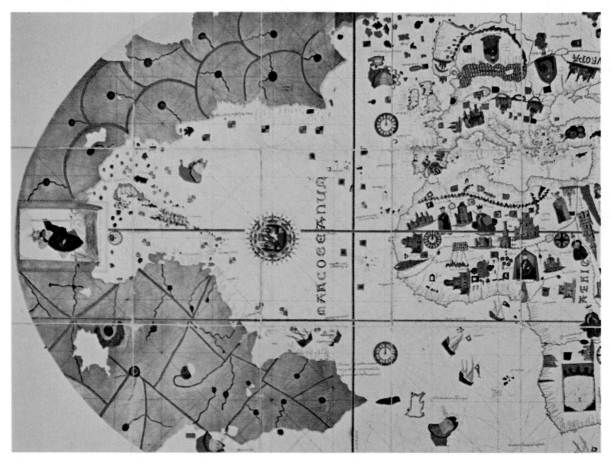

Compared with the French, they were less successful in allying themselves with Indians and in controlling the settlers. Yet the English colonies became the most successful of all those in America.

# The Lure of the New World

The area where the English and the French started their colonies seemed at the time the least promising for settlement. The Spaniards had passed it by because it did not seem to contain riches they could get quickly. In 1529, a Spaniard wrote on part of a map showing what is now the northeastern United States, "Trees and fruits like those of Spain abound, and turbot, salmon, and pike. They found no gold." The Spanish did not want to waste their people and their money on areas that were like Spain. "What need have we of these things which are common with all the people of Europe?" asked a Spanish official. "To the South, to the South . . . they that seek riches must go, not unto the cold and frozen North."

The English, having little choice, went to "the cold and frozen North." To interest settlers, the English tried to make people think they could instantly become rich in North America by picking up gold, growing mulberry trees to feed silkworms, or planting vines to produce fine wines. A church official in 1609 declared that Virginia would produce a great amount of "whatsoever . . . England wanteth." While glowing reports about America were spreading throughout England, the first settlers in Virginia were starving.

Could discuss the uses and abuses of propaganda.

An English play, *Eastward Ho,* made fun of the wild talk of instant wealth in America:

> *Scapethrift:* But is there such treasure there, captain, as I have heard?
>
> *Seagull:* I tell thee, gold is more plentiful there than copper is with us; and for as much red copper as I can bring, I'll have thrice the weight in gold. Why, man, all their dripping pans and their . . . pots are pure gold; and all the chains with which they chain up their streets are massy gold; all the prisoners they take are [chained] in gold; and for rubies and diamonds, they go forth on holidays and gather 'em by the sea-shore. . . .

*Colonizing the New World*

38　　　Many of the claims about the New World were like this satire, but there was a point to them. These wild stories might offset the grim tales of sickness, no food, and Indian attacks. They might persuade more English people to become colonists.

# An Extension of England

London merchants hoped that the North American colonies would help England and themselves in many ways. The colonies were expected to send raw materials like tobacco and tall pine trees for ships'

EUROPEAN CLAIMS
IN NORTH AMERICA 1650
☐ FRENCH ☐ BRITISH ☐ SPANISH
☐ DUTCH ☐ SWEDISH

Stress importance of water routes for travel and trade. Note French control of access to interior.

masts to England. In return, the colonists would buy large amounts of British goods—woolens, pots and pans, china, and hardware. The colonies would also be a place for those English seeking new opportunities outside England. Those who wanted freedom of religion would find it in the colonies. The unemployed and poor in England would be able to find land and become useful workers in the New World.

The English colonies, then, were meant to be more than small outposts in a foreign land. Rather, they would be overseas extensions of England, with towns and countrysides much like those in England. English people going to America would take their sheep, cattle, pigs, seedlings from their orchards, household goods, and more important, their ways of life and their laws.

The first English attempts to start colonies in North America failed. In 1583, Sir Humphrey Gilbert left a small group of people on the bleak shores of Newfoundland. This small colony soon disappeared. The second attempt was made by Sir Walter Raleigh, who hoped to found a colony on Roanoke Island. Over a period of two years, he sent three groups of people to settle and explore the area. John White, the leader of the third group, made excellent drawings of the plants, animals, and Indians, giving the people in England their first clear idea of the new lands. In 1587, White returned to England. He left behind a small group of colonists, including his own granddaughter, Virginia Dare, the first English child born in America. When he came back in 1591, the colonists were gone, never to be found.

Unlike the French and Spanish, the British moved in large numbers to their colonies with the intention of staying permanently.

# Joint Stock Companies

The first successful English colonies were started by joint stock companies. King James I would not provide money for starting colonies, but he would allow private companies to do so. Since most individuals did not have enough money to start colonies, joint stock companies were formed. The head of a joint stock company would get a charter from the king. A charter was an official paper that gave permission to settle in a certain region and the right to establish a government there. It also allowed the selling of shares of stock in the company. The money for colonizing came from the investors who bought the stock.

In 1606, King James I gave charters to two joint stock companies to settle the land claimed by England in North America. One company was the Virginia Company of London which was to settle the southern half of this land, part of which is now Virginia. The Virginia Company of London, also called the London Company, was made up mostly of wealthy merchants and nobles who hoped to make large profits in the New World.

# Jamestown

*Economic, political, and religious reasons led to heavier British colonization.*

In 1607, the London Company sent 104 settlers to Virginia. The first settlement was called Jamestown in honor of the king. These first settlers were adventurers, nobles, and others who were eager to make a quick fortune and just as eager to avoid hard work. They thought that they could get rich by trading with the Indians and finding gold mines. The settlers soon fell upon hard times. They were kept alive and together only by the firm hand of their leader, Captain John Smith, and by the food that he was able to get from Powhatan, the powerful chief of the Virginia Algonquin Indians.

Captain John Smith

# Pocahontas

The story of Pocahontas has become an American legend. Even as a child, she was a symbol of friendship between the Indians and the settlers at Jamestown. In his writings, Captain John Smith once told how she saved his life when her father, Chief Powhatan, was going to kill him. She was only about twelve years old at the time. Pocahontas became a favorite of Captain Smith, whom she came to think of as a second father. The name Pocahontas meant playful or frolicsome, and Smith described her as having wit and spirit. Many times, she persuaded Powhatan to trade with the settlers rather than kill them.

Captain Smith made a trip back to England in 1609. While he was gone, fighting broke out between the Indians and the settlers. In 1613, a trading ship sailed up the Potomac River. Learning that Pocahontas was in the area, the captain invited her on board and then held her captive. He took her to Jamestown where the settlers hoped that, by keeping her there, they could persuade Powhatan to make peace.

Pocahontas easily became used to the life in Jamestown. She learned to speak English, wore European clothes, and became a Christian. One of the settlers, John Rolfe, began spending much time with her. In 1614, when Pocahontas was seventeen, they were married. After the wedding, Powhatan sent word that he was old and wished to end his days in peace. He gave a plot of land to Pocahontas and John and did not make war on the settlers again.

In 1616, John Rolfe, Pocahontas, and their son Thomas sailed for England. Pocahontas was an instant success there and was presented to the king and queen. Just before they were to sail for home in 1617, she became ill and died.

Pocahontas had been admired and respected by those who knew her. Her son Thomas inherited land from his father and from his grandfather, Powhatan. He later became an important leader in Virginia, and the heritage of Pocahontas was passed to a long line of descendants.

That first summer, the Jamestown colonists grew wheat, pumpkins, potatoes, and melons. However, there was not enough food to keep them alive for the winter. The London Company sent more settlers, but this meant more mouths to feed. Smith's skill in trading copperware, knives, and fishhooks with Chief Powhatan for more food was all that kept the colonists alive.

Smith and the colonists did not completely trust Powhatan. They were always ready for any trouble and kept their weapons at hand. Powhatan ruled over about two hundred Indian villages. He could have crushed Captain Smith and the handful of settlers at Jamestown during the first difficult years. Instead, he chose to trade rather than to make war. Smith and the settlers lived through their "starving time" because of this trade. Their demands were heavy. Later, when they had enough food and the Indians were starving, the English set very heavy terms before giving them four hundred bushels of corn. This kind of treatment did not help relations with the Indians.

As time went on, the London Company began to send more farmers who grew food and raised animals on large plots of land which they got from the Indians. A settler named John Rolfe began raising tobacco. It soon became an important crop because it could be sold in England for a good price. Until 1619, Virginia prospered. Then for five years disease raged, killing four thousand settlers. During the epidemic, the Indians under Powhatan's successor massacred several hundred colonists. The Indians fought for over ten years, but slowly the Virginians pushed them back. By the 1630's, the colony was firmly established.

*Help students realize a time without "instant communication" of daily newspapers, radio, TV, and easy travel.*

# Government in Jamestown

During the early years, a lasting kind of government began to take form in Virginia. The owners of the London Company in England gained the right to name a governor and a council to run the colony. All land belonged to the company, and the settlers worked as its servants. These policies did not work, and in 1618, the company began granting land to individuals. The settlers were given a voice in the running of the government, and in 1619, they elected representatives to serve in a legislature, or lawmaking body, called the House of Burgesses. These representatives could pass laws, but the laws could be vetoed, or put aside, by the governor or taken away by the London Company. Limited though its power was, the House of Burgesses was a representative form of government.

The Virginia Company of London never made any profit from the Jamestown colony. The investors ran the company badly and quarreled bitterly among themselves. In 1624, James I took away their charter and brought Virginia under royal control. From then on, the king named the governor, who always came from England, and the members of the council, who were always important Virginians. The House of Burgesses continued as the elected legislature.

*By the 1630's, Jamestown was well established. Trade with the Indians and the firm leadership of John Smith had helped it survive.*

The Virginia colony provided a model for the settlement of other English colonies. The mistakes made by the London Company were a lesson for those who followed. Only hardworking people could make a success of a colony. People worked hardest on land that was their own. Easy riches were not to be found, but for those willing to work and to take the chance, the opportunity for a new life might be found in the New World.

Most lower and middle class British considered work among the highest virtues and placed great value on utility.

# Pilgrims at Plymouth

The settlement of New England became the undertaking of the Virginia Company of Plymouth, England. It was given its charter in 1606, the same time as the Virginia Company of London. In 1620, the Plymouth Company became the Council for New England, gaining the right to grant land to settlers for colonies. Attempts at settlement before 1620 had not been successful, but descriptions of New England by Captain John Smith, who had explored its coastline, brought new interest. Also, news that an epidemic had killed most of the Indians along the coast meant that the area could be settled without fear of war.

In 1620, 102 settlers sailed on the *Mayflower* from Plymouth, England. These people, known as the Pilgrims, had actually been heading for Virginia. However, strong winds in that wintry season had blown their ship farther north. They landed in New England on the shores of

*The ship that the Pilgrims used, the* Mayflower, *had three masts and two decks. It was about ninety feet long and landed at Cape Cod after sixty-five days at sea.*

*Colonizing the New World*

Cape Cod, in what is now Massachusetts. They were a group of poor men and women who were hoping to make enough profit in the New World to pay off the English merchants who had invested money in their passage and had granted them land. They had been treated badly because of their religious beliefs. They were called Separatists for their desire to separate themselves from the Church of England. King James I of England allowed them to migrate to America and promised that they would not be bothered if they lived in peace. This promise was important because it opened the way for great numbers of people seeking religious freedom to migrate to the English colonies.

*The first colonists were seeking religious freedom for themselves, not religious tolerance for all.*

When the *Mayflower* anchored in the harbor at the tip of Cape Cod, the Pilgrim leaders realized that they had not reached Virginia. Some of the people were upset, saying that they had only been given the right to govern in Virginia. In order to stop any possible trouble, forty-one of the passengers signed a compact, or agreement, to set up a civil government and to obey its laws. The Mayflower Compact was the basis for government in the colony.

*Could discuss written vs. oral agreements.*

# THE MAYFLOWER COMPACT

*In the Name of God, Amen. We, whose names are underwritten, the Loyal Subjects of our dread Sovereign Lord King James, by the Grace of God, of Great Britain, France, and Ireland, King, Defender of the Faith, &c. Having undertaken for the Glory of God, and Advancement of the Christian Faith, and the Honour of our King and Country, a Voyage to plant the first colony in the northern Parts of Virginia; Do by these Present, solemnly and mutually in the Presence of God and one another, covenant and combine ourselves together into a civil Body Politick, for our better Ordering and Preservation, and Further-ance of the Ends aforesaid; and by Virtue hereof do enact, constitute, and frame, such just and equal Laws, Ordinances, Acts, Constitutions, and Offices, from time to time, as shall be thought most meet and convenient for the general Good of the Colony; unto which we promise all due Submission and Obedience. In witness whereof we have hereunto subscribed our names at Cape Cod the eleventh of November, in the Reign of our Sovereign Lord King James of England, France, and Ireland, the eighteenth and of Scotland, the fifty-fourth. Anno Domini, 1620.*

*Colonizing the New World*

In December, 1620, the Pilgrims began building houses in a small settlement on a fine harbor. They called it Plymouth after the town in England from which they had sailed. Their first winter was a hard one, and half of them died from the cold, illness, or the lack of food. In the spring, their fortunes improved. They began to plant the large fields left by the Indians who had died in the epidemic. They received help from Squanto, a Pawtucket Indian, who had lived in England. He joined the Pilgrims and taught them useful Indian ways of living in the wilderness. The settlers also made a peace treaty with Massasoit, the chief of the nearby Wampanoag Indians. It lasted for over forty years.

In time, the Pilgrims got a land grant from the Council for New England, and they governed themselves for seventy years with almost no outside control. They had become a small, independent republic in New England with their own elected governor and council. Life never became very easy in Plymouth, but the settlers made a fair living by farming, fishing, and trading. The colony slowly grew until 1691 when it became part of the Massachusetts Bay Colony.

# Massachusetts Bay Colony

The largest and most powerful settlement in New England was Massachusetts Bay Colony, founded in 1630. It was started by a number of educated, wealthy leaders of the Puritans in England. Like the Separatists who settled Plymouth, the Puritans did not like the Church of England. Unlike the Separatists, they wanted to improve or purify the Church, not leave it. They hoped to establish a model community in the New World as an example of the type of society—both a civil and church government—in which they so strongly believed.

In 1629, a group of these Puritans received a charter and land grant for the Massachusetts Bay Company. John Winthrop was the leader of those Puritans who wished to go to America. The group took the charter, and thus the government of the colony, with them to America. They did not want to be controlled by people in England, as the colonists in Jamestown had been by the owners of the London Company. If the charter remained in England, their enemies might buy stock and gain control of the company. The Puritans wanted to be independent and to govern themselves according to their own ideas.

These Puritan groups were much larger than any previous attempts at white settlement.

A thousand Puritans arrived in Massachusetts in 1630. They founded Boston and several other towns and elected John Winthrop

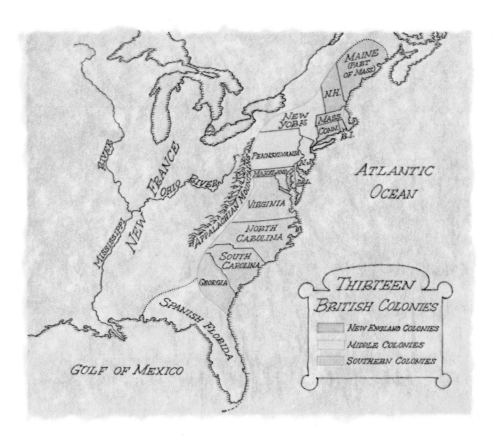

Map labels: RIVER, Great Lakes region, NEW FRANCE, OHIO RIVER, MISSISSIPPI, APPALACHIAN MOUNTAINS, MAINE (PART OF MASS), N.H., NEW YORK, MASS., CONN., R.I., PENNSYLVANIA, N.J., MARYLAND, DEL., VIRGINIA, NORTH CAROLINA, SOUTH CAROLINA, GEORGIA, SPANISH FLORIDA, ATLANTIC OCEAN, GULF OF MEXICO

THIRTEEN BRITISH COLONIES
- NEW ENGLAND COLONIES
- MIDDLE COLONIES
- SOUTHERN COLONIES

governor of the colony. The first winter was difficult. They lived in sail-cloth tents and bark huts and became ill from lack of food. They finally received supplies, and soon they were building sturdy houses. They began tilling fields and building boats for fishing.

While the Puritans wished to be independent of English rule, they had no thought of starting a democracy in Massachusetts. Winthrop and the other Puritan leaders hoped to keep the Massachusetts government in the hands of a small group of important Puritans. Yet when a group of settlers asked to be admitted as voting shareholders of the company, they were given this right. To keep the ordinary people from gaining control of the government, the legislature (called the General Court) passed a law that only certain members of Puritan churches could become voters. Since it was difficult to become a church member, the number of voters was quite limited. Beginning in 1634, the voters of each town elected two or three deputies to represent them in the General Court. It was a representative government, but it represented only some of the people.

Rule by the elite was still the accepted custom of the day, even to the "ordinary people."

*Colonizing the New World*

# Rhode Island, Connecticut, New Hampshire, and Maine

Differences on ideas of religion and government among early colonists led to establishment of other colonies.

With so many restrictions on life in Massachusetts Bay Colony, many of the new settlers did not wish to stay there. The Puritans forced new settlers to practice Puritanism, did not give them certain rights, and would not grant them good land. As a result, many settlers moved on to found new settlements which later became colonies.

A young Puritan minister, Roger Williams, was banished from Massachusetts and founded Rhode Island in 1636. He had shocked the Massachusetts leaders with his belief that people should worship as they please, without government restrictions. Church and State should be separate, he believed. Williams and his followers settled at Providence, where they established freedom of religion and a representative

*Touro Synagogue, a Jewish place of worship, was built in Rhode Island over two centuries ago.*

government in which most colonists were able to vote. In 1638, Anne Hutchinson, another settler who left Massachusetts, also established a town in Rhode Island. Roger Williams got a charter for the colony in 1644. It became a place where Quakers, Jews, and members of other religious groups could have freedom of religion.

Connecticut was settled by the Reverend Thomas Hooker in 1636. He and his followers found their way into the rich lands of the Connecticut River Valley where they established Hartford. Their government, the Fundamental Orders of Connecticut, allowed more voters and was thus more representative than the government of Massachusetts. Other Puritans started the town of New Haven. In 1662, the king gave a charter uniting New Haven with Hartford and establishing the Connecticut colony.

*Fundamental Orders of Connecticut are sometimes called the first written constitution in America.*

*Thomas Hooker and his followers moved into Connecticut in 1636. They were unhappy with life in the Massachusetts Bay Colony.*

Some of the colonists driven out of Massachusetts went north in 1638 to begin towns in New Hampshire. Other Puritans and members of the Church of England also settled there. In 1641, Massachusetts took over control of the New Hampshire towns. Finally in 1679, New Hampshire became a separate colony under royal government.

Clarify Maine as part of Massachusetts during the Revolutionary period.

The land that is now Maine was originally owned by Sir Ferdinando Gorges, who founded several settlements there. In 1691, Massachusetts was given a new charter which included Maine. From then until 1820 when it became a state, Maine was part of Massachusetts.

# Maryland

Sir George Calvert, a Catholic, persuaded Charles I to grant him the unsettled northern part of Virginia. There his son, Lord Baltimore, started a settlement in 1634. The colony of Maryland became a place for Catholics to find freedom of religion. It also became known for allowing other Christians to practice their own faiths.

# Colonies Started Under Charles II

English politics had a lot to do with what happened in the colonies. Before 1640, many colonies were started in the New World. Then, during a civil war in England in the 1640's, no new colonies were founded. In 1660, Charles II became king, and colonizing began again. In the next twenty-five years, the English established several new colonies along the Atlantic coast. The proprietors, or rich nobles who owned the colonies, usually failed to make money from these lands. But they were able to bring large numbers of settlers to the New World.

# The Carolinas

Eight proprietors were granted a charter to the land of Carolina in 1663. They hoped to make money as landlords and to develop large estates which would produce olives, wine, silk, turpentine, and pitch. The proprietors failed to make money in this way. However, they did establish the city of Charleston in the southern part of their land. In 1719, this section of the colony broke away from the proprietors and became the royal colony of South Carolina. Finally in 1729, the king bought back the whole grant, and North Carolina also became a royal colony.

# TIME

Understanding the concept of *time* is important in understanding history. The following time line covers the period from 1492 to 1900 and shows the period in which the English colonies were established. How many centuries elapsed after Columbus and before the first colony? How long has it been since the last English colony was started?

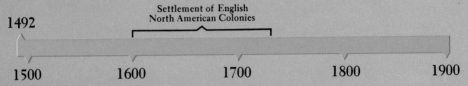

The following time line shows when each of the English colonies was founded. Which colony was started first? Which was last? In what century were most of the colonies founded?

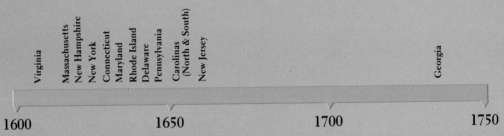

Time in relation to people is often expressed in generations. The following time line is about the Adams family of Massachusetts during the period the colonies were being established. It begins with Henry Adams in England and continues to the birth of John Adams, who became the second President of the United States. How many generations of the Adams family lived during this time? How was John Adams related to Henry Adams?

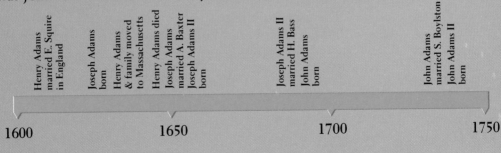

Understanding the concept of time is very important to students' successful study of history. Might review second, hour, day, week, year, decade, etc.
Clarify meanings of century and generation with students.

*Colonizing the New World*

# New York

During the first wave of settlement in the early seventeenth century, the Netherlands and Sweden built several small settlements in the area between Maryland and Connecticut. They traded with the Indians there for furs. The Dutch began settlements at present-day Albany and New York City in 1624. In 1625, New Amsterdam was founded on the tip of Manhattan Island. The settlements were weak. Because of this, Charles II in 1664 had no difficulty in renewing English claims to the area and in taking over the Dutch settlements. He gave the whole area to his brother James, Duke of York, in whose honor it was named New York.

# Pennsylvania, Delaware, and New Jersey

The colony of Pennsylvania was started by William Penn. He was a great religious thinker and was clever in business. He became a Quaker and wanted to found a colony where the people of this faith would be free to practice their religion. Charles II owed a large sum of money to Penn's father who was head of the king's naval office. After his father died, Penn asked for a land grant in the New World as payment. The king gave him the land in 1681 and named it Pennsylvania in honor of Penn's father. Philadelphia was founded that same year and quickly became one of the most important towns in the colonies.

Because Pennsylvania had no seacoast, Penn received another grant of land from the Duke of York. This area, known as Delaware, became part of Pennsylvania. Then in 1704, it became a separate colony.

The Duke of York granted New Jersey to two proprietors in 1664. One soon turned over his area to Quakers, and in 1676, it became West Jersey. Settlers in East Jersey were mostly Puritans who did not get along with their proprietor. Many troubled years passed until finally, in 1702, New Jersey was united again and became a royal colony.

# Georgia

The last of the English colonies along the Atlantic coast was Georgia. It was founded in 1733 as a military defense against any

*The colony of Pennsylvania was started by William Penn on land given to him by the king of England. Penn insisted on also buying some of the land from the Indians, whom he considered the rightful owners. For many years, there was no trouble between the colonists and the Indians in Pennsylvania. While Penn was interested in making a profit, he thought of his colony above all as a "Holy Experiment."*

trouble from Spanish Florida and French Louisiana. James Edward Oglethorpe, the founder of the colony, was a British officer who was interested in helping people in debtors' prisons. He hoped to make these debtors into hardworking colonists. They would pay their debts by becoming soldier-settlers in Georgia. He also welcomed German Protestants who were seeking religious freedom. Because of the nature of the colony, rum, slaves, and large plantations were not allowed. After Georgia became a royal colony in 1751, however, it came to be run by owners of large plantations as the other southern colonies were.

Within a very few years of their beginnings, each of the thirteen English colonies began to take on its own character. The companies and proprietors who had started them found that they could not make money from them. Nor were the Puritan founders of the New England colonies able to keep tight religious control over their colonies for long. Planters and merchants were rising to power, but small farmers and artisans could also find a place of their own in the lands of the New World. All of these people were helping to form what was becoming a new American civilization.

Might discuss practice of placing debtors in prison until they or someone else paid their debts.

# The Thirteen Colonies

| Colony | Permanent Settlement | Original Founders | Government |
|---|---|---|---|
| Virginia | 1607 | English | Charter–1606<br>Royal–1624 |
| Massachusetts | 1620 | English | Self-governing–1620<br>Charter–1629<br>Royal–1691 |
| New Hampshire | 1623 | People from Massachusetts | Charter–1629<br>Royal–1679 |
| New York | 1624 | Dutch | Dutch rule–1624<br>Proprietary–1664<br>Royal–1685 |
| Connecticut | 1633 | People from Massachusetts | Self-governing–1636<br>Charter–1662 |
| Maryland | 1634 | English | Proprietary–1632<br>Royal–1692<br>Proprietary–1715 |
| Rhode Island | 1636 | People from Massachusetts | Self-governing–1663 |
| Delaware | 1638 | Swedish | Proprietary–1664 |
| Pennsylvania | 1643 | Swedish, English | Proprietary–1681 |
| North Carolina | 1653 | People from Virginia | Proprietary–1663<br>Royal–1729 |
| New Jersey | 1660 | Dutch | Proprietary–1664<br>Royal–1702 |
| South Carolina | 1670 | English | Proprietary–1663<br>Royal–1719 |
| Georgia | 1733 | English | Proprietary–1732<br>Royal–1753 |

# Chapter 3 in Perspective  See Teacher's Manual, page 66T.

## Identify

London Company
Captain John Smith
Powhatan

House of Burgesses
Pilgrims
Separatists

Mayflower Compact
Puritans

# Explain

joint stock company
charter

legislature
compact

proprietors

## Check Your Memory of the Facts

1. Why did the English settle the Atlantic Coast of North America instead of farther south?
2. When did the English settlements along the coast of North America begin?
3. What advantages did England expect to gain from its colonies?
4. What part did John Smith play in the success of the settlement at Jamestown?
5. How did the Indians help in the successful start of the colonies of Jamestown and Plymouth?
6. What religious groups played a part in the establishment of the English colonies?

## Check Your Understanding of the Ideas

1. In what ways did the English and Spanish colonies differ?
2. What is the importance of the Mayflower Compact? Why did the Pilgrims agree to obey it?
3. What was the Puritan attitude toward religious freedom?
4. How did royal colonies and proprietory colonies differ?

## Expand Your Knowledge

1. Write a general description of the people who settled the first English colony in North America. What kind of work had they done in England? What was their religion? Why did they leave their homeland?
2. Prepare a chart showing the length of time needed to travel from Europe to North America or from Africa to North America at various times between the first voyage of Columbus and the present.

# Plymouth 1620-1650

After sixty-five days at sea, the *Mayflower* reached the coast of America at the beginning of winter in 1620. The passengers, knowing they were too far north, sailed down the coast toward the Virginia lands. The weather was so terrible that they turned back to Cape Cod Bay.

Using small boats from the ship, some of the passengers explored the land for a place to live. They finally found an area they named Plymouth where much of the land had already been cleared by Indians. It had a river and a hill where they could build a fort for safety. The passengers decided to settle there.

The *Mayflower* stayed for the rest of the winter because of the weather and the need for repairs. Many of the passengers lived aboard the crowded ship while they were building houses on the land. Among those settlers who came to Plymouth in 1620 were:

*Mr. John Carver, Katherine his wife, Desire Minter, and two manservants, John Howland, Roger Wilder. William Latham, a boy, and a maidservant and a child that was put to him* [to bring up] *called Jasper More....*

*Captain Myles Standish and Rose his wife....*

*Francis Cooke and his son John; but his wife and other children came afterwards....*

*Mr. William Mullins and his wife and two children, Joseph and Priscilla; and a servant, Robert Carter....*

## The Pilgrims

Most of the *Mayflower* passengers were Separatist Puritans, a small group of poor people seeking religious freedom. Others, called Strangers by the Separatists, had been included so there would be more workers for the new settlement. These people, Separatists and Strangers, were called Pilgrims because they were travelers in a strange land. All of them were looking for a better life in the New World.

## A Record

William Bradford, a Separatist, was chosen by the Pilgrims to be governor of Plymouth in 1621. He wrote a history, or record, of the many years of hardship that the Pilgrims faced in America. That history still exists today, and from it, people can learn who the Pilgrims were and what happened to them. Bradford was a leader in the

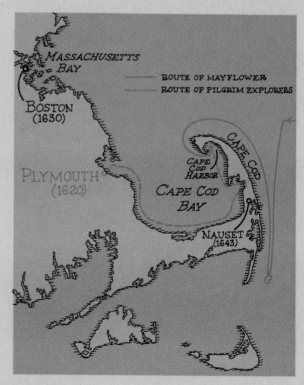

*The landing of the Pilgrims*

settlement for more than thirty-five years. Much of the information on the following pages comes from his record.

## A Hard Beginning

The settlers had a very hard time at first. They had only a few small boats, and the winter winds and rains made the harbor's water very rough. It was not easy to move their goods to land, and it took weeks to get their small houses built.

*But that which was most sad . . . was, that in two or three months' time half of their company died, especially in January* *and February, being the depth of winter, and [needing] houses and other comforts; being [sick] with . . . diseases which this long voyage . . . had brought upon them. So as there died some times two or three of a day . . . of 100 and odd persons, [only about] fifty remained. . . .*

*As this [sickness] fell among the passengers . . . [they] were [sent] ashore. . . . The disease began to fall amongst [the ship's crew] also, so as almost half of their company died before they went away. . . .*

*All this while the Indians [were watching] them, and would sometimes show themselves . . . but when any approached near them, they would run away. . . .*

*Samoset meeting the Pilgrims*

## Spring

*But about the 16th of March, a certain Indian came boldly amongst them and spoke to them in broken English, which they could well understand. . . . His name was Samoset. He told them also of another Indian whose name was Squanto . . . who had been in England and could speak better English. . . .*

Samoset came to visit the Pilgrims again and brought Squanto, Chief Massasoit, and others with him. The Pilgrims and the Indians exchanged gifts and made speeches which Squanto translated. The visit ended after a peace treaty with Massasoit was signed. When the other Indians returned to their homes, Squanto stayed with the Pilgrims to help them learn about the new land.

## New Ways for New Land

The Pilgrims were not very skilled in farming and fishing at first. For example, Plymouth Harbor was filled with fish, but they had not brought hooks small enough to catch them. Squanto taught the Pilgrims Indian ways to fish and farm. He showed them where and how to trap and catch fish. He also taught them how and when to plant corn in hills, using fish for fertilizer. Governor Bradford wrote about Squanto's ways.

*All which they found true by trial and experience. Some English seed they sowed, as wheat and pease [peas], but it came not to good, either by the badness of the seed or lateness of the season or both, or some other [trouble].*

*Houses in Plymouth*

## Celebration

Bradford's first wife, Dorothy, had died soon after the *Mayflower* reached land. In 1623, he married the widow Alice Southworth who had come to Plymouth on a later ship. Their Indian friends were invited to join in the celebration. The Plymouth Company's agent wrote to his brother in England about it.

*. . . Massasoit was sent for to the wedding, where came with him his wife, the queen, although he hath five wives. With him came four other kings and about six score men with their bows and arrows—where, when they came to our town, we saluted them with the shooting off of many muskets and training our men. And so all the bows and arrows was brought into the Governor's house, and he brought the Governor three or four bucks [deer] and a turkey. And so we had very good pastime in seeing them dance, which is in such manner, with such a noise that you would wonder. . . .*

*And now to say somewhat of the great cheer we had at the Governor's marriage. We had about twelve pasty venisons, besides others, pieces of roasted venison and other such good cheer in such quantity that I could wish you some of our share. For here we have the best grapes that ever you say [saw]—and the biggest, and divers [many different] sorts of plums and nuts. . . .*

## Earning a Living

In a small village like Plymouth, everyone had to work hard for food—hoeing corn and other crops in the summer, digging clams and catching fish in the winter. About 1623, one of the Pilgrims made up a song which was passed down in their families for many years.

The place where we live is a wilderness wood,
Where grass is much wanting that's fruitful and good:
Our mountains and hills and valleys below
Being commonly covered with ice and with snow;
And when the northwester with violence blows,
Then every man pulls his cap over his nose;
But if any's so hardy and will it withstand,
He forfeits a finger, a foot, or a hand.

When the spring opens we then take the hoe,
And make the ground ready to plant and to sow;
Our corn being planted and seed being sown,
The worms destroy much before it is grown;
And when it is growing, some spoil there is made
By birds and by squirrels that pluck up the blade;
E'en when it is grown to full corn in the ear
It is often destroyed by raccoons and deer.

And now our garments begin to grow thin,
And wool is much wanted to card and to spin;
If we can get a garment to cover without,
Our other in-garments are clout upon clout
   [patch upon patch];
Our clothes we brought with us are often much torn,
They need to be clouted before they are worn;
But clouting our garments they hinder us nothing,
Clouts double, are warmer than single whole clothing!

If flesh meat be wanting to fill up our dish,
We have carrots and pumpkins and turnips and fish;
And, when we've a mind for a delicate dish,
We repair to the clam-bank and there we catch fish.
Instead of pottage and puddings and custards
   and pies,
Our pumpkins and parsnips are common supplies;
We have pumpkin at morning and pumpkin
   at noon;
If it was not for pumpkin we should be undoon.

## More Problems

Since they were poor people, the Pilgrims had needed help to come to the New World. The Plymouth Company's investors had paid for the voyage and for supplies. But, in return, the settlers had to spend their first seven years working for the company as a group, with common land and property. All of the profits, or extras, from their farming, fishing, and trading went back to London. And the Pilgrims did not like working common fields to fill a common warehouse, with no time to work for themselves and their families.

*For the young men, that were most able and fit for labour and service,* [were unhappy] *that they should spend their time and strength to work for other men's wives and children without any* [extra credit]. . . . *this was thought* [unfair]. . . . *And for men's wives to be commanded to do service for* [others] . . . *they deemed it a kind of slavery.* . . .

In 1623, the common use of land began to change. That year, each family was given a piece of land for planting corn. Bradford wrote that:

*This had very good success, for it made all hands very* [busy], *so as much more corn was planted than otherwise.* . . . *The women now went willingly into the field, and took their little ones with them to set corn; which before would* [make believe] *weakness and inability.* . . .

Beginning to divide the land among families settled one problem. The trouble of paying back the Plymouth Company lasted for years. The settlers were not good enough at fishing to make a lot of profit, although the demand for dried cod was great in Europe. Most of their profit came from fur

trading with the Indians from Cape Cod to Maine. In 1626, their debt was set at about $9,000. By the time they finally paid it off in 1648, the Pilgrims had sent the Plymouth Company furs and other goods worth about $100,000!

## Growing

Plymouth, though small, was becoming a stronger settlement by 1627. The chief trading agent of the Dutch West India Company was very pleased with it during his visit that year. He reported that:

*New Plymouth lies on the slope of a hill stretching east towards the sea-coast.* . . . *The houses are constructed of clapboards, with gardens also enclosed behind and at the sides with clapboards, so that their houses and courtyards are arranged in very good order, with a stockade against sudden attack; and at the ends of the streets there are three wooden gates. In the center, on the cross street, stands the Governor's house, before which is a square stockade upon which four patereros* [guns] *are mounted, so as to enfilade* [cover] *the streets. Upon the hill they have a large square house, with a flat roof, built of thick sawn planks stayed with oak beams, upon the top of which they have six cannon, which shoot iron balls of four and five pounds, and command the surrounding country. The lower part they use for their church, where they preach on Sundays and the usual holidays.*

## Troubled Times

In the 1630's, many Puritans came to settle in the Boston area. The Pilgrims did make some money by selling cattle and other goods to the new people. But the growth of towns to the north of Plymouth, around the better Boston Harbor, also had a bad effect on the Pilgrim settlement. Soon, fewer ships came into their harbor, and trade fell off. Their fields, worked by the Indians long before the Pilgrims had arrived, were not so rich as some of the newer land. And as children grew up, there was no more land for them near their parents. Some of the first settlers and many of their children began to move farther away. New towns and churches were started in other parts of the settlement. In 1644, the people talked about moving the whole settlement to better land on Cape Cod. Finally, some of the Pilgrim families did move to a place called Nauset. Governor Bradford wrote:

*And thus was this poor church* [Plymouth] *left, like* [a] *mother grown old and forsaken of her children . . . her* [older people] *being most of them worn away by death, and these of later time being like children* [married] *into other families, and she like a widow left only to trust in God. Thus, she that had made many rich became herself poor.*

## Catching Up

In 1650, Bradford reported again on the families who had first come to Plymouth:

*Mr. Carver and his wife died the first year, he in the spring, she in the summer. Also, his man Roger and the little boy Jasper died before either of them, of the common infection. Desire Minter returned to her friend and proved not very well and died in England. His servant boy Latham, after more than 20 years' stay in the country,*

*went into England and from thence to the Bahama Islands in the West Indies; and there with some others was starved for want of food. His maidservant married and died a year or two after, here in this place. His servant John Howland married the daughter of John Tilley, Elizabeth* [also a *Mayflower* passenger], *and they are both now living and have ten children, now all living, and their eldest daughter hath four children; and their second daughter one, all living, and other of their children marriageable. So 15 are come of them. . . .*

*Captain Standish his wife died in the first sickness and he married again and hath four sons living and some are dead. . . .*

*Francis Cooke is still living, a very old man, and hath seen his children's children have children. After his wife came over with other of his children; he hath three still living by her, all married and have five children, so their increase is eight. And his son John which came over with him is married, and hath four children living. . . .*

*Mr. Mullins and his wife, his son and his servant died the first winter. Only his daughter Priscilla survived, and married with John Alden* [a *Mayflower* passenger]; *who are both living and have eleven children. And their eldest daughter is married and hath five children. . . .*

Governor Bradford himself died in 1659, but Plymouth did continue. The town grew slowly and, in 1691, became part of the larger Massachusetts Bay Colony. As for the children of the Pilgrims, they also continued to grow in number. Some of them moved out into every part of America.

# America Is... Independence

For the Independent Journal.

## The FŒDERALIST. No. I.

To the People of the State of New-York.

AFTER an unequivocal experience of the inefficacy of the subsisting Fœderal Government, you are
called upon to deliberate on a new Constitution for
the United States of America. The subject speaks
its own importance; comprehending in its consequences, nothing less than the existence of the UNION,
the safety and welfare of the parts of which it is composed, the fate of an empire, in many respects, the
most interesting in the world. It has been frequently remarked, that it seems to have been reserved to
the people of this country, by their conduct and example, to decide the important question, whether so-
cieties of men are really capable or not, of establishing good government from reflection and choice, or
whether they are forever destined to depend, for their
political constitutions, on accident and force. If there
be any truth in the remark, the crisis, at which we
are arrived, may with propriety be regarded as the
æra in which that decision is to be made; and a wrong
election of the part we shall act, may, in this view,
deserve to be considered as the general misfortune of
mankind

This idea will add the inducements of philanthropy
to those of patriotism to heighten the sollicitude, which
all considerate and good men must feel for the event.
Happy will it be if our choice should be decided by a judicious estimate of our true interests,

# Colonial Society

**4**

Aim: to increase understanding of the conditions of colonial life which led to the maturing of a separate American culture.

Colonial populations were a mix of geographical, social, and economic backgrounds.

During the seventeenth and eighteenth centuries, the colonists in the New World gradually became Americans. For the most part, their culture was that of England, and they came to speak a common language, English. But some of their ways of doing things came from other European countries, from Africa, and from the American Indians. In

*A map of New Haven, Connecticut, was drawn in 1748. It shows the names and jobs of the people who lived there. The plan of the town was typical of most New England towns during the colonial period.*

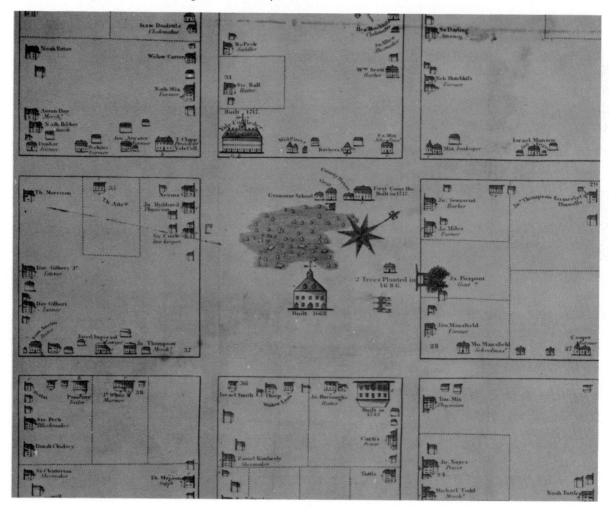

addition, living conditions were very different in the New World, and the newcomers had to change their style of life to meet these conditions. In some ways, they began to live and act as Americans do today.

# Coming to the New World

The difficulty of getting to the New World, as well as the length of the voyage, helped set it off from the Old World. The passage to America was an ordeal. Most ships were very small and overcrowded. People were not fed well and often were the victims of epidemics. In the early 1700's, a group of four thousand German Protestants set sail for New York. Seventeen hundred died on the voyage or shortly after landing. The slave ships were especially crowded, giving each person a space only 5½ feet long and 16 inches wide. Sanitary conditions were so terrible that sometimes the ships could be smelled before they could be seen. Early in the period of slave trading, almost one fourth of the blacks died before reaching America. Later, this death rate on board ship was still as high as one tenth. Because of the difficulty of the crossing, only the very strong usually survived it. The hardy people who made it were the basis of colonial society.

Most people came to the New World voluntarily to improve their ways of life. Many came to escape religious oppression. Puritans, Quakers and Catholics from England, Protestants from France, Germany, and Austria, and Jews from many European countries, all fled to gain freedom of worship. Others wanted to escape extreme poverty and the cruelty and humiliation that went with it. In some cases, these people came to the colonies as indentured servants. This usually meant that they voluntarily agreed to work for a person for a limited number of years in payment for the cost of the trip to America.

Not all people who arrived in America came of their own free will. A common punishment for criminals and debtors was to take them to the New World where they were sold as indentured servants. They usually had to work for five to seven years before they gained their freedom. Gottlieb Mittelberger, who crossed the Atlantic Ocean from Germany in 1750, described the buying of indentured servants from his country:

> This is how the [sale of] human beings on board ship takes place. Every day Englishmen, Dutchmen, and High Germans come . . . on board the newly arrived vessel that has

Labor was more difficult to secure than land in British colonial America.

Many people, white and black, were brought to the colonies against their wills.

brought people from Europe and offers them for sale. From among the healthy they pick out those suitable for [their] purposes. . . . Then they [bargain] with them as to the length of the period for which they will go into service in order to pay off their passage, the whole amount of which they generally still owe. When an agreement has been reached, adult persons . . . bind themselves to serve for three, four, five, or six years, according to their health and age. The very young, between the ages of ten and fifteen, have to serve until they are twenty-one, however.

*An indentured servant's contract*

Many parents . . . must . . . sell their children as if they were cattle. Since the fathers and mothers often do not know where or to what masters their children are to be sent, it frequently happens that . . . parents and children do not see each other for years on end, or even for the rest of their lives.

The author of this description is Oloudah Equiano. See p. 78.

# Slave Ships

During the height of the slave trade, Africans of all ages were sold as slaves. Here is a description of the trip to America on a slave ship. The author was only eleven years old when he was kidnapped in Africa and taken to Virginia.

*I was not long suffered to indulge my grief; I was soon put down under the decks, and there I received such a [greeting to] my nostrils as I had never experienced in my life: so that with the [sickening] stench and crying together, I became so sick and low that I was not able to eat, nor had I the least desire to taste anything. . . . but soon, to my grief, two of the white men offered me eatables, and on my refusing to eat, one of them held me fast by the hands . . . and tied my feet while the other [beat] me severely. . . . In a little time after, amongst the poor chained men I found some of my own nation, which in a small degree gave ease to my mind. I inquired*

*of these what was to be done with us; they gave me to understand we were to be carried to these white people's country to work for them. I then was a little revived, and thought if it were no worse than working, my situation was not so desperate: but still I feared I should be put to death, the white people looked and acted, as I thought, in so savage a manner. . . . The stench of the hold while we were on the coast was so intolerably [sickening] that it was dangerous to remain there for any time, and some of us had been permitted to stay on the deck for the fresh air; but now that the whole ship's cargo were confined together it became absolutely [deadly]. The closeness of the place and the heat of the climate, added to the number in the ship, which was so crowded that each had scarcely room to turn himself, almost suffocated us. . . . The shrieks of the women and the groans of the dying [made it] a scene of horror. . . .*

Many Africans came to America during this period as indentured servants. Often they had been captured in wars, kidnapped by slave traders, or sold to the traders by their own people. These black indentured servants were supposed to work out their service and then get their freedom, just as white servants did. Conditions for them worsened in the seventeenth century, however, and a cruel system of slavery developed in America.

As slavery spread, the demand for Africans became greater than for European indentured servants or Indian slaves. Blacks did not always receive their freedom after a set number of years. In addition, they

Free and enslaved Africans were in North America before British settlement began.

*Colonial Society*

That same year, David Dove opened a private school for teaching girls some of the more advanced subjects. His school was very successful. Three years later, Anthony Benezet convinced the leaders of the Academy to permit girls to study the same subjects that the boys were offered, but in a separate building.

Benezet was also a pioneer in education for black people. A few black children had been attending the Quaker church schools. In 1750, Benezet opened an evening school for them in his home and paid for the supplies himself. He continued these classes until a group of Quakers took over the costs. They opened a free school to teach reading, writing, and arithmetic to black children in 1770. By the 1790's, Philadelphia had schools for black students taught by black teachers.

## City Improvements

The rapid growth of business pushed the city's boundaries outward. The price of land within the city grew higher, and the noise of city traffic grew louder. To avoid the higher land costs, many smaller merchants moved to the edges of town. To avoid the noise and traffic, many of the richer families built their homes in areas outside the city. By the 1770's, Philadelphia had grown from a trade town to a metropolitan city with suburbs, or outlying districts of homes and small businesses.

Although many lived in the suburbs, the people worked to improve the appearance of the city. They supported many plans for the general public. Franklin and the members of the Junto were often involved in these projects. In his writings, Franklin described their "first project of a public nature."

*Those who lov'd reading were oblig'd to send for their books from England. . . . [In 1731] I propos'd to render the benefit from books more common, by commencing [beginning] a public subscription library. . . . So few were the readers at that time in Philadelphia, and the majority of us so poor, that I was not able, with great industry, to find more than fifty persons, mostly young tradesmen, willing to pay down for this purpose forty shillings each, and ten shillings per annum [year]. On this little fund we began. The books were imported; the library was opened one day in the week for lending to the subscribers, on their promissory notes to pay double the value if not duly returned. The institution soon manifested [showed] its utility [usefulness], was imitated by other towns, and in other provinces.*

Fires were a problem in the city, and there was no organized way to fight them. In 1737, Franklin wrote and printed a paper about the different causes of fires. He also wrote about ways to avoid them.

*This . . . gave rise to a project, which soon followed it, of forming a company [the Union Fire Company] for the more ready extinguishing of fires, and mutual assistance in removing and securing of goods when in danger. Associates in this scheme [plan] were presently found, amounting to thirty. Our articles of agreement oblig'd every member to keep always in good order, and fit for use, a certain number of leather buckets, with strong bags and baskets (for packing and transporting of goods), which were to be brought to every fire; and we agreed to meet once a month [to discuss] the subject of fires, as might be useful in our conduct on such occasions.*

were not as successful in attempts to run away or as likely to die from the settlers' diseases as were enslaved Indians. But throughout all the colonies, the buying and selling of human beings was common. Here are two advertisements that appeared in the *Boston News Letter* in 1714:

Might discuss results of discrimination by skin color upon victims' attitudes. Could help students understand a campaign like "Black is Beautiful."

An Indian Boy aged about sixteen Years, and a [black] man aged about twenty, both of them very likely and fit for any service, they speak very good English: to be sold: Enquire at the Post Office in Boston.

For Sale: several Irish Maid Servants . . . most of them for Five Years one Irish Man Servant who is a good Barber and Wiggmaker, also Four or Five Likely [black] Boys.

# The People

While the English, Scotch, and Scotch-Irish made up the majority, people from many other lands added to the growth of colonial America. In 1608, people from Poland and Germany who could build sawmills and make glass arrived in Jamestown. Jonas Bronck from Denmark owned a farm which is now the area of New York City known as the Bronx. In 1643, a visitor to New Amsterdam (New York) reported that eighteen languages were spoken there. Other nationalities among the early colonists were Italians, Portuguese, Spaniards, Norwegians, Finns, Bohemians from present-day Czechoslovakia, and Walloons from present-day Belgium.

The population of the English colonies was thus a mixture of peoples of different geographic, social, and economic backgrounds. There were only a few people of high birth and great wealth. In the South, a society of owners and slaves developed which made many planters wealthy. A number of merchants were also becoming wealthy in the English colonies. The great majority of Americans, however, were farmers who worked their own land.

# The Land

Abundant land was the economic base of colonial America. Early dreams of finding gold and silver mines, or Indian treasures like those of Mexico and Peru, were soon gone. The search for a northwest passage to East Asia and its riches lasted much longer but was fruitless.

# Anne Bradstreet

Born in England in 1612, Anne Dudley was the daughter of a wealthy family. She received a good education and was reared according to the strict religious beliefs of her family. At sixteen, she married Simon Bradstreet and, two years later, sailed with her husband and her parents to Massachusetts Bay Colony.

It was not easy for Anne Bradstreet to adjust to life in a new settlement on the edge of a great wilderness. She later wrote, "I . . . came into this Country, where I found a new world and new manners, at which my heart rose [in dread and dismay]. But after I was convinced it was the way of God, I submitted to it. . . ."

Amid her household duties and bringing up eight children, Anne Bradstreet found time to write verse. Her early poems reflected her formal Puritan upbringing and religion. Then, when she was older, she wrote some poems of a more personal sort. In 1666, her home burned, destroying the precious possessions brought from England. She wrote of the house:

> Here stood that Trunk, and there that chest:
> There lay that store I counted best:
> My pleasant things in ashes lye,
> And them behold no more shall I.
> Under thy roof no guest shall sitt,
> Nor at thy Table eat a bitt.

In a poem praising Queen Elizabeth I, she expressed some thoughts on being a woman.

> She hath wip'd off the aspersion [slander] of her Sex,
> That women wisdom lack to play the Rex [ruler]. . . .

In 1650, a book of poems written by Anne Bradstreet was printed in London. *The Tenth Muse Lately Sprung Up in America* was the first volume by an American poet to be published. In that and later books, Anne Bradstreet's verse shows a special quality that is still appreciated today.

Some money could be made by the fur trade with the Indians, but the French in Canada were more successful at this than the English. It was the land that proved to be the wealth of the English colonies.

*Plantations, like Rice Hope, developed in the South. The few large ones had many slaves; most were small with less than five slaves.*

Could discuss idea of "plenty" leading to "waste" in light of current concerns for resource conservation.

Because land was cheap or sometimes free, many people could get it in large amounts. Workers were greatly needed, and wages began to rise. This created the demand for indentured servants and, especially in the South, for slaves as cheaper sources of labor. With so much land and so few workers, most of the colonists wasted the soil. They cut around the bark of trees to kill them, burned underbrush and fallen logs, and planted corn and other grains around the dead trees and stumps. At first, the rich soil grew unusually large crops. Then, since the colonists seldom had money for fertilizer, the harvest got smaller as the land wore out. Only the German settlers in Pennsylvania and a few others continued the careful practices of the Old World (crop rotation and fertilization). General use of better farming methods was introduced slowly in the colonies.

As the land wore out, people moved west and cleared fresh land. Generation by generation, the line of settlement moved farther inland, first along the rivers and valleys. By the 1770's, the colonists had established farms in much of the area from the Atlantic coast to the Appalachian Mountains. Many people were eager to move into the rich lands on the other side of these mountains. Daniel Boone took the first party of settlers into Kentucky in March, 1775.

At the end of the eighteenth century, Timothy Dwight, president of Yale College, described the process of settlement during the colonial period. He wrote the following:

A considerable part of all those who *begin* the cultivation of the wilderness may be [called] *foresters or pioneers.* . . .

They . . . cut down some trees and [kill] others; they furnish themselves with an ill-built log house and a worse barn, and reduce a part of the forest into fields, half enclosed and half cultivated. The forests furnish [leaves of plants and trees], and their fields yield [coarse grass]. On this scanty provision they feed a few cattle, and with these [few] products of their labor, [along with] hunting and fishing, they keep their families alive.

. . . The [pioneer] is always ready to sell, for he loves this irregular, adventurous, half-working, and half-lounging life, and hates the sober industry and [careful] economy by which his bush pasture might be changed into a farm. . . .

The second [owner] is commonly a *farmer*, and with an industry and spirit deserving no small [praise] changes the desert into a fruitful field.

Might discuss advantages to farmer who got pioneered lands.

*Most of the people in the New England colonies had small farms. They first cleared the land of trees and underbrush. Then they planted corn, grain, and other crops, usually with the help of their children.*

# Farming in the Colonies

Most of the people in the colonies had small farms. They tilled the land by themselves, usually with the help of their children. In New England, the land produced little more than the owners used themselves. New England farmers often added to their income by fishing, lumbering, shipbuilding, or manufacturing things at home. Many of the children, when they were grown, moved west in search of better lands of their own.

Could assign student research on regional climate, soil, water conditions for class discussion.

The more fertile lands of the Middle Colonies produced more than enough crops for the people. The farmers there exported their surplus goods. That is, they sent the goods out of the country for sale. The extra grain and flour, as well as cattle and horses, were sent to the West Indies and other places. In addition to farming, home manufacturing was important in the Middle Colonies, although not as important as it was in New England.

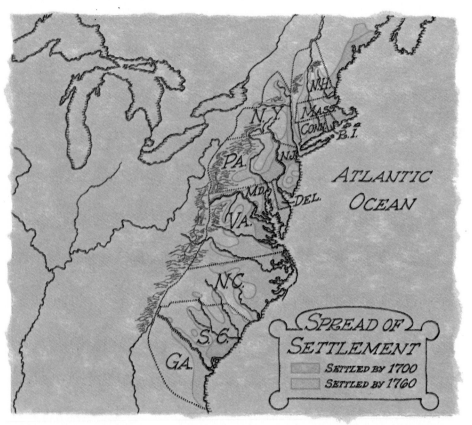

Might compare to map on p. 47.

Farming was by far the most important way of life in the Southern Colonies. Although most of the farmers there worked their own land, a handful of large planters ruled southern life. They controlled agriculture and most of the business of exporting and of importing, or bringing in goods from other countries to sell. The most important export of colonial America, tobacco, was grown on their plantations. The planters could sell tobacco at a good profit because they worked large fields with slaves or indentured servants. They sold it to British merchants and imported British manufactured goods. Often they bought the produce of small farmers and sold it to the British at a higher price. They ran many businesses on their plantations, from brick-making to distilling. They sometimes traded with the Indians, bought and sold slaves, and invested in western lands.

# Towns and Cities

Since most people lived in the country, towns and cities throughout the colonies were small. In spite of their size, however, they were important. They were the centers of cultural life. Through them flowed the trade with other British colonies and England. They contained the shops of the artisans and the homes of the wealthy merchants. Although colonial cities were smaller than most European cities of the eighteenth century, they were growing much faster. By 1775, Philadelphia was a very large city for that time. It was larger than any city in England except London. New York was also a fast-growing city. The secretary of a new royal governor was surprised by his first view of the city in 1753. He wrote, "This populous and well built Town with the Fort in front, with the many steeples of its Churches, . . . and the [great amount] of Shipping with which it is [always crowded], makes a very striking appearance and altogether as fine and as pleasing a View as I ever saw."

Merchants were the key figures in the cities. They bought American-built ships and sent them from the northern ports across the seas on many different kinds of business. Much of the trade was with the islands of the West Indies. Colonial merchants sold lumber, food for slaves, and new slaves from Africa to the sugar planters of these islands. These things were exchanged for sugar, some of which was distilled into rum. Both sugar and rum could be used for trading with the Indians

When diagramed on map, the Triangle Trade appears. Great wealth for some white settlers resulted in North from slave trade and in South from African labor.

and for buying slaves in Africa. The slave-sugar-rum trade route was just one of the many patterns of trade. The merchants bought and sold wherever they could make a profit.

Some of the money the merchants earned in trading was invested in mills and factories. They also started small iron-making furnaces, and soon the colonies produced more pig iron, or crude, unrefined iron, than England. Much of this pig iron was made into nails, tools, and cast-iron kettles, despite a British law of 1750 which forbade this and other kinds of manufacturing. Skilled artisans in the towns made fine shoes, excellent furniture, and beautiful silverware. The most famous and one of the finest of the silversmiths was Paul Revere. He was also a dentist and made false teeth. In later years, he started a foundry and invented a process for rolling sheet copper.

British colonial trade laws based on theory of mercantilism. More on p. 88.

*Although most colonial cities were small, they were very important centers of trade and cultural life. New York was one of the most important towns in the English colonies and was growing faster than many European cities. In a few years, it became one of the largest cities in the world.*

## Population of Colonial Cities

|      | Boston | New York | Philadelphia | Charleston |
|------|--------|----------|--------------|------------|
| 1690 | 7,000  | 3,900    | 4,000        | 1,100      |
| 1710 | 9,000  | 5,700    | 6,500        | 3,000      |
| 1730 | 13,000 | 8,600    | 11,500       | 4,500      |
| 1760 | 15,600 | 18,000   | 23,750       | 8,000      |
| 1775 | 16,000 | 25,000   | 40,000       | 12,000     |

See Teacher's Manual, page 24T.

# Social Classes

Social classes of people were clearer during the colonial period than in later years. The rich southern planters and the northern merchants were like the nobles of England. The middle class was the largest group in America. Along with the small farmers, it was made up of professional people, skilled workers, and artisans. Unskilled workers and indentured servants were part of the lower class. At the bottom were the slaves, who were often thought of as property, not people.

These classes of people were not rigid, and it was possible to move from one class to another. Some families lost their money; both planting and trading were risky. Other families rose rapidly in wealth and power. For example, Daniel Dulany, who had studied at the University of Dublin in Ireland, arrived in Maryland as an indentured servant in 1703. He was sold to work as a clerk in a law office. After serving his term, he became a rich lawyer and planter and made more money buying and selling land. He was the founder of one of the powerful families of the Maryland colony.

Classification is used to make easier the study of ideas, customs, power, etc., held by different groups of people.

*Colonial Society*

*Oloudah Equiano*

Oloudah Equiano, also called Gustavus Vassa, was able to break the class lines, too. He had been kidnapped in Africa when he was eleven and brought to the West Indies as a slave. After many adventures, he was sold to a Philadelphia merchant and was able to earn enough money to pay for his freedom. He moved to England where he became well known in the British antislavery movement. In 1789, he wrote his autobiography, which was read in America and in England.

During the eighteenth century, more and more colonists, especially those who were white, were able to rise above their class. Most people (except for the slaves) had a better way of life than they would have known in the Old World. Their life was more secure, and they enjoyed freedom of religion. The colonists had already become Americans and were proud of their ways of life.

*Intolerance was prevalent in colonies, but there was also greater opportunity to escape it.*

# *Chapter 4 in Perspective* See Teacher's Manual, page 68T.

## Identify

New England Colonies
Middle Colonies

Southern Colonies
Paul Revere

Daniel Dulany
Oloudah Equiano

## Explain

indentured servant

export

import

# Check Your Memory of the Facts

1. From what countries in Europe did people come to settle in the English colonies?
2. For what reasons did people come to the New World?
3. Why was the demand for blacks to be slaves so great? Why was it greater than for Indians or Europeans?
4. Which was more difficult to get in the colonies, land or labor?
5. Where in North America were most Africans located? Why?
6. What different kinds of work were done by people living in the English colonies?

# Check Your Understanding of the Ideas

1. Why did people living in the colonies develop characteristics different from those of people remaining in Europe?
2. Why was the trip to the New World difficult? For what group was it most difficult? Why?
3. Why did the colonists treat African and European servants differently?
4. What was the effect of the abundance of land on methods of farming used in the colonies?
5. How is the life of a teenager different today from what it was in colonial America?
6. How did farming differ in New England, the Middle Colonies, and the Southern Colonies?
7. What were the major colonial cities? What features did they have in common?

# Expand Your Knowledge

1. Imagine that you are a teenager who, with your parents, made the trip from Europe or Africa to one of the colonies. Create a diary that might have been kept by such a person.
2. Draw up a list of the daily activities of a colonial family which would not be part of the daily life of a family today. Draw up a second list of present-day activities which would have been unknown to a colonial family.
3. Make a list of the various manufactured products made in colonial America. Prepare a second list of the major manufactured products made today. What can you say about the differences between the two lists?

*Colonial Society*

# Philadelphia 1700-1790

William Penn laid out the plans for his Pennsylvania "city of brotherly love" in 1682. He located Philadelphia on the west banks of the Delaware River, not far from the Atlantic coast. The city grew quickly and, by the middle of the eighteenth century, was the largest and richest city in the American colonies.

The first settlers of Philadelphia were English Quakers, or members of the Society of Friends. They allowed all other Christians to come there and worship as they pleased. That freedom of religion drew many different groups of people from Europe, and the city's population continued to grow. By 1740, there were more Presbyterians, Anglicans, Lutherans, Baptists, Methodists, Roman Catholics, and other Christians in Philadelphia than there were

Quakers. Several Jewish families also lived in the city, and many people did not belong to any particular church. The Quakers, however, continued to be a strong influence in the development of the city.

## Earning a Living

Philadelphia quickly became a center of business for Pennsylvania and the other colonies. There were ironworks, flour mills, yards for building and repairing ships, carriage and wagon shops, and many different ways for people to earn their livings. Farmers brought produce from their rich fields to market. In the city's shops, they purchased candles, shoes, tools, and other goods.

Shipping and trade were the base of Philadelphia's economic growth. A visitor to the city in 1759 reported on what he saw.

*There is belonging to this town a great Number of Ships, and from hence [here] a very Extensive trade is Carrd [carried] on to all the English Islands in the west Indies for Bread, Flour, Porke, Hams, Indian Corn, Buckwheat Oats, Apples . . . Shingles, Hoops, Bar Iron . . . also live Stock as Sheep, Geese, Turkeys, Ducks & fowles in great Plenty; But Some of their Chiefe men . . . drive on a very large & Contraband [against the law] Trade with the French . . . for Sugar And Molosses, to the great damage of the Honest And fair Trader.*

*They have also a good trade for wheat, Staves [and other things], to Madeira, Lisbon, And Several parts of Spain, to Say Nothing of that Extensive trade between them & their Mother Country [England] for Black wallnut and other valuable wood of different kinds. . . .*

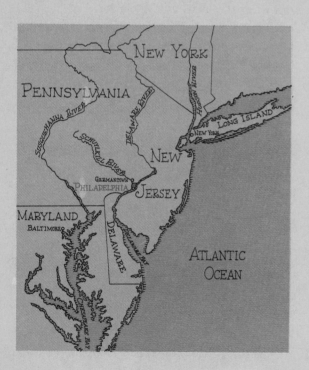

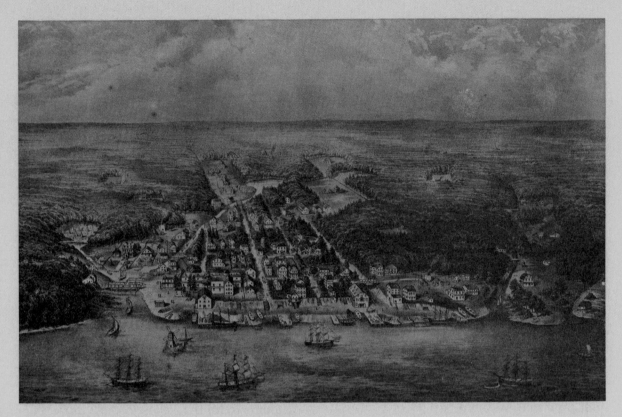

*Philadelphia in 1702, located on the Delaware River*

Such a busy city could support workers with special skills. Painters, weavers, silversmiths, and cabinetmakers made things that were beautiful as well as useful. There was a need, too, for printed business and legal forms, government notices, and other useful items. By the time Benjamin Franklin arrived in 1723 to look for work, there were already two printers in Philadelphia. He went to work for one of them and, in a few years, became the city's most famous printer. Franklin, as others did, printed a newspaper, pamphlets, and a yearly almanac.

Families often continued to work in the same trade or profession for generations. The Bradfords, for example, were Philadelphia printers for more than a hundred years. Cornelia Bradford, in 1740, became the first woman to be a successful printer and bookseller in the city. By the 1770's, presses were turning out seven different newspapers and thousands of books and pamphlets. Philadelphia's printers played a very important part in the exchange of ideas among the American colonists.

## Self-improvement

Many of the people in the city enjoyed sharing ideas. Clubs were sometimes formed for "mutual improvement," as Franklin said of the Junto, a club that he and eleven of his friends started in 1727.

*. . . we met on Friday evenings. The rules that I drew up required that every member, in his turn, should produce one or more*

*queries* [questions] *on any point of Morals, Politics, or Natural Philosophy, to be discuss'd by the company; and once in three months produce and read an essay of his own writing, on any subject he pleased. Our debates were . . . to be conducted in the sincere spirit of inquiry after truth. . . .*

According to the social traditions of the times, only men belonged to these clubs. But women were sometimes the topic of the meetings. Carl Bridenbaugh, historian of colonial Philadelphia, wrote about a club that met in October, 1766. Its members had chosen to discuss the question of women in politics.

*After an animated and extremely serious discussion, in which it was conceded* [agreed] *that women have natural abilities equal to those of men, which might be improved by education, that their lively imaginations would "throw a subject into new lights," that their natural timidity* [lack of boldness] *would make for prudent* [wise] *decisions, and that Queen Elizabeth had proved an able ruler, the question was decided in the negative, on the grounds that the use of beauty and female arts would prejudice the public good and that active participation by the ladies* [in politics] *would "destroy the peace of Families."*

## Education

Education for women was not a common idea in all of the colonies. But the Quakers believed in a practical education for both boys and girls. Reading and writing were taught without charge if the children's parents were too poor to pay. Those who could pay were expected to do so. Philadelphia's first schools were started by the Quakers and other church groups. Within a

Just imported in the Ship **Myrtilla**, Captain **Bolithr**, from London, and to be sold by

### HANNAH BREINTNALL,

At the Sign of the Spectacles, in Second-street, near Black-Horse Alley,

A Great Variety of the finest Chrystal Spectacles, set in Temple, Steel, Leather or other Frames. Likewise true Venetian green Spectacles, for weak or watery Eyes, of various Sorts. Also Concave Spectacles, for short sighted Persons; Magnifying and Reading Glasses; and an Assortment of large and small Spy glasses and Bone Microscopes, with magnifying and multiplying Glass, &c. &c. Pocket Compasses, of different Sizes. &c.                    || 10 s. Tbctf.

*Advertisement for Hannah Breintnall's shop*

few years, night schools opened for young workers eager to advance in business. Good private teachers could always find enough students to fill their classes.

In 1751, the Philadelphia Academy opened for the city's young men. It had been a special project of Franklin's, and he helped decide the subjects that were taught. Families from the lower and middle classes wanted their sons trained for business with English, bookkeeping, and other such practical courses. Upper-class families wanted their sons trained in the arts with foreign languages, philosophy, and classics. As a compromise, Franklin wrote:

*. . . it would be well if they could be taught everything that is useful and everything that is ornamental. But art is long and their time is short. It is therefore proposed that they learn those things that are likely to be most useful and most ornamental, regard being had to the several professions for which they are intended.*

*. . . this went on, one new company being formed after another. . . . The small fines that have been paid by members for absence at the monthly meetings have been apply'd to the purchase of fire-engines, ladders, fire-hooks, and other useful implements [tools] for each company, so that I question whether there is a city in the world better provided with the means of putting a stop to beginning conflagrations [fires]. . . .*

More than twenty-five years after his first public project, Franklin was still working for the general good of the city. He had convinced the city leaders to keep the streets cleaned and patrolled at night for safety. But he believed that there was more to be done.

*Our city, tho' laid out with a beautiful regularity, the streets large, strait [straight], and crossing each other at right angles, had the disgrace of suffering those streets to remain long unpav'd, and in wet weather the wheels of heavy carriages plough'd them into a quagmire [deep mud], so that it was difficult to cross them; and in dry weather the dust was offensive. . . .*

*After some time I drew a bill for paving the city, and brought it into the Assembly.*

*Downtown Philadelphia in the 1790's*

84

*It was just before I went to England, in 1757 [on colonial business], and did not pass till I was gone . . . with an additional provision for lighting as well as paving the streets, which was a great improvement. It was by a private person, the late Mr. John Clifton, his giving a sample of the utility of lamps, by placing one at his door, that people were first impress'd with the idea of enlighting all the city.*

## Social Improvements

As Philadelphia grew into a rich city, many of its successful people were interested in helping those who were not successful. At first, the Quakers were the strongest influence in this work. Soon church groups, business and social clubs, and many individuals were involved. They supported buildings to house and care for the old, the poor, the widows, and the orphans. They also collected money, food, and clothing for others when it was most needed.

Dr. Thomas Bond, helped by Franklin, opened a hospital to care for the sick and the insane in 1751. Bond needed Franklin's help to raise money because the idea of a hospital was new to most people. Many families of the lower and middle classes never went to doctors, and even the upper classes usually tried old family cures first.

Philadelphia also became a center of resistance to slavery. The Quakers taught that every individual had special dignity and that blacks were people, not property. Their ideas influenced others in the city. In 1775, the people of Philadelphia started the first antislavery society in America.

# Gaining Liberty 5

Aim: to increase understanding of economic and political factors which led to war between Britain and the British American colonies.

Before Americans became independent from Great Britain, they had more than a hundred years of experience in trying to govern themselves. Most of them had come to the New World seeking freedom of worship and the chance for a better life. Because they basically governed themselves, they were able to get and keep these benefits. By the second half of the eighteenth century, the people in most of the colonies looked upon self-government as a right.

*The House of Burgesses was the first elected representative government in America. Its members met in this building in Williamsburg to make laws for the Virginia colony.*

After many generations, the colonists had become Americans. They were proud to be different from Europeans. Michel Guillaume Jean de Crèvecoeur, a French settler in New York, described the ideals of the colonists in the years just before the Revolution:

> What then is the American, this new man? . . . *He* is an American, who leaving behind him all his ancient prejudices and manners, receives new ones from the new [way] of life he has [taken on], the new government he obeys, and the new rank he holds. . . . Here individuals of all nations are melted into a new race of men, whose labours and posterity will one day cause great changes in the world. . . .
>
> Europe contains hardly any other [classes] but lords and tenants; this fair country alone is settled by freeholders, the [owners] of the soil they cultivate, members of the government they obey, and the framers of their own laws, by means of their representatives.

Crèvecoeur used "man" generically, according to custom of his day. Clarify with students.

As proud as they were of being Americans, the colonists also felt that they were subjects of the British king. Being his subjects meant that they had all the rights of English people. The British government defined these rights in one way. The colonists came to define them in another way. When Britain challenged them, the colonists fought to keep the rights they felt had always been theirs.

Might have student investigate and report on Canadian colonies' relations to Britain at this time for comparison.

# Government Before the Revolution

By the end of the seventeenth century, the power of the English government was divided between the king and the people's elected representatives in Parliament. The king was supposed to obey the Bill of Rights of 1689. This limited his powers and made him subject to Parliament. Actually, few English people could vote for the members of Parliament, which was made up of nobles who owned large estates. These people were not very active in government, and most of the governing was left to the king. Since the colonies had been founded under royal authority, the king governed them as he pleased.

The colonial governments were modeled after that of England. Each had a legislature like Parliament, with an upper house and a lower house. The upper house in colonial governments was an appointed council which advised the governor. The lower house was an assembly elected by the colonists. The governor of the colony was usually appointed by the king and represented royal authority.

In reality, the colonial assembly was more representative of the people than Parliament was. The governor was responsible to the king and vetoed bills that were against British policy. However, the lower house frequently fought with the governor. It tried to limit the governor's authority by refusing to agree to taxes unless he gave in to their wishes.

For more than a hundred years before the Revolution, the colonial governments struggled against royal control. Some were more successful than others. Rhode Island and Connecticut had almost completely representative self-government. Their governors were elected by the colonists. Other colonial governments, like New York, had very little power against the rule of the royal governor.

# Quarrels Over Economics

To understand British viewpoint, students should understand theory of mercantilism.

The quarrels between the colonists and England were most often over two problems: economics and European wars. Economically, the problem was the wealth to be made in the New World. The British government followed the policy of mercantilism. Like other countries, they tried, through tight controls, to make the colonies profitable for the founding country. If mercantilism had worked in America, most of the wealth made in the New World would have gone into the pockets of the British.

According to mercantilism, the colonists were to produce raw materials which were not found in England. They were supposed to sell these goods only to England. Thus, for example, the British urged the colonists to grow tobacco. They insisted it all be sold to British merchants (even for resale in Europe) and would not allow tobacco to be grown in England.

Many laws were passed to control colonial trade. The Navigation Acts of the 1660's listed products such as tobacco, cotton, indigo, and turpentine which the colonists could export only to Britain. They also ruled that the colonists could import only British goods. All goods traded between the colonies and England had to be carried on British, Irish, or colonial ships. One of the most profitable businesses in the colonies was the sugar trade. In an effort to control this trade, Britain passed the Molasses Act of 1733. This act made colonists pay more for sugar, molasses, and rum imported from any place outside British territory.

*Under the policy of mercantilism, the colonies were encouraged to grow tobacco but were only allowed to sell it to England. People were brought from Africa to be used as slaves on the plantations.*

Mercantilist laws included colonial manufacturing. The colonies were not to make anything they could buy from Britain. The Woolen Act of 1699 did not allow the colonists to export wool or woolen cloth. The Hat Act of 1732 and the Iron Act of 1750 also limited manufacturing. These acts were designed to keep colonial manufacturers from competing with British manufacturers.

Luckily for the colonists, these laws were not well enforced. The success of the colonies came from their avoiding the mercantilist laws. They could get higher prices for some of their goods if they sold them directly to European countries. Goods bought directly from other countries cost them less than those bought through England. The Molasses Act could have wrecked the sugar trade between New England and the French West Indies. As it was, laws like the Iron Act did hurt manufacturing. On the other hand, mercantilism benefited the colonies in many ways. They enjoyed a monopoly on the sale of several major crops. Their merchants took part in a trade which was closed to other nations, and during that era of almost constant war, colonial ships were protected by the powerful British navy.

# Quarrels Over European Wars

Almost constant European wars were also a great problem for the colonists. Each time the British and the French began fighting in Europe, the war naturally involved their colonies. This meant Indian raids on the frontier and attacks against colonial shipping. The British colonists would join Britain's cause. In King George's War, they were able to capture the great French stronghold on Cape Breton Island in Canada. This French fortress was a threat to New England ships and fishing waters, and the colonists were glad to finally have control of it. However, at the peace talks to end the war, Britain agreed to give it back to France. The colonists resented this kind of treatment after fighting in a war that, in the beginning, had little to do with them.

The last of these European wars involving the colonists was the Seven Years' War. In the colonies, it was called the French and Indian War. The English colonists defended their lands against the French

*In 1758, the English colonists joined the fighting against the French and Indian soldiers at the Battle of Rogers' Rock in New York.*

and their Indian allies in North America. There were many reasons for fighting England's old enemy in North America. The colonists wished to end the threat of the Indians on the frontier who, for the most part, sided with the French. They wanted to move onto the fertile western lands of the Ohio Valley which were held by the French. The colonists also wanted to take over the fur trade from the French.

The war began in 1754. The governor of Virginia sent Colonel George Washington, who was twenty-one years old, to drive the French out of the new forts which they had built from Lake Erie to the Ohio River. Washington's troops were defeated. British General Edward Braddock and his troops were sent against the French in 1755. Braddock and his forces marched along to the beat of drums, wearing bright red coats. The French surprised them, firing from behind trees and bushes. The British were defeated, and Braddock was killed. In the full-scale war that followed, the colonists fought bravely when their own lands were in danger. At other times, they did little to help. They even went on trading with the enemy in the French West Indies. Finally, the British won the French and Indian War, and the long struggle with the French in North America was over.

There was great rejoicing in the colonies over the end of the French and Indian War. Canada now belonged to England. There was no longer a threat from the French. Colonists could settle in the Ohio Valley. The young British king, George III, was hailed by everyone. Yet in the next dozen years, events in America led rapidly to war with England.

To survive the European invasion, Indian groups made alliances with French or British as necessary at particular times. In this period, the French seemed less threatening to many Indians than the British who exhibited such desire for lands.

European warfare practices were based on formations of troops advancing toward each other and firing their guns at close range. These tactics did not work well in America's heavily wooded areas.

# The "New Colonial Policy"

With the addition of the territory gained from France, Britain's holdings in North America were vast. The English government realized the great responsibility it had to govern these lands. At the same time, it became more aware of the importance of the colonies along the Atlantic Coast. The population of these colonies was growing rapidly, and the colonists were developing their own ways of life. These colonies had become too important to England to be allowed to run themselves. If Britain was to keep its rule over them and gain the wealth that was to be made in North America, some changes needed to be made in its colonial policy. Britain decided to tighten its controls over the colonies by establishing the "new colonial policy."

The Proclamation of 1763 was a blow to wealthy colonists, including Washington, Franklin, and Henry who had speculated in the "western lands."

This new policy was intended to make the colonies more profitable to England and to keep them from becoming too independent of British rule. The colonists were not to have a share in the spoils of the French and Indian War. This meant they could not join in the fur trade and, by the Proclamation of 1763, they could not settle in the lands west of the Appalachian Mountains. The colonists were also supposed to pay a large part of what the war had cost. Troops were sent to the colonies, and the colonists were told that the purpose was to protect them from the Indians. Actually, the troops were there to control trouble-making colonists and make sure the law was obeyed. By enforcing the old economic laws and by making new ones, Britain hoped to make mercantilism work. Such was the plan of the members of the British government, most of whom had never been to the colonies.

# More Conflicts

The British laws hurt the economic interests of the colonists. In addition, if the colonists obeyed them, they could no longer say that they had all the rights of English people, including the right of self-government. The liberties of the colonists were at stake, and one crisis followed another.

Enforcement was the main cause of colonial distress over Sugar Act. Frequency of payment was the cause with the Stamp Act which covered many daily and weekly types of transactions.

Two of the new laws passed by Britain were the Sugar Act of 1764 and the Stamp Act of 1765. The Sugar Act replaced the Molasses Act which the colonists had been avoiding for years. It put a smaller tax on sugar imported from outside British territory, but it provided for strict enforcement to stop the smuggling. The Stamp Act put a tax on certain kinds of printed papers which had to bear a stamp to prove the tax had been paid. This tax was designed to raise money to help pay the cost of keeping the troops in the colonies.

Throughout the colonies, there was an uproar against these measures. Patrick Henry of Virginia attacked them as taxation without representation. Massachusetts called for a meeting to talk about the problems. Representatives from nine of the colonies met at the Stamp Act Congress of 1765 and drew up a Declaration of Rights and Grievances. This declaration stated that it was against the rights of the colonists as English people to be taxed without their consent or that of their representatives. Since the colonists were not represented in Parliament, they felt they should only be taxed by their own colonial governments.

In many towns, people formed secret protest groups called the "Sons of Liberty." These groups rioted against tax officials and got merchants to stop importing goods from Great Britain. The British government was more upset by the riots and the boycott of—refusal to buy or

*Many of the colonists protested the passage of the Stamp Act in 1765. Some of the people in Boston gathered to burn the British tax stamps in bonfires.*

use—British goods than by the Declaration of Rights and Grievances. Parliament repealed, or withdrew, the Stamp Act and the Sugar Act but passed a Declaratory Act. This act stated that Parliament had the right to make laws "to bind the colonies and people of *America* . . . in all cases whatsoever."

In 1767, a British official, Charles Townshend, ordered a new set of taxes. These were duties that the colonists had to pay on paper, glass, lead, paint, and tea that they imported. The money from these duties would be used to pay the soldiers, the governors, and the judges in the colonies. These officials were sure to enforce the laws that would pay their salaries. The British sent more soldiers to New York and Boston. They also sent home the colonial lawmakers in New York and Massachusetts, so that they could not make any more laws. The colonists began to wonder whether they had any right of self-government which the British would respect.

As the conflicts between the British and the colonists increased, the people divided into two groups. Those colonists who supported a break with Britain were called patriots. Those who remained loyal to England were called loyalists. The patriots boycotted British goods and began to tar and feather loyalist tax officials. In March, 1770, a group of angry British soldiers in Boston fired into a mob of patriots who had

# Crispus Attucks

On March 5, 1770, a street fight took place in Boston between a crowd of angry colonists and a squad of British soldiers. The colonists resented the heavy taxes set by England and the presence of the soldiers. Tension had been growing on both sides. Finally that night, the two groups clashed.

One of the leaders of the mob of colonists was Crispus Attucks. Not a great deal is known about his early life. He was tall and muscular, a former slave who had run away twenty years earlier to become a sailor. Waving a cordwood stick, Attucks was part of the crowd shouting insults and throwing snowballs at the soldiers. In the confusion, the soldiers fired into the group of colonists. Three people were killed instantly; one of them was Crispus Attucks. Eight others were wounded, and two of them died later.

The citizens of Boston were very angry about the killings. A few colonists used the event to stir up hatred for the British throughout the colonies. Although it was five years before war actually broke out, the Boston Massacre was one of the events that led to the Revolution. Attucks and the other victims have been thought of as the first martyrs in the struggle against England.

been teasing them. Five colonists were killed, and many others were wounded. The news of the "Boston Massacre" was spread to patriots all over the colonies.

At the same time, for reasons of its own, Parliament repealed the duties which Townshend had set up. Only the duty on tea was kept. The colonists boycotted the British tea and drank smuggled, cheaper tea that came from Holland. Matters seemed to improve for a while. Then in 1773, a more serious crisis happened, again over tea. That year, Parliament passed a new tea act. It allowed the British East India Company to sell tea in the colonies at a bargain price, less than the tea from Holland. Colonial merchants dealing with Holland faced ruin from this direct competition. From Charleston to Boston, there were riots and even destruction of East India Company tea. The Boston Sons of Liberty, dressed as Indians, dumped the tea cargo from three ships into Boston Harbor. This famous "tea party" was the patriots' response to the British tax on tea.

"Boston Massacre" offers another opportunity to discuss uses and abuses of propaganda.

Lawyer John Adams successfully defended British soldiers in following court case. Might have student investigate and report on trial.

Some colonists claimed that the bargain price was a trick to get them to pay the tax which they had resisted.

# The Coming of the Revolution

The angry British Parliament passed laws to punish the people of Boston for the "tea party." These measures closed the port of Boston to shipping until the people had paid for the tea they had destroyed. Parliament also put Massachusetts under control of the royal governor and British troops. The Quebec Act stated that lands west of the Appalachian Mountains belonged to Canada, not to the American colonies. It was designed to keep the colonists from moving into the western lands with their ideas of representative self-government. All these acts quickly became known as the "Intolerable Acts." As a result, the colonists joined together in protest. They held mass meetings and protested to their colonial legislatures. The Virginia House of Burgesses asked each colony to send delegates, or representatives, to a Continental Congress which could plan the next move.

Explain "intolerable."

Delegates from every colony except Georgia met in the First Continental Congress at Philadelphia in September, 1774. They were deeply worried by the British actions but were divided in their ideas for meeting the crisis. Some like John Jay of New York and Joseph Galloway of Pennsylvania hoped to ask the king for help. If George III would aid them, they would remain in the British Empire. They believed there were still some advantages to being tied to England and

Georgia's strong, Loyalist governor, James Wright, managed to keep opinions divided among colonists for some time.

under Parliament's rule. Other patriots like Samuel Adams and John Adams of Massachusetts and Patrick Henry of Virginia took the view that Parliament had no power over the colonies. Even these patriots, however, were willing to try to make peace before starting to fight.

The Continental Congress took two major steps. As some patriots wished, a letter of grievances was sent to the king. The letter admitted that Parliament might govern colonial trade, but it asked Parliament to repeal the laws which had been made since 1763. These were the laws to which the colonists objected.

To satisfy those who wanted more extreme action, the Congress created a Continental Association. The association was to enforce a boycott of British goods until Parliament repealed the Intolerable Acts. Patriots tarred and feathered loyalists who would not join the boycott and burned British goods. Imports from England dropped to

Students should understand the difference between primary and secondary sources.

# Paul Revere's Ride

Historians depend on many different kinds of sources for information about the past. From these sources, they establish facts and interpret their meaning. Among the most important sources are written records. These may be written at the time an event happens, or they may be written later.

The two selections that follow tell about Paul Revere's part in the battles of Lexington and Concord. The first one is from the poem "Paul Revere's Ride," written by Henry Wadsworth Longfellow in 1860.

Listen, my children, and you shall hear
Of the midnight ride of Paul Revere,
On the eighteenth of April, in
    Seventy-five;
Hardly a man is now alive
Who remembers that famous day and
    year.

He said to his friend, "If the British
    march
By land or sea from the town to-night,
Hang a lantern aloft in the belfry arch
Of the North Church tower as a signal
    light, —
One, if by land, and two, if by sea;
And I on the opposite shore will be,
Ready to ride and spread the alarm
Through every Middlesex village and
    farm,
For the country folk to be up and to
    arm."

How long after the battles of Lexington and Concord was this poem written? How reliable in specific details do you think this poem is as a source? How valuable do you think this poem is as a source of history?

Another source of information about the battles of Lexington and Concord is the writing of Paul Revere himself. This is how he described his ride:

Might bring in Emerson's poem on "the shot heard 'round the world" and relate to Longfellow poem on Revere's ride.

almost nothing, but George III would not give in to the colonists. Tensions rose on both sides, and it seemed that the only way out would be war.

# Independence

The Revolutionary War began at Lexington and Concord, Massachusetts, on April 19, 1775. Earlier that month, British General Thomas Gage in Boston planned to send a force of soldiers to arrest several patriot leaders in Lexington and to capture arms that Massachusetts patriots were storing in Concord. The patriots received advance news of this and warned others that the redcoats were coming. One of those who spread the alarm was Paul Revere of Boston.

*I set off upon a very good Horse; it was then about 11 o'Clock, [and] very pleasant. After I had passed* Charlestown Neck, . . . *I saw two men on Horse back, under a Tree. When I got near them, I discovered they were* British officers. *One tryed to git a head of me, [and] the other to take me. I turned my Horse very quick, [and] Galloped towards* Charlestown neck, *and then pushed for the* Medford Road. *The one who chased me, [trying] to cut me off, got into a clay pond, near where the new Tavern is now built. I got clear of him, and went [through]* Medford, *over the Bridge, [and] up to* Menotomy. *In* Medford, *I awaked the Captain of the Minute men; [and] after that, I alarmed almost every House, till I got to* Lexington. *I found . . .* Hancock [and] Adams *at the* Rev. Mr. Clark's; *I told them my errand, [and] inquired for* Mr. Daws [who was also spreading the alarm]; *they said he had not been there; I related the story of the two officers, [and] supposed* that He must have been stopped, as he ought to have been there before me. After I had been there about half an Hour, Mr. Daws *came; we refreshid our selves, and set off for* Concord, *to secure the stores . . . there.*

Which of the two previous accounts do you consider a more reliable report about the actual events? Why?

*The battles of Lexington and Concord marked the beginning of the Revolutionary War. As the British troops retreated from Concord, some of the colonists fired at them from behind trees and walls.*

When the English arrived at Lexington, seventy minutemen—patriot soldiers who could be ready for duty at a moment's notice—stood on the village green, ready to meet them. Shooting broke out, and eight minutemen were killed. At Concord, there was more firing, but the fighting was over by noon and the British were turned back to Boston. Meanwhile, all the minutemen of the countryside had been called to arms. On the fifteen-mile march back to Boston, they shot at the British from behind trees and stone walls. Their march became a retreat.

Even after the fighting had begun in Massachusetts, it was hard for the colonists to cut the remaining ties with England. The Second Continental Congress met in Philadelphia in May, 1775. It had become a government for the patriots in revolt. For the sake of those still hoping for peace, the Congress sent to King George III one last appeal—the

Georgia delegates attended the Second C. C. meeting. Other colonies had boycotted Georgia trade to add pressure.

"olive branch petition." King George would not accept it, and in August, he declared that the colonists were rebels. The time for appeals was over.

# Thomas Paine

One of the most effective writers on behalf of the patriot cause was Thomas Paine. He had come to America in 1774 from England. He became a Philadelphia journalist, writing appeals to ordinary people in the struggle against England. In 1776, Paine published a pamphlet, *Common Sense*, in which he argued that the rebelling colonists should cut their ties with England. Here is one of his arguments:

The infant state of the Colonies, as it is called, so far from being against, is an argument in favour of independence. We are sufficiently numerous, and were we more so we might be less united. . . .

Youth is the seed-time of good habits as well in nations as in individuals. It might be difficult, if not impossible, to form the Continent into one government half a century hence. The vast variety of interests, occasioned by an increase of trade and population, would create confusion. Colony would be against colony.

*Common Sense* became the most widely read pamphlet in the colonies. It persuaded many Americans to favor independence. During the war, Paine helped to lift the patriots' spirits by writing a series of papers titled *The Crisis*. The first of these began:

These are the times that try men's souls. The summer soldier and the sunshine patriot will in this crisis, shrink from the service of his country; but he that stands it NOW, deserves the love and thanks of man and woman. Tyranny, like hell, is not easily conquered; yet we have this consolation with us, that the harder the conflict, the more glorious the triumph.

After the colonies had won their independence, Paine looked elsewhere for causes to champion. He returned to Europe in 1787. In the 1790's, Paine was banished from England for urging a revolt against the monarchy. He was also briefly a hero in revolutionary France. Thomas Paine spent his last years in the United States and died in 1811.

While the Second Continental Congress had been sending its last appeal to the king, it had also been signing up soldiers for the Continental Army. As a symbol of unity, it chose a southerner, George Washington of Virginia, to lead the army. The new army showed its ability even before Washington arrived to take charge. It made the British pay dearly for their victory over the patriots in the bloody Battle of Bunker Hill near Boston. The Continental Army kept up their siege of Boston, and in the spring of 1776, the British finally left the city.

During the first winter of the war, the patriots began to see that they should cut any remaining ties with England. The Continental Congress began to act as a new central government. Royal governors fled, and colonial assemblies created new governments for their colonies. In January, 1776, Thomas Paine printed a pamphlet called *Common Sense*. It was read widely and convinced many that the colonies

*Many colonists felt that the time had come for a complete break with England. On July 4, 1776, the formal Declaration of Independence was adopted by the Continental Congress in Philadelphia.*

should be independent. But only slowly did the colonists come to feel that they should declare their independence from England.

In June, 1776, the Continental Congress finally named a committee to draw up a statement of independence. It resolved ". . . That these United Colonies are, and of Right ought to be Free and Independent States." Thomas Jefferson wrote the statement with the help of John Adams and Benjamin Franklin. On July 4, 1776, the Declaration of Independence was adopted by the Continental Congress. It became a model for people throughout the world who wanted to have self-government.

See annotated Declaration on pages 524-528.

# The Revolutionary War

The war was run by the Continental Congress and George Washington, the commander-in-chief of the army. The Congress had a hard time raising money to carry on the war. It did not put taxes on imports because Americans were fighting the British to protest these very things. The Congress tried asking the colonial governments for money but was not successful. As a result, it printed its own paper money which lost value very rapidly. By 1781, Continental currency was worth less than what it cost to print it.

The Declaration of Independence resulted from strong minority efforts. Some colonists remained loyal to Britain, and many others were apathetic.

It was only through the remarkable ability and determination of General Washington that the Continental Army was kept in the field. About 300,000 men, five thousand of them blacks, served in the army. Yet, Washington never had more than a few thousand troops under his command at any one time. It was an army of farmers who fought for a few months at a time and tried also to provide for their families back home. Washington usually had to train an almost new army before each season of fighting. However, as long as Washington could keep his army together, the American cause was not defeated.

Might raise and discuss the contradiction of fighting a revolution for freedom while maintaining a slave system. Some colonies paid part of their officers' salaries by giving them slaves.

Few women took active part in fighting the war. Deborah Sampson, a white woman, disguised herself as a man and served in the Continental Army for many months. Deborah Gannet, a black woman, also fought and was later cited for bravery. Some women joined their husbands in camp and on the battlefield to cook and care for the ill and wounded. Most women at home worked hard to care for the farms, plantations, and shops while the men were gone.

The most that could be said about the ability of the Continental Army from 1776 to 1777 was that it survived a number of defeats from the British. The Continental Army did have one major victory in the

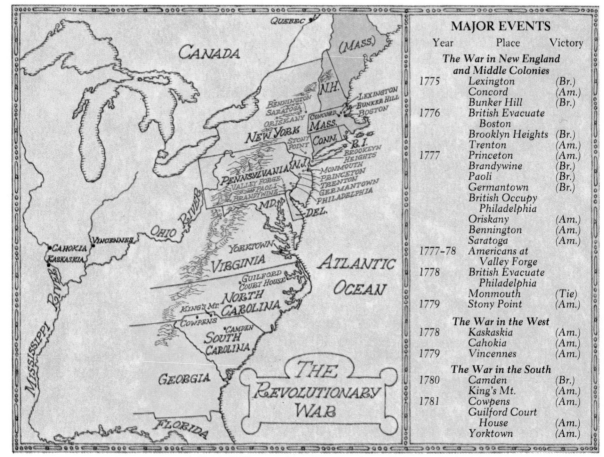

| MAJOR EVENTS | | |
| --- | --- | --- |
| Year | Place | Victory |
| *The War in New England and Middle Colonies* | | |
| 1775 | Lexington | (Br.) |
| | Concord | (Am.) |
| | Bunker Hill | (Br.) |
| 1776 | British Evacuate Boston | |
| | Brooklyn Heights | (Br.) |
| | Trenton | (Am.) |
| 1777 | Princeton | (Am.) |
| | Brandywine | (Br.) |
| | Paoli | (Br.) |
| | Germantown | (Br.) |
| | British Occupy Philadelphia | |
| | Oriskany | (Am.) |
| | Bennington | (Am.) |
| | Saratoga | (Am.) |
| 1777–78 | Americans at Valley Forge | |
| 1778 | British Evacuate Philadelphia | |
| | Monmouth | (Tie) |
| 1779 | Stony Point | (Am.) |
| *The War in the West* | | |
| 1778 | Kaskaskia | (Am.) |
| | Cahokia | (Am.) |
| 1779 | Vincennes | (Am.) |
| *The War in the South* | | |
| 1780 | Camden | (Br.) |
| | King's Mt. | (Am.) |
| 1781 | Cowpens | (Am.) |
| | Guilford Court House | (Am.) |
| | Yorktown | (Am.) |

Might assign individual reports on particular battles like Trenton, Saratoga, and King's Mt.

fall of 1777. The British had been planning to gain control of the Hudson River Valley in New York. To do this, British General John Burgoyne was marching his forces from Canada toward New York City. Hearing of this, New England farmers rushed to the aid of the Continental Army and forced Burgoyne to surrender at Saratoga. It was the first great American victory of the war.

Students might investigate and report on contributions of foreign officers like LaFayette, von Steuben, Kosciusko, Pulaski, and de Kalb.

The victory at Saratoga was a spectacular triumph for the American forces because it brought France into the war on their side. Benjamin Franklin, who was a colonial representative to France at the time, used the news of victory to persuade the French to enter the war. From this point on, the French, who had already given secret aid to the Americans, began helping them openly.

In the latter part of the war, most of the fighting was in the South. There the Americans and French won many battles. The fighting ended in 1781 when the British under General Cornwallis moved into

Yorktown on their way north. Yorktown was a trap. Washington, with American and French troops, blocked Cornwallis on land. French and American ships kept him from escaping by sea. In October, 1781, he surrendered, and the fighting was over.

The Treaty of Paris of 1783 ended the war. According to its terms, Great Britain recognized the independence of the United States. The land that George Rogers Clark, a Virginia patriot, had captured in the western territories was given to the United States. The important right to sail on the Mississippi River was also included in the treaty. The new nation's boundaries now stretched from the Great Lakes to Florida, from the Atlantic Ocean to the Mississippi River. There was plenty of room in which to grow and become strong. The United States had proven it could exist. It still faced the task of becoming unified at home and developing a strong government.

*Treaty of Paris of 1763 had given Spanish Florida to England; this treaty of 1783 returns it to Spain.*

See Teacher's Manual, page 71T. *Chapter 5 in Perspective*

## Identify

| | | |
|---|---|---|
| Navigation Acts | Stamp Act | Intolerable Acts |
| George III | Patrick Henry | George Washington |
| Sugar Act | Charles Townshend | Benjamin Franklin |

## Explain

| | | |
|---|---|---|
| mercantilism | Sons of Liberty | loyalists |
| French and Indian War | boycott | minutemen |
| "new colonial policy" | patriots | Treaty of Paris of 1783 |

## Check Your Memory of the Facts

1. What actions by the English led to the end of good relations with the colonies?
2. Why did the colonists oppose the Sugar Act and the Stamp Act?
3. What was Patrick Henry's position on taxation?
4. What was the cause and the result of the Boston "tea party"?

*Gaining Liberty*

5. Which colonies sent representatives to the First Continental Congress? Which did not?
6. Who were the leading colonists opposed to the English policy toward the colonies?
7. What country aided the colonists in the war against England?

## Check Your Understanding of the Ideas

1. What were the immediate and the long-range causes of the Revolution?
2. What different views of English policy existed among colonists before the start of the war?
3. Why did France come to the aid of the colonies?
4. How were the thirteen English colonies able to win independence from a much stronger England?
5. What were the major provisions of the Treaty of Paris of 1783?

## Expand Your Knowledge

1. Are there examples today of colonial control of one group of people by another? Compare the problems of such people with the problems faced by the American colonists on the eve of the Revolution.
2. Locate information which shows how heavy the tax burden was on the colonists in 1774. Compare this with the taxes paid in the United States today. Were colonial taxes more or less?
3. Prepare a chart comparing England and the colonies in 1776. Include size, population, size of army, size of navy, value of trade, and any other information which shows the chances for success of each side. Based on your chart, what statements can you make about the war?

# The Use of Freedom

Aim: to help students understand the evolution of ideas over time which resulted in ratification of the Constitution and Bill of Rights.

The American people had won the right of self-government through the American Revolution. They had a democracy, or a government that is run by the people who live under it. Before the Revolution, Americans claimed that they had the right to govern themselves and to worship as they pleased. After the Americans won their independence, they made laws to protect these rights.

## The Effects of Independence

The people of the United States gained their political independence through the Revolution. Each of the former colonies was now a state, and together, they had become a nation. Yet the future of the country was far from certain. It was still to be determined how well

*People from the United States began to settle as far west as the Mississippi River after the Revolutionary War.*

Americans would be able to put their freedom to use. Four million colonists, living along a coast stretching twelve hundred miles from Georgia to Maine, had to learn to govern themselves as United States citizens. There had been democracies before in ancient Greece and in fifteenth-century Italy. None though had ever had so many people scattered over so large an area as the United States.

The Revolution helped to spread democracy more quickly through American society. By the Treaty of Paris which ended the war, the United States gained more land. Americans were no longer kept from crossing the Appalachian Mountains. They could settle all the way to the Mississippi River. More land meant more opportunity to get ahead. After the war, there were still rather strict class lines in some states, but they were never as important as before. There were still laws which allowed only some white men to vote or hold office. Usually, these men had to own a certain amount of property. By the 1830's, these property laws were almost all gone for white men.

Women had hoped the war for independence would bring greater rights for them, too. It was a serious concern of Abigail Adams, although she wrote a rather joking letter to her husband John at the Continental Congress.

> . . . Remember the Ladies, and be more generous and favourable to them than your ancestors. Do not put such unlimited power into the hands of the Husbands. Remember all Men would be tyrants if they could. If perticuliar care and attention is not paid to the Laidies we are determined to foment a Rebelion, and will not hold ourselves bound by any Laws in which we have no voice, or Representation.

Despite the hopes of many women, they still could not vote or hold office in the years after the Revolution. In most states, the husbands of married women held legal control over their property and children. Black men and women in America, most of whom were slaves, were unable to take part in public life for some time. However, antislavery groups began to try to stop the slave trade and to work for freedom of slaves.

# Establishing New State Governments

The thirteen colonies were very successful in forming their own governments. The new governments after the Revolution were different from each other in small ways. But they did share certain ideas.

Might discuss differences between direct and representative democracies, asking students what practical bearing the number of citizens has on the form chosen.

Women, in fact, faced more restrictions and found less opportunity to participate in community economic life as the nation's population and productivity increased.

*After independence was won, state governments were set up. They adopted constitutions based partly on English law.*

The colonists had been using English law and political ideas even before the Revolution. So it was natural for them to base their own governments in part on the English system, which was slowly becoming more representative. They also drew on the political ideas of the great thinkers of the eighteenth century, especially those in England.

The first state governments had very limited powers because the patriots had feared the power of the British government. They did not want their own governments to become too strong. In many states, the office of the governor was weak, and most power was in the lower house of the legislature. Some of the state governments were under the control of a small group of wealthy people. In others, voting and political power were in the hands of the great majority of people who were farmers or skilled workers.

After a few years, political leaders in many states felt stronger governments were needed. More power was given to the governor and to the upper house of the legislature. State leaders increased the amount of property needed by an individual in order to hold office or to vote for members of the upper house. Therefore, although they differed from state to state, these governments were often less representative.

Might discuss the idea with students of whether government is to represent the citizens who are voters, or the citizens in general.

*The Use of Freedom*

# The National Government

Just as the leaders limited the powers of the first state governments, the Second Continental Congress limited the powers of the first national government. This, too, was because of the colonial fear of strong government. During the Revolution, the members of the Continental Congress had drawn up a plan for a federal, or central, government. Known as the Articles of Confederation, the plan went into effect as the new government in 1781.

Congress, under the Articles of Confederation, had little more power than the Continental Congress. That is, it had only those powers which the colonists had been willing for the king to have before the Revolution. The Congress could declare war, make peace, and maintain an army and navy. It could carry on business with foreign countries. It was given the power to make coins and paper money and to borrow money. It also ran a mail service. However, Congress did not have the power to tax and could only ask states to give it money.

In some ways, the Confederation government did act as a united, central government. It stated that there was a national citizenship. Citizens of any state were free to travel and trade throughout all the states. Also, it said that courts in one state must respect the findings of courts in other states. In other ways, the Confederation government seemed more like an agreement among many countries working together. Each state sent representatives to the Confederation Congress. They were paid by their states and told how to vote. Each state had one vote in the Congress.

A few representatives actually ran the Confederation government. The president was only in charge of conducting the Congress. Committees of Congress, made up of a few powerful people, ran foreign affairs, the treasury, the armed forces, and the post office.

# The Northwest Territory

After the Revolution, the lands beyond the Appalachian Mountains were settled quickly, and the Confederation Congress had to make laws for these areas. The Confederation government wanted these lands to become states equal to the original thirteen states, not colonies under their rule. Already, thousands of settlers had crossed the mountains into Tennessee and Kentucky. No plans had been made for those lands or for the huge area north of the Ohio River, called the Northwest Territory. Settlers also began to move into this land, and they soon needed some form of government to keep order. To answer this need, Congress passed two important ordinances, or rules.

The Land Ordinance of 1785 stated that the Northwest Territory would be surveyed, or examined and measured. The surveyors would then divide it into pieces that could be bought by settlers. The lands in Kentucky and Tennessee had been divided at random. In contrast, the Northwest Territory would be divided along north-south and east-west lines into townships thirty-six miles square. Each township would be made up of sections 640 acres, or a square mile, in size. Interest in education was shown by the fact that Section 16 in each township would be rented or sold to raise money for schools.

Land in the Northwest Territory would be sold at auction in 640-acre lots at a price of at least a dollar an acre. This was more money than most settlers had and more land than they could work. Before the

*The Northwest Ordinance provided for an orderly plan of government in the new territory west of the mountains. Towns and cities like Cincinnati, Ohio, grew quickly as centers of trade and commerce.*

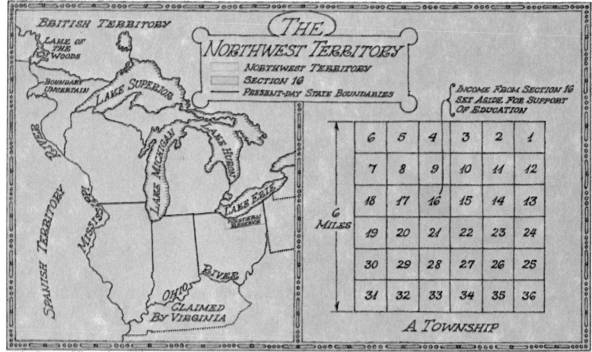

Map: THE NORTHWEST TERRITORY — BRITISH TERRITORY, LAKE OF THE WOODS, BOUNDARY UNCERTAIN, LAKE SUPERIOR, LAKE MICHIGAN, LAKE HURON, LAKE ERIE, SPANISH TERRITORY, MISSISSIPPI RIVER, WESTERN RESERVE, OHIO RIVER, OHIO CLAIMED BY VIRGINIA. Legend: Northwest Territory, Section 16, Present-Day State Boundaries. Income From Section 16 Set Aside For Support Of Education.

A Township (6 Miles), numbered grid:

| 6 | 5 | 4 | 3 | 2 | 1 |
| 7 | 8 | 9 | 10 | 11 | 12 |
| 18 | 17 | 16 | 15 | 14 | 13 |
| 19 | 20 | 21 | 22 | 23 | 24 |
| 30 | 29 | 28 | 27 | 26 | 25 |
| 31 | 32 | 33 | 34 | 35 | 36 |

Might discuss different forms of presenting information — maps, charts, and narratives so that students realize all people do not find the same forms useful for remembering data.

public sale of the lots, huge amounts of land were bought by two groups of investors calling themselves the Ohio Company and the Scioto Company. They bought the land for only a few cents an acre, hoping to make a profit by selling it in small sections to settlers. The Confederation government had agreed to sell the land to these companies for such a low price because it needed money.

# The Northwest Ordinance

The investors of the Ohio Company and the Scioto Company, some of whom were members of Congress, wanted strong governments in the territories to protect their property. To do this, Congress passed the Northwest Ordinance of 1787. It outlined steps that would lead to statehood for the areas in the Northwest Territory.

1. Congress would choose a governor, a secretary, and three judges to control the Northwest Territory.

2. When there were five thousand free adult men in the Northwest Territory, they could elect a legislature, but the governor could veto any laws it passed. A representative could be sent to Congress but could not vote there.

3. The Northwest Territory would be divided into not less than three nor more than five territories. When there were sixty thousand free settlers in a territory, they could write a constitution and apply to Congress for admission as a state.

The Northwest Ordinance was a model of the steps to statehood for all the territories that were to become part of the United States. The ordinance guaranteed freedom of worship and speech to the settlers. It gave the right to trial by jury and encouraged public education. It was also important because it did not allow slavery in the Northwest Territory. This was the first national legislation forbidding slavery.

# Weaknesses of the Confederation

Few other important things were done by the Confederation government. It is remembered most for its weaknesses. The settlers in the West complained that the Confederation government was not strong enough to protect them from the Indians and the British who still held trading posts on American soil. In addition, each state taxed goods that came across its borders from other states. This was very harmful to trade within the country, but the central government did not have the power to stop it. People also wanted the government to help win respect for American merchants in foreign countries.

For these reasons, many people began to feel that the United States needed a stronger central government. This feeling became even more urgent after 1786. In that year, Daniel Shays, a soldier in the Revolution, had led some farmers from western Massachusetts in a revolt against high taxes. Shays' Rebellion was stopped by the state troops, but people were afraid that there might be new revolts. It seemed clear that the Confederation government did not have the power to keep order in the country.

Student could research and report on Daniel Shays or Shays' Rebellion.

# The Constitutional Convention

Leading Americans came together at Annapolis, Maryland, in 1786 to talk about the problems of the Confederation government. They agreed to invite representatives of all thirteen states to meet at a convention the next year in Philadelphia. Their purpose would be to amend or change the Articles of Confederation so that the federal government could meet the needs of the nation.

*Delegates to the Constitutional Convention met in Philadelphia in 1787. George Washington was in charge of the meetings as the representatives worked on the new Constitution.*

When the representatives at the Constitutional Convention met in the summer of 1787, they decided that it would be useless to try to amend the Articles of Confederation. Instead, they would draw up a new frame of government. It would be a difficult job. The interests of small states conflicted with the interests of large states. There were also serious differences between the southern states and the northern states.

# Compromises

Rhode Islanders were afraid of losing their state rights to tax imports and to use state currency.

All these great differences were worked out by important compromises in which each side gave up part of what it wanted. The success of these compromises was due to the great skill of the fifty-five delegates to the Constitutional Convention. They came from every state but Rhode Island and included Alexander Hamilton, who was thirty-two years old, and Benjamin Franklin, who was eighty-one. Most of them were young planters, lawyers, or merchants. The delegates drew up a Constitution which gave some strong powers to the federal government. Other important powers were left to the states.

The question of representation in Congress was a difficult one. If each state had equal representation, the states with more people would be hurt. If representation was based on the number of people in each state, the states with fewer people would be hurt. This question was settled by the "Great Compromise." There would be two houses of Congress: the Senate, or upper house, and the House of Representatives, or lower house. Every state would send two senators to the Senate. The small states, therefore, would have a voice in the Senate equal to the large states. The number of representatives in the House would be decided by the number of people in each state. The states with the most people, therefore, would have a stronger voice in the House. An act would have to pass *both* houses of Congress before it could become law.

# SYSTEM OF CHECKS AND BALANCES

Veto legislation
Call special sessions of Congress
Control patronage

**LEGISLATIVE BRANCH**

**EXECUTIVE BRANCH**

Overrule President's veto
Refuse to ratify treaties
Refuse to confirm appointments
Impeach and remove President

Declare
laws
unconsti-
tutional

Declare
laws or
executive
acts
unconsti-
tutional

Impeach and
remove judges
Fix number of judges
Establish lower courts
Propose amendments
to overrule
judicial decisions

Appoint
federal
judges
Pardon or reprieve
federal
offenders

**JUDICIAL BRANCH**

Within the "Great Compromise" was a second compromise which grew out of the conflict between slave and free states. Southern states wanted to count all slaves when determining the population for setting the number of representatives. Northern states wanted none of the slaves counted. It was decided that three fifths of the number of slaves should be counted in determining the population for representation.

Other compromises were also made. In fact, the Constitution has been called a "bundle of compromises." Since such agreements were possible, it seemed likely that the new federal government would work. The bitter debates between North and South, however, were a sign of the troubles that would remain with the Union, finally causing the Civil War.

The 3/5 compromise indicates the strength of the slaveholders who thereby gained extra representation. Might discuss the contradiction of claiming a slave was property while claiming a slave was 3/5 of a person for population counts.

# James Madison

In the years after the Constitutional Convention, James Madison was frequently given credit for being the main author of the document. He protested this, saying it was "not the off-spring of a single brain," but "the work of many heads and many hands." It is true, however, that the young Virginia lawyer was one of the key figures at the convention.

Madison was a leader of the group who favored a strong central government. He also planned the system of checks and balances for the three branches of government. His detailed notes are the only record of the important debates at the convention.

No one was clearer or more effective than Madison in explaining the meaning of the new Constitution. During the debates over ratification, he worked hard in support of it. Madison wrote many of the essays in *The Federalist*. He also wrote letters to Thomas Jefferson, persuading him to approve the Constitution. At the Virginia ratifying convention, Madison's quiet reasoning overcame the lively, colorful arguments of the leading Anti-Federalist, Patrick Henry.

Virginia elected James Madison to the first House of Representatives in 1789. There, too, he was a leader. He helped establish new executive departments and proposed taxes on imports and exports. Madison also wrote the draft for the first ten amendments to the Constitution, the Bill of Rights.

# Federalists and Anti-Federalists

Lively debates took place all over the country as state after state called conventions to ratify, or approve, the Constitution. These debates were very important because they helped people understand the Constitution. Those who wanted the new Constitution were called Federalists because they were for a strong federal government. Three members of the group—James Madison, Alexander Hamilton, and John Jay—worked for ratification. They wrote a number of essays explaining the new Constitution. These appeared in a newspaper and later were printed in a book called *The Federalist*.

For the Independent Journal.

The FŒDERALIST. No. I.

To the People of the State of New-York.

AFTER an unequivocal experience of the inefficacy of the subfisting Fœderal Government, you are called upon to deliberate on a new Conftitution for the United States of America. The fubject fpeaks its own importance; comprehending in its confequences, nothing lefs than the exiftence of the UNION, the fafety and welfare of the parts of which it is compofed, the fate of an empire, in many refpects, the moft interefting in the world. It has been frequently remarked, that it feems to have been referved to the people of this country, by their conduct and example, to decide the important queftion, whether focieties of men are really capable or not, of eftablifhing good government from reflection and choice, or whether they are forever deftined to depend, for their political conftitutions, on accident and force. If there be any truth in the remark, the crifis, at which we are arrived, may with propriety be regarded as the æra in which that decifion is to be made; and a wrong election of the part we fhall act, may, in this view, deferve to be confidered as the general misfortune of mankind.

This idea will add the inducements of philanthropy to thofe of patriotifm to heighten the follicitude, which all confiderate and good men muft feel for the event. Happy will it be if our choice fhould be decided by a judicious eftimate of our true interefts,

In these essays, the Federalists said that the powers of government should be divided between the federal and state governments. The federal government could do only what the Constitution said. Limited as it was, the federal government would have the important powers which the earlier Confederation government had lacked. These were the powers to tax and to look after trade among the states and with other countries. At the same time, the new government would be strong enough to protect American borders and American ships at sea.

# Sources of History

The attitudes of Americans toward the Constitution are described in a variety of sources. Some are firsthand, or primary, sources which tell the author's own ideas. Others are secondhand, or secondary, sources which tell about other people's ideas. Which seems most important as a source?

James Madison of Virginia reported his own speech on the Constitution.

*In order to judge of the form to be given to this institution, it will be proper to take a view of the ends to be served by it. These were, first, to protect the people against their rulers, secondly, to protect the people against [brief] impressions into which they themselves might be led. A people [thinking] in a [calm] moment, and with the experience of other nations before them, on the plan of government most likely to secure their happiness, would first be aware, that those charged with the public happiness might betray their trust. An obvious precaution against this danger would be, to divide the trust between different bodies of men, who might watch and check each other. . . .*
Primary source

Madison also reported a speech made by Benjamin Franklin.

*I confess that there are several parts of this Constitution which I do not at present approve, but I am not sure I shall never approve them. For having lived long, I have experienced many instances of being [made] by better information, or fuller consideration, to change opinions even on important subjects, which I once thought right, but found to be otherwise. . . . On the whole, sir, I cannot help expressing a wish that every member of the Convention who may still have objections to it, would with me, on this occasion, doubt a little of his own [rightness], and to make [clearly known] our [total agreement], put his name to this instrument.*
Secondary source

George Mason of Virginia, in a letter to George Washington, explained one of his objections to the Constitution.

*There is no declaration of rights: (a bill of rights for individuals and states) and the laws of the general government being [higher than] the laws and constitutions of the several states, the declarations of rights in the separate states are no security.*
Primary source

Finally, the Preamble to the Constitution explains the purpose of the new plan of government.

*We The People of the United States, in Order to form a more perfect Union, establish Justice, insure domestic Tranquility, provide for the common defence, promote the general Welfare, and secure the Blessings of Liberty to ourselves and our Posterity, do ordain and establish this Constitution for the United States of America.*
Primary source

More subtle distinctions here than examples on pp. 96-97. Might bring out in class discussion the factors of time and distance when evaluating reliability of secondary sources.

*The Use of Freedom*

Those against approving the new Constitution were called Anti-Federalists. They all had different ideas about how strong the central government should be. Some even wanted to keep the Confederation government. Eventually, the Constitution was ratified in spite of these objections.

See annotated Constitution on pages 529-555.

## Powers of the Government

| STATE POWERS | STATE AND FEDERAL POWERS | FEDERAL POWERS |
|---|---|---|
| Regulate intrastate commerce | Collect taxes | Regulate interstate and foreign commerce |
| Grant return of criminals and suspects | Set criminal laws | Establish lower courts |
| Regulate voting laws and procedures | Borrow money | Coin money |
| Make marriage and divorce laws | Take property for public purposes | Make citizenship laws |
| Make traffic laws | Charter banks | Set weights and measures |
| Establish and maintain public education | | Run postal system |
| Make corporation laws | | Regulate copyrights and patents |
| | | Declare war |
| | | Establish and support armed forces |

See Teacher's Manual, page 27T.

# The Bill of Rights

One of the most important objections to the Constitution was that it did not include a list of definite personal rights. Laws which limited the power of the government over the individual had been written into the Constitution. Yet there were those who felt that these personal rights should also be spelled out. Before many of the states would ratify the Constitution, they insisted that such a list be added to it. Soon after the new government began, these rights were drawn up by Congress, approved by the states, and added as amendments to the Constitution. These first ten amendments are called the Bill of Rights.

The new Constitution was ratified in June, 1788. No one was quite sure how well it would work. Some delegates to the convention did not approve of the document when it was finished. Others signed the Constitution only hoping that it would work. Benjamin Franklin had

Order of ratification:

| | | |
|---|---|---|
| DE | 12/07/87 | Unanimous |
| PA | 12/12/87 | 46-23 vote |
| NJ | 12/18/87 | Unanimous |
| GA | 1/02/88 | Unanimous |
| CT | 1/09/88 | 128-40 |
| MA | 2/06/88 | 187-168 |
| MD | 4/28/88 | 63-11 |
| SC | 5/27/88 | 149-73 |
| NH | 6/21/88 | 57-46 |
| VA | 6/25/88 | 87-76 |
| NY | 7/26/88 | 30-27 |
| NC | 11/12/89 | 187-77 |
| RI | 5/29/90 | 34-22 |

Might have students investigate state histories and report on the close votes, VA's early claim for honor of 9th to ratify, and disputes postponing ratification in NY, NC, and RI.

*The Use of Freedom*

stated, "Thus I consent, Sir, to this Constitution, because I expect no better, and because I am not sure that it is not the best." Franklin had pointed to the sun painted on the back of the chair in which the presiding officer at the convention, George Washington, had sat. Franklin remarked, " . . . now at length I have the happiness to know that it is a rising and not a setting sun."

*The rising sun noticed by Benjamin Franklin was painted on the chair used by George Washington at the Constitutional Convention. Franklin saw the sun as a symbol of the dawn of a new nation.*

# Chapter 6 in Perspective See Teacher's Manual, page 75T.

## Identify

| | | |
|---|---|---|
| Articles of Confederation | Shays' Rebellion | Anti-Federalists |
| Northwest Territory | Federalists | |

## Explain

| | | |
|---|---|---|
| democracy | Northwest Ordinance | ratify |
| federal government | "Great Compromise" | Bill of Rights |

# Check Your Memory of the Facts

1. What did the Revolution achieve for the American people?
2. What things did the new state governments established after the Revolution have in common?
3. What were the powers of Congress under the Articles of Confederation?
4. What were the chief weaknesses of the Articles of Confederation?
5. What provisions for new states were made in the Northwest Ordinance?
6. What powers were given to the federal government under the Constitution?

# Check Your Understanding of the Ideas

1. How did the American experience with the British government influence the kind of state and federal governments created after the Revolution?
2. What groups in America did not secure full citizenship rights after the Revolution?
3. Were the Articles of Confederation able to provide the government needed by Americans? Why or why not?
4. Was the federal government under the Constitution more like the colonial government under Britain than it was like the government under the Articles of Confederation? Why or why not?
5. What caused some people to oppose the Constitution?
6. What was the purpose of the Bill of Rights?

# Expand Your Knowledge

1. Examine the constitution or rules of one of your school organizations. Prepare a report showing the following information:
   a. Who has the executive power
   b. Who has the legislative power
   c. Who has the judicial power
   d. How a person becomes a member of the group
   e. How the chief executive is elected
   f. What power the chief executive has
   g. What the purpose of the organization is
2. Organize a debate on the following question. Resolved: that the creation of the Constitution represented a return to the same kind of strong central government against which the colonies had fought in the American Revolution.

*The Use of Freedom*

# America Is... Democracy

# Testing the
# New Government

# 7

Aim: to clarify the main structures of U.S. federal government.

Might discuss Washington's use of word "experiment," stressing that these Americans had no guarantees and few guidelines from history.

The first twenty years of the new federal government were very difficult ones. No one could be sure that the new Constitution would work. It was not certain that the still weak American nation could last in a world of powerful, unfriendly countries. George Washington voiced these worries when he said, " . . . the preservation of the sacred fire of liberty and the destiny of the [democratic] model of government . . . [depend] on the experiment intrusted to the hands of the American people."

During these first years, the new government was being tested. Most of its leaders were the same ones who had led the American Revolution and had formed the new state and federal governments. Now their job was to help the American people prosper and become united. They also had to keep the country from getting into war with European powers. The United States was not yet strong enough to defend itself. Because these leaders succeeded, the nation was able to weather these trying years.

## Washington as President

Student reports, see note p. 117, might provide answers to whether or not NC and RI attended this Congress.

See Art. II, Sec. 1, of Constitution on presidential electors.

As soon as the Constitution had been ratified, the new government started to work. The first members of the Senate and the House of Representatives were elected. They came to New York, the capital at that time, and met in Congress early in 1789. The state legislatures chose electors whose task was to choose the President. All the electors voted for George Washington, and they chose John Adams to be Vice-President.

The authors of the Constitution had been thinking of Washington when they created the presidency. No one else in the United States seemed to have so much experience as an executive as he did. He had shown how able he was by the way he ran his large plantation and by his command of the Continental Army. Washington was an ideal person to serve as the nation's first President. He was patient, hardworking, and careful. He brought to the presidency a dignity and honor that few

George Washington was a skilled military leader. As President, he was also commander-in-chief of the armed forces.

Testing the New Government

other Americans could. The authors of the Constitution had wanted to create a strong presidency which also had certain limits. Washington carried out their plans.

During his first months as President, Washington knew that what he did would set an example for Presidents who followed him in office. One of the most lasting things he did was to meet with the heads of his departments to talk about their problems and to ask their advice. These people, then, became his Cabinet, or body of advisers. He gave a

Cabinet is not mentioned in Constitution, but following Presidents continued the practice.

*The members of Washington's first Cabinet were Henry Knox, Thomas Jefferson, Edmund Randolph, and Alexander Hamilton.*

From left to right: Secretary of War Knox, Secretary of State Jefferson, Attorney General Randolph, Secretary of the Treasury Hamilton, President Washington.

*Testing the New Government*

lot of power to his Cabinet officers and made sure that they reported only to him. Washington, in turn, informed Congress of the progress in each department. If the Cabinet officers had reported directly to the Congress, the President would have been much less powerful.

Washington thought of himself as the chief executive. It was his task to execute, or carry out, the policies made by Congress. In theory, that was how it was supposed to happen. In practice, the President also became a maker of policy, especially in the field of foreign affairs. Because of one meeting with Congress, Washington gained for the presidency more power over foreign affairs than the Constitution had clearly provided. It said that the President should negotiate, or work out, treaties with other countries with the advice and consent of the Senate. While Washington was negotiating a treaty with a group of Indians, he took the papers to the Senate to get advice and approval. The senators would not discuss the treaty while he was present. They wished to talk it over in private. Washington left, and from then on, he and the Presidents who followed him have negotiated treaties as they think best. Then they have sent the treaties to the Senate to ratify or reject as it sees fit.

Note the relationship between the U.S. government and American Indian groups which were considered outside, sovereign nations.

# A New Court System

One of the most important goals of the framers of the Constitution was to make a strong court system. It would protect the rights of the people and keep them from being harmed by governments or by other people. Congress soon began passing laws to make the new government work and to set up a court system. The Judiciary Act of 1789 created a system of courts that is still working, although sometimes the number of the courts has changed. The act set up three levels of courts:

1. The federal district courts, set up throughout the United States, were established as the first level of the court system. These courts hear cases involving federal law, the law made by Congress.

2. The federal circuit courts were the next level of courts. They hear cases which are taken to them, or appealed, because the district court might have made a mistake or been unfair.

3. The Supreme Court was the highest court in the federal court system. It was established to cover legal problems between the states. It also hears cases that are beyond the powers of the states as they are written in the Constitution and cases that come to it from the lower courts. The Supreme Court is the last court of appeal.

The federal court system can also decide if a state law or a federal law goes against the Constitution. The power to judge whether or not a law is unconstitutional is called judicial review. This is only done if the law comes up in a court case. The use of judicial review made the federal courts very powerful.

# Early Economic Policies

An economic program was also important if the government were to help the nation prosper. Those who were forming the new government wanted it to be powerful. If it were to keep order at home and be respected in other countries, the government had to have a secure economy. It must be able to collect taxes, pay its debts, and keep its armed forces strong. It also had to have a supply of money that would keep its value. The United States would not be strong if the value of its money fell until it was almost worthless, as the Continental dollar had done during the Revolution.

Hamilton's *Report on Manufactures*, 1791, presented plan for future development of American industry in the North to be supplied with raw materials by agricultural South and with labor by European immigration.

Alexander Hamilton, the secretary of the treasury, drew up an economic program for the country. He proposed legislation that would bring money into the government's treasury through taxes. He thought that these and other measures would help the nation prosper. Even more, the program would be particularly profitable for the wealthy business people in the country. Hamilton meant to favor these people in order to make sure of their support for the new government.

Import duties and excise taxes were harder on farmers than on those in trade. Plantation owners also strongly resented secondary role assigned them in Hamilton's plans for U.S. economic independence.

There was sharp disagreement over Hamilton's ideas. Most of those who had been for the new Constitution wanted his plan. But many other people were against it because it favored the rich. James Madison from Virginia, where many people did not want to see Hamilton's program pass, led the fight against it. Most everyone, however, agreed with one part of Hamilton's program. The government should pay back the money that had been borrowed from foreign countries during the Revolution.

Federal assumption of state war debts led foreign countries to look to the central government as authority rather than to state governments.

Another main argument over Hamilton's program focused on the war debts of the states. Hamilton wanted the federal government to take over the state debts from the Revolution. The southern states had, for the most part, already paid their debts. Southerners in Congress felt that citizens of their states should not be taxed to help pay the debts of other states. A compromise was finally reached. The southerners agreed to vote for the federal government to take over the state debts. In return, northerners in Congress agreed to vote for the new capital of the

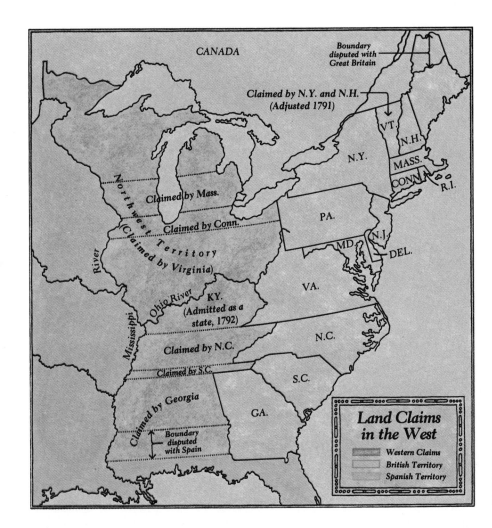

CANADA

Boundary
disputed with
Great Britain

Claimed by N.Y. and N.H.
(Adjusted 1791)

VT.

N.H.

MASS.

CONN.

R.I.

N.Y.

Claimed by Mass.

Claimed by Conn.

PA.

N.J.

MD.

DEL.

VA.

KY.
(Admitted as a
state, 1792)

N.C.

Claimed by N.C.

Claimed by S.C.

S.C.

Claimed by Georgia

GA.

Boundary
disputed
with Spain

Mississippi River

Ohio River

North West Territory
(Claimed by Virginia)

**Land Claims
in the West**

Western Claims
British Territory
Spanish Territory

Compare to maps on pp. 47
& 74. Review land claim
transfers from French to
British, pp. 91-92, and from
British to American, p. 103.

United States to be built in the South. A new city, to be named Washington, would be built on the banks of the Potomac River in the new federal District of Columbia. During the years it was being planned and built, the capital would be Philadelphia.

# The Bank of the United States

People also disagreed over the last point of Hamilton's program—setting up a Bank of the United States. Money taken in by the government would be deposited there, and the Bank would issue the secure paper money which businesses needed. Hamilton's program would put

*Testing the New Government*

U. S. Bank resented by southern and western farmers for its tight credit policies and by smaller banks for its direct competition. Bank's loan policies favored eastern business. See also p. 179.

large amounts of money into the hands of the people who could help develop the nation's industry and trade. It would make these people look to the federal government for help in their businesses. And it would give them a secure money system with which to do their business. Hamilton believed that all of this would strengthen the nation's economy.

When the bill to set up the Bank of the United States passed Congress, it came before President Washington. He asked Secretary of State Thomas Jefferson and Secretary of the Treasury Alexander Hamilton whether it was constitutional or not. Jefferson thought it was not,

*The first Bank of the United States was built in Philadelphia in 1791. Although Jefferson opposed it, Hamilton thought it would create a secure money system for the country.*

because the powers that the Constitution gave to Congress did not include the power to set up a bank. Although Congress was given the power "to make all laws necessary and proper" to carry out its work, Jefferson felt that all this could be done without a bank. Hamilton, on the other hand, said that a bank was necessary. He felt that the "necessary and proper" clause of the Constitution gave Congress the power to set up a bank.

President Washington finally accepted Hamilton's views and signed the bill setting up the Bank of the United States. The debate over whether the Bank bill was constitutional or not has had lasting effect. It marked the beginning of two different ways of understanding the Constitution. Jefferson understood the Constitution to mean only what it specifically said. His view was called a narrow or strict interpretation of the Constitution. Hamilton understood the Constitution to mean much more than it said. This view was called a broad interpretation of the Constitution. These two views have been brought up again and again over the years.

Might discuss the disagreements between Hamilton and Jefferson in light of the regional viewpoints they held as New Yorker and Virginian.

# Foreign Affairs

There were also debates over foreign affairs during Washington's term. Hamilton and his followers usually took one side, while Jefferson, Madison, and their followers took the other side. When war broke out in Europe between England and France, these debates became bitter. President Washington feared that it would be dangerous for the United States to become involved in the European war. He followed the advice of neither Jefferson, who favored the French, nor Hamilton, who favored the British. Instead, he issued a proclamation of neutrality —the United States would not take sides.

U.S. had signed a Franco-American Alliance of 1778 still officially in effect. See p. 102.

As time went on, quarrels over foreign policy became even more bitter. British troops still held trading posts in the American Northwest. Also, the British had been capturing some American trading ships in the West Indies. Americans started calling for war against Britain. To settle these problems, Washington sent John Jay, the Chief Justice of the Supreme Court, to England where he negotiated a treaty.

Jefferson and his followers were bitterly against the treaty that was made. According to it, the British agreed to remove their trading posts from American soil. Americans could only send very small ships to trade in the British West Indies. To many Americans, it seemed that

*Although the Jay Treaty avoided war with Great Britain, many people were against it. Angry mobs burned a dummy labeled "Jay."*

*Testing the New Government*

England was still giving the orders. To the French and their allies, the Spanish, it looked as if the United States had taken the side of the British.

Although many people were against it, the Jay Treaty was passed by the Senate. That led Spain to agree to a treaty that favored the United States. The Spanish were afraid that the United States would join the British and attack its lands in the New World. Under the Pinckney Treaty of 1795, Spain gave Americans the right to carry goods down the Mississippi River to New Orleans or ship them abroad. This made it possible for western farmers to get their goods to eastern and foreign markets without having to carry them across the mountains, a very costly practice. The treaty also fixed the northern boundary of Florida where the United States had claimed it should be.

# Political Parties

The authors of the Constitution had not expected national political parties to develop, even though there had been such parties in the colonies and the states. After the quarrels over the Jay Treaty, however, the two sides began to form two political parties, the Federalists and the Republicans. Adams, Hamilton, some members of Congress, and some state leaders formed the Federalist party. Jefferson, Madison, other members of Congress, and state leaders who were against the people in power in the government formed the Republican party.

This Republican party is also known as the Democratic-Republican party which split later into Democratic-Republicans and National-Republicans. It is not the forerunner of the current Republican party which developed in the 1850's.

The feelings between the two parties were made worse by the Whiskey Rebellion of 1794. Pennsylvania frontier people rose up in arms against a federal tax on the whiskey they made. Hamilton wanted to show that the new government could control such protests. To do that, a large army was sent to capture the leaders of the rebellion. After the Whiskey Rebellion, these frontier people, most of whom were Republicans, said that the Federalists were a party of merchants, bankers, and important people who did not care about small farmers or planters. Actually, neither party was made up of one class of people from one part of the country. But many frontier people, small farmers, and southern planters were angered by Hamilton's actions.

Washington, who had been easily reelected in 1792, had expected to be President of all the American people. He felt that separate political parties were dividing the country and was unhappy about their development. He did not join either party, but his political ideas were

*Testing the New Government*

*During the Whiskey Rebellion, angry farmers tarred and feathered a federal tax collector and forced him from his burning house.*

Jefferson became Vice-President but opposed much of Adams' administration. See also KY Resolution next page.

close to those of the Federalists. In 1796, Washington decided not to run again, and the presidential election that year was the first between two parties. Hamilton's economic program was working, and business was good. Because of the prosperity of the country, many Republicans decided to vote for Federalists. Federalist John Adams was elected over Republican Thomas Jefferson.

# The XYZ Affair

Soon after John Adams became President, the French began capturing American ships. They had been angered by the Jay Treaty with the British, and soon an undeclared war at sea began. Adams sent representatives to France to settle the problem. Three French officials met with them and said there could be no more talks unless the Americans gave them a large sum of money. Adams called these French officials X, Y, and Z in his report to Congress. This became known as the XYZ Affair.

Popular slogan at time of XYZ affair was "Millions for defense but not one cent for tribute."

The American people were greatly angered when they learned of the XYZ Affair. They backed President Adams when he sent American ships to fight the French at sea. They probably would even have supported an all-out war, but Adams wanted to avoid it. He blocked Hamilton's efforts to build a strong army and, in 1799, sent other representatives to France who finally settled the matter.

Convention of 1800 guaranteed American neutrality at sea and formally ended the Franco-American Alliance of 1778.

# The Alien and Sedition Acts

While Americans were still involved in the trouble with France, Federalists in Congress passed a number of laws harmful to the Republicans who opposed them. These laws were the Alien and Sedition Acts of 1798. The Alien Acts were aimed at hurting aliens, or foreigners, many of whom agreed with the Republican party. The acts gave the President the power to send out of the country any foreigner he felt was dangerous. The Sedition Act said that anyone guilty of "false, scandalous and malicious writing or writings" against the government should be fined up to two thousand dollars and put in prison for up to two years. Many Republican news writers were punished under this act.

Alien and Sedition Acts were passed with two year limits.

The Republicans were frightened by such laws that seemed to go against the personal rights stated in the Constitution. James Madison for Virginia and Thomas Jefferson for Kentucky drew up what came to be known as the Virginia and Kentucky Resolutions. These resolutions said that the Alien and Sedition Acts were unconstitutional and, therefore, could not be upheld by the states. They also said that the state governments had the right to judge any law passed by Congress to be unconstitutional.

The Alien and Sedition Acts were a way for the party in office to fight the other party. Although they did not last, they were laws made at a time when some people thought that strong political actions against the party in office were disloyal and illegal. Slowly people began to understand that party opposition was not only legal but valuable as a control over the party in power.

# Point of View

The Federalists had the most power in Congress before 1800, and they wanted to keep this advantage. One way they tried to do this was by passing the Alien and Sedition Acts. The Federalists thought that aliens might support the Republican party if they became citizens. So, the Alien Act made it difficult for aliens to obtain citizenship. The Federalists also feared that the Republican press might stir up opposition to the Federalist government. The Sedition Act made it illegal to criticize the government. Congress made these laws only ten years after the Constitution was ratified and seven years after the Bill of Rights was passed. Many people felt that these laws went against the principles of the original documents.

The following selections from the Bill of Rights and from the Sedition Act reflect the points of view of the supporters of each piece of legislation. How do the views expressed in the two selections differ? How could members of Congress have such different views on the issue of personal liberty within such a short time?

## Bill of Rights

*Congress shall make no law . . . abridging the freedom of speech, or of the press; or the right of the people peaceably to assemble, and to petition the government for a redress of grievances.*

## Sedition Act

*That if any person shall write, print, utter, or publish . . . any false, scandalous and malicious writing or writings against the government of the United States, or either house of the Congress of the United States, or the President of the United States . . . or to excite against them . . . the hatred of the good people of the United States . . . or to excite any unlawful combinations therein, for opposing or resisting any law of the United States . . . then such person, being thereof convicted . . . shall be punished by a fine not exceeding two thousand dollars, and by imprisonment not exceeding two years.*

# The "Revolution of 1800"

The political pendulum swung toward Jefferson and the Republicans in the election of 1800. The Hamilton wing of the Federalist party was furious with Adams because of the way he ended the trouble with France. Not only were the Federalists split, but the voters were unhappy because taxes had increased. In the election, Jefferson and a Republican Congress were elected by a small margin of votes.

The results of the election were in question for a while. The electors each had two votes and were to choose a President and a Vice-President from among four candidates. The one who received the most votes would be President. The one who got the next largest number of votes would be Vice-President. Each elector who voted Republican cast one vote for Jefferson and one vote for Aaron Burr. Jefferson was

Might assign student research and report on Burr.

*Thomas Jefferson became the third President of the United States in 1800.*

Hamilton supported his usual opponent Jefferson over Burr. Student investigation and report could reveal that Hamilton also blocked Burr's attempt to become NY governor in 1804. Burr's increasing emnity resulted in famous duel and Hamilton's death.

the party's choice for President, but the election had ended in a tie between Jefferson and Burr. The tie was settled in the House of Representatives where Jefferson was elected President. In 1804, the Twelfth Amendment was added to the Constitution to keep this from happening again. It said that the electors would vote separately for the President and for the Vice-President.

Jefferson liked to call his election the "Revolution of 1800." It proved that, in the United States, one political party could be defeated and the opposition party could take power peacefully. In his inaugural address, Jefferson was friendly toward the Federalists, saying, "We are all Republicans, we are all Federalists." His election showed that the common goals of both parties were larger than the differences separating them. It also proved that the new government was strong and could survive change.

So far as policies were concerned, Jefferson's election was by no means a revolution. He continued the Bank of the United States and most of the policies of the Federalists. The biggest change he made was to cut government costs sharply, mostly by cutting down on the money spent on the army and the navy.

President Jefferson believed in states' rights. This was the idea that the states had the right to judge the acts of the national government and decide whether to follow them or not. Although Jefferson was a strong believer that the powers of the federal government should be limited, he was also a strong nationalist. He believed that the federal government should be able to help the nation grow larger and stronger. He saw the United States growing into an "empire of liberty."

# The Louisiana Purchase

Anticipating defeat by British, Louis XV gave these lands to his Spanish cousin Charles III in 1762. Napoleon forced Spain to return them in 1800.

One of Jefferson's most important acts as President showed his nationalist feelings. This act was the doubling of the size of the United States through the Louisiana Purchase, a piece of land stretching from the Mississippi River to the Rocky Mountains. Soon after he became President, Jefferson learned that Napoleon of France was taking over Louisiana from Spain. The people of the West depended on the Mississippi River and New Orleans, the gateway to the sea, to get their goods to market. They were afraid that the French would close the Mississippi River and New Orleans to American use.

To keep this from happening, Jefferson sent representatives to France to buy New Orleans and the land along the Gulf of Mexico.

*Sacajawea, a Shoshone Indian, was born in what is now Idaho. She served as guide and interpreter for Lewis and Clark on their explorations through the Northwest to the Pacific Ocean.*

Napoleon, who was about to go to war in Europe, needed money. He offered to sell all of Louisiana to the United States. In 1803, Jefferson agreed, even though the Constitution did not specifically give him power to get new territory. For fifteen million dollars, he bought an area larger than the entire United States at that time.

In 1804, Jefferson sent Meriwether Lewis and William Clark to explore this huge area. Guided by Sacajawea, a Shoshone Indian woman, they made their way up the Missouri River and through the wilderness beyond. Crossing the continent, they reached the mouth of the Columbia River at the Pacific Ocean in 1805. Soon many American fur traders were pushing into the Rocky Mountains. The people in the West no longer had to worry about the use of the Mississippi River, and a whole new frontier was opened to American settlement.

Might refer students to Jefferson's view of Constitution, p. 129, and compare with this pragmatic action.

Might assign investigation of different aspects of Lewis and Clark expedition to several students—routes, people met, plant or animal life discovered, etc.

*Testing the New Government*

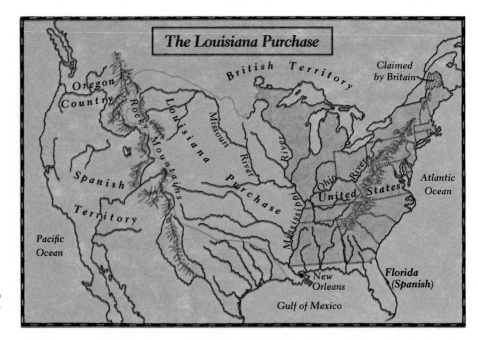

**The Louisiana Purchase**

Note Spanish territories to set background for further U.S. acquisitions.

# Jefferson and the Supreme Court

Students should understand that these cousins were often political opponents. See sketch on Federalist Marshall next page.

Judicial review defined p. 126. Primary source research on court cases difficult for average students. *Marbury v. Madison,* 1803, established Supreme Court review over acts of Congress; *Fletcher v. Peck,* 1810, over acts of state legislatures; *Cohens v. Virginia,* 1821, over state courts.

While Jefferson was doubling the size of the nation, his cousin, John Marshall, was serving as Chief Justice of the Supreme Court. Marshall and the other Supreme Court judges made the judicial branch of the government more powerful through the decisions they made on a number of cases. In the case of *Marbury v. Madison* (1803), the Supreme Court had established for itself the right to decide if a law passed by Congress was unconstitutional. In later decisions, the Marshall Court said that the powers of the federal government were above those of the states in cases of federal law or constitutional law. All of these decisions made the judicial branch of the government as strong as the executive and legislative branches.

# Years of Prosperity

Jefferson's years as President saw the nation prosper. Jefferson knew good times would remain if he could, like Washington, keep America out of war. At first, this was not too difficult, and the booming nation reelected Jefferson in 1804. Throughout the country, the Republicans were gaining strength, and the Federalists were no more than a weakening New England party. Yet in his second term, Jefferson faced such big problems that, at the end of his eight years in office, he was happy to retire. He had done much to help the American nation. In its first twenty years under Federalist and Republican Presidents, the new nation had become firmly established.

# John Marshall

John Marshall was born in Virginia in 1755. Like his cousin, Thomas Jefferson, he grew up the son of a planter on the Virginia frontier. Marshall was an eager patriot and served as an officer in the Continental Army. He studied law only briefly in school but learned much by his own experiences and by watching other lawyers. His success as a lawyer probably came from the simple, direct, and very logical arguments he gave in court.

In 1801, President John Adams appointed Marshall as Chief Justice of the Supreme Court. Adams and the Federalists soon went out of office. The appointment of Marshall, a strong Federalist, had a great effect on the development of the United States. Because of his powerful leadership, the Supreme Court ruled in keeping with Marshall's Federalist views for many years.

The American legal system had not been firmly established when Marshall became Chief Justice. It had only been a few years since the Revolution, and Americans did not want to follow the example of the British legal system. There were few American examples to follow. So Marshall was able to establish some of the basic principles of American law. In one Court decision, he said that the Supreme Court has the power to decide if an act of Congress is unconstitutional. He believed that the federal government must be strong for the United States to be successful. In conflicts between the federal and state governments, Marshall ruled that the federal government must be supreme. These decisions made the federal government stronger and gave the states less power. In this way, Marshall helped create a single nation out of many states.

At the time of Marshall's appointment, the Supreme Court had little power. Many people felt that it would never decide important issues. At the end of his thirty-four years as Chief Justice, John Marshall had made the federal judicial system a strong and equal branch of the government.

# Chapter 7 in Perspective See Teacher's Manual, page 78T.

## Identify

Judiciary Act of 1789   Pinckney Treaty   Alien and Sedition Acts
Alexander Hamilton   Whiskey Rebellion   Louisiana Purchase
Thomas Jefferson   John Adams   John Marshall
Jay Treaty

## Explain

Cabinet   neutrality   Twelfth Amendment
negotiate   Federalists   states' rights
judicial review   Republicans

## Check Your Memory of the Facts

1. What were the major concerns of the new government as the United States began operating under the Constitution?
2. What three levels of federal courts were formed by the Judiciary Act of 1789?
3. What were the main parts of Hamilton's economic policy?
4. Where was the first capital of the United States? What other city served as capital before Washington, D.C.?
5. What were the first two national political parties started in the United States?
6. Why were the Alien and Sedition Acts passed?
7. How did the United States buy Louisiana?

## Check Your Understanding of the Ideas

1. Why did George Washington become the first President?
2. Why is a strong court system important for a nation?
3. What were the economic advantages of the Bank of the United States?
4. Why did the United States decide not to support France in its war with Britain?
5. In what way did the Pinckney Treaty help the United States?

6. Why did political parties form in the United States?
7. In what ways were the supporters of the Virginia and Kentucky Resolutions like those who opposed the ratification of the Constitution?
8. What was the significance of Thomas Jefferson's election in 1800?

## Expand Your Knowledge

1. Several new countries have come into existence since 1950. Choose one of these, and compare the way it has handled its economic problems with Hamilton's program.
2. Check on the treatment of opposition political parties in newly established countries today. Write a report on the information you find.

# Washington, D.C. 1800-1825

The United States government moved to the new federal city of Washington in 1800. In that year, the young city was a clear example of the difference that can exist between dreams and reality. In the dreams of government leaders, Washington was a magnificent capital with lovely parks, beautiful public buildings, and grand avenues. In reality, it was a small village of rough fields, half-finished buildings, and muddy paths.

There had been years of debate in Congress over the location of the nation's capital. No state wanted any other state to have special influence over the federal government. Congress had met in eight different cities, four different states. Moving became more difficult as the quantity of needed records grew. A compromise was finally reached that settled the question of a permanent location for the capital city. When southerners agreed to let the federal government assume the state debts of the Revolution, northerners agreed to have the capital located along the banks of the Potomac River.

Two states gave land to the government to form the federal District of Columbia. There, only Congress had control. The District was free of any single state's influence. The capital, built in the District, was available to people from the North, the South, and the rapidly growing West.

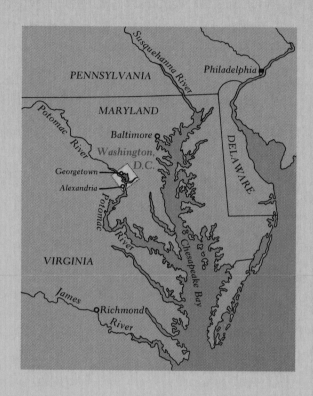

## Plans

President Washington selected the French engineer, Pierre Charles L'Enfant, to design the federal city in 1791. L'Enfant had come to America to serve in the Revolution. He wanted very much to design a great capital for the new nation. And on paper, his plans for the city of Washington were beautiful.

The survey work of marking the District's boundaries was done by Americans Andrew Ellicott and Benjamin Banneker. Banneker, a free black from Baltimore, was also an astronomer, mathematician, and scientist. The boundaries of the District of Columbia included the cities of George Town in Maryland and Alexandria in Virginia. The capital city itself was located next to George Town, on the Maryland side of the Potomac River.

L'Enfant planned Washington so that the three branches of the federal government were located in three separate areas of the city, according to their different constitutional duties. The building for the legislature, the Capitol, was on the highest point of land. A mile and a half away was the President's House, in the center of the executive area. From both of these, streets went out into the rest of the city. Pennsylvania Avenue was planned as a broad, stately connection between them. It would serve for ceremonial processions and would add dignity to the communication between the Congress and the President. The judicial building was to be in a third section of the city, away from these two main areas of traffic. The different buildings would be designed by different architects. By law, there could be no slave labor used to build the capital. Some slaves were hired out to do this work and earned money to buy their freedom.

## Money Problems

President Washington and the early sessions of Congress did not set aside any money for building the city because they thought it would pay for itself. Government leaders expected many people to move into the area and buy expensive lots for their homes and businesses. Profits from those sales would be used to pay for the public streets and buildings. That idea did not work. Few people came to the city at first, and even fewer of them invested their money in it. The total number of people working for the federal government at that time was very small. It was not easy for others to earn a living in Washington. There was not much business in providing for the needs of those who worked for the government. Carpenters, stonemasons, and people in the building trades even had difficulty finding steady work. Life in the new federal

city was certainly not as pleasant or profitable as it was in Philadelphia and the older American cities.

## Moving In

With only three months left to serve in his term, John Adams moved into the President's House in 1800. Abigail, his wife, arrived in November and described the city in a letter to her sister.

*As I expected to find it a new country, with Houses scatterd over a space of ten miles, and trees [and] stumps in plenty with, a castle of a house—so I found it—The Presidents House is in a beautifull situation in front of which is the Potomac. . . . The country around is romantic but a wild, a wilderness at present.*

*I have been to George Town. . . . It is only one mile from me but a quagmire [deep mud] after every rain. Here we are obliged to send daily for marketting; The capital is near two miles from us. . . . but I am determined to be satisfied and content, to say nothing of inconvenience. . . .*

Determined as she was, Abigail did mention some of the problems of living in a huge, unfinished house in another of her letters.

*The house is upon a grand and superb scale, requiring about thirty servants to attend and keep the apartments in proper order, and perform the ordinary business of the house and stables. . . . The lighting [of] the apartments, from the kitchen to parlours and chambers, is a tax indeed [so many candles are needed] . . . we are obliged to keep [fires going] to secure us from daily agues [chills and fevers]. . . . bells [to call the servants] are wholly [wholely] wanting, not one single one being hung through the whole house, and promises are all you can obtain. This is so* great an inconvenience, that I know not what to do, or how to do it. . . . if they will put me up some bells, and let me have wood enough to keep fires, I design to be pleased. I could content myself almost anywhere three months. . . . We have, indeed, come into a new country.

You must keep all this to yourself, and, when asked how I like it, say that I write you the situation [location] is beautiful, which is true. The house is made habitable, but there is not a single apartment finished. . . . We have not the least fence, yard, or other convenience . . . and the great unfinished audience-room [the East Room] I make a drying-room of, to hang up the clothes in. The principal stairs are not up, and will not be this winter.

## The Capitol

Members of Congress arrived in Washington after the fall harvest season. They found an unfinished Capitol with a few boarding houses close by it. One wing of the new building was almost completed. Its rooms were shared among the Senate, the House of Representatives, the Supreme Court, the courts of the District, and the new Library of Congress.

Unlike the members of the executive branch, the lawmakers usually came to their sessions alone. They left their families behind since Congress met for only a few months of the year. Most of the members lived in the boarding houses, and their social life generally centered around the dinner tables there. Travel around the city was difficult during the day and dangerous at night. There were no real streets, only fields and a few paths. In most areas, the ground was not even leveled to make walking easier.

*The Capitol from Pennsylvania Avenue in 1812*

Margaret Bayard Smith, wife of the city's first newspaper editor, wrote a letter that described the dangers of traveling at night. Thomas Law, a friend, had built a new house:

*This out-of-the-way-house to which Mr. Law removed, was separated from the most inhabited part of the city by old fields and waste grounds broken up by deep gulleys or ravines over which there was occasionally a passable road. The election of President by Congress was then pending, one vote given or withheld would decide the question between Mr. Jefferson and Mr. Burr. Mr. Bayard from Delaware held that vote. He with other influential and leading members [of Congress] went to a ball given by Mr. Law.*

*The night was dark and rainy, and on their attempt to return home, the coachman lost his way, and until daybreak was driving about this waste and broken ground and if not overturned into the deep gullies was momentarily in danger of being so, an accident which would most probably have cost some of the gentlemen their lives, and as it so happened that the company in the coach consisted of Mr. Bayard and three other members of Congress who had a leading and decisive influence in this difficult crisis of public affairs, the loss of either, might have turned the scales . . . and Mr. Burr [would have] been elected to the Presidency. . . .*

## Slow Growth

During Jefferson's administration, Congress did provide three thousand dollars to improve Pennsylvania Avenue and to plant trees along it. In general, however, little progress was made in completing the city. Poverty and unemployment were serious problems in Washington from its beginning. By 1802, over 40 percent of the city's funds were put into helping the poor.

The city's founders had expected a very rapid growth in population, especially by people with money to invest. But in twenty years' time, the total number of people who lived in the capital had increased by just ten thousand people, most of them poor. Free blacks were the only group within Washington that grew quickly in number. The city did allow slavery, and most citizens did not seem to have strong antislavery feelings. But Washington did not force slaves to leave the area when they were freed, as most of the southern states did. The city also had not made laws that stopped the growth of independent churches and schools for blacks. In general, most free black families felt safer in Washington than in other southern American cities. By 1820, the number of free blacks almost equaled the number of slaves. By 1840, their number was four times larger than the number of slaves.

The commerce and industry that was expected by the city's planners did not develop. George Town and Alexandria competed for most of the business in the District. Congress seldom provided funds for work on the public properties. The experiment of establishing a magnificent federal city seemed to be a failure. Political scientist James Sterling Young suggests that the main problem was a lack of interest on the part of most Americans in a government that was located out of their way.

*For the government of Jeffersonian times was not, by any candid [honest] view, one of the important institutions in American society—important as a social presence or important in its impact upon the everyday lives of the citizens. It was, for one thing, too new, an unfamiliar social presence in a society whose ways of living and whose organization of affairs had developed over a century without any national governmental institution. . . .*

*What government business there was was not, most of it, of a sort to attract any widespread, sustained [long lasting] citizen interest.*

Growth was so slow for the capital that some people continued to believe that the federal government should move back to a larger city. To many people, the burning of Washington's government buildings by the British forces in 1814 seemed to be the final blow. Margaret Smith expressed those feelings in her writings:

*The Capitol after the fire in 1814*

Thursday. . . . This morning on awakening we were greeted with the sad news, that our city was taken, the bridges and public buildings burnt, our troops flying in every direction. Our little army totally dispersed [scattered].

. . . I do not suppose Government will ever return to Washington. All those whose property was invested in that place, will be reduced to poverty. . . .

Tuesday [August] 30. Here we are, once more restored to our home. . . . The blast has pass'd by, without devastating this spot. . . . The poor capitol! nothing but its blacken'd walls remained! 4 or 5 houses in the neighbourhood were likewise in ruins. . . . We afterwards look'd at the other public buildings, but none were so thoroughly destroy'd as the House of Representatives and the President's House. Those beautiful pillars in that Representatives Hall were crack'd and broken, the roof, that noble dome, painted and carved with such beauty and skill, lay in ashes in the cellars. . . . In the P.H. [President's House] not an inch, but its crack'd and blacken'd walls remain'd. That scene, which when I last visited it, was so splendid . . . was now nothing but ashes. . . .

## Recovery

But the government did return to Washington. That same September, President and Mrs. Madison moved into a house in the city, and the President worked from there. Members of Congress came back to the city for a special session. They met in the only government building that had not been damaged, the Post Office. There, after three weeks of debate, the House of Representatives voted eighty-three to fifty-four that the federal government would stay in Washington. City bankers offered a loan to start the work of rebuilding. Three and a half months later, the Senate finally agreed.

## Adams to Adams

In 1818, James and Elizabeth Monroe moved into the White House, as it was beginning to be called. Its outside walls had been freshly painted white to cover the marks from the British fire. Both wings of the Capitol were finished by then. Work had begun on the center section. Washington still had no street lights, no sewer system, no city water system. Water was carried from wells in the center of the city or from the nearby creek. There were still open fields where cattle and hogs ran free. But there was a stronger feeling that the federal capital of Washington, D.C., was in place to stay.

John Quincy Adams moved into the White House just twenty-five years after his parents had lived in it. There was still no fence, but the grounds had been made smoother for walking. Most of the White House rooms were finished enough to be used. Louisa Adams, unlike Abigail, could use the great "audience-room" for public receptions instead of drying the family's clothes in it. A quarter of a century had passed since the government first moved to the District of Columbia. There was still a very strong contrast between the original dream and the reality of the capital city, but a beginning had been made. Washington, as a city, would move a little closer to the dream in the years to come.

*The city of Washington, D.C.*

# Americans All

Aim: to improve student understanding of sectionalism and nationalism as both uniting and dividing forces.

In the years following the Revolution, a new generation was taking over in America. By 1809, most Americans were young people who had little or no memory of the hard times faced before and during the Revolution. They were ambitious, hopeful, and proud Americans, certain of being able to get ahead in their growing nation. The thought of war did not frighten them. Many were ready to follow the so-called "War

*In the early 1800's, many Americans felt a growing sense of unity as the new nation became strong. Independence had been established, and they were governing themselves. There were strong feelings of pride, hope, and adventure. The spirit of this period is shown in the painting by George Caleb Bingham, "Jolly Flatboatmen in Port."*

Hawks," John C. Calhoun, Henry Clay, and others. These people believed that war was the answer to the problem of protecting American neutrality.

Might discuss the irony in idea of war as solution to protecting neutrality.

# Weakening American Neutrality

The long war between the British and the French had brought both prosperity and problems for the United States. During Jefferson's presidency, both sides allowed American merchant ships to trade with their West Indian islands. Both sides also bought American goods in Europe. Yet, each side tried to keep the United States from trading with the other. The British and the French were slowly hurting the American merchants by capturing ships that were trading with the other side.

The British angered the Americans in another way. They stopped American ships and took members of the crew whom they said were British. These sailors were made to serve on British warships. The removal of sailors from their ships in this way was called impressment. Often the sailors were British, but sometimes they were Americans. Many Americans had to serve for long terms before they were freed.

Royal Navy was losing about 2,500 sailors a year through desertion.

In 1807, the British fired on a ship of the American navy, the U.S.S. *Chesapeake,* and forced some of its sailors into the British navy. Many American people were so angry about the impressment that they would gladly have gone to war. President Jefferson, however, tried to avoid war, and he asked Congress to pass the Embargo Act of 1807. The embargo was an order that forbade American ships from leaving for any foreign port. Jefferson was trying to deal with the British (and the French) just as the colonists had in the days before the Revolution. He hoped he could force them to respect America by refusing to sell them American goods.

The embargo actually harmed American farmers and merchants even more than it did other countries. It was such a failure that Congress ended it just before Jefferson left office. New laws were passed that allowed Americans to trade with any nations except England and France. Then in 1810, Congress decided to allow trade with either England or France if either of them agreed to respect American rights. When that happened, Americans would promise not to trade with the other country. Napoleon and the French pretended to go along with this, and the United States cut off trade with Britain. By 1812, England was so hurt by the American boycott that it repealed its laws against American shipping.

# Pressure for War

The people of the United States were determined to protect American rights on the sea. But much of the pressure for war also came from the western and southern frontiers which were not on the coast. Protecting national pride was one reason that these frontier settlers wanted war. But they had other reasons as well. These were hard times for farmers. Some settlers wanted to take over the good lands held by Spain in the South, by Britain in the North (Canada), and by the Indians in the West.

During this time, settlers were rapidly moving across the Appalachian Mountains, pushing the Indians off land which was wanted for farming. As they were pushed westward, groups of Indians were crowded against each other and frightened of losing their individual

## Tecumseh

Tecumseh, the son of a Shawnee chief, was born in Ohio in 1768. His name meant shooting star. He soon rose to become a leader of the eastern American Indians.

Tecumseh was concerned because white settlers in America were rapidly taking Indian lands. He believed that all land, like water and air, belonged to all Indians and could not be sold by one group. In 1808, Tecumseh and the Prophet, with their followers, were forced by white settlers to move into Indiana. A gifted speaker, Tecumseh urged Indians to join together in a confederation. In this way, they could work together to return to Indian ways of life and to prevent more loss of Indian lands.

The Indians established a large camp in Indiana. American troops fought and defeated them there in 1811 at the Battle of Tippecanoe. When the War of 1812 began, Tecumseh believed that the British would support the Indians' desire to keep their lands. So he and his followers joined the British. The next year, American forces defeated them in the Battle of the Thames. Tecumseh was killed in that battle, and his confederation was destroyed.

Tecumseh was described as a tall man with intense eyes. He was forty-five years old when he died. His life had been filled with acts of strength, courage, pride, and compassion.

ways of life. Tecumseh, chief of the Shawnees, and his brother, the Prophet, tried to bring all the Indians together in 1811. To resist further losses, the Indians along the northern and southern frontiers joined to form a confederation.

*Tecumseh*

Along the frontier, the settlers were afraid that they would be attacked by the Indians. They thought that England was encouraging the Indians to fight and that the Spanish were also backing the Indians. Frontier forces under General William Henry Harrison fought and defeated the Indians in the Battle of Tippecanoe in western Indiana. The "War Hawks" in Congress blamed the British for the trouble with the Indians and called again for war against England.

Tecumseh was not in camp when the Prophet led the Indians into this battle.

# The War of 1812

In June, 1812, President James Madison finally asked Congress to declare war against Britain. The vote was seventy-nine to forty-nine in the House of Representatives and nineteen to thirteen in the Senate. If Congress had known that the British were repealing their laws against American shipping, it probably would not have voted for war. When the news finally did arrive, the war had already started. Because the British were still taking American sailors from American ships, the United States let the war continue. Besides, Americans still wanted to conquer Canada.

The War of 1812 did not go well for the United States. The first moves against Canada failed, and the British soon took over Detroit. Not until the following year was there an American victory, in a battle

*American forces held out against heavy bombing at Fort McHenry. They inspired Key to write the "Star Spangled Banner."*

fought on Lake Erie. Captain Oliver H. Perry and his crews of young white and black sailors defeated a British fleet there. The next month, General Harrison defeated the British and the Indians in the Battle of the Thames, north of Lake Erie in Canada. In that battle, Tecumseh was killed, and so was any chance of a strong Indian confederation.

There were few other land victories, but the U.S.S. *Constitution* thrilled Americans with its great success at sea. Nicknamed "Old Ironsides," the ship won many battles against the British. Then, in 1813, the British blocked the American coasts with their strong navy, and American ships were bottled up in the harbors.

More British troops sailed to America in 1814 after the defeat of Napoleon in Europe. The new forces attacked Washington, D.C., and burned the Capitol and the White House. When the British tried to enter Baltimore, American volunteers at Fort McHenry turned them back. During that three-day British bombing, Francis Scott Key wrote the "Star Spangled Banner," which later became the national anthem of the United States.

Many people in New England were against the war from the start. During the first year, they went on trading with the British. In the fall of 1814, New England Federalists met at the Hartford Convention. There they voiced their dislike of the way President Madison was running the war. Later, it was falsely charged that they had planned to leave the Union.

It was at this low point that a treaty of peace was signed. The British, tired of fighting wars in Europe for twenty years, were eager for peace. America needed to begin trading with Europe once again. So in Ghent, Belgium, on December 24, 1814, a treaty was finally signed. It returned all land boundaries to what they had been when the war began, but it said nothing about American rights on the sea.

Before the news of the peace treaty could reach the United States, American forces under General Andrew Jackson fought and won the Battle of New Orleans. General Jackson had been fighting Indians in

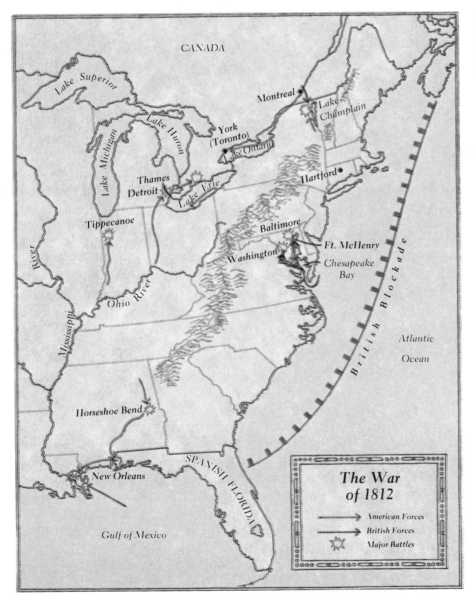

Could assign reports on individual battles. Note blockade area. Later compare to Union blockade, map p. 251, to show growth of U.S.

the Mississippi Territory in 1814. He had defeated the Creek Indians in the Battle of Horseshoe Bend and went on to take over Pensacola in Spanish Florida. At the end of 1814, Jackson and his troops moved west to defend New Orleans. The British troops were well trained and experienced from the war against Napoleon. Most of the soldiers that Jackson was able to gather, including two black battalions, had little experience in battle. The British thought they would have no trouble, but everything went wrong for them. In the end, while two thousand British were killed or wounded, less than a hundred American lives were lost.

# Results of the War

Because of the Battle of New Orleans, Americans thought they had won the War of 1812. Even though they gained no land, they felt much had been won. The power of the Indians east of the Mississippi River had been crushed. Settlement of the lands there could go ahead quickly. Nothing had been done about American neutrality rights, but in the years of peace that followed, this was no longer a problem.

The War of 1812 is sometimes called the "Second War of American Independence." For a century after 1812, the absence of European wars which involved America gave the people and the country a chance to develop. The close of the war began a period of strong national pride under the direction of the Republican party. The war had one other result. The Federalist party was looked upon as disloyal because of the Hartford Convention. The party weakened, and soon it was gone.

# Nationalism and Sectionalism

In the years after the war, two opposing forces developed in America which worked to both unite and divide the country. These forces were nationalism and sectionalism. Nationalism is a feeling of pride in the nation as a whole and loyalty to its goals. Sectionalism is a feeling of pride in a particular part of the country and loyalty to its goals. Sometimes sectionalism works against the good of the nation. Americans were proud of their success in the War of 1812 and in the country's growth and development. Each section of the country, however,

# Nationalism

Mary Jane Watson came to live in America with her parents in the early 1820's. She wrote a letter to her grandparents in 1825, expressing her confidence in the future of America.

*... It would be very agreeable for me to see my English friends, but I don't wish to return to England again. I like America much the best; it is a very plentiful country. . . .*

*My father is doing very well and is ... satisfied to stay in this country. He has got a cow ... and nine hogs. . . .*

*I have been very fortunate. I have got good clothes, and I can dress as well as any [upper-class woman] in Sedlescomb. I can enjoy a silk and white frock and crepe veil. . . . You cannot tell the poor from the rich here; they are dressed as good as the other. . . .*

*Any respectable person may get a good living by industry. It is a good place for young people; they can get good wages for their work. . . .*

*The people here are very good about education, much more so than they are in England.*

had its own special interests. People were often more concerned with the interests of their section than with those of the nation.

A spirit of nationalism was behind the program that President Madison presented to Congress in 1816, at the close of the war. He asked for a new Bank of the United States, a protective tariff, and federal grants to build roads and canals. All of these were designed to help the country as a whole, but different sections either favored or opposed them.

## A New Bank

A new Bank of the United States was needed because the charter of the first Bank had run out before the war. Without the Bank, the federal government had no safe place to deposit its money. Also, there was no way to make sure that the state banks issued secure paper money. These banks did not always have enough gold or silver to back up their paper money. Merchants across the country had to read lists which told how much a state bank's money was really worth before they would accept payment with it.

Congress passed a bill chartering a new Bank for a period of twenty years. The Bank was strong and had many branches in different states.

*McCullock v. Maryland, 1819*, decision was that states could not tax federal enterprise because "the power to tax involves the power to destroy." Also supported implied powers view of Constitution: since Congress was given authority to coin money, authority to establish bank was implied.

The money it issued was secure, and it had control over the less stable state banks. Like the first Bank of the United States, it helped business prosper and strengthened the country's economy.

The state banks, both the weak ones and the strong ones, did not like the wealth and power of the Bank of the United States. State governments tried to drive out branches of the Bank by demanding heavy taxes from it. The Supreme Court, which was following a policy of nationalism, decided that it was unconstitutional for state governments to tax the Bank.

# The Tariff of 1816

A protective tariff is a tax on imported goods. To pay for this tax, either the foreign seller or the American merchant must raise the price of the goods. The tax or tariff protects a country's industries because it encourages people to buy goods made at home since they usually cost less than the imported goods whose price included the tariff.

During the War of 1812, when British imports had been cut off, many new factories were started, primarily in New England. After the war, the British sent great amounts of cotton, woolen, and iron goods to the United States, hoping to force the new American factories out of business. Owners of New England cotton and woolen mills, iron manufacturers from Pennsylvania, and western suppliers of these new factories demanded a protective tariff. Congress passed the Tariff of 1816 which protected cotton, woolen, and iron manufacturing.

Sections of the country were split on their feelings about the tariff. Daniel Webster, from New England, said that the tariff would hurt American trade with other countries. John C. Calhoun, from South Carolina, was for the tariff because he hoped to see factories started in his state. Yet other southerners, who sold their crops in England, were against the tariff.

# Roads and Canals

The third part of Madison's plan was a program to build national roads and canals. Better transportation would improve trade and manufacturing. Factories could get raw materials and could send their products to market cheaper and faster. Calhoun, at this time a strong nationalist, and people from the West fought hard for this program.

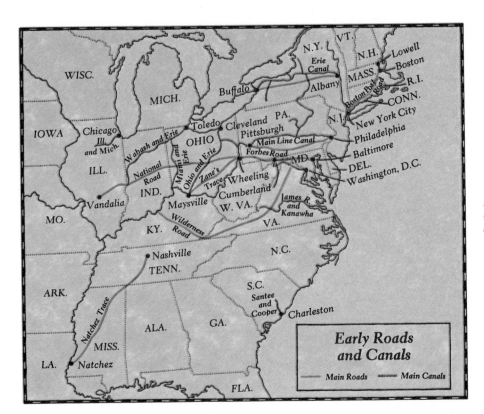

Modern state boundaries are shown in dotted line for convenience.

*A canal in Ohio was located near a river. The canal boats were pulled by horses or mules.*

People from New England where there already were good roads did not want to pay taxes to help build roads in other parts of the country. New York favored the program because it wanted federal money to help build the Erie Canal connecting New York City to the Great Lakes.

The road-building program moved ahead slowly. Only one important route to the West was finished. This was the Cumberland Road which was first planned in 1806. By 1818, it joined the Potomac River with the Ohio River. The Cumberland Road was also known as the National Road, and work on it continued into the 1840's. It slowly moved west, past the Ohio River, through Columbus, Ohio, and Indianapolis, Indiana, to Vandalia, Illinois.

State and sectional differences affected each part of the national program, and later on, some sections changed their points of view. The people of New York opposed federal aid for state programs after the Erie Canal was finished. The New England states later favored aid because better roads would improve their trade with the West. The South, not wishing to see New England trade with the West, went against federal aid for the states. Thus, the sections and the states switched their positions as their own economic needs changed.

Remind students that "the West" is a relative term, here meaning the lands west of Appalachian Mts.

*The National Road helped tie the West with the East in the early 1800's. The Fairview Inn was a typical stopping place on the road where travelers could rest and find refreshment.*

# Era of Good Feelings

While all this was going on, there was only one strong party in national politics, the Republicans. During the War of 1812, it had been strong enough to reelect President Madison. In 1816, its choice was one of the last of the leaders of the Revolution, James Monroe of Virginia. He easily won and, in 1820, was reelected with only a single electoral vote against him.

Because there was only one strong political party, Monroe's presidency has been called the "era of good feelings." It is not really a very correct name for these years. Although it was a time of national progress, sectionalism was beginning to divide the country.

# The West, Another Section

The West was settled rapidly after the War of 1812. Large numbers of Americans moved into the rich farmlands and booming towns. Great numbers of covered wagons carried trade goods and even whole families along the National Road to the Ohio River. From there, the goods and the settlers traveled by flatboats or steamboats. In 1807, Robert Fulton had built the first successful steamboat, and by 1830, there were nearly two hundred steamboats on western waters.

The quick settlement of the West helped increase feelings of both nationalism and sectionalism. Feelings of national pride grew strong. But Americans moving westward gave up their old state and sectional loyalties for new ones. Both north and south of the Ohio River, the new settlers felt they were westerners with interests that were different from those of easterners.

This difference was seen clearly in the Panic of 1819. After the War of 1812, many people bought large amounts of land in the West by paying for only part of the cost. Most settlers had large loans from western banks. By 1818, the new Bank of the United States, which had been losing money in its own deals, called on the state banks for the money they owed it. The banks did not have large amounts of cash on hand, and they had to call in the loans owed by the settlers. Many of the settlers could not pay and lost all they had. The western banks were forced to close. Westerners believed this Panic was caused by the Bank of the United States and eastern businesses. They felt a loyalty to their section and blamed their troubles on the East.

Two main factors of Panic were overextension of credit and wild land speculation.

# Slavery: A Growing Issue

Cotton was minor crop until the cotton gin. (See p. 219.) By 1825, it had become the nation's leading export. There were about 700,000 slaves in 1790. By 1860, there were almost 4 million, about 60% of whom worked in cotton growing or processing.

The growth of the West also made worse the sectional differences between the South and the North, the slave states and the free states. With the spread of cotton growing, slavery became more and more important to the South. During these same years, slavery was less important in the more industrial North. Representatives of the slave and free states in Congress had always protected the interests of their own sections. There was an uneasy balance of power in the Senate where slave states and free states had been admitted in equal numbers. In 1819, there were twenty-two senators from the North and twenty-two from the South. Things were different in the House of Representatives. By 1820, the faster growing North had 105 representatives while there were only 81 from the South.

When Missouri applied for admission as a slave state in 1819, Congress saw that it would upset the balance that existed in the Senate. Representative James Tallmadge of New York asked for an amendment to the Missouri Statehood Bill. It said that slaves could not be brought into Missouri and the children of slaves already there would become free at the age of twenty-five.

Slavery also existed in parts of the North until the 1860's.

The proposed Tallmadge Amendment led to bitter debate in Congress. Southerners attacked it because it was likely to stop the western spread of slavery. Northerners in Congress called slavery morally wrong, and southerners defended it. The debate became so hot that Speaker of the House Henry Clay said, "The words civil war and disunion are uttered almost without emotion."

# The Missouri Compromise

Clay was able to work out a solution to the immediate problem. It is called the Missouri Compromise. According to it, Missouri was admitted as a slave state. To balance Missouri, Maine, which had been part of Massachusetts, entered the Union as a free state. Most important was the part of the compromise about the future of slavery in the West. A line was drawn west from the southern border of Missouri. Slavery was not allowed in the territory north of this line. South of it, slavery was allowed.

In the territory divided by the line, there was room for many free states but only one slave state, Arkansas. Because of this, southerners were not happy over the compromise. Many Americans, both in the North and the South, felt that the slavery problem had not been solved. They believed that Missouri was only the beginning of serious conflict over slavery. Jefferson said the slavery debate was like a "fireball in the night . . . the knell [funeral bell] of the Union."

# Foreign Affairs

Americans agreed more often about national policies in foreign affairs. Northerners were pleased by the Rush-Bagot Agreement of 1817 with Great Britain. In it, both the United States and England agreed to limit their navies on the Great Lakes. Eventually, forts on both sides of the border between the United States and Canada were closed.

*This treaty began the eventual demilitarization of entire U.S.-Canadian border. Might tie in to "arms limitation talks" of today.*

Other problems with Britain were also settled in later agreements. The northern boundary of the United States was set along the forty-ninth parallel from Lake of the Woods in Minnesota to the top of the Rocky Mountains. The great Oregon Country stretched beyond, and both the United States and Britain claimed it. The two countries agreed to hold Oregon jointly for ten years.

Southerners were pleased when Florida was added to the United States in 1819. Spain had only weak control over the area. Planters in the South said that bands of unfriendly Indians and escaped slaves were crossing the border from Spanish Florida and attacking them. In 1816, General Jackson fought the Indians and the blacks there in the first Seminole War. He put to death two British persons who were helping the Seminoles and captured the Spanish capital at Pensacola. Secretary of State John Quincy Adams upheld Jackson's actions. Adams warned Spain it must police Florida or give it to the United States. In 1819, Spain turned over Florida to the United States which, in return, gave up its weak claims to Texas. The United States government also agreed to pay, for Spain, five million dollars worth of the claims that Americans held against the Spanish government.

*Spanish Florida came to the U.S. through Adams-Onís Treaty. Mexico declared independence from Spain in 1821. Florida organized as U.S. territory in 1822 with Andrew Jackson appointed governor.*

# The Monroe Doctrine

Americans were pleased when President Monroe stated an American policy which later became known as the Monroe Doctrine. Many South American countries had recently won their independence from Spain. Some European nations were thinking of helping Spain reconquer these lands. Monroe's statement was a warning to European powers to keep "hands off" the South American countries. It was also a warning to Russia not to try to move into the area along the Pacific

*European monarchies especially interested because of threat these new republics represented to their forms of government.*

Coast below Alaska, which Russia already held. President Monroe stated this policy in a message to Congress in December, 1823. He said that the Americas "are henceforth not to be considered as subjects for future colonization by any European powers." The United States would not enter into any European quarrels. European governments must, therefore, not interfere with the nations in the New World.

Americans were proud of Monroe's policy statement, but at the time, it was not greatly respected in Europe. European nations left the Latin American nations alone mostly because the British, too, had warned them to keep away. British warnings were backed by a strong navy. It was not until a generation later that the Monroe Doctrine came to be a powerful force in American foreign policy that was respected outside the Americas.

The forces of nationalism and sectionalism were at work during these years. Most often, the national forces won over the sectional ones. The country was growing rapidly, and national habits were forming. In the way they earned their livings, governed themselves, talked, worshipped, and in their confidence in the future of the country, the people of this generation were proving themselves Americans all.

# Chapter 8 in Perspective  See Teacher's Manual, page 81T.

## Identify

| | | |
|---|---|---|
| Tecumseh | John C. Calhoun | James Monroe |
| James Madison | Erie Canal | Henry Clay |
| Battle of New Orleans | National Road | Seminole War |

## Explain

| | | |
|---|---|---|
| War Hawks | nationalism | Panic of 1819 |
| impressment | sectionalism | Missouri Compromise |
| embargo | protective tariff | Monroe Doctrine |

# Check Your Memory of the Facts

1. Who were the leaders who urged the United States to go to war to solve the problem of neutrality rights?
2. What actions by the British and the French angered Americans?
3. What happened to the U.S.S. *Chesapeake?* How did Americans react?
4. Why did the United States go to war against Britain in 1812?
5. Who were the American military leaders in the War of 1812?
6. Why was a new Bank of the United States needed?
7. What were the major routes taken by travelers to the West?
8. What was the main point of the Monroe Doctrine?

# Check Your Understanding of the Ideas

1. How successful was President Jefferson's plan to force the British and French to respect American neutrality rights?
2. What did the United States gain in the peace treaty ending the War of 1812?
3. How did the War of 1812 affect the two major political parties, the Federalists and the Republicans?
4. What were the reactions of the sections of the United States to the issues of the Bank, the protective tariff, and federal grants to build roads and canals?
5. What changes were made in the boundaries of the United States in the years following the War of 1812?
6. What actions by Americans during the period reflect strong feelings of nationalism? What actions reflect strong sectionalism?

# Expand Your Knowledge

1. Dramatize a meeting of Tecumseh and William Henry Harrison to discuss their differences. Three or four students should represent each side. Prepare a speech to show your point of view.
2. Prepare a report on changing fashions for men and women from the colonial period to the beginning of the nineteenth century. Illustrate your report with pictures or drawings of the typical styles.
3. Between 1810 and 1824, several Spanish colonies in Latin America established their independence. Find information in the library on the dates, the leaders, and the government organized in each new country. Compare these revolutions with the American Revolution.

# New Orleans 1840-1855

By the middle of the nineteenth century, New Orleans was the busiest port city in the southern United States. It was located on the banks of the lower Mississippi River, about one hundred miles north of the Gulf of Mexico. People from France made the first permanent settlement there where American Indian trade routes crossed. The United States government bought New Orleans and the whole Louisiana Territory in 1803. By 1840, New Orleans was the third largest city in the country.

## The Levees

The city was built on low land, almost as low as the river level in some areas. When northern snows melted in the spring, the river overflowed its banks and flooded many parts of the city. Early settlers began building walls of earth, or levees, to keep back the spring floods. In later years, more earth was added to the levees, and the walls grew high and wide. As the levees got wider, roads and warehouses were built on them. Ships and boats of all kinds were tied up at the docks along the levees. There the cargoes, or goods from the ships, were picked up or deposited. In New Orleans, the richest cargoes were usually those like Kentucky tobacco, Ohio flour, and cotton and sugar from plantations in Mississippi, Georgia, and Louisiana. Workers, called stevedores, moved the goods between the ships and warehouses. From New Orleans, the cargoes were carried in larger ships to the West Indies, Central and South America, Europe, and Africa. Goods brought to New Orleans from other countries were loaded onto steamboats and carried up the Mississippi River to other parts of the United States and to Canada.

Visitors always found the levee exciting. Oakey Hall, from New York, wrote a description of the activity there in 1851:

*A wilderness of ships and steamboats skirt it—if 'tis early morning. If but one short hour after sun-rise, the decks and wharfs are all astir, processions of loaded drays [heavy wagons] are going by. . . . Thousands of hogsheads [barrels], bales, and bags and packages . . . sailors; stevedores; steamboat hands; clerks; planters; wealthy merchants too; running to and fro with [many] projects in their head. . . . A million dollars could not buy the articles of traffic [trade goods] taken in at one glance; articles of traffic that before twenty-four hours have gone by will all have disappeared. . . . Above the tornado noise and bustle can be plainly heard the hailing among water craft; the bell-ringings of arriving and outgoing steamboats. . . .*

*The levee in New Orleans*

"How do you like the city?" inquires an old resident. While you hesitate for an answer, himself replies:

"Excellently, of course; fine commercial advantages, eh?—the store-house of the Mississippi Valley—great destiny ahead."

## Things French

Immigrants as well as visitors came in large numbers to New Orleans. Irish, German, Mexican, Italian, West Indian, and other people came to escape from starvation or political dangers in their home countries. Some stayed a short time in the city and then moved on to live in other places. Many chose to live in New Orleans or could not afford to leave it. They added their customs and languages to the culture of the city.

The culture of New Orleans was different from most other cities in the United States. In other large cities, the most powerful groups in social and political life were the Anglo-Americans. These were the people whose first language was English and whose customs were most like the Anglo-Saxon people of Great Britain. In New Orleans, the main influence over the general culture was held by the French Creoles. Creoles were the children and grandchildren of the early French and Spanish settlers.

In general, many people copied Anglo business ideas and Creole social ways. French was the language used by the rich. Legal cases were handled more often in that language than in English. Many who could afford it sent their children to schools in Paris. People bought French furniture for their homes and tried to dress in the latest French fashions. There was strong competition between the Creoles and the Anglos to build bigger and better homes, hotels, theaters, restaurants, and amusement or vacation areas. Other peoples' ways also influenced the Creoles and Anglos. For example, the most famous food served in restaurants was often seafood from the Gulf of Mexico, cooked in French ways and seasoned with American Indian and West African spices.

By the time of the Civil War, Creole influence had weakened, and New Orleans had become more English (or Anglo). The poet Walt Whitman was in New Orleans in 1848. Some years later, he wrote:

*Sundays I sometimes went forenoons to the old Catholic Cathedral in the French quarter. I used to walk a good deal in this* [area]; *and I have deeply regretted since that I did not cultivate, while I had such a good opportunity, the chance of better knowledge of French and Spanish Creole New Orleans people. (I have an idea that there is much and of importance about the Latin race contributions to American nationality in the South and Southwest that will never be put with sympathetic understanding and tact on record.)*

## Blacks in the City

New Orleans was one of the main slave markets in the United States. Black people were traded between plantation owners and sent to work in Georgia, Mississippi, and other southern states. Most of the slaves who lived in the city were house servants. The owners, who were whites and sometimes free blacks, made money by having their slaves trained in skilled work and then hiring them out to work for others. As a result, some slaves were more highly skilled than many of the white immigrants who came to the city looking for jobs. In the 1840's and 1850's, whites had laws passed that limited the types of jobs blacks could hold.

Sunday was a holiday for slaves in New Orleans. Many of them spent their time in Congo Square where they sang and danced in West African tradition. Some blacks in New Orleans continued to practice non-Christian religions brought from Africa and the West Indies. Most blacks attended Christian churches, usually Catholic, sometimes Baptist and Methodist. The Catholic church services were attended by whites and blacks together. In other services, blacks usually were separated from whites. New Orleans also had a few churches that were only for blacks.

There were about ten thousand free blacks living in the city. Some of them were very successful in business and the arts. Cecee Macarthy started an import business that was worth more than $150,000 by the time she died in 1845. Armand Lanusse was a famous poet, and inventions of Norbert Rillieux were of value to the sugar industry.

As individuals, free white and black people in New Orleans often respected each other. Free blacks lived on the same city streets as whites. When they could afford it, they sent their children to private schools in America and France. As a group, however, the whites had almost all of the power and wealth. By the 1850's, more laws were passed to limit the free blacks.

## The Young People

Eliza Ripley wrote a book about her life as a child in New Orleans. Her story has many examples of what it was like to grow up in that city.

"Children should be seen and not heard." Children were neither seen nor heard in the days of which I write, the days of 1840. They led the simple life. . . .

Children's clothes were homemade. A little wool shawl for [a girl's] shoulders did duty for common use. A pelisse [a long cloak with fur trim] made out of an old one of mother's, or some remnant found in the house, was fine for Sunday wear. . . . Our dresses were equally simple and equally "cut down and made over. . . ."

Every woman had to sew. There were well-trained seamstresses in every house; no "ready-mades," no machines. Imagine the fine hand-sewing. . . . I can hear my mother's voice now, "Be careful in the stitching . . . take up two and skip four," which I early learned meant the threads of the linen.

## Fun and Games

Our amusements were of the simplest. My father's house on Canal Street had a flat roof, well protected by [walls], so it furnished a grand playground for the children of the neighborhood . . . where all could romp and jump rope to their heart's content. . . . It could not have been much beyond Claiborne Street that we children went

*The French Market*

*crawfishing in the ditches . . . for we walked, and it was not considered far. . . .*

*Sometimes I was permitted to go to market with John, way down to the old French Market. We had to start early, before the shops on Chartres Street were open, and the boys busy with scoops watered the roadway from brimming gutters [to settle the dust]. John and I hurried past. Once at market we rushed from stall to stall, filling our basket, John forgetting nothing that had been ordered, and always carefully remembering one most important item, the saving of at least a picayune [Spanish nickel] out of the market money for a cup of coffee at Manette's stall. I drank half the coffee and took one of the little cakes. John finished . . . the cup, and with the remark, "We won't say anything about this," we started toward home. We had to stop, though, at a bird store, on the square above the Cathedral, look at the birds, [tease] the noisy parrots, watch the antics of the monkeys, and see the man hang up his string of corals and fix his shells in the window, ready for the day's business. We could scarcely tear ourselves away, it was so interesting; but a reminder that the wax head at Dr. De Leon's dentist's door would be "put out by this time," hurried me to see that wonderful [thing] open and shut its mouth, first with a row of teeth, then revealing an empty cavern. How I watched, wondered and admired that awfully artificial wax face! These occasional market trips—and walks with older members of the family—were the sum of my or any other child's recreation.*

## School and Private Lessons

*. . . there have always been schools and schools. . . . not that I ever entered one of them, but I had girl friends in all [of them]. In the [1830's, Mister] St. Angelo had a school on Customhouse Street. . . . His method of teaching may have been all right, but his discipline was objectionable; he had the delinquent pupils kneel on brickdust and tacks and there study aloud the neglected lesson. . . .[He] retired from the business before the forties. . . .*

*In 1842 there was a class in Spanish at Mr. Hennen's house. . . . I was ten years old, but was allowed to join with some other members of my family, though my mother protested it was nonsense for a child like me and a waste of money. Father did not agree with her, and after over sixty years to think it over, I don't either. . . . years and years thereafter . . . while traveling in Mexico, some of the señor's teaching came [like a miracle] back to me, bringing with it enough Spanish to be of material help in that stranger country.*

Eliza and her friends also had private lessons in music, singing, and dancing. Teachers were hired to give children lessons in polite manners. They were expected to learn how to walk gracefully and how to bow and curtsy properly. Eliza later wrote:

*Is it any surprise that the miscellaneous education we girls of seventy years ago in New Orleans had access to, [ended] by fitting us for housewives and mothers, instead of [also teaching us to be] writers and platform speakers, doctors and lawyers. . . ?*

## The Homes

*People had candelabras. . . . The candles in those gorgeous stands and an oil lamp on the [usual] center-table were supposed to furnish abundance of light for any occasion. . . . Two candles without shades—nobody had heard of shades—were [enough] for an ordinary tea table. . . . People sewed, embroidered, read and wrote and played*

The city of New Orleans on the Mississippi River

chess evenings by candlelight, and except a few near-sighted people and the aged no one used glasses.

... Everybody in my early day had black haircloth furniture; maybe that was one reason red curtains were preferred. ... However, as no moth [ate] it, dust did not rest on its slick, shiny surface, and it lasted forever, it had its advantages. [Many people had] a haircloth sofa, with a couple of hard, round pillows of the same ... too slippery to nap on. ...

Butler's pantry! My stars! Who ever heard of a butler's pantry, and sinks, and running water, and faucets inside houses? The only running water was a hydrant in the yard [connected to the city water pipes]; the only sink was the gutter in the yard; the sewer was the gutter in the street. ... To be sure there was a cistern [tank] for rainwater,

and jars. ... Those earthen jars were [refilled] from the hydrant. ...

Of course, every house had a storeroom ... lined with shelves. ... We had wire [boxes] on the back porch and a [metallined] box for the ice. ... Ice was in general use but very expensive. It was brought by ship from the North. ...

For the kitchen there were open fireplaces with a pot hanging from a crane, skillets [frying pans] and spiders [skillets with legs]. ...

There were [steel knives] and they had to be daily scoured with "plenty of brickdust on your knife board". ... There [were] few pictures, nothing ornamental in the parlors.

... I feel I am going way back beyond the [memory] of my readers, but some of the grandmothers ... can recall just such a life, a life that will never be lived again.

# Forming American Habits

**9**

Many of the qualities now called "typically American" could be seen in the people of the United States between 1820 and 1840. Ordinary, average Americans, from city workers to farmers, became the center of attention in political and social life. Laws were made or changed to give more people a vote in local and national elections. Opportunities for education became available to more people. The works of writers, artists, and musicians showed scenes from everyday life. Many

*In the early 1800's, many Americans were interested and involved in politics for the first time. John L. Krimmel reflected the excitement of the period in his painting, "Election Day at the State House, Philadelphia."*

people in the United States gained a new feeling of influence and power in the affairs of their country. In the 1830's, Alexis de Tocqueville wrote:

Might remind students of de Tocqueville, p. 3.

> . . . in the United States . . . society governs itself for itself. . . .
> The people reign in the American political world. . . . They
> are the cause and the aim of all things; everything comes
> from them, and everything is absorbed in them.

# Practice in Democracy

In the early 1800's, all of the women, Indians, slaves, and most of the free black men in the United States could not vote or hold public office. Politics and government were controlled by educated, rich people. Older state laws had limited voting to only those white men with property or who belonged to a certain religion. In the territories, however, a person's ability was more important than property, religion, education, or family ties. As the territories became states, their laws allowed almost any white male citizen to vote or hold office. Slowly, the laws of older states also were changed to agree with those of the new states. The states also changed the way they chose the electors who voted for President and Vice-President. The electors had been picked by the state legislatures. Under the new laws, citizens voted directly for the electors. The total number of voters in the United States had grown by the 1830's, and their influence had increased.

Rule of elite based on attitude that general public lacked judgment and information.

Refer to p. 122 on electoral system. Winner of popular state vote usually took all of state's electoral votes. Might use mock election results to help students understand that a candidate can win majority of popular vote and lose office by electoral vote.

State political leaders paid close attention to these new voters. They often praised "average Americans" in speeches to win their support and votes. Different opinions among the leaders and voters led to new rival parties within the states. These groups became organized and nominated candidates for local offices. When a party won an election, its leaders often rewarded party workers with government jobs. This practice of replacing job holders with members of the winning party is called the spoils system.

# The Election of 1824

In national politics at this time, Congress picked the candidates for President and Vice-President. The Republican party was the only party in Congress, and senators and representatives held a private meeting, or caucus, to decide their party's choices. By 1824, this method was not satisfactory to many leaders.

That year, some state leaders felt that the caucus choice, William Crawford of Georgia, would not help their interests. These states chose their own candidates. Leaders in New England were most interested in manufacturing and shipping. They wanted John Quincy Adams for President. Western leaders wanted better transportation and cheaper land prices for settlers. Some of them chose Henry Clay, and others picked Andrew Jackson. Southern leaders supported the caucus choice, Crawford. They wanted lower taxes on imported goods and more land for planting cotton.

None of these candidates won a majority of votes in the election. The House of Representatives had to choose the President from the top three, according to the plan in the Constitution. Jackson had received the largest number of votes. His supporters, the Jacksonians, expected him to be named President. But Clay, who came in fourth, encouraged his friends in the House to vote for Adams. Both Clay and Adams wanted a new protective tariff. The money from it would be used for canals and roads to join the different sections of the country.

With Clay's support, Adams was named President. Jacksonians in Congress were very angry. They worked against the new President and blocked almost all of his plans. Near the end of Adams' term in office, Congress did pass a high protective tariff on certain raw materials and woolen goods. This tariff of 1828 upset southern cotton growers even more than the earlier tariffs. Again, their direct trade with England was strongly affected.

# National Political Parties

Political disagreements like the one over the tariff helped to divide the Republican party further. The Jacksonians called themselves Democratic-Republicans. Others, including President Adams, used the name National-Republicans. These groups began to act more like separate parties when they selected their candidates for election.

In 1828, Adams and Jackson were the only candidates for President. Jacksonians worked hard to get people interested in the election, especially the "average American" voters. They held rallies and parades to make Jackson known to the people. At a time when many people were looking to the west, Andrew Jackson of Tennessee was an example of the western or frontier spirit. He had fought against the Indians to get their lands for white settlement. He was a military hero who, with Indian help, had defeated the British at the Battle of New Orleans. Three times more people voted in 1828 than had voted in 1824. Jackson won the election with a clear majority. His followers claimed his victory as the victory of the common people.

# Jackson as President

Andrew Jackson appealed to many voters because of his courage and daring in military battles. As leader of his party, he had an iron will in political battles, too. Jackson was a very strong President and had great influence on national politics. He used his veto power to control Congress. Before him, Presidents had vetoed bills only when they thought the bills were unconstitutional. Jackson did this, but he often gave strong political reasons as well. He vetoed more bills than all of the earlier Presidents. People who disagreed with Jackson called him "King Andrew."

Those who supported Jackson, the Democratic-Republicans, soon dropped the word Republicans. They have been known ever since as the Democrats. Those who were against Jackson, including the

Might compare Adams' difficulties with Congress, p. 172, to Congress' difficulties with Jackson for general discussion on political bargaining and compromise.

*More than ten thousand average Americans came to the capital for Jackson's inauguration.*

National-Republicans, found that they were most against the way he used his power as President. They thought of themselves as being like the Whig party in England which was against the royal power of the king. So, they began calling themselves Whigs.

Spoils system defined p. 171.

The Whigs claimed that Jackson, as President, brought the state spoils system of filling jobs to the national government. Jacksonians had asked the President to fire those against them and give the jobs to Democrats. Jackson agreed to some changes, but during his eight years as President and party leader, he actually changed only about one fifth of the officeholders. The spoils system was not used for a complete turnover in jobs until the 1840's.

Whigs also attacked Jackson for not spending federal money to help the states make improvements, mostly in transportation. In 1830, the President vetoed a bill that was supposed to help build a national road system. That bill, Jackson said, only covered a piece of road that would be completely inside the state of Kentucky. He thought federal aid for a state road was unconstitutional. Jackson did, however, sign many bills for river and harbor improvements. He spent much more federal money than earlier Presidents for interstate programs, or ones that crossed state lines.

As major issues came up, Jackson's views became known to the people. Sometimes, he supported the side of the states against the federal government. Other times, he decided that the federal government's rights were stronger. Whatever his decision, Jackson acted with great firmness to enforce it.

# Jackson and the Indians

Note double standard applied to principle of rights of private ownership by Euro-Americans when dealing with Indian lands. Hundreds of legally binding treaties were broken by state and federal governments.

From the eastern seacoast to the Mississippi River, Indian forests and hunting grounds were giving way to farms, plantations, and cities. The United States had said from the time of the Constitution that it would respect Indian rights of property and self-government. By the 1820's, the ideas behind that policy were changing. White Americans did not need the Indians as friends and as allies against foreign countries as they had before. They also felt that the Indians were in the way of white settlement.

Jackson was the first President from a frontier state. He told Congress that all Indians still living east of the Mississippi River should be moved to the Great Plains in the West. In 1830, Congress gave Jackson

# The Trail of Tears

Cherokee Indians owned and lived on a large area of rich land within the state of Georgia. Their rights to that land were guaranteed by treaties with the federal government. They had been promised, as the Treaty of Hopewell said in 1785, that:

*The hatchet shall be forever buried, and the peace given by the United States, and friendship re-established between the said states on the one part, and all the Cherokees on the other, shall be universal. . . .*

In the years after these treaties were made, the Cherokee Indians adopted many of the ways of the white settlers. They worked large farms and built permanent towns with houses, schools, stores, and Christian churches. They developed an alphabet and published the first newspaper using an American Indian language. The Cherokee people governed themselves as an independent nation within the borders of Georgia. They adopted a constitution and a form of government similar to that of the United States.

In the early 1800's, the number of white people in the state of Georgia was growing rapidly. Land for white settlement became scarce. Settlers began to demand the Cherokee land for themselves, especially after gold was discovered there. In 1829, the Georgia legislature passed an act that added the Indian lands to the state and cancelled all Indian laws.

To protect their land and way of life, the Cherokee Indians went to the Supreme Court of the United States. Chief Justice John Marshall wrote:

*. . . the Indian nations possessed a full right to the lands they occupied . . . established by treaties; that within their boundary, they possessed rights with which no State could interfere. . . . the acts of Georgia are repugnant [opposed] to the constitution, laws, and treaties of the United States.*

The Cherokee nation rejoiced at the news of the decision. The governor and legislature of Georgia, however, refused to accept the Supreme Court opinion. The Indians then appealed to President Jackson to support the federal treaties and to carry out the Court's ruling. Jackson refused to help. He said the Indians would be better off living west of the Mississippi River.

Without the support of the President, the Cherokee people soon lost their lands to the state of Georgia. Some of the Indians fled into the mountains, but most of them were forced to pack their belongings and leave their homeland. White settlers moved in as groups of Cherokee families moved out to begin the thousand-mile trip west. More than four thousand people died on this long, hard journey from cold, lack of food and shelter, and disease. Because they had to stop every few miles to bury their dead, the Cherokee journey west became known as "the trail of tears."

In *Cherokee Nation v. Georgia*, 1831, Supreme Court claimed no jurisdiction on grounds that Indian groups were not, in fact, foreign nations. In case brought by citizen missionaries, *Worcester v. Georgia*, 1832, Court held Georgia laws over Cherokee lands invalid because Indians were under the jurisdiction of the federal government.

*Forming American Habits*

the power to negotiate land exchanges with the Indians for this purpose. The Indian Removal Act did not say that the army could be used to carry out the plans. However, few white Americans spoke out against the use of state or federal troops to crush Indian resistance.

# The Indian Removal

Removal was aimed at several Indian groups in the Great Lakes area and especially at those in the southeastern part of the United States. Over the next ten years, the Chippewa, Menominee, Iowa, Sioux, Ottawa, and Winnebago Indians signed treaties giving their lands to the government and moved west of the Mississippi River.

*The Indians had very little choice about signing the treaties.*

In the Southeast, the states of Georgia, Mississippi, and Alabama passed laws claiming authority over the Indians and Indian lands within their state borders. The laws were aimed at the Creek, Chickasaw, Choctaw, and Cherokee nations. When these Indians claimed their rights from treaties with the federal government, President Jackson answered that the states had stronger rights in this matter. By 1836, the Choctaw, Chickasaw, and Creek Indians were moved west under the Indian Removal Act. The Cherokee Indians were the last to sign over their land. They had appealed their case to the Supreme Court of

*The painting, "Trail of Tears," shows the long and often fatal journey of the Cherokees.*

the United States and had won. The President, however, agreed with the government of Georgia and would not support the Supreme Court. The Cherokees began their journey west in 1838.

In the Florida territory, many of the Seminole Indians refused to leave their homeland. Under their leader, Osceola, and with the help of escaped slaves, they fought against the federal troops. After seven hard years of war, they were finally pushed into the southern swamps of the Everglades. Those who surrendered were sent west. In 1842, the government agreed to allow the few hundred people still deep in the Everglades to remain there. During the years of the Indian Removal, more than 100,000 Indians were forced from their homes to lands in the West. They were promised that they could stay on their new lands there forever.

Osceola was taken when he arrived for peace talks requested by Gen. Sidney Jessup at St. Augustine.

# "A Little Farther"

Speckled Snake, a Creek chief, spoke to his people in 1829 about advice they had received from President Andrew Jackson.

Brothers: We have heard the talk of our Great Father; it is very kind. He says he loves his red children. . . .

When the first white man came over the wide waters, he was but a little man . . . very little. His legs were cramped by sitting long in his big boat, and he begged for a little land. . . .

When he came to these shores the Indians gave him land, and kindled fires to make him comfortable. . . .

But when the white man had warmed himself at the Indian's fire, and had filled himself with the Indian's hominy, he became very large. He stopped not at the mountain tops, and his foot covered the plains and the valleys. His hands grasped the eastern and western seas. Then he became our Great Father. He loved his red children, but he said: "You must move a little farther, lest by accident I tread on you. . . ."

On another occasion he said, "Get a little farther . . . there is a pleasant country." He also said, "It shall be yours forever."

Now he says, "The land you live upon is not yours. Go beyond the Mississippi; there is game; there you may remain while the grass grows and the rivers run."

Will not our Great Father come there also? He loves his red children, and his tongue is not forked.

Brothers! I have listened to a great many talks from our Great Father. But they always began and ended in this— "Get a little farther; you are too near me." I have spoken.

*Forming American Habits*

# Jackson and Nullification

See KY and VA Resolutions, p. 133, for idea of nullification. Calhoun, who had resigned as Vice-President and entered the Senate, was proposing a process to support the nullifcation concept.

On the question of Indian rights, Jackson favored the power of the states. At the same time, he firmly defended the power of the national government, especially on the issue of the tariff of 1828. Southern states, particularly South Carolina, were strongly against the tariff. John C. Calhoun of that state wrote a proposal that was like the Virginia and Kentucky Resolutions of 1798. Like the resolutions, it said that final power in the country was found in the states, not in the federal government. But Calhoun's plan went even further. He said that each state had the right to nullify, or cancel, a federal law if the people thought it was unconstitutional. To get the law passed over nullification, three fourths of the states would have to ratify it as an amendment to the Constitution.

Southerners tried to win western support for nullification in 1830, during a debate in the Senate over western lands. Westerners were angry because of a proposed bill which would stop the sale of these lands. Robert Hayne of South Carolina suggested that western states could nullify the bill if it became law. Daniel Webster of Massachusetts argued against the idea of nullification. He said that only the Supreme Court had the right to decide if a law was constitutional.

The Webster-Hayne debates did not settle the nullification issue. Most important, no one was sure which side the President would support. The President's view became known in April at a dinner honoring Thomas Jefferson. Jackson faced Calhoun and proposed this toast: "The *Federal* Union—*It must be preserved.*"

The test of nullification came in 1832 when Jackson signed into law a new high tariff. A special convention in South Carolina nullified the tariff in that state. President Jackson replied that "our present happy Constitution was formed . . . in vain" if the idea of nullification was accepted. He prepared to send troops against South Carolina. Henry Clay set up a compromise to lower the tariff little by little. Other southern states agreed to the compromise, and South Carolina could not stand alone against federal power. The idea of nullification died. In later years, however, many people in the South would be willing to withdraw from the Union to protect their states' rights views.

# The Bank War

One of Jackson's biggest political battles was fought over the Bank of the United States. Like many other westerners, the President had lost money in the Panic of 1819 and blamed the Bank. Jackson thought of the Bank as a monopoly that made a few rich people richer. It was a private company run by its directors as they saw fit. The government owned one fifth of the Bank's stock but had very little control over it. The Bank kept tight control of the amount of money and credit available to the state banks.

Henry Clay planned to run for President in 1832. He advised the Bank's president to ask Congress to pass a bill renewing the Bank's charter. The original charter would not end until 1836, but Clay believed that Jackson would veto the new bill. He thought that Jackson's veto would be so unpopular with the voters that Jackson would lose the election. Congress passed the bill, and the President did veto it. Many voters, however, were pleased by the veto. In the election, Jackson was reelected by a wide margin.

After the election, Jackson set out to destroy the Bank. He ordered all the government's money taken out of the Bank of the United States. It was put in several state banks that became known as Jackson's pet banks. These banks used the money to start a credit boom. They loaned much of it to business people who used it to buy western land from the government land offices. The land offices then deposited the money back into the pet banks. More money and credit became available to more people. There was a heavy increase in land buying, especially by speculators who buy land to sell again at a big profit.

Before Jackson left office in 1836, he tried to slow down the heavy buying of land on credit. He issued a plan that allowed only the people who settled on the land to use paper money to pay for it. Everyone else had to pay in hard money, meaning gold or silver.

# A Depression

Martin Van Buren, Jackson's choice, was elected President in 1836. By the next year, results from Jackson's hard money plan began to show. In the Panic of 1837, many banks did not have enough gold or silver to cover the paper money they had issued. The amount of credit given was much larger than the amount of available hard money. Jackson's plan had stopped the heavy land buying, but it soon led the country into a depression. Banks called in loans, and people could not pay all that they owed. Many people lost their land, especially the speculators. Prices dropped and business slowed because people were buying fewer products. Many people, especially in cities, lost their jobs since fewer products could be sold. Many businesses and banks failed.

Refer to causes of Panic of 1819, note on p. 159. Similar situation in 1837 compounded by overextension of canal and railroad building.

Students should begin to recognize economic interrelationships.

*In the Panic of 1837, paper money was worthless, and people could not get gold from banks. People were out of work, and businesses failed.*

An Independent Treasury was established in 1840, abolished by Whigs in 1841, restored by Democrats in 1846, and remained in force until the Civil War's National Bank Act of 1863.

Van Buren had agreed with Jackson's economic plans and continued them. The situation grew worse. The new President also believed that his duty was to cut government spending. Without federal aid, railroad and canal building almost stopped. Van Buren was against efforts to set up a new Bank of the United States. He believed that the government should handle its own money and not favor any banks. In 1838, Congress repealed the hard money plan. That helped, but it was several years before the country recovered from the depression.

# The Election of 1840

Because of the problems during Van Buren's term, Whigs believed that their party had a good chance to beat Van Buren and the Democrats in the election of 1840. They chose William Henry Harrison as their candidate for President. Harrison, a wealthy Ohio farmer, was also well known from the Battle of Tippecanoe. The Whigs said that he, like Jackson, was the friend of the average American and fought for white settlement. They called Harrison a cider-drinking settler who lived in a log cabin. At the same time, they called Van Buren a rich aristocrat. The campaign was full of slogans, banners, rallies, and parades. It was the depression as well as the campaign, however, that swung the voters to Harrison and the Whigs.

Harrison died within a month after becoming President. With him died the Whig hopes of building a program to help the nation out of the depression. The Vice-President, John Tyler, became the President. Tyler had been a Democrat but had broken his ties with Jackson. As the new President, Tyler still held Democratic views. He often vetoed Whig bills and did not get along with Whig leaders or Congress.

Might have student investigate and report on Harrison's death by pneumonia since he was first President to die in office.

# American Education

The spirit of democracy that was changing politics in America was also affecting ideas about schools. In the South, general education for blacks was not allowed, although some slaves learned to read and write. There were also some independent schools for free black children. Most schools of the early 1800's, however, were only for white children. Elementary schools were usually church schools where children learned to read and write about their religions. Private schools, called academies and seminaries, were mostly for training young men as church, government, and business leaders. Private schools and colleges were too expensive for most people. Local and state governments were willing to set land aside for schools. But they did not often vote any tax money to help run them.

Multiple opportunities for student research and reports over topics in following six pages of text. Research on aspects of education might result in lively class discussions through comparisons.

By the 1830's, costly schools no longer fit in with the democratic political ideas of average Americans. Voting citizens needed to read and write and to understand the issues. Many people began to agree that schools should be free to all children, rich and poor. Slowly, leaders like Horace Mann of Massachusetts received backing for some new ideas. One idea was that a basic education for all children should be paid for by taxing all the people of the town. Another idea was to offer all students the same beginning subjects. That, people thought, would give all children an equal chance for success. These ideas were not put into general practice for some time, but agreement about them spread.

Women had not often been allowed to enter the academies, seminaries, and colleges. Emma Hart Willard and Mary Lyon were among those people who tried to change that. At Troy, New York, Willard opened a Female Seminary in 1821. There, women were offered an

*Forming American Habits*

education equal to that of men. Lyon traveled through New England to collect money for the school that she finally opened in 1836. In Massachusetts, her Mount Holyoke Female Seminary was a school that average families could afford. Some other schools for women were started, and a few colleges, like Oberlin in Ohio, began to allow women to take some courses. It took a long time, however, for most people to accept the idea of higher education for women.

The books used by teachers and students were also changing. Noah Webster is sometimes called the "schoolmaster to America." In 1828, his dictionary and speller taught people a common, American style of English words. Thousands of the "Old Blueback" spellers were sold all over the country. Webster and others, like the McGuffey brothers, also published thousands of readers that had stories praising American life.

# American Literature

Children and adults found many opportunities for reading during this period. New libraries were opened, and newspapers became cheaper to buy. Magazines used more articles and stories by American writers. These writers were turning toward American settings and ideas in their poems, essays, and novels. Since Americans were generally proud of their country, these works were widely read.

At first, American writers closely followed the style of English writing to tell American stories. Washington Irving and James Fenimore Cooper did that. Irving's "Legend of Sleepy Hollow" and "Rip Van Winkle" were popular tales of life in the lower Hudson Valley. Cooper's books, like *The Last of the Mohicans*, were exciting stories of Indians and frontier people in early New York. Edgar Allan Poe was the best-known southern writer. He often used English traditions like old castles and secret passages. His stories were full of mystery, suspense, and horror. He was one of the first to write detective stories. Poe also wrote beautiful, sad poems like "Annabel Lee" and "The Raven."

In the West, writers gave accounts of life on the small farms and on the frontier. These stories were often very realistic, telling of strength and courage. But they sometimes stretched the truth. From this part of the country came some of the boasting stories called "tall tales." They delighted readers with their humor.

Many of the things people read had a strong influence on their social and political opinions. Some authors wrote about the unpleasant

*In a scene from Irving's "Legend of Sleepy Hollow," the "headless horseman" is chasing schoolteacher Ichabod Crane.*

side of life. Nathaniel Hawthorne's *The Scarlet Letter* and Herman Melville's *Moby Dick* were stories in which people fought evil and cruelty. Other writers were more hopeful about goodness in life. They believed, like Ralph Waldo Emerson, in individual independence and self-responsibility. Margaret Fuller stressed these ideas as a writer for a New York newspaper. She also wrote a book titled *Women in the Nineteenth Century*. Henry David Thoreau practiced living a simple life close to nature and wrote about it in *Walden*. His most famous essay is "On the Duty of Civil Disobedience." In it, Thoreau said that governments must act from high moral principles; citizens should not support governments when they believe them to be wrong.

# American Art and Music

Artists in America were also turning away from English styles. They painted scenes of common life on the farms, the riverboats, and the prairies. One group, known as the Hudson Valley School, was famous for landscape paintings of forests, mountains, and streams. Many artists followed the advice of William Sydney Mount who said, "Paint for the many, not the few." The public paid attention to these painters. More Americans attended art shows and bought paintings.

People also enjoyed the lighter side of cultural life. Almost every large city had more than one theater. Companies of players visited smaller towns, performing in barns, tents, or log cabins. Plays and musicals were usually a part of any steamboat trip on western waters. Families bought pianos to play the tunes of American songwriters. Stephen Foster songs like "My Old Kentucky Home" and "O Susanna" were played, sung, or hummed by thousands. American music, like American literature and art, was created for all the people to enjoy.

# Reform Movements

Americans had seen great change and growth in the first fifty years of their new nation. They had confidence in the future of their country. Many of their religions added the belief that people and society could become perfect with enough hard work. Ralph Waldo Emerson expressed the spirit of the times in his essays and books. Emerson believed that people were basically good. They, as well as society in general, could become perfect if people would give up the things in their lives that hurt others. That meant that each person should decide and act as an individual and not follow the crowd.

Some Americans thought that the best way to practice these ideas was to withdraw from society into smaller groups. These people tried to form perfect communities where all property and work were shared. Some of them, such as Brook Farm in Massachusetts and New Harmony in Indiana, did not last long. Shaker communities, where religion joined the people together, and new religious groups like the Mormons and the Adventists were more successful.

Other Americans believed that they should stay in society but work to reform, or improve, it. Most reform leaders were average Americans with strong religious beliefs; several of them were women. One leader, Dorothea Dix, visited jails and hospitals herself. Then she reported to lawmakers about the horrible conditions she found there. Insane people, for example, were being treated like animals. They were often kept in chains or cages. Sanitary conditions were terrible. Dix's reports helped to get laws passed for better treatment of these people.

Reformers worked to change many things. New religions developed; older religious groups made changes. Thousands of people were won over to the idea of temperance, or self-control, in drinking liquor.

# Margaret Haughery

Born in Ireland in 1813, Margaret Gaffney came to Maryland with her parents when she was five years old. Her parents died four years later. She was brought up by a neighbor who could not afford to send her to school, and she never learned to read or write. In 1835, Margaret Gaffney married Charles Haughery, who was also from Ireland. They moved to New Orleans, but he soon left her and their sick baby daughter to return to Ireland. Within a few months, the baby died.

Margaret Haughery went to work doing laundry and helping at a Catholic orphanage in New Orleans. With money she saved, she bought several cows and began to sell milk. She gave milk to those who could not pay for it. By 1840, Haughery had a dairy with forty cows. In time, she used her profits to help build a home for orphans. During her lifetime, she helped establish ten other homes for children and for the elderly.

In 1858, Haughery gave up the dairy and enlarged a bakery she owned. She bought new, steam-powered machinery for it, and it became the first bakery run by steam in the South. Soon it was the city's largest export business, making and selling packaged crackers. Despite her business success, Margaret Haughery's way of life did not change. She liked to sit outside her office, wearing an old shawl, quietly giving help to people in need. When she died in 1882, she left large sums of money to continue this help.

The remarkable career of Margaret Gaffney Haughery symbolizes both the drive for business success and the spirit of reform in America during this period. In tribute, the citizens of New Orleans raised money to build a statue of her. She is shown sitting in a chair with her arm around a child. On the base of the statue is the name by which everyone knew her, "Margaret."

*Camp meetings were common in the 1830's. People gathered to celebrate their religions and encourage others to join them.*

Laws were passed so that people were no longer put in jail for owing money. Some programs were started for teaching the blind and the deaf. One of the main ideas behind these reforms was to help Americans make use of the many opportunities in the United States.

Some reforms were made quickly. Other changes took years of hard work. Two general reform movements of this time created violent feelings and produced great conflict among Americans. These were the movements for ending slavery and for equal rights for women. By 1860, the entire country was involved in settling the question of slavery. The question of equal rights for women, and all Americans, in politics, education, and economic life has taken much longer.

# *Chapter 9 in Perspective* See Teacher's Manual, page 85T.

## Identify

| | | |
|---|---|---|
| Andrew Jackson | Martin Van Buren | Mary Lyon |
| Democrats | William Henry Harrison | Margaret Fuller |
| Whigs | John Tyler | Hudson Valley School |
| Osceola | Horace Mann | Dorothea Dix |

# Explain

| | | |
|---|---|---|
| average American | Indian Removal Act | pet banks |
| spoils system | nullification | depression |
| caucus | Webster-Hayne debates | reform |

## Check Your Memory of the Facts

1. How were President Jackson's reasons for vetoing bills different from those of earlier Presidents?
2. When did President Jackson act as a nationalist? As a supporter of states' rights?
3. Over what issue was the idea of nullification tested? What was the result?
4. What political party supported John Tyler for President?
5. What kinds of things did the reformers of this time period help change?

## Check Your Understanding of the Ideas

1. How did voting become more democratic by 1830?
2. Why did Henry Clay support John Quincy Adams for President?
3. How was the President of the United States elected in 1824?
4. How could the Southeast Indians lose their lands if treaties protected their rights of ownership?
5. Why did Jackson want to destroy the Bank of the United States?
6. What connection was there among the works of American authors, artists, and musicians of this period?
7. What ideas did Horace Mann want people to accept?
8. What connection was there between American religions and American reform movements? Between the reform movements and the spirit of democracy?

## Expand Your Knowledge

1. Prepare a collection of newspaper articles on reforms that interest people today. How do these compare with the reforms of Jackson's time?
2. Organize a debate on the following question. Resolved: that all adult members of the community shall be taxed to provide a basic education for all children of the community.

*Forming American Habits*

# America Is... **Expansion**

# Ocean to Ocean 10

In the 1840's, large areas of land in the West were added to the United States. Its boundaries extended all the way from the Atlantic Ocean to the Pacific Ocean. Except for a small area in the Southwest and the lands of Alaska and Hawaii, the United States grew to its present size during these years.

## A Manifest Destiny

John L. O'Sullivan, the *Democratic Review*

In 1845, a newspaper editor first used the term Manifest Destiny. He wrote that it was manifest destiny, or certain fate, for the United States to stretch from ocean to ocean. Many people in both the North and the South agreed. Merchants wanted ports on the Pacific coast

*An America spanning the length of the continent, from the Atlantic to the Pacific, was an exciting idea in the 1840's. Lines of wagon trains stretched out over the plains as Americans moved west.*

where American ships could stop on their way to trade with Asia. Settlers wanted to live on the northwest lands of Oregon and California. Some southerners wanted the land in the Southwest for growing cotton.

There were also political reasons for the idea of Manifest Destiny. Southern state leaders hoped to have the new territories opened to slavery. New slave states would mean more people in Congress who favored the South. Northerners wanted to expand into the Northwest to bring more people who favored the North into Congress. Many northerners hoped to get laws passed to stop the spread of slavery. Most Americans also did not want the British to control any part of the Oregon territory, California, or Texas. They wanted to prevent any European nations from taking over these areas.

Manifest Destiny became a popular slogan for expansion as a "national duty" to spread the democratic experience and as a rationalization of desire for land.

# The Western Indians

Many different Indian groups lived in the lands that attracted Americans. In the Great Basin between the Rocky Mountains and the Sierra Nevada Mountains were the Shoshone group and the Paiute Indians. In the Southwest were the Pueblo Indians and the quite different Navaho and Apache groups, who had come several hundred years earlier from northern Canada. California had more different kinds of Indians than almost anywhere else. There were 105 different groups and subgroups, speaking dialects that belonged to six different major language families.

Great Basin groups are noted for extraordinary folklore.

Like the territories in which they lived, these Indian groups were different in many ways. On the plains and in the mountains, most of them hunted and gathered wild food. The Northwest Indians maintained their way of life through fishing. The Pueblo Indians and some other groups were farmers; the Navaho people became herders. The Indian peoples not only had many different languages, but also different religions, customs, and crafts.

Zuni and Hopi Pueblo groups developed North America's earliest known irrigation systems.

Navaho groups also adopted Spanish and Mexican practices of silversmithing.

# The Spanish Territory

Many of the Indian peoples had lived on these lands for hundreds of years. But the vast territory of Oregon between Alaska and California was also claimed by both the United States and Great Britain. The rest of the area, including California, New Mexico, Texas, and all the land in between, had been claimed by Spain since the sixteenth century. Spanish explorers had come, searching in vain for gold. In 1541, Coronado had explored the Great Plains as far north as present-day Kansas, hoping to find a "city of gold."

In the seventeenth and eighteenth centuries, a small number of Spanish missionaries built missions from Texas to California. They converted thousands of Indians to the Catholic faith and put them to work on the lands owned by the missions. Soldiers and settlers established small outposts like the one at Santa Fe, New Mexico. This area also had huge ranches and some mines. They were run by a few rich Spanish owners and their workers. The number of white people in this territory remained small. The area mainly served as a border to protect the lands of central Mexico. The Spanish government did not allow people in New Mexico to trade with the United States. However, they did allow a few Americans to live in eastern Texas.

# Changes in Indian Life

The contact between the Spanish and the Indians brought changes in the way of living for both. One of the most important changes came from the introduction of horses into North America. The Spanish had brought horses with them when they explored the Great Plains in the sixteenth century. Through raids and trading with the Spanish and each other, many groups of Indians came to own and to breed horses. This meant that they could hunt buffalo for food and skins more easily. Horses also helped them travel over larger areas of land than before.

The Kiowa Indians were one group who gained wealth and power by using horses. They occupied the plains of western Oklahoma and southwestern Kansas. In the 1830's, they had come into conflict with the Cheyenne Indians, a group who had moved toward the southern Great Plains from the north. The two sides clashed in 1838 at the Battle of Wolf Creek in what is now Oklahoma. They fought to a draw with great losses on both sides. The two groups later decided to make peace rather than to fight again. In 1840, the Cheyenne Indians and their Arapaho allies met with the Kiowa Indians and their Comanche allies. Near Bent's Fort on the Arkansas River, the four groups exchanged gifts and agreed not to fight each other any more. They did not make plans for acting together to stop the spread of white settlement in their hunting lands.

George Catlin became famous for his study and paintings of Indian peoples. This 1832 scene is called "The Cheyenne Brothers Starting on Their Fall Hunt."

# The Land of Mexico

In 1821, Mexico won its independence from Spain. The areas that later became the states of Texas, Oklahoma, New Mexico, Arizona, Utah, Nevada, and California were part of Mexico. The Mexican government opened a large part of their northern territory to trade with the United States. People from the United States eagerly began to trade and to settle there.

Might refer students to map on p. 138, and see note p. 161 on Florida.

In the 1820's and 1830's, traders carried goods by wagon a thousand miles across the plains and mountains from Missouri to Santa Fe. This proof that wagons pulled by horses could travel over the rough lands of the West made people in the eastern United States more interested in these areas. Men, women, and children packed up their belongings in covered wagons and started the long, hard journey west.

*A covered wagon served as a home on wheels during the long westward journey.*

# Texas

Of all the Mexican territory, Texas most interested the people in the United States because of its rich soil. In the early 1820's, Stephen Austin started a settlement on the Brazos River in Texas. Under an agreement his father had made with the Mexican government, each of the three hundred families Austin brought to Texas received over thirteen thousand acres of land. Each family had to swear to obey the Mexican government. In 1825, Mexico began to accept all settlers who would swear their loyalty to Mexico and who would practice the Catholic religion. Texas' population grew rapidly. By 1830, some eight thousand settlers were living there. Almost all of them were from the southern United States, and many of them had slaves.

Slavery and other troubles soon led to quarrels between the people in Texas and the Mexican government. The Mexicans ended slavery in their country. But Americans living in Texas kept the slaves they had brought with them. At the same time, the Mexicans began to wonder if the true loyalty of the Texas settlers was to the United States rather than to Mexico. They tried to stop more American settlers from coming into Texas by placing customs officers and troops along the border.

In 1835, General Antonio López de Santa Anna became the Mexican president. He ordered new laws which limited the freedom of Texans even more. The Texans rebelled, declared their independence, and set up their own government like that of the United States. Mexico sent a large army under General Santa Anna to put down the rebellion. At the Alamo, an abandoned mission in San Antonio, a small force of Texans held out for several days against nearly four thousand Mexican soldiers. Finally, the Mexicans killed every Texan at the Alamo, among them the famous Jim Bowie and Davy Crockett. Later, with the cry "Remember the Alamo," the Texans won many battles. Their final victory came when they defeated the Mexican army at San Jacinto.

Could have student investigate and report on Sam Houston, leader of Texan forces at San Jacinto and first president of Republic of Texas.

Mexico did not recognize the independence of Texas, but the government no longer had any control over it. For several years, the people of the Republic of Texas governed themselves. In 1837, Texas applied to be annexed, or added, to the United States. President Andrew Jackson refused the request because he thought it might cause a war with Mexico. Northern political leaders also spoke against annexing Texas

Might remind students of continuing question at this time of balance of power in U.S. Senate.

Jackson, with Congress' approval, did recognize the independence of the Lone Star Republic in March, 1837.

*Stephen Austin established several colonies like this one in Texas. Many Americans went to settle there.*

# Debate Over Texas

The question of the annexation of Texas was debated many times by many people. The following selections are taken from the debate in Congress in 1844. What opinion about annexation is expressed in each? What reasons were given for annexing Texas? What reasons were given for rejecting Texas?

On April 22, 1844, President Tyler sent the following message to the Senate:

*The country thus proposed to be annexed* [Texas] *has been settled . . . by persons from the United States, who* [came there] *on the invitation of both Spain and Mexico, and who carried with them into the wilderness . . . the laws, customs, and political and domestic institutions of their* [home] *land. They are* [well instructed] *in all the principles of civil liberty, and will bring along with them . . . devotion to our Union. . . . The country itself thus obtained is of* [large] *value in an agricultural and commercial point of view . . . and is destined at a day not distant to make large contributions to the commerce of the world. . . . The question was narrowed to the simple* [point of] *whether the United States should accept the boon* [benefit] *of annexation upon fair and even terms, or, by refusing to do so, force Texas to seek refuge in the arms of some other power. . . .*

Members of the Congress said the following during the debate:

## Rep. Joshua Giddings of Ohio

*. . . admit Texas, and we shall place the balance of power in the hands of the Texians themselves. They, with the southern States, will control the policy and the destiny of this nation; our tariff will then be held at the will of the Texian* [supporters] *of free trade.*

## Senator Jacob Miller of New Jersey

*. . . I cannot conceive how we are to get rid of slavery through the process of annexing foreign slave States to the Union, by opening new and more profitable fields for its employment.*

## Senator Sidney Breese of Illinois

*The soil and climate of Texas are very desirable, and her productions rich and varied.* [Texas is] *a planting state, a producer of our great staple—cotton—and of one of the great necessaries of life—sugar,—she will, united with us, greatly* [increase] *her power of production, and add largely to the number of consumers of the bread-stuffs and provisions we in the West raise in such abundance, and for which it is an object to open new markets, so that* [good] *prices for our labor can be obtained. To the manufacturing industry of the North, additional* [buyers] *of their . . . fabrics will be found in* [growing] *numbers, giving to their shipping interest also additional and profitable employment.*

because they did not want another slave state added to the Union. As the Lone Star Republic of Texas, the area was settled by many German, French, and American people who grew cotton on the rich land.

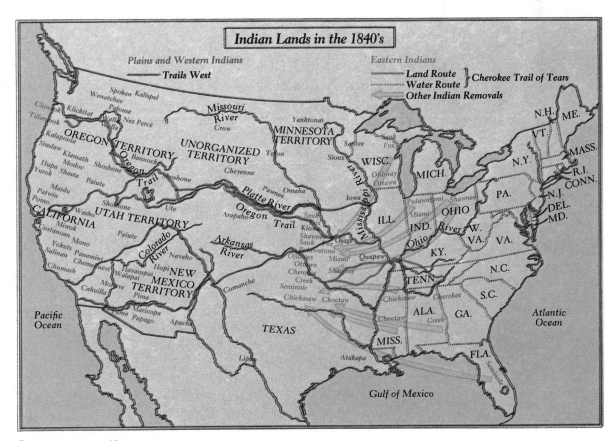

Mexico did not recognize Texas' independence although France and England encouraged it to do so, hoping to keep Texas out of U.S. for trade reasons.

# The Indians' Loss of Land

The western migration of settlers during this time meant the loss of more land by the Indians of the West. First, some groups such as the Kickapoo, Winnebago, Delaware, Sauk, Fox, and Shawnee Indians had been forced to move from east of the Mississippi River to these lands west of the river. Some of these groups had been forced to move several times. The Indian groups became more crowded together. In the 1840's, Indians west of the Mississippi River felt the direct pressure of white settlement for the first time.

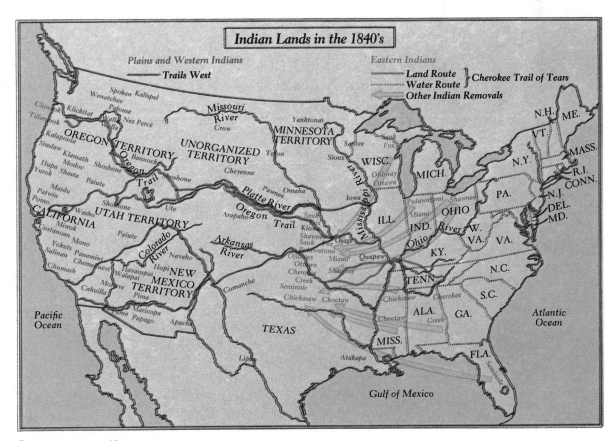

**Indian Lands in the 1840's**

*Plains and Western Indians*
— Trails West

*Eastern Indians*
— Land Route } Cherokee Trail of Tears
— Water Route
← Other Indian Removals

Compare to map p. 13.

*Ocean to Ocean*

The Comanche Indians lived on the Great Plains of Texas and New Mexico. In 1840, they asked the government of Texas for a treaty that would protect their lands against white settlement. The Texans rejected the request. They believed that any land that was not already owned by a white settler was open to settlement. So the Comanche people began raids against Texas settlers. At one point, Comanche warriors went as far as the Gulf coast. The Texans raised troops to fight the Comanche Indians and stopped them at the Battle of Plum Creek.

The year 1840 marked the peak of power for the Plains Indians. Trade and the flow of settlers increased quickly on the Santa Fe trail between Missouri and New Mexico. The trail cut through the lands of the Kiowa and Comanche Indians. Gradually, most of the Indian groups were pushed off their lands onto reservations, separate areas set aside or reserved for them by the government.

Might have students investigate and report on reservation life where lands were often unfertile with little game, annuities and supplies usually insufficient, laws barred tribal religions, and children sent to far off schools where their heritage was denounced and they learned white ways.

# California

*Presidio* established at San Diego in 1769.

In the early 1800's, the white population of California was still small. Spain had established a colony in California in 1769. Missionaries of the Catholic Church had built missions throughout much of the area. They hoped to convert the Indians there to the Catholic faith and to teach them Spanish ways of life. The missionaries put many Indians to work in fields belonging to the Church. When Mexico won its independence in 1821, the lands of the missions were turned over to the government. The Indians were supposed to receive a part of the lands, but in fact, they got very little. Many died from disease and lack of food. Their population dropped from more than one hundred thousand to fewer than fifty thousand.

In the 1840's, more settlers from Europe and the United States came to live in California. John Sutter, a Swiss settler, built a fort on the Sacramento River. A few Americans made their way overland to the fort and became ranchers in the area. Others arrived aboard whaling ships and trading vessels. In a few years, several hundred Americans were living in California. There was talk of adding California as a state.

Thomas Larkin, who had a business in California, became the American representative in Monterey in 1843. He told the Spanish-speaking people in California that there were more advantages to living under the American government than under the Mexican government. Some Mexicans in California, like Colonel Mariano Vallejo, who once had been governor of Spanish California, were not happy with Mexican rule. In 1846, an expedition led by Captain John Frémont of the

Could have student investigate and report on John Frémont as the great "Pathfinder."

# Mariano Guadalupe Vallejo

In 1808, Mariano Guadalupe Vallejo was born in Monterey, California. When he was fifteen, he became a cadet at the military post there. As a young army officer, Vallejo was in command of a hundred other Mexican soldiers and a number of Indian allies. In 1829, he led them to the San José mission, where they put down an Indian rebellion against the missionaries. Later when the missions were closed, Vallejo helped the Indians to settle on some of the former mission lands.

In the 1830's, Vallejo became the commander of a military post at Sonoma, north of San Francisco. His duty was to keep out settlers from the United States and to watch the Russian fur traders along the northern border. He also had to protect California settlers from Indian warriors farther north. Vallejo owned a large section of land near Sonoma. Because of this and his position as military commander, he became one of the most powerful leaders in northern California. However, he still could not put a stop to the many settlers coming in from the United States. Finally, since he could not stop them, he decided to help the people settle in his territory.

While the United States was fighting the war with Mexico in 1846, some American settlers in Mexican California rebelled and proclaimed the Bear Flag Republic. Vallejo and his brother were arrested and held prisoner for two months. After the war ended and California became a state, however, Vallejo became an important state leader. He was a delegate to the state constitutional convention in 1849 and served in the new state senate.

In his later years, Vallejo lived in his large home in Sonoma, although he had lost much of his lands and fortune. He spent his time writing about the history of early California. He died there in 1890. During his life as a military and political leader, Mariano Vallejo saw California change from a thinly settled Spanish outpost into a well-populated American state.

United States Army helped to start a rebellion in California. Many Spanish-speaking people in California resisted the rebellion and fought the American settlers. However, the rebels declared California to be independent from Mexico and adopted a flag with a picture of a bear on it as their symbol. The rebellion became known as the Bear Flag Revolt, and California became the Bear Flag Republic.

The Sonoma-based republic lasted about a month with Frémont as president before the U.S. flag was raised at Monterey and California was proclaimed a part of the U.S.

# Oregon

Remind students of British-U.S. agreement to occupy jointly, p. 161.

Cayuse and Yakima Indian resistance of this period put down by army.

During these same years, Oregon was the goal for several thousand settlers from the United States. Through the 1820's, the only white people in Oregon were fur traders, most of them working for the British Hudson's Bay Company. Dr. John McLoughlin ran the company's business from a fort on the Columbia River. In the 1830's, Protestant missionaries from the United States led by the Reverend Jason Lee began to arrive. Dr. McLoughlin helped them settle on the rich soil of the Willamette Valley. The missionaries grew fine crops but converted few of the Nez Percé Indians to Christianity. Farther east on the Columbia River, the Reverend Marcus Whitman and his wife Narcissa founded a mission at Walla Walla.

The efforts of the missionaries attracted much attention back in the United States. In 1841, settlers in covered wagons began pouring into Oregon. They traveled along the Platte River, crossed through a break in the Rocky Mountains at South Pass, and followed the Snake River to the Columbia River. Their route was called the Oregon Trail. Soon there were over five thousand people from the United States in Oregon, all of them living south of the Columbia River. In 1843, they organized themselves into the Oregon Territory. These settlers were eager for the United States to stop sharing control of the area with Great Britain and to claim all of Oregon for itself.

# The Election of 1844

Until the middle of the 1840's, political leaders had stayed away from the issue of adding new lands to the country. They felt it might split their parties. Northerners and southerners were both against adding new territories that would help the other section. As the time for the election of 1844 neared, the likely candidates were Henry Clay and Martin Van Buren. Both of them were against the annexation of Texas for fear that it would lead to war with Mexico.

Then, public opinion began to change. The Whigs stayed with their candidate, Henry Clay. The Democrats switched from Martin Van Buren to James K. Polk of Tennessee. Polk promised to annex Texas and to secure Oregon for the United States. Clay, fearing the loss of southern votes, also promised to annex Texas if it could be done without war. The election was close, but it was Polk who won. Although many people had opposed it, Polk set out to obtain the new territories. "I regard the question of annexation," he said as a warning to Mexico, Britain, and France, "... as belonging exclusively to the United States and Texas." In 1845, Texas became a state.

Polk had also promised that he would try to obtain all of the territory from California to Alaska. There were no American citizens, however, living north of the Columbia River. To demand all this territory could have meant war because the British felt they had more right to it. Polk threatened the British anyway. They offered to divide the land at the forty-ninth parallel, except for the tip of Vancouver Island. Polk finally accepted the offer. The land below this line later became the states of Oregon and Washington.

See note p. 197 on British and French interests in Texas as a wedge between the U.S. and Latin America, an independent source of cotton, sugar, and tobacco.

A joint resolution, supported by outgoing President Tyler, was passed by Congress on Feb. 28, 1845. Its offer of annexation and statehood was promptly accepted by Texas.

# War With Mexico

After Texas became a state, Mexico stopped formal government relations with the United States. Conflict grew between the United States and Mexico over the Texas-Mexico border. The United States backed the Texas claim that its southern boundary was the Rio Grande. Mexico believed the Texas border was much farther north and east along the Nueces River.

President Polk sent an agent to Mexico to talk about the border dispute and to try to buy California and part of New Mexico. When Polk heard that Mexican officials would not meet with the agent, he ordered General Zachary Taylor and his troops to the north bank of the Rio Grande. Polk began preparing a message asking Congress to declare war on Mexico for refusing to meet his representative. Before he could send the message, word came that Mexican forces had crossed the Rio Grande and had attacked the American soldiers. The President then sent a new war message to Congress. He wrote, "Mexico has passed the boundary of the United States, has invaded our territory, and shed American blood on American soil." On May 12, 1846, Congress declared war on Mexico.

The American forces won victory after victory in the war. General Zachary Taylor, known to the troops as "Old Rough and Ready," fought the Mexican army with little planning but with great courage. In a short time, he forced it to withdraw from northern Mexico. Other American troops marched through New Mexico and captured Santa Fe. They continued to California. Volunteer forces and the United States Navy controlled most of California at the time, so the newly arrived army quickly completed the conquest.

Taylor, in crossing the Nueces River, broke a traditional boundary more than a century old. Even the Lone Star Republic had not tried to exercise authority beyond the Nueces.

Polk's message implied that the boundary was settled. The Mexican government had not agreed, so the U.S. forces were on Mexican soil from their point of view.

Many Whig leaders charged that this war was a land grab plotted by southern planters to gain new slave states.

The American forces were more successful than the Mexican ones, and the United States held northeastern Mexico, New Mexico, and California. However, the Mexicans did not give up. Polk decided to send General Winfield Scott, a careful planner nicknamed "Old Fuss and Feathers," to lead an army into the center of Mexico. Sailing to Veracruz on the Mexican coast, this army marched to Mexico City, winning battles on the way. In September, 1847, Mexico City was conquered. Months went by, however, before Mexican officials agreed to peace terms.

Among the last to fall in defense of the Mexican flag were 100 teenage cadets honored by Mexicans today as *Los Niños*, The Boys.

# New Territory

As the American forces pushed into Mexico, some people in the United States demanded more and more territory. A few even wanted to annex all of Mexico. Most Americans were not so demanding, but they did want to annex California and New Mexico. The government also wanted Mexico to agree that Texas was part of the United States.

Trist lost his job over the treaty because he followed Polk's original instructions and ignored a letter of recall. Might have student investigate and report on Trist.

Polk's agent in Mexico, Nicholas Trist, arranged a treaty that included some of these terms. The Treaty of Guadalupe Hidalgo was signed in 1848. The United States paid Mexico fifteen million dollars for all the land north of the Rio Grande and the Gila River. The land included California, Texas, and most of New Mexico. Several years later, the United States found that the best southern railroad route to the

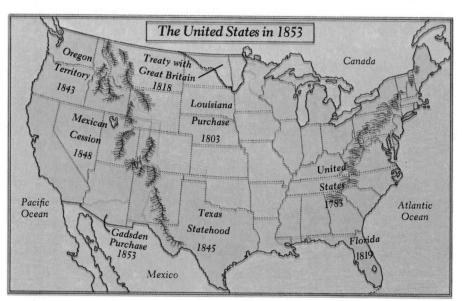

The United States in 1853

Oregon Territory 1843

Treaty with Great Britain 1818

Louisiana Purchase 1803

Mexican Cession 1848

Canada

United States 1783

Pacific Ocean

Atlantic Ocean

Texas Statehood 1845

Gadsden Purchase 1853

Florida 1819

Mexico

Compare to map on p. 197. Mexico lost more than half its territory to the U.S. Modern state boundaries shown by dotted lines for ease of comparison.

*Ocean to Ocean*

Pacific Ocean was south of the Gila River. In 1853, the United States paid Mexico ten million dollars for the strip of land that now forms the southern part of New Mexico and Arizona. This was called the Gadsden Purchase.

James Gadsden was the railroad magnate sent to negotiate the purchase.

# The Mormons at Salt Lake

Immediately after the Mexican War, settlers from the United States began to rush into the new territories. Some of them, known as Mormons, were members of the Church of Jesus Christ of Latter-Day Saints. They moved into what is now Utah, looking for a place where they could settle and practice their religion.

The Mormons were a religious group founded by Joseph Smith in New York in 1830. They were persecuted by other Americans for their beliefs and were forced to move many times to escape cruel treatment. After living briefly in Ohio and Missouri, they settled in Illinois and formed a close, successful community. The Mormons' success was envied by their neighbors. The fact that Mormon men were allowed to have more than one wife also upset many people. In 1844, Joseph Smith was killed by an angry mob.

Brigham Young became the new leader of the Mormons. He decided to move the whole community to the West where he believed they could live in peace. The Mormons established Salt Lake City in Utah in 1847. During the next few years, they founded many more towns, raised crops on irrigated fields, and brought in thousands of new members from the eastern United States and Europe.

Might have student investigate and report on Mormon troubles in Nauvoo, Illinois, where Smith was murdered.

Issue of polygamy, first sanctioned by Smith in 1843, prevented Utah statehood until church officially renounced it in 1896.

# The California Boom

In 1848, James Marshall accidentally discovered gold in California on the property of John Sutter. Word spread rapidly, and by 1849, adventurers from all over the world were coming to California to look for gold. That year, more than eighty thousand people came, and they were known as forty-niners.

At first, there seemed to be a lot of gold in the streams and mountains of California. But only a few people actually became rich. Many of the gold seekers were disappointed and returned home. Some hurried off to try their luck in other gold or silver booms in Nevada, Colorado, and later in Montana. Others settled down to farming or business. The real wealth in California was to be found in its fertile land.

*People came from many parts of the world to look for California gold in the late 1840's.*

# Effects of Westward Movement

In the growing United States, the addition of western lands brought many problems. For the Indians, these problems were often deadly. White settlers poured into Texas after the territory was admitted as a state in 1845. The discovery of gold in California brought a stream of people to the West that was too great for the Indians to halt. In the 1840's, more and more Indian groups were moved from their own land and onto other Indian lands. For the United States government, the addition of new territories made the question of slavery even more difficult. Once the former Mexican lands were brought into the United States, the problem of balancing the interests of the North and the South grew worse.

# Chapter 10 in Perspective See Teacher's Manual, page 89T.

### Identify

Stephen Austin
John Sutter

John McLoughlin
James K. Polk

Zachary Taylor
Joseph Smith

# Explain

| | | |
|---|---|---|
| Manifest Destiny | reservations | Mormons |
| the Alamo | Oregon Trail | forty-niners |
| annexed | Gadsden Purchase | |

## Check Your Memory of the Facts

1. What reasons did people give to support the idea of Manifest Destiny?
2. What were some of the Indian groups originally living west of the Mississippi River?
3. What did the Mexican government ask of Americans who wanted to settle in the territory of Texas?
4. What happened to the Spanish missions in California after Mexico gained its independence from Spain?
5. Why were the Mormons persecuted? Where did they finally settle?

## Check Your Understanding of the Ideas

1. Why did the Spanish explorers come to western North America?
2. What changes did horses make in the lives of some of the Indians?
3. Why was Mexico's independence from Spain in 1821 important to people in the United States?
4. Why did the Texans want to be independent from Mexico?
5. Why did the candidates for President in the 1844 election agree or disagree with annexing Texas?
6. In what ways did the westward movement affect the government? The Indians? The settlers?

## Expand Your Knowledge

1. Choose an Indian group that lived in the West in the 1840's. Prepare a report on that group. Include where they lived, what language they used, how they got their food, to what other groups they were related, and what changes they went through in the 1840's. Find out how the group lives today, and make a comparison.
2. Find out the size of covered wagons of the 1840's and what equipment they had. Make a list of important items that people needed for a move west. What kind of things could they buy, hunt, or trade for along the way?

# San Francisco 1845-1855

In 1776, the English colonists along the eastern coast of North America signed their Declaration of Independence. That same year, the Spanish started a settlement halfway up the coast of California. There were two parts to the settlement: a *presidio*, or army post, and a mission. Soldiers at the Presidio protected Spanish California from the claims of England, France, Russia, and the United States. Priests at the mission taught the Pomo and other Indian people about Christianity.

The soldiers and priests in California made the Indians work on the mission lands. These Indian workers produced food and trade goods for the people living in the area. Their work was not easy. Many of the mission Indians died from the hard work, punishments, and diseases brought by the white people. When the number of workers was low, the soldiers rode out and captured more Indians for the mission.

## Village of Saint Francis

In the following years, a small village grew up near the mission. It was named Yerba Buena, after the "good herb" that grew in the hills nearby. The mission priests belonged to a group started by Saint Francis of Assisi, and the village was sometimes called the village of Saint Francis, or *pueblo de San Francisco*.

The Presidio, Mission Dolores, and San Francisco were built on an arm of land that reached out between the Pacific Ocean and a beautiful bay. Whaling and cargo ships entered and left the village harbor through the Golden Gate, a name given to the natural

channel of deep water that connected the bay to the ocean. This arrangement of land and water made San Francisco one of the finest and safest harbors in the world.

In 1821, Mexican soldiers raised the flag of Mexico over the Presidio to show their new independence from Spain. In the 1830's, the Mexican government took back the lands that the Spanish had given to the mission. Most of it was given to ranchers in the area. Many Indians had completely depended on the mission for food, shelter, clothing, and jobs. With the mission lands gone, they had very little land of their own for farming and hunting. Some of the Indians moved away, but many Indians died.

## International Port

At San Francisco, there had been Spanish and Mexican laws against trading with other countries. In spite of these laws, the harbor served sailors and merchants from around the world. The largest amount of trade was with the United States. During the 1840's, more and more people from the United States moved west. They soon discovered the pleasing weather and rich soil of California. At the end of the Mexican War in 1848, Mexico turned over California and other territories to the United States.

## Eureka!

In the spring of 1848, the quiet growth of San Francisco exploded into noisy activity. People in the village finally believed the stories that gold had been found in the nearby Sierra Nevada Mountains. The stories described huge amounts of gold dust, thin gold flakes, and lumps or nuggets of gold to be found in the mountain streams and gravel beds.

San Francisco's *Californian* newspaper printed its last issue in May. In it, the owners wrote that the paper was closing down because they could not find anyone to work on it. Almost all of the eight hundred people living in the town had gone off to look for gold.

*The whole country . . . resounds with the sordid [greedy] cry of <u>gold</u>! GOLD!! GOLD!!! —while the field is left half planted, the house half built, and every thing neglected . . . one man obtained one hundred and*

*The village of Yerba Buena in 1847*

twenty-eight dollars' worth of the real stuff [gold] in one day's washing, and the average for all concerned is twenty dollars per diem [day]!

Cries of *Eureka!* (Greek for "I've found it!") carried across the country and around the world. By the beginning of 1849, nearly two thousand people lived in San Francisco. At the end of that year, the number was higher than twenty-five thousand. Most of the newcomers were young men looking for adventure as well as for gold. They came from the United States, Mexico, Canada, South America, Europe, Australia, and Asia.

## Golden Opportunities

As thousands of people came to California, new towns were started, and older towns became large cities. Those people who came by sea often landed first at San Francisco. Merchants in the city soon made it a supply center for the miners. One historian wrote in 1855:

*A short experience of the mines had satisfied most of the citizens of San Francisco that . . . all was not gold that glittered, and that hard work was not easy. . . . They returned very soon to their old quarters, and found that much greater profits, with far less labor, were to be found in supplying the necessities of the miners. . . .*

The miners' work was, in fact, hard and uncomfortable. They usually stood in cold streams for hours to wash, or separate, the gold from the mud and gravel. After the loose gold was taken up, the miners had to dig for the rest of it. They often slept on the ground at night and seldom cooked a good meal at camp. Most miners suffered from sore hands, sore feet, and sore stomachs. So

they came into town for company and comfort, as well as for supplies and news from home.

In a short time, there was more gold in San Francisco than there were goods to buy with it. Storekeepers charged very high prices, and people paid them. Many people made very large fortunes without a bit of "washing" or digging. Everyone who sold anything kept scales on hand to weigh the gold, valued at sixteen dollars an ounce.

One person from New York named Levi Strauss arrived in San Francisco in 1850. He had a roll of canvas cloth and some new ideas for making strong work pants. In a few years, miners and farmers alike were buying the famous "Levi's" work clothes.

It was a rare thing to find people doing the same kind of work in San Francisco that they had done before coming to California. People who had been farmers or bankers could as easily earn money as bakers and storekeepers. There seemed to be many different ways to get rich.

## Women and Children

A Massachusetts woman wrote home to a friend about other opportunities in the days of the gold rush.

*The demand for marriageable women seems to be as great as for goods. This is the only country in the world where women are properly appreciated. . . . By all means [get] Peggy to come here by the first vessel. . . . she would be readily taken [married] . . . in the present brisk state of the market.*

T. A. Barry and B. A. Patten wrote a book about San Francisco as they remembered it. There were so many more men in the city that they wrote:

*A new arrival in San Francisco*

We remember the day, when a woman walking along the streets of San Francisco was more of a [rare] sight than an elephant or a giraffe would be today. Men lingered [waited] to see them pass, crowded to the wharves when they arrived, and followed them along the streets to their dwellings, and stared . . . [at] the house's front. . . .

Judge S---- told us that when he arrived in 1849, and walked up from the ship, with his wife and several little children, men crowded about the children, asking permission to kiss them, to shake hands with them, to give them gold . . . following them

a long way, as if fascinated by the sight of their child faces and voices. . . . The boys and girls of San Francisco in that time, who were not spoiled, were remarkable children. The sight of their faces touched tender places in the hearts of men [so far away] from their own little ones. . . .

The old signal station on Telegraph Hill was a very important feature in [those] days . . . to tell thousands of anxious husbands, fathers and lovers that the steamer, bearing news of hope and happiness, or of the death of loved ones, was then in sight. How that signal . . . did wake up the street! All along the line of stores were men out upon the walk, their faces all turned in one direction, looking at the signal. . . . The idea of news from wife, children or sweetheart to a man, thirty days' distance away, made him ignore business at once.

## All That Glitters

According to some San Francisco historians, "the place and habits of the people" were odd or different because there were so few women and children.

There was no such thing as a <u>home</u> to be found. . . . Both dwellings and places of business were either common canvas tents, or small rough board shanties [poorly built sheds], or frame buildings of one story. Only the great gambling saloons, the hotels, restaurants, and a few public buildings and stores had any pretensions [claims] to size, comfort or elegance. . . .

In those miserable apologies for houses, surrounded by heaps and patches of filth, mud and stagnant [bad] water, the strange mixed population carried on business, after a fashion. It is not to be supposed that people could or did manage matters in the

209

strict orderly manner of older communities. . . . The streets and passages, such as they were, and the inside of tents and houses, were heaped with all sorts of goods and lumber. There seemed no method in any thing. People bustled and jostled [bumped] against each other . . . cursed and swore, sweated and labored . . . and somehow the work was done. . . . Heaps of goods disappeared, as if by magic, and new heaps appeared in their place. Where there was a vacant piece of ground one day, the next saw it covered with half a dozen tents or shanties. . . .

While wages and profits were so high, and there was no comfort at their sleeping quarters, men spent money freely . . . at drinking bars, billiard rooms and gambling saloons. . . . A concert or a lecture would at other times help to entertain. . . . But of all . . . the gambling saloons were the . . . best patronized [attended].

## City Government

City leaders could not keep up with San Francisco's population growth. Local government was in such confusion that there were three different city councils in 1849. Each of them claimed to be the official one. A newly elected leader described the city's problems.

At this time we are without a dollar in the public treasury, and it is to be feared the city is greatly in debt. . . . You are without a single police officer or watchman, and have not the means of confining [holding] a prisoner for an hour; neither have you a place to shelter, while living, sick and unfortunate strangers who may be cast upon our shores, or to bury them when dead. Public improvements are unknown in San Francisco. In short, you are without a single [thing] necessary for the promotion of prosperity, for the protection of property, or for the maintenance of order.

When California became a state in 1850, elections were still a problem for the city. Many people lied about their citizenship so that they could vote. Some cheated in other ways when casting their ballots. The court system did not work often or well because the city leaders had trouble working together. When trials were held, jury members were often more influenced by bribes than by words from witnesses.

## Law and Order

There was no clear authority to establish order or to enforce laws. San Francisco was sometimes a very frightening city in which to live. Cheating, stealing, mugging, and murder were common. Criminals were not often caught and even less often punished. Fires were a constant danger in a city of so much canvas and wood. Many people believed that some of the fires had been started just to cover up other crimes. At different times, whole sections of the city had burned to the ground in a few hours.

Fear and anger led groups of citizens to enforce the laws themselves. Twice in the 1850's, they formed a Vigilance Committee to rid the city of "the ballot box stuffers, jury packers, swindlers, thieves and villains generally." The committees captured, tried, and hanged several well-known criminals. They forced many others to leave the country and scared hundreds from the city. Several thousand citizens supported the work of the two Vigilance Committees who brought some peace and safety to San Francisco.

*San Francisco, a busy seaport in 1850*

There were also serious complaints against these groups because they had ignored the established system of law. But no legal action was brought against the committee.

## Gold to Goods, Again

By the middle of the 1850's, the California miner working alone had little chance of finding a rich strike. The gold was too deep in the earth to be taken out by hand. San Francisco had based its growth on the miners' gold. For a few years, the city suffered a panic and a depression as the supply of new gold grew smaller. Some miners went on to other western territories. Some returned, with or without gold, to their former homes. Many brought their families west and settled down in farming or business.

In the early years of the gold rush, the city was a wild and rough place. But almost overnight, San Francisco had changed from a quiet village into a major center of banking and trade. Ship captains from around the world continued to come to its excellent harbor. And the newly populated western lands continued to offer opportunities to people seeking adventure.

# New Ways to Make a Living

# 11

Aim: to help students understand the continuing development of different regional economies through presentation of contributing factors.

In the years before 1860, many people in the United States wanted to remain apart from problems in Europe. They wanted their economy to be independent, and they worked to provide their own goods and services. On land bought or taken from Indians, railroads were built, and more farms were settled. As the use of machines became more common, the number of factories grew, and cities became larger. Most of the railroads and factories were located in the North. Water resources there provided enough force for running machines. During this

*As America grew during this period, so did its economy. Industry was constantly improving in the mid-1840's, and settlements around large factories soon turned into thriving cities.*

period, the South remained a farming society. The soil and climate there were very suited to growing cotton. So differences between the North and South grew in the 1800's.

# A Working People

In 1815, there were eighteen states in the Union. Only four of them lay west of the Appalachian Mountains. By 1850, there were thirty-one states, and fifteen of them were west of these mountains. Americans seemed to be always on the move. Most Americans believed that, with hard work, they could give more comforts to their families. Moving west to richer lands often gave them a new chance to improve their lives. Thomas Nichols, a New Jersey doctor, wrote:

The sheer quantity of land and their continuous discovery of its resources gave most of these Americans an unusual faith in the future.

> Every one is tugging, trying, scheming to . . . get ahead. . . . all are troubled and none are satisfied. In Europe, the poor man, as a rule, knows that he must remain poor, and he . . . tries to make the best of it. . . . Not so in America. Every other little ragged boy dreams of being President or millionaire. The dream may be a pleasant one while it lasts, but what of the . . . reality?

The reality was that only a few became very wealthy or famous. But more people than ever were able to make a good living. To do this, they still had to work hard and long hours. In the early 1800's, it was difficult to find anyone to hire to help with the work. So people in families and communities often helped each other. Soon, other solutions were developed as new machines and factories were introduced.

# The Growth of Industry

People began to develop new and better tools as another way to get more work done. Sometimes, efforts to improve tools led to the development of machines. Very often, the machines were based on ideas or discoveries of Europeans. Americans made practical use of the ideas. Industry, or the making and selling of goods, grew with the development of machinery.

*New Ways to Make a Living*

*Men, women, and children worked in the textile mills, often as much as fourteen hours a day. More mills and a good supply of cotton reduced the need for cloth imported from Europe.*

Francis Cabot Lowell established the first mill to combine operations of carding, spinning, and weaving under one roof at Waltham, MA, 1814.

As machines began to be used, products were made in factories instead of by one person at home or in a small shop. In the past, the people of the United States had mainly produced raw materials such as cotton, lumber, iron, and wheat. And until the 1800's, artisans like blacksmiths used hand tools to make their products. Shoes, saddles, hats, wagons, nails, flour, and books were all made by hand. People in England had carefully guarded their knowledge of manufacturing. Machinery or plans for it were not allowed to be taken out of the country.

Samuel Slater came to the United States from England in 1789. He had memorized the plans for the textile, or cloth-making, machines he had used there. He built similar machines and, in 1790, started the first textile mill at Pawtucket, Rhode Island. Soon, New England mills were making cloth for most of the country.

Americans not only copied European machines, they also developed new and improved machines. The growth of the textile mills resulted in the production of large amounts of cloth. In 1846, Elias Howe invented a machine which could sew the cloth faster than a person could by hand. Isaac Singer improved the sewing machine in 1851. Soon hundreds of these machines were used by people at home and in factories to make clothing, shoes, and other goods.

# Lucy Larcom

Lucy Larcom, the ninth of ten children, was born in Beverly, Massachusetts, in 1824. Her father was a merchant and a former sea captain who died when she was small. After his death, there was not enough money to support the large family. So her mother took them to Lowell, Massachusetts, where she supervised a group of girls who worked in the textile mill.

Lucy Larcom worked in the mill for many years along with her older sisters. She began writing poems, and some of them were published in the mill girls' magazine, the *Lowell Offering*. In 1846, she went to Illinois and became a teacher. After a few years, Larcom returned to the East and spent most of her time writing and editing. She died in Boston in 1893.

One of Lucy Larcom's best-known books was *A New England Girlhood*. In it, she remembers her life in Massachusetts. The book has great value for its picture of life in a small New England town before the Civil War.

The sea was its nearest neighbor, and penetrated to every fireside. . . .

It was hard to keep the boys from going off to sea before they were grown. No inland occupation attracted them. "Land-lubber" was one of the most [scornful names] heard from boyish lips. . . .

And there were wanderers from foreign countries . . . [who] became familiar in our streets,—Mongolians, Africans, and waifs from the Pacific islands. . . . Families of black people were scattered about the place. . . .

We had great "training-days," when drum and fife took our ears by storm; when the militia and the Light Infantry . . . marched through the streets. . . .

The town used to wear a delightful air of drowsiness. . . .

Her spirit was that of most of our Massachusetts coast-towns. They were transplanted shoots of Old England.

*New Ways to Make a Living*

# The Factory System

The number of mills and factories increased in New England during this time. It was the start of the factory system, or the bringing together of workers to make goods by machines. Two ideas were very important in the factory system. First, making a product could be divided into separate tasks. Instead of having one artisan or trained worker do them all, each task could be done by a person with less training. Women and children, and later people from foreign countries, provided a lot of this unskilled labor, especially in the cloth mills.

The second idea in the factory system was the use of machines to make interchangeable, or standard, parts for an item. Machines could turn out parts exactly alike so that they could replace each other. Standard parts were first used widely in making firearms. If one part of a gun was damaged, a matching part could fit in its place. This was much easier and less costly than having to replace the whole gun. Interchangeable parts were also very important in making machines.

Together, these two ideas of separate tasks by unskilled workers and interchangeable parts made it possible for manufacturers to produce large quantities of goods in a short time for a low price. People demanded more and more manufactured goods. By the 1840's, many kinds of machinery, from clocks to farm equipment, were made by factory workers from standard parts.

# Transportation

Improved ways to move people and goods added to the changes in American life. Transportation on land began to improve with a system of roads and highways. By 1820, more than nine thousand miles of hard-surfaced roads were in use. By 1860, there were over eighty-eight thousand miles, built with private, state, and federal funds. The roads meant that farmers on the frontier could buy and sell goods in the markets in the eastern states. Unfortunately, moving goods by wagons was still slow and costly.

Canals provided the first low-cost transportation between the Atlantic coast and the newly settled land farther west. Then in the early 1800's, steamboats became popular. They moved faster and carried bigger loads than boats on canals. They could also maintain a good speed upstream as well as downstream. Steamboats which traveled from New

Refer to map on p. 157.

Hard-surfaced roads were covered with rocks, stone, or gravel. Corduroy roads had logs or planks laid across the roadbed. Development and conditions of early roadways are good topics for student research and report to modify image of "roads" as modern highways and city streets.

*There was friendly rivalry between steamboats on the Mississippi River. They often raced each other to various ports.*

Orleans up and down the Mississippi and Ohio rivers could meet and trade cargoes with ships from northern and eastern ports. With this network of water transportation, manufacturers could send more products a long distance to trade centers and still make a profit.

Railroads, developed in England in the early 1800's, were an even greater improvement in transportation. They moved goods and people over long distances faster than wagons or steamboats. Railroads could be built through the mountains. They could also serve areas that were not close to water routes. The first successful steam railroad in the United States was started in Baltimore, Maryland, in 1828. More and more railroads were built, and by 1860, there were over thirty thousand miles of tracks, mostly in the North and Midwest.

Might remind students that improvements in transportation are directly related to improved speed of communication.

# Communication

Better ways to send news and messages helped the growth of industry. In 1844, Congress provided money for the world's first telegraph line. It went from Washington, D.C., to Baltimore, Maryland. Samuel

**Transportation in 1860**

Principal Roads
Canals
Railroads

Morse sent the first message, "What hath God wrought," using his important dot-dash code. The telegraph made it possible for people to send and receive news and market reports quickly. The use of the telegraph also helped improve railroad service. Messages could be sent from station to station giving the arrival and departure times of trains. Many more telegraph lines were built, usually along the railroad routes. By the time of the Civil War, there were thousands of miles of telegraph lines.

# New Ways of Farming

Just as machines improved manufacturing, they also brought changes in methods of farming. One machine in particular affected farming in the South. Most crops grown there, especially cotton, were planted, picked, and treated by hand. The cotton gin, invented by Eli Whitney in 1793, made it easier and faster to separate the cotton seeds from the cotton fiber. The demand for cotton was growing because the textile mills in the North were making more cloth than before. The cotton gin helped get the cotton ready for the mills faster. However, people were still needed to plant and pick the crop. Cotton growers in the South often bought more slaves to solve that problem.

In the North and Midwest, new machines brought great changes in farming methods. A steel plow invented in 1830 helped farmers cut through the tough prairie sod. A year later, Cyrus McCormick introduced a mechanical reaper. With this harvesting machine, farmers could gather five times more wheat in a day than without one. In 1860, McCormick sold eighty thousand improved reapers.

As farmers bought steel plows, reapers, other inventions, and more slaves, they were able to work larger sections of land and produce more crops. They also began to raise only one or two crops or kinds of animals to sell on these larger farms. Raising only one or two items, or specializing, cost less and took less work than raising several different kinds. By specializing and using low-cost transportation, farmers were able to make more profit from their work. The country got large amounts of food at low prices. These things all changed the pattern of farming in the United States.

See note on cotton, p. 160.

Import slave trade officially ended in 1808, but smuggling rampant. Internal slave trade increased to meet demands brought by cotton gin. Most major southern cities had slave markets.

Mechanical reaper marks beginning of more extensive use of animal power. Might have student research and report on McCormick who pioneered or perfected several business techniques including field trials, testimonials, and installment sales.

*Cyrus McCormick's reaper made harvesting grain much easier. Farmers were able to plant many more acres each year.*

New Ways to Make a Living

# Work on the Farms

Use of time-saving machinery also increased acre-yield since there was less crop loss to damage by elements.

Farm families in the early 1800's had to grow or make almost everything they needed in order to live. To do this, they worked from dawn to dark six days a week. They had to know how to do everything themselves. Even after machines were invented that helped farmers, they worked hard. The time saved by using machines was usually spent making farms bigger and better.

Most people in the United States lived on farms, and most farms were small, even in the South. Actually, only a few white people there owned large plantations. There were four million slaves in the South in 1860, and over half of them lived on the few large plantations. Such large amounts of land could not be farmed by a single family. Most plantation owners could not pay the number of workers they needed. So, the plantation system depended on slaves. Although conditions did vary, Solomon Northup, an escaped slave, told about work on one cotton plantation:

> The hands are required to be in the cotton fields as soon as it is light in the morning, and, with the exception of ten or fifteen minutes, which is given them at noon . . . they are not permitted to be a moment idle until it is too dark to see, and when the moon is full, they often times labor till the middle of the night. . . .
>
> The day's work over in the field, the baskets are . . . carried to the gin-house, where the cotton is weighed. . . . no matter how much he longs for sleep and rest—a slave never approaches the gin-house with his basket of cotton but with fear. If it falls short in weight . . . he knows that he must suffer. And if he exceeded it by ten or twenty pounds . . . his master will measure the next day's task accordingly.

# Work in the Factories

Women's family responsibilities had given them long experience in these industries.

By 1860, about one million people worked in factories; one fourth of them were women. Two thirds of the workers in the shoe, cloth, and clothing industries were women. A few of the workers in factories were slaves hired out by their owners. About one slave in ten lived in a town or city, as a servant or skilled worker.

The people in factories worked from dawn to dark just as those on farms did. Machine-made goods and specialized farming lowered the prices of most products. Even so, factory workers, who were often trained in very specific tasks, could barely earn enough money to cover living costs. A few workers tried to improve their situation by joining together to form labor unions. Through these unions, they tried to bargain with factory owners for better conditions. During times when prices went up faster than wages, workers in some unions would strike. They refused to work until the owners agreed to higher pay and shorter working hours. However, during times of depression when jobs became scarce, many workers were afraid of losing the jobs they had and did not always support the unions.

Earliest unions were of skilled workers. By 1830's, more than 30,000 members. Panic and depression of 1837 had almost ruinous effect on unionizing; not revitalized until rapid economic growth and labor shortages following Civil War.

*A worker on an assembly line did the same task all the time. Even meat packers used this method of production.*

The courts were very hard on union members who went on strike. Judges often sent strikers to jail. There were old state laws that made it illegal for anyone to keep business or trade from taking place. In 1842, the United States Supreme Court ruled that it was no longer illegal to strike in some cases. It took time, however, before laws were passed to protect the strikers.

# The Growth of Cities

Factories were usually built on rivers, canals, or near railroad lines. Towns grew up around them because people wanted to live close to where they worked. These towns became centers for trade and transportation. More workers were needed as more factories were built. People

*New Ways to Make a Living*

came from farms and small towns to live in the busy cities. Only a few cities were very large at this time. Between 1840 and 1850, however, the total number of people in all cities in the United States grew from less than two million to more than three and a half million people.

Many workers came to American cities from foreign countries. From 1790 to 1815, about 250,000 of these immigrants arrived. During the 1830's, more than half a million people came. In the 1840's, the number was three times that figure. Most of the immigrants of the 1840's and 1850's were from Ireland and Germany. Crop failures and political troubles caused most of them to leave their countries.

The immigrants settled mainly in two areas, the Atlantic Coast and the upper Midwest. Those with industrial skills often settled in cities which used their trades. Farmer immigrants chose areas like the ones they had left. They often took over farms whose owners wanted to go west. Workers without special skills became porters, waiters, house

*Traveling conditions were often crowded and uncomfortable for the people coming to America from foreign countries. The voyages were long, and sometimes food was scarce. But thousands of immigrants poured into cities in the United States during the 1840's.*

*New Ways to Make a Living*

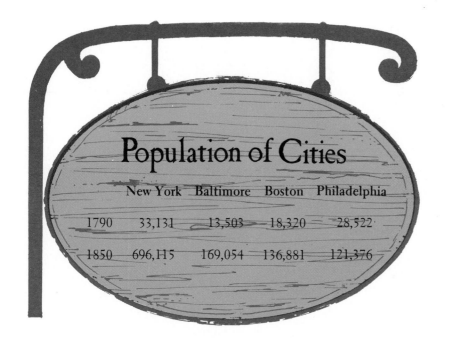

## Population of Cities

|      | New York | Baltimore | Boston  | Philadelphia |
|------|----------|-----------|---------|--------------|
| 1790 | 33,131   | 13,503    | 18,320  | 28,522       |
| 1850 | 696,115  | 169,054   | 136,881 | 121,376      |

Help students relate population growth to text's presentation of ways to earn living.

servants, and builders. Many were important in digging canals and building railroads. With the moving from farms to factories and the immigration from Europe, the number of people in cities grew rapidly.

# Together and Apart

National pride seemed to grow as more goods were made and more land was settled. Along with this pride was a concern that the unity brought by better transportation might be weakened. Many changes had come with economic growth. Some people feared changes like the growing numbers of slaves and immigrants. Both of these groups added to the growth and development of the nation. Different feelings about them, however, caused division among the sections of the country.

There was often resentment of the immigrants because they would accept work for lower wages at a time when American-born workers were beginning to demand higher pay. Religious differences added to this resentment. Most Americans were Protestants. Many of the immigrants from Ireland and Germany were Catholics. They wanted their own schools in order to teach their children the Catholic religion. Some of their priests ran for office in local elections. Protestant Americans feared that the Catholics might become a strong political group.

*New Ways to Make a Living*

# Fact and Opinion

The factory system was a faster way of producing goods. It also brought new problems. During his lifetime, Josiah Quincy became a member of Congress, the mayor of Boston, and the president of Harvard University. In 1801, he visited Slater's mill in Rhode Island and described his reactions.

*All the processes of turning cotton from its rough [form] into every variety of marketable thread . . . are here performed by machinery operating by Water-wheels, assisted only by children from four to Ten years old, and one [supervisor]. Above an hundred of the [children] are employed, at the rate of from 12 to 25 cents for a day's labor. Our attendant was very [enthusiastic about] the usefulness of this manufacture, and the employment it supplied for so many poor children. But an [argument] was [given] on the other side of the question . . . which called us to pity these little creatures, [working] in a [crowded] room, among [fast machinery], at an age when nature requires for them air, space, and sports. There was a dull dejection in the [faces] of all of them. This, united with the deafening roar of the falls and the rattling of the machinery, [satisfied] our curiosity.*

Notice that different kinds of information were included by Quincy. What facts did he give about workers in the factory? What was his opinion about using children as workers? What other opinion was expressed? How can you tell what is fact and what is opinion?

# Division

Conflicts over slavery were promoted largely by white extremists in both North and South. Many white Americans, including political leaders, tried to ignore or bury the issue, hoping that time would gradually resolve it.

During this period, the differences between the North and the South grew more serious. The main conflict was over slavery. The North depended more and more on machines to produce goods, and the South continued to depend on slaves. Northerners moving west usually went to the northern part of the frontier. Southerners settled in the southern part of the western lands. These people took their ways of life and ideas, especially about slavery, with them to the new lands. So the differences between North and South grew as the country grew.

Many people in the North were not against the slavery already in the South, but they did not want to see it spread into the new territories and states. Other northerners became more active in their opposition to slavery. They often joined antislavery groups. Southern leaders spoke in favor of slavery. They called it a secure life and a good way for black and white people to live together.

While white southerners told of the benefits of slavery, many of the slaves themselves did not agree. They were owned by another person who could make any demands and give any punishment. Many slaves tried to run away to escape. Some joined together in revolts like the one in Virginia led by Nat Turner in 1831. Turner and his followers killed sixty whites before state and federal troops stopped them. More than one hundred blacks were killed; some of them had not even been part of the revolt. Nat Turner was captured and put to death. Fear of other slave revolts led white southerners to tighten controls over slaves.

*The southern economy depended on the slavery system. Many slaves were used to pick cotton, one of the main crops of the South.*

Be sure that students are not assuming that abolition of slavery will mean freedom with political rights.

Even free blacks had very little chance for equality. They often faced discrimination, or unfair treatment because of a person's race, religion, nationality, or sex. Few northern states allowed blacks to vote. Most schools were for white or black children but not both. Blacks were made to sit in separate areas on trains or boats. Their opportunities for work were mostly the lowest paying or hardest jobs. Some states passed laws to keep free blacks from living within their borders.

Because the population of the North was growing more rapidly than that of the South, the balance of power in Congress began to change. Many southerners felt that the North would soon gain control. Sectionalism became very strong, and no easy solutions were in sight.

# Chapter 11 in Perspective See Teacher's Manual, page 92T.

## Identify

| | | |
|---|---|---|
| Samuel Slater | Eli Whitney | Nat Turner |
| Elias Howe | Cyrus McCormick | |

## Explain

| | | |
|---|---|---|
| industry | interchangeable parts | strike |
| textile machines | cotton gin | immigrants |
| factory system | labor unions | discrimination |

## Check Your Memory of the Facts

1. Who started the first textile mill in the United States? Where was it located?
2. Which section of the United States developed more factories in the years before 1860?
3. What methods of transportation and communication developed?
4. What new farm machines were invented?
5. From what countries did most of the immigrants come in the 1840's and 1850's?
6. How many slaves were there in the South in 1860? How many of them worked on large plantations?

# Check Your Understanding of the Ideas

1. What two ideas were important to the factory system? Why?
2. What things contributed to the growth of cities?
3. Why were labor unions formed?
4. How did some people feel about the immigrants?
5. What were some of the attitudes of slave owners toward slaves? Of slaves toward slavery?

# Expand Your Knowledge

1. Prepare a chart comparing the North and the South in the 1850's on each of the following: population, labor supply, farm production, industrial production, and railroad mileage.
2. Find out two or three crops that today are grown and harvested by machine and two or three which depend on hand labor. Who provides the hand labor? What are the working conditions?
3. Make a list of five inventions since 1960 which make it possible for people to produce more or to do something better. Explain how these inventions influence your life. Compare your list with others in your class.

# America Is... **Division**

# A Divided Nation

In the mid-1800's, the United States experienced great national growth. The number of people increased, and the country's borders stretched from coast to coast. People were settling the frontier in both

*William Lloyd Garrison fought against slavery with his newspaper. He published it until slavery ended in 1865.*

the South and the North. The settlers in these areas agreed on some
things, but many of them had different ideas on the question of slavery.
The split between the two sections grew wider.

231

# The Growth of Abolition

From the beginning of the nation, some people had wanted to
abolish, or put an end to, slavery. These abolitionists spoke against
slavery at a time when most people in the United States accepted it.
The abolition movement grew stronger in the nineteenth century. In
1831, William Lloyd Garrison began publishing a newspaper called
*The Liberator.* Garrison demanded immediate freedom for all slaves.
The American Anti-Slavery Society was founded in 1833. Members of
this group mailed pamphlets all over the country and sent letters to
Congress asking for an end to slavery.

Many free blacks worked against slavery. Frederick Douglass, a former slave, gave powerful speeches which turned people against slavery.
Sojourner Truth had been a slave on a farm in the state of New York
and was set free by a state law in 1827. She traveled around the North
to speak for the rights of women as well as blacks.

For many years, abolitionists were as unpopular in the North as
they were in the South. One reason for this was the prejudice of many
white Northerners against all black people. Prejudice is an attitude or
opinion about a person, group, or race, which is unfair and not based on
sound reasoning. Most Northerners wanted only to keep slavery out of
the new territories of the West. Crowds stopped meetings of abolitionists in big cities like Boston and New York. In 1837, a mob killed an
abolitionist publisher in Alton, Illinois. Slowly people began to agree
with and join the abolitionist groups. Their numbers remained small
even in the early 1860's.

Might review definition of discrimination on p. 226 and relate to prejudice.

Elijah Lovejoy was the Alton publisher killed.

# The Election of 1848

After the Mexican War, members of Congress could not agree
whether to allow slavery in the new lands won from Mexico. Early in
the war, a member of Congress had suggested the Wilmot Proviso. It
stated that slavery would not be allowed in any territory that might be

David Wilmot, Democratic Representative from PA, had borrowed the phrasing of his amendment from the Northwest Ordinance of 1787.

*A Divided Nation*

taken from Mexico. Antislavery Northerners supported the Wilmot Proviso. Senator John C. Calhoun and other Southerners took a different view. They felt that slaves were property and that the Constitution

# Frederick Douglass

Frederick Douglass was born a slave in Tuckahoe, Maryland, in 1817. When he was eight years old, Douglass was sent to be a house servant for relatives of his owner. He secretly learned to read and write there, and he began to think about escaping to freedom.

In 1833, Douglass was sent to work in the fields. Three years later, he and four other slaves made plans to run away, but they were captured as they got ready to leave. Although Douglass spent some time in jail as punishment, he continued to think about freedom. In 1838, he was able to escape to New York City and later went to Massachusetts. Douglass attended antislavery meetings there. He spoke to one group in 1841 about what freedom meant to him. He soon became a speaker throughout the Northeast about his life as a slave. Douglass also fought against unfair treatment of blacks on trains and against religious discrimination.

Frederick Douglass wrote his autobiography in 1845. Because of his growing fame, he was concerned that some people might try to send him back to slavery. So Douglass went to Europe for two years and spoke to abolitionist groups in England and Ireland. With money to buy his freedom, he returned to the United States in 1847 and settled in Rochester, New York. Douglass continued to be a part of the abolitionist movement and started an antislavery newspaper, the *North Star*. He fought against the discrimination he and other blacks faced in the free states. Once officials on a train tried to force Douglass to move from the part reserved for whites to a separate section for blacks. He held onto the seats so tightly that several pulled loose as he was physically dragged away. Douglass helped many slaves escape to the North. During the Civil War, he worked to get blacks accepted as soldiers in the Union army. He discussed the problems of slavery with President Lincoln and, after the war, worked for rights for the freed slaves. In later years, Douglass held several offices in the federal government.

Frederick Douglass fought tirelessly for equal rights for black people. He also believed that women should have the right to vote. His powerful speeches and writings inspired many people. Douglass supported these causes for liberty and justice until his death in 1895.

gave Americans the right to own and protect their property. So, citizens should be able to keep slaves on any land in the United States. Because of these different opinions, the Wilmot Proviso was voted down each time it was brought up in Congress.

Proviso was an amendment on bill to provide funds for purchase of land from Mexico. Passed in House 1846 and 1847. Final funding bill passed by Senate and House did not mention slavery issue.

Many people in the country did not agree completely with either side. Some of them liked a plan suggested by Senator Lewis Cass of Michigan. According to it, the settlers in each area could decide for themselves whether or not slavery would be allowed there. This plan became known as popular sovereignty.

During the campaign for the 1848 presidential election, both the Democrats and the Whigs tried to avoid open conflict over the issue of slavery. Lewis Cass, the Democratic candidate, hoped to win both Northern and Southern votes with his idea of popular sovereignty. The Whig candidate was Zachary Taylor, a general in the Mexican War. He was a Southerner from Louisiana who owned a plantation and some slaves. No one was sure, however, what he would do about slavery in the territories. Antislavery people were unhappy with both candidates. They formed the Free Soil party and nominated Martin Van Buren.

Confirm students' understanding of popular sovereignty which was also issue in Lincoln-Douglas debates, see p. 241.

Zachary Taylor won the election by a narrow margin. Although Taylor was a slave owner, he did not defend slavery and was strongly opposed to sectionalism. His years as an army officer on the frontier had led him to become a strong nationalist. Taylor cared more about the growth of the nation than about the growth of slavery. As President, he favored the idea of popular sovereignty for the new territories.

# *Debate Over Slavery*

Soon after President Taylor took office in 1849, people in both California and New Mexico drew up constitutions and applied for statehood. Taylor supported the admission of both territories. He thought that they were likely to enter the Union as free states because few people from the South had settled there. Southerners worried that more free states would give the North too much power in the Senate.

The presence of a thriving slave market in the capital of the "land of the free" was also source of acute embarrassment when dealing with some foreign visitors.

Other issues became part of this quarrel. Some citizens from the North wanted slavery stopped in the District of Columbia. They also wanted blacks who were accused of being runaways to be given a jury trial. People who owned slaves wanted slavery continued in the District of Columbia. They also demanded a strict national law to make people return runaway slaves. Another problem existed between Texas, a slave

Review Constitution, Art. IV, Sec. 2, on state laws and runaway slaves.

state, and New Mexico, a possible free state. They both claimed the same land around Santa Fe. Antislavery people did not want to see Texas gain more land.

# The Compromise of 1850

Henry Clay suggested a plan early in 1850 which he hoped would please everyone. Many members of Congress wanted to satisfy both sides, but they were not sure that they could support all the parts of Clay's plan. President Taylor, as well as leaders in Congress who had strong feelings about these problems, did not want to compromise. Taylor wanted to admit both California and New Mexico and then let them decide about slavery for themselves.

Then in July, President Taylor died suddenly. Vice-President Millard Fillmore of New York became President. Fillmore gave his support to compromise. Because Clay was sick, Senator Stephen A. Douglas of Illinois took over the fight to pass Clay's plan in Congress.

*Artist Eastman Johnson portrayed a slave family fleeing to the North in the painting, "A Ride for Liberty."*

# Escape From Slavery

For a slave, the decision to stay or to try to escape was a very hard one. Twice Frederick Douglass made such a decision. In later years, he described his thoughts and feelings in an autobiography. What does he give as the major reasons for his decision? What made it difficult for him to leave? Why, according to Douglass, did most blacks not try to escape?

*In coming to a fixed determination to run away, we did more than Patrick Henry, when he [decided] upon liberty or death. With us it was a doubtful liberty at most, and almost certain death if we failed. For my part, I should prefer death to hopeless bondage [slavery].*

*. . . I thought the matter over . . . and finally [decided] upon the third day of September, as the day upon which I would make a second attempt to secure my freedom. . . .*

*Things went on [around me] very smoothly indeed, but within [myself] there was trouble. It is impossible for me to describe my feelings as the time of my . . . start drew near. I had a number of warm-hearted friends in Baltimore,— friends that I loved almost as I did my life,—and the thought of being separated from them forever was painful beyond expression. It is my opinion that thousands would escape from slavery, who now remain, but for the strong cords of affection that bind them to their friends. The thought of leaving my friends was decidedly the most painful thought with which I had to [deal]. The love of them was my tender point, and shook my decision more than all things else. Besides the pain of separation, the [fear] of a failure exceeded what I had experienced at my first attempt. The [awful] defeat I then [suffered] returned to torment me. I felt assured that, if I failed in this attempt, my case would be a hopeless one—it would seal my fate as a slave forever. I could not hope to get off with any thing less than the severest punishment, and being placed beyond the means of escape. . . . The [misery] of slavery, and the blessedness of freedom, were [always] before me. It was life and death with me. But I remained firm, and, according to my [decision], on the third day of September, 1838, I left my chains, and succeeded in reaching New York without the slightest interruption of any kind.*

Douglas divided the plan into separate bills and managed to get each one passed. This group of laws formed the Compromise of 1850. The compromise included these parts:

1. California was admitted as a free state. The territories of New Mexico and Utah were to decide about slavery for themselves. New Mexico voted to become a slave territory, and Utah voted to be free.

See map on p. 239 for territories under discussion.

*A Divided Nation*

2. The slave trade, or selling slaves at a public auction, was stopped in the District of Columbia. Slavery, however, was still allowed.

3. The Fugitive Slave Act was passed. According to it, federal officers were to be used to capture runaway slaves. Any citizen could be required to help slave owners get back their slaves.

4. The land claimed by both New Mexico and Texas became part of New Mexico. Texas received ten million dollars from the federal government for giving up its claim.

The Compromise of 1850 seemed to be a success. Most people in the North and South accepted the compromise as a whole, even if they disliked some parts of it. Feelings were eased for a time, but the plan did not settle the issues forever.

# The Fugitive Slave Act

One part of the Compromise of 1850 upset people in the North more than any other. Many of them who opposed slavery felt that the Fugitive Slave Act was too harsh. Slave owners had demanded the law because they felt that troublemakers were persuading their slaves to run away to the North. They believed that abolitionists were robbing them of their property by helping slaves to escape. After the act was passed, it was easier to return blacks to slavery. They were not allowed a jury trial, and they could not even speak in court to defend themselves.

The Fugitive Slave Act also made life more hazardous for free blacks, thousands of whom also fled to Canada.

People in several states helped slaves escape to the North or to Canada after the Fugitive Slave Act was passed. These secret groups were known as the Underground Railroad. They hid slaves in their homes during the day. At night, when it was safer to travel, they directed them to another station, or safe home, along the route. Some three thousand slaves escaped to Canada in the months following the passage of the Fugitive Slave Act. Harriet Tubman was one of the most famous conductors on the Underground Railroad. Born into slavery in Maryland, Tubman escaped to Pennsylvania in 1848. She later returned to slave states nineteen times to lead over three hundred people to freedom.

Many runaway slaves were captured and returned to their owners. In 1854, a mob in Boston tried to keep a runaway slave, Anthony Burns, from being returned to South Carolina. They did not succeed. Burns, guarded by a sheriff and more than fifty soldiers, was put on a ship in the Boston harbor and sent back. But more and more people were beginning to resist the Fugitive Slave Act.

*Many abolitionists provided food and shelter for escaping slaves. Levi Coffin's farm in Newport, Indiana, was used as a station on the Underground Railroad. Many slaves stopped there on their way north.*

# An American Best-seller

The stories of runaway slaves did much to increase the sympathy of white Northerners for black people. In 1852, Harriet Beecher Stowe wrote *Uncle Tom's Cabin*. This novel described the severe and cruel conditions of the slave system. It was a dramatic story of how slavery broke family ties and caused great suffering for black people. Southern whites felt strongly that the book was not a true picture of slavery. But over 300,000 copies of it were sold in the first year. People who had never been a part of the abolition movement were very moved by the story. Many of them joined the fight against slavery. Because of its emotional effects, *Uncle Tom's Cabin* has been called one of the most important American novels ever published.

Stowe's novel presented the antislavery argument as the cause of absolute good against unmitigated evil.

*Harriet Beecher Stowe*

# The Kansas-Nebraska Act

The city at the eastern end of the railroad route would become the "gateway to the West" for trade. Douglas wanted Chicago to be that city. Other cities contending were St. Louis, Memphis, and New Orleans. Reference also the Gadsden Purchase, pp. 202-3, which favored a southern route.

See Missouri Compromise, p. 160.

A new law split the leaders of the North and South even more. It was written to organize the lands of the Great Plains into territories. This land lay between the eastern half of the United States and the areas of California, Oregon, Utah, and New Mexico. Senator Stephen Douglas of Illinois wrote the bill which was passed by Congress. Douglas was an investor in railroads. He wanted a railroad to be built to California. Once the area of the Great Plains was divided into territories, the federal government could give land to companies to build railroads. The railroads could then sell some of the land to settlers. And these settlers would provide the railroad with more business.

The Kansas-Nebraska Act divided the land into two territories called Kansas and Nebraska. It also repealed the Missouri Compromise which had not allowed slavery in this area. The question of allowing slaves there was to be decided by popular sovereignty.

Kansas became the center of a great battle over slavery. Both proslavery and antislavery groups sent people to live in Kansas. During elections, many people from Missouri, a slave state, crossed the border to vote for proslavery candidates. At one time, there were two governments in Kansas, one proslavery, one antislavery. Things in Kansas became violent as people on both sides were shot and killed. Throughout the 1850's, the territory became known as "Bleeding Kansas."

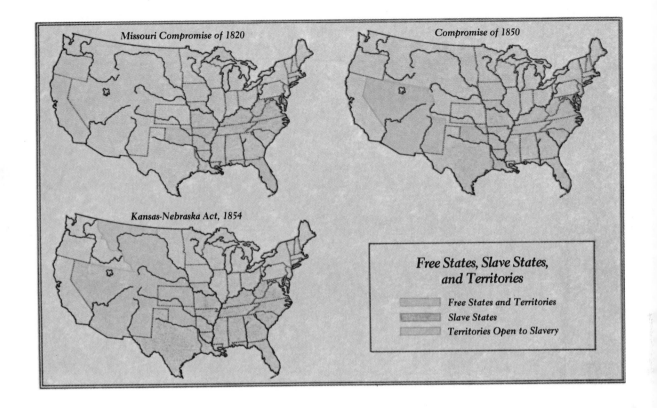

Missouri Compromise of 1820

Compromise of 1850

Kansas-Nebraska Act, 1854

**Free States, Slave States,
and Territories**

Free States and Territories
Slave States
Territories Open to Slavery

# New Political Parties

A new political party, called the Know-Nothing or American party, was formed during this period. Because the party members tried to be a secret group, they answered "I know nothing" when asked about the goals of the party. The Know-Nothings united many people in both North and South who opposed the large number of immigrants entering the country. They gained seats in some state governments and won control of the Massachusetts government in the election of 1854. They soon split up over the issue of slavery. After a short time, the party disappeared.

A Republican party was started during the arguments over the Kansas-Nebraska Act. Members of this party included antislavery people from the Whig party, the Democratic party, and the Free Soil party. Support for the new Republican party was widespread in the North. In state after state, Republicans organized campaigns in time for the 1854 elections to Congress. That year, they won a majority of seats in the House of Representatives.

See also note p. 131. This Republican party is the first to clearly represent one section of the country.

*A Divided Nation*

The Republicans soon became a new major power in America. They were a Northern party and favored the programs the South had been voting down for years. These were a protective tariff, free land for farmers, and land grants to help build railroads. Most important to the party was its opposition to the spread of slavery. In the presidential election of 1856, Republicans nominated John C. Frémont, the soldier and explorer. The Democratic candidate, James Buchanan of Pennsylvania, won the election, but Frémont made a strong showing. Southern leaders saw the Republican party as a serious threat to their interests.

# The Dred Scott Decision

When President Buchanan came into office, there was fear across the nation that the Union was splitting apart. Leaders in the South and North could not agree about slavery in the new territories of the West. To both South and North, the Supreme Court seemed to offer hope of a solution. The Court was considering an important case from a Missouri court about a slave named Dred Scott.

Scott had been "sold" to an abolitionist, and *Dred Scott v. Sandford*, 1857, was a deliberate test case. Scott was "freed" by Sandford three days after Taney's decision.

Scott was the slave of an army doctor who lived in Missouri. He had been taken by the doctor into a free state, Illinois, and into a territory (later Minnesota) where Congress had forbidden slavery. Finally, they returned to Missouri. Scott believed that, since he had lived on free soil, he was no longer a slave. His case for freedom was heard in Missouri courts and appealed to the United States Supreme Court.

The Chief Justice of the Supreme Court, Roger B. Taney of Maryland, wrote for the majority. He denied Scott's claim that he was free. The decision said that Scott was a slave and did not have the right to take cases to court. Taney wrote that slaves were property and that the Constitution protected a person's right to own property. He also stated that Congress had no right to prohibit slavery in the territories.

Republicans and many Northern Democrats were outraged at the Dred Scott decision. The Kansas-Nebraska Act had said that voters could decide about slavery. This case suggested that slavery could not be kept out of the territories, even by voting against it.

# The Lincoln-Douglas Debates

In 1858, Abraham Lincoln, a Republican, ran against Stephen Douglas, a Democrat, for election to the Senate from Illinois. Many Democrats, in both North and South, hoped to see Douglas run for

President in the future. In a series of debates, these two candidates covered the important issues of the spread of slavery, popular sovereignty, and the Dred Scott case. Lincoln challenged Douglas to the debates, hoping to win voters to his side. The whole nation read about the debates in the newspapers.

See definition of popular sovereignty on p. 233.

Lincoln was deeply against the spread of slavery. The Dred Scott decision had suggested that the territories did not have the right to decide about slavery. But popular sovereignty was the base of Douglas' Kansas-Nebraska Act. Lincoln hoped to trap Douglas. So he asked if the Dred Scott case did mean that popular sovereignty could not be used by new territories. If Douglas spoke against popular sovereignty, he was likely to lose the election in Illinois. If he spoke for it, he would lose the backing of Southern Democrats. Douglas stated that the people could keep out slavery if they wished. If they did not pass laws to protect slavery, it could not survive.

*In the election of 1858, Abraham Lincoln ran against Stephen Douglas for senator from Illinois. Lincoln and Douglas met in a series of debates that were followed by people across the country.*

Some Northerners had turned against Douglas as presidential material because they considered the Kansas-Nebraska Act a sell-out to Southern slave interests.

Douglas' view satisfied many people in Illinois, and he was re-elected. His position did not satisfy the Southern Democrats. They did not trust him as a candidate for President in 1860. Lincoln, on the other hand, had stated clearly that slavery was wrong. Republicans began to consider him for the presidential nomination.

# John Brown

Brown had been an abolitionist activist for several years and had contributed to the civil war in Kansas by leading a raid, the "Potawatomi massacre," in which 5 proslavery settlers were murdered in 1856.

The bitterness between the North and South became even greater in the fall of 1859. Abolitionist John Brown planned to operate a fort in the Allegheny Mountains of Virginia. From there, he would give weapons to slaves and start a war for freedom. Brown organized a small band of blacks and whites. To get guns, they attacked the federal arsenal, a place where weapons are kept, at Harpers Ferry, Virginia. United States Marines under Colonel Robert E. Lee soon captured Brown, who was tried and hanged. While the Dred Scott case had angered many Northerners, the events at Harpers Ferry upset many Southerners. They feared that other abolitionists would encourage uprisings to free the slaves.

*This poster was used by Lincoln and Hamlin in the presidential election campaign of 1860.*

# The Election of 1860

The Democrats met in Charleston, South Carolina, in the spring of 1860 to choose a candidate for President. Northern and Southern Democrats could not agree on a person who would represent both sections. Each group met separately and chose its own candidate. The Northern Democrats chose Stephen Douglas. The Southern Democrats chose John C. Breckenridge of Kentucky.

With the Democratic party divided in this way, Republicans hoped to win. At their convention, the Republicans nominated Abraham Lincoln. They considered Lincoln a compromise candidate. He wanted to stop the spread of slavery, but he did not demand that slaves in the South be freed. The party pictured Lincoln as a humble man with firm moral beliefs. Lincoln's image in the South was different. Southerners saw him as a monster who would destroy their way of life. In the election, Lincoln won every free Northern state except New Jersey. That was enough electoral votes to win the presidency.

New Jersey's electoral votes were split, part of them going to Douglas.

Lincoln won only 39% of the popular vote, but those were distributed strategically enough to give him a majority of electoral votes.

# The Confederate States of America

To some powerful Southern leaders, secession, or withdrawing, from the Union seemed the only answer to Lincoln's election. They felt that the Republicans would soon control the entire government of the United States. Northern policies would hurt the South. After the Republican victory in 1860, several Southern states decided to secede.

There was no Southern state in which the sentiment for secession was universal, and there was considerable opposition to it in GA, AL, VA, and TE for some time.

Secession was a popular idea throughout the South, although not everyone agreed with it. Some leaders had spoken about secession during the arguments of the 1850's. Others had asked Southern states to try to heal the differences with the North. Every year, however, more and more Southerners had thought of secession as the final solution to their problems. South Carolina was prepared for it. Soon after news of Lincoln's election arrived, that state acted to secede. Delegates attended a convention in December, 1860. They voted to take South Carolina out of the federal Union. Mississippi, Florida, Alabama, Georgia, Louisiana, and Texas soon followed. All seven states sent delegates to Montgomery, Alabama, in February, 1861. There they drew up a constitution much like the Constitution of the United States. They made Jefferson Davis, a former United States senator, president of the Confederate States of America.

President Buchanan expressed his disapproval of secession as he left office, but had considered himself legally unable to stop it.

*Jefferson Davis had served in the Mexican War and was an experienced politician. He had been a member of Congress and the secretary of war.*

During these months, some people tried to find a compromise. Lincoln promised that, as President, he would leave slavery alone where it already existed, unless the states themselves voted otherwise. But neither he nor the Republican party would agree to the spread of slavery. Lincoln's promises and the compromise plans of other leaders had little effect on the new Confederate States. Confederate leaders were determined to build their own nation. The only question that remained was whether or not the North would let the South secede in peace.

# *Chapter 12 in Perspective* See Teacher's Manual, page 95T.

### Identify

| | | |
|---|---|---|
| William Lloyd Garrison | Stephen A. Douglas | Abraham Lincoln |
| Frederick Douglass | Harriet Tubman | John Brown |
| Sojourner Truth | Harriet Beecher Stowe | Jefferson Davis |

# Explain

| | | |
|---|---|---|
| abolition | popular sovereignty | Kansas-Nebraska Act |
| prejudice | Fugitive Slave Act | Dred Scott decision |
| Wilmot Proviso | Underground Railroad | secession |

## Check Your Memory of the Facts

1. What position did Zachary Taylor take on the issues of the 1848 election?
2. What were the main parts of the Compromise of 1850?
3. What events led to "Bleeding Kansas"?
4. What issues did Stephen Douglas and Abraham Lincoln debate in the race for senator from Illinois?
5. What helped the Republicans win the presidential election of 1860?
6. Which states joined to form the Confederate States of America?

## Check Your Understanding of the Ideas

1. What were the main issues in the conflict over slavery at this time?
2. What was the purpose of the Compromise of 1850? Did it succeed?
3. What was the significance of *Uncle Tom's Cabin?*
4. Why was the Kansas-Nebraska Act written? What effect did it have on the nation?
5. What effect did the Dred Scott decision have?
6. Why did the Republican victory in the 1860 election lead to the secession of several Southern states?

## Expand Your Knowledge

1. Even though abolitionists wanted to free the slaves, they all did not use the same methods. Prepare a brief report comparing John Brown's actions with the way the Underground Railroad worked.
2. Write a brief statement showing how each of the following persons might have reacted to news about the Supreme Court decision in the Dred Scott case: a slave owner, an abolitionist, a free black person, and a slave.
3. Find out why the Lincoln-Douglas debates were important to both candidates. How were the debates planned and announced at the arranged places? How would you compare these political meetings to those of today?

*A Divided Nation*

# The Civil War

# The Civil War

13

Aim: to present students with military and nonmilitary factors involved in the Civil War and the eventual success of the Union forces.

The Civil War caused more death, suffering, and property damage for the people of the United States than any other war in the nation's history. It decided the issue of the federal government's power over the individual states. Slavery was ended, but most freed blacks were left

*In April, 1861, Confederate troops opened fire on the Union forces at Fort Sumter. The people of nearby Charleston, South Carolina, watched from rooftops as the long war began.*

without homes or jobs. The war brought an increase in business for many industries in the North, but it left the South with a ruined economy. The Civil War caused important changes in the country, but it created very serious problems.

# One Nation or Two

Seven states seceded and, in February, 1861, formed the Confederate States of America. The North could have let the Southern states leave the Union in peace. At first, some Northern leaders wanted to do that. But by March, most people in the North agreed that secession should not be allowed. They felt that the American people had been one nation since before the Constitution was written. North and South had the same language and culture. Trade flowed back and forth between the two sections. Northerners also pointed out that a long border between the United States and the Confederacy could lead to trouble. The South had to be kept in the Union, even if it meant war.

Southern leaders had a very different view. They thought that their own rights under the Constitution, especially those about property and slaves, were threatened. Many Southerners believed their culture and economy were different from and better than those of the North. A depression in the country at the end of the 1850's had not affected the South as much as the North. Cotton prices remained high in the English market. Southern leaders felt they did not need the North in order to be prosperous. They thought that they had a right to secede and form their own government.

Remind students of the very old arguments on the nature of the Union and the issue of states' rights. Review colonial difficulties over Declaration and states' problems over ratification of Constitution, KY and VA Resolutions, Webster-Hayne debates and nullification crisis, etc.

# Two Governments

The Confederacy set up a new government based on the ideas that their leaders had fought for in the Union. The Confederate constitution was modeled after the Constitution of the United States. However, it did contain two important changes. The Confederate congress could not pass any law against slavery, and it could not enact tariffs to protect industry. Before secession, Southern leaders had argued that states' rights were more important than the power of the federal government. Under the Confederate government, most power remained with the states.

Help students note use of phrase *Confederate* States as an expression of states' rights view of government.

*The Civil War*

The government of the United States continued to place more importance on its powers over those of the states. The Republicans in the North took advantage of their new party power in Congress and in the presidency. In the next few years, they passed laws the South had blocked for so long. Kansas was admitted as a free state. Colorado, Nevada, and Dakota were admitted as free territories. Manufacturers got a protective tariff. Farmers got the Homestead Act which gave settlers 160 acres of land without charge. The government gave huge grants of land to build a railroad from Nebraska to California. To help finance the war, a system of national banks was developed.

See note on p. 180 for banking.

# The Beginning of the War

Early in 1861, the Confederacy had taken over nearly all forts and navy yards in the South. Fort Sumter, on an island off Charleston, South Carolina, was one of the few that remained under Union control. When Lincoln became President, one of his first acts was to try to protect that fort. He announced that he was sending supplies there. This alarmed Southern leaders, who thought he might also send more soldiers. On April 12, 1861, Confederate cannons began firing on Fort Sumter. It was forced to surrender within two days.

The firing on Fort Sumter helped to unite people in the North for war. On April 15, 1861, President Lincoln asked for seventy-five thousand volunteers for the army. The South saw this as a declaration of war. Many Southerners who had been against secession felt that they were forced to defend their states. Jefferson Davis, president of the Confederacy, also called for volunteers to fight.

Four of the slave states that had not seceded earlier—Virginia, Arkansas, Tennessee, and North Carolina—chose to leave the Union and join the Confederacy. The western part of Virginia refused to secede and later became the separate state of West Virginia. Four other slave states—Missouri, Kentucky, Maryland, and Delaware—remained part of the Union. As the war began, the Confederacy included eleven states and the Union twenty-three.

It took some time for the United States and the Confederacy to raise and drill armed forces that would be ready for battle. The army of each side was much larger than any before in the nation's history. The commanders of both the Union and Confederate forces had to learn to control and direct 100,000 soldiers and more. In the first year of the

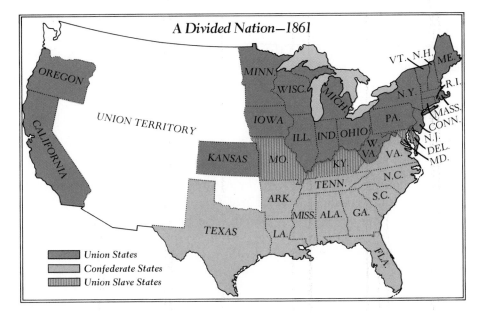

A Divided Nation—1861

UNION TERRITORY

OREGON

CALIFORNIA

MINN.

WISC.

IOWA

KANSAS

MO.

ILL. IND. OHIO

KY.

TENN.

ARK.

TEXAS

LA.

MISS. ALA. GA.

S.C.

N.C.

FLA.

MICH.

N.Y.

PA.

W. VA.

VA.

MD.

DEL.

N.J.

CONN.

MASS.

R.I.

N.H.

VT.

ME.

Union States
Confederate States
Union Slave States

Compare with map on p. 239.

war, there was little heavy fighting. One important battle was fought at Bull Run in Virginia. The Union forces there, who had expected an easy victory, suffered a surprising defeat. Leaders in both the North and the South decided that long-range plans were needed to win the war.

# Southern Plans

At first, the leaders of the Confederate States planned for a defensive war. They expected to defend their territory until the United States wearied and recognized it as an independent country. There were advantages to keeping the fighting in the South. The Confederate army would be close to its own cities and could get supplies easily. The soldiers would know the land and roads where they were fighting. Many of the army officers in the Confederacy had gained experience before the war in the armed forces of the United States. These officers, like Robert E. Lee and A. S. Johnston, gave the Confederate army an early advantage over the Union army.

One of the biggest hopes for a Confederate victory was to get help from Europe, especially France and Great Britain. In particular, the Confederates hoped to use their cotton trade to influence Great Britain. Southerners believed that the British textile mills depended

By the 1850's, more than 80% of Britain's cotton supplied by America. But by spring of '61, English market 50% oversupplied and Confederate decision to withhold only gave England chance to work off surplus. Both Britain and France also increased cotton trade with Egypt and India.

*The Civil War*

heavily on Southern cotton supplies. The British would have to aid the Confederate States in the war to keep that trade open. Their mills, however, were able to find other sources for cotton. It soon became clear that neither Great Britain nor France would be of great help.

# Northern Plans

The main goal of the leaders of the United States was to restore the Union. They planned to send troops southward to divide and occupy the Confederate territory. There were two other important parts to the Union plan. One was to keep other countries from entering the war on the side of the South. The other was to blockade, or close off, the South by using the strong Union navy. After the firing on Fort Sumter, a blockade was established along the Southern coast, especially around the chief ports.

*The U. S. Military Railroad Field Hospital at City Point, Virginia, was photographed by Mathew Brady.*

Early in the war, most things seemed to favor the North. It had a store of weapons and materials and the factories to produce more. The South depended on buying many manufactured goods from Europe. The North also had better means of transportation. The New England states and the Midwest had nearly twenty-one thousand miles of railroad tracks. The South had only about nine thousand miles of tracks. Many sections of tracks in the South were not directly connected to each other. The North had over twice the population of the South and so could raise a bigger army.

Southern rail system was collection of short lines with different gauges which meant that one line's cars had to be unloaded and reloaded into another's to move supplies over greater distances.

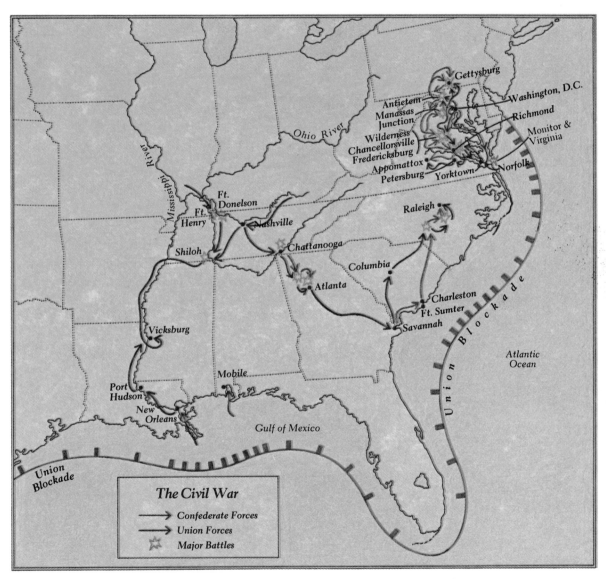

The Civil War

Confederate Forces
Union Forces
Major Battles

Might compare Union blockade with British blockade, see map on p. 153, to reinforce understanding of nation's growth in unity and division.

*The Civil War*

# From Plans to Action

The *Merrimac* had been a U.S. steam frigate before the Confederates outfitted it as the first ironclad vessel ever put to sea.

The blockade was the most successful part of the Union plan at the start of the war. It cut off the South and stopped much Confederate trade. The Confederacy tried to break through the blockade in 1862, using an ironclad ship, the *Merrimac*, renamed the *Virginia*. A Union ironclad, the *Monitor*, battled it to a draw, and the blockade remained tight.

The Union forces won some victories in the West in 1862. They gained control of the upper Mississippi River north of Memphis, Tennessee. Confederate troops were forced out of Kentucky and most of Tennessee. The Union navy gained control of the important port of New Orleans. In the East, the armies battled back and forth between Washington, D.C., and Richmond, Virginia. Each side hoped to capture the capital of the other side. In 1862, General Robert E. Lee took command of the main Confederate army. Under his leadership, Confederate forces began to win more battles in the East.

# Preserving the Union

President Lincoln believed that the Civil War was being fought to preserve the Union, not to abolish slavery. There were people throughout the North who were not interested in emancipation, or freeing slaves. Lincoln felt that making abolition the main goal of the war might divide the North. He did not want the slave states of Delaware, Maryland, Kentucky, and Missouri to leave the Union.

As the war progressed, antislavery forces became stronger. Abolitionists wanted to make the war a fight to end slavery. As they gained strength, Lincoln took action to hold their support and achieve his goal of saving the Union. In 1862, he wrote:

> My [main] object in this struggle *is* to save the Union, and is *not* either to save or to destroy slavery. If I could save the Union without freeing *any* slave I would do it; and if I could save it by freeing *all* the slaves I would do it; and if I could save it by freeing some and leaving others alone I would also do that. . . . I have here stated my purpose according to my view of *official* duty; and I intend no [change] of my oft-expressed *personal* wish that all men every where could be free.

*A group of slaves listen to a Union soldier read the Emancipation Proclamation.*

# The Emancipation Proclamation

Lincoln decided that freeing slaves in at least part of the South would help unite the North and hurt the Confederacy. He wrote a proclamation, or an official announcement, freeing Confederate slaves. Then, believing it would be better to make the announcement after a Union success, he waited to tell the public.

In September, 1862, the Union and Confederate armies clashed at the Battle of Antietam in Maryland. More soldiers died there on September 17 than in any other single day of the war. Neither side won the battle, but the Confederate army was stopped from invading the North. Because of this, President Lincoln saw it as a victory. He announced that on January 1, 1863, "all persons held as slaves" within the lands under Confederate control "are, and henceforward shall be, free." This statement is known as the Emancipation Proclamation.

The Emancipation Proclamation did not apply to slaves in states and territories in the Union. It did not affect areas that had joined the

More than 23,000 total casualties at Antietam.

Since it could not be enforced in areas not held by Union forces, the Proclamation mainly served to "dignify" the war as a crusade for human liberty.

*The Civil War*

Confederacy but had already been won back by Union forces. But as Union troops took over additional areas in the South, thousands of slaves in those areas were freed. Nearly 200,000 blacks joined the Union forces, but they were not treated equally. They received lower pay and were often given jobs away from the actual fighting. However, during the last two years of the war, black soldiers took part in most of the major battles.

# Clara Barton

Clara Barton's long career of helping others began when she was very young. At eighteen, she became a teacher in a school near her home in North Oxford, Massachusetts. Barton founded the first "free" or public school in New Jersey thirteen years later in 1852. She became a clerk in the Patent Office in Washington, D.C., in 1854 and was probably the first regular woman employee of the federal government.

After the start of the Civil War, Clara Barton began taking food and first-aid supplies to the people in the army. She nursed wounded soldiers, even under fire, and soon became known as the Angel of the Battlefield. She wrote about her mission:

> Men have worshiped war till it has cost a million times more than the whole world is worth, poured out the best blood and crushed the fairest forms the good God has ever created.—Deck it as you will, war is—'Hell'. . . . The war side of war could never have called me to the field. . . . Only the desire to soften some of its hardships and [relieve] some of its miseries ever [convinced] me. . . .

At the war's end, Barton started a group who tried to find information on the thousands of soldiers who were missing.

In 1882, Clara Barton founded the American Red Cross. She had worked with the International Committee of the Red Cross in Europe and was impressed by their work. For twenty years under her leadership, the American Red Cross raised money and sent aid to victims of floods, fire, disease, and other disasters. By the time that Barton gave up control of the Red Cross, it was a large, well-established organization. The American Red Cross continues to provide the relief services for which it was founded. Clara Barton was ninety-one years old when she died in 1912. She was one of the most honored women of her time.

# *People at Home*

For people in both the South and North, it was a terrible war. They were shocked by the large number of soldiers killed in the battles. Prices of most goods rose quickly everywhere. Most families could not afford to buy the things they needed. They tried to repair what they had and make or grow what they needed at home.

As more men went off to war, many women were left alone to run farms, plantations, and businesses. Women in both South and North volunteered to help the armies, especially as nurses. At first, their offers were turned down because most men did not think it proper for women to work as nurses. But Clara Barton, who later founded the American Red Cross, replied:

> When our armies fought on Cedar Mountain [Virginia, August 9, 1862], I . . . went to the field.
> . . . And if you chance to feel, that the positions I occupied were rough . . . for a *woman*—I can only reply that they were rough . . . for *men*. But under all, lay the life of the nation. . . . I felt that some return was due from me and that I ought to be there.

In order to get enough soldiers into the army, both the North and the South had to start drafts, or the selection of men who would be

*Nearly everyone on both sides contributed to the war effort. Many women volunteered to sew uniforms for the soldiers.*

Early in the war, "bounty" payments were offered as inducements to enlist. Volunteers could sometimes collect from county, city, state, and federal government.

forced to serve. On both sides, a wealthy man could pay someone else to serve for him. Soldiers complained that it was "a rich man's war and a poor man's fight." Many people in cities rioted against the draft.

# Effects on the Economies

The war was slowly destroying the Southern economy. The need for food and manufactured goods increased, and the South could not supply all of these things alone. Trade with Europe was needed, but the Union blockade prevented it. Because much of the fighting took place in the South, there was great destruction of land and property. There were not enough people or money to keep up fields, buildings, or railroads. The Southern economy was not able to meet the demands the war put on it.

The North experienced a growth in its economy during the war. More farms were developed in the Midwest. The demand for food increased because of the need to feed the Union army. Also, crop failure in parts of Europe during 1862 and 1863 created markets there for food from the United States. Farmers bought more farm machines to take the place of workers who had gone to war. Some Northern industries were hurt. Others, like the weapons, iron, steel, and textile industries which supplied the army, grew to meet the greater demands.

# A Desperate Struggle

As an important commander in the Confederate army, General Lee felt that the South could not plan only to defend its land. He decided that his troops should invade the North and force the Union to agree to independence for the South. In late June, 1863, the Confederate army of seventy-five thousand soldiers moved north. The Union army, with ninety thousand troops commanded by General George Meade, moved to stop them. The two armies met near Gettysburg, Pennsylvania, on July 1, 1863. For three days, the Confederates attacked the Union lines south of town. But they were unable to defeat the Union troops and finally retreated south.

Although they had not gained much territory in the East, the Union army was winning important battles in the West. General Ulysses S. Grant took over command of Union forces there. While the

Union troops were winning at Gettysburg, Grant forced the surrender of Vicksburg, Mississippi, after a six-week siege. This victory opened the entire Mississippi River to Northern use. It divided the South into two parts. The eastern states of the Confederacy were completely cut off from Louisiana, Texas, and Arkansas.

Many people felt that the battles of Gettysburg and Vicksburg were the most important ones of the war. Both sides suffered heavy losses. But while Union forces were still strong, the Confederate army was shattered. There were not many more soldiers to replace those who had been killed. Supplies were running out, and there was no longer hope for aid from Europe. The defeat of the Confederate troops at Gettysburg and Vicksburg became the turning point in the war.

Might assign student research and report on civilian suffering during siege situations, focusing on Vicksburg.

# The Gettysburg Address

On November 19, 1863, President Lincoln went to the dedication of a cemetery on the battlefield of Gettysburg. There he gave this short speech.

*Four score and seven years ago, our fathers brought forth on this continent, a new nation, conceived in Liberty, and dedicated to the proposition that all men are created equal.*

*Now we are engaged in a great civil war, testing whether that nation or any nation so conceived and so dedicated, can long endure. We are met on a great battle-field of that war. We have come to dedicate a portion of that field, as a final resting place for those who here gave their lives that that nation might live. It is altogether fitting and proper that we should do this.*

*But, in a larger sense, we can not dedicate—we can not consecrate—we can not hallow—this ground. The brave men, living and dead, who struggled here, have consecrated it, far above our poor power to add or detract. The world will little note, nor long remember what we say here, but it can never forget what they did here. It is for us the living, rather, to be dedicated here to the unfinished work which they who fought here have thus far so nobly advanced. It is rather for us to be here dedicated to the great task remaining before us—that from these honored dead we take increased devotion to that cause for which they gave the last full measure of devotion—that we here highly resolve that these dead shall not have died in vain—that this nation, under God, shall have a new birth of freedom—and that government of the people, by the people, for the people, shall not perish from the earth.*

*The Civil War*

# Splitting the South

After the Battle of Vicksburg, General Grant was put in command of all Union forces. He planned to lead the Union troops in the East in an attack on the Confederate capital in Richmond, Virginia. General William T. Sherman was in charge of the troops in the West. He was to move through Georgia, capture Atlanta, and continue to the Atlantic Ocean. Four railroads and several factories were located in Atlanta, and it was very important to the Confederacy. Sherman's route to the sea would again divide the Confederacy.

In May, 1864, Sherman began his advance through Georgia. On the way, the Union troops took horses, supplies, and whatever else they needed from the people in the area. They completely destroyed almost everything else—railroads, bridges, buildings, crops, and animals. They left behind a path of destruction nearly three hundred miles long and sixty miles wide. In late December, 1864, Sherman captured Savannah, Georgia, on the Atlantic Ocean.

By the spring of 1865, the Confederacy was nearly defeated. Sherman had turned north from Savannah into the Carolinas. He put pressure from the south on Confederate forces in Virginia. Grant had led his soldiers in a long attack on Richmond. Lee and the Confederate soldiers were finally forced out of the city. But with Union troops on both sides, the Confederate army could not retreat very far. On April 9, 1865, General Lee surrendered his army to General Grant at Appomattox Court House, Virginia. The surrender of other Confederate units soon followed. The Civil War was over.

# "With Malice Toward None"

Abraham Lincoln had been reelected President of the United States in 1864. As the war ended, he faced the very difficult task of rebuilding the nation. He spoke of his plans in his second inaugural address.

> With malice toward none, with charity for all, with firmness in the right as God gives us to see the right, let us strive on to finish the work we are in, to bind up the nation's wounds, to care for him who shall have borne the battle and for his widow and his orphan, to do all which may achieve and cherish a just and lasting peace among ourselves and with all nations.

*Crowds gathered in Springfield, Illinois, to see the wagon carrying Lincoln's body.*

Lincoln was never able to put these ideas into practice. On April 14, 1865, only five days after Lee surrendered, Lincoln was shot by John Wilkes Booth, an actor who believed that he was helping the Confederacy. The death of Abraham Lincoln caused great sadness and bitterness in the North.

The Civil War had been cruel to both sides. Sorrow had touched almost every family in the nation. About 2,400,000 soldiers had served in the two armies. Nearly 200,000 of them were killed in the fighting. Another 400,000 soldiers had died from disease and other causes. As the military battles came to an end, political battles began in the search for "a just and lasting peace."

Through World War I, the major number of war deaths resulted from poor sanitation and medical ignorance.

See Teacher's Manual, page 97T. ## Chapter 13 in Perspective

## Identify

Robert E. Lee
Clara Barton

Gettysburg
Ulysses S. Grant

William T. Sherman
John Wilkes Booth

*The Civil War*

# Explain

blockade                    Emancipation Proclamation                    drafts

## Check Your Memory of the Facts

1. Why did the South want to leave the Union?
2. Why was the North unwilling to let the South leave the Union?
3. How did the constitutions of the Confederate States and the United States differ?
4. Which slave states did not leave the Union?
5. Where did the first military action of the Civil War take place?
6. How did the South and the North compare in population and railroads?
7. Which slaves were freed by the Emancipation Proclamation?

## Check Your Understanding of the Ideas

1. Why did the South claim it had a right to withdraw from the Union?
2. How did Southerners try to use cotton to influence Great Britain to support them in the war? Why were they unsuccessful?
3. What were the Confederate military plans for the war? The Union plans?
4. How did Lincoln's actions to end slavery relate to his goal of preserving the Union?
5. What attitude toward the South was expressed by Lincoln in his second inaugural address?

## Expand Your Knowledge

1. Prepare a report on one of the following topics: the treatment of prisoners of war in the South and the North; black soldiers during the Civil War; medical care during the Civil War.
2. Locate several poems written during or about the Civil War. Select one or two which express something you think is important about the war, and read them to the class.
3. Choose a state or territory—California, New Jersey, or Colorado, for example—that was not part of the battleground of the Civil War. Find out how the people in that area were affected by the war.

# New York 1860-1865

A group of American Indians sold an island off the northeastern coast of their lands to the Dutch West India Company in 1626. The Company had established a fort and trading post at the tip of the island which was located in a large bay. The island was named Manhattan after the Indians who sold it. The Dutch called the settlement New Amsterdam.

In 1664, New Amsterdam came under the rule of the English who changed its name to the City of New York. The English held it until the end of the Revolutionary War. The new government of the United States took its first census, or population count, in 1790. By that time, Manhattan was home to more than thirty-three thousand people. Under Dutch, English, and American rule, the city had grown as a center of trade.

In 1860, on the eve of the Civil War, New York was the biggest, richest city in the entire United States. More than 800,000 people lived on Manhattan, and hundreds of thousands more lived in nearby cities like Brooklyn, Queens, and the Bronx. Almost half the people living on the island had come to the United States from other countries. The City of New York was the biggest center of immigration in America.

## A City Map

One visitor to New York found an easy way to remember the pattern of its many avenues and streets. Edward Dicey wrote:

*The plan of the city is wonderfully simple.... If you suppose that the skeleton of a sole [a*

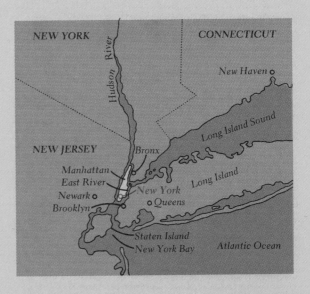

*kind of fish] had a number of cross-bones parallel to the back-bone, you will have an exact idea of the plan of New York. The back-bone is the Broadway; the parallel cross-bones are the Avenues; and the bones at right angles to the back-bone are the Streets, numbered [in order] from the sole's mouth. The system is not perfect, because the streets in the old part of the city have names of their own. . . . The lower end of the island, corresponding to the sole's mouth, is the commercial part, the "city" of New York. Broadway is the great thoroughfare, where all the chief stores and shops are situated; and Fifth Avenue, with the streets running across it, is the fashionable quarter. . . . Across the middle of the island stretches the Central Park; and beyond that, towards the tail of the sole, are long straggling suburbs, which threaten . . . to cover the whole island of Manhattan.*

## First Impressions

In the spring of 1861, an English news writer visited the United States to report on the possibility of war between the North and South. William Russell's visit took him first to New York and then to other cities in the North and South. Russell returned to New York in July, after the war had started.

*... the first thing which struck me was the changed [look] of the streets. Instead of peaceful citizens, men in military uniforms [crowded] the pathways, and [so many] United States' flags floated from the windows and roofs of the houses as to [give] the impression that it was a great holiday festival. ... [In March,] it was very rarely I ever saw a man in soldier's clothes. ... Now, fully a third of the people carried arms, and were dressed in some kind of martial garb.*

*... An outburst of military tailors has taken place in the streets; shops are devoted to militia equipments; rifles, pistols, swords, plumes, long boots, saddle, bridle, camp beds, canteens, tents, knapsacks, have [taken] the place of the ordinary articles. ...*

*... I [saw a] crowd of women, some with children in their arms standing in front of a large house and gazing up earnestly and angrily at the windows. I found they were wives, mothers, and sisters, and daughters of volunteers who had gone off and left them destitute [without support]. ...*

*The change in manner, in tone, in argument, is most remarkable. I met men to-day who last March argued coolly ... about the right of Secession. They are now furious at the idea of such wickedness. ...*

## Reactions

Once the question of war was decided, the people of New York joined in support of the Union cause. They acted quickly to organize and equip the soldiers, and they gave help to the families of those who volunteered to serve. There were thousands of volunteers, especially among the immigrant groups. To the poorest of them, army service

*Union troops marching in New York City*

A Union army hospital

meant pay. To most of the immigrants, it was also proof of loyalty to their new country.

Through religious, social, and government organizations, the people of the city played an important part in the war. They raised money for special payments to those who volunteered to join the army. They arranged for improved health care and sanitary conditions in the distant army camps. By the spring of 1862, people realized that "the show time of the war has passed away, and it has become a matter of sober business." Edward Dicey also wrote:

*In many a house that I have been into, I have found the ladies busy in working for the army . . . but there is little talk or fuss made about it. There are few balls or large parties this season, and the opera is not regularly open. . . . but work is plentiful, and the distress, as yet, has not gone deep down.*

## Young People

The daily lives of the younger people in the city changed little during the war years. Most of them kept up their studies, and Dicey was very impressed by the schools they attended.

*The instruction is entirely [free]—everything, down to the pens and ink, being provided by the State. Education is not compulsory [required by law]; but the demand for it is so great that . . . the school benches are always more than filled. . . . The teachers in all the classes, except two or three . . . are women. . . . Reading, writing, ciphering* [arithmetic], *geography, grammar, history, book-keeping for the boys, and moral philosophy* [the study of right and wrong] *for the girls, were the* [main subjects]. . . . *What struck me most was the look of intelligence and the orderly behavior of the children. . . .*

*Besides the State schools, there are several free public schools, kept up by voluntary contributions* [from church members]. *. . . In the classes I went through . . . were representatives of almost every foreign nation . . . the majority were Germans, Irish, and* [blacks]. *. . . they learn to read and write* [American English]. *. . .*

## The Cost of Living

By the summer of 1863, the slow and deadly progress of the war had changed life for many of the city's people. Some of those in business became very rich from war trade. But the pay of ordinary soldiers was quickly spent by families as the cost of living increased. Taxes rose, rents went up, and food became very expensive. One writer reported on clothing:

*A lady's bonnet—a little piece of velvet and a flower . . . now costs one hundred dollars. . . . Gloves are worth what was formerly considered a week's salary for many people, while other styles of dress have increased* [also]. *. . .*

Even the lowest-paying jobs became very important to the city's immigrants who held most of them. The Emancipation Proclamation had upset many workers, especially the Irish who had most of the unskilled, low-paying jobs. These people were afraid that freed blacks would come north to find work. Many of the workers had been the first to volunteer to fight for the Union. They were not so willing, however, to fight for the freedom of slaves.

## The Draft Riot

Some political leaders and news writers in the city did not agree with the way President Lincoln ran the war. In 1863, they especially attacked the order to draft soldiers. The first list of drafted men was published on Sunday, July 12. It was made up mostly of poor people; many of them also supported the Democratic party. Some Democratic party leaders had claimed that it was unconstitutional for the government to force a state citizen to serve in a federal army. They charged that the number of Democrats on the draft list was too high.

Monday morning, a large crowd of people gathered in front of the draft office. Some of them believed that men had been drafted for political reasons. Others were afraid of losing their jobs to blacks. Many were tired of high prices and low pay.

By Monday afternoon, the crowd had changed into a violent mob. Men, women, and some children began to attack the draft office. They set fire to the records, books, and furniture. They beat the people who tried to stop them. From the draft office, the mob went to attack the shops and homes of antislavery leaders. They caught black people on the street and beat them, sometimes killing them. A home for black orphans was burned to the ground, and one child died in the fire.

After four days, the riot was finally ended with the help of federal and state soldiers and special groups of volunteer citizens. Many people had lost their lives, and over $1,500,000 worth of property had been destroyed.

## Joy and Sorrow

In some sections of New York, many people were making a great deal of money from the war. They enjoyed spending it. New theaters opened, and large new houses were built. Richly dressed men and women rode in expensive carriages along Fifth Avenue to Central Park.

George Templeton Strong, who lived on Manhattan all his life, recorded some of the events of April, 1865, in his diary. Strong was walking down Wall Street on April 3 when the news came that Richmond had been captured by Union troops.

*An enormous crowd soon blocked [the street]. . . . Never before did I hear cheering that came straight from the heart . . . given because people felt relieved by cheering and hallooing. . . .*

*I walked about on the outskirts of the crowd, shaking hands with everybody. . . . Men embraced and hugged each other . . . retreated into doorways to dry their eyes and came out again to flourish their hats and hurrah. . . .*

*April 15. . . . LINCOLN . . . ASSASSINATED LAST NIGHT!!!! . . . Tone of [angry] feeling [is] very like that of four years ago when the news came of Sumter.*

*. . . No business was done today. Most shops are closed and draped with black and white muslin [cloth].*

## Homecoming

As the war came to an end, soldiers who were not given other duties were allowed to go home. A news writer reported on their return to New York.

*Some came by sea, but most by railways to Jersey City, and thence across the ferry to Pier No. 1. They landed near the open space by the Battery [the old Dutch fort area] and marched up town. . . . [Some freed blacks], acting as water-carriers, [walked] in the rear. . . . Regiments known in the city were of*

New York City after the war

*course more warmly greeted than strangers passing through. . . . Heavy losses had been sustained. . . . The New York 52nd regiment, for example, came back less than three hundred strong, having had on its muster rolls, during the war, two thousand six hundred names.*

Many families had lost their fathers, brothers, and husbands. Some soldiers returned from the war badly wounded or crippled. These families faced a difficult future. Others looked at the rebuilding of the South as a new business adventure. They faced the future with confidence. The lives of the people of New York had been changed by the war in many ways.

# Atlanta 1860-1865

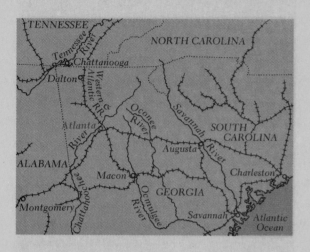

By the late 1830's, the state of Georgia had taken the Indian land on both sides of the Chattahoochee River. Business and political leaders used some of the land to improve the state's transportation routes. In 1836, the legislature created a state-owned railroad company. The route they chose for this new Western & Atlantic Railroad was "from some point on the Tennessee line near the Tennessee River . . . to some point on the southeastern bank of the Chattahoochee River." State leaders also encouraged owners of private railroad companies in Georgia to make their lines longer and connect them with the Western & Atlantic.

## Poster Power

In 1845, the Georgia Railroad Company announced its newly finished connection to the Western & Atlantic line at Marthasville. On advertising posters, the company called the town where the railroads met "Atlanta," a form of the railroad name Atlantic. In 1846, the state legislature made the name Atlanta official.

Another important railroad connection was completed in 1846. Atlanta began to grow very quickly. Property sales multiplied as new people came to start businesses. There was a medical college, but Atlanta did not have a public school system. White children attended private schools or took private lessons. There were very few free black families in the city, and slave children were not allowed to study. There were churches, factories, warehouses, banks, hotels, and restaurants. Doctors and lawyers settled in Atlanta, and newspaper offices opened. By 1860, Atlanta had a population of nearly six thousand people and was one of the most important cities in the South.

## Civil War Service

Atlanta was the chief supply center for the Confederate army during most of the Civil War. Its factories made many of the weapons used by the South. The four main railroad lines through the city carried soldiers and supplies to the front lines of the war. Some of Atlanta's people had moved north when the war first started. Many more of them stayed, raising money for weapons and supplies and caring for wounded soldiers. As the war dragged on, Atlanta grew so important to the Confederate cause that it became a main target of General Sherman's Union troops.

Early in the summer of 1864, Union soldiers pushed the Confederate troops into Georgia and across the Chattahoochee

River. By July, General Hood's outnumbered troops prepared to defend Atlanta. Hood encouraged most of the families in the city to leave. Many of them did, and merchants and bankers sent their extra supplies to other cities for safekeeping. In August, Sherman's Union guns opened fire on the city.

## Surrender

After several weeks of Union attack, the Confederates were forced to abandon Atlanta. Before leaving the city, Hood ordered his soldiers to burn all the army supplies that they could not carry with them. He did not want to leave weapons for the enemy to use. Sherman's soldiers entered Atlanta on September 2, 1864. Historian Franklin M. Garrett wrote about that day.

*. . . Atlanta for the first and last time in its history, was surrendered to an invading army.*

*By noon the whole line of Marietta Street was blue with Union soldiers, and the citizens of Atlanta [showed their] mixed emotions. Some, tired of the war . . . greeted the Federals with a show of enthusiastic welcome; others took [few] pains to conceal the fact that they regarded the Northern [soldiers] as "vandal invaders."*

Sherman ordered the citizens to leave their homes and turned Atlanta into an armed Union camp. The city had been captured, but the war was not over. By November, Sherman's plans for marching through Georgia to Savannah were complete. He ordered his troops to destroy the railroad and telegraph lines and the bridges into northern

*Citizens leaving Atlanta*

Georgia and Tennessee. Atlanta was not to serve the Confederates as a supply base again.

When the Union troops prepared to leave the city, they gathered cattle and food supplies to take with them. Sherman told his officers that the army of more than 62,000 soldiers would have to "live off the land" when those supplies were gone. Orders were given to burn warehouses and factories before leaving the city. A Union soldier wrote about that day.

*. . . it soon became* [clear] *that these fires were but the beginning of a general* [blaze] *which would sweep over the entire city and blot it out of existence . . . the soldiers* [took] *what they wanted before it burned up. . . . new fires began to spring up . . . noises rent the air . . . soldiers on foot and horseback raced up and down the streets while the buildings on either side were solid sheets of flame. . . . The night, for miles around was bright as mid-day; the city of Atlanta was one mass of flame. . . .*

## Coming Home

Three weeks after the Union army had burned Atlanta, General W. P. Howard of the Georgia troops came to inspect the damage. He reported to the governor:

*Could I have arrived ten days earlier, with a guard of 100 men, I could have saved the State and city a million dollars.*

*There were about 250 wagons in the city on my arrival, loading with pilfered plunder* [stolen goods]; *pianoes, mirrors, furniture of all kinds, iron, hides without number, and . . . other things, very valuable at the present time. This exportation of stolen property had been going on ever since the place had been abandoned by the enemy.*

Sherman's troops leaving Atlanta

*. . . About fifty families remained during the occupancy of the city by the enemy, and about the same number have returned since its abandonment.*

Kate Massey from Atlanta wrote about some of the difficulties that families faced upon their return to the city.

*People lived in anything they could find. Some families were housed in old freight cars. Some used discarded army tents. . . .*

*. . . A young woman* [who needed a new dress] *took several old ones, ripped, raveled, carded, spun, and wove them into new material. Then she made her dress. . . . Some children's shoes were made with wooden soles. One mother of two small daughters of approximate age and size managed to get for them one pretty outfit. . . . They wore it on alternate Sundays. . . .*

A few people found their homes unburned when they reached the city. Octavia Hammond wrote to neighbors about the condition of their property.

*Your flowers are still alive and I think the grass lots have a notion to come up. If it were possible to* [find] *material we would* have your lots enclosed for you to save them from wagons, horses and cattle. But the plank is not to be had. . . . We have no garden at all, but I am afraid Ma will plant the front yard in cabbage, onions and peas. If she does I will [give you some]. . . .

. . . Bacon is five dollars a pound, butter six, flour a dollar and a half, syrup twenty a gallon, eggs six [dollars] a dozen, potatoes twenty a bushel and meal the same.

## Action!

Enough people had returned to Atlanta by December that regular elections were held for mayor and city council. The council then elected people to jobs like tax collector, city doctor, and police officers. The newly-elected treasurer reported that the city had less than two dollars in cash. Supplies of money and goods were low, but the people of Atlanta had energy and courage. A visiting news writer reported on their activities a few months later.

From all this ruin . . . a new city is springing up with marvelous [speed]. . . . streets are alive from morning till night with . . . hauling teams and shouting men,—with loads of lumber and loads of brick and loads of sand,—with piles of furniture and hundreds of packed boxes . . . with carpenters and masons,—with rubbish removers and house-builders . . . all bent on building and trading and swift fortune making.

## Union Blue Again

By early spring, a few private schools had opened, and the medical college was preparing to hold classes again. But April was a month filled with bad news for the citizens of Atlanta. On the ninth, they learned

Union troops back in Atlanta

that General Lee had surrendered to General Grant. On the twenty-sixth, General Johnston surrendered to General Sherman. For Atlanta, and for the whole South, the Civil War was over. Early in May, the city again became a military post for the United States army. This time, citizens were encouraged to stay and to continue rebuilding the city.

In many ways, the Union troops were helpful to the people of Atlanta. They were a strong influence on law and order, and they brought Northern money to the city. In the months that followed, the federal government was a great help to the poor of the city. Atlanta's leaders were concerned about the large numbers of Southerners who came to the city for help. The editor of the Atlanta *Daily Intelligencer* wrote in September about these people.

*There is a population in and on the suburbs of this city . . . of families who have been stripped of everything, and whose [working men] went into the war and have never returned. . . . they simply exist. . . . With barely food [enough] to keep soul and body together. . . .*

*Others . . . were driven from their homes in other states and places, and have never been able to return to them. . . . These people may be seen in any direction on the outskirts of town, and in the hurry and bustle of business it becomes us not to forget them. Strained, as our people are . . . surely something may be spared [for these others]. . . .*

*Another [group], larger and increasing . . . are huddled together in most [awful poverty]. . . . our feelings are not so keenly aroused in their behalf. We [mean] the recently liberated slaves. . . .*

*. . . the good of society, and the [lessening] of crime, demand . . . [we do something for them] speedily!*

## Freedom

Almost all groups of people faced hardships after the war. The recently freed slaves also faced terrible prejudice. Some white Southerners supported the ideas of freedom for blacks. Very few of them were willing to accept the idea that any blacks should have full voting rights as citizens of the United States.

To most black people, freedom meant joy mixed with fear. Many came to the city because they had nowhere else to go. As Frederick Douglass said, "They were sent away empty-handed, without money, without friends and without a foot of land to stand upon."

A few black people had been trained in skills or as household servants. They often found work in the city, although they did not receive the same pay as white workers. Thousands of blacks had known only field work. They came to the city because they were curious or to find family and friends. Many came from fields ruined by war, and they needed the food that was given out by the army and the government.

Even with the terrible hardship and discrimination they faced, blacks preferred their new roles as free people. One former slave explained when asked about it:

*What do I like best, to be slave or free? . . . Well, it's this way, in slavery I own nothing and never own nothing. In freedom I can own the house and raise the family. All that causes me worry—and in slavery I had no worries—but I take the freedom.*

# Rebuilding the Union

# 14

Aim: to help students understand the complex political, social, and economic problems facing Americans after the Civil War.

The job of reconstruction, or rebuilding the country after the Civil War, was a long and difficult one. The Union had been preserved, but the war had created many serious problems. Ways had to be found to work with the defeated South and the freed slaves. The United States tried to solve these issues in the years from 1865 to 1876, known as the Reconstruction period. However, the rebuilding never returned things to the way they had been before the war. The Civil War had a lasting effect on the nation.

Students should understand that Reconstruction years given are general, as with most designated "eras."

*Destruction of Southern railroads by the Union army helped guarantee the North's victory. It cut off the South's communication and transportation and prevented the movement of food and other supplies in the South.*

*Rebuilding the Union*

# The Problems

Most of the battles during the war had been fought in the South. Several important cities, like Atlanta and Richmond, had been nearly destroyed. There were signs of ruin everywhere. Cities, towns, homes, and farms had been badly damaged. Railroads, roads, and bridges were torn up, and many could not be used. The supply of food was low because crops had been taken or destroyed by both armies. Business, industry, and banking had to be restored, and Confederate paper money was worthless.

Before the war, much of Southern life centered around the plantations and the slave system. After the war, plantation owners did not have slaves. The men and women who had been slaves, called freedmen, had received their legal freedom but little else. Neither Southern nor Northern whites were willing to consider them as equals. Most of them had no food, no homes, and no property. They heard stories that each freedman would be given forty acres of land and a mule. No such help ever came.

# Lincoln's Plan

Government leaders had different views about how to deal with the defeated Southern states. One group felt that these states had never really left the Union. According to them, certain people who were disloyal to the United States government had led a rebellion. The states themselves, however, were still part of the Union. Another group believed that the states which had seceded were no longer a part of the United States. They had to apply to Congress to be admitted as states just as new territories did.

Long before the end of the war, President Lincoln had been concerned about what would happen to the South. He thought that a defeated South would face much confusion, with no state governments and no money. Lincoln had wanted to make it easy for the seceded states to return to the Union. In 1863, he had offered a plan to the South that he hoped would help end the war.

According to Lincoln's plan, the Confederate states could begin to start new state governments in the Union if 10 percent of the voters took an oath of loyalty to the United States. The states also had to accept the Emancipation Proclamation. Four Southern states—Louisiana, Arkansas, Tennessee, and Virginia—had set up new governments following the President's plan. Lincoln had approved these governments before his death in 1865. But they were still waiting to be approved by Congress where there was disagreement over Lincoln's plan.

# Charlotte Forten

Charlotte Forten was born in Philadelphia, in 1837. Her grandfather James Forten, the great-grandson of a slave, owned a large sailmaking business and was a famous anti-slavery leader. The members of Charlotte Forten's family were all active in the abolition movement. She grew up with a strong desire to prove that black people were as capable of learning as white people.

In 1854, Forten was sent to study in Salem, Massachusetts, where there was no discrimination in the schools. She wanted to be a teacher and graduated from the Salem Normal School in 1856. For two years, Forten taught in an elementary school in Salem. Then in 1858, she returned to her family in Philadelphia because of her poor health.

During the Civil War, Charlotte Forten took the opportunity to help blacks in the South who had been slaves. In late 1861, Union forces had taken over a group of islands off the coast of South Carolina and Georgia. Thousands of slaves had been left there as their owners fled the Union army. Many government leaders and abolitionists saw this as a chance to show that former slaves could live successfully as free citizens. The Port Royal Experiment was started to give educational and medical aid to the freedmen on the islands. Forten was one of the teachers who volunteered to help. She taught there from 1862 to 1864.

Charlotte Forten kept a journal of her years in Philadelphia, Salem, and Port Royal. In it, she expressed her feelings as a young black woman growing up in a world that was mostly white. Published long after her death in 1914, it pictures her strong commitment to help blacks. She wrote:

> This morning a large number—Superintendents, teachers and freed people, assembled in the little Baptist church. It was a sight that I shall not soon forget—that crowd of eager, happy black faces from which the shadow of slavery had forever passed. "Forever free!" "Forever free!" Those magical words were all the time singing themselves in my soul. . . .

# The Reaction of Congress

One group in Congress led those people who felt the South was out of the Union and had to apply to be admitted again. The members of the group were called Radical Republicans because they wanted to make major, or radical, changes. They wanted to protect the rights of the freed slaves and to increase the power of the Republican party in the North and the South. These leaders did not think the terms of Lincoln's plan were hard enough on the South. They felt that policies for reconstruction should come from Congress and not from the President.

The Radical Republicans formed their own plans for rebuilding the South. They were concerned that slavery still existed in some parts of the country. In January of 1865, they proposed the Thirteenth Amendment to the Constitution. It was a bill to abolish slavery throughout the United States. Most members of Congress wanted each Southern state to approve this amendment before returning to the Union. By the end of the year, most of the Northern states and eight of the Southern states had ratified the amendment, and it became law. The status of the Southern states, however, was still in question. Congress had not yet approved their new governments.

Another part of the Radical Republican plan unfolded in March, 1865. Congress created a Bureau of Refugees, Freedmen, and Abandoned Lands. Commonly known as the Freedmen's Bureau, its purpose was to provide food, clothing, fuel, and land to poor or homeless people, black or white. Agents of the Bureau traveled throughout the South, giving help to those in need.

Clarify with students that slavery was abolished by this Amendment, not by the Proclamation.

Note pragmatic acceptance of Southern states' ratification of 13th Amendment by Congress although question of state or territory still unresolved.

# Johnson's Plan

Lincoln and Johnson had run on the Union party ticket, a temporary party of Republicans, Democrats, and others who supported the war.

When Abraham Lincoln died, Vice-President Andrew Johnson became President. The struggle over reconstruction continued between Congress and the new President. Johnson had been a Democratic senator from Tennessee who disliked rich planters. He had refused to follow that state out of the Union and had remained in the Senate. But Johnson still believed strongly in states' rights. He thought that the federal government should not interfere very much with the new state governments. He was not concerned with how the new governments would treat black people.

Johnson's plan for reconstruction was much like Lincoln's. It applied to the seven seceded states which had not yet followed Lincoln's plan. According to Johnson, a certain number of people (probably a

*The government helped set up schools for free blacks. Some abolitionist groups and churches provided teachers and supplies.*

majority of voters) in a state had to take an oath of loyalty. Then a state constitution could be written, and a new state government could be set up. Johnson announced his plan while Congress was not meeting. When Radical Republicans and others in Congress opposed his plan, he refused to compromise. The remaining Southern states—South Carolina, North Carolina, Alabama, Mississippi, Florida, Georgia, and Texas—set up new governments under Johnson's plan. But these states, like the four under Lincoln, still had to be approved by Congress.

# Black Codes

Many war leaders of the South were leaders again in the new state governments. These people took steps to restore their former ways of life. In most states after the war, black people could legally own property, make contracts, and be legally married. The new state governments, however, passed laws called Black Codes which limited most opportunities for blacks. In some states, the codes left freedmen not much better off than they had been as slaves. Blacks were kept from serving on juries or testifying against whites at trials. The codes limited the kinds of jobs blacks could hold. They also said that freed slaves who did not have jobs could be forced to work for their former owners.

Many Northerners were alarmed by the number of former Confederate officials who were serving in the new Southern governments. Many believed that this plus the Black Codes were signs that Johnson's plan left the South almost as it had been before the Civil War. The

Under some of these laws, black Americans could be arrested and jailed for "breaking contracts" if they quit their jobs.

# View of the South

David Macrae, a well-known Scottish writer and church leader, toured the United States in 1867 and 1868. He later wrote a book called *The Americans at Home*. The following selections from that book describe the lives of some white Southerners and former slaves in the years after the Civil War. What are the important points that Macrae makes about the people?

*The South had not only wasted her population, but her material resources. I visited districts where the people . . . had dug up every potato in their fields, pulled every apple from their orchards, taken even the blankets from their beds, to make up and send to the . . . army.*

*. . . I heard of one lady who in January 1865 had 150,000 dollars in Confederate paper [money], and owned slaves that would have sold in 1860 for 50,000 dollars more in gold. . . . she had to go . . . to the [Freedmen's] Bureau shed . . . to get bread to keep her children from starvation.*

*. . . Men who had held commanding positions during the war had fallen out of sight and were filling humble [jobs]. . . . One of the most prominent men of the Confederacy was trying to earn a living in the pea-nut business; a cavalry commander was keeping a boarding-school. . . .*

*The old planters were . . . so poor that they were trying to sell a portion of their land in order to pay the tax upon the rest. . . .*

*All this talk about the [blacks] being happier in slavery I heard amongst the white people, but rarely if ever amongst the [blacks] themselves. Many of the poorest of them told me that they had to put up with coarser food . . . and poorer clothing . . . and that they had a hard struggle even for that; but the usual wind-up was,—"But thank the Lord, we're free, anyhow. . . ."*

*I made inquiries also amongst those whom I found swarming into cities and towns, instead of staying in the country where their labour was needed. I found that, while some had come to eat the bread of idleness, many had come for safety; others to get their children to school; others to seek for work that would be paid for.*

Republican majority in Congress refused to accept any of the representatives from former Confederate states when Congress met in December, 1865. They repeated that only Congress, and not the President, could decide about the admission of these states. This meant that all eleven of the Southern states would have to start over to get back in the Union.

Might assign student research and reports on Thaddeus Stevens, PA leader of Republicans in the House, and Charles Sumner, Republican senator from MA.

# Radical Reconstruction

Early in 1866, the Republicans in Congress fought the Black Codes. Led by the Radicals, they passed the Civil Rights Act of 1866. This act said that states could not discriminate against a person because of race or color. President Johnson vetoed the bill. He believed it was against the constitutional rights of the states. Congress, however, passed the act over Johnson's veto. Until this time, Congress had not been able to pass bills over the vetoes of Johnson.

Some moderate Republicans had hoped for conciliation with Johnson and hesitated to override his vetoes.

In June, 1866, Congress voted for the Fourteenth Amendment. Based on the Civil Rights Act, it clearly stated that blacks were citizens of the United States. When a state did not allow all male citizens over twenty-one years of age to vote, it would lose part of its representation in Congress. The bill also made it very difficult for people who had been officials in the Confederate government to be elected to Congress. Of the eleven Southern states, only Tennessee ratified the Fourteenth Amendment. It then became the first Southern state to be returned to the Union with the approval of Congress. The Fourteenth Amendment was approved by enough states to be added to the Constitution in 1868.

Citizenship was not defined in the main body of the Constitution although Congress was given power to make naturalization laws. Review 14th Amendment with class. In it, for first time, citizenship is defined and citizens' rights of life, liberty, and property are specifically placed under the protection of the federal government.

During the elections of 1866, the Radicals gained so much power in Congress that they could pass any bills they wanted over Johnson's vetoes. As a result, Congress could control the reconstruction of the South, rather than the President. Early in 1867, the Radical Republicans passed laws for their plan of reconstruction. These laws applied to all the states which had been part of the Confederacy, except Tennessee. The states were placed under the rule of the army. They had to hold constitutional conventions to create new state governments. All men who swore their loyalty to the federal government, except certain former Confederate officials, could vote for delegates to these conventions. Their new constitutions had to give black men the right to vote. Before being taken back into the Union, the new state governments had to ratify the Fourteenth Amendment.

# Impeachment of Johnson

Many of the Radicals were most interested in establishing the supremacy of Congress in the American system of government.

President Johnson did not like the new reconstruction plan, but he carried it out. The Radical Republicans felt that Johnson was not doing as much as he could to put the laws into practice in the South. They wanted to remove him from office. Under the Constitution, a President who is impeached, or charged by the House of Representatives with crimes while in office, then has a trial in the Senate. The members of the Senate act as judge and jury. A President who is found guilty is removed from office.

*President Johnson was handed his notice of impeachment. Although found not guilty, he lost most of his political power.*

Congress had passed a law in 1867 called the Tenure of Office Act. This law said that the President could not remove members of the Cabinet from office without asking the approval of the Senate. The Radicals hoped to keep some people in the Cabinet who agreed with them on reconstruction. Edwin Stanton, the secretary of war, was one Cabinet member who sympathized with the Radicals. Because of this, President Johnson removed him from office. The Radicals then charged the President with breaking the law. In the spring of 1868, the House of Representatives voted to impeach President Johnson.

During Johnson's trial, many members of the Senate as well as people across the country felt that the President was really being tried because he disagreed with the Radicals. The final vote came in the Senate on May 16, 1868. It was 35 to 19, just one vote short of the two-thirds majority needed to convict the President. Johnson served the rest of his term in office, but he had lost almost all of his influence.

Might review with students the presidential powers stated in Constitution and hold mock election on constitutionality of law requiring Senate approval for removing Cabinet member. Tenure of Office Act not invoked again and repealed in 1887. Supreme Court retroactively found it unconstitutional in *Myers v. U.S.* (1926).

Had Johnson been found guilty, precedent would have been established for removing President for political reasons, not for "high crimes and misdemeanors" as required by Constitution.

# New Southern Governments

In 1868, six states were returned to the Union under the reconstruction plan of the Congress. North Carolina, South Carolina, Alabama, Arkansas, Louisiana, and Florida set up governments that were approved by Congress. Along with Tennessee, this brought the total of approved states to seven out of the eleven which had seceded.

At first, the Republican party controlled all the new governments in the Southern states. It was supported by the large numbers of blacks who were allowed to vote for the first time. Many blacks were elected or appointed to office in the new governments. P.B.S. Pinchback became lieutenant-governor of Louisiana and served for a short time as governor. Blacks outnumbered whites in the lower house of the South Carolina legislature in 1868, but whites kept most of the seats in the state senate. Blacks did not gain full control of any of the legislatures of the new Southern governments.

Several blacks were elected to serve in the federal government during this period. Hiram Revels had been born in North Carolina and had attended Knox College in Illinois. He became the nation's first black senator when he was elected from the state of Mississippi in 1870. In 1874, Blanche K. Bruce, a former slave who had studied at Oberlin College in Ohio, was elected to the Senate from Mississippi.

*Rebuilding the Union*

# Scalawags and Carpetbaggers

The Republican party received support from some Southern whites. Enemies often called these people scalawags, a word meaning scamp or rascal. Usually, scalawags had been in business or had owned plantations. They wanted to control black voters as they had controlled their slaves. Many Northern whites who supported the Republicans also came to the South during this period. They were often called carpetbaggers by Southerners. They saw these people only as adventurers carrying all they owned in a bag made from pieces of carpet. The carpetbaggers actually came for many reasons. Some planned to buy land or start new businesses. Others wanted to help the freedmen.

Many white Southerners were upset with the new state governments and blamed them for many problems during this period. They did not like the idea of blacks and white Northerners having any power in their states. The Southerners claimed that the state governments were very corrupt and were bitter about higher taxes that were passed. State governments were trying to rebuild roads and railroads and expand the public school system. Higher taxes brought in the money needed to do this. Some people in office did take tax money for themselves. In South Carolina, for example, some officials kept money that was supposed to be used to buy land for black farmers.

# The Election of 1868

In the presidential election of 1868, the Republicans chose Ulysses S. Grant, the commander of the Union armies in the Civil War, as their candidate. They hoped that the voters would see Grant as a war hero and elect him to lead the nation in peace. The Democrats chose Horatio Seymour, former governor of New York, as their candidate. He attacked the way the Radicals were handling reconstruction. Large numbers of Northerners and many new black voters in the South supported Grant, and he won.

Many Republicans saw that the votes of blacks could be very important to the future of the party. In the North, many states had chosen not to let blacks living there vote. But the new governments in the South had been forced to do so. After the election, Republicans wanted to make sure that they would get the support of black voters again. They proposed the Fifteenth Amendment in February, 1869. This bill said that no state could keep a person from voting because of color. The amendment was approved by enough states to become law

*Black men received the right to vote in 1867. Here a former slave casts his ballot in a state election that same year.*

on March 30, 1870. Virginia, Georgia, Texas, and Mississippi were required to vote for it before they could return to the Union. These states approved the amendment by July, 1870. With this, all of the seceded states were once again part of the Union.

# Democratic Power in the South

A short time after the new state governments were set up, certain groups of Southern whites began working to regain control of them. Most of these white Southerners belonged to the Democratic party. They wanted to rid the South of carpetbaggers and to keep the blacks from gaining any more power in the government. Several things helped the Democrats return to power in the South. Many Northerners had not wanted blacks in the North to be allowed to vote. Others were losing interest in the Southern blacks and their problems. Voters no longer elected to Congress as many representatives who pressed for the rights of black people.

In the South, groups were formed which threatened blacks and their friends and kept them from voting. The Ku Klux Klan, formed in Tennessee in 1866, was started by former Confederate soldiers to oppose the state government of Republican Governor William Brownlow. Although some members were against violence, others began a campaign of terror against black and white Republicans. They also tried to scare teachers of the freedmen's schools and others who helped blacks. While Congress passed the Radical reconstruction acts, the Ku Klux Klan spread to other states in the South. Blacks were kept from voting by threats and sometimes by killings. In 1871, Congress ordered federal troops to stop the violence. Many arrests were made, and the Klan began to lose its power.

In the long run, Southern Democrats were also able to regain power because they controlled so much of the land and the money in the South. They could refuse to lend money, to rent or sell land, or to give jobs to blacks. Slowly, the new governments returned to the control of the Democrats. Blacks were once more discouraged from taking part in the government.

*Little effort was made toward establishing an economic base for black Americans upon which they could build their political rights. In the few cases of land distribution accomplished, blacks proved to be successful farmers and organizers of civil government.*

*Members of the Ku Klux Klan often wore ghostlike costumes. They frightened and even killed blacks and sometimes whites who helped blacks.*

# Political Scandals

Several events took place in the government under President Grant that also turned people's attentions from reconstruction. In 1872, it became known that some members of Congress had accepted stock in a company called Crédit Mobilier. This was a separate construction company set up by the directors of the Union Pacific Railroad. The directors then gave contracts to their own company to build the railroad lines. Since the Crédit Mobilier charged very high prices for the work, the directors and some members of Congress received large profits. Because the Union Pacific had to pay the high prices, it did not make much profit. So, the stockholders of the Union Pacific received little or no money in return for their investments.

In 1875, employees of the Treasury Department were caught in dealings with the Whiskey Ring. This was a group of whiskey manufacturers who were not paying the full amount of taxes they owed. President Grant's own personal secretary was involved, and the government had been cheated out of thousands of dollars. These and other scandals caused many people to doubt the honesty of the people leading the United States government.

# The Election of 1876

In the election of 1876, both the Republicans and the Democrats chose candidates who promised to reform the government. Governor Rutherford B. Hayes of Ohio was the Republican candidate. Governor Samuel J. Tilden of New York was the Democratic candidate. Both wanted honest government; neither pressed for the rights of blacks.

When the electoral votes were counted, a problem arose. Both the Democrats and Republicans claimed the electoral votes of Louisiana, South Carolina, and Florida. In addition, an elector in Oregon was dismissed because he did not meet the proper qualifications. Twenty electoral votes were in question. No one could prove clearly that they had been cast for Hayes or for Tilden. Tilden had won a narrow majority of the popular vote, and he needed only one more electoral vote.

For months, the House of Representatives could not agree on a winner. Finally, the leaders of the two parties made a deal among themselves. The Republicans promised to remove the federal troops from the three Southern states still under Republican control. They were also to support a bill for federal aid to build a railroad from the

See p. 171 to review electoral system. This election has also been called the "Great Swap" and the "Stolen Election." Country faced constitutional crisis of a vacant presidency. Electoral commission was made up of 5 members each from the House, the Senate, and the Supreme Court.

South to the Pacific Ocean. In return, the Democrats would agree to have Republican Hayes as President. A special electoral commission was set up. It gave all twenty of the votes in question to Hayes.

# After Reconstruction

Black people were the real losers in the election of 1876. White rule again became the way of life in the South. In a few areas, blacks were still allowed to vote because some Democrats could control those votes to defeat the whites who worked small farms. Few rights were gained in the North to give blacks full and equal citizenship. The attention of white voters and government leaders in both the North and the South turned to other issues.

# Chapter 14 in Perspective See Teacher's Manual, page 100T.

## Identify

Andrew Johnson          Blanche K. Bruce          Rutherford B. Hayes
Hiram Revels

## Explain

reconstruction          impeach          Ku Klux Klan
freedmen               scalawags        Crédit Mobilier
Black Codes            carpetbaggers

## Check Your Memory of the Facts

1. What years were known as the Reconstruction period?
2. What were two views about returning the seceded states to the Union?
3. What did the Radical Republicans want to do?

4. Which states responded to Lincoln's plan for reconstruction?
5. Which states responded to Johnson's plan for reconstruction?
6. What was the Freedmen's Bureau? What did it do?
7. Which was the first state to return to the Union with the approval of Congress? What did Congress ask of the seceded states at that time?
8. What did Congress ask of the seceded states applying to return to the Union after 1869?

## Check Your Understanding of the Ideas

1. What were the important differences between the plans for reconstruction of Lincoln, Johnson, and the Radical Republicans?
2. What actions by Southern governments showed that their attitudes toward blacks were the same as before the Civil War?
3. What was an important result of the election of 1868?
4. What events caused Northern voters to lose their concern for protecting the rights of blacks?
5. How was the presidential election of 1876 finally decided?
6. How did the Civil War affect blacks?

## Expand Your Knowledge

1. Find out how, if at all, Indian groups were affected or involved in the Civil War and the Reconstruction period.
2. During the years immediately after the Civil War, a number of schools and colleges were started for blacks. Some of these still exist. Prepare a report on one of the following institutions: Fisk University, Talladega College, Hampton Institute, Howard University, or Atlanta University. Include how the school was founded and for what achievements some of the students are known.
3. Be prepared to debate the issue of whether or not the South had actually left the Union.

# America Is... **Growth**

# A Changing Nation 15

As the United States recovered from the Civil War in the 1870's, its people faced many changes, and its economy grew very rapidly. New methods of farming were developed, and millions of acres of land were farmed for the first time. Old industries expanded, and many new industries began. The war had a lasting effect on the lives of people, as some began to change their ideas about freedom and equality.

## Rights for Women

Many women had played an important role in the abolition movement. During the Civil War, they served as nurses, worked on farms

*Houses made of large chunks of grass and earth dotted the Great Plains. Although they had few comforts, the settlers found that their sod houses were cool in the summer and warm in the winter.*

and plantations, and raised money for soldiers and their families. Because of these activities, a growing number of people felt that women had again shown themselves to be capable citizens and should have the same legal rights as men. These rights were such things as owning property, being legal guardians of their children, and voting in all elections. Most white men had the right to vote before the Civil War. After the war, the Fourteenth and Fifteenth Amendments were passed so that black men would not be denied this right. But women still were denied suffrage, or the right to vote.

One of the most important leaders in the women's rights movement at this time was Elizabeth Cady Stanton. She and Lucretia Mott, both abolitionists, had organized the first women's rights convention at Seneca Falls, New York, in 1848. After the Civil War, Stanton and Susan B. Anthony gave speeches, wrote articles, and organized meetings for women's rights. Stanton argued against states ratifying the Fifteenth Amendment, saying that it would not protect voting rights for women, only those of black men. She said she would support the amendment only if it were rewritten to include women.

These efforts to change the Fifteenth Amendment failed. Later, people tried to establish that the Fourteenth Amendment guaranteed women the right to vote. In 1872, Virginia Louisa Minor, encouraged by her husband Francis, tried to register to vote in Missouri. When she was turned down, Minor took her case to the state courts, claiming that the Fourteenth Amendment guaranteed her the right to vote. The case later went to the Supreme Court which said that neither the Fourteenth Amendment nor the Constitution itself gave anyone suffrage. The Constitution only made clear who could not be denied the right to vote by the states.

The *Minor v. Happersett* decision was that suffrage was not coextensive with citizenship and that women's political rights were controlled by their states.

Although women did not gain the right to vote on a national level, they did win the right to vote on school issues in the states of Kentucky, Kansas, Michigan, and Minnesota by 1865. The territory of Wyoming gave women full voting rights in 1869. People continued to work for suffrage and other legal rights for women.

Wyoming wanted to encourage female settlers to increase its population as needed for achieving statehood.

# *Sharecropping*

Changes were made in the way many of the South's farms were run after the Civil War. Some plantation owners sold part of their land to have enough cash to pay taxes or buy equipment. Many white and some black people bought a few acres of this farmland. Other plantations were completely taken over by bankers or merchants.

290

Many people who wanted to farm did not have the money to buy land. Most plantation owners did not have the cash to pay wages to workers who replaced the slaves. A system of sharecropping developed. Under this system, landowners provided farmers and their families with cabins, mules, some supplies on credit, and a section of their land to work. In return, they received a share, usually half or more, of the harvested crops.

Landowners, as well as local merchants who also gave credit to the farmers, wanted a crop that was guaranteed to sell. To be sure that they always had enough cotton, mill owners signed contracts with the landowners for their cotton crops before they were harvested. This helped the landowners to be sure they could get cash for their crops. But the contracts made it impossible for the farmers to change to different crops. So cotton continued to be the most important crop in the South. This led to worn-out soil, poor harvests, and low profits.

Some whites and many blacks became farmers under the sharecropping system. At first, the Freedmen's Bureau approved of the system. It seemed to help many freed slaves who had some experience in farming and no experience in factory work. Sharecropping did not always help the farmers, however. In years of bad harvests, farmers often had to borrow the next year's supplies on credit without being able to pay that year's bills. Many farmers were constantly in debt.

*Southern sharecroppers did not own their land and depended upon the owners for their cabins. Many cabins were small and had few comforts.*

The sharecropping system of tenant farming generally benefited only those with capital, either money or land. For most blacks, it established the failure of Reconstruction before the federal troops withdrew in 1877.

American emancipation was landless for blacks and without compensation for the loss of their labor to whites. Help students understand that the *methods* used in freeing the slaves, not the freedom itself, increased economic and social stress.

# Sharecropping

The following selections are taken from the writings of three authors who wrote about farming in the South in the 1870's and 1880's. What main points does each make about the system of farming in the South? What was the main difference between conditions for white and black farmers? How did the sharecropping system affect the farm worker? The landowner? The land?

A visitor from England came to the South after the Civil War. He described part of what he saw there.

*The intermixture of white labour in the cotton culture of the South is already large . . . yet the general [difference is that] large plantations [are worked by blacks] under white employers, and small farms [are worked] chiefly by white people. . . . [It] remains a [clear] feature of the new state of things. . . .*

A second writer noted the effects of sharecropping on the farmer.

*At the close of the war, added to the renting of small farms to the [black] man by whites, to be paid in certain [shares] of the crop, was the system of making advances to this class of farmers of such necessary farming [tools] and . . . food and clothing. . . . The poor . . . are forced to pay [very high] interest, frequently of fifty per cent and not unusually of seventy or ninety per cent. A coat which cost the merchant one dollar, was frequently sold for two; a pound of meat that cost six cents was sold for twelve . . . so likewise with shoes and other things. . . . I have also seen the taking of all the crop by the merchant, and also, the horse or mule and other [things] which were given as . . . security for the debt in making a crop in one year.*

Writing of the landowner, one author said:

*He is, of course, interested in the improvement of his land; but to supply the fertilizers for a large plantation, when he [farms] it by hired labor, would cost more than he usually has to [spend], and where the share system, or that of renting, [is common] he is still further removed from personal care of the land. . . .*

*In addition to these, the system of advances or credit, so [common] throughout the cotton-producing parts of the state, is not without its evil influence, for the laborer, and too often the owner of the land, is [forced] to get advances of [supplies] from their merchants . . . and as cotton is the only crop which will always bring ready money, its planting is usually insisted on by the merchants making the advances and selected by the farmer as a means of providing for payment. In this way cotton comes to be the [most important] crop, and there is little chance for rotation with other things. . . .*

# Changes in Industry

The increasing use of steam-powered machinery helped to make new industry locations possible.

After the Civil War, southern leaders encouraged people to build mills and factories in the South. Many people there were looking for jobs, so manufacturers were able to hire the workers they needed at low wages. The manufacturers also saw the advantages of building factories near the natural resources and farm areas which provided the needed materials. In 1871, a steel mill was started in Birmingham, Alabama, near coal and iron mines. That mill became one of the largest iron and steel producers in the industry. The market for cotton goods was still important across the country. By 1880, there were more than 150 textile mills in the South.

Throughout the United States, there was an increased supply of goods from farms, mines, and lumber mills. These goods were often exported, bringing in the money needed to build new factories. The local, state, and federal levels of the government helped industry. They kept taxes low and passed protective tariffs.

Population growth played an important role in the country's increased production. The number of people in the United States grew by about eight million between 1860 and 1870 and by another eleven million by 1880. People often had large families, and immigration brought in nearly three million people between 1870 and 1880. So there were more people to make goods, and there were more consumers, or people buying goods. More people had money to spend in the United States than in most other countries. American industries were able to make and sell more goods than ever before.

# The Importance of New Inventions

Students should recognize that new inventions are often the result of combined efforts or of building on others' ideas. They should begin to understand the relationships among ideas, practical application development, manufacturing, and marketing of new products and the job opportunities that different phases represent.

Inventors in the United States worked to make production easier or faster. Many of the improvements were the work of people like Thomas A. Edison. He was most interested in ideas that would make things easier for people in their daily lives. Edison developed an electric light that was soon used all over the country. He also improved the telegraph system.

Other new inventions made it possible for people to communicate faster, which especially helped people in business. A typewriter was developed in 1867 by Christopher Sholes. Six years later, the Remington Company was manufacturing them on a large scale. The telephone, invented by Alexander Graham Bell, was introduced in Philadelphia in

1876. In only three years, people in fifty-five cities in the United States were using more than fifty-five thousand telephones.

Sometimes inventions brought about whole new industries, and inventing became a business itself. Edison set up a laboratory in Menlo Park, New Jersey, where he brought other inventors to work. By joining their skills and knowledge, they were able to improve upon each other's ideas and inventions.

# New Ways With Natural Resources

New ways to get and use the country's natural resources added to the greater production in the 1870's. People used the small amounts of oil that seeped out of the ground before the 1850's. As the demand for oil grew, Edwin Drake set out to find a way to collect larger amounts of it. He drilled a well near Titusville, Pennsylvania. When this first well proved successful in 1859, more people came to the area to drill for oil. Before long, drilling began in Ohio and West Virginia. In 1865, over two million barrels of oil were produced.

American Indians used surface petroleum as medicine hundreds of years before arrival of whites. Colonists adopted such use and also used it to waterproof ships and lubricate axles and machinery. By the mid-1800's, the dominant use of petroleum was as kerosene fuel for lighting.

*Discovering many uses for oil products, people began to drill for oil everywhere. Railcars took the crude oil to refineries.*

Gasoline was an unwanted by-product of kerosene manufacture until the internal combustion engine created a market for it at the turn of the century.

Before the crude oil could be used, it had to be refined, or broken up by heat into lighter products such as kerosene. Only a small part of the lighter products were used, however. The rest were considered waste. Soon people found ways to change the waste into new products like hair oil, waxes, and the base for chewing gum.

The making of steel was an industry that became more important after the Civil War. Henry Bessemer of England and William Kelly of the United States had developed similar ways of making steel from iron ore. In 1866, their methods were joined into the Kelly-Bessemer process, which was much faster and easier than other methods. More steel could be made at a lower cost to the manufacturer. Steel became very important in making supports for buildings and bridges, rails for trains, and heavy machinery.

*The Kelly-Bessemer process for making steel from iron ore helped make the production of steel an important industry. Giant furnaces were needed to melt the iron ore in order to mix it with other materials.*

# Carnegie and Steel

Andrew Carnegie was an important leader in the rapid growth of the steel industry in the United States. In 1864, Carnegie set up his own iron business. He was very successful, partly because he was willing to try new ideas. His factory in Braddock, Pennsylvania, was one of the first to use the Kelly-Bessemer process. Carnegie also bought companies that supplied the coal and iron ore needed to make steel. He built his own railroad and bought boats for shipping these materials from mines in Michigan and Minnesota to the steel mill. In this way, Carnegie did not have to compete with other buyers for iron ore and coal or pay someone else to ship his materials. His costs were lower, and he could afford to sell steel for a low price.

# Rockefeller and Standard Oil

At the end of the Civil War, John D. Rockefeller and some partners set up a small refinery, or plant where crude oil is changed to get other purer products, in Cleveland, Ohio. Many people were building refineries in Cleveland and other eastern cities. To avoid competition, Rockefeller began to buy out these other oil businesses. In 1867, he organized the Standard Oil Company, and it was soon making high profits. By 1871, Standard Oil owned most of the other refineries in Cleveland.

Rockefeller made special deals with the railroad companies which shipped the crude oil to Cleveland and then took the oil products to the markets. Because Standard Oil shipped larger amounts than any other company, Rockefeller asked for lower rates from the railroad owners. Instead, they agreed to give back a certain amount of the rate, called a rebate, if Rockefeller shipped a certain amount of oil products. This low shipping cost and other ways of saving money allowed Standard Oil to charge low prices. Smaller companies could not compete successfully. They either sold out to Standard Oil or went out of business. Soon the Standard Oil Company had a monopoly controlling over 90 percent of the oil refining business in the country.

# Hetty Green

One of the great American fortunes in the years after the Civil War was made by a woman. Hetty Robinson Green, born in 1834 in New Bedford, Massachusetts, was the only daughter of wealthy Quaker parents. Hard work, thrift, and honesty were stressed by her family. "I was forced into business," Green said later. "I was the only child of two rich families and I was taught from the time I was six years old that I would have to look after my property." As a child, Green read the financial pages of newspapers to her grandfather. She went with her father to visit his whaling and shipping businesses. By the time Green was thirty, she had inherited over a million dollars from her family.

Hetty Green and her husband Edward, also a millionaire, went to England in 1867. A son and a daughter were born during their seven-year stay. By the 1870's, Hetty Green's main concern was making her fortune grow. She invested in government bonds and railroads. Green also bought large amounts of land in fast-growing cities across the country.

In later years, Green was famous not only for her wealth but also for the strange way she lived. She was always afraid that people were trying to cheat her or that she would be murdered for her money. Green lived in cheap rooms and wore old clothing. She argued with storekeepers over prices and tried to get free medical care. News writers called her "the witch of Wall Street." By 1910, Green had arranged for her son to help manage her money. Six years later, at age eighty-one, Hetty Green died. The fortune she left to her children had grown to more than $100,000,000.

# Corporations and Trusts

The term "trust" is here applied to industrial monopolies. "Trust" as a banking term is not explained to avoid confusion.

As oil, steel, and other companies were growing, some people found it very hard to start new businesses in these areas. They needed large amounts of money and business experience to compete against the big companies. Joint stock companies had been formed to get enough money to start the colonies. More business people also organized this way after the Civil War. They formed corporations, or groups of investors who buy shares of stock.

Most often, a board of directors is chosen by the stockholders to run the business. The stockholders receive a certain part of the profits, based on the number of shares they own. If a corporation fails and there are no profits, the people lose only the money they pay for shares. When a company or corporation owns enough stock in other companies to control the making and selling of a product, the organization is called a trust. In the years after the Civil War, both the oil and steel businesses were organized into trusts, and several other products as well were controlled by trusts.

Over the years, the courts greatly enhanced the usefulness of corporate form of business by ruling that corporations may act as individuals in making contracts, bringing suits, and being sued.

# Growth of the Railroads

Most industries of the 1870's would not have been able to grow so fast if the railroad industry had not also grown. After the Civil War ended, railroad companies began to repair their damaged lines and to build new ones to many cities. Leaders in business and government had talked for several years about the need for a transcontinental railroad—one that connected the East and the West. Congress granted a charter to the Union Pacific Railroad Company in 1862 to build a line west from Omaha, Nebraska. California granted a charter to the Central Pacific Railroad to build one east from Sacramento. It was to meet and connect with the Union Pacific, becoming the transcontinental line.

Note that Congress was no longer constrained by proponents for a southern line since this followed secession.

After the charters were granted, one of the first steps was to find people to build the lines. There were few settlers in the areas where the railroads were to be built. So the Central Pacific brought large numbers of Chinese workers to the United States, as well as smaller numbers of Japanese and Mexicans. The Union Pacific hired mostly Irish and German immigrants, Mexicans, and blacks.

The route of the Central Pacific went through the rugged Sierra Nevada Mountains of California. The Union Pacific had easier going. But as many as twenty thousand workers on the railroads endured heat, snowstorms, and attacks from Indians who were trying to protect their lands. In May, 1869, the two lines were joined at Promontory Point, Utah. The Union Pacific Company had laid over one thousand miles of track and the Central Pacific Company almost seven hundred miles.

To emphasize unifying effect of railroad transportation, might compare this map with land acquisition map on p. 202.

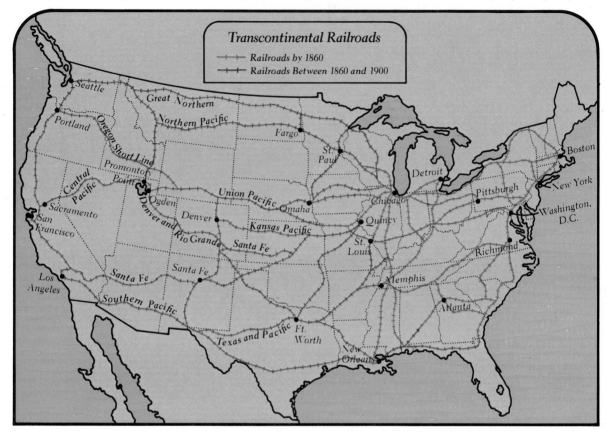

**Transcontinental Railroads**

- ┼┼ Railroads by 1860
- ┼┼┼ Railroads Between 1860 and 1900

Seattle
Portland
Great Northern
Northern Pacific
Oregon Short Line
Fargo
St. Paul
Boston
Detroit
Pittsburgh
New York
Promontory Point
Central Pacific
Union Pacific
Chicago
Washington, D.C.
Sacramento
Ogden
Denver
Omaha
San Francisco
Denver and Rio Grande
Kansas Pacific
Quincy
St. Louis
Richmond
Los Angeles
Santa Fe
Santa Fe
Santa Fe
Memphis
Southern Pacific
Atlanta
Texas and Pacific
Ft. Worth
New Orleans

Might have student research and report on George West-inghouse's air brake, pat-ented 1869, and George Pullman's sleeping car, pat-ented 1864, as significant improvements in railroad safety and comfort.

Many other railroad lines were planned, and rivalries began. The railroad companies competed with each other for routes which had the most traffic, those into the larger cities in the Northeast and Midwest. Four companies—the Pennsylvania, the New York Central, the Baltimore and Ohio, and the Erie—bought up smaller companies to stop competition. These four railroad companies grew bigger than any others during the 1870's.

# Settling the Frontier

To speed up construction of the transcontinental railroad, the government had given the companies land grants along the route. Railroad owners organized companies to sell the land for profit. Agents traveled around the United States and to Europe to tell people about rich farmland at low prices. Thousands of immigrants, especially farmers from

Scandinavian countries, Germany, and Bohemia, came to settle the frontier. Thousands of other people came from the Midwest and other parts of the United States. Millions of acres of land were settled and farmed for the first time.

The people who came to the Great Plains faced a shortage of rainfall, blizzards in winter, and swarms of grasshoppers that could wipe out crops in summer. Since there were few trees for wood, the settlers made houses out of sod. They began to use barbed wire to fence out cattle and wild animals. In the years of drought, they used windmills to pump water from underground so that they could at least grow vegetables to eat. Machines made it possible to farm large areas of the hard, dry land. Wheat and other grains grew well on the Great Plains, and it was not long before this area became very productive.

Could have student research and report on barbed wire. Use of it drastically changed patterns of ranching. Joseph F. Glidden patented a machine for producing barbed wire in 1874 and by 1878 was selling 80 million pounds of it a year.

# The Cattle Industry

Long before people came to farm the West, cattle ranchers had grazed their herds on large sections of the open land. In the early 1800's, cattle were raised in Ohio and Kentucky and then driven to Baltimore, Philadelphia, or New York to be sold. As people settled farther west, the cattle industry moved beyond the line of settlement. The largest herds of cattle grazed on the open range lands of Texas. These Texas longhorns were a cross between the cattle brought to that area by the Spanish and a breed brought later by the Anglo-Americans.

The Texas ranchers found it very difficult to get their cattle to the distant markets in the East. When the Kansas Pacific Railway was built through Kansas in the late 1860's, ranchers were then able to drive their herds to the railroad, a much shorter distance. The railroad then shipped the cattle to meat-packing plants in Kansas City, St. Louis, Chicago, and Cincinnati.

# Mining in the West

In the 1870's, new discoveries of gold and silver were found that brought many people to the frontier. The largest silver strike during these years was made at Leadville, Colorado. The largest gold strike was in the Black Hills in Dakota Territory. Thousands of people moved

The Black Hills were sacred to the Sioux Indians and guaranteed to them by Fort Laramie Treaty of 1868.

*Many miners and huge equipment were needed to get the ore deep in the earth. Large mining companies built towns at the camps.*

Have students consider the costs of deep mining to understand the possible advantages of forming corporations.

west hoping to strike it rich. Miners started camps in the Rocky Mountains, the Black Hills, Nevada, and in the Southwest.

At first, some of the metals were found close to the surface of the ground. But the thick veins of ore ran deep into the hard rock. Heavy machinery and large numbers of miners were needed to reach those veins. Large companies were set up to do this mining, and many miners went to work for them. Others went elsewhere in the West to farm, ranch, or start businesses. As the smaller mines were worked out, people left the mining camps, and many of them became ghost towns.

# Indians and Settlers

Plains Indians referred to here are those who lived in skin teepees and hunted buffalo, not the Eastern Woodland groups who were farmers and general hunters.

The movement of farmers, miners, ranchers, railroad workers, and their families into the frontier brought more conflict between Indians and settlers. Not only did the building of railroads cross Indian lands, but it also led to the killing of thousands of buffalo. This took away the main source of food and clothing for many Plains Indians. Some hunters killed the animals for food for the railroad workers. Buffalo hides also became popular in the East for blankets in sleighs, and some people shot the buffalo for sport. In a few years, the large herds were reduced to a few animals.

A long series of wars were fought between the Indians and the United States army during this period. Shortly after the Civil War, the army tried to build a road across Sioux Indian lands in present-day Montana for miners on their way to a gold discovery there. The Sioux warriors attacked the soldiers and builders. The United States government then agreed that the lands in part of what are now South Dakota and Montana belonged to the Indians. The Indians also demanded the right to hunt from there to the Bighorn Mountains in the territory of Wyoming. The government agreed and promised that this land would be protected from settlers and miners. But when gold was discovered in the Black Hills, miners came by the hundreds. In 1875, the government broke its promise to the Sioux people and opened the Black Hills to settlement.

Many Sioux Indians, joined by some Cheyenne and Arapaho people, left their lands and camped near the Little Bighorn River in Montana Territory. There were over twenty-five hundred warriors led

The high plains groups included Blackfeet, Assiniboine, Crow, Western Dakota Sioux, Cheyenne, Arapaho, Comanche, and Kiowa. In addition to Indian heros in text, students might research and report on Red Cloud, Geronimo, and Gall.

*White settlers forced American Indians onto pieces of land called reservations.*

Battle of the Little Bighorn was brought about by broken treaty, rush for gold, and overconfidence of ambitious Custer who tried a surprise attack against the Indian encampment of more than 10,000 people including the women, children, sick, and aged.

Chief Joseph was also an extraordinary speaker. If possible, some of his speeches should be brought in and read to the class.

by Chiefs Sitting Bull and Crazy Horse. The government ordered the Indians to return to their lands. When the Indians did not go, the army sent out soldiers to force them to do so. One group of soldiers commanded by Colonel George Custer advanced against the Indians in a valley near the Bighorn River. Custer and his command, about 225 soldiers, were killed.

The Indians had few victories after this. The United States government continued to send troops to force the Indians onto reservations. In 1877, a group of Nez Percé Indians led by Chief Joseph fought against an attempt to force them onto a small reservation. They did not succeed and, like most other Indian groups, were forced to live on a reservation.

# Concern Over Growth

Citizens of the United States were proud of the growth of the nation during the 1870's. A large part of the population enjoyed a higher living standard than ever before. At the same time, a depression occurred from 1873 to 1878. Many small businesses failed, and most workers and farmers were faced with hard times.

There were other problems as well. Range wars were beginning between ranchers and farmers over the use of the land. Ranchers wanted their cattle and sheep to graze over large open areas. Farmers put up barbed wire around their land to protect the fields from grazing herds. Throughout the country, there were growing feelings that something was needed to bring about balance, not only in the economy, but between differing groups of Americans. People began to look to the government for answers.

# Chapter 15 in Perspective See Teacher's Manual, page 103T.

### Identify

| | | |
|---|---|---|
| Elizabeth Cady Stanton | Edwin Drake | Chief Sitting Bull |
| Virginia Louisa Minor | Andrew Carnegie | Colonel George Custer |
| Thomas A. Edison | John D. Rockefeller | Chief Joseph |

# Explain

| suffrage | consumers | corporations |
|----------|-----------|--------------|
| sharecropping | rebate | trusts |

## Check Your Memory of the Facts

1. What economic changes took place in the South after the Civil War?
2. How did the organization of some businesses change in the 1870's?
3. What steps did Carnegie and Rockefeller take to gain control of the steel and oil industries?
4. What is an advantage of a corporation?
5. What effects did the transcontinental railroad have?
6. What problems did the farmers and ranchers face on the Great Plains?
7. What events led to renewed conflict between the Indians and the settlers?

## Check Your Understanding of the Ideas

1. What things led to the rapid growth of production in the 1870's?
2. Why did women organize to gain the right to vote?
3. What does the Constitution say about suffrage?
4. What were the advantages and disadvantages of sharecropping for the landowner? For the farmer?
5. What things about a monopoly helped or hurt the consumer? The monopoly itself? The smaller competitors?
6. How did the railroad companies help settle the Great Plains?

## Expand Your Knowledge

1. Locate information on the conflict between western farmers, sheep ranchers, and cattle ranchers. Report on what caused the conflict and how it was resolved.
2. Natural gas was usually found near oil wells. Find out what oil producers did with the gas at first and when natural gas became used as an energy source. Find out what some of the by-products of oil, coal, and natural gas are today.

See Teacher's Manual, page 43T.

# Abilene 1865-1875

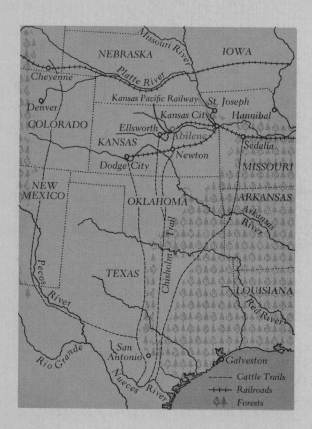

*Abilene in 1867 was a very small, dead place, consisting of about one dozen log huts, low, small, rude affairs, four-fifths of which were covered with dirt for roofing; indeed, but one shingle roof could be seen in the whole city. The business of the [town] was conducted in two small rooms, mere log huts, and of course the inevitable saloon also in a log hut, was to be found.*

Joseph G. McCoy so described Abilene, Kansas, as he first saw it in 1867. McCoy and his brothers were in the livestock business. One brother took care of the animals in Springfield, Illinois, and another brother sold them in New York. McCoy had come west on the Kansas Pacific Railway that passed through Abilene. He was looking for more livestock to buy, but he also had another idea for making money.

In the late 1860's, railroads helped supply the needs of settlers in the West by shipping goods to them. The trains returning to the East, however, were often empty. Joe McCoy wanted to use the railroads to ship cattle to the East. Supplies of meat there and in the Midwest were low after the Civil War. At the same time, the herds of cattle in Texas had grown very large. These Texas longhorns would bring a high price if they could be brought to the eastern markets. McCoy began visiting Kansas towns along the railroad line. He chose dusty little Abilene as the place where the cattle drivers and the railroads would meet.

McCoy bought 250 acres of land just outside Abilene to use as stockyards. He began making plans for building up the town so that it could take care of the cattle and people that would be coming. Then he contacted Texas cattle drivers, and even though it was late in the season, thirty-five thousand cattle reached Abilene in 1867. McCoy bought some cattle for his family's business, but he made more money from the railroad. The Kansas Pacific Railway paid him five dollars for every carload of cattle that was shipped out of Abilene.

## The Long Drive

Bringing the cattle north from Texas was called the long drive. It started in the spring, and the hardest work—caring for and moving the cattle—fell to the cowhands, or drovers. They were usually young men and had often been soldiers in the Civil War. Many of them were Mexicans or blacks; some were Indians. The trail boss bought Texas cattle, hired six to eight cowhands for every thousand cattle, and got six to ten horses for each cowhand. The drive north started slowly at first. After a week of routine, the cattle could be driven faster.

The cook rode in front of the herd and had each meal ready by the time the cowhands stopped to eat. The chuck wagon carried food and equipment. Then came the herd, spread out along the trail for perhaps a mile. Some cowhands rode at the head of the herd, some brought up the rear, and some rode on each side. At night, some stood on guard.

In the morning, at noon, and at dusk, the cattle grazed. It was important that they did not lose too much weight on the trail. So the drive had to be through good grass country. Most of the cattle drives from Texas to Abilene followed a famous route known as the Chisholm Trail.

## Life on the Trail

Being a cowhand meant hard work and loneliness. There were many dangers on the trail.

*Great hardships attended driving that year [1867] on account of Osage Indian troubles, excessive rain-storms, and flooded rivers. The cholera [a disease] made sad havoc with many drovers, some of whom died ... and many suffered greatly. The heavy rains caused an immense growth of grass, too*

*Texas longhorns in the Abilene stockyards*

coarse and washy to be good food for cattle or horses, and but little of the first years' arrivals at Abilene were fit to go to market.

Sometimes, trail bosses set up strict rules for their cowhands while they were on the drive.

First, You can't drink whiskey and work for us.

Second, You can't play cards and gamble and work for us.

Third, You can't curse and swear in our camps or in our presence and work for us.

The cowhands worked long hours, but they also had time for fun. One of them wrote about life on the Chisholm Trail:

After supper the [cowhands] not on herd would tell yarns, sing songs, wrestle, and act generally like a bunch of kids, which mostly we were. Like many of the outfits, ours had a fiddle, and while some artist in spurs "made it talk," we often put the end gate of the chuck wagon on the ground and then took turns dancing jigs upon it. . . .

Some people say that the reason [cowhands] sang to the cattle was to prevent their being frightened by any sudden or irregular noise. . . . One lazy old . . . steer . . . seemed particularly fond of "One Evening in May"—a waltz tune. . . . Pleasant it was on a warm, clear night to circle slowly around a herd of cattle that were bedded down quiet and breathing deep and out there to catch the strains of song or fiddle coming from camp, where the fire was like a

*Relaxing on the long drive*

*A dance hall in Abilene*

*dim star. . . . As long as a* [cowhand] *heard music he knew that all was well.*

## Boom Town

The cattle trade had an electric effect on dusty, quiet Abilene. Almost overnight, it became a boom town. Its success came mostly from supplying the needs of the drovers. Many of Abilene's merchants became rich by doing this. Mayer Goldsoll, a Russian immigrant, was one of them. He built the Texas Store in 1871. There Goldsoll sold everything from fancy clothing to guns and ammunition.

One of the first new buildings in Abilene was the Drover's Cottage. It was built in 1867 by Joe McCoy as a hotel for the Texas cattle drivers and the buyers. Three stories high, it had a billiard parlor, a saloon, and a carriage house. The dining room served turkey with oyster sauce, raspberry tarts, and other special dishes.

During the spring and summer when the herds of cattle arrived, the population of Abilene grew to about three thousand people. Most of the newcomers were the dusty, thirsty, pleasure-seeking cowhands. After two or three months on the trail, the cowhands first got shaves, haircuts, baths, and new clothes. Then they often spent the rest of their pay drinking and gambling.

A letter written in Kansas during the cattle-drive days describes these cowhands:

*The typical* [cowhand] *wears a white hat, with a gilt cord and tassel, high-top boots, leather pants, a woolen shirt, a coat, and no vest. On his heels he wears a pair of jingling Mexican spurs, as large around as a tea-cup.*

*When he feels well . . . the average* [cow- hand is hard] *to handle. Armed to the teeth, well mounted, and full of their favorite beverage, the* [cowhands] *will dash through the principal streets of a town, yelling. . . . This they call "cleaning out a town."*

The cowhands spent much of their time in Abilene's saloons, gathering there to drink and gamble. One of the most popular saloons in Abilene was the Alamo.

*The Alamo . . . was housed in a long room with a forty-foot frontage on Cedar street, facing the west. There was an entrance at either end. At the west entrance were three double glass doors. Inside and along the front of the south side was the bar with its . . . carefully polished brass fixtures and rails. From the back bar arose a large mirror, which reflected the brightly sealed bottles of liquor. . . . Covering the entire floor space were gaming tables, at which practically any game of chance could be* [played]. *The Alamo boasted an orchestra, which played forenoons, afternoons, and nights. In the height of the season the saloons were the scene of constant activity. At night the noises that* [came] *from them were a combination of badly* [played] *popular music, coarse voices . . . laughter and Texan "whoops," punctuated . . . by gun shots.*

## Law and Order

During the cattle boom, Abilene became known as the wildest town in the West. No one did very much to keep order. People with businesses thought the cowhands might spend their money in other towns if Abilene set up strict rules.

Then the settlers who lived in and around Abilene began to establish stricter laws. At first, the cowhands rebelled. Early in 1870, the new jail was torn down before it was even finished. Posters stating that guns could not be worn in town were shot so full of holes that they could not be read.

The mayor of Abilene hired Thomas J. Smith as marshal, hoping that he would be able to bring order to the town. Smith had served on the New York police force and had worked on the Union Pacific Railroad. As marshal, he worked to enforce the law forbidding guns in town. Even though Smith wore his own gun, he rarely used it. Instead, he used his fists on several cowhands who refused to obey the law. After that, cowhands did not wear their guns in the streets of Abilene.

Tom Smith's rule over Abilene lasted only five months. On November 2, 1870, he was killed by a farmer who was accused of murder. James Butler Hickok, known as Wild Bill, became the next marshal. He served from April to December, 1871. Hickok kept the town under control, but he was never as respected as Smith. People like Tom Smith and Wild Bill Hickok created a new sense of order in Abilene.

This new respect for the law grew as more settlers began to arrive. Two of the settlers who came to Abilene in 1871 were A. J. and Florence Bingham. She described her first sight of the town:

*"As the train came in sight of Abilene, such a lonesome feeling came over me,"* she reported to the historical society years later. *"The country and town looked so different from the East where every farm had its wood lot, and I had never seen a prairie before; then the fear of what we would find in this wild western country which was settled with* [cowhands], *longhorns, Indians and such men as Wild Bill."*

The Binghams bought ten acres of land and built a small house.

*Abilene, a booming cattle town*

"I was a little timid at first," she recalled, "as north of us, on the prairie, lots of cattle were pastured and the [cowhands] rode past our house many times a day, shooting their revolvers and yelling. However, they never came to our house, never said anything to us and paid strict attention to their own business."

## End of the Boom

By 1871, many people like the Binghams were settling in Abilene. They wanted to farm the land and raise their own livestock. The farmers did not like the wild life of the cowhands nor the large herds of Texas cattle moving through the area. In February, 1872, they published this statement:

*We the undersigned members of the Farmers' Protective Association and Officers and*

*Citizens of Dickinson county, Kansas, most respectfully request all who have [thought about] driving Texas Cattle to Abilene the coming season to seek some other point for shipment, as the inhabitants of Dickinson [county] will no longer submit to the evils of the trade.*

That year, the Texas cattle drovers headed for other towns in Kansas. The cattle trade in Abilene was over. One Kansas news writer described the town:

*Its glory has departed from it, and so have the cattle, and the streets that were once filled with life . . . are growing up with grass. The principal business street is almost entirely deserted, and over two-thirds of the business houses are closed.*

A small group had brought about this change, though many people had been against the cattle trade for years. One person with strong influence was Theodore C. Henry. His business was land. He was one of the first in 1867 to see what the cattle trade would do for the dusty little town of Abilene. Between 1868 and 1871, he had sold more real estate than all the other Abilene land agents combined.

T. C. Henry had known that the cattle boom would not last in Abilene. While he continued to sell land to the new settlers, he also began to plant wheat on the Kansas prairie. In the fall of 1871, at the end of the cattle season, he planted several hundred acres of wheat. By 1875, he owned five thousand acres of farmland covered with wheat.

The city of Abilene started in 1867 with a dozen log huts. Within three short years, it had become one of the wildest cattle boom towns in the West. By the mid-1870's, Abilene was growing into a world wheat center, and Kansas was becoming the "bread basket of the world."

# New Ideas, New Roles

# 16

Americans took pride in the industrial growth of the nation and in the higher living standard it brought to most of them. Not all of them shared as fully as they would have liked in the better life. Some groups organized to seek reforms that would improve their living standards. They had not especially favored government regulation, but they began to demand that the government help them solve some of their problems.

## Business and Government Ideas

Most Americans in the nineteenth century agreed with a set of ideas called laissez-faire. This French term means to let people do as

*The F. W. Woolworth Company opened the first "Dime Store" in America in 1879.*

they please. In general, laissez-faire means that the government does not regulate, or make rules for, business. Its duty is to keep the country at peace and to protect property rights of citizens. Sometimes in practice, Americans supported government action like protective tariffs or road building. But one of the main ideas in laissez-faire is that without government regulation there is a lot of competition and lower prices for the public.

Companies like the railroads and Standard Oil did not fit the ideas of laissez-faire. Those companies often provided more services or produced more goods at lower costs, so they could sell them at lower prices. They also had grown so large that they controlled whole industries and had little competition. Under trusts, prices could be raised, and people would have to pay them. Some Americans began to call for government action to regulate the size and power of these trusts as a way of restoring competition.

Confirm that students understand the relationship discussed between competition and price.

# Buying and Selling

Manufacturers would sell at lower prices to store owners who bought large amounts. Store owners could make big savings in the cost of products if they could find ways to sell more goods to more people. In 1859, the Great Atlantic and Pacific Tea Company (the A & P) introduced the idea of chain stores. Chain stores are two or more of the same kind of store owned and managed by one company. The F. W. Woolworth Company changed American selling ideas in 1879 by opening a store where every item cost ten cents or less. The company made great profits by selling large amounts of low-priced goods. In twenty years, Woolworth had a chain of more than one thousand stores.

In the early 1800's, most Americans shopped at specialty stores or general stores. Specialty stores carried only one kind of product. General stores carried more kinds of products but in small amounts that gave customers little choice. Between 1860 and 1880, people like Alexander Stewart and R. H. Macy in New York, Marshall Field in Chicago, and John Wanamaker in Philadelphia developed the idea of the department store. Their buildings were several stories high. They had large amounts of many kinds of products, grouped in different areas or departments. The department store offered the same service and prices to all customers. These giant general stores were very successful in cities where large populations meant many customers.

In 1872, Aaron Montgomery Ward carried the idea of the department store to America's farm population. He bought large amounts of

Large orders helped manufacturers plan resource allocation and production schedule more efficiently, aiding in cost control.

Review with students the idea of high volume sales at low individual-item profit resulting in large overall profit, in addition to volume buying resulting in low cost of individual item.

Success of department store policy of single service and single price marks beginning of decline of price bargaining in individual's daily affairs.

For a look ahead, might have student research and report on rural free delivery (passed in 1893) and parcel post (1913) in connection with success of mail order business or related to improved communication for agricultural community.

different products at low costs. Then he offered these items at lower prices than those charged by the general stores in most farm areas. Ward sent out a sheet with pictures and descriptions of the goods and instructions for buying them with cash through the mail. The idea was so successful that Ward's sheet of items soon grew into a catalog, or book. The Montgomery Ward catalog, and later the Sears, Roebuck catalog, became very important books to most American farm families.

# Agriculture

Remind students of high cost of farmers' investments in land and machinery.

At these given prices, a farmer would have to produce almost 3 times as much corn in 1889 to match the amount received in 1869. Crop prices dropped faster than prices on goods purchased. Farmers' tendency to specialize also meant that more goods needed to be purchased, sometimes including family food.

It could be cheaper for farmer to ship by rail between cities farther apart than those closer together if the longer route was served by several competing railroad companies.

Farmers were producing more crops than ever before, but most of them were making little profit. The amounts of farm products were increasing in many parts of the world because of new lands and the use of machines. American farmers competed against each other and against farmers in Canada, Australia, Russia, and other countries. The prices they received for their crops kept going down. In Chicago in 1889, the price for a bushel of corn was only 28¢. It had been 75¢ in 1869. The price for a pound of cotton in 1886 was 9¢, down from 31¢ in 1866. Many farmers in the Midwest, Great Plains, and South were deeply in debt.

Most farmers believed that their problems were caused by high costs, not by too much competition. They especially blamed the high costs of railroad rates. In the 1860's, farmers had supported railroad building. Twenty years later, the railroads also owned many of the warehouses and grain elevators where crops were stored for shipping. In areas where the railroad had a monopoly, it charged higher rates than those in areas where it competed with other lines or warehouses. Farmers wanted the government to regulate fair and standard railroad rates.

# Organizations

Farm supporters had organized the National Grange of the Patrons of Husbandry in 1867. Grange is another word for a farm, and husbandry means farming. Most early Grange activities were educational and social. Farmer members learned that they shared many of the same problems. By 1875, when the Grange had more than 800,000 members, local groups had turned to self-help programs and politics. Some members set up their own businesses in farm machinery, insurance, and warehousing. They hoped to sell these goods and services at

# Visual Evidence

From the Sears, Roebuck catalog of the late 1890's, people can gain an idea of the things Americans used then in their everyday lives. Historians call this type of information visual evidence.

From the evidence shown, decide which items are not familiar today. Which are still used but look a little different? Are any the same today? How do prices compare to those of today?

314

lower prices than those charged by others. Some of these efforts succeeded, but they did not keep crop prices from falling.

Grange members, especially in the Midwest, tried to force railroads to charge fair, standard rates through state regulations. Local groups worked to elect judges and members of state legislatures who favored their ideas and would pass laws to help them. For a few years, these new state laws worked. In 1877, the United States Supreme Court upheld an Illinois law that regulated grain elevator rates. It also upheld a later Wisconsin law that regulated the rates of a railroad that carried goods into another state. Although these laws regulated costs, crop prices continued to fall. Eventually, Granges turned back to educational and social interests.

*Munn v. Illinois (1877)*

Farmers formed other organizations in the 1880's. In Kansas, Nebraska, Iowa, Minnesota, and the Dakota territory, they joined the Northwestern Alliance. In the South, white farmers joined the Southern Alliance. Black farmers formed the Colored Farmers Alliance and

*Grange meetings meant a chance for farmers to get together and discuss problems they faced. Members worked on self-help programs and political changes important to them.*

Cooperative Union. These groups tried many of the political and business ideas used by the Grange. They, too, supported certain candidates in state and national elections.

# The Interstate Commerce Act

A new railroad rate case came before the Supreme Court in 1886. This time, the Court said that the state could not set rates for the railroad because it carried goods through several states. Only Congress had the power to make laws for interstate trade, or commerce. Farmers then demanded that Congress take action.

*Wabash, St. Louis and Pacific Railway Company v. Illinois (1886)*

Congress passed the Interstate Commerce Act in 1887. This law said that railroads must charge reasonable rates, could not give rebates, and must publish their rates for all to read. It also established the Interstate Commerce Commission to check into railroad businesses and to take lawbreaking companies to court. The law did not say what rates were reasonable. For several more years, cases brought to the Supreme Court were decided in favor of the railroad companies. Farmers' problems continued to grow.

# National Labor Unions

Industries had been made up of many small businesses run directly by their owners in earlier years. In the new larger companies, managers ran the business and reported to the owners. Workers were finding it harder to believe that anyone was concerned with their problems. The increased use of machines and the growth of large companies led more workers to turn to labor groups for help.

The National Labor Union was organized in 1866 by several local unions, some farm groups, and some people who favored women's suffrage. Leaders of the union tried to gain reforms by having their own candidate run for President in 1872. Their candidate received few votes, and the union lost influence. During the depression of 1873, when many people were out of work, the National Labor Union broke up.

Another national union had been organized in 1869. It was called the Noble Order of the Knights of Labor. Leaders of the Knights invited all workers, including blacks and women, to join them. Mother

*Knights founded by Uriah S. Stephens, a Baptist preacher.*

Might have student research and report on Mary Harris Jones (1830-1930) who was extraordinary crusader for workers' rights, especially active in union organization of miners.

Mary Jones, a woman who joined the Knights in Chicago, wrote about her decision:

> I learned that in 1865 . . . a group of men met in Louisville, Kentucky. They came from the North and from the South [and] a year or two before had been fighting each other over the question of . . . slavery. They decided that the time had come [for] a program to fight another brutal form of slavery—industrial slavery. Out of [their] decision had come the Knights of Labor.
>
> . . . I decided to take an active part in the efforts of the working people to better the conditions under which they worked and lived. I became a member. . . .

Terence Powderly was elected leader of the Knights in 1879. He hoped that workers could establish their own mines, factories, and railroads by working together as a community. Powderly was against strikes because he felt that they hurt all members of the community. But, strikes became more common in the 1880's because a few local unions carried them out successfully.

Many of the strikes were related to extreme economic hardships following the depression of 1873.

*Railroad strikes because of wage cuts kept trains from running in many cities and caused much damage to railroad property.*

# Strikes and Union Membership

The idea of striking for improvements was not new to American workers. Strikes by unskilled people had not been successful because companies could easily find new workers. Strikes by skilled people, who were harder to replace, had more influence on owners. The decision to strike by any group, however, often led to danger.

Following the depression of 1873, some companies looked for ways to cut their costs. In 1877, the Baltimore and Ohio and other railroad companies cut their workers' wages. These skilled workers went on strike and stopped the trains from running in most cities of the East and Midwest. A riot broke out during the strike in Pittsburgh, and more than one hundred locomotives were destroyed. Strikers blamed the destruction on the state troops who had been called in to stop the riot. Many others blamed the strikers for the violence and property ruin. People viewed strikers with anger and fear.

Several other local unions had successful strikes and won higher wages, shorter hours, or better working conditions. Workers on the Missouri Pacific Railroad won a strike in 1885. The Knights of Labor received much of the credit even though national leaders did not approve of striking. More workers became interested in the union movement. By 1886, the Knights had over 700,000 members.

# Haymarket Square

One major improvement workers wanted in the 1880's was a shorter work day—from ten or twelve hours to eight. The Knights led the campaign for the eight-hour day from Chicago in 1886. A strike was also in progress there against the McCormick Harvesting Machine Company. Strikers, strikebreakers, and police had clashed in a street fight on May 3. A striker was killed. Union leaders called for a meeting the next day in Haymarket Square to protest the striker's death. Anarchists, or people who believe in doing away with government, attended the meeting and made speeches to the crowd. The police started to break up the meeting, and someone threw a bomb. It killed several police officers and wounded many people. The police fired into the crowd and killed four more people. The anarchist leaders were later tried and found guilty in court although no evidence connected them directly with the bomb. Four of the anarchists were hanged.

This national union first formed as Federation of Organized Trades and Labor Unions in 1881. Name changed to AFL in 1886. Gompers served as president from 1886-1895 and 1896-1924.

*Samuel Gompers served as the first president of the American Federation of Labor, a national union founded in 1886.*

All over the country, people were upset by the news of the violence in Chicago. Many blamed the labor union. They believed that unions were trying to overthrow the government. Support for the Knights and their ideas quickly disappeared. Several later strikes failed, and Powderly was not a strong leader. Within a few years, the Knights of Labor lost many members and much influence. Some of the skilled workers joined the new American Federation of Labor. It was founded by Samuel Gompers, president of the cigarmakers' union, as a national union for skilled workers. Some unskilled workers continued to fight for improvements, but for a long time, no national union was able to provide these people with leadership.

First unions in the AFL were those of printers, carpenters, glassworkers, iron and steelworkers, molders, and cigarmakers.

# Local Government

In the 1880's, the farm population of the United States grew by four million people. The population of its cities grew by twice that number. Such quick growth created many problems in local government. Services to people in the cities, like water and sewer and transportation lines, had to be provided for health and safety. Many local governments did not have the money or number of workers to do these jobs quickly and well.

In some cities and states, local political leaders called bosses had gained power during the 1860's and 1870's. The political parties of the bosses were called machines because their workers could perform the same task time after time, like winning election after election. The bosses gained and kept their power by using the spoils system to fill new city jobs. Another way they gained power and money was to give contracts for city work to the companies which gave them the highest bribes. Some bosses, like William Tweed of New York, allowed the companies to overcharge for the work they did. Most of the extra money charged was given to the boss. Many cities had honest political leaders who worked hard to provide fair government. But some of the largest were controlled by bosses and their political machines. As news of their corrupt deals reached the people, many Americans gave their support to reform ideas.

Might have student research and report on development of police departments which, at this time, were noted for lack of training, corruption, etc., and were often controlled by machine politics in large cities. Contrast with today's entrance exams, training, etc.

Machine politics sometimes beneficial to city's poor because of welfare services and some jobs supplied to win support and votes.

This cartoon shows the Tweed Ring, run by the political boss, William Tweed. They robbed the people of New York of millions of tax dollars.

"WHO STOLE THE PEOPLE'S MONEY?" — DO TELL . N.Y.TIMES.          'TWAS HIM.

# National Government Reform

Review spoils system if necessary, pp. 171-74.

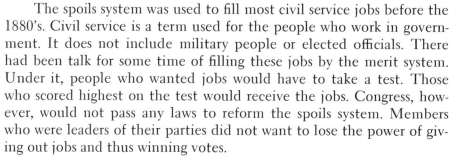

The spoils system was used to fill most civil service jobs before the 1880's. Civil service is a term used for the people who work in government. It does not include military people or elected officials. There had been talk for some time of filling these jobs by the merit system. Under it, people who wanted jobs would have to take a test. Those who scored highest on the test would receive the jobs. Congress, however, would not pass any laws to reform the spoils system. Members who were leaders of their parties did not want to lose the power of giving out jobs and thus winning votes.

Pressure to reform the spoils system grew much stronger after President James Garfield, who was elected in 1880, was killed by an angry job seeker in 1881. With the support of the new President, Chester Arthur, Congress passed a national civil service law in 1883. It was sponsored by Senator George Pendleton of Ohio. The Pendleton Act established a Civil Service Commission to give tests for government jobs. It also required that a certain number of jobs be given on merit. At first, only about 10 percent of the nearly 120,000 federal jobs were given through the merit system. Most Presidents after 1883, however, increased the number. Garfield was shot by Charles J. Guiteau and died 80 days later. Guiteau was tried, convicted, and hanged.

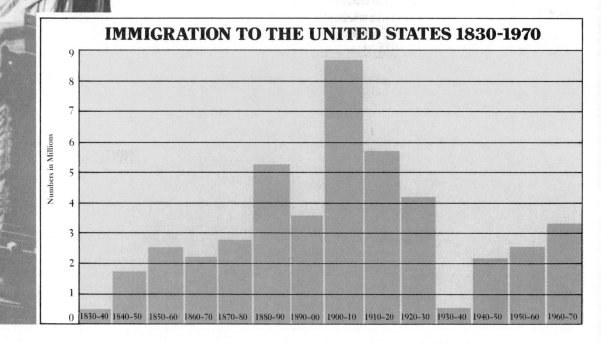

## IMMIGRATION TO THE UNITED STATES 1830-1970

Numbers in Millions

1830–40 | 1840–50 | 1850–60 | 1860–70 | 1870–80 | 1880–90 | 1890–00 | 1900–10 | 1910–20 | 1920–30 | 1930–40 | 1940–50 | 1950–60 | 1960–70

*Many immigrant families came to find the freedom promised in the United States.*

# Immigration Regulation

In addition to their demands for regulation of trusts and for government reform, some Americans also wanted government action on immigration. Between 1880 and 1890, more than five million people came to the United States. Unlike earlier years, many of these immigrants were from eastern and southern Europe. Some Americans were prejudiced against them because their languages, customs, religions, or skin colors were different. Workers continued to dislike immigrants who accepted low pay. They were especially angered if the immigrants took jobs of American workers on strike.

Students should recognize that work at low pay is usually preferred to starvation. For many, survival was the key. Because of discriminatory laws in some areas, many blacks and new immigrants could find work *only* as strikebreakers.

Might compare Chinese immigration of about 300,000 between 1820 and 1882 with the 221,000 Irish who immigrated in 1851 alone or the 215,000 Germans in 1854.

In *US v. Wong Kim Ark* (1898), the principle was established that a person born of parents residing in U.S. is automatically a U.S. citizen, except for children born of foreign sovereigns or their ministers, and children born of foreign enemies during hostile occupation of U.S. territory.

The Chinese Exclusion Acts were not repealed until 1943 when U.S. and China were allied for WW II. At that time a quota of 105 per year was established as a "goodwill" gesture.

Although the Chinese people came in much smaller numbers than most immigrant groups, prejudice against them was very strong. Some had come to the United States during the California gold rush. Others came to work on the Central Pacific Railroad. Many stayed to work in the mines and in businesses in California, Nevada, and other western states. Sometimes local laws were passed against the Chinese. Like the laws and local customs against black people, the Chinese people were not allowed to have certain jobs and were separated from whites.

In 1882, Congress passed the Chinese Exclusion Act. It said that Chinese workers were excluded from, or could not be admitted to, the United States for the next ten years. The law also said that courts could not give citizenship to any Chinese people already in the country. A few months later, Congress passed another immigration law which placed a tax of fifty cents on each immigrant. That law also stated that the United States would not admit convicts, insane people, and those who might not be able to support themselves. From the 1880's, the United States was no longer open to all people.

# Susette La Flesche Tibbles

Susette La Flesche Tibbles was a famous speaker and writer for Indian rights in the 1880's. Her Indian name was Bright Eyes. She was born near Bellevue, Nebraska, in 1854. Her father was chief of the Omaha Indians there. Bright Eyes learned English at the mission school on the reservation. She was a very good student and went to college in New Jersey when she was fifteen. Bright Eyes later returned to the Omaha Indians as a government school teacher.

In 1879, Chief Standing Bear of the nearby Ponca Indians came to the Omaha Indians for help. The government had forced the Ponca people to leave their land. Bright Eyes wanted to help the Ponca Indians. She wrote newspaper stories to tell about their problems. While working to help the Ponca Indians, she married Omaha newspaper writer Thomas Tibbles.

In 1883, Bright Eyes and her husband took Chief Standing Bear to the East to talk about Indian rights. They toured the East and Europe for five years giving speeches at colleges and social gatherings. Bright Eyes' strong arguments won many supporters for Indian rights and the Ponca cause. After she returned to Nebraska, Bright Eyes kept working for Indian rights until she died in 1903.

*New Ideas, New Roles*

# American Indian Policy

American Indians were not American citizens. The federal government policy had been to treat each group as a separate nation. The two groups in government who dealt most with the Indians were the Bureau of Indian Affairs and the army. The Bureau's agents received their jobs through the spoils system. Most of them did not understand Indian ideas or ways of life. Many of the agents were corrupt and cheated the Indians out of the food and supplies paid by the government for the lands taken from them. The army dealt mostly with forcing Indians out of the way of white settlement.

In 1881, Helen Hunt Jackson wrote a book called *A Century of Dishonor*. In it, she told of the many times that the federal government had broken its lawful treaties with the American Indians. Her book helped make other Americans aware of the injustice done to the Indians. In answer to demands by supporters of Indian rights, Congress passed the Dawes Act in 1887. Through it, the federal government tried to make Indians become individual landowning farmers, following white settlers' ways of life. After twenty-five years, the Indians would become citizens of the United States. Individual ownership of property was against the beliefs and customs of most Indians. Although many were also not farmers, they were forced to accept the Dawes Act. The reservation lands that had been returned by treaties to Indian groups were divided into lots and given to individual Indian families. The "extra" land left over was offered for sale or given to white settlers, ranchers, and business people. The Indians, under the Dawes Act, lost more than 60 percent of their remaining lands.

Bureau established as commission in War Department in 1832, transferred to Interior Department in 1849. Duties were to control trade, supervise removal to West, organize and run reservations, and hand out annuities and supplies.

Emerson considered Helen Fiske Hunt Jackson (1830-1885) the best woman poet in America in the 1870's. Jackson sent a copy of this book at her own expense to every important official connected to Indian affairs and to members of Congress.

# Changing Roles

Local and national government was slow to answer the demands of citizens. Their lobbies, or efforts to influence legislation and government policy, were not always successful. The government answers were not always successful, either. But in the 1880's, the Interstate Commerce Act did establish the idea of national rules for big business. The Pendleton Act was a start toward trained workers in government, and it weakened the power of the spoils system. The role of the government was changing in answer to the demands of its citizens.

"Lobbies," as old as the government, were so called because the halls, or lobbies, outside the legislative chambers were the easiest places to meet the lawmakers.

Might hold class discussion on ways the needs of citizens become known to government leaders who respond to the "demands."

*New Ideas, New Roles*

# Chapter 16 in Perspective See Teacher's Manual, page 106T.

## Identify

| | | |
|---|---|---|
| the Grange | Mother Mary Jones | James Garfield |
| Aaron Montgomery Ward | Haymarket Square | Chester Arthur |
| Knights of Labor | Samuel Gompers | Helen Hunt Jackson |

## Explain

| | | |
|---|---|---|
| laissez-faire | anarchists | Chinese Exclusion Act |
| regulation | merit system | Dawes Act |
| Interstate Commerce Act | Pendleton Act | lobbies |

## Check Your Memory of the Facts

1. What did farmers want the government to do about railroads?
2. What changes took place in the way goods were sold or marketed?
3. Terence Powderly wanted the members of the Knights of Labor to do what kinds of things?
4. How did some party bosses gain power?
5. From what new areas did many immigrants come in the 1880's?

## Check Your Understanding of the Ideas

1. Why would there be lower prices under laissez-faire?
2. Why did some people want the government to regulate trusts?
3. Why did the changes in the way goods were sold and marketed come about?
4. Why did the Interstate Commerce Act fail to help the farmers immediately?
5. Why did the Supreme Court say that only Congress had the power to make laws for interstate commerce?
6. What conditions caused labor unions to grow? What actions caused unions to lose members?
7. How did population growth affect cities and their governments?
8. What was the effect of the Dawes Act?
9. What were the reforms people asked of the government? For each reform, why was it demanded? Which group of people were to be helped? Which group or groups were hurt?

# Expand Your Knowledge

1. Find out how lobbies started. What kinds of lobby groups exist to-day? How, or how not, does lobbying reflect the ideas of democracy at work?
2. Make a bar graph showing the number of immigrants for each ten-year period between 1840 and 1890. Provide information about where they were from and why they came. How does this information relate to the difference in the number of immigrants from one ten-year period to another?
3. Doing library research, compare farm prices of 1960 to farm prices of 1970.

# A World Leader 17

Aim: to help students relate factors of increasing industrial power in the U.S. to governmental policy of overseas expansion at the turn of the century.

The United States became the world's leading industrial nation in the 1890's. Yet, a large number of Americans felt that they were not sharing in the country's wealth. Farmers and workers who had organized in the 1880's formed their own political party. Many black Americans knew that their opportunities were being limited. They did not agree on the best way to improve their situation. Many Americans traded with people all over the world. They became more interested in

*Constant progress and change are seen in the use of both railcars and horse-drawn wagons in this picture of New York City in the 1890's. America was rapidly changing into the leading industrial nation of the world.*

foreign issues and lands. Near the end of the nineteenth century, the United States gained several new territories overseas. Economic, political, and religious interests in these lands led many Americans to new ideas about their country's role in world affairs.

# A New Party

A group of people dissatisfied with government policies formed a new political party in 1892. It was called the National People's party, and its members were called Populists. Most of the Populists were white and black farmers from the western and southern Alliances. Others were miners, industry workers, and owners of small businesses. They held a convention in Omaha, Nebraska, and chose James B. Weaver of Iowa as their candidate for President. The Populists also issued a program calling for many reforms. There were three main changes demanded in the Populist platform, or program. They wanted the coinage of silver dollars, an income tax, and the election of United States senators by popular vote.

# Money and Taxes

The Populists wanted the federal government to increase the supply of money. They hoped to make their debts easier to pay and bring about higher crop prices. The government had stopped using silver to make coins and to back paper money in 1873. After that year, only gold was used. Populists wanted the government to go back to a two-metal system. Farmers were supported in this demand by silver miners and their friends in the silver mining states in the West.

Money to run the government came mostly from tariffs. The Populists believed that raising tariffs was unfair to poor people. They could not afford higher costing goods. When more money had been needed by the government during the Civil War, a tax was placed on everyone's income, or money earned. The income tax was dropped in 1872, but the Populists wanted to bring it back. They wanted a graduated income tax, or one that was applied in different steps. People with low incomes would pay a low percent of tax, those with higher incomes would pay higher percents. Most rich people were not in favor of the idea.

Help students understand that an increase in the money supply would result in money of lower value which benefited debtors who had incurred debts when money had higher value.

Mine owners had almost ignored the Coinage Act of 1873 (see pp. 299-300 for mining strikes of the 1870's) because they had been getting higher prices for silver on the open market.

Have students investigate and report on today's income tax system and rates for comparison.

# Voting Power of the People

Remind students that business and profit are very important to country's economy and beneficial to citizens. Arguments arise over listing of priorities and differences of opinion on profit excess.

According to the Constitution, members of the state legislatures chose the people who became members of the United States Senate. Many Populists believed that state legislatures were controlled by trust and corporation business interests. They wanted the law changed so that senators were chosen by the direct votes of each state's citizens. Two other ideas supported by the Populists would give individual voters more influence on state lawmaking. One was initiative, a way that citizens can propose laws without the legislature. They must have a certain number of voters sign a petition, or request, to bring the proposed law before the people for a vote. The other idea was referendum. That is a way, through petition, for placing a law that already exists before the voters to approve or disapprove of it. Populists felt that this allowed citizens more power to make decisions about their government.

# The Elections of 1892

Might recall earlier debates over protective tariffs on pp. 156, 172, 178, 240, 247-8.

Benjamin Harrison had been elected President in 1888. The Republicans chose him as their candidate again in 1892. The Democratic party chose Grover Cleveland, who had been the President before Harrison. The main difference between the two major parties was that the Republicans wanted a higher tariff to protect American industry. Only the Populist party wanted major changes in the government.

Cleveland won the election with 227 electoral votes against 145 for Harrison and 22 for Weaver. In elections for other offices, however, the Populist party had some success. They elected three governors, five U. S. senators, and ten members of the House of Representatives.

# Southern Populists

The common problems of black and white farmers led to some cooperation between them in the South. The farmer Alliances had tried to bring the two groups together. Nearly one hundred black people had attended the Populist convention in 1892. Tom Watson of Georgia, a white Populist, made speeches favoring free schools for blacks and their right to vote without trouble. H. S. Doyle, a black preacher, made speeches favoring Watson.

In the North Carolina elections of 1894, Populists and black Republicans won control of the state legislature. By 1895, the state had appointed about three hundred blacks as judges. While the cooperation of blacks and whites in other states was not so successful, the example of North Carolina upset many white leaders in other southern states. The Democratic parties there fought to keep whites from joining the Populists. In some states, white voters who agreed with Populist ideas stayed with their own party rather than give any power to blacks.

# Thomas Watson

Thomas E. Watson was born in 1856 into a family of Georgia planters. He became a successful lawyer, regaining much of the land the family had lost in the Civil War. In 1882, he was elected to the Georgia legislature. Watson sought prosperity for the southern farmers. He did not want the farming economy of the South to change into a business and industry economy like the North. He ran for Congress in 1890 as a member of the Populist party. Watson won the support of the Farmers' Alliance. He became the speaker for Populist ideas in Congress. His work there helped farmers and working people.

In 1892, the shape of Watson's district changed. With a different number of voters in his district, Watson lost his next election. He lost again in 1894, but farmers still supported his ideas. In 1896, he ran as the Populist party candidate for Vice-President. Democrat William Jennings Bryan ran for President. Many Democrats did not want a Populist Vice-President with Bryan. Without their support, Bryan and Watson lost the election. Watson left politics for eight years.

Watson returned to politics in the 1900's with different ideas. He spoke against Catholics, Jews, Socialists, and blacks. He was also against the United States fighting in World War I. Watson lost many supporters with these ideas. In 1920, he finally decided to support minorities and labor. He was elected to the Senate that year. Watson died in office in 1922. A few years later, people were still singing the "Thomas E. Watson Song." It was about "a man of mighty power" who "fought and struggled" but failed.

# The Election of 1896

The depression was foreshadowed by a continuing decline in farm prices and a rash of strikes. Principle causes were 1) overexpansion of railroad building, 2) speculation by overly optimistic business people, and 3) gold drain caused by sales of American bonds by European investors worried by unstable conditions in agriculture and industry.

A depression began in 1893. By the next year, nearly four million people were out of work. President Cleveland believed that the government should not be involved in the social or economic lives of the people. He gave little support to those out of work. He also did little about the silver issue. The Democratic party chose another candidate for President in 1896.

Members of the Democratic party who supported silver coinage were in control at the convention. They chose William Jennings Bryan to run for President and put many Populist ideas in their platform. The Republicans chose William McKinley of Ohio. The Populists disagreed among themselves about supporting the Democrats, but they finally also chose Bryan as their candidate.

Review electoral system if necessary to relate electoral vote with popular vote.

McKinley won the election with 271 electoral votes. He had been supported most by business and newspaper people. Bryan had won nearly every state in the South and West. They had less population, however, and so had fewer electoral votes. In a short time, the silver issue lost importance because prices for American crops began to rise.

*In the elections of 1896, William McKinley was one of the candidates for the office of President. Here he campaigns from his porch.*

That was partly because of crop failures in Europe. In addition, gold was discovered in Alaska. An increase in the money supply backed by gold was possible. As a result of these changes, the Populists soon lost their importance as a separate party.

# Losing the Right to Vote

The cooperation shown between white and black Populists caused great concern to other white leaders in the South. They worked to find ways to stop blacks from voting. The states began to pass laws that limited voting, often making them part of new state constitutions. In Mississippi's constitution of 1890 were laws requiring a poll tax and a literacy test. The tax had to be paid by anyone voting at the polls, or election places. The literacy test meant that voters had to prove that they could read and explain any part of the state constitution. The voting officials, mostly white people, decided if the voter did that correctly. After 1890, most black citizens could not vote in Mississippi.

By the middle of the 1890's, many southern states began to write a "grandfather clause" into their constitutions. According to it, even if people could not pass the literacy test or pay the poll tax, they could still vote if they, their fathers, or their grandfathers had been allowed to vote on January 1, 1867. Thus, many poor whites were allowed to vote while most blacks could not because their fathers had been slaves.

Such discriminatory laws were frequently sanctioned by the courts. See note on *Minor v. Happersett*, p. 289. Might have students reread 15th Amendment and note that grandfather clause not declared unconstitutional until 1915 in test case brought by NAACP.

# Segregation

At the same time most southern states were limiting the right to vote, they also passed laws to segregate, or separate, blacks from whites in everyday life. There were separate sections on trains and boats, and in restaurants, hotels, and theaters. In many areas by 1885, separate schools were required for black children. Hope for a change from these policies by action from the federal government was lost in a court case known as *Plessy v. Ferguson*. In 1896, Homer Plessy brought a case against a Louisiana judge who had ruled that it was legal for a state to require people to sit in separate railway cars because of their color. The United States Supreme Court heard the case and ruled in favor of the

In 1883 Civil Rights Cases, Supreme Court paved the way for these "Jim Crow" laws of segregation by declaring unconstitutional the Federal Civil Rights Act of 1875 which had mandated that all public accommodations must be open to all.

Might have students investigate and report on Justice John Marshall Harlan (1833-1911), a former southern slave owner, who wrote the dissenting opinion in the 8-1 decision of *Plessy v. Ferguson*.

*A World Leader*

See p. 469 for 1954 case of *Brown v. Board of Education of Topeka* brought by NAACP resulting in reversal of Plessy decision. These two cases are important milestones in history of black Americans.

Louisiana law. The Court said that states could maintain "separate but equal" facilities for blacks. In many areas, black people had no voting power and no money to make sure that their schools and other facilities would be equal to those of whites.

# Booker T. Washington

Washington's speech became known as the Atlanta Compromise.

During the late 1890's and early 1900's, Booker T. Washington became one of the most important black persons in the United States. He was able to do so largely because his views were accepted by whites. Washington believed that education for blacks should mean learning a trade or the skills of farming. He used these ideas when he was invited to Alabama to run the school at Tuskegee. Washington was very successful in raising money for the school. In a few years, Tuskegee had more than a thousand students. Washington was asked to make a speech at the Cotton States Exposition in Atlanta in 1895. The speech he made became famous among white people as the view of all black people on questions of work and civil rights. In part of his speech, Washington said:

> The wisest among my race understand that [fighting for] social equality is . . . folly, and that progress in the enjoyment of all the privileges that will come to us must be the result of . . . constant struggle rather than [by force]. . . . The opportunity to earn a dollar in a factory just now is worth [much] more than the opportunity to spend a dollar in an opera house.

Washington's speech was widely reported in the newspapers in both the North and South. Because many whites did not want blacks to have equal rights, they felt that Washington had said that blacks did not want that either. Washington did not openly press for the rights of black people. He did help pay for court cases aimed at fighting for their rights. At times, Washington also secretly wrote to white leaders asking them for support.

# William E. B. DuBois

There were other important black persons who disagreed strongly with Washington's views and actions. William Monroe Trotter, a

*In the late 1800's, Tuskegee Institute stressed practical education for blacks. Students learned farming and other skills.*

*William E. B. DuBois was a black leader who fought for full equality of opportunity for blacks in every field.*

newspaper owner in Boston, said that Washington betrayed black people by not speaking out for their rights as American citizens. Another leading critic was William E. B. DuBois, a graduate of Fisk and Harvard universities. In 1903, DuBois wrote a book called *The Souls of Black Folk.* In it, he spoke against Washington's views on education for blacks and wrote of justice. DuBois pointed out that without higher education for blacks, schools like Tuskegee would not be able to stay open. There would be no trained black teachers. By reading DuBois' book, some white people learned that Washington did not represent the views of all black people.

# Overseas Territories

American interests were not limited to problems at home during this period. In the late nineteenth century, the United States gained control of territories in other parts of the world. These new lands were not connected to the United States, most of them were islands. Americans in business thought of them as sources of raw materials and as markets for American goods. Military leaders saw them as needed bases where American ships could stop for repairs and fuel. They said that a strong navy was needed to protect American trade. Some people believed that they had a duty to convert the people to Christianity.

Vocal opponents of overseas expansion included House Speaker Thomas Reed, philosopher William James, writer Samuel Clemens, educator Charles Eliot, and millionaire industrialist Andrew Carnegie.

Many Americans had argued against overseas expansion. Some pointed out that new territories would mean more money for a larger army and navy to protect them. Others were prejudiced against the island peoples and did not want the United States to be involved with them. Some Americans said that gaining land overseas meant taking it away from others. As a democracy, the United States should allow other people to decide their governments for themselves.

# Early Interests

Russians recent defeat in Crimean War lessened their interest in burden of defending Alaska where fur trade was declining.

People of the United States had been trading with the people of Europe, China, and countries in the Western Hemisphere from colonial days. Trade with Japan was established after a fleet of United States warships visited that country in 1853 under the command of Matthew Perry. In 1867, Secretary of State William Seward arranged to buy Alaska from Russia because of the natural resources he believed to be there. Congress approved the purchase of Alaska and the annexation of the Midway Islands. These were two small islands in the Pacific Ocean at the end of the Hawaiian island chain. By 1878, the government also had a treaty with Samoa in the Southwest Pacific. It allowed the United States to have a coaling station for ships at Pago Pago.

First big "boom" in American Alaska was the Yukon gold rush of 1890's.

## Hawaii

The United States government was interested in Hawaii from the time that Americans began to trade with China in the late 1700's. The islands were important stops for the sailors and ships of many nations.

Verify that students understand that Hawaii is a chain of some 1,400 coral and volcanic islands in the North Pacific.

*Queen Liliuokalani lost power in 1893 and was the only ruling queen of the Hawaiian Islands.*

*A World Leader*

American missionaries came to Hawaii to try to convert the people to Christianity. Other Americans came to grow sugar and to trade. They soon became rich and gained influence in the Hawaiian government. When the new ruler, Queen Liliuokalani, came to the throne in 1891, she wanted to rid the government of outside influences. The Americans there led a successful revolt against the queen. They had the help of the American government representative and the United States marines. The Americans set up a new government and asked the United States to annex Hawaii. Congress refused to do so, but it recognized the government and did not try to return the islands to Hawaiian rule.

# Spanish Cuba

Might have students investigate and report on comic strip "Battle of the Yellow Kids" which led to the term "yellow journalism" for the circulation boosting tactics used by Joseph Pulitzer's New York World and William Randolph Hearst's New York Journal.

Nineteenth-century Spain controlled an empire which included Cuba and Puerto Rico in the Caribbean and the Philippines in the Pacific. The people of these islands had tried many times to break Spain's rule and become independent. The Cubans had revolted in 1868 and tried again in 1895. Some Americans, with large amounts of money invested in sugar and other industries there, paid close attention to the revolt of 1895. Others became familiar with it as a result of American newspaper reporting. The papers competed with each other to see which one could report the most shocking tales of cruelty. Their stories increased Americans' sympathy for Cuba and hatred for Spain.

Feelings between the United States and Spain grew worse when a letter stolen from a Spanish official in 1898 was printed in a New York newspaper. In it, the official called President McKinley a crowd pleaser and hinted that he was a poor politician. Americans were angered by the insult. The situation became more dangerous in February. The American battleship *Maine* exploded while in the harbor at Havana, Cuba. More than 250 crew members died. The cause of the explosion was not known, but newspaper headlines and many political leaders blamed the Spanish. The cry, "Remember the *Maine*," was heard everywhere. By early April, Congress recognized the independence of Cuba and demanded that the Spanish leave the island. The Spanish refused, and on April 25, Congress declared war on Spain "to free Cuba."

Prior to the war with Spain, Congress had declared that it would not annex Cuba.

# The Spanish-American War

While the disagreement with Spain began over Cuba, the fighting started in the Philippines. Before war was declared, Assistant Secretary

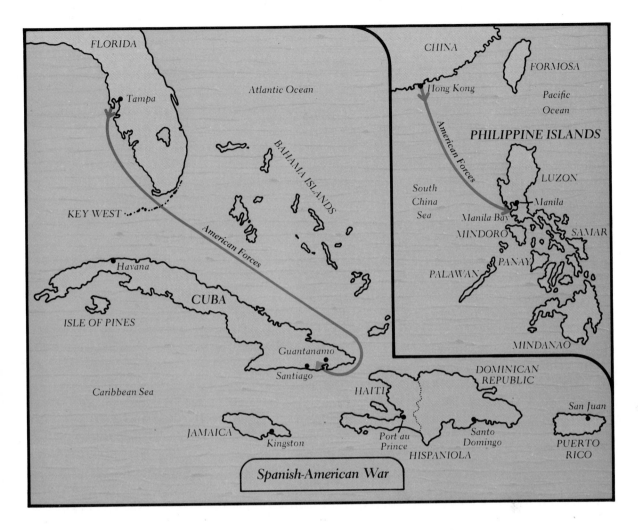

**Spanish-American War**

of the Navy Theodore Roosevelt had secretly ordered Commodore George Dewey to take the American fleet in the Pacific to the Philippines. Dewey was to take over the Philippines in case of war with Spain. In early May, Dewey's fleet of new steel ships destroyed the Spanish fleet in Manila Bay after a brief fight. The Spanish finally surrendered the city of Manila to the Americans in August.

Spain had controlled the Philippines for more than three hundred years. The Filipinos had revolted many times against Spanish rule without success. A stronger revolt in 1896 had been halted because the Spanish promised reforms. No reforms were made, and the Filipinos began fighting again. After the Spanish-American War, they expected their independence.

In the Caribbean, the United States sent an army of seventeen thousand troops to Cuba. They landed near Santiago in June and were

There is some evidence that the Filipinos might have succeeded in their revolt if the United States had not intervened and that Spain chose to surrender to the Americans instead.

*A World Leader*

*American troops in Cuba fought a short war with*
*Spain for Cuban independence.*

opposed by only a small part of the Spanish forces in Cuba. Santiago was captured, and the Spanish fleet there was destroyed. The island of Puerto Rico was also soon occupied by the American army. Like the Filipinos and the Cubans, the people of Puerto Rico had fought against Spain for their independence. Under the leadership of Ramon Emeterio Betances, they had revolted in 1868 and declared the Republic of Puerto Rico. That revolt failed, as did another in 1897.

# The Treaty of Paris

On August 12, 1898, agreement was reached to end the fighting. Representatives from Spain and the United States met in Paris to discuss the settlement. There were no representatives from the countries in the Pacific or the Caribbean which had been involved. According to the treaty signed by Spain and the United States, Cuba received its independence. Puerto Rico and the island of Guam in the Pacific were given to the United States. The Philippines were sold to the United States for the sum of twenty million dollars. In addition to these lands taken from Spain, Congress had annexed Hawaii to the United States in July of 1898.

The American army remained in Cuba following the defeat of the Spanish. They were to protect American businesses. In 1900, the Cubans held a convention to write a constitution for their country. The United States put great pressure on members of the convention for certain additions to the constitution. The Cubans had to agree to sell or lease land to the United States for naval bases. They also had to allow the United States the right to interfere in their affairs, when necessary, to preserve Cuba's independence and to maintain law and order on the island. The American army was withdrawn in 1902.

# Imperialism

The policy of extending one nation's rule over another country is called imperialism. Following the Spanish-American War, Filipinos fought against American soldiers in their country who represented American rule. In the United States, many citizens argued both for and against extending American rule over the Philippines.

President William McKinley later explained how he arrived at the decision to favor rule over the Philippines.

*When . . . I realized that the Philippines had dropped into our laps I confess I did not know what to do with them. I sought counsel from all sides—Democrats as well as Republicans—but got little help. I thought first we would take only Manila; then Luzon; then other islands, perhaps, also. I walked the floor of the White House night after night. . . .*

*And one night late it came to me this way—I don't know how it was, but it came: (1) That we could not give them back to Spain—that would be cowardly and dishonorable; (2) that we could not turn them over to France or Germany— our commercial rivals in the Orient— that would be bad business . . . ; (3) that we could not leave them to themselves— they were [not ready] for self-government—and they would soon have anarchy and misrule over there worse than Spain's was; and (4) there was nothing left for us to do but to take them all, and to educate the Filipinos, and . . . do the very best we could by them. . . . And then I went to bed . . . and the next morning I sent for the chief engineer of the War Department . . . and I told him to put the Philippines on the map of the United States . . . and there they are, and there they will stay while I am President!*

See Teacher's Manual, page 46T.

The first civil governor of the Philippines was William Howard Taft. Filipinos did not gain independence until 1946.

When the Filipinos realized that they were not going to gain their independence, they revolted against the American troops there in February, 1899. The number of American soldiers was raised to seventy thousand. The Filipinos continued to fight under General Emilio Aguinaldo until 1902. Many of them died during the war against American rule. The President of the United States appointed a governor and commissioners, all Americans, for the Philippines. The commissioners acted as the upper house of the legislature, and Filipinos elected members to the lower house.

Puerto Ricans had mixed feelings about American rule. Leaders like Betances were against it, but many business people were in favor of it. A new government was set up for Puerto Rico in 1900. The President of the United States appointed an American governor with complete veto power over the legislature elected by the Puerto Ricans.

# Toward the Twentieth Century

The United States was the leading industrial country in the world. Other nations also saw it as one of the leading colonial and military powers. The citizens of the United States joined the people of other nations in concern over world issues. At home, Americans carried many of the problems of the nineteenth century into the twentieth, but they found new opportunities as well. The people who saw problems in sharing the wealth and opportunities of the nation also believed that there were solutions to those problems.

# Chapter 17 in Perspective See Teacher's Manual, page 109T.

## Identify

| | | |
|---|---|---|
| Benjamin Harrison | Booker T. Washington | Theodore Roosevelt |
| William Jennings Bryan | William E. B. DuBois | Emilio Aguinaldo |
| William McKinley | | |

# Explain

National People's party     initiative     *Plessy v. Ferguson*
Populists     referendum     segregation
platform     grandfather clause

## Check Your Memory of the Facts

1. What were three main changes the Populists demanded in their platform?
2. How successful were the Populists in the elections of 1892?
3. How did some states keep black people from voting?
4. How did Alaska and Hawaii become American territories?
5. What events led to the Spanish-American War?
6. What were the peace settlements of the Spanish-American War?

## Check Your Understanding of the Ideas

1. What reasons did the Populists give for their platform demands?
2. How did black leaders differ in their ideas about how to gain rights for black people?
3. Why did the Populists lose their importance as a separate party?
4. Why did some people favor overseas expansion? Why did others oppose it?
5. Why was the Spanish-American War a short one?
6. How did the people in the territories gained by the United States react to the peace settlements of the war?
7. How did the United States govern its new territories?

## Expand Your Knowledge

1. The territories gained by the United States as a result of the Spanish-American War were not all given the same status in relation to the United States government. Find out how, if at all, the relationship between the governments of Cuba, Puerto Rico, or the Philippines and the United States has changed over the years.
2. Choose an article from a current newspaper or magazine that seems to be fair in its approach to a problem. Find another article which tries to shock people into demanding action on a certain issue. Identify the key phrases in both articles. How can the press influence public opinion?

# The Progressive Era  18

Aim: to help students understand the American people's response to the increasing industrialization and urbanization of American life in the early 1900's.

In the early years of the twentieth century, there were more opportunities for the average citizen than ever before. Even so, a general reform movement swept across the United States. Many average Americans saw and read about serious problems in their country and tried to deal with them. These reformers believed that their ideas would lead to progress and a better way of life for more Americans. They were called Progressives, and the time when they were most active is called the Progressive Era.

## New Opportunities

For better perspective, have students relate these figures to the U.S. Census figures for 1870 (38.6 million) and 1900 (76.0 million).

Might have student investigate and report on the Morrill Act provisions. The act represents earliest major action taken by the federal government in the field of education.

Opportunities were limited for people who lived on farms and for those crowded into the poor neighborhoods of American cities. But for many average citizens, there were more opportunities to attend school, to take part in free-time activities, and to work toward improving their lives. The growth of educational opportunities in the United States had followed the growth of the economy. In the 1870's, some states and territories began to require that children attend school for a certain part of the year. By 1900, thirty states had passed laws to require some amount of time to be spent in school.

The number of new colleges grew at a rapid rate in the late nineteenth century. Congress had passed the Morrill Act in 1862 which gave land for the establishment of state colleges. The total number of colleges grew from about five hundred in 1870 to nearly one thousand in 1900. In addition to colleges that admitted blacks and whites, there were over thirty colleges especially for blacks by 1900. Over two thousand blacks had graduated from college by then. Also by 1900, nearly 100,000 women were attending colleges or schools for teacher training. The growth of education provided the country with many people trained for different professions.

## More Free Time

The growing number of machines used at work and at home made it possible for people to have more free time. This time was spent in a

*Women and men enjoyed bicycle rides on beautiful afternoons. A safer bicycle made cycling a popular sport in the 1880's.*

number of ways. People attended popular sports events like horse racing, boxing matches, and baseball games. Baseball had developed into a professional sport after the Cincinnati Red Stockings team was formed. Teams from eight cities organized a league, called the National League, in 1876. The American League was formed in 1900. The first World Series to determine the best team from the two leagues took place in 1903. Basketball, the only major sport that started in the United States, was first played in 1891. It soon became important as an indoor team sport for both men and women.

A safer bicycle was developed by 1888. It had two rubber tires of the same size filled with air. Older bicycles had had metal rimmed wheels, a large one in front and a small one in back. They had been difficult and dangerous to ride. Thousands of people took up riding the new bicycle. Clubs were formed, magazines carried articles on cycling, and roads were improved for riding.

Many people enjoyed musical events. Thousands went to see Victor Herbert's "Babes in Toyland" written in 1903 and "The Red Mill" written in 1906. Herbert was one of the first important American composers of theater music. John Philip Sousa and his band thrilled thousands with their rousing marches like "The Stars and Stripes Forever" and "The Washington Post March." Sousa had been a director of the

*All of America enjoyed the humorous adventures of Mark Twain's characters. His simple style and love of travel created memorable books.*

United States Marine Corps Band. He formed his own band in 1892 and took it on tour to cities in Europe and across the United States. Scott Joplin, a black composer of ragtime music, had his first hit in 1899 with "Maple Leaf Rag." Even though he became wealthy through his music, Joplin died a disappointed man. Ragtime had not been accepted as a serious form of music.

More Americans were finding time to read. Bret Harte, Louisa May Alcott, and Samuel Clemens, who wrote under the name of Mark Twain, were popular authors of the late 1800's. Harte wrote adventure stories of the West, and Alcott based her stories on the lives of young people in New England. Clemens traveled widely and wrote humorous and witty stories which reflected life as "Mark Twain" saw it. Newspapers were a part of nearly every American's life. They were printed in large and small cities, often in several languages. There were also special newspapers for different organizations such as labor unions.

As average Americans read more, they became aware of poor conditions in cities. Danish immigrant Jacob Riis published a book in 1890 entitled *How the Other Half Lives*. It contained photographs of overcrowded apartment houses and writings about the lack of food and poor health conditions in large cities. Hundreds of articles appeared in newspapers and magazines around the country.

Ragtime, featuring syncopated rhythms played against a steady beat, laid the foundation for jazz.

# The Social Justice Movement

Increasing awareness of the needs of others led many Americans into a movement for social justice. The reforms from this movement made up a large part of the Progressive Era. Social justice reforms included creating better opportunities for education and jobs, as well as improving health and living conditions. Many reformers were teachers, lawyers, social workers, or church leaders. Some were people in business or politics. People in the social justice movement worked hard to help poor people living in American cities.

The cities continued to grow at a fast rate with thousands of people moving there to find jobs. In the early 1900's, a large number of black people moved from farm areas to cities. They were the majority of citizens in Charleston, South Carolina, Montgomery, Alabama, and other southern cities. Blacks also moved to New York, Baltimore, Washington, D.C., and Philadelphia. Besides the people moving to cities from farms, immigrants continued to settle in the cities in large

Social justice efforts, different and more widespread than the legal justice efforts of the time, aimed at more equitable distribution of opportunity and power.

Might remind students of the severe depression of 1893, p. 330.

*The Progressive Era*

# The Triangle Shirtwaist Fire

Fire was one of the many dangers factory workers faced in the early twentieth century, especially in the clothing industry. Many of the companies were located in buildings without much fire protection. The City of New York had one of the best equipped fire departments in the United States. Yet its equipment could not reach the tops of tall buildings.

The Triangle Shirtwaist (a type of blouse) Company was located on the eighth, ninth, and tenth floors of the Asch Building. The Asch Building had been built in 1901 and met all of New York's safety laws. It had only one fire escape which ended on the second floor. Workers did not practice fire drills.

On March 25, 1911, a fire broke out in the Triangle Company and spread quickly among scraps of cloth. Max Rothen, a worker at the company, described attempts to stop the fire:

. . . there were cries of "fire" from all sides. The line of hanging patterns began to burn. Some of the cutters jumped up and tried to tear the patterns from the line but the fire was ahead of them. The patterns were burning. They began to fall on the layers of thin goods underneath them. Every time another piece dropped, light scraps of burning fabric began to fly around the room. They came down on the other tables and they fell on the machines. Then . . . the whole string of burning patterns fell down.

To escape the fire, the workers pushed and shoved their way to one of the two stairwells in the building. Others crowded onto the elevators or to the fire escape. Finally, people began to jump from the windows to keep from being burned to death. More than 140 people died from the fire or from jumping.

The owners of the Triangle Company were charged with manslaughter and placed on trial. The charge was based on the fact that a ninth floor door to one of the stairwells had been locked. Several witnesses testified that the door was often locked. This was to keep workers from leaving the building without being seen as they sometimes took shirtwaists with them. However, it could not be proven that the owners knew that the door had been locked on the day of the fire. They were both set free.

People were shocked by the disaster and demanded reform of factory safety laws. On June 30, 1911, the New York legislature created the Factory Investigating Commission. It was to check for fire hazards, unsafe machines, and poor health conditions. In the first year, the commission checked nearly two thousand factories.

numbers. Nearly nine million new immigrants entered the country between 1901 and 1910 with another five million in the ten years after that. Many of these people had been farmers and had few of the skills needed for factory work.

# Organizations in the City

Settlement houses were one way that reformers helped people. These were places where people could come for help finding jobs, learning the English language, or receiving proper medical care. The first settlement house had been set up in London, England, in 1884. Stanton Coit set up the first American settlement house in New York City in 1886. Others were soon established in Chicago, Pittsburgh, Boston, and most other large cities around the country.

One of the most famous settlement houses was Hull House in Chicago. Jane Addams started it in 1887. In New York, Lillian Wald set up Henry Street Settlement. Wald was especially interested in providing nursing care for people who could not afford to go to hospitals. Under her leadership, nurses were soon making thousands of visits to homes and schools in New York.

Other organizations were formed especially to help black people adjust to living in the city. Jane Edna Hunter, a black woman from South Carolina, set up the Working Girls' Home Association in Cleveland, Ohio. There she helped other black women coming to the city find jobs. In 1911, the National Urban League was formed. The league helped train black social workers. Because of discrimination in housing opportunities, groups were formed in several cities to provide money and information on homes for blacks.

Most of the people in the social justice movement believed that laws would have to be passed to help the poor. They brought the government into their fight. Reformers talked to government leaders to get rules for inspecting apartment houses and to force owners to repair them. They especially pressed for laws that would require owners to provide running water and indoor toilets to improve health conditions.

# Improving the Lives of Children

Many of the reforms wanted by Progressives were aimed at helping children. Thousands of children were working sixty or more hours every week. Children were employed in coal mines, textile mills, and factories. Sweatshops, or buildings where many people worked under poor conditions, involved children. Often, entire families sewed clothes at home to earn money. Reformers believed that children needed more time to go to school and to take part in free-time activities.

Settlement house workers did many things especially for children. They pressed city governments to build parks and playgrounds. Jane Addams felt that children should not be treated like adults when they got into trouble with the law. Her influence helped pass the first state law that set up juvenile courts. In 1912, with help from Lillian Wald, the Children's Bureau was established in the federal government. Julia Lathrop, trained at Hull House, was its first director. The bureau investigated conditions of health, education, and work involving children. It made recommendations to Congress for laws to protect them.

First state juvenile court law passed in Chicago in 1899. Juvenile justice might be very good topic for student research and report to produce class discussion on constitutional rights of those citizens under their state's legal age of adulthood.

# Reforms of City Government

Might have students research and report on city government movement for home rule. City government was not provided for in Constitution and was controlled by state legislatures. Students should investigate local area's type of government.

People were turning to the government for answers to problems. There was also a continuing effort to reform all levels of government. At the local level, Progressives hoped to give people more services and to take the control away from corrupt officials. Before the 1900's, many American city governments were run by a mayor and a city council elected by the people. Other important jobs were given out as political favors through the spoils system. During the early 1900's, two new forms of government were being used by many cities.

One new kind of government was started in 1901 in Galveston, Texas. The city had been hit by a tidal wave, and mayor and council failed to provide needed services after the disaster. A commission was then set up with five members. As a group, commission members made laws for the city. Each of the commissioners was in charge of a city department, such as water services. This system allowed each person to work on one area of government rather than having one person, the mayor, working on them all.

Another new form of government was used in Staunton, Virginia. A city manager was hired there in 1908. The manager had been trained in city planning and was hired for ability. The city manager's job was to administer the laws made by the city council in a businesslike way. It was not long before four hundred cities had commission governments and some forty others had hired city managers.

*In the 1880's, there was more awareness of child labor abuses. Children worked long hours in factories from an early age.*

# Reforms of State Government

Progressive leaders wanted to make state governments more democratic. They wanted to increase the power of the voters to make decisions and to limit the power of the legislatures. Progressives believed, as the Populists had, that many members of legislatures were under the control of people who put the interests of business first. Reformers in many states wanted to use the referendum and the initiative. Some states also made laws for recall to increase voters' control over elected leaders. Recall meant that the voters could remove elected leaders from office if the voters felt that they were not doing a good job. Some members of Congress were against the recall of judges, and they

Reference p. 328 for definitions of referendum and initiative. Recall movement led by Oregon (1902) as part of series of reform measures called the Oregon System.

blocked the admission of Arizona territory as a state until it got rid of that law. After Arizona was admitted in 1912, along with New Mexico, the voters put the recall of judges back into their state laws.

# Progressives and the Federal Government

United States senators were still elected by members of state legislatures. Like the Populists, Progressives believed that many of them represented the industries rather than the people of their states. The Senate was called a "Millionaire's Club." Many people felt that most

*When Theodore Roosevelt became President, he strongly supported the creation of national parks. Here he enjoys a beautiful scene with John Muir, a noted naturalist and one of his advisers.*

members of the Senate did not know or care about the problems of average workers, farmers, or the poor. One of the most successful Progressive reforms at the federal level was about this issue. In 1912, Congress passed the Seventeenth Amendment which provided for the election of senators by the direct vote of the people. It was ratified by the states and became law in 1913.

# Conservation of Natural Resources

Protection of natural resources was another goal of many Progressives. The first national park had been established at Yellowstone, Wyoming, in 1872. In 1891, the National Forest Reservation Act gave the President the power to set aside public forests. Theodore Roosevelt, who became President when William McKinley was assassinated in 1901, strongly supported the creation of national parks and forests. He set aside over 200 million acres of land for federal reserves. They included forest lands and those with important minerals or sources of power. Under the Newlands Reclamation Act of 1902, money from the sale of land in the West was used to build dams for electric power and canals to take water to dry fields. Settlers who benefited from these projects paid a small fee to help build more projects. By 1915, twenty-five projects were being built.

# Regulation of the Economy

Most Americans, including reformers, were proud of the position the United States had as the leading industrial nation in the world. They saw the benefits of living at a time when so many products made life easier. But for many Progressives, regulation of the country's economy was more important than any other reform. They wanted to make laws to control monopolies and trusts. They believed this would help to limit depressions in the economy.

Might review definitions of trust and monopoly on pp. 297 and 311.

Progressives wanted to stop what they felt were unfair business practices by large companies. Congress had passed the Sherman Antitrust Act in 1890. This law made it illegal for companies which sold products in more than one state to form monopolies or trusts. But since the law failed to say how much control of an industry made a monopoly, it was hard to enforce. By 1904, there were over three hundred trusts. Oil, steel, copper, tobacco, sugar, and meat packing were only a few of the industries controlled by trusts. Nearly 95 percent of the nation's railroads were controlled by six companies. Bankers, led by J. P. Morgan of New York, provided money to these large companies and so had gained a strong voice in their control. Morgan bought Andrew Carnegie's steel company for about 400 million dollars. He then helped to organize the first billion dollar corporation—United States Steel—in 1901. Morgan or one of his partners served on the boards of directors of seventy-two different companies. So much control by so few people alarmed many Americans. Progressives felt that a fulltime government office was needed. It would make regulations for large businesses or bring cases to court to break the trusts into smaller companies.

# "Trustbusting"

President Roosevelt understood that large businesses could often produce more goods at lower prices than could small companies. He

*This political cartoon shows the feelings of Progressives who thought senators represented industries instead of people.*

wanted Congress to make rules for them rather than to stop their growth. During President Roosevelt's term, Congress passed a law that set up a Bureau of Corporations. This bureau checked into the organization and operation of big businesses. It brought court cases against those who broke antitrust laws. Roosevelt became famous as a "trust-buster" because of one case in particular. He ordered the attorney general to bring a case against the Northern Securities Company. The company was made up of three different railroads. The Supreme Court ruled that Northern Securities was organized in violation of the Sherman Antitrust Act. It ordered the company to be broken up into three separate companies again.

Other suits were also brought to court with success, but most large companies remained untouched by the government. By 1911, the Supreme Court decided that the large size of some companies was not always against the antitrust laws. It began to consider whether breaking up a large business would do more harm to the public than good. Many such companies produced goods or services cheaper than any smaller ones could. The justices of the Court came to feel that there were "good" and "bad" trusts. The "bad" ones were those which government leaders felt were charging too much or went too far in putting others out of business. The Presidents following Roosevelt in office—William H. Taft elected in 1908 and Woodrow Wilson elected in 1912—agreed with his policies toward large businesses.

Could note for students that mergers have been influenced by changes in attitudes. Today's Burlington Northern Railroad includes those companies involved in the breakup of the Northern Securities Company.

Might have student investigate and report on the "Great Dissenter" Justice Oliver Wendell Holmes (1841-1935) whose opinion in the Northern Securities case was that mere bigness itself was not illegal. Many of Holmes' dissents became the Court's majority opinions in later years.

# Banking Reform

One of the most important economic reforms of the Progressive Era was the Federal Reserve Act of 1913. This law set up the Federal Reserve banking system. Twelve reserve banks were established around the country. National banks were all required to join the federal bank in their area. Each member bank had to put a certain amount of its money into the federal bank as a reserve. When a large number of people wanted to withdraw their savings, fewer banks were ruined because they had this reserve. At times when people needed more money, such as when farmers needed to pay extra workers at harvest time, federal banks lowered the requirement for the reserve amount. This made more money available for loans. This was an improvement over the old banking system because more money was available when it was needed.

See pp. 178-179 for National Bank controversy under President Jackson.

State chartered banks were invited to join upon fulfillment of membership requirements.

The Reserve Banks act as Bankers' Banks by doing for member banks what they do for the public: hold deposits, make loans, and influence the economy by regulation of interest rates.

*The Progressive Era*

# Income Taxes

The Constitution (Art. I, Sec. 8) called for *uniform* taxation with everyone paying the same amounts.

The fight the Populists had started for an income tax continued with the Progressives. In 1901, Congress passed the Sixteenth Amendment which was ratified by the states in 1913. This amendment gave Congress the power to tax personal and corporate income in different degrees. Congress then quickly passed the Revenue Act of 1913. It placed a 1 percent tax on all income over three thousand dollars and an additional tax on incomes over twenty thousand dollars. Most citizens were not affected by this tax.

Total receipts from the tax were less than 5% of total federal revenues.

# Workers and the Progressive Movement

Strike leaders were jailed for contempt of court.

One of the main reasons workers were unable to make more progress in organizing unions was the attitude of the courts. Judges could force people to stop a strike by issuing injunctions, or special court orders. If the leaders of a strike did not obey the injunction, they could be arrested and put in jail. During the coal strike of 1902, however, President Roosevelt brought the owners and the workers together. Their talks resulted in a pay increase for the miners. In 1912, the American Federation of Labor supported Woodrow Wilson for President hoping to get laws passed to protect labor unions from the courts. Courts had been treating labor unions as they treated trusts. President Wilson did support the Clayton Antitrust Act. This law stated that unions were not organizations keeping trade from taking place in the same way that trusts limited trade. However, judges continued to issue injunctions against strikers.

Trusts and unions were both considered as "conspiracies in restraint of trade."

Progressives tried to get laws passed to limit the number of hours for workers. Several states passed laws limiting the working hours of children and women. The Supreme Court, however, was not very sympathetic to these laws. In 1904, the Court ruled that a New York law setting hours for bakery workers was unconstitutional. The Court said that it interfered with people's right to work as many hours as they pleased. By 1908, the Court was presented with a large amount of evidence about what long hours did to people's health and to the well-being of families. That year, it ruled in favor of an Oregon law that limited the hours of women workers to ten a day. Two laws to do away with child labor were passed during President Wilson's terms, but they were later declared unconstitutional.

*These people risked a court order forcing them back to work. Many strikes failed when leaders ignored injunctions and were jailed.*

# Outside the Progressive Movement

There were large groups of people in the United States who benefited very little from the reforms of the time. The Progressives were mainly concerned about the conditions of people in the cities because most of the reformers lived and worked there. The problems of city industries could be clearly seen. Poor people living in farm areas received much less attention.

Large numbers of Mexicans began coming to farm areas in the southwestern part of the United States in the early twentieth century. They came for many reasons. Some opposed the Mexican government and wanted to avoid being put into jail. Others came because European and American businesses were buying up large pieces of land in Mexico. It was growing harder to compete with them. Some Mexicans took jobs as farm workers in the United States. Others went to work in the mines and on the railroads. They often settled in areas where descendants of Mexican and Spanish people had lived for many years.

The border had little historical or cultural meaning at this time; not patrolled until mid-1920's.

Mexican government under President Porfirio Diaz had encouraged foreign investment and speculation in railroads, mining, oil, and land. This was a period of political unrest in Mexico which led to revolution in 1910.

*The Progressive Era*

For most farm workers, wages were low and housing conditions were poor. They moved with the growing season and thus had little chance to attend school or to form organizations to help themselves. In railroads and mines, Mexicans and Mexican Americans were often paid lower wages than other workers. Mexican-American workers led a strike in Arizona copper mines in 1903. The strike was broken when the leaders of the strike were arrested and put in jail. Mexican and Japanese

Some U.S. business people actively recruited Mexican laborers because of lower wages.

# Ellen Richards

Ellen Swallow Richards was a chemist and founder of the study of home economics. Born in 1842, she showed an early skill as both a housekeeper and storekeeper for her parents. Richards worked for years saving money to enter college. She was twenty-five before she began studying science at Vassar College in 1868.

Richards finished Vassar College in two years. Then she entered the new Massachusetts Institute of Technology to study chemistry. Richards was the first woman student in any scientific school. She worked for a Doctor of Science degree but did not receive one. She said, "the heads of the department did not wish a woman to receive the first D.S. in chemistry." Even without the degree, Richards followed her interest in chemistry. She married a metal and mining engineer in 1875 and became a chemist partner in his work. Later she became the first woman member of the Institute of Mining Engineers.

Richards helped other women find jobs in science. She trained women to teach science in high schools. She started a woman's laboratory at Massachusetts Institute of Technology. Then she turned her interests to public health and consumer problems. Richards worked as a chemist for the Massachusetts Board of Health in 1878. She tested foods and consumer products for purity. By 1900, she was also an expert on the chemistry of air and water.

During the 1890's, Richards worried about family life in the cities. She feared that children did not know enough about health and housekeeping. Richards raised public support to teach these in school. She also helped schools and hospitals plan low-cost, balanced meals. In 1899, Richards and her followers named their work "home economics." Richards was elected the first president of the American Home Economics Association in 1908. A year before her death in 1911, Smith College honored Richards with the Doctor of Science degree.

farm workers won the right to talk with farm owners about wages after a strike in Ventura, California, in 1903. Some attempts to improve the lives of Mexican Americans were successful, but many were not. They continued to receive low pay and had little opportunity for education. Most of them were forced to live in separate areas of towns.

# The Rights of Black People

Conditions for black Americans grew worse in many ways. Trouble between black and white Americans increased in both the North and the South. Riots between blacks and whites took place in Brownsville, Texas, in Atlanta, Georgia, and in Springfield, Illinois, among others.

In 1905, a group of black people met in Niagara Falls, Canada, to form an organization to work for the rights of blacks. William E. B. DuBois was an important member of the group. Booker T. Washington feared that the group would cause trouble with whites and tried to keep them from having their views printed in papers.

Remind students of text material on DuBois and Washington, pp. 332-33.

In 1909, a group of white reformers and blacks from the Niagara Movement met to organize the National Association for the Advancement of Colored People (NAACP). DuBois was the only black person elected as an officer. He edited the group's newspaper called *Crisis*. The NAACP brought cases to court against laws that kept blacks from voting or receiving equal treatment. In 1915, they won a case when the Supreme Court said that a law in Oklahoma was unconstitutional because it kept blacks from voting. The NAACP continued to bring other cases to remove laws that discriminated against black people.

See note on grandfather clause, p. 331.

# Results of the Progressive Era

Americans had always tried to improve their government. The years of the early twentieth century were different because so many reforms were also tried in the economy and in how people lived. Reformers were not successful in everything they tried to do. They did go a long way toward making all levels of government more responsible for the health, education, and security of the people. Some Progressives, like President Wilson, felt that what they had done at home could be done in other countries. Many Americans agreed that their system of government was best for everyone. This belief shaped the ideas of Americans in dealing with nations overseas.

*The Progressive Era*

# Chapter 18 in Perspective See Teacher's Manual, page 112T.

## Identify

| | | |
|---|---|---|
| Victor Herbert | Jacob Riis | J. P. Morgan |
| Louisa May Alcott | Jane Addams | Woodrow Wilson |
| Mark Twain | | |

## Explain

| | | |
|---|---|---|
| Progressives | National Urban League | Bureau of Corporations |
| Morrill Act | recall | injunction |
| settlement house | Federal Reserve Act | Clayton Antitrust Act |

## Check Your Memory of the Facts

1. What were some of the reasons for increased spare-time activities? What were some of the activities?
2. Who were the reformers? What did they start out to do?
3. What were some of the reforms tried in the area of social justice?
4. How were children affected by reforms?
5. What new forms of city government were introduced? What was important about them?
6. What reform ideas of the Populists were realized in the Progressive Era?
7. What groups of people were not affected by the reforms of the Progressive Era?
8. What was the purpose of the NAACP?

## Check Your Understanding of the Ideas

1. How did increased opportunities for education affect reform movements?
2. What was important about the conservation policies of the Progressives?
3. Why was there a change in attitude toward trusts after 1911?
4. What was important about the Federal Reserve Act?
5. How do the reforms of the Progressive Era show that the actions of individuals are sometimes regulated for the good of others? Give

some examples. Are the reforms of the Progressive Era different from those demanded in the 1870's and 1880's?

## Expand Your Knowledge

1. Using your local newspaper, find out what reforms are being demanded in your area. What groups of people will benefit? What groups of people might not? How do these reforms compare to those of the Progressive Era?
2. Read or reread a story by Bret Harte, Louisa May Alcott, Mark Twain, or another writer of the late 1800's or early 1900's. What kinds of conditions illustrated in the story would cause people of that time to demand reforms?

# Chicago 1870-1890

In the 1830's, the United States bought a piece of land at the southern tip of Lake Michigan from the Potawatomi Indians. Much of the land was a muddy swamp, and the air above it had an odd smell. The Indians called it Chicagou, or "place of the skunk." Ten years earlier, William H. Keating had described the area in a report to the government:

*We are greatly disappointed. Fertile soil? . . . 90 men cannot [live] on the grain raised in this country! The village . . . consists of a few huts. . . . As a place of business it offers [nothing] to the settler, for the whole amount of trade on the lake did not exceed a cargo of five or six [ships]. . . .*

The opening of the Erie Canal in 1825 had connected the eastern part of the country to the Great Lakes and the Midwest. Chicago was located on Lake Michigan, and it had river connections to trade on the Mississippi River. Settlers began coming into the area, and Chicago started to grow.

## A City

By 1870, Chicago had grown from a small town into the fourth largest city in the nation. It connected East and West not only by water but also by rail. The lines of four major railroad companies spread out from the city's center. By the end of the Civil War, Chicago was a leading trade center for the corn, wheat, lumber, and meat-packing industries.

The city that had grown from the small town looked very different. Mud was no longer a serious problem. The streets had been drained, raised on supports nearly twelve feet high, and paved. Some buildings stayed at the lower level, while others were built at the new level. Wooden sidewalks were put down in front of each building. The difference in levels made walking down the street much like climbing stairs.

It was easy to get lumber from the nearby forests in Michigan and Wisconsin. Many of the buildings at this time were made of wood, and fire was a serious threat. In the fall of 1871, this threat became real.

## The Great Chicago Fire

Chicago had been without rain for almost three months. About 9:30 P.M. on Sunday, October 8, a fire started. Firefighters had little hope of stopping it. Most of their equipment had been destroyed in a fire the night before, and they were very tired. This new fire was out of control in two hours. It raged on until the morning of October 10, when rainfall finally put it out.

The path of the fire had been almost five miles long and one mile wide. It went through the heart of the business district.

grain was shipped from the area as in 1869. By 1875, meat-packing companies owned by Nelson Morris, Gustavus Swift, and Philip Armour controlled the entire industry. New methods of shipping meat—using cans or refrigerated railroad cars—extended their market throughout America and Europe.

Much of the economy of Chicago was based on food products needed by other Americans. For this reason, the people of Chicago got through the depression of 1873 better than people in other cities. Many people from faraway places heard stories of jobs to be found in Chicago's meat-packing, lumber, and grain industries.

## The Heart of Chicago

Tens of thousands of people came to Chicago during the late 1800's. They included thousands of immigrants from Germany, Ireland, Italy, Greece, and many other countries. Black people moved there from southern states. The newcomers seldom found things as they had hoped. Jobs were hard to get. Work was not steady, and many people had to do jobs they had never done before. Pay was very low for working days that were sometimes ten to sixteen hours long.

Housing was a serious problem. Most immigrants lived close to the business districts. The buildings in these districts were not kept in very good condition. The only water for some came from a pump in the yard. Garbage and waste matter often sat in the alleys behind the buildings. Still, owners charged high rents. Sometimes several families lived together in one room to help pay the rent. Others took in boarders.

## More Building

The population of Chicago grew, and the need for more living space became a big problem. Tall apartment buildings, called tenements, were built by landowners to house more people. These buildings were put close together with only narrow walks and alleys between them. The rooms were often dark and had little fresh air. There was almost no privacy. Many times boarders lived in dark basements or in closets made into sleeping spaces.

Construction was not limited to tenement buildings. The wealthy people of the city had beautiful homes with handcarved woodwork, marble floors, and treasures in art and furniture. They were responsible for building new schools, clubs, factories, stores, restaurants, and hotels. Few people thought about the problems of the immigrants.

## A Helping Hand

Jane Addams wanted to help the newcomers. In 1889, she started one of the first settlement houses in Chicago, called Hull House. There newcomers to the area could learn how to handle the problems they were facing. Working parents could have a place to leave their children during the day. Adults could come together for social and educational activities. Immigrants learned to speak American English, and many learned new job skills.

The efforts of Jane Addams to help the newcomers did not stop at Hull House. She had a great respect for the immigrants and joined many groups to help change living conditions. She told of a Greek fruit seller and his impression of the people of Chicago:

*For three years, in Greece, while he was saving money to come to America, he used to make drawings of ancient Athens, of which he was very fond. He was a graduate of the Institute of Technology [in Greece], and drew very well. He had collected a large book of drawings and photographs. He thought that when he came to America, where we had no ruins, that we would be interested to hear about them. . . . He said he had sold fruit to Americans for years in Chicago, and that although he often had tried to lead the conversation to his beloved Acropolis* [an ancient ruin in Athens], *no one had ever seemed interested. He came to the conclusion no one in Chicago had heard of ancient Greece, nor knew that it had a wonderful history. . . . That man was disappointed and Chicago was losing something he could have given to it. I did not like to tell him we had become so snobbish in America that it did not occur to* [us] *that a shabby-looking foreigner selling apples could have his mind and heart full of the deathless beauties of ancient Greece. . . .*

## Working Conditions

Mary McDowell also helped people in Chicago. While living and working in a settlement home in the late 1880's, she wrote:

*. . . the Settlement home was upstairs over a Day Nursery; every morning when it was barely light in the winter, I would be wakened by the cry of the little children who wanted the mother to stay at home and not go to work. Here again for the first time in my life I saw the meaning of the job and how wage-earning women had to carry two burdens—that of the home and that of the wage-earning world. In that day there was no child-labor law and the packing industry found useful the boys and girls of eleven years of age, and men and women and children had no limit to their day's work.*

Women and children often had to work in sweatshops to help their families live. These shops were usually found in the run-down tenement buildings surrounding the business districts. The bad lighting, lack of fresh air, and poor plumbing made working there very difficult. Some girls, ten to fifteen years old, worked in clothes sweatshops. They averaged fifty cents a week for sewing on buttons or pulling out threads. If they did those jobs well, they sometimes moved up to sewing articles by hand and earned $2 or $2.50 a week as the older women did. Boys of the same age generally had jobs as messengers or errand runners.

Holding the same job for many years did not guarantee that a worker would keep that job. Mary McDowell wrote:

*One of my best friends was a German cattle butcher who began work at eleven years of age on the "killing floor," where he worked for twenty-five years until his right arm began to shake from the constant* [use] *of a huge cleaver, more like a battle axe.*

*. . . after going twenty-five years on a "killing bed," where he had been one of the few skilled workers, receiving forty-five cents an hour, he* [was] *suddenly* [fired] *without any reason given by the boss, except that his right arm was shaking and that he was unable to keep up with the "pace maker,"* [leader] *who was a giant. . . . "I understand now," he said, "why men are not sure of a job always, and why they organize, for at thirty-five I have reached my old age limit."*

## Change

Recognizing the problems of the workers, Jane Addams, Mary McDowell, and others worked to get new laws passed. Jane Addams wrote:

*There was at that time* [1890] *no . . . information on Chicago industrial conditions, and Mrs. Florence Kelley . . . suggested to the Illinois State Bureau of Labor that they*

*Jane Addams, founder of Hull House in Chicago*

*investigate the sweating system in Chicago with its . . . child labor. . . .*

*As a result of . . . investigations, [a special committee] recommended to the [Illinois] Legislature the provisions which afterwards became those of the first factory law of Illinois, regulating the sanitary conditions of the sweatshop and fixing fourteen as the age at which a child might be employed.*

By the 1890's, America was moving into a new age. The city of Chicago was an example of this progress. Most newcomers had to be told that the city had been in ashes only twenty years before. There was a rapid growth of population and industrialization in Chicago. It had erased memories of the fire of 1871 as well as of the small town near the swamp.

# America Is... Conflict

**FOOD WILL WIN THE WAR**

You came here seeking Freedom
You must now help to preserve it

**WHEAT is needed for the allies**
Waste nothing

**COAL**

The coal you are
going without is
forging the key to

**VICTORY**

# A World at War 19

The ideas of the Progressives were aimed at making life better for all the people of the United States. Many government leaders used these ideas in their dealings with countries in the Western Hemisphere. Sometimes they tried to help set up new governments that would be more democratic. At other times, they claimed that the United States government had the right to step in and manage some

*Almost all Americans played a part in World War I. Those at home saved things needed for the troops overseas. War posters were used to remind people of the necessity for this savings program.*

FOOD WILL WIN THE WAR
You came here seeking Freedom
You must now help to preserve it
**WHEAT** is needed for the allies
Waste nothing
UNITED STATES FOOD ADMINISTRATION

COAL
The coal you are going without is forging the key to
VICTORY

affairs in other countries. By 1914, United States government leaders were more concerned about the growing conflict in Europe. It threatened to involve the world.

# The Open Door

By the end of the 1800's, several countries had become very interested in China. It was rich in natural resources, and China's large population made it a growing market for manufactured goods. Some of the Chinese people were not pleased at this interest. Because there were many wars at this time among the Chinese people, China's government was not strong enough to keep others out.

Some outside governments claimed trade monopolies in China for their people. Great Britain, Germany, Russia, Japan, France, and Italy each claimed different areas. Business people in the United States wanted to increase their trade in China, too. American government leaders hoped to bring about a balance of power among the outside nations. Secretary of State John Hay offered a plan called the Open Door Policy to those countries. Under it, all nations would agree to respect the trading rights of others and would not form monopolies. Most of the nations accepted the idea.

Some of the Chinese people were strongly against the changes in their country that came from trade with others. These Chinese, called Boxers by Europeans and Americans, started a revolt in 1900 against all outsiders. The United States and several other countries sent soldiers to put down the revolt. Then these countries made the Chinese government pay them for the damages done to their citizens by the Boxers.

The American view of the power and authority of the Chinese government at this time is evidenced by the Chinese Exclusion Acts. Might compare to the slightly greater respect accorded the Japanese government evidenced by the fact that anti-Japanese legislation never actually referred to the Japanese by name.

# Relations With Japan

Most countries had agreed to the Open Door Policy, but they did not work to make it successful. In 1904, Japan and Russia went to war over control of the rich resources in Manchuria, an area in northern China. The Japanese defeated the Russians. Other nations worried about the Japanese becoming the only outside power in Manchuria.

In 1905, President Theodore Roosevelt arranged a peace meeting between the Japanese and the Russians. At the meeting, a treaty was signed to end the war. Roosevelt later won the Nobel Peace Prize for his work. But the treaty did not improve relations between the United States and Japan. Some Japanese leaders felt that their country had not gained enough benefits from the treaty after they had defeated the Russians. The Japanese government also was upset at the way Japanese people who lived in the United States were treated.

Japanese immigration to the United States had grown after the Chinese people were no longer allowed to enter the country. Plantation owners in Hawaii brought workers from Japan for their fields. Many of these workers later moved to the West Coast of the United States. There they farmed, opened small businesses, or did other work. They were not allowed to become citizens. Some Americans began to demand that the federal government stop Japanese immigration as it had Chinese. People in some cities and towns passed laws against the Japanese and other Asian people. In 1906, for example, a San Francisco law made Asian and Asian-American children attend separate schools from white children.

During 1907, President Roosevelt worked out an agreement with the Japanese government. It was called the Gentlemen's Agreement. In it, the government of Japan agreed to stop letting workers leave their country, and Roosevelt agreed that the Japanese people already in the United States would be treated fairly. Congress did not act to support the President. No federal laws were passed to protect the Japanese from discrimination. Life in the United States continued to be very hard for Japanese and other Asian peoples.

*Although not specifically named, the Japanese were subjected to the same discriminatory policies and laws as the Chinese who had been declared "ineligible for citizenship" by a Federal District Court in 1867 (which became law in the Exclusion Act of 1882).*

# The Panama Canal

During this time, the United States government was most interested in the countries of the Western Hemisphere—those in the North, Central, and South Americas and on islands in the Caribbean Sea. Military leaders felt that these areas were very important to the country's defense. Business people in the United States also had invested large amounts of money in those countries.

For more than fifty years, people had talked of building a canal through some part of Central America. Such a waterway would shorten the route between the Atlantic and Pacific oceans by nearly seven thousand miles. People in the United States believed that a canal would not only help trade but would also make naval defense of their country easier.

*France started construction on the Panama Canal in the late 1870's. The United States completed the project in 1914.*

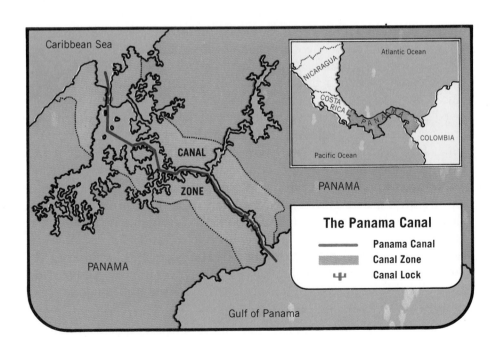

A World at War

In the late 1870's, a French company had begun to dig a canal through the Isthmus of Panama. The Isthmus was a narrow strip of land under the rule of the South American country of Colombia. Building the canal through swamp and jungle was very difficult, and the company ran out of money before it was finished. In 1903, the United States offered to buy the rights to the canal. It also wanted Colombia to give the United States a strip of land along both sides of the route for the sum of 10 million dollars. The Colombian government turned down the offer.

In November of 1903, a group of people in Panama who favored the offer started a revolt for independence from Colombia. Roosevelt sent United States warships to the area. They kept Colombian soldiers from landing to stop the revolt. The United States then recognized the new Republic of Panama and signed the treaty for the canal with its government. The treaty said that ships from all countries would be allowed to use the canal, but the canal and strip of land would be leased to the United States forever. After several more years of work to overcome health and building problems, the Panama Canal opened in 1914.

Because of current interest in the Panama Canal, students should be able to find enough information to stage debate on military value of Canal to U.S., trade shipping value, etc. Might have them act as members of Congress voting on ratification of latest Treaty.

# The Caribbean Islands

Business people from Europe also had invested money in countries of the Western Hemisphere. Some of these countries could not pay their debts. Several of the European governments decided to try to collect the money by force. Some of the island governments were not strong enough to keep these powers out. Leaders in the United States feared that, if the Europeans moved in soldiers to collect what was owed them, the Europeans would stay to take over those countries. To prevent this, Roosevelt announced another view of the Monroe Doctrine. His view is called the Roosevelt Corollary. The President said that the United States would act, if it appeared necessary to protect its interests, as a police power in the Western Hemisphere.

Following Roosevelt's policy, soldiers from the United States were sent to the Dominican Republic in 1905, to Nicaragua in 1912, and to Haiti in 1915. They took over the collection of tariff and tax money to be used to pay back the Europeans. In Haiti and the Dominican Republic, the American army actually ran the governments. Many of the people in these countries believed that the United States had no right to step into their affairs.

Although troops were withdrawn, the U.S. retained control over Dominican Republic's customs until 1941. Might have student research and report on 1965 action of President Johnson to send U.S. troops to intervene in civil war in Dominican Republic.

*This cartoon on the Roosevelt Corollary reminds people that President Roosevelt liked to quote a well-known saying from West Africa, "Speak softly, and carry a big stick, you will go far."*

# The United States and Mexico

People in the United States generally believed that others should have the same political rights that they had. President Woodrow Wilson was elected in 1912 and acted on this idea when he stepped into Mexico's affairs. He wanted to help its government become more democratic. That country had recently suffered several revolutions. Victoriano Huerta, a general of the Mexican army, became president of Mexico after a revolution in 1913. Wilson believed that Huerta was a dictator, or a leader who rules with total power.

In 1914, Wilson ordered the navy to the Mexican city of Veracruz to stop a shipment of guns to Huerta's soldiers. There was a battle in which 126 Mexican and 19 United States soldiers and sailors were killed. Wilson's action was not popular in Mexico or in the United States. Leaders from Argentina, Brazil, and Chile helped to arrange peace between the two countries.

In 1916, there was trouble again. General Francisco (Pancho) Villa began to attack and kill citizens of the United States. He hoped to win support from the Mexican people and become president. Villa's soldiers killed eighteen people working in northern Mexico. They then crossed into the United States and killed sixteen more in New Mexico. Some people in the United States wanted President Wilson to go to war against Mexico. Instead, Wilson ordered General John Pershing to capture Villa. Pershing's soldiers chased Villa back into Mexico but did not catch him. In 1917, Wilson ordered the soldiers back to the United States because of serious troubles in Europe.

# European Alliances

Several countries in Europe were industrial nations like the United States and had strong armies and navies. There was much conflict among these countries as they competed for new lands and resources. By the early 1900's, many of these nations had made promises to defend each other in case of war. There were two main groups or alliances. The group called Allied Powers by Americans was made up of Great Britain, France, Russia, and their friends. The Central Powers were Germany, Austria-Hungary, Italy, and their friends. Most American leaders believed that relations among these countries were very dangerous and could lead to war. Many people did not want the United States to join or favor either group.

# The Beginning of World War

Archduke Franz Ferdinand, next in line to be king of Austria-Hungary, was killed by a Serbian student in June of 1914. Austria-Hungary blamed the government and declared war on Serbia in July. Russia came to the aid of its ally, Serbia. Germany, as an ally of Austria-Hungary, then declared war on Russia. By 1915, war was being fought by Germany, Austria-Hungary, Bulgaria, and the Ottoman Empire (Turkey) against Great Britain, France, Russia, Italy, Belgium, Rumania, Greece, Serbia, and Montenegro. The policy of the United States government was to remain a neutral nation, although many European-Americans sympathized with the countries of their ancestors.

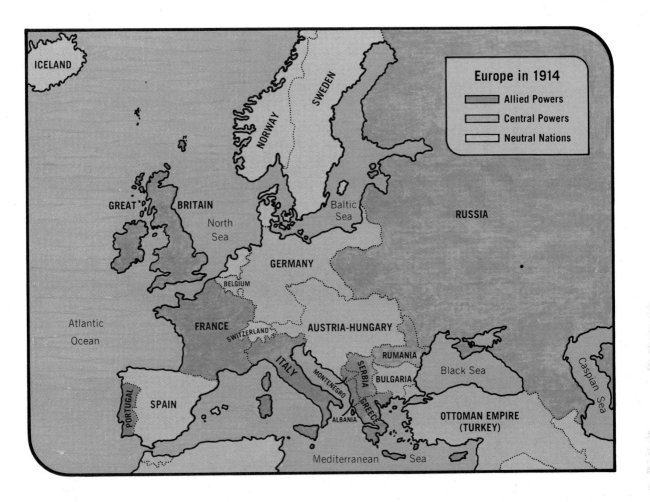

Europe in 1914

Allied Powers
Central Powers
Neutral Nations

ICELAND

NORWAY

SWEDEN

GREAT · BRITAIN

North Sea

Baltic Sea

RUSSIA

GERMANY

BELGIUM

Atlantic Ocean

FRANCE

SWITZERLAND

AUSTRIA-HUNGARY

ITALY

MONTENEGRO

RUMANIA

SERBIA

BULGARIA

Black Sea

Caspian Sea

PORTUGAL

SPAIN

ALBANIA

GREECE

Mediterranean    Sea

OTTOMAN EMPIRE (TURKEY)

# A Neutral Nation

One of the first effects of the European war on the United States was a slowing down of overseas trade. Then quickly, trade increased as the countries at war needed more food and clothing than they could produce themselves. As a neutral nation, the United States was supposed to be able to trade any goods but weapons with any other country. That policy did not work out. The British used their very powerful navy to stop supply ships from reaching Central Power countries. The Germans, in turn, used submarines to sink ships bound for Great Britain and France. In May, 1915, a German submarine sank a British passenger ship, the *Lusitania*. There were 128 American citizens among the more than 1,000 people killed in the attack. President Wilson sent

The British waged a heavy propaganda campaign to win American interest and support.

strong protests to the German government, and it agreed to stop sinking passenger ships. Even though the United States was a neutral nation, President Wilson did not protest the British naval actions as he did those of Germany.

*German submarines did much damage in World War I. Americans used submarine chasers and the convoy system to fight them.*

# Entering the War

The German government announced that it would begin again to attack all ships bound for enemy countries in February, 1917. That same month, the British gained possession of a note from the German government to the government of Mexico. They sent it to President Wilson. In the note, Germany asked for Mexico's help in case it declared war on the United States. Mexico was promised the lands it had lost to the United States in 1846 for its help. Wilson made the note public, and many people in the United States became very angry. Relations with Germany grew worse. In March, news came that Germany had sunk three American ships. On April 2, 1917, President Wilson asked Congress for a declaration of war against Germany. Four days later, Congress agreed.

Mexico did not rise to the bait offered in the "Zimmerman note" affair and remained neutral.

# Preparing for War

The United States had begun to prepare for possible war before 1917. Ideas that had brought about new inventions and improved others were used to make new military machines. The automobile had been developed by many people in the late nineteenth century. By 1917, it was greatly improved. Knowledge gained from making cars was put to use in making trucks, tanks, and ships called submarine chasers. Orville and Wilbur Wright had made the first successful airplane flight in 1903. Since then, knowledge for making and flying airplanes had grown. World War I was the first time that military plans included the use of airplanes.

Changes in the ways of manufacturing goods also helped industries meet new military needs. Before the growth of the automobile industry, people worked separately on different parts of the product. These parts then were carried to another place to be assembled, or added to the final product. By 1917, many factories used moving assembly lines where belts carried the parts from one worker to another until the product was finished. This method saved a great deal of time which could be used to make more products.

To make sure that the country would be able to supply the armed services as well as the people at home, the government set up agencies with power to regulate the economy. The Railroad Administration, for

*Eddie Rickenbacker was one of the best-known
American pilots in World War I.*

example, took over control of all the nation's railroads. It ran them without competition as one system. The Food Administration planned ways to increase the amount of food grown. Herbert Hoover, its director, announced that the government would buy the entire crop of wheat grown in 1917 at $2.20 a bushel. Farmers felt that the price was a good one for them, and more wheat was grown that year.

Before the United States declared war on Germany, the army had only eighty thousand soldiers. Congress passed the Selective Service Act, or draft law, in 1917. Under it, all male citizens between the ages of twenty-one and thirty had to register with their local draft boards. They were then selected by chance from the register lists to serve in the army. With this system, plus those who volunteered, the number of soldiers grew to two million.

# Labor Changes

Thousands of jobs became available as more people joined the armed services. Large groups of people began to move to new areas of the country to fill these jobs. Thousands of black people left the South and were hired by industries all over the North. They worked in steel mills, coal mines, meat-packing plants, and other industries. More than twelve thousand blacks worked on the Pennsylvania Railroad during the war. Mexican Americans, who had lived mostly in the Southwest, moved to cities in the Midwest for the first time. They also worked in mills, mines, and plants. By 1920, nearly 70,000 Mexican Americans were living east of the Mississippi River, and 700,000 lived in western states. Many blacks and Mexican Americans also served in the armed forces.

# Carrie Chapman Catt

Carrie Chapman Catt was a leader in the women's right to vote movement in the 1900's. Born in Wisconsin in 1859, she grew up on a frontier farm in Iowa. Catt went to Iowa State College in 1877. After college, she wanted to be a lawyer and worked in a law office for a while. Then in 1881, she accepted a job as a high school principal. Later she became superintendent of schools in Mason City. Catt married a newspaper editor in 1885. She worked on his newspaper until he died a year later.

Catt joined the Iowa Woman Suffrage Association in 1887. She married a second time in 1890. Her husband supported women's right to vote, and Catt worked for the movement several months each year. She tried to win the vote in state after state during the 1890's. Catt's husband died in 1905, and she began to work for the movement full time. Catt became president of the National American Suffrage Association in 1915. She developed a three-way plan to give women the right to vote. Her plan supported an amendment to the Constitution. It also called for amending state constitutions and for gaining voting rights in state party primary elections.

Some members of the movement wanted to put off these plans when the United States entered World War I. Catt and other leaders wanted to continue their work to get the vote. They thought that if women helped in the war, it would be harder for the government to deny them the vote. President Wilson finally came out in favor of a suffrage amendment. After the war ended, Congress approved the amendment and sent it to the states. In 1920, the amendment was passed by enough states to become law. Catt had worked for thirty years to see women gain their right to vote. She lived many years longer working for world peace until she died in 1947.

Both men and women served in the armed forces during the war. However, men who served as combat, or fighting, soldiers were in the majority. Many women took over the work in factories that had been done by men. They were also hired in new industries to make supplies especially for the military. Between 1915 and 1918, more than one million women had taken jobs outside their homes. Those who had already been working in business and industry before the war were able to move more easily into better jobs.

# Public Support

President Wilson set up a Committee on Public Information to explain to citizens the reasons that the United States was in the war. The committee hired speakers, writers, and artists to give out this information. Congress and state legislatures passed laws to keep people from speaking out against the war. The Espionage Act of 1917 had set fines and prison terms for citizens found guilty of spying, destroying government war property, or other actions against the United States war efforts. Courts were allowed to decide what actions interfered with the war. A. Philip Randolph and Chandler Owen were sentenced to two and a half years in prison for writing an article in their newspaper that urged other black people not to support the war. Eugene Debs was sent to prison for speaking out in favor of pacifism, or remaining peaceful instead of fighting.

In some places, German Americans were suspected of supporting Germany in the war. Some cities and citizen groups passed rules against playing German music or teaching the German language in schools. Their libraries burned books written in German or about Germany. German foods were given new names. Sauerkraut was called "liberty cabbage," and hamburger was often called "liberty sausage."

# Immigration

The number of Europeans coming to the United States had slowed down when the war began in Europe. Congress passed a law in 1917 that further limited the number of all immigrants. The law set up a special zone including India, Siam, and Indochina. Persons from this zone were not allowed to come to the United States as immigrants.

A tax of eight dollars and the ability to read were required of all others.

The need for workers grew as the war continued. Food growers in the West forced Congress to allow farm workers to enter the country without limits. These growers then brought Filipinos to work in their fields in Hawaii, as well as Mexicans to California and other areas. The country gained much from their labor, but little was done to make sure that these immigrants received fair wages or lived and worked under fair conditions.

# American Contributions

The United States Navy played a very important role in the war. Its first job was to make sure that supplies as well as soldiers crossed the Atlantic Ocean without being sunk by German submarines. Before the United States entered the war, the Allied Powers were losing ships faster than new ones could be built. American navy leaders developed a

*The Selective Service Act boosted the number of American soldiers to two million at the start of the war. Many did not come home.*

plan called the convoy system. Under it, warships traveled along with supply ships to protect them from attack. The warships carried weapons to use against submarines when they were sighted. This system was very successful, and it badly damaged German naval plans.

When American soldiers arrived in Europe to help, the Allied armies were in trouble. Early in 1918, Russia surrendered to Germany, and the French and British armies were being pushed back in France. The American soldiers, under General Pershing, were first used to replace Allied soldiers who had been killed or wounded. Then American troops were grouped together to fight. They were a major force in stopping the German drives toward Paris, France, and bringing an end to the war. As German attacks failed, their government finally asked for an armistice, or end to the fighting. On November 11, 1918, the fighting stopped.

All the countries at war had suffered heavy losses of people and money. Russia, France, Austria-Hungary, and Germany each lost over a million soldiers. Several times that number of private citizens had died from wounds, disease, and hunger. Nearly a million British had been killed, and Italy, Rumania, and Turkey lost hundreds of thousands of people. Most of these countries were deeply in debt at the end of the war from buying guns and other military supplies. Although the United States had been in the war for less than two years, more than 100,000 Americans had died, and more than 200,000 had been wounded.

# A Plan for Peace

Before the war ended, President Wilson had written a plan for peace called the Fourteen Points. It was supported by large numbers of Americans and by the German government which expected it to be the basis for a peace treaty. Among other things, the plan stated that countries all over the world should be free to use the oceans without fear and to trade. People would be free to choose their own kinds of governments. Armies and navies would be made smaller. Finally, the plan called for an association of all countries in the world—a League of Nations. In the League, countries would work together for the independence and freedom of all. President Wilson believed that the League of Nations was the most important part of his plan. He soon learned, however, that the Allies had made plans among themselves to punish Germany and to divide its overseas lands.

# Points of View

Philip Gibbs was a visitor from England in 1919. He wrote about his views of the American people and their feelings toward World War I and the peace that followed.

*. . . the people I met were not so much [excited] with the sense of victory as [unsure] and anxious about the new responsibilities which they would be asked to fulfill. . . . I received an immense number of letters "putting me wise" as to the failure of the President to gain the confidence of the American people and their [doubts] that he was [giving] away the rights and liberties of the United States, without the knowledge or support of the people. . . .*

*. . . above all it was the fear of being "dragged in" to new wars, not of their concern, which made them deeply suspicious of the League of Nations. . . .*

*. . . Nevertheless, it became more clear to thinking minds in America that the days of "isolation" were gone, and that for good or evil the United States is linked up by unbreakable bonds of interest and responsibility with other great powers of the world. . . . If another great [war] happens in Europe, American troops will again be there. . . .*

Professor Moritz Bonn, a German, wrote about his views of American feelings in an Austrian newspaper article in 1920.

*When the World War started, America, except for a very small section of its people, was inspired by a single wish: to keep out of the [war]. Business interests, followed later by financial ties . . . dragged the nation constantly closer to the whirlpool. . . .*

*Our [Germany's] decision to [renew] an unrestricted submarine campaign wrecked the project of making peace.*

*. . . politics [later] awakened the first opposition to America's entering the League.*

*. . . So it has turned its attention to matters at home. It will have nothing to do with a continent which merely irritates and [misleads] it.*

What reasons do these writers give for the Americans rejecting the League of Nations? Compare what each says about how the United States will act toward Europe in the future.

President Wilson and his advisers went to Paris to discuss the peace treaty to end the war. He compromised with Allied plans in order to get them to accept the idea of the League of Nations. The Versailles Treaty included some of Wilson's Fourteen Points. It also stated that (1) Germany alone was responsible for starting the war, (2) Germany was to pay money to the Allies for war damage, and (3) the size of the German army and navy would be greatly reduced. The German leaders signed the treaty, but their people were shocked because they had expected better treatment under Wilson's original plan.

# Reaction at Home

Several members of the United States Senate did not want to ratify the Versailles Treaty. One group opposed the League of Nations because that part of the treaty included a promise to come to the aid of other countries if they were invaded. These senators felt that part could mean that Americans would have to fight in wars for other countries' interests. Such a promise would interfere with United States foreign policies. Other senators were upset because the President had not asked their advice. They wanted some changes in the treaty before they would support it. President Wilson refused to compromise, and the Senate refused to accept the Versailles Treaty.

See also note on League, p.457.

Wilson was ill and chose not to run again for President in 1920. The Democrats chose James Cox, a former governor of Ohio, to run against the Republican candidate Warren Harding who was also from Ohio. Cox spoke in favor of the League of Nations while Harding did not make his stand on it clear. Instead, Harding spoke of returning the country to the ways of life enjoyed before the war.

Harding won the election by a large number of votes. The idea of the United States as a member of the League was ended. Congress passed a resolution in 1921 that declared an end to the war between the United States and Germany. American lives had been greatly changed by the war. Many had lost members of their families, and many had taken new jobs in new parts of the country. The people of the United States began to turn their attention away from Europe.

# Chapter 19 in Perspective See Teacher's Manual, page 116T.

## Identify

| | | |
|---|---|---|
| Boxers | Allied Powers | Herbert Hoover |
| Manchuria | Central Powers | General Pershing |
| Isthmus of Panama | *Lusitania* | Warren Harding |

# Explain

| | | |
|---|---|---|
| Open Door Policy | moving assembly line | armistice |
| Gentlemen's Agreement | Selective Service Act | Fourteen Points |
| Roosevelt Corollary | convoy system | Versailles Treaty |
| dictator | | |

# Check Your Memory of the Facts

1. Why were other nations interested in China?
2. What two issues made the Japanese government unhappy with the United States?
3. What United States military actions came from the policy of the Roosevelt Corollary?
4. What German actions led the United States to enter World War I?
5. How did the United States prepare for war? What were some of the changes that came from this preparation?

# Check Your Understanding of the Ideas

1. What did the United States government try to do through the Open Door Policy?
2. Why was a canal through Central America important to people in the United States?
3. What events made poor relations between the United States and Mexico? How did they influence the United States' decision to declare war on Germany?
4. How was Wilson's plan for peace accepted by the Germans? By the Allies? By the United States Senate?
5. What did the election of 1920 seem to say about the general atti tude of the people of the United States toward other countries?

# Expand Your Knowledge

1. Choose one of the following countries and report on its interests and needs for defense between 1900 and 1915: China, Japan, Russia, Mexico, Colombia, Austria-Hungary, Serbia, Great Britain, Italy, France, Belgium, Greece, Bulgaria, or Turkey.
2. Find out what the Nobel Peace Prize is and how it started. How many Americans have been given this prize and for what reasons?

# Detroit 1900-1920

People who visited Detroit at the end of the nineteenth century saw a comfortable, midwestern town on a beautiful river. One visitor wrote:

*The Detroit River . . . is one of the most beautiful water avenues west of the Hudson. It is from half a mile to a mile wide, [and] is always of a clear blue color. . . . It is, with reason, the pride of the city, and the ferry boats [moving] between Detroit and Windsor [in Canada] are of the most attractive type. In summer . . . musicians are engaged for the regular trips. . . . Whole families spend the day on the river . . . taking their dinner in baskets, as . . . a picnic. . . .*

*Detroit has been called, with reason, one of the most beautiful cities of the West.*

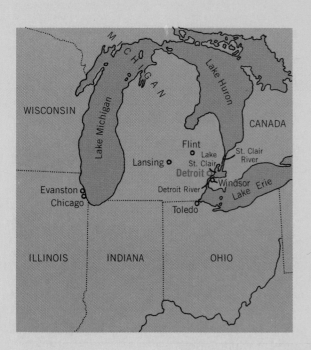

## Memories

George Stark recalled his childhood during this time in Detroit.

*We children were always told to [keep] our play to our own back yards, so we seldom played in our own back yards. We went "out in front." Mother never worried much about this small disobedience, because there was no danger of us being run down by automobiles. There weren't any. . . .*

*In the late 1890's, the bicycle craze was at its peak. . . . The more daring of the ladies wore divided skirts, making it possible for them to ride men's bicycles, which, for some strange reason, were supposed to be faster. But what difference did it make, when the police would grab you if you went more than fifteen miles an hour. That was our speed limit. If you exceeded it, you were called a "scortcher" and the "scortcher cops" might get you. . . .*

*But what would one remember from the early days. . . . [We] would remember . . . the . . . chug of the horseless carriage which churned up the dirt roads in our neighborhood. . . . We didn't know that we were looking at the dawn of the machine age. . . .*

The machine age in transportation soon changed Detroit into one of the leading industrial cities of the world.

## Right Place, Right Time

In 1900, Detroit was a rapidly growing city of 285,000 people. It was well known for iron and steel production. Detroit factories

*The city of Detroit*

were also producing furniture, tobacco products, drugs, men's clothing, flour, and other goods. There were twenty shops in which 318 workers made wagons and carriages.

Because of its location near the Great Lakes, Detroit had developed as a center for building gasoline boat engines. The city had many workshops where people made engines and engine parts. Others in the city were interested in transportation. Michigan was not on a major railroad line, and the lakes were frozen four or five months of the year. Some people living in Detroit had made great fortunes in mining, shipping, and lumber. At the end of the nineteenth century, their children were looking for new ways to make more money.

This was the time, then, when the people of Detroit were interested in transportation. Many of them had the parts and the skills needed to make machines. Others

had the money to finance new ideas. The people of Detroit were ready for a new industry—the manufacturing of automobiles.

## A New Machine

Toward the end of the nineteenth century, people in Detroit began to hear stories about horseless carriages in Europe. Some people in France had started putting engines on buggy frames. These carriages were called automobiles. The name came from the Greek word *auto*, meaning *self*, and the French word *mobile*, meaning *moving*. But they were costly machines, and only the rich could afford them. In the early 1890's, American inventors were working in their barns, backyards, cellars, and workshops. More than three hundred Americans were also trying to build automobiles powered by electricity, steam, or gasoline.

One young inventor, Henry Ford, spent much of his time experimenting with engines. After he moved to Detroit in 1891, he completed his first automobile. It was not the first in the United States or even in Detroit. The year before, a round-trip automobile race was run from Chicago to Evanston, Illinois. Six automobiles had run the 52 mile course. The winning car averaged 6.6 miles per hour.

## Early Success

One of the most successful early automobile manufacturers was Ransom Olds. Using mass production in his Detroit plant, he produced 425 small, three-horsepowered Oldsmobiles in 1901. A fire destroyed the factory that year, and Olds started work again in Lansing, Michigan. After a sensational trip by an Olds test driver over cow paths and poor roads, the Oldsmobile was

*Henry Ford and his first automobile*

automobile manufacturers was high. William Durant, a Michigan wagonmaker, formed the General Motors Company. To cut down on competition, Durant bought David Buick's company. Using the Buick company for financial backing, Durant then bought the Cadillac, the Oakland (later known as Pontiac), the Oldsmobile, and the Chevrolet companies. By 1919, the company was called General Motors Corporation.

In later years, another automobile manufacturer, Walter Chrysler, sought to cut down on competition, too. He bought the Dodge Company and made it the Dodge division of the Chrysler Corporation. But all companies, large and small, had the same problem—how to produce more cars at lower costs.

## Putting Ideas to Work

From 1903 to 1909, Henry Ford's company produced several different models of cars. His biggest success was the Model T or "Tin Lizzie." The advantage of the Model T over any car produced at that time was its simplicity. Ford had said:

*We must make the cars simple. I mean we must make them . . . so that people can operate them easily, and with the fewer parts the better.*

The popularity of the Model T made it easier for Ford to use another idea:

*The way to make automobiles is to make one automobile like another automobile, to make them all alike, to make them come through the factory just alike. . . .*

Ford announced to his workers in 1909 that they were going to produce one car—the Model T. The body would be exactly the same for all cars, and "*any customer [could] have a car painted any colour, so*

suddenly the best known car in America. Orders rose to 3,300 in 1902, and the autos sold for $650 each. Olds quickly became one of America's first automobile millionaires.

The young inventor, Henry Ford, started the Ford Motor Company in 1903. At first, he did not have controlling interest of the company. There were problems between Ford and his financial backers, but he slowly gained control. The Ford family owned the entire company by 1919, and it grew rapidly.

## Too Much Competition

Other companies also grew. By 1908, competition among American and foreign long as it [was] *black.*" Ford then began to concentrate on making more cars instead of more models.

## The Moving Assembly Line

Slowly, Ford and other automobile manufacturers developed methods for mass production. Many of their ideas were later used in other American factories. Ford explained how he developed one idea, the moving assembly line, in his plant.

*In the beginning we tried to get machinists* [people who run or repair machines]. *As the necessity for production increased it became* [clear] . . . *that skilled* [workers] *were not necessary. . . .*

*. . . In our first assembling we simply started to put a car together at a spot on the floor and* [workers] *brought to it the parts as they were needed in exactly the same way that one builds a house. When we started to make parts it was natural to create a single department of the factory to make that*

*Hazards for early drivers*

389

*An automobile assembly line*

part, but usually one [worker] *performed all the [jobs] necessary on a small part. The [need for more] production made it necessary to [think of ways] that would avoid having the workers falling over one another. . . .*

*The first step forward in assembly came when we began taking the work to the [people] instead of the [people] to the work. . . .*

*The principles of assembly are these:*

*(1) Place the tools and the [workers] in the [order] of the operation. . . .*

*(2) Use work slides or some other form of carrier . . . and if possible have gravity carry the part to the next [worker].*

*(3) Use sliding assembling lines by which the parts to be assembled are delivered at convenient distances.*

*The net result . . . is [less need] for thought on the part of the worker and [fewer] movements. . . . [Each person] does*

*as nearly as possible only one thing with only one movement. . . .*

*It must not be imagined, however, that all this worked out as quickly as it sounds. The speed of the moving work had to be carefully tried out. . . . The idea is that [people] must not be hurried . . . [they] must have . . . not a single unnecessary second.*

### Five Dollars a Day

Average auto plant workers had been paid $1 a day for unskilled labor and $3.50 a day for skilled labor. Workers in other countries as well as Americans in other jobs usually made less. Ford announced in January, 1914, that he would pay his workers five dollars a day. People from as far away as Europe packed their belongings and headed for Detroit hoping to find jobs in its growing automobile industry.

The added number of people moving to the city put a strain on living conditions. In 1918, a geographer wrote:

*As the town grew, and more business was centered in the business sections, the value of land increased, ground rents became higher, and only business houses came to occupy the central sections. [Living] quarters were driven farther and farther from the center. The well-to-do left first. They went to the outskirts . . . of the city. The old mansions came to be tenement houses; for by crowding, the laboring people were able to reduce the rent per [person]. As a result of this process the worst housing conditions are to be found about the business section. . . .*

Detroit manufacturing grew during World War I. Many of the city's factories were changed to include the production of weapons. The war stopped immigration from Europe. Southerners, both white and black, came to take jobs in the factories. They moved into the tenements of the already overcrowded business section.

## A Difference

By 1915, automobiles had changed a great deal. They had steel-enclosed bodies instead of open carriages. The driver's seat was on the left side, and electric starters had replaced the outside crank. Automobiles were painted different colors, not just black. The market for American automobiles had also changed. In 1900, there were eight thousand autos registered in the United States. That number increased to 2.5 million in 1915.

The automobile city of America had also changed. Through mass production, Detroit became one of the most important cities in the world. The sound of its first chugging automobile had turned into the booming roar of an industrial empire.

*One day's output—one thousand cars*

# Life in the Twenties

Aim: to help students understand the social, political, and economic changes in American life following World War I.

There are many opportunities for individual student research and reports on following chapter pages. Assignments should be geared to students' local interests and daily activities.

When World War I ended, the people of the United States faced the task of making a living in an economy that no longer needed to make war materials. Soldiers returning home had the challenge of finding jobs. This could mean the same ones as before the war or taking new ones. People who had taken jobs left by the soldiers during the war faced the possibility of losing them as soldiers came home. The growth of the economy during the war brought an increase in prices. Many workers wanted higher wages. Companies wanted to keep costs down so profits and businesses could grow. Because of the changes brought about by the war, it was not possible for most people to return to the life that they had known before 1917.

## Radio, Jazz, and Movies

At the end of World War I, people seemed to be confused and dissatisfied with the results of the peace treaties. They wanted a peaceful way of life that held some enjoyment. People welcomed new and

*Family entertainment in the 1920's often meant an evening listening to the radio.*

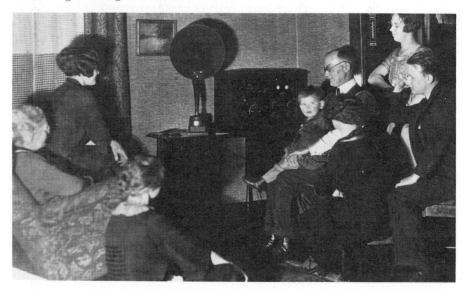

*These "Ziegfield Girls" were famous because they took part in the huge 1920's musical productions called the Ziegfield Follies.*

different ideas. New fashions, like short skirts and short hair for women, were accepted in large and small towns alike.

New forms of entertainment appeared. The radio had been used by the government during the war to send and receive messages. It was soon thought of as a way to inform and entertain large numbers of people at once. In 1920, two stations—WWJ in Detroit, Michigan, and KDKA in Pittsburgh, Pennsylvania—began regular broadcasting. Soon the National Broadcasting Company (NBC) organized a group of stations into a network. By 1930, twelve million of the total twenty-six million families in the country owned radios.

Newspapers and magazines continued to be important as sources of news and entertainment. *Saturday Evening Post* was still one of the best-selling magazines. *Time* was a widely read news magazine while the *Reader's Digest* printed articles and shortened stories from best-selling magazines and books. F. Scott Fitzgerald was a popular writer of novels about rich young people. Ernest Hemingway wrote about people in times of war and praised those who faced danger and death.

Black writers like Langston Hughes and Claude McKay wrote stories about black people. Sometimes they wrote of discrimination. At other times, their writings showed humor and happiness in the daily lives of black Americans. Because many black writers lived and worked in an area in New York City called Harlem, their work was called Harlem Renaissance. Renaissance means a time when there is much artistic and intellectual activity.

A new form of music called jazz became popular with thousands of Americans. Jazz is original American music. It grew out of the early music of the slaves and of the ragtime of the 1890's. Created by black musicians in New Orleans, jazz was soon played by bands in Chicago, Harlem, and other places.

The movies were still another form of entertainment that grew during the twenties. For a five-cent admission in the early 1900's, people could see a short movie like *The Great Train Robbery*. At first, the movies had no sound. In 1927, the first "talkie" was made with the sound played on a phonograph. Soon, millions of Americans were going to the movies every week.

# Prohibition

People's lives were changed in other ways. The Eighteenth Amendment, proposed by Congress in 1917, was ratified in 1919. It was a law to keep people from making, selling, or shipping alcohol to drink. Groups such as the Women's Christian Temperance Union (WCTU) had worked hard for the amendment. They believed temperance, or doing without alcohol, would make home life happier for everyone. But this prohibition of alcohol was not accepted by all. Thousands of Americans began to make liquor and beer at home. Some smuggled it into the United States from Canada and other nearby countries. Night-club owners sold liquor illegally to customers.

In a short time, gangsters took over most of the alcohol trade. They fought against each other for the power to sell the alcohol in certain areas or cities. Because many city government officials were against prohibition, they did little to stop this traffic. The federal government was not able to patrol the whole border of the United States and was largely unsuccessful in stopping the illegal traffic of alcohol.

# Health and Education

Ideas for "progressive education," influenced by John Dewey, became popular at this time. Dewey insisted that what students learned in school should have something to do with their future lives. He also believed that they should try out different ideas and learn by doing rather than by drilling on memorized facts. There were also great improvements in treating sickness. Doctors were able to reduce the number of babies who died in their first year, the most critical time. People who had been born in 1900 could expect to live an average of 47.3 years. By 1930, that number had risen to 59.7 years.

In another area, Helen Keller was doing important work for handicapped people. Keller had become blind and deaf at the age of two. She learned to speak at the age of sixteen and later attended college. Keller, an example of how training could help handicapped persons, wanted to help other blind people live normal lives. When the American Foundation for the Blind was formed in 1921, she went on a tour of the country speaking to people to raise money for the foundation. The money was used to buy books printed in braille—a special writing that

Helen Adams Keller (1880-1968) is an excellent subject for biographical research and report.

*"Learning by doing," these students in a hat-making class are learning how to handle their equipment and materials. This was part of the "progressive education" movement in the 1920's.*

is read by touch. It also paid for hospitals and workers to help handicapped people. Keller said of her work: "I long to accomplish a great and noble task, but it is my chief duty to accomplish small tasks as if they *were* great and noble." She believed that progress came from the work of many people, not just from single achievements of a few.

# Civil Rights

Because of the important contributions women made to the wartime economy, some people pushed harder for them to have the same rights as male citizens. President Wilson asked Congress to propose a women's suffrage law. The Nineteenth Amendment was proposed in 1919 and ratified in 1920. It says that states cannot keep people from voting because of their sex.

Curtis (1860-1936) also served as Vice-President under Hoover from 1929 to 1933.

In 1924, Congress passed an act giving citizenship to all Indians who were not already citizens. Senator Charles Curtis of Kansas, who had some Kaw and Osage Indian ancestors, wrote the bill. Two thirds of the Indians living in the United States had become citizens before 1924. They had done so through treaties, marrying white citizens, the Dawes Act of 1887, or by joining the armed services during World War I. When the Indians became citizens, they were subject to taxes and local laws. Many had lost their lands as new citizens because they could not pay their property taxes. This, and the fear that their own religions, languages, and ways of educating children would be lost, caused some Indians to try to stop the move to make them citizens. Eight Indian nations protested the Curtis law to Congress and later to the League of Nations. Their protests failed, and they had to accept citizenship.

World War I caused many Americans to become more aware of the country and its opportunities. Mexican Americans, because of their work as soldiers and in the arms factories, expected to be treated as well as other Americans. Instead, they found that many jobs were closed to them after the war. Those that were open did not offer chances to move up to better jobs. Continued immigration from Mexico brought competition for unskilled jobs. Those who did find jobs most often worked for low pay, especially as farm laborers.

Returning soldiers of Mexican-American background worked to help their people learn more about their political and legal rights as citizens. They were important in forming organizations such as the Order of the Sons of America. The Order was founded in San Antonio,

# Ynes Mexia

Ynes Mexia was a plant scientist in the 1920's. She was born in Washington, D.C., where her father worked as a representative for the Mexican government. Mexia grew up in Texas and went to school in Pennsylvania and Maryland. She was married in Mexico City in 1907. Her husband died only a year later, and Mexia moved to San Francisco as a social worker.

In 1921, Mexia entered the University of California. She studied the science of plants called botany. In 1925, she went with another plant scientist to the Mexican desert. They were looking for new kinds of plants. Mexia returned with almost five hundred kinds of plants. She decided to spend her life as a plant explorer.

Mexia was the leader of many more plant study trips. She worked for the University of California and other groups and sold her rare plants to pay for her trips. Mexia discovered many new plants. She found mosses in Alaska and tropical plants in Mexico, Ecuador, and Peru. Mexia traveled as far as the Andes Mountains and the Straits of Magellan to look for plants. Another plant scientist said this about her: "She was the true explorer type and happiest when independent and far from civilization." Many plants that Mexia discovered in the 1920's are named in her honor.

Texas, in 1921. It worked, through political action, for greater educational opportunities for people of Spanish and Mexican background. This and other organizations spread to areas of the country where there were large numbers of Mexican Americans.

# Dignity and Pride

Many black Americans who had served the country in wartime also expected better chances for education and jobs. For some, the end of the war meant less work, however, as returning white soldiers asked for their old jobs back. Other black people tried to earn their livings by starting neighborhood businesses. When their neighbors began losing jobs, many of these new businesses failed.

Marcus Garvey, born on the island of Jamaica, started a movement in the United States that became popular among thousands of black people during the 1920's. Garvey believed that black people should become independent from whites. He encouraged black people to look to Africa to find out about their backgrounds. Through his newspaper, *Negro World*, Garvey told his readers about the history and the achievements of the people of Africa. At least 500,000 people became members of his Universal Negro Improvement Association (UNIA). In 1923, Garvey was tried and found guilty by the federal

*With the rise in production and wages after World War I, many Americans moved their families to industrial cities in the North. They hoped to find better opportunities for jobs and education there.*

*Life in the Twenties*

courts for using the United States mail to trick people into giving money to the UNIA. Two years later, he was pardoned by the President but was deported, or sent out of the country. Garvey's ideas of pride and dignity and his organization have lasted.

The National Association for the Advancement of Colored People (NAACP) gained importance when it won two important court cases in the 1920's. A white mob attacked a black dentist, Dr. O. H. Sweet, for buying a home in a white neighborhood in Detroit, Michigan. Gunfire from the house killed one of the attackers. A court later ruled that Dr. Sweet had the right to defend himself when threatened with harm. In another case in 1927, the Supreme Court ruled that states could not keep black voters from taking part in primary elections. These are elections to decide who will be a party's choice for a political office. In many areas of the South, black people had not been allowed to vote in primary elections. When there was only one strong party, as was the case in most areas, this meant that black people did not really have a choice in the general election. The primary winner's name was the only one that appeared on the ballot.

# Labor After the War

During the war, manufacturers had generally been willing to talk to workers in labor unions about working conditions and raising wages. The government had wanted to be sure that goods were produced on time to help the war effort. It put pressure on employers to meet workers' demands. Wages in many industries rose during the war, as did the profits of many businesses. The cost of living also went up and kept on rising once the war ended. During 1919, several million workers who were demanding raises in pay went on strike in different industries around the country.

One of the largest strikes involved the steel workers around the country. On September 22, 1919, over 250,000 workers went out on strike. The companies, with the help of local officials in the steel towns, moved quickly to end the strike. Newspaper advertisements appeared telling the people to return to work. Spies were hired by the companies to discover union plans, and strikebreakers were brought in to work. The people out on strike were soon out of money. The strike ended in defeat for the workers and so did the attempt to form a strong steel workers union at that time.

# Fighting the Unions

A series of other strikes took place in the 1920's. Many business leaders joined together to stop labor unions from forming in their companies. One such group was the National Association of Manufacturers (NAM). NAM set up a plan that was to keep the open shop—no labor unions—in their businesses. Lists were kept of workers who were known as organizers of labor unions. NAM members set up a special fund for hiring strikebreakers. Workers in many NAM companies had to sign a contract, called a yellow-dog contract, before being hired. It stated that the worker would not join a labor union. Labor unions had often refused to admit blacks, Mexican Americans, or women, and some employers took advantage of this. They stopped strikes by hiring one group against another as strikebreakers. By the end of the 1920's, the number of union members was far below what it had been at the end of the war—from over five million to less than three million people.

# The Red Scare

The Communist party in the U.S., formed in 1919, has never made headway against the practice of capitalism and the general prosperity of the American economy. Its greatest popularity was evidenced by the polling of 102,000 votes out of 40 million cast in the presidential election of 1932.

The large number of strikes after the war was upsetting to many Americans. They also worried about the spread of communism. The Communist party had won a revolution in Russia in 1917. Once in power, these leaders in Russia, or the new Soviet Union, ran the government without average people being fully involved. Newspapers carried stories that Communists were helping to start the strikes that were taking place around the United States. Because Communists were known as "reds," this became known as the Red Scare. The attorney general of the United States, A. Mitchell Palmer, began arresting people in this country who were known or suspected to be Communists. During this Red Scare, more than five hundred people were deported.

# New Immigration Laws

Many Americans felt that thousands of people from Europe would want to come to the United States after the war. They feared this would create too much competition for jobs or bring in too many Communists. In 1921, Congress passed a law that set a quota, or certain number, for people who could come from each country overseas. The quota system was for all countries except most of those in the Western Hemisphere. Immigration from Asia was still very controlled, and prejudice remained strong against immigrants from eastern and southern Europe. In 1924, another immigration law was passed by Congress to allow more people from western and northern Europe. It also lowered the numbers for other areas. Few immigrants were coming from western and northern Europe at the time. So the law had the effect of greatly lowering the total number of all people immigrating to the United States.

Japanese immigration had been limited by the Gentlemen's Agreement in 1907. Most of the Japanese immigrants before then had

*401*

Many countries in western and northern Europe offered jobs for their people in their own increasingly industrialized economies.

*The government greatly lowered the number of immigrants coming into the United States in the 1920's. Many Americans feared new immigrants would take what few jobs were available and that many Communists would come into the country. Laws were passed to slow down immigration.*

been young men seeking jobs. The agreement of 1907 stopped this immigration but did not stop wives and children of immigrants from joining them in the United States. Some Japanese-American men went to Japan to marry and then returned to the United States with their wives. Other Japanese women came to the United States after their families had arranged a marriage.

The immigration law of 1924 stopped women and men from coming to the United States from Japan. It was against the law in many states for Asians to marry white Americans. Many Japanese families also did not approve of such marriages. So, many Japanese men were unable to find wives and establish families. This almost stopped the growth of the Japanese-American population in the United States.

# Immigrants from the Philippines

When Japanese immigration was stopped, a shortage of workers on sugar plantations and farms followed. Owners of large plantations in Hawaii then began to encourage Filipino immigration. Some Filipinos also came as students to study at colleges in the United States. They often returned to the Philippines to work, mostly in the government. Still others came as a result of serving in the United States Navy.

By 1930, there were about forty-five thousand Filipinos in the United States and sixty-three thousand in Hawaii. In addition to working on farms, they held jobs in the canning and fishing industries on the West Coast. Prejudice against Japanese and Chinese immigrants was often directed at Filipinos as well. When there were local laws which kept Asians from marrying white Americans or owning or renting land, they often included Filipinos.

# Return of the Ku Klux Klan

Refer students to p. 282 for earlier KKK information.

Prejudice and fear led to the organization of another Ku Klux Klan in 1915. It was modeled after the Klan of the 1870's. This time, the organization also declared itself against Catholics, Jews, and all people from foreign countries. The new KKK grew rapidly in the 1920's and by 1924 claimed nearly five million members. They worked to elect people to state governments and often used threats and violence against voters. Black people who owned businesses were threatened to keep them from competing with Klan members. Japanese and Chinese people on the West Coast were sometimes forced to sell their land at

*A new Ku Klux Klan was organized in 1915. The Klan said it was against not only all blacks but also all Catholics, Jews, and all people from foreign countries. Here the Klan parades in full costume before the Capitol Building in Washington, D.C.*

*Life in the Twenties*

low prices. After the conviction of a Klan leader for murder and investigations by the government, membership began to decline. By 1930, the Klan had lost most of its power.

# The Growth of the Economy

The economy of the United States improved and continued to grow after a short depression in the early 1920's. More goods were produced than in any earlier period of the nation's history. Making automobiles became one of the fastest growing and most important industries. By the end of the twenties, three million people were making or selling automobiles or parts for them. The number of Americans who owned cars increased as quickly. By 1930, there were twenty-three

# Statistics

One source historians use to discover information about the past is collections of numbers called statistics. Many statistics are gathered by various government offices. They are kept for such things as the number of people living in a city or in the country, the number of cars people own, or the amount of money that people have in savings accounts in any one year. The tables below are some examples of the statistics that have been kept for the 1920's.

Table I shows the number of motor vehicles that were registered, or recorded, for use on the highways in the

United States. How many years are covered for each item? During what time did the number of cars go over the one million mark? Why might it be useful to have such information? What do these statistics tell us about the automobile industry in the 1920's?

**TABLE I**

**Motor Vehicle Registration**

| Year | Automobiles | All Motor Vehicles |
|------|------------|--------------------|
| 1900 | 8,000 | 8,000 |
| 1910 | 458,377 | 468,500 |
| 1920 | 8,131,522 | 9,239,161 |
| 1930 | 23,034,753 | 26,749,853 |

million cars and four million trucks and buses in the United States. Over 75 percent of all families owned a car.

Aviation, or air transportation, became an important industry in the 1920's. In 1927, Charles Lindbergh piloted his small plane, the *Spirit of St. Louis*, from New York to Paris alone without stopping. His was the first solo flight across the Atlantic Ocean. Large crowds gathered to see Lindbergh land in Paris and a huge parade for him was held when he returned to New York City. His trip helped to make air travel popular. More planes were built by Americans in following years. Between 1928 and 1930, the number of people traveling by airplane rose from 1,400 to 32,000.

For a majority of Americans, the 1920's offered good opportunities for jobs and for making money in business. Many people earned more money than they had ever been able to do. It allowed them to buy automobiles, radios, houses, and other goods. People thought that the economy would continue to grow as fast as it had from 1919 to 1929.

Table II shows the average amount of money paid in a year to a worker. What groups of workers had the highest wages? What group the lowest? In what years did wages go down from the year before? For whom? What could such information tell about the economy in general?

## TABLE II

### Workers' Average Yearly Wage

| Year | Farming | Manufacturing | Government | Average for all Workers* |
|------|---------|---------------|------------|--------------------------|
| 1919 | $725    | $1264         | $1151      | $1220                    |
| 1920 | 830     | 1497          | 1375       | 1424                     |
| 1921 | 567     | 1306          | 1429       | 1311                     |
| 1922 | 551     | 1255          | 1473       | 1294                     |
| 1923 | 614     | 1372          | 1510       | 1382                     |
| 1924 | 629     | 1394          | 1515       | 1394                     |
| 1925 | 642     | 1417          | 1545       | 1421                     |
| 1926 | 651     | 1442          | 1593       | 1450                     |
| 1927 | 648     | 1467          | 1642       | 1459                     |
| 1928 | 646     | 1500          | 1673       | 1478                     |
| 1929 | 651     | 1508          | 1703       | 1489                     |

* This also includes wages of workers in mining, trade, construction, finance, transportation, and services.

*Life in the Twenties*

But the growth of the economy did not continue, and the worst depression in the country's history began in 1929. To millions of Americans, the changes and the problems of the 1920's seemed mild compared to the new ones they faced in the 1930's.

# Chapter 20 in Perspective See Teacher's Manual, page 119T.

## Identify

| | | |
|---|---|---|
| F. Scott Fitzgerald | John Dewey | Dr. O. H. Sweet |
| Ernest Hemingway | Helen Keller | A. Mitchell Palmer |
| Langston Hughes | Marcus Garvey | Charles Lindbergh |

## Explain

| | | |
|---|---|---|
| prohibition | open shop | deport |
| yellow-dog contract | Red Scare | quota system |

## Check Your Memory of the Facts

1. What were some new forms of entertainment in the 1920's?
2. What does the Nineteenth Amendment cover?
3. In what ways did Indians become citizens? What reasons did some Indian groups give for not wishing to be citizens?
4. What was the purpose of the Order of the Sons of America?
5. What were some important cases won by the NAACP in the 1920's?
6. What kinds of things did business leaders do to stop unions from forming? How did these things affect unions?
7. What new group of immigrants came to the United States in the 1920's? What were their reasons for coming?
8. How was prejudice against some groups of Americans expressed?

## Check Your Understanding of the Ideas

1. How was prohibition accepted by American citizens?
2. What does the average life expectancy tell about living conditions?
3. Why did certain groups of Americans feel they deserved better treatment after World War I?

4. What ideas about black people were made popular by Marcus Garvey?
5. Why was the quota system for immigration created?
6. What kinds of information show the huge growth of the economy during the 1920's?

## Expand Your Knowledge

1. Bring to class records of songs that were popular in the 1890's and of jazz music of the 1920's. Play them for the class and discuss the differences.
2. Make a list of sports figures of the 1920's for baseball, track, football, and swimming. List their important sport records and compare them with records today. Do any of the records of the 1920's still stand?
3. Find pictures from magazines or family albums that show how people lived in the 1920's. Share them with the class.

# The Depression and the New Deal

# 21

Aim: to help students relate the economic effects of the depression of the 1930's to the changed relationship between government and business.

The economic growth of the 1920's ended with a depression that began in 1929. The depression, which lasted through the 1930's, was the worst in American history. Because the effects of the depression were so bad for so many people, ideas about the relationship between government and business were greatly changed. The federal government began to accept far more responsibility for the lives of the people. More

*The depression of the 1930's caused many people to wander around the country in search of work and food. Many built shacks out of cardboard and tin so they might have some place to sleep.*

than ever before, it tried to find ways to help people have chances to make good livings.

*409*

# Confidence in Business

As the economy grew quickly during the 1920's, the ideas of laissez-faire again became popular. Many Americans felt that government regulation of the economy, such as in the Progressive Era and World War I, was no longer needed nor wanted. People were certain that American business would be able to make enough goods to meet the needs of the people and to give workers jobs.

The three Republican Presidents of the 1920's were also confident about American business. When President Harding died in 1923, Vice-President Calvin Coolidge became the new President of the United States. Coolidge, reelected in 1924, decided not to run again in 1928. That year the Republican candidate, Herbert Hoover, easily won the election. Like both Harding and Coolidge, Hoover was against having any large programs of government control.

Remind students of laissez-faire presentation, pp. 310-11.

# The Stock Market Crash

Confidence in American business and in the economy led many people to buy stock in companies. These stockholders expected to make a profit over a long period of time from their investments. There were also people buying stock only to sell it when the price went up. This is called speculation. There were a large number of speculators in the stock market by 1929. With so many people wanting to buy from a limited amount of stock, the prices of stocks rose quickly. Banks made a large number of loans to speculators.

In early 1929, some people thought that the economy would not keep growing so quickly. They began to sell their stocks because they believed the price would soon go down. Others began to sell their stocks. Soon more people wanted to sell than wanted to buy. Prices of stocks began to fall. Banks who had loaned money to people to buy stock asked for payment. Many people soon found they could not get enough money to pay back the loans. Many investors lost all they owned. Banks began to fail because their loans were not repaid.

Might review other depressions, especially 1873 and 1893, with students.

Speculative favorites in the stock market of the 1920's were the new and developing industries like radio, air transportation, and public utilities in which spectacular growth was anticipated.

*People outside the New York Stock Exchange in 1929 anxiously wait for news about the stock market crash.*

At first the stock market "crash," as it was called, did not have any immediate effect on the general economy. But by late 1930 and early 1931, a major depression had begun. Since people did not have money to invest, companies could not buy new equipment or even stay open. The number of people out of work began to grow.

# Causes of the Depression

The stock market crash was only the beginning of the depression. There were other problems in the economy which most people had failed to see. Farmers had been in a depression since the end of World

War I. Prices for farm products were low, and farmers had little money to buy factory-made goods. Factory workers' pay had not risen as fast as the profits of business. Like farmers, these workers were not able to buy as many goods as were being made.

Trade with Europe, which might have made up for the lack of goods sold in the United States, had begun to decline. Since World War I, most European countries were in debt to the United States. They could not pay for imports, so they began to buy less. Eventually, investors with large amounts of stock assumed that many businesses would have to cut back on production. This would mean lower sales and profits which would lead to lower stock prices. These things all played a part in the stock market crash and in the depression.

Verify with class discussion that students recognize the interrelationships among various sections of the national economy.

# Effects of the Depression

The depression of the 1930's was not like anything many Americans had ever known. The number of people out of work soon rose to over twelve million—nearly 25 percent of the work force. Thousands of others worked only a small number of hours each week. The depression

*Farmers were hit hard by the depression of the 1930's. Many lost their farms and had to move when prices dropped because they had grown more food than people were able to buy.*

*The Depression and the New Deal*

Some students may have grandparents or other relatives who could provide students with firsthand accounts of daily life during the depression and New Deal which could be shared in general class discussion.

hit unskilled workers very hard. They were usually the first to lose their jobs. Poor people who had made little money before 1929 saw all hopes disappear for improving their lives.

Thousands of people began to wander around the country in search of work and food. Some young men and women joined the movement because their families were no longer able to support them. Families began moving to other areas in search of jobs or better land. Many moved to California. Cities around the country soon had areas where poor people had built shacks out of cardboard or tin. Local governments as well as groups of private citizens raised money to buy food and clothing for these people. Other towns began to post signs telling travelers to keep moving because there were no jobs there. In the mid-1930's, a drought in the southern Great Plains, which became known as the "dust bowl," ruined the farmland there.

Federal and local governments wanted to reduce the number of people seeking jobs or needing relief. One way was to send Mexicans in the United States back to Mexico. Those who volunteered to return were often given free transportation. However, many Mexicans did not wish to leave. Local governments sometimes refused to give relief aid to them. Between 1930 and 1940, over 250,000 people were sent to Mexico. While most of the adults were Mexican citizens, many had children born in the United States who were American citizens. The children had to leave with their parents.

Several members of Congress wanted to restrict immigration to help American workers without jobs. They passed the Tydings-McDuffie bill in 1934. This act called for the independence of the Philippines in ten years. It also set a quota on Filipino immigration to the United States of fifty people a year. During the depression, more people left the United States than came in as immigrants.

# Hoover and Roosevelt

President Hoover believed that businesses as well as state governments should help themselves during the depression as much as possible. With his support in 1932, Congress set up the Reconstruction Finance Corporation to loan money to banks, businesses, and railroads in danger of going out of business. He also encouraged states to create jobs through public works projects like building roads. He met with business leaders to encourage them not to cut wages and to keep people working. Through a Farm Board, the government bought some surplus crops but not enough to keep the prices up.

Some leaders in Congress wanted more effective aid to farmers. They also wanted more help for the unemployed. President Hoover did not think the federal government needed to go so far to help end the depression. The United States had suffered depressions before which had lasted only a few years. Hoover believed that the economy would soon get better. Many people who believed that business could take care of itself and the country began to worry, however, as this depression grew worse.

For the 1932 election, the Republicans chose President Hoover to run again. The Democrats nominated the governor of New York, Franklin Roosevelt. During the campaign, Roosevelt promised the American people a "New Deal" to put people back to work and to provide help for people out of work. Roosevelt won the election, and the Democratic party won control of both houses of Congress.

# The New Deal

President Roosevelt hoped to develop plans that would help the economy grow and also put people back to work. While he had few definite plans in mind when he took office, he was willing to try new ideas from his advisers. Many of these people were believers in the reforms of the Progressive Era for government regulation of the economy. Among the advisers were Harry Hopkins, a former social worker, and Frances Perkins who was named the secretary of labor. Perkins was the first woman ever to hold office in a President's Cabinet. Eleanor Roosevelt, the First Lady, also made suggestions to the President for helping people through the depression. She traveled around the country and won support for the government's programs among the people.

Eleanor Roosevelt was the niece of Theodore Roosevelt. She worked for civil rights for women and minority groups most of her life and represented the United States at the United Nations from 1945 to 1952 and from 1961 to 1962.

One of the first programs passed under the New Deal helped farmers get higher prices for their goods. In 1933, Congress passed a law to set up the Agricultural Adjustment Administration (AAA). Crop prices were low because the farmers were growing more food than people had the money to buy. The AAA tried to reduce farm production so that what was left for sale by the farmers would bring better prices. The government paid farmers to plant fewer acres of basic crops like cotton, wheat, and corn, and to raise fewer pigs. It also bought and stored farm products, giving much of this food and cotton to people on relief. The

Farmers had destroyed crops and livestock at times to limit the amount of products for sale and to avoid selling them at lower-than-cost prices.

AAA plan helped many farmers by raising crop prices, but it did little for the people who worked on but did not own the land. Farm workers often lost their jobs when fewer crops were grown. They added to the number of poor people moving around the country and living in the cities without jobs.

*Franklin D. Roosevelt, shown here with his wife Eleanor, offered a New Deal to the depression-weary people of America. Elected President in 1932, he served for 13 years.*

# Mary McLeod Bethune

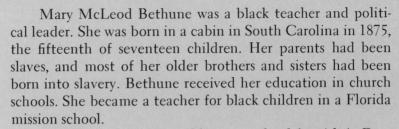

Mary McLeod Bethune was a black teacher and political leader. She was born in a cabin in South Carolina in 1875, the fifteenth of seventeen children. Her parents had been slaves, and most of her older brothers and sisters had been born into slavery. Bethune received her education in church schools. She became a teacher for black children in a Florida mission school.

In 1903, Bethune started her own school for girls in Daytona Beach, Florida. She had little money of her own, but many people gave to help the school grow. Bethune taught job training and religion in her school. As the school grew, it also offered other courses. In 1928, it joined with a school for boys to become Bethune-Cookman College.

By the 1920's, Bethune was a well-known black leader. She was president of the National Association of Colored Women. President Franklin Roosevelt made her a member of the advisory committee of the National Youth Administration, an organization to help young people.

President Roosevelt was impressed by Bethune's work. He made a separate Division of Negro Affairs in the National Youth Administration and asked her to lead it. Bethune used her power to make sure the organization gave education and job training for black young people. Bethune also started the Federal Council of Negro Affairs, which told the government about the needs of black people.

Eleanor Roosevelt invited Bethune to a White House tea party in 1937. She was the only black woman there. Bethune wrote about it in her diary:

> While I felt very much at home, I looked about me longingly for other dark faces. . . .
>
> Then I thought how vitally important it was that I be here, to help these others get used to seeing us in high places. . . .
>
> I know so well why I *must* be here, *must* go to tea at the White House. To remind them always that we belong here, we are part of this America.

# The NRA

A second major part of the New Deal program helped businesses and industrial workers. The problem for business was how to raise prices to make it profitable for companies to keep making goods. This would keep people working. Both government and business leaders agreed on the need to cut competition. In 1933, Congress passed the National Industrial Recovery Act. The act permitted businesses to set up codes, or rules, so that several companies in the same industry could prohibit unfair price-cutting without violating antitrust laws. The government tried to prevent the fixing of standard prices or the raising of prices, but that was what resulted. Under this new law, the National Recovery Administration (NRA) was formed. Its task was to settle disputes and enforce the codes.

In addition to the codes for business, the NRA established a minimum wage for workers in industry. Businesses covered by the codes had to pay each worker at least forty cents an hour. The law also did away with child labor because it stated that only persons at least sixteen years of age could be hired to work in industry.

One part of the National Industrial Recovery Act stated that workers had the right to form labor unions of their own choosing. Because many labor leaders felt that the NRA still did not give enough support to unions, they asked for a stronger law. Senator Robert Wagner of New York wrote a bill that was passed by Congress in 1935. It gave government protection to workers who wanted to form unions. The Wagner Act set up the National Labor Relations Board (NLRB).

*The WPA started by Roosevelt in 1935 created jobs for the unemployed. They built bridges, roads, hospitals, and airports.*

The NLRB had the authority to look into complaints against employers who tried to stop unions from being formed. It could also take cases to court to enforce the law.

To put more people back to work, the federal government set up several different agencies. One of these, the Civilian Conservation Corps (CCC), gave jobs mostly to young people. They planted trees in forests, built small dams to stop soil erosion, fought forest fires, and stocked lakes and rivers with fish. The Works Progress Administration (WPA) was started in 1935. Its funds were used to pay unemployed people to work on such projects as building roads, airports, bridges, and hospitals. It also provided work for artists and writers.

Because the funds of many cities and towns to buy food and clothing for poor people did not last long, the government set up the Federal Emergency Relief Administration (FERA). The FERA gave money to states and cities to buy food and clothing and in some cases gave money directly to people in need.

## Social Security

Several countries in Europe had established pensions, or retirement pay, for their citizens long before the 1930's. Others also provided some payments to people without jobs. Frances Perkins thought there should be similar programs in the United States. In 1935, Congress passed the Social Security Act. This law gave federal government money to states which set up programs to help people have security if they could not work. The state government could then provide a certain amount of money to retired workers and handicapped people. The act also established programs to be run by the states for mothers and children without support and workers without jobs.

Might have student investigate and report on original aims of and changes in Social Security system because of current concerns.

## Other Recovery Efforts

An old issue that came before Congress at the beginning of the New Deal was the prohibition of alcoholic beverages. The Eighteenth Amendment was hard to enforce because many people failed to support it. Some people believed that it was a good law and should be kept. Many thought if it were repealed, the sale of liquor would help recovery. Taxes on it would help the federal and state governments pay

*418*

for relief. Congress and the states settled the issue with the Twenty-first Amendment which was ratified in 1933. This law repealed the Eighteenth Amendment and left to each state the question of controlling the sale and use of alcohol.

# Good Neighbors

Another way of fighting the depression was to encourage foreign trade. For this reason, the United States recognized the government of

## Political Cartoons

All cartoons in a newspaper do not appear on the comic page. Some, like political cartoons, are usually found on the editorial page. They are used to tell

"Yes, You Remembered Me"

A WISE ECONOMIST ASKS A QUESTION

the reader what the artist thinks about some subject of interest in the news. These cartoons become important sources for historians looking at the past.

See Teacher's Manual, page 53T.

*The Depression and the New Deal*

the Soviet Union in 1933. However, little trade resulted. Through improving relations with Latin-American countries, Roosevelt did help increase trade with them. In his inaugural address, Roosevelt introduced his Good Neighbor Policy. "In the field of world policy I would dedicate this nation to the policy of the good neighbor—the neighbor who . . . respects the rights of others." By 1934, Roosevelt had pulled United States soldiers out of Haiti. He gave up the right to send forces into Cuba if there was disorder there. The government raised the yearly payments to Panama for the Panama Canal. The United States also signed new trade treaties with a number of Latin-American countries.

During the 1930's, some of the favorite subjects for political cartoonists were the depression and the New Deal. Study each of the following cartoons. What is the artist trying to say in each? In the second cartoon, why do you think the cartoonist used a squirrel? In the other two cartoons, which one is for and which one is against the New Deal? Who is the sick man in the last cartoon? Who is the forgotten man in the first cartoon? What are some advantages of creating cartoons over writing about the same subject? Some disadvantages?

*The Depression and the New Deal*

# Effects of the New Deal

The New Deal committed the federal government to forceful action through direct intervention in almost every area of economic life from farm prices to the stock market as a policy for preventing future economic disasters.

The most important effect of the New Deal laws was that, under them, many people were able to at least get some food and clothing. The laws did not help the economy recover fully. The NRA codes for business did not work out as expected. Large companies often controlled the making of codes in their industry. Monopolies and trusts kept growing in spite of the efforts of the federal government.

As an outcome of the Wagner Act, larger numbers of workers in many industries began to form unions. Many of these local unions tried to join the American Federation of Labor (AFL). But the leaders of the AFL wanted the workers to organize according to their craft or skill. This often left out many unskilled workers who worked on assembly lines. A group in the AFL, led by John L. Lewis of the United Mine Workers, formed the Committee for Industrial Organization (CIO). This group organized all skilled and unskilled workers in the same industry into the same union. The CIO was very successful in the steel, automobile, textile and clothing, meat-packing, and electrical industries. Both the AFL and the CIO grew quickly after the passage of the Wagner Act. The number of Union members was soon over seven million. Disagreements among the leaders of the two organizations led to the CIO being forced out of the AFL. The CIO members formed a separate national union as the Congress of Industrial Organizations.

AFL expelled 10 unions in Committee group in 1937. They reorganized as Congress in 1938 with Lewis as president. Lewis pulled UMW out of CIO in 1942, and it has remained separate. AFL and CIO merged in 1955 with Walter Reuther (UAW) as president.

# Indians and the New Deal

As part of a large plan to improve the lives of Americans, Congress passed the Indian Reorganization Act in 1934. This new act allowed Indians to form corporations for the purposes of holding land and governing their people as a group. The law required that a council be elected by the adult members of each group. Money was set aside by the federal government to buy back Indian land that had been sold to others. Some money was set aside for the education of Indian children. In both cases, the money was too little for the needs of the people.

The Indians felt that they should not have to buy the land back since it was rightly theirs. Large numbers of Indians did not take part in the elections for council governments because it was not the way that their leaders had been chosen in the past. The Indian Reorganization Act returned some control over their lives to American Indians, but it gave final power to overrule council governments to the federal secretary of the interior. Under this act, some Indian lands were recovered.

*Under the Wagner Act of 1935, these pickets were given government protection to belong to a union.*

The living conditions for most Indians, however, did not improve. They continued to be the poorest group in the United States.

# The Supreme Court and the New Deal

There were many people in the country who did not agree with New Deal programs. Business people said that they favored workers. Others felt that too much power in the hands of the government might lead to loss of their freedom. But because supporters of the New Deal were in the majority in Congress, those against it had no way of changing the program. In 1935, however, a case came before the Supreme Court challenging the NRA codes, and the Court ruled that they were unconstitutional. In a 1936 case, the Supreme Court also ruled that parts of the AAA were unconstitutional.

To supporters of the New Deal, these decisions seemed to ruin their work of the last three years. President Roosevelt, reelected by a large majority in 1936, believed that most Americans favored the New Deal. He wanted to change the Supreme Court by appointing more

The NRA case was *Schnechter Poultry Corporation v. U.S.;* grounds were that Congress could not give President power over trade and commerce nor attempt itself to regulate purely intrastate trade. The AAA case was *United States v. Butler;* grounds were that major parts of the act violated rights reserved to the states by the Constitution.

members who would be favorable to the New Deal. The number of members of the Supreme Court had been changed by Congress before, but this time people from both major parties spoke out against the plan. Congress refused to pass a law to increase the number of people on the Supreme Court. However, in 1937, the Court began to rule in favor of some New Deal programs. In cases against the Wagner Act and the Social Security Act, the Court ruled that both were constitutional. Congress eventually passed new laws much like the AAA and the NRA. In the next few years, several of the members of the Supreme Court retired, and President Roosevelt replaced them with people he felt were favorable to the New Deal.

# New Problems Overseas

The plans of the New Deal did not bring an end to the depression in America. By 1940, there were still eight million people without jobs. But the programs of the 1930's helped many Americans through a difficult time. People who would have had no job found some work on government projects. Poor families were able to find food and clothing through government aid. Social Security became a permanent responsibility of the federal government.

The depression seriously affected countries all over the world. Partly because of it, the governments of several countries came under the control of military or political dictators. These changes alarmed many Americans. A majority of the voters in the 1940 presidential election wanted Roosevelt to continue as the leader of the United States. For the first time in the nation's history, its citizens chose the same President for a third term in office.

# Chapter 21 in Perspective See Teacher's Manual, page 121T.

## Identify

Calvin Coolidge       Frances Perkins       John L. Lewis
Franklin Roosevelt

# Explain

speculation                New Deal            Social Security Act
stock market crash         Wagner Act          Indian Reorganization Act
Good Neighbor Policy

## Check Your Memory of the Facts

1. What kinds of government action did President Hoover support to ease the depression?
2. What did the Tydings-McDuffie Bill of 1934 do?
3. What American government actions followed President Roosevelt's "Good Neighbor" speech?
4. What was a major difference between the AFL and the CIO?
5. How did the Supreme Court rule on cases involving New Deal legislation?

## Check Your Understanding of the Ideas

1. Why did people have great faith in American business in the 1920's?
2. What happened to cause the crash of the stock market?
3. What problems in the economy led to the depression?
4. How were people affected by the depression?
5. What were some of the programs in the New Deal? How did they work? How were they different from President Hoover's plans?
6. Why did President Roosevelt want to add members to the Supreme Court?

## Expand Your Knowledge

1. Find out about a project done under the Works Progress Administration to relate to the class.
2. Interview someone who was old enough to work during the time of the depression. What problems were faced, and what kind of community help was available?

# Muncie 1920-1935

Muncie is located on the White River in the rich farm lands of east central Indiana. By 1865, it had grown into a small city. Deposits of natural gas were discovered there in the 1880's, and industries came to the area to use the gas for fuel. These industries caused Muncie to change from a farming community to an industrial city in the early 1900's. For this reason, it was like thousands of other small American cities at that time.

## Middletown

In the 1920's, the supply of goods from mass production caused changes in American customs. People had new ideas about ways to earn their livings, keep house, and enjoy more free time. Sociologists, or those people interested in recording the way others live and work together in groups, were studying these changes. In 1925, two sociologists named Robert and Helen Lynd decided to study one city in America. By studying a "typical" city, the Lynds hoped to record a general picture of what most American cities were like. Muncie was chosen for their study because it had "many features common to a wide group of communities." They called the study, *Middletown*.

## Earning a Living

By 1920, Muncie was an industrial city of almost thirty-seven thousand people. Over three hundred different products were made by over one hundred different companies. These products included glass jars, auto parts, batteries, wire, and other metal products.

The Lynds noted that this production caused changes in the way people earned their livings in Muncie. Skilled artisans were often replaced by machines which did similar jobs but at faster speeds. The Lynds said:

*And in modern machine production it is speed and endurance that are* [needed]. *A boy of nineteen may, after a few weeks of experience on a machine, turn out an amount of work greater than that of his father of forty-five. . . . It is not uncommon for a father to be laid off during slack times while the son continues to work.*

So more young people were beginning to take jobs in the factories. Many people left farms in the area to take jobs in the city.

Most city people worked ten hours a day, averaging fifty-five or sixty hours a week. Working hours were usually during the day, but some factories also had night shifts. Work was generally steady in business, but some factories had slack times, and workers had times of unemployment.

In the 1920's, families worked hard to earn money to buy the new machines which made life easier and more enjoyable. The Lynds discovered:

*This* [desire for] *the dollar appears in the . . . growing tendency among younger* [workers] *to* [trade future job interests] *for immediate "big money."* [Supervisors] *complain that* [Muncie people] *entering the shops today are increasingly less interested in being moved from job to job until they have become all-around skilled workers, but want to stay on one machine and run up their production so that they may quickly reach a maximum wage scale.*

## Home Life

Home life in Muncie was also changing in the 1920's. The Lynds wrote:

*Several hundred homes are heated . . . by furnace, steam or oil, although most of the* [factory workers] *still live in the . . . unheated-bed-room era. . . .*

*There was no running water* [before] *1885, and by 1890 not more than 20 per cent. of . . . the city's streets* [were] *underlaid with water mains. . . . For approximately ninety-five families in each hundred, "taking a bath"* [in those days] *meant lugging a heavy wooden or tin tub into a bedroom, or more usually the warm kitchen, and filling it half full of water from the pump, heated on the kitchen stove. Today all new houses, except the very cheapest, have bathrooms, and many old houses are* [adding] *this improvement rapidly. . . . It is not uncommon to observe* [old] *and* [new]

*habits . . . side by side in a family with primitive back-yard water or sewage habits, yet using an automobile, electric washer, electric iron, and vacuum cleaner.*

The use of prepared foods, canned goods, and refrigerators meant a change in eating habits. More fruits and vegetables were eaten during the winter months. Families started buying bread instead of making their own. Meat was eaten at least twice a day in many homes. A greater variety of foods could be bought and kept for longer periods of time without spoiling.

There were many changes in clothing, too, in the 1920's. As the Lynds reported:

*A well-dressed Muncie woman of the 1920's*

*. . . clothing plays more than the . . . role of protecting the body against* [the weather]. . . .

*In this era of furnace-heated houses and enclosed automobiles the* [use] *of clothing* [for protection only] *is declining.*

*. . . Among women and girls . . . skirts have shortened from the ground to the knee and the lower limbs have been emphasized by sheer silk stockings; more of the arms and neck are* [shown]. . . .

*. . . Every step in this change had been greeted as a violation of morals and good taste.*

There was a clear difference in the traditional activities of men and women in Muncie. The Lynds wrote:

*This is especially marked in the . . . activities known as "housework," which have always been almost exclusively performed by the wife, with more or less help from her daughters. In the growing number of . . . families in which the wife helps to earn the family living, the husband is beginning to share directly in housework. Even in* [other] *families . . . activities of the wife in making a home are being more and more replaced by goods and services* [supplied] *by other agencies in return for . . . money . . . throwing ever greater emphasis upon the money-getting activities of the husband. . . .*

*Smaller houses, easier to "keep up," labor-saving* [machines], *canned goods, baker's bread, less heavy meals, and ready-made clothing are among the places where . . . time* [is] *saved today. . . .* [Homemakers] *repeatedly speak, also, of the use of running water, the* [change] *from wood to coal fires, and . . . linoleum on floors as time-savers.*

## Education

One of the biggest changes noted by the Lynds was the sharp increase in the number of students in higher education. Only a few Muncie children went to high school before the 1900's. By the 1920's, most of them went to high school, and some of those went to college. The most important reason given for dropping out of school was lack of family money. Yet parents often gave up "extra things" to afford more education for their children. One mother said:

*If children don't have a good education they'll never know anything except hard work. Their father wants them to have just as much schooling as he can afford.*

The schools in Muncie changed to meet the needs of the people of the community. Classes were added in the high school to train students for specific jobs in homes, offices, and factories.

The city also had a community college. The owners of the Ball Corporation, which made glass canning jars, bought a private school on the edge of the city. They gave it to the state, and it then became a part of the state college system.

## Free Time

When asked to comment on the changing times, one lifelong resident of Muncie said, "Why on earth do you need to study what's changing this country? I can tell you what's happening in just four letters: A-U-T-O!"

About two out of every three families in Muncie had an automobile. Some families bought automobiles before they bought bathtubs. The automobile was making free time enjoyment an everyday happening rather than an occasional event. As one woman said, "We just go to lots of things we couldn't go to if we didn't have a car." To have a picnic in a park or nearby woods could be decided in a moment.

Automobiles were also influencing the practice of vacations as part of free time activities. People could go farther away from home in automobiles, so they were interested in a shorter working time. Owners of companies began taking more time off, especially in the summers. Slowly, they also began allowing managers and supervisors to take vacations with pay. But factory workers, if allowed to take vacations, took them without pay.

Movies also created a change in the habits of Muncie people. Many went to movies for fun and entertainment. Comic films, starring Charlie Chaplin or Buster Keaton, and "Wild West" films starring Tom Mix or Hoot Gibson drew the biggest crowds.

Radios were rapidly becoming a "necessity" in the homes of many. Although it was another form of entertainment, the radio also brought the people of Muncie into contact with the ideas and events of the rest of the nation. Muncie was becoming more like other American cities. As the Lynds pointed out:

*The rise of large-scale advertising, popular magazines, movies, [and] radio . . . are rapidly changing habits of thought as to what things are essential to living. . . .*

## Effects of the Depression

In 1935, the Lynds returned to Muncie to study it again. They wanted to see how the national depression of the 1930's had affected the lives of the people. The Lynds

*A picnic by the roadside*

*Young people in Muncie in touch with the world by radio*

found that the depression had shaken the city, but not shattered it. By the time they arrived to begin their new study, business leaders of Muncie were saying that the depression was over. But many merchants had lost their businesses, and others were still doing poorly. Many workers had lost their jobs. Young people were very hard hit. They often could not afford to continue in college or to marry. Many could not find jobs.

City money for aid to the poor and unemployed had been only a small problem in Muncie in the 1920's. But during the depression, relief payments completely used up funds from private groups and were a heavy drain on city funds. During the worst of the depression, relief payments had to be cut because of the lack of funds. One woman wrote to the newspaper:

*Our slip called for two dollars a week and [those in charge] thought [anyone] could prepare forty-two meals a week on a dollar-fifty for two people. So we got fifty cents taken from the two dollars.*

*. . . We haven't had a tube of toothpaste in weeks and have to check off some item of needed food when we get soap. I can only do my washing every two weeks, because that is as often as I can get oil for the oil stove to heat wash water and laundry soap with which to do my washing.*

But the people of Muncie had less trouble than many people in other American cities. Ball Corporation, one of the largest industries in the city, had been able to keep up the sales of their glass canning jars. Throughout the depression, the increase in gardens and home canning had created a bigger market for their product. They tried to keep as many workers on the payroll as possible.

The people of Muncie had had to face some important questions about their values during the depression. The Lynds wrote:

*A city* [used to] *the question, "How fast can we make even more money?" was startled by being forced to shift its central concern for a period of years to the stark question, "Can we manage to keep alive?"* . . .

*A city living by the faith that everyone can and should support himself lived through a period of years in which it had to confess that at least temporarily a quarter of its population could not get work. . . .*

*A city committed to faith in education as the key to its children's future has had to see many of its college-trained sons and daughters* [without work], *and to face the question as to what education is really "worth. . . ."*

*A city still accustomed to having its young assume . . . the values of their parents has had to listen to an increasing number of its young speak of the world of their parents as a botched mess.*

Nevertheless, the Lynds found that the depression had done little to change the basic views of most Muncie people:

*On the surface* [Muncie] *is meeting such present issues and present situations as it cannot escape by attempting to* [go back] *to the old* [ideas]: *we must always believe that things are good and that they will be better. . . . The system is fundamentally right and only the persons wrong; the cures must be changes in personal attitudes, not in the institutions themselves.*

The people of Muncie had been through a bad time, but they thought of it as temporary. They had only been "interrupted" in their race to make more money in order to buy more things. Muncie was a growing American city.

The Ball brothers, Muncie's industrial leaders in the 1920's

# War Again

Aim: to help students understand the factors which contributed to the involvement of the United States in a second world war.

During the depression of the 1930's, the attention of most Americans and their government had been on matters inside the United States. In Japan, Italy, and Germany, dictators built strong armies and navies and began to expand their countries. Toward the end of the

*After winning one of the hardest battles of the war, American soldiers raised the flag at Iwo Jima, 750 miles from Tokyo, Japan.*

*War Again*

1930's, their actions threatened to lead to another major war. Americans began to pay greater attention to the rest of the world and to worry about their country's future.

# Japan, Italy, and Germany

The League of Nation's failure to take strong action against the aggression of Japan, Italy, and Germany contributed to its demise.

The people of the Japanese islands were ruled by Emperor Hirohito although most government matters were decided by a prime minister and advisers. In the 1930's, military leaders took over the Japanese government. They favored taking land on the continent of Asia to get needed raw materials. In 1931, the Japanese army invaded and conquered the Chinese in Manchuria, renaming the area Manchukuo.

In Italy, Benito Mussolini and the Fascist party gained control of the government. Mussolini promised to end the depression in Italy and to make the country a great power. He intended for Italy to build an empire in Africa and the Mediterranean area. In 1935, the Italian army invaded and conquered Eritrea, now a part of Ethiopia.

Adolf Hitler and the Nazi party formed a dictatorship in Germany in 1933. Hitler promised the people to regain land taken from their country at the end of World War I. In his speeches, Hitler blamed Germany's Jewish people for the country's troubles. He said that they controlled the banks in Germany and other countries and had caused the depression. He also blamed them for Germany's defeat in World War I. There had been prejudice in Germany for some time against Jews, so many people believed Hitler without asking any questions. Under the Nazi party, the government passed laws taking civil rights away from German Jews. Their synagogues and businesses were destroyed by Nazi gangs. Finally, the Nazis forced the Jews from their homes and sent them to prisonlike concentration camps.

Hitler announced that he wanted to unite all the German-speaking people of Europe into one country. In 1938, his soldiers occupied Austria, making it part of Germany. Hitler then claimed the German-speaking people of Czechoslovakia. By 1939, a large part of Czechoslovakia was occupied by the German army.

# Avoiding Conflict

Throughout the 1930's, the policy of the American government was to avoid trouble with other countries. The League of Nations had

*Adolf Hitler, dictator of Germany, believed that the Germans were a superior people whose mission was to conquer Europe.*

passed a resolution to stop countries from shipping oil to Italy after its victory in Africa. The United States did not support the resolution because American leaders did not want to upset the Italian government. Isolationists—people who want to isolate, or close off, their country from outside problems—had strong support throughout the United States. Congress passed the Neutrality Act in 1935. This act made it against the law for Americans to sell arms to any country at war.

# Changing American Views

Several events took place in the late 1930's and early 1940's which changed the isolationist views held by many Americans. Japan attacked eastern China again in 1937 and conquered large areas of the country.

*War Again*

In September, 1939, Hitler and Joseph Stalin who was head of the government of the Soviet Union made an agreement not to attack each other. Germany then invaded western Poland, and the Soviet army moved into the eastern part of the country. France and Britain, who had made agreements to help Poland, declared war on Germany. They were not able to send troops there in time to stop the invasions.

Early in 1940, the Germans quickly defeated and occupied Denmark and Norway. In May, they took Holland and Belgium and attacked France. France had a very strong army and received aid from the British, but by June, the German army had defeated the French. In September of 1940, Germany began dropping bombs on Britain.

President Roosevelt and many Americans were very alarmed by these German victories and by the growing power of Italy and Japan. In 1939, Roosevelt had pointed out that the Germans could send 1,500 planes to the Western Hemisphere and that the United States would have only 80 planes to fight them. From that time, Congress and the President prepared to defend the country in case of such an attack. Congress passed a law for the first peacetime draft in the country's history in 1940. The American army, which had only 170,000 soldiers in 1939, was soon over one million in number.

Germany's effective use of airplanes and motorized vehicles to move troops and supplies quickly allowed them to win many victories without becoming bogged down in the trench warfare problems of World War I.

# Lend-Lease

President Roosevelt favored helping Britain fight the Germans. He believed, however, that most Americans were against becoming directly involved in the war. The Neutrality Act of 1935 had kept the United States from shipping arms to the British. The Johnson Act passed in 1934 had stopped loans to countries which had not paid their debts from World War I, including Britain. The President got around these laws by proposing the Lend-Lease Act which Congress passed in 1941. This law allowed the President to loan arms and other war supplies to any country he believed was important to the defense of the United States. The supplies were to be returned later.

Supporters of Lend-Lease recognized that the supplies were not likely to be returned.

The President wanted to help the British move the lend-lease materials without the United States actually entering the war. He announced a defense zone for the United States as far as Greenland to be patrolled by the American navy. Later, the area was changed to reach Iceland, and the navy used its convoy system to protect supply ships. The Germans knew that the American navy was helping Britain move war supplies, and battles between the navies of the United States and Germany began. In June of 1941, Germany invaded the Soviet Union, breaking the treaty between them. The United States then gave Lend-Lease aid to the Soviets for their fight against the Germans.

# *Japan and Pearl Harbor*

After the French were defeated by Germany, they were too weak to keep the Japanese from building air bases in French Indochina. These bases and the continued advance of the Japanese army in China caused as much alarm in the United States as the victories of the Germans.

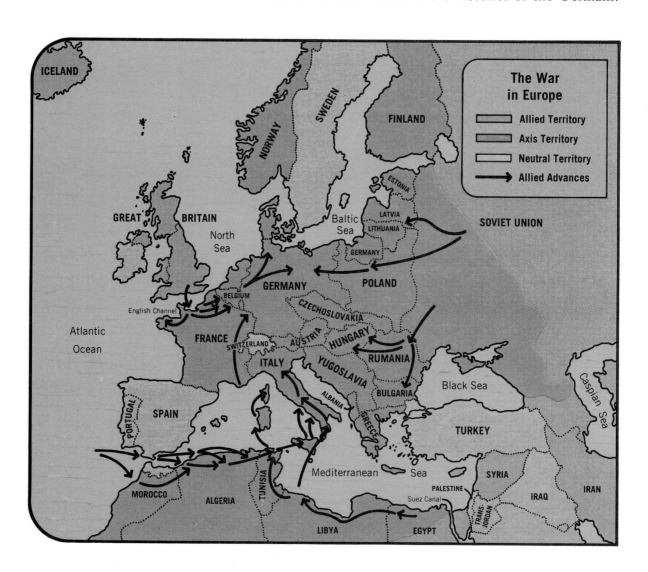

The United States government quickly approved a loan to help the Chinese government buy arms. In the summer of 1941, Japan joined the Axis alliance with Germany and Italy. The United States then announced that it would no longer export oil, airplane fuel, steel, and other metal to Japan. Without these goods, the Japanese had a harder time building ships and making other war supplies for its armed forces.

On December 7, 1941, Japan attacked Pearl Harbor in Hawaii. Pearl Harbor was the largest American navy base in the Pacific Ocean. The United States Navy and Army were caught completely by surprise. Japanese planes sank six battleships and destroyed over one hundred planes on the ground. More than two thousand Americans were killed.

Many Japanese leaders felt that war with the U.S. was inevitable if Japan was to gain control of East Asia without interference. They hoped to seriously cripple American military power with a surprise attack.

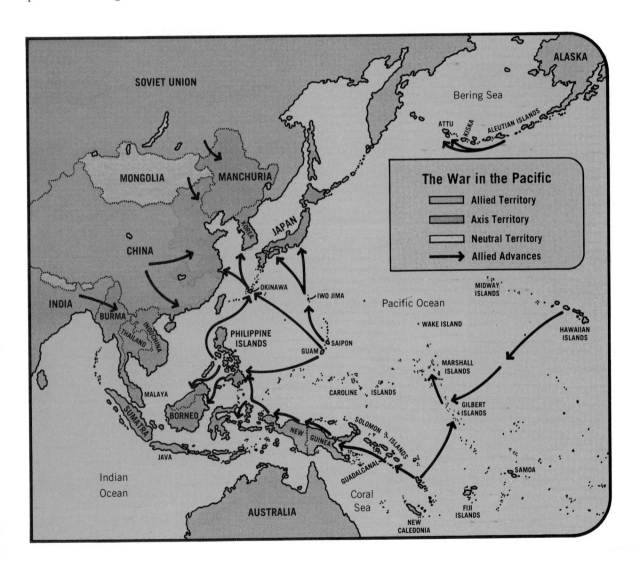

The War in the Pacific

- Allied Territory
- Axis Territory
- Neutral Territory
- → Allied Advances

The next day, President Roosevelt asked Congress to declare war on Japan:

> Yesterday, December 7, 1941—a day which will live in infamy—the United States of America was suddenly and deliberately attacked by naval and air forces of the Empire of Japan. . . .
>
> I ask that the Congress declare that since the attack . . . by Japan . . . a state of war has existed between the United States and the Japanese Empire.

Congress approved the declaration of war against Japan that same day. Because of the Axis alliance, Germany and Italy declared war on the United States on December 11.

*Japanese attacked the largest American navy base in the Pacific at Pearl Harbor on December 7, 1941. Six battleships and over one hundred planes were destroyed. Over two thousand Americans lost their lives.*

# The Allies and the Atlantic Charter

The United States entered at once into an alliance against the Axis countries. This alliance of Allied countries included not only the United States, Great Britain, and Russia but also twenty-three smaller nations. Twenty more countries joined the Allies before the end of the war. All of these nations agreed to a set of war aims known as the Atlantic Charter. It had been drawn up by President Roosevelt and Prime Minister Winston Churchill of Great Britain.

In the Atlantic Charter, the United States and Great Britain declared that they were not seeking additional lands. They were against any land changes "that do not accord with the freely expressed wishes of the peoples concerned." Further, "they respect the right of all people to choose the form of government under which they will live." It was necessary for the Allies to gain military victory, however, before the aims of the Atlantic Charter could be put into practice. In January of 1942, that victory seemed very far away.

# Preparing to Fight

After the declarations of war, more Americans were drafted into the armed services. Many men and women volunteered for duty. Women served in nonfighting roles in all service groups. They made maps, operated radios, worked in offices and medical laboratories, and were teachers. More than 100,000 women served in the Women's Army Corps alone.

As in World War I, American industries cut down the production of goods for the public so that they could make more war goods for the United States and its allies. Congress set up agencies to make sure that the right materials were sent to these industries at the right times. Other rules were set up for many industries. Men's pants, for example, were made without cuffs and women's dresses without ruffles to save cloth. This time the government also rationed many of the goods bought by the public. Rationing goods means to set the amounts that any one person can buy. Sugar, coffee, canned foods, butter, shoes, tires, gasoline, and oil were some of the goods that were rationed. The government gave out ration books which had stamps showing how often and how much of a rationed item a person could buy.

# Plans for Cash

To help pay the costs of the war, Congress passed new tax laws. One law raised the income tax rate to 6 percent. Married people making $1,200 a year and single people making $500 had to pay income taxes. Additional taxes were set on a scale from 13 to 82 percent for incomes from $2,000 to $200,000. People with taxable incomes over $200,000 paid even higher rates. This scale was set to keep people from making huge profits from the war. Other taxes were placed on such things as telephone service, telegraph messages, movie tickets, travel fares, and some alcoholic drinks.

The new or higher taxes paid 40 percent of the cost of the war. The government raised more money through the sale of war bonds. People could loan the government small or large amounts by buying bonds. The government paid interest on this borrowed money. Many students bought savings stamps through the schools for ten cents to one

*Relocation centers for the Japanese Americans in the United States were like prison camps.*

dollar. When a book of savings stamps was filled, it could be traded for a war bond. Through newspapers, radio messages, and door-to-door appeals, people were urged to buy government bonds.

# The Removal of Japanese Americans

There was some fear that people of Japanese backgrounds living in America would aid the Japanese army in an attack against the United States. Some people began to demand that they be moved from the West Coast. Prejudice there was very strong against Japanese and Japanese Americans, and it was the main reason for the demand. The President ordered some 110,000 people to be moved from their homes to relocation centers, which were much like prison camps. Ten camps were set up in California, Arizona, Wyoming, Utah, Arkansas, and Idaho. Over 70,000 of the people moved were American citizens. Many lost their land and their homes as a result of the move. In spite of this treatment, over 33,000 Japanese Americans fought in the war for the United States. German Americans and Italian Americans also suffered from prejudice, but they were not taken from their homes nor was their property taken from them.

Many Japanese-American families were forced to sell their homes and businesses at low rates and few received compensation when they returned in January of 1945.

# The War in Africa and Europe

The United States faced two major wars at the same time. One was against Japan in and across the Pacific Ocean, and it would need mostly naval and air power. The other was against Germany and Italy across the Atlantic Ocean. It would need mostly army and air force action. American leaders believed that Germany was the most dangerous enemy because of its strong industries and able scientists who might develop new weapons. So, the United States made it a policy to use its strongest power against the Nazis.

America's industries were able to equip its armed forces rapidly. Military leaders studied the question of where to attack the Nazis first, since Germany was fighting both in Africa and in Europe. After the defeat of France, the Soviet Union was the only country still able to fight the Germans in eastern Europe. The Nazis had driven into Russia

# The Normandy Invasion

General Dwight Eisenhower of the United States Army was made the commander of all Allied forces in western Europe. After the Allied decision was made to land on the Normandy peninsula in France, it became his responsibility to make the final decision of when to begin the invasion. The following selections are from Eisenhower's book, *Crusade in Europe.* What things did he have to consider in making the decision?

*I left the United States on January 13 to undertake the organization of the mightiest fighting force that the two Western Allies could muster. . . .*

*In order to obtain the maximum length of good . . . weather, the earlier the attack could be launched the better. Another factor in favor of an early attack was the continuing . . . efforts of the German to strengthen his coastal defenses. Because of weather conditions in the* [English] *Channel, May was the earliest date that a landing attempt could be successfully undertaken. . . .*

*Two considerations . . . combined to postpone the target date from May to June. The first and most important one was our insistence that the attack be on a larger scale than that originally planned by the staff. . . .*

*Another factor that made the later date* [better was the plan for] *the air force. An early attack would provide the air force with only a minimum opportunity for* [planning] *pinpoint bombing of* [important] *transportation centers in France. . . .*

*Experience in Mediterranean warfare had* [shown] *that each of our reinforced divisions . . .* [used] *about 600 to 700 tons of supplies per day. . . . On top of all this we had to provide for bringing in the heavy engineering and construction material needed to . . . refit captured ports, to repair railways, bridges, and roads, and to build airfields. A further feature of the . . . plan, and a most important one, provided for the speedy removal of wounded from the beaches. . . .*

*At three-thirty the next morning our little camp was shaking and shuddering under a wind of almost hurricane* [strength]. *. . . The mile-long trip through muddy roads to the naval headquarters was anything but a cheerful one, since it seemed impossible that in such conditions there was any reason for even discussing the situation. . . .*

[The weather staff announced] *that by the following morning a period of . . . good weather, heretofore completely unexpected, would* [begin], *lasting probably thirty-six hours. . . .*

*. . . I quickly announced the decision to go ahead with the attack on June 6. The time was then 4:15 a.m., June 5. No one present disagreed and there was a . . . brightening of faces as, without a word, each went off to his . . . post of duty to flash out to his command the messages that would set the whole* [plan] *in motion.*

during 1942, and they seemed near victory. The Russians asked the United States and Britain to attack the Germans from the west.

In Africa, the Germans had landed to help the Italians fight against the British in Libya and in Egypt. There, the important Suez Canal was in danger. The United States continued to send arms to the Russians, but it decided to use its armies first to help the British. More than 500,000 American soldiers landed in northern Africa in November of 1942. The British attacked the Axis forces from Egypt in the east, and the British and American forces attacked them from the west. By May, 1943, the German and Italian armies in Africa surrendered.

From Africa, British and American soldiers invaded Sicily, an island at the southern tip of Italy. By the middle of August, Sicily was in the hands of the Allies. From Sicily, the Allies attacked Italy at Salerno and began moving slowly north. After defeats in Africa and Sicily, Mussolini was forced to leave the Italian government. The other Italian leaders began to talk to the Allies about surrendering. When the Germans learned of this, they sent troops to take over Italy to fight the Americans and the British. On October 13, 1943, the Italians declared war on Germany. The German army was able to set up strong defenses that slowed the advance of the Allies through Italy.

Thousands of other American, British, and Canadian troops were preparing to invade France from England. In June, 1944, General Dwight Eisenhower, commander of all Allied troops there, decided that they were ready. On June 6, the Allies invaded Normandy in France. American and British planes controlled the skies, and bombers made raids against nearly all large enemy-held cities. The Allied troops moved quickly across France. One last attack by the Germans failed in December, 1944, at the Battle of the Bulge.

The people of Soviet Russia had succeeded in holding off the German army in their country. Soviet troops were pushing the Germans back into western Europe. The Allied armies continued their advance from France and Italy toward eastern Europe. On April 25, 1945, the Soviet and American armies met in victory at Torgau in eastern Germany. That month, Adolf Hitler killed himself in Berlin. On May 7, other German leaders signed the Allied surrender terms, and the war in Europe was over.

American industrial production of war items gave the Allies a great advantage.

German military leaders were aware of Allied plans to invade the Atlantic coast of Europe from England but did not know exactly where the attack would take place.

# The War in the Pacific

After the attack on Pearl Harbor, the Japanese had begun attacking countries in other areas of the Pacific Ocean. They soon took the

Philippines, Thailand, Burma, Malaya, and the Dutch East Indies. By the middle of 1942, the Japanese were near the border of India and were also preparing to attack Port Moresby in New Guinea, not far from the coast of Australia.

Under the leadership of General Douglas MacArthur, American forces in the Pacific planned to keep the Japanese from taking more islands. They also intended to take back many of the islands that the Japanese armies held. A strong navy was needed to carry out these plans. The United States had already begun to build new ships, especially those which could carry airplanes. In their final plans, Americans intended to use the Pacific islands as air bases from which they would attack Japan with bombs.

In June, 1942, the American navy stopped the Japanese from taking the Midway Islands. In August, American marines and soldiers landed on Guadalcanal in the Solomon Islands in the southwest Pacific Ocean. After six months of fighting, the Americans cleared the island of Japanese soldiers, most of whom fought to their deaths rather than surrender. Then, the troops of the United States captured the Gilbert, Caroline, and Mariana islands by 1944.

On October 20, 1944, the United States Army landed in the Philippines. Filipinos had continued to hide and fight against the Japanese after Japan had occupied their country. They joined with the American forces to drive the Japanese from their islands. The largest naval battle in history took place in Leyte Gulf. In three days of fighting there, the American navy destroyed a large part of the Japanese fleet. The Japanese were unable to replace the ships and planes lost in the battle.

In the early part of 1945, United States Marines landed on Iwo Jima in the Bonin Islands, only 750 miles from Tokyo, Japan. They fought and won one of the hardest battles of the war there. Over six thousand Americans were killed. American planes were soon taking off from Iwo Jima to bomb Okinawa, which was just 350 miles south of Japan. The army and marines landed on Okinawa in April of 1945, and the fighting went on there until July.

# A Change of Command

In the United States, President Roosevelt had been elected for a fourth term in 1944. A short time later, on April 12, 1945, he died. No other American President had served for so long, and the American

*The terrible destruction of the atomic bombs dropped on Hiroshima and Nagasaki by American bombers forced the Japanese to surrender on September 2, 1945, and brought an end to World War II.*

people were shocked by his death. Vice-President Harry Truman of Missouri became the new President. Roosevelt had given scientists his approval to begin working on an atomic bomb. President Truman was told about this after Roosevelt's death. On July 16, 1945, the first atomic bomb was successfully tested at Alamogordo, New Mexico. The bomb was more powerful than any weapon ever invented. Besides a huge explosion with extreme heat, an atomic bomb leaves radioactive fallout which can cause sickness or death to anyone exposed to it.

# The Last Effort

After Okinawa was taken by the Americans early in July, the next step was to invade Japan. Because the Japanese soldiers had fought so fiercely in the past, American military leaders feared that the United States would suffer huge losses. President Truman asked the Japanese government to give up or face complete destruction. When the Japanese refused, President Truman ordered the army air force to prepare the atomic bomb to be used against Japan.

# Albert Einstein

Albert Einstein was born in Germany in 1879 and studied mathematics and physics in Switzerland. In 1905, when he was twenty-six years old, Einstein wrote five papers for a German science magazine. They explained his theories about space and time, light, and energy. His theories were so different they started research around the world. In 1915, Einstein wrote another paper about his theory of relativity. This theory changed ideas about gravity that scientists had held since Newton's time.

During the early 1930's, the Nazi party came to power in Germany. It stopped the work of artists and scientists who did not agree with the government. While Einstein was visiting England and America in 1933, Nazis took away his property and citizenship. The Institute for Advanced Study in Princeton, New Jersey, invited Einstein to join their school. He accepted and stayed in the United States.

Einstein's theories were used as the basis for the most powerful weapon in World War II, the atomic bomb. During the 1930's, European scientists discovered how to break the atom into parts, giving off energy. In 1939, these scientists and Einstein wrote a letter to President Roosevelt. They warned him that it was possible to build an atomic bomb and that the Nazis were probably already working to make one. Germany failed to make such a bomb, but the United States was successful. Einstein was very saddened when he heard of the destruction caused by the atomic bombs in Japan. He spoke to people and wrote articles about the dangers of atomic war until his death in 1955. Einstein was one of the world's greatest scientists.

On August 6, 1945, the first atomic bomb ever to be used in war was dropped on Hiroshima, Japan. The blast killed over 60,000 people and destroyed four square miles of the city. Three days later, a second bomb was dropped on the city of Nagasaki, killing over 35,000 people. On August 14, the Japanese government informed the United States that it would accept terms for surrender. Allied and Japanese officials signed the treaty aboard the American battleship *Missouri* in Tokyo Bay on September 2, 1945. World War II was over. The war cost the United States government more than 300 billion dollars. More than

# After the War

An important Allied aim during the war had been to destroy many of the industries in Germany and Japan so that those countries would have a hard time starting another war. After the war ended, some Allied leaders and the people of their countries also wanted certain Axis leaders punished for what they had done during the war.

More than six million European men, women, and children of Jewish backgrounds had been murdered by the Nazis in their concentration camp gas chambers. Millions of Europeans had been forced to work as slaves in Nazi factories. Many of these people had died from starvation and lack of medical care. Entire cities and towns in countries occupied by Nazi forces had been totally destroyed. Throughout 1945, top Nazi officials were tried for war crimes by a special Allied court in Nuremberg, Germany. Ten were found guilty and were hanged. Others were sentenced to prison terms.

In Japan, American military leaders took control of the government and began to remove all Japanese military officials. There, too, trials were held against Japanese leaders for war crimes. Prime Minister Hideki Tojo and six others were found guilty and were executed.

# Troubles Between Allies

During World War II, the United States and the Soviet Union had cooperated with each other only to defeat the Nazis. The two countries were based on very different beliefs about government, and their leaders did not fully trust each other. Roosevelt, Churchill, and Stalin had held a meeting at the beginning of 1945 at Yalta on the Black Sea. There, the leaders talked about postwar control in central Europe and about the war with Japan. The Americans expected to follow the aims of the Atlantic Charter in central Europe. The meeting was friendly and gave promise of future cooperation between the Americans and the Soviets. Even before the war in Europe ended, however, the Russians failed to keep some of the Yalta agreements. By the end of the war, it was clear that the Russian view of control in central Europe was very different from the Atlantic Charter aims. The two most powerful countries to survive World War II found it more and more difficult to cooperate with each other. The United States and the Soviet Union began to compete against each other to spread their ideas of democracy and communism.

*Churchill, Roosevelt, and Stalin attended the Yalta Conference in February, 1945.*

# *Chapter 22 in Perspective*  See Teacher's Manual, page 124T.

## Identify

| | | |
|---|---|---|
| Benito Mussolini | Winston Churchill | Douglas MacArthur |
| Adolf Hitler | Dwight Eisenhower | Harry Truman |
| Joseph Stalin | Pearl Harbor | Hiroshima |

## Explain

| | | |
|---|---|---|
| isolationists | Axis alliance | rationing |
| Lend-Lease | Atlantic Charter | |

# Check Your Memory of the Facts

1. What was the United States' policy toward other nations in the 1930's?
2. What action did the United States take in 1935 to avoid conflict with European nations?
3. How did the United States prepare for war?
4. What roles did women have in the armed services?
5. How did the government raise money to help pay for the war?
6. What was the major effort of the Allies in Europe?
7. What were the military plans of the United States for the Pacific area?
8. What was the last action taken against Japan?

# Check Your Understanding of the Ideas

1. Why did Japan take land from China?
2. Why did Italy invade Africa?
3. What reasons did Hitler give for Germany's plans for Europe?
4. What events or situations made many Americans change their minds about the policy of isolationism?
5. Why were people in America of Japanese backgrounds placed in relocation centers?
6. What was an important aim of the Allies regarding the Axis powers?
7. Why was there an Allied meeting at Yalta?
8. How much cooperation was there between the United States and the Soviet Union after the war?

# Expand Your Knowledge

1. Find figures that show how many lives were lost by the Allies and by all the countries involved in the war. Compare these with the casualties of the United States. Compare the figures with those from World War I.
2. Prepare a report on the way people with German, Italian, or Japanese backgrounds were treated during World War II.
3. Prepare a report on some helpful or harmful uses of technical knowledge in the United States since the Civil War.
4. Find out about the women's groups of the armed services: WACs, WAVEs, SPARs, WASPs, and Women's Marines. Where and how did they serve, and what veteran's benefits did they receive?

# Los Angeles 1940-1955

*To the Easterner . . . after the long trip across deserts and mountains, southern California is like a new world, a world set off by itself, with definite geographic boundaries of mountain ranges and sea. Los Angeles . . . is like the capital of an empire in miniature; a land that has its own [French] Riviera, its [Swiss] Alps, and its [African] Sahara; a domain that is richer . . . than many an American state. . . . Los Angeles County alone is nearly as large as Connecticut. . . .*

*To many [newcomers in the 1950's], Los Angeles is a modern Promised Land. It amazes and delights [them], and thaws [them] out physically and spiritually. There is a . . . fragrance in the air, and a spaciousness of sky and land and sea that gave [strangers to the city] a new sense of freedom and tempt [them] to taste new pleasures, new habits of living, new religions.*

## Early Days

These feelings of Los Angeles as a "Promised Land" seem to date back to the founding of the city. Spanish Catholic priests under Father Junipero Serra chose the site of a Shoshone Indian village for their San Gabriel Mission in 1771. It was near a river and had rich soil. There was plenty of wild fruit and game. Felep de Neve, the new governor of California, followed Spanish colonial policy by establishing a town at the mission in 1781. Forty-four people who had Indian, African, and European backgrounds were the first settlers.

By 1800, 350 people made up the farming community of *Nuestra Señora la Reina de Los Angeles,* or Our Lady the Queen of the Angels. Their main business was raising cattle. But their town soon developed into the trading, shopping, and social center of southern California. Huge *ranchos* (ranches) run by Spanish *dons* (nobles) grew around the town.

The discovery of gold in northern California in 1848 caused a great demand for the beef raised in southern California. Many of the *dons* prospered for a time, but by 1857, cattle prices dropped. A drought also caused many cattle to die. Some of the Spanish and Mexican ranchers were deeply in debt by the time Anglo-Americans arrived from the East and Midwest to buy up the land. The

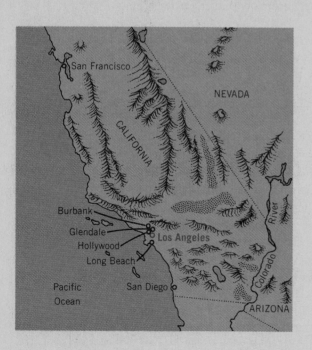

1860's brought an end to much of the *rancho* life around Los Angeles.

## American Control

California had become a state in 1850. Its first Anglo-American legislature divided the state into counties, established county governments, passed new laws, and set up new courts. The Spanish town of Los Angeles gradually took on the look of an Anglo-American city. Houses made of adobe, or sun-dried earth and straw, gave way to houses made of red brick or wood. Formal gardens and white picket fences also appeared. By 1870, horse-drawn streetcars and carriages had taken the place of Mexican wagons.

Railroad connections with San Francisco, and therefore with the nation, were established in 1876. By 1885, the Santa Fe Railroad also reached Los Angeles. Its one dollar fare from Kansas City brought people to the area in great numbers.

A real estate boom in the 1880's caused land prices to rise. New communities like Hollywood, Burbank, Glendale, and Long Beach appeared around the city of Los Angeles. The citrus fruit, olive, walnut, and grape industries in the area grew rapidly. Another real estate boom occurred in the 1920's, and half a million more Americans came to Los Angeles, many of them by automobile. Houses began to fill the valleys and climb the hillsides.

During the depression, droughts, and dust storms of the 1930's, thousands of people moved to California from central, southern, and eastern states. Many of them hoped that Los Angeles would be their "Promised Land."

*The city of Los Angeles*

## Job Opportunities

Some of these people found work in the oil and shipping industries. Sunkist, one of California's citrus fruit industries, offered jobs to others. The aircraft industry was also growing in Los Angeles. By World War II, Los Angeles aircraft plants employed one third of the workers in the city. These workers produced one third of the planes being built in the United States. All of the "big four" rubber companies—Goodyear, Goodrich, Firestone, and United States Rubber—operated plants in the city. There were also several assembly plants owned by major companies in the automobile industry.

Workers in an aircraft plant

## A Mixture of Backgrounds

By 1940, more than one and a half million people lived in Los Angeles. Most of them were "newcomers."

*Only a handful of the inhabitants are descended from pioneer Mexican and American families. Only a small number of adult Angelenos [citizens of Los Angeles] were born in the city. The majority of the inhabitants have come here in recent years, mostly from the Middle West. . . . In addition to American settlers, Los Angeles has attracted immigrants of many races. . . . Mexicans, Japanese, Chinese, Filipinos.*

More black Americans were also seeking that "Promised Land" found in the job market of Los Angeles. The wartime prosperity that brought more people to the city uncovered old problems of prejudice and created new ones. Under the pressures of competition for jobs and housing, people began to lose control of their feelings.

## Mexican-American Problems

Some of these feelings were shown in the "zoot suit riots" of 1943. Several Mexican-American young men had joined together into groups and wore "zoot suits" as a symbol of their unity. This outfit included a flat hat with a wide brim and a long coat worn over baggy pants with tight cuffs. A long key chain hanging from the pants pocket was usually part of the outfit.

In April and May, there had been some minor clashes between these young men and soldiers who were waiting to go overseas. Growing tensions led to serious rioting by early June. Soldiers and sailors roamed the streets looking for and attacking those people they thought were "zoot-suiters."

The federal government feared that the riots were being used in war propaganda against the United States. It insisted that military police settle the trouble quickly. Military passes were canceled, and strict controls were placed on the soldiers and sailors. The street fighting gradually stopped, and order was restored. A citizen's committee was set up by Governor Earl Warren to investigate the causes of these riots. The committee reported that the riots had been caused mostly by racial prejudice against Mexican Americans. Poor police actions and bad newspaper reporting had made matters worse.

## Japanese Americans

The Japanese Americans living in Los Angeles at this time also suffered under prejudice. Some people of the city believed that the Japanese Americans were trying to take over the farming interests in the area. These Japanese had been very successful in farming because they were willing to work hard and do without many comforts in order to build up their farms. When war with Japan had been declared, some people claimed that the Japanese Americans on the West Coast would help Japan. There was no evidence that they would do so. Most of these Japanese were American citizens, and many had been born in this country. Yet, under the fear and excitement of war, many people believed that people in California of Japanese background would betray America. In 1942, the Japanese Americans were moved to relocation camps. They were surrounded by armed guards and barbed wire.

Most of the people forced into these camps were from Los Angeles County. After the war, many of them returned to find that their homes and businesses were gone. A few received some government payment for what they had lost. Full repayment, however, was never made.

*Hindu workers in Los Angeles*

## The Good Life

In the 1950's, many people still came to Los Angeles to find the "good life." This meant having homes in the suburbs, owning cars, having swimming pools in backyards, and having jobs that allowed enough money to enjoy weekend free time. It also meant:

*. . . strange new industries and new agricultural products: movie studios, oil fields, almond orchards, vineyards, olive and orange groves. . . . new and exotic types of people: movie actors and sombreroed Mexicans, kimonoed Japanese and turbaned Hindus. . . . things that are novel and exciting, from Chinese herb doctors to Indian medicine men . . . from a wine-colored stucco dwelling to a restaurant shaped like a hat.*

## Hollywood

One of the first places new people looked for in Los Angeles was Hollywood. Leo Rosten described the magical world of the movie kingdom:

*The legendary Hollywood is . . . full of . . . dazzling maidens, and men like gods. Everyone has flashing white teeth, shapely limbs, three bank-accounts, and a sun tan. Marble swimming pools abound . . . and champagne flows everywhere. Every lawn boasts a [Russian wolfhound], every living room a fireplace, every garage two Cadillacs and a station wagon. The skies are always bejeweled with stars and the blaze of preview lights. Romance breathes from the very stones, and each golden sunset is the [beginning of an unbelievable] night life. . . .*

*[People] have always loved the Cinderella story and have always dreamed of magical success. . . . One reason for Hollywood's stars becoming national idols is that they represent a new type of hero in American experience. Hollywood's children of fortune are not the thrifty newsboys . . . honest, [hardworking], pure of heart; here, instead, are [people] known to be spendthrift and Bohemian [out of the ordinary], people believed to lack impressive brains and given to [wasteful] ways. Yet they have been rewarded with great [wealth] and honored throughout the land. They represent a new type of folk-hero in a society whose [ideal] rests upon hard work and virtuous [behavior]. Furthermore, the public sees the actors at their trade; it sees how they earn their living. The public never sees . . . [Henry] Ford making cars; but it does see Robert Taylor making faces. The visual evidence of the films offers the waitress a chance to compare herself to the movie queen; it gives the shoe clerk a chance to match himself against the matinee idols. It provokes the thought, "Say I could do that . . ." No other industry presents so simple an invitation to the ego.*

## The Only Way to Go

In 1941, a historian wrote:

*The Los Angeles of the future is likely to evolve [develop] along highways. Already there is a vast network of superb roads. In [public transportation], however, Los Angeles is outranked by many a smaller town. . . . old-fashioned trolleys still rattle through the streets. . . . Busses and a few lightweight streamlined trolleys have been introduced. . . . Travel on public [systems] is often a distinct inconvenience because of long waits and overcrowding. In some instances the city has left outlying districts [without] any method of travel except by automobile or on foot.*

By 1950, more than a million automobiles were registered in Los Angeles, and thousands of freeway miles connected the city to its sprawling suburbs. To citizens who were looking for jobs or houses, access to the freeways and to parking spaces was most important. To almost all automobile owners in Los Angeles, cars meant freedom to seek the "good life."

For all Los Angeles residents, however, the increased number of cars meant more pollution of the city's air. In recent years, government leaders had been working on a problem new to the city—smog. This smoke-like fog would sometimes cover the city. It caused people to sneeze and their eyes to burn. Many had difficulty breathing freely. Through the early 1950's, smog alerts became more common. City leaders passed laws to control some of the causes of pollution. They believed that the problem would soon be solved. This was Los Angeles, the "Promised Land" where everything good was possible.

*Los Angeles, the "Promised Land"*

453

# America Is... Challenge

# Cold *W*ar and Crisis     23

By tradition, Americans would have returned to isolationism after World War II, but many believed that it was no longer possible. The oceans would not protect the country in an age when atomic weapons could be taken to targets anywhere in the world by air. Leaders of the government turned to new military and economic policies with other countries. To protect American democratic government, they decided that the United States must help other non-Communist countries defend themselves against communism. Americans feared communism overseas and worried about it in their own government.

The return to a peacetime economy was not easy, although America was the strongest industrial country in the world. People in business,

*In the United Nations, the members can talk over world problems and try to prevent another world war.*

industry, and agriculture all faced changes in their lives. The general economy of the United States continued to grow, and people increased the attention they gave to democracy. Many groups of Americans from all backgrounds began to demand their full share of the country's economic growth and their full rights as its citizens.

# The Cold War

Following World War II, several countries throughout the world gained their independence. Both the United States and the Soviet Union tried to influence these new nations to set up governments that were friendly to them. This competition became so strong that it was called the cold war, or a conflict of ideas and actions without military battles. The cold war threatened at times to lead to a hot, or shooting, war. A hot war with atomic weapons could destroy a large part of the world. It might make life on earth impossible. The growing strength of the Soviet Union and the threat of atomic war had a very strong influence on American leaders in their dealings with other countries.

# The United Nations

Representatives from fifty nations, including the United States and the Soviet Union, met at San Francisco, California, in 1945. They met to draw up a charter for an organization which they hoped would keep the world from future wars. The charter established a United Nations (UN), with a General Assembly where all members could meet to talk over world problems. Smaller groups were formed to study world health problems, world trade, population growth, education, and many other areas of interest. The charter also set up a Security Council whose major task was to prevent war. The five great world powers—the United States, the Soviet Union, France, Great Britain, and China—were permanent members of the Council. Six other nations were elected for two-year terms. Each member of the Security Council had the right to veto any plan that was offered. All UN members agreed that the Security Council could use force to see that accepted plans were carried out.

The UN charter allowed each member to make any other treaties for defense that it wished. As a permanent member of the Security

The League of Nations was officially disbanded in April of 1946 although it had already lost most of its support and influence before and during the war.

Might refer students to League arguments pp. 382-84.

Council, the United States could also veto any plan it disliked. So, many Americans felt that the UN did not threaten the power and rights of the United States as they believed the League of Nations had following World War I. Members of Congress quickly voted to join this new world organization.

# Peacetime Economy

The federal government had made rules to hold down wages, prices, and the amounts of consumer goods in the United States because of the need for weapons and military supplies. During the war, workers had generally received better wages than at any time since the 1920's. There were high employment rates and much overtime pay in most industries. With fewer consumer goods available, many Americans had saved large sums of money. When the war ended, they wanted to spend that money on the things they had been doing without, like refrigerators, radios, and automobiles. Industries were changing over to peacetime products. Manufacturers, however, could not produce goods fast enough to keep up with the flood of money to buy them. This brought about inflation, or a continuing rise in prices.

The general cost of living had risen during the war even with some government controls. Soon after the war ended, many workers in the steel, automobile, mining, and other industries went out on strikes. They hoped for wage raises to help them keep up with the rising cost of living and to make up for lost overtime pay. The federal government approved agreements made in some industries to raise the hourly pay of workers and also the price charged for the product. The cost of living for average Americans continued to go up.

President Truman and Congress did not agree on when to end the wage and price controls and how to stop inflation. When Congress passed a weak bill, Truman vetoed it, and controls ended in June of 1946. Prices for most items rose about 25 percent. The next month, Congress passed a law for new price controls. Some people complained that the set prices for their products were not high enough. When government controls were later removed, prices rose again.

# Truman's Fair Deal

President Truman wanted to continue and to improve many of Roosevelt's New Deal programs. In the fall of 1945, he asked Congress to pass bills for higher Social Security payments and a higher minimum wage. He also asked for a Fair Employment Practices Act to help blacks and other minority groups receive government jobs. Truman called his program the Fair Deal. Congress, however, passed few of the laws that Truman wanted, especially if they meant spending more government money.

In 1947, Congress passed the Labor Management Act, which is also called the Taft-Hartley Act after the members of Congress who offered it. The Taft-Hartley Act made it possible for companies to sue unions for broken contracts. Companies were also to be given sixty-days notice before a strike could be held in industries with interstate trade. Nearly all labor leaders were against the act, and President Truman vetoed it. Congress passed the act over the President's veto. Some workers who had turned against Truman because of inflation and wage controls began to support him again.

Most people seemed sure that the Republican candidate, Thomas Dewey of New York, would defeat Truman in the election of 1948. Truman, however, made a long train tour and gave more than three hundred speeches to people all over the country. In them, he attacked Congress for not passing the Fair Deal programs. Truman won the election by more than two million popular votes.

One newspaper's early edition went on sale with the headline of "Dewey Defeats Truman."

*President Truman's campaign for reelection in 1948 depended heavily on his long train tour across the country.*

In 1949, Congress passed several parts of Truman's program. It increased Social Security payments, raised the minimum wage to 75 cents an hour from 40 cents, and passed the National Housing Act. This act provided money for building 810,000 housing units. Money was also set aside to help families with low incomes pay their rents.

# Economic Aid Overseas

Poverty and starvation faced millions of people in war-torn Europe and other parts of the world after the war. The industries in many countries had been destroyed or badly damaged. The people of the United States quickly sent food, clothing, and other aid to these areas. They sent more than eighteen million tons of food in 1946 and 1947.

In 1947, Secretary of State George Marshall offered a plan in which the United States could give long-range help. Countries in Europe who wanted aid would draw up plans telling how they would use the money. After their plans were approved by the United States, the money was loaned to them. American leaders believed that the Marshall Plan would not only help the economies of European countries to grow, but it would also improve the economy of the United States by increasing world trade. They believed, too, that stronger economies in those countries would help stop the spread of communism. Communism seemed to be most popular in areas where people felt they had no hope of earning a good living.

In 1948, Congress passed Marshall's plan as the European Recovery Act. Within three years, the United States loaned over twelve billion dollars to countries of western Europe to buy machinery, tools, food, and to build roads and factories. Some countries in eastern and central Europe had shown interest in the plan. They did not ask for aid because of pressure from Soviet Russia.

# Central Europe and NATO

At the end of World War II, the Russians occupied Poland, Hungary, Czechoslovakia, Rumania, Bulgaria, Yugoslavia, and the eastern half of Germany. The western Allies—the United States, Great Britain, and France—occupied the western part of Germany. Berlin, the capital and largest city in Germany, was inside the Russian zone. The city was divided into four zones and occupied by each of the four main powers. The western powers, especially the United States, did not agree with Russia over the kind of new German government which should be set up after the war.

In 1948, the western Allies invited the Germans in their zones to elect representatives for their own government. The Russians had hoped that Germany could be united under a government that favored the Soviets. On June 24, 1948, the Russians closed all ground and water

*American and British planes airlifted supplies to West Berlin when the land and sea supply routes were closed in 1948.*

routes into West Berlin. They hoped to force the Allies into giving up control of that part of the city.

President Truman and other government leaders decided not to risk war by ordering the army to reopen the routes by force. Instead, they ordered an airlift of supplies to the people of West Berlin. American and British planes landed with tons of food, clothing, coal, and other supplies for the people in the western section of the city. The plan was a complete success. By May 12, 1949, the Russians ended the blockade and reopened the routes into West Berlin.

American and western European leaders began to feel they needed to cooperate with each other in defense against the Russians. In April, 1949, leaders from the United States, Canada, Great Britain, France, the Netherlands, Luxembourg, Denmark, Norway, Iceland, Italy, and Portugal signed the North Atlantic Treaty. Under it, the countries agreed that their armed forces would work together to stop any possible attack from the Soviet Union. Later Greece, Turkey, and the German Federal Republic (West Germany) also joined the North Atlantic Treaty Organization (NATO).

# Changes in Asia

Changes had been taking place in Asia that influenced American policy toward the countries there. The people of China had suffered greatly from wars with Japan, and in the 1930's, a Communist movement gained strength. Communist leader Mao Tse-tung had the support of many people in the Chinese countryside. The government at that time was under the control of the Nationalist party, led by Chiang Kai-shek.

During World War II, the Nationalists and Communists fought each other as well as the Japanese. When Japan was defeated, the two groups began a civil war for control of the country. The United States gave arms and supplies to the Nationalists while the Soviet Union supplied the Communists. In 1949, the Communists forced the Nationalists out of mainland China. They retreated to the island of Taiwan and continued to receive aid from the United States.

The United States refused to recognize the Communist government of the People's Republic of China and changed its policy toward Japan. American leaders began to see Japan as a possible friend against Communist China. Like West Germany, Japan had a new government based on democracy. The United States helped it to rebuild industries.

In 1951, Japan and the United States signed a treaty that ended the American military occupation but allowed the United States to keep bases in Japan.

# The Korean War

Shortly after the Communist victory in China, a war broke out in Northeast Asia which brought the United States and Communist China into direct conflict. Korea had been ruled by Japan from 1910 until the end of World War II. After Japan's surrender, Russian troops occupied the northern half of Korea, and American troops occupied the southern part. The Russians set up a Communist government in

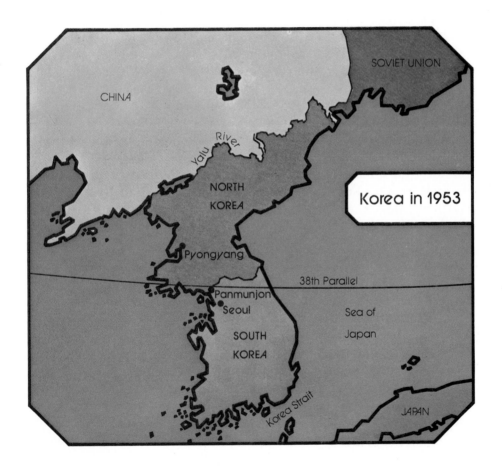

*Cold War and Crisis*

North Korea and built a strong military force there before leaving. Elections held in South Korea set up a representative government and American troops were withdrawn early in 1948.

On June 25, 1950, North Korea invaded South Korea. On June 27, the UN Security Council voted to send forces to stop the invasion. The Russian representative was not at the Council meeting and so could not veto the plan. General Douglas MacArthur was made commander of the UN forces. Most of his soldiers were American and South Korean with small numbers from other UN countries.

The UN forces landed in Korea in September of 1950 and won back the South Korean capital of Seoul. They pushed the North Koreans back across the thirty-eighth parallel, which was the temporary dividing line between North and South Korea. The UN action to stop the Communist invasion succeeded. General MacArthur believed that the UN forces could also defeat the Communists, free North Korea, and unite the country. UN forces moved farther north and captured the North Korean capital of Pyongyang in October. They were soon at the Yalu River border of China. MacArthur believed that the Chinese would not enter the war, but if they did, UN forces could defeat them. In November of 1950, large numbers of Chinese soldiers suddenly crossed the Yalu River and attacked the UN forces. They drove the UN soldiers back across the thirty-eighth parallel into South Korea. In March, 1951, UN forces recaptured Seoul and once more crossed the thirty-eighth parallel.

MacArthur received a hero's welcome upon his return to the U.S. and was allowed to speak before Congress. Most top-ranking American military officers, however, agreed with Truman.

General MacArthur wanted to bomb China and held news meetings where he criticized President Truman for not allowing it. Truman did not want a major war with China. He felt that it would lead to a third world war. Truman replaced General MacArthur with General Matthew Ridgeway. The war continued, but talks began with the North Koreans and the Chinese to find a way toward peace. The talks dragged on for some time.

# The Election of 1952

The states had ratified the Twenty-second Amendment to the Constitution of the United States in 1951. Under this new law, no person would be allowed to run for a third full term as President. President Truman was specifically not bound by the law, but he decided not to run for office again. For the election of 1952, the Democrats chose

Adlai Stevenson of Illinois to run against Dwight Eisenhower, the Republican candidate.

Eisenhower was known to millions of Americans as a winning general of World War II, and he easily won the election. During the campaign, Eisenhower promised to end the war in Korea. He worked toward that goal, and an armistice was signed on June 27, 1953. In the Korean War, over 30,000 soldiers from the United States had died, and more than 100,000 had been wounded. Many Americans were upset by the war because the United States had not won a clear victory after three years of fighting.

American troops continued to be stationed in South Korea. Might have student investigate and report on President Carter's 1977 announcement of a plan to withdraw all of them.

# The Domino Theory

President Truman had declared that the United States would help other nations of the world fight the spread of communism. Under President Eisenhower, an idea about the spread of communism called the "domino theory" became accepted by many American leaders. This theory held that countries were lined up touching each other like the pieces of a game called dominoes. If one country fell to communism, then the countries touching its borders would soon fall also. There was strong Communist activity in Indochina in Southeast Asia, and American leaders feared that the Philippines and Australia might soon be threatened.

At the end of World War II, the French had regained control of their colonies on the peninsula of Indochina. But the peoples of Laos, Cambodia, and Vietnam wanted their independence from France. In Vietnam, the movement for independence was led by Ho Chi Minh and the Communist Vietminh. War had broken out between the French and the Vietminh in 1946. A meeting was held in Geneva, Switzerland, in 1952 to settle the fighting.

Leaders at the conference agreed to give independence to Laos and Cambodia and to divide Vietnam into North and South Vietnam at the seventeenth parallel. North Vietnam was to be controlled by a Vietminh government and South Vietnam by a non-Communist government. It was also agreed that elections would be held to decide which of the two governments would finally rule the whole country. The elections were not held because the South Vietnamese were afraid that the Communists would win.

American leaders had favored the French during the war because they feared a Communist victory in Vietnam. According to the domino theory, the rest of Indochina would then soon fall to communism. When the French army left Vietnam, the United States began to give economic and military aid to the South Vietnamese government.

# McCarthy and Communism

Many Americans were upset by the Communist victories in China, North Korea, and North Vietnam. They feared communism overseas and were hearing stories of communism at home. Under President Truman, the attorney general had been given the power to decide if a

*Senator Joseph McCarthy tried to "sweep" the government clean of Communists in the 1950's. He had no proof for many of his charges.*

government worker's actions were against the interests of the country. Under President Eisenhower, workers were to be fired if their bosses believed they could not be trusted. No evidence of wrongdoing was needed. In 1950, Senator Joseph McCarthy of Wisconsin charged that the United States government, especially the Department of State, was full of American Communists. Members of Congress who spoke out against McCarthy for not proving his charges were also accused of being Communists. Between 1953 and 1954 alone, more than seven thousand government workers lost their jobs.

In 1954, McCarthy began making charges that there were Communists in the army. A Senate committee was set up to check into the charges, and the committee hearings were seen by hundreds of thousands of Americans on television. They saw and heard McCarthy claim that government workers had to give him information even if it was classified, or secret. They also saw that McCarthy gave no evidence to back up his charges. The Senate voted to condemn McCarthy's actions, and public opinion also turned against him. McCarthy lost much of his influence, but not before thousands of Americans came to feel that the government had taken away or ignored many of the civil rights belonging to American citizens.

Note for students the growing influence of television programming.

# *Immigration Laws*

The fear of communism stirred up during the McCarthy period was shown in part of the McCarran-Walter Act of 1952. Under this immigration law, the attorney general could deport people whose actions he felt were not in the country's interests. The law did not define the interests of the United States. The McCarran-Walter Act, however, ended the exclusion of Asian immigrants. It said that people of Japanese background who had been born outside of the United States would be allowed to become citizens. Chinese people born outside the United States had been allowed this in 1943. Similar laws were made for immigrants from India and from the Philippines which had become independent in 1946. The immigrant quotas given to Asian countries were much lower than those for Europe. President Truman had vetoed the bill because of this and because of the powers given to the attorney general to deport people. Congress, however, passed the bill over his veto.

For laws on persons born in the U.S., see 14th Amendment and *U.S. v. Wong Kim Ark* note, p. 322.

# Other Newcomers

In addition to those people who entered the United States under new general immigration laws, thousands entered under special laws during this time. Congress welcomed over 400,000 Europeans into the United States from war-torn countries under the Displaced Persons Act of 1948. In 1953, Congress passed the Refugee Relief Act for the entrance of people escaping from Communist governments. Acts like it were passed again in 1957 and 1958.

Nearly 500,000 people from Puerto Rico came to the United States in the 1950's. Puerto Ricans had been citizens of the United States since 1917, and some had come to the mainland earlier. In 1952, Puerto Rico became a commonwealth of the United States. As a commonwealth, Puerto Rico had self-government, was joined to the United States, but had no vote in Congress. Although some of these newcomers held jobs as social workers, teachers, lawyers, and politicians, most of them had a very hard time earning a living. Earlier groups coming to America had been able to find jobs as unskilled workers. The use of machinery had done away with many of those jobs by the 1950's. Prejudice added to their troubles.

# Era of Good Feelings

Unlike Presidents Roosevelt and Truman, Eisenhower did not believe that it was his duty to give Congress a set plan for government action. He hoped to bring about a new "Era of Good Feelings" in place of the tension Americans had suffered during the depression, World War II, and the cold war. Eisenhower supported several bills to help workers and older citizens. He proposed and Congress passed a law giving money for the building of the interstate highway system to improve transportation. Eisenhower supported other bills passed by Congress including raising the minimum wage to one dollar an hour and changing Social Security to cover more people.

# The Rights of Citizens

President Eisenhower did not press for support of civil rights demanded by black Americans and other groups, but several events took place during his terms that started a great movement toward equality. In 1954, the NAACP brought a court case against the school board of Topeka, Kansas, to admit a young black girl to an all-white school. The Supreme Court ruled in *Brown v. Board of Education of Topeka* that "separate but equal" facilities, which had been approved by law since 1896, had no place in the United States. The Court, under Chief Justice Earl Warren, stated that such facilities would always result in black people getting unequal treatment.

See also *Plessy v. Ferguson*, p. 332.

In May, 1955, the Supreme Court ordered an end to segregated schools. Many white leaders announced that they would not obey the order. In 1957, President Eisenhower ordered soldiers to Little Rock, Arkansas, to keep peace and to enforce a federal court order when eighteen black students entered Central High School there. Desegregation took place slowly in some places and not at all in others, but the Supreme Court ruling of 1954 gave blacks hope that they could win other civil rights denied them since Reconstruction.

In 1955, Rosa Parks, a black woman, refused to give up her seat near the front of a bus in Montgomery, Alabama. She was arrested. In the South, blacks were expected to sit at the back of buses. Black people in Montgomery, led by Martin Luther King, Jr., refused to ride the buses at all until segregation of seating was ended. A year later, the Supreme Court ruled that segregation of bus transportation was unconstitutional. In 1960, young black students refused to leave a lunch counter in Greensboro, North Carolina, until served. This method of protest is called a sit-in. Blacks and some whites staged other sit-ins all over the South to end different kinds of segregation.

In 1957 and 1960, Congress passed the first civil rights acts since the 1870's. Both laws were to help blacks register to vote. The 1957 law created the Commission on Civil Rights to study voting and other rights of citizens and to make suggestions to Congress for new laws.

# *The Continuing Cold War*

While the nation dealt with its troubles over civil rights, the cold war against Russia continued. The war in Korea had brought the possibility of a third world war and one that might involve atomic weapons. Before 1949, the United States was the only country with an atomic bomb. In that year, however, the Russians successfully tested their own. Both nations began to develop rockets and then guided missiles to carry atomic explosives to targets in distant areas.

In 1952, the United States tested a hydrogen bomb which was even more powerful than the atomic bomb. The Russians developed

*The threat of total destruction of the world by atomic war has caused government leaders to work together to maintain peace.*

their own hydrogen bomb the next year. Both nations developed long-range missiles to carry atomic and hydrogen bombs—nuclear weapons. In addition to weapons, the United States and the Soviet Union moved to increase their military strength in other areas. In 1953, a separate agreement was made between the United States and Spain for American military bases there. The Soviet Union set up an organization like NATO in eastern Europe. The Warsaw Pact was signed in

# Daniel James

General Daniel James was born in Pensacola, Florida, in 1920. He was the last of seventeen children in a poor family. James grew up during a time of segregation when there seemed little hope he could reach his dream to be a pilot. He washed airplanes at the Pensacola airport in exchange for rides. His mother wanted him to get a good education and taught him herself at home through the eighth grade. James went to Tuskegee Institute in Alabama in 1937.

During World War II, James learned to fly. He was good and became a flight teacher in the Army Air Corps, James was assigned to an all-black flying group. He joined the Air Force after the war. When President Truman ordered the armed forces desegregated, James had the chance to prove his skill. He flew more than one hundred combat missions in the Korean War and sixty-eight in the Vietnam War.

James received many important assignments. He was a flight leader in a bomber squadron and later was commander of a fighter interceptor squadron. In 1975, James became the first black four-star (top-ranking) officer in the United States military. He was also appointed the commander-in-chief of the North American Air Defense Command (NORAD), which protects Canada and the United States from a surprise air attack.

Secretary of Defense Harold Brown said, at the time of James' death in 1978, that he had "fought for equal rights as he fought for his country, even when doing so was not popular." In his many public speeches, James had emphasized his faith in America and in civil rights. He had worked for racial equality throughout his life, and General Daniel James hoped that his success would inspire other black Americans.

1955 by Poland, Czechoslovakia, Hungary, Rumania, Bulgaria, Albania, the German Democratic Republic (East Germany), and the Soviet Union.

# The Space Race

In 1957, the Soviet Union announced that it had built the first Intercontinental Ballistic Missile (ICBM). This missile could be launched from the Soviet Union to nearly any place on the earth. The competition between the United States and the Soviet Union to build more and better weapons grew stronger. Both countries had the technical ability to reach into outer space. Each began to realize that control of outer space could give a nation a large advantage over enemies. Both nations began work to send a satellite, or container carrying scientific instruments, weapons, or people, into orbit around the earth. The United States was certain that its scientists were years ahead of the Russians in knowledge of missiles to carry satellites.

The American people were shocked when the Soviet Union sent the first successful satellite, called Sputnik, into orbit around the earth in October of 1957. The United States successfully launched its own smaller satellite the next January. People both in and out of government service demanded that American schools teach more science and mathematics so that future American scientists would be the best trained in the world. In 1958, Congress passed the National Defense Education Act to give federal funds directly to colleges around the country. The money was to be spent to build new buildings and to begin projects, mostly in science and research. Later, money was used to help many students attend college through government loans. In the "space race" that followed, the Russians led for several years. But Americans were proud that their satellites were of higher quality.

# Taking Stock

The United States was a very prosperous nation in 1960 by any general measure. Weekly paychecks of factory workers were 15 percent higher than in 1947. More than 65 percent of American families were buying their own homes. The nation had also grown in size as Alaska and Hawaii joined the Union in 1959. The gross national product

(GNP), or the value of all the goods and services produced in the country, had doubled in the last twenty years. But in 1960, millions of Americans still had only a small part of this great prosperity.

*Alaska became a state in 1959. In later years, rich oil fields were discovered there. A pipeline was built to get the oil to the rest of the United States.*

# Television

The first regular television operation began in New York in 1941. Growth of the industry was slowed by World War II. But after the war, stations were built all over the country, and people bought televisions by the millions. By 1960, 88 percent of the nation's families owned television sets; this was more than owned bathtubs or telephones.

John Floherty wrote a book in 1957 about the beginning of television. He described some of the problems with the live shows of early broadcasting.

*Because television was so young it still suffered from childish [problems]. . . . A microphone boom, swinging across stage during a production, knocked an actor cold in sight of millions of viewers. A goat that was supposed to add realism to a scene, destroyed [it] by proceeding to [eat] the scenery. A . . . scientist, demonstrating certain . . . chemical reactions, got his ingredients mixed and nearly suffocated in dense clouds of . . . smoke. The corpse in a [mystery show got] a violent case of hiccups. . . .*

*In its early days television was limited to a [small area] in covering sports because of the . . . weight of its . . . equipment. . . . it used generously long-focus lenses which were nothing more than . . . a telescope through which the camera brought distant objects into close view.*

Floherty interviewed Dr. Vladimir Zworykin, who developed many of the electronic instruments that made television possible. Zworykin gave his views of the future of television:

*. . . I can only give you my personal views for what they are worth. Even in its present adolescent state, it is proving to be [a learning device] of extraordinary power. While it is not yet required equipment in the classroom, I believe the time is not far distant when it will solve many of the economic . . . problems that [are in] our schools and colleges.*

# *Chapter 23 in Perspective*

### Identify

| | | |
|---|---|---|
| NATO | Joseph McCarthy | Rosa Parks |
| Matthew Ridgeway | Earl Warren | Martin Luther King, Jr. |

*Cold War and Crisis*

# Explain

| | | |
|---|---|---|
| cold war | Marshall Plan | Refugee Relief Act |
| Security Council | domino theory | sit-in |
| inflation | McCarran-Walter Act | Warsaw Pact |
| Taft-Hartley Act | Displaced Persons Act | gross national product |

## Check Your Memory of the Facts

1. What conditions brought about inflation after World War II?
2. What parts of Truman's Fair Deal program were passed into law?
3. What events created the need for the Berlin airlift?
4. What led to the Korean War?
5. What was an outcome of the Senate hearings regarding McCarthy's actions?
6. How did Puerto Rico's position change in 1952?
7. What information shows the general economic standing of the United States in 1960?

## Check Your Understanding of the Ideas

1. Why were Americans more interested in joining the UN than they had been the League of Nations?
2. Why did American leaders support the Marshall Plan?
3. Why did the United States, in the late 1940's, change its policy toward Japan? What resulted from the change?
4. How was the Korean War settled?
5. How did the United States become involved in the fighting in Vietnam?
6. Why did President Truman veto the McCarran-Walter Act?
7. Why did President Eisenhower feel the country was ready for an "Era of Good Feelings"?
8. What is important about the Supreme Court ruling in the case of *Brown v. Board of Education of Topeka*?
9. How did the American people react to Sputnik?

## Expand Your Knowledge

1. General Douglas MacArthur was the head of the United States occupation forces in Japan after World War II. Find out what steps were taken there to prepare Japan for democratic self-government.
2. Bring in magazine or family pictures, magazine articles, or examples of music to illustrate American life in the 1950's.

# *A* Time of Discontent  24

The cold war between the United States and the Soviet Union continued into the 1960's. American support to the government of South Vietnam increased but without full public agreement. In the midst of major scientific achievements and national prosperity, there were other problems. Many young people were not following social patterns accepted by their parents. The civil rights movement took on new aims. Like blacks, other minority groups who formed a large part of the poor were demanding better chances for good educations and jobs.

*John F. Kennedy, shown here with his daughter Caroline, was one of the first Presidents to use television effectively in American politics. Kennedy's strength and sense of purpose, as well as his family's energy and appeal, stirred the emotions of many people around the world.*

Sometimes their protests for changes were mixed with violence, often by people against the changes. Even so, there was great progress made in gaining civil rights for many citizens. The 1960's were a time of hope and discontent.

# The Election of 1960

President Eisenhower's second term ended in 1960. That year, the Republicans chose Vice-President Richard Nixon to run for President. The Democrats chose Senator John Kennedy of Massachusetts. In one of the closest elections in American history, Kennedy defeated Nixon by 100,000 popular votes. Kennedy believed in being an active leader. He offered a program for government action which he called the New Frontier. Kennedy said that the New Frontier was a challenge to the people of the United States to honor the civil rights of all Americans, to work toward prosperity for all, and to remain strong in the face of communism. In his inaugural address, President Kennedy told Americans to "ask not what your country can do for you—ask what you can do for your country. . . ."

Kennedy received 34,227,096 popular votes to Nixon's 34,108,546 votes, a difference of less than one percent.

# The New Frontier

In some ways, President Kennedy's program continued other Presidents' ideas. In other ways, it was very different. Kennedy and his brother, Attorney General Robert Kennedy, were quite active in pressing for the civil rights of people of minority groups. President Kennedy offered Congress a civil rights bill. This bill covered more than the civil rights voting laws of 1957 and 1960. It would end discrimination for people seeking homes, educations, and services at public facilities. Congress did not support all of the President's ideas, and his civil rights law was not passed. An amendment to the Constitution, however, made it illegal to charge poll taxes in federal elections. The states ratified the Twenty-fourth Amendment by 1964. Congress refused to pass other Kennedy bills for federal aid to schools, money to build city transportation facilities, and aid to older Americans for medical care.

# Herman Badillo

Herman Badillo, who served as a member of the House of Representatives from New York, was born in Puerto Rico. When he was seven, he got a job mopping out a local theater. When he was eleven, Badillo came to New York to live with an aunt. When she lost her job, he went to live with an uncle in Chicago. He later lived in Burbank, California, where he sold newspapers and mowed lawns.

Badillo returned to New York and worked two jobs while he went to high school. He was a pinsetter in a bowling alley and a dishwasher at a restaurant. Badillo remembers that his restaurant job "didn't pay much, but the meals were free." He later cleared tables and did short-order cooking. He finally quit those jobs because he made the most money as a pinsetter in the bowling alley.

Badillo went to City College of New York to study accounting. He got an accounting job and went to law school at night. After he graduated from law school in 1954, Badillo practiced law and entered politics. During the 1960's, there was much tension between Puerto Ricans, blacks, and whites in New York. Badillo listened to their problems and won their respect. He was successful in combining their support in his election to borough president of the Bronx in 1965. Badillo was elected to the House of Representatives from New York in 1970.

Congress did raise the minimum wage to $1.25 an hour, included more people in the Social Security program, and passed a bill for federal aid to build more houses and apartments. Because many workers were unemployed, Congress lengthened the time they could receive unemployment payments from the federal government. Congress also passed a bill that created a program to train unemployed workers so they could get other kinds of jobs.

# Kennedy and Foreign Affairs

President Kennedy spent much of his time on foreign affairs. He continued the foreign policy of the United States government to stop the growth of communism by being strong, by helping weaker countries meet their needs, and by working toward peaceful solutions to world problems. Kennedy established the Peace Corps to help smaller and poorer countries help themselves. Through it, hundreds of Americans went overseas to train people in other countries to work in teaching, farming, medicine, and other areas. President Kennedy also gave strong support to the space program. He established a national goal that Americans would land on the moon by 1971. An important step toward this goal was reached on February 20, 1962, when John Glenn became the first American to orbit the earth in a space satellite.

Glenn's spacecraft orbited the earth three times in 4 hours, 55 minutes. Two Soviet cosmonauts had orbited the earth in separate missions the year before.

There was great pressure to end the arms race with the Soviet Union. Many people in the UN, including Bernard Baruch of the United States, had worked hard for that since 1945. They wanted to set a policy that would keep the nuclear weapons from being tested in the atmosphere because of the dangers of radioactive fallout. The Soviet Union ended above-ground testing in 1958, and the United States soon followed. However, talks to end testing failed, and the Russians began testing above ground again in 1961. President Kennedy then ordered American scientists to do the same.

# Trouble Over Cuba

In 1959, Fidel Castro had led a successful revolution against the Cuban dictatorship of Fulgencio Batista. At the time, many Americans were friendly toward Castro. But Castro soon set up a Communist government and took over control of American-owned businesses. He received military and economic aid from Russia, and the American government turned against him.

Nearly 600,000 Cubans who opposed Castro left the country and came to the United States. A few of them planned to return to Cuba to try to defeat Castro's government. They were given secret aid by the United States. Kennedy learned that plans had been made for the invasion after he became President. He agreed to let the invasion go ahead but would not allow the American military to give any direct help. The invasion force landed at the Bay of Pigs in Cuba in April of 1961. It was quickly defeated by the Cuban army, and many of the invading troops were captured. Nations all over the world, especially the countries of Central and South America, criticized the role of the United States in the invasion.

*A Time of Discontent*

*United States ships were ordered to Cuban waters to search Russian ships for missiles going to Cuba. The world held its breath as America and Russia worked out the problems of the Cuban missile crisis.*

# A Threat of Nuclear War

Radar devices in Canada and the U.S. would give enough warning to allow the American military to prepare defenses. Missiles launched from only 90 miles away would cut down that warning time drastically.

On October 16, 1962, the President was told of photographs taken from American spy planes which proved that the Russians were building guided missile bases in Cuba. The missiles would be able to hit targets in the United States much more quickly than missiles launched from the Soviet Union. Some of the President's advisers wanted him to order the air force to bomb the missile sites. He refused, fearing an immediate war with the Soviet Union. Instead, he ordered the United States Navy to Cuban waters to search approaching Soviet ships for missiles. Both nations prepared their armed forces for war. Kennedy threatened to invade Cuba if the Russians did not remove their missile bases. The United States asked for a meeting of the UN Security Council to discuss the problem. Many Americans watched the Council meetings on television. Never had the world been so close to nuclear war. Finally, Soviet Premier Nikita Khrushchev ordered the missiles to be removed, and relations between the two countries became less tense for a time.

# *Kennedy's Last Months*

Kennedy did not want to deal with another situation like the Cuban missile crisis. He sought, with much public support, a nuclear testing agreement among the United States, Great Britain, and the Soviet Union. They agreed in July of 1963 to stop testing nuclear weapons in the atmosphere, in outer space, and under water. Over one hundred other nations also signed the treaty, even though most had no nuclear weapons. Neither France nor China signed it.

A step to prevent an accidental war was taken in 1963. A "hotline" was set up between Washington, D.C., and Moscow, the Soviet capital. On this special telephone line, leaders of the two great powers could talk to each other when a crisis threatened to bring about war.

The better relations with the Soviet Union were in contrast to the unrest among people in the United States. Violence had broken out in the South as whites fought against the desegregation of schools ordered by the Supreme Court ruling of 1955. Federal soldiers were used to be sure that James Meredith, a black student, would be admitted to classes at the University of Mississippi. In June of 1963, Medgar Evers, head of the Mississippi NAACP, was murdered at his home.

President Kennedy pressed harder for the civil rights cause, and he again placed bills for it before Congress. To let Congress know of their support and demand for those civil rights laws, several black leaders organized a march on the capital in Washington, D.C., in August of 1963. Martin Luther King, Jr., A. Philip Randolph, and Roy Wilkins, who was head of the national NAACP, were among those who led over 200,000 people in one of the largest demonstrations ever held in the United States. In spite of the urging of President Kennedy and the civil rights march, Congress did not pass the bills. Violence grew worse in the South. That same year, four black children were killed when a bomb exploded in a Birmingham, Alabama, church.

Kennedy believed that making personal appearances as President would help him gain support for New Frontier ideas. On November 22, 1963, while in a parade in Dallas, Texas, he was assassinated. The

*Martin Luther King, Jr., spoke to the crowd during the march on Washington in 1968.*

Amid charges that Oswald was part of a conspiracy, President Johnson named Chief Justice Earl Warren head of a commission to investigate the assassination. The commission reported that Oswald had acted alone.

American people were shocked and filled with grief. The youngest President ever elected to office had also become the youngest to die. Within two hours, Vice-President Lyndon Johnson of Texas was sworn in as President of the United States by Judge Sarah Hughes. Later, Lee Harvey Oswald was caught and accused of Kennedy's murder. Before he could be brought to trial, Oswald was shot and killed by Jack Ruby, a Dallas nightclub owner.

# The Continuing Work

At the time of Kennedy's death, Congress had passed only a small part of the New Frontier program. According to public opinion surveys, more people had come to believe that the nation should seek these new goals. Lyndon Johnson had served in Congress for twenty-five years, and he was very skillful in getting bills passed. As President, Johnson used this experience to continue the plans of John Kennedy. Soon after taking office, he convinced Congress to pass a bill giving over one billion dollars for new college buildings around the country. He won the support of both business and labor people for a cut in taxes. The economy improved in 1964, and the unemployment rate dropped.

# The Great Society

In the 1964 presidential election, Johnson ran against Republican Senator Barry Goldwater of Arizona. Johnson won by more popular votes than any candidate ever received in United States history. President Johnson intended to continue the Kennedy program, but he also presented his own plan. He told Americans that his administration was declaring war on poverty so that the United States would be not only a prosperous society, but also a great society.

Much of Johnson's program was passed by Congress in 1964 as the Economic Opportunity Act. This law set up government agencies like the Job Corps, Volunteers in Service to America (VISTA), and Head Start. The Job Corps trains young people for work. VISTA is like a Peace Corps for Americans living in poor areas of the United States. Head Start is a program to help the young children of low-income families prepare for school. Congress set up the Office of Economic Opportunity to run these programs. It also set aside more than 300 million dollars for communities to use for local improvements.

Congress passed other major bills supported by President Johnson. Medicaid was set up in 1965 to help families with low incomes pay medical expenses. Both the states and the federal government share the cost of the program. Medicare, also set up in 1965, gives aid to older people to help pay their medical bills. The Elementary and Secondary Education Act of 1965 gave federal aid to schools to help pay for books and other needs.

# Civil Rights and Immigration

President Johnson gave further support to laws promoting equality and enforcing civil rights. Congress passed the Civil Rights Act of 1964 which made it against the law to discriminate against anyone using

# I Have a Dream

On August 28, 1963, over 200,000 people took part in a march on Washington, D.C. They wanted to let Congress know of their support for the civil rights movement. Near the Lincoln Memorial, Martin Luther King, Jr., made a speech to the crowd in which he stated many of his hopes for the future.

*Fivescore years ago, a great American, in whose . . . shadow we stand today, signed the Emancipation Proclamation. This . . . came as a great beacon light of hope to millions of . . . slaves. . . .*

*But one hundred years later, the [black person] still is not free; one hundred years later, the life of the [black person] is still sadly crippled by the mannacles [bonds] of segregation and the chains of discrimination; one hundred years later, the [black person] lives on a lonely island of poverty in the midst of a vast ocean of material prosperity. . . .*

*I say to you today, my friends, so even though we face the difficulties of today and tomorrow, I still have a dream. . . . I have a dream that one day this nation will rise up and live out the true meaning of its creed, "We hold these truths to be self-evident, that all men are created equal." I have a dream that*

*one day on the . . . hills of Georgia, sons of former slaves and the sons of former slave owners will be able to sit down together at the table of brotherhood. . . . I have a dream that my four little children will one day live in a nation where they will not be judged by the color of their skin, but by the content of their character. . . .*

*So let freedom ring from the . . . hilltops of New Hampshire; let freedom ring from the mighty mountains of New York; let freedom ring from the . . . Alleghenies of Pennsylvania; let freedom ring from the snow-capped Rockies of Colorado; let freedom ring from the . . . slopes of California. But not only that. Let freedom ring from Stone Mountain of Georgia; let freedom ring from Lookout Mountain of Tennessee; let freedom ring from every hill and molehill of Mississippi. From every mountainside, let freedom ring.*

*And when this happens . . . we will be able to speed up that day when all God's children, [black and white], Jews and gentiles, Protestants and Catholics, will be able to join hands and sing in the words of the old . . . spiritual: "Free at last. Free at last. Thank God Almighty, we are free at last."*

public services such as hotels, gas stations, and parks. Discrimination was also against the law in any program receiving federal money. The Equal Employment Opportunity Commission (EEOC) was set up by law to help women and people of minority groups fight discrimination in job hiring. Congress also passed the Voting Rights Act of 1965 which added to the laws of 1957 and 1960. The law kept states from using a literacy test as a means of deciding who could vote. It also gave federal officials the power to register voters in areas where local authorities were keeping blacks and others from voting.

A new immigration law was passed in 1965 to end quotas favorable to western Europeans. Under it, no more than 20,000 immigrants a year could come from any country. The immigration law of 1965 also set up quotas for hemispheres. Immigration was limited to 120,000 people a year from the Western Hemisphere and to 170,000 a year from the Eastern Hemisphere.

President Truman had vetoed the McCarran-Walter Immigration Act in 1952 because it continued preferential treatment for European immigration. See p. 467.

# Mexican-American Rights Movements

Black Americans were not the only group working toward better conditions. The Community Service Organization (CSO) campaigned in the 1950's to get Mexican Americans in the Los Angeles area to register to vote. Organizations such as the Mexican-American Political Association worked to elect Mexican Americans to political offices.

César Chávez was an early leader of the CSO and a worker for civil rights. He became a strong leader in a nonviolent movement to raise the standard of living for farm workers, most of whom were Mexican Americans. Chávez helped organize the National Farm Worker's Association. Its members joined a strike begun by Filipinos of the Agricultural Workers Organizing Committee (AWOC). These two groups joined the AFL-CIO as the United Farm Workers Organizing Committee (UFWOC). The UFWOC organized strikes and boycotts against large companies that grow grapes and lettuce. Union members demanded the right to talk with the growers to bargain for higher wages and better working conditions. After several years, most of the growers had agreed to union terms. This victory and the leadership of Chávez helped call attention to the problems of Mexican Americans.

Mexican Americans formed other groups to fight for different needs. In New Mexico, the Alianza was begun by Reies López Tijerina. Much of its work has been to regain families' deeds to lands lost to the federal government through treaties such as the Treaty of Guadalupe Hidalgo. In Colorado, Rodolfo (Corky) Gonzales formed the Crusade for Justice mainly to gain civil rights. Jóse Angel Gutiérrez set up a new political party called La Raza Unida in Texas. These groups grew and spread to other areas. They have used different ways at different times to reach their goals. Sometimes, they have used force. At most other times, they have followed the nonviolent example of Chávez.

*César Chávez shook hands with a grape grower after signing a three-year contract. Chávez, a leader of the UFWOC, stresses nonviolence.*

# War in Vietnam

The early years of the New Frontier and Great Society were filled with hope. It seemed that the American people could solve any problem facing them. American leaders believed that the United States military could help defeat the Communists in Vietnam. There was still worry over the domino theory in Southeast Asia. Under President Kennedy, ten thousand American military advisers and much equipment had been sent to South Vietnam. Shortly after Lyndon Johnson became President in 1963, the United States troops became directly involved in the fighting.

The Vietcong—Vietnamese Communist guerrillas—began fighting the South Vietnamese government. Instead of having a full-time army in the field, guerrillas carry out bombings and ambushes against government forces and then return to their homes or hideouts. The Vietcong were difficult to find in the thick jungles and were difficult to stop. Much of South Vietnam outside the major cities was controlled by the Vietcong. They received arms and ammunition from North Vietnam and other Communist countries. Regular North Vietnamese troops also entered South Vietnam to aid the Vietcong.

In 1964, President Johnson announced to Congress that American warships cruising in the Gulf of Tonkin near the coast of North Vietnam had been attacked by North Vietnamese gunboats. He asked to be allowed to use whatever force was necessary to stop any more attacks. Congress passed the Gulf of Tonkin Resolution giving the President this power in Southeast Asia. Johnson ordered the air force and navy to bomb North Vietnamese ports. By the end of 1965, nearly 180,000 United States troops had landed in South Vietnam.

Congress had not declared war against North Vietnam and had only given approval for a limited use of power under the Tonkin Resolution. Any greater use of power would have risked a third world war. Because of this and the ability of the guerrillas to cause great damage with their surprise attacks, the military forces were not able to defeat the Vietcong or the North Vietnamese troops. As the United States became more involved and as more Americans lost their lives, the war lost some of its support from the public.

The United States considered the North Vietnamese responsible for attacking the South Vietnamese and saw the war as a war between two countries. The Communists claimed it a civil war and said that Americans had no right to interfere.

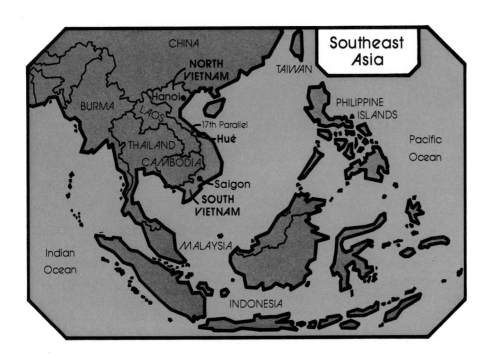

*A Time of Discontent*

# The Generation Gap

Many Americans, mostly young people, were beginning to voice their feelings about the war and the way things were going for the country in general. Many young people were not satisfied that the technical and scientific progress of the 1960's was the answer to the country's troubles. In fact, they thought it was only bringing more. Exciting achievements in space were contrasted to the fact that the possibility of nuclear war was very real. The use of chemicals designed to make farm products grow better sometimes ruins the lakes and rivers and can be harmful to wildlife. The use of bigger and faster automobiles was adding more pollution to the air as were the machines used in large factories. To many young people, too much stress was being placed on owning electric dishwashers, air conditioners, and ownership of goods in general.

The youth showed their dissatisfaction in many ways. Many young men let their hair grow long. Communes were set up to show that friendship and cooperation were valued over material goods. Communes are small communities whose members have the same interests, own property jointly, and share the work. Groups of "flower children," or those who wore or gave out flowers to show they wanted peace instead of war, were found in many cities.

There were many adults who responded to the youth and their ideas. However, there were outcomes which created conflicts among family members and society as a whole. Some youth, in the process of "doing their own thing," broke the law. Some said that real satisfaction in life could only be found by using drugs. The gap between the beliefs and values of separate generations was very great.

# Black Power

By the middle of the 1960's, such large problems troubled the nation that the mood of the people turned from hope to frustration and discontent. Many blacks, especially in northern cities, felt that the civil rights movement was doing little for them. Riots broke out in black neighborhoods. In 1964, there was one in the Harlem area of New York City. In August of 1965, a riot started in the Watts area of Los Angeles which lasted for six days. Thirty-five people were killed, and eight hundred were injured. Buildings were looted and set on fire. While businesses owned by whites were often the target of blacks' frustration, many black people also lost all they owned. Riots took place in Cleveland, Detroit, and several other large cities.

President Johnson appointed a commission to study the cause of the riots. The commission, headed by Illinois Governor Otto Kerner, reported that the riots were the result of frustration over bad housing, overcrowding, high unemployment rates, and the general lack of opportunity. Indeed, the gap between blacks and whites was growing bigger rather than smaller. The average income of black families was less than $5,000; for white families it was well over $8,000. Living conditions for blacks crowded into the central areas of American cities were far from satisfactory.

In the late 1960's, many black leaders began pressing for blacks to have a greater voice in making decisions about their communities. They called this "black power." They wished to see more businesses owned by blacks and neighborhood organizations like schools run by black people. Blacks urged schools and colleges to offer courses in the history of black people. There was increased interest and study in African customs and culture. The "soul" music of performers like Stevie

The idea of black power was debated among black leaders. Some considered it a means of unity and greater cooperation among blacks to reach common goals, others felt that it threatened established cooperation with whites and implied black supremacy.

*In the 1960's, the frustrations in seeking equality for living standards, education, and jobs caused many people in minority groups to riot. Street scenes, such as the one here, occurred frequently.*

Wonder and Aretha Franklin appealed especially to young blacks. Some groups said that they would use violence to protect the rights of black people. This often led to trouble between those groups and the police.

# Martin Luther King, Jr.

Some black leaders, including Martin Luther King, Jr., were against the use of violence and opposed to the separation of black and white people. They did, however, support some of the other goals of black power groups. King was especially concerned about raising the standard of living for poor people. To demonstrate their needs, he planned another march on Washington in 1968. King also went to Memphis, Tennessee, to support a strike of sanitation workers, most of whom were black. They were demanding higher pay. While there, on April 4, 1968, King was shot and killed on the balcony of his hotel room. The American people were shocked and saddened by his death. Riots broke out in several black communities after the news.

James Earl Ray, a white man, was accused of the murder and later arrested. He was found guilty and sentenced to serve ninety-nine years in prison for the crime. Without the leadership of King, the civil rights movement began to lose its unity and effectiveness. Congress passed the Civil Rights Act of 1968 outlawing discrimination in the renting or selling of houses, but it cut spending in the community improvement and Head Start programs.

# On the Way Out

Besides trouble in the United States over civil rights, more problems arose over the war in Vietnam. More troops were being sent there, and by 1968, more than 500,000 American soldiers were fighting in that war. Many young people were refusing to be drafted to fight. People who opposed the war wanted Congress to stop allowing money to be used for it. They said that the war was not legal. It had not been declared by Congress, which was necessary according to the Constitution.

Johnson was upset about the war effort and was also saddened by the violence over civil rights. He announced in 1967 that he would not run again for President. Before he left office, Johnson worked very hard for a treaty to stop the spread of nuclear weapons. Such a treaty was finally signed by the United States, the Soviet Union, and over one hundred other countries in 1968. The powers who had nuclear weapons agreed not to sell or give them to others. Countries without nuclear weapons agreed not to buy or try to make them.

# The Election of 1968

In 1968, three Democrats fought for their party's presidential nomination. Vice-President Hubert Humphrey campaigned on his past experience as Vice-President and as senator. He was a strong supporter of Kennedy's and Johnson's plans. Senator Eugene McCarthy of Minnesota drew support mainly from young people by calling for an immediate end to the war in Vietnam. Senator Robert Kennedy also drew

The "flower children" seen here are demonstrating their belief in the idea of brotherly love and peace instead of war. Many other Americans did not understand them or their chosen life-style.

much support from those opposed to the war and from supporters of the civil rights movement. Before a candidate could be chosen, Robert Kennedy was shot and killed by Sirhan Sirhan on June 5, 1968. An Arab immigrant from Jordan, Sirhan was against Kennedy because he had favored United States support for Israel. Sirhan was tried and found guilty of the murder.

When the Democratic convention was held later, Humphrey was nominated. The Republicans chose former Vice-President Richard Nixon as their candidate. Both of these candidates said they would end the war. Humphrey, however, lost support because he was associated with President Johnson's policies in Vietnam. Nixon further promised to bring law and order to the country after the riots and war protests. George Wallace of Alabama was the candidate of a third party called the American Independent party. He drew support from many whites who were against the desegregation of schools.

Nixon won the close election by 31.7 million popular votes to 31.2 million for Humphrey, with 10 million for Wallace. As the 1960's were coming to an end, Nixon promised that, as President, he would bring the nation back together. Many of the major problems of the 1960's, however, continued to divide the American people in the 1970's.

# Chapter 24 in Perspective See Teacher's Manual, page 131T.

## Identify

| | | |
|---|---|---|
| John Kennedy | Nikita Khrushchev | César Chávez |
| John Glenn | James Meredith | Robert Kennedy |
| Fidel Castro | Lyndon Johnson | Richard Nixon |

## Explain

| | | |
|---|---|---|
| New Frontier | Medicare | Gulf of Tonkin Resolution |
| Peace Corps | guerrillas | black power |
| Head Start | | |

# Check Your Memory of the Facts

1. What type of legislation was passed from President Kennedy's New Frontier program?
2. What problems did the United States have with Russia over Cuba?
3. Near the end of Kennedy's administration, what are some examples of easing of tensions between the United States and Russia?
4. What legislation did Congress pass from the New Frontier and Great Society programs under President Johnson?
5. What immigration laws were passed in the 1960's?
6. How were some Americans reacting toward the Vietnam War by 1968?
7. What agreements were signed by the United States, Russia, and other nations in the 1960's?

# Check Your Understanding of the Ideas

1. How did President Kennedy deal with the Cuban missile crisis?
2. What progress did the civil rights movement make in the 1960's? Make a list showing advances and setbacks.
3. How did Americans become more involved in the Vietnam War?
4. What were some differences in ideas that created a "generation gap"?
5. What were some of the causes of the riots in black neighborhoods in the 1960's?

# Expand Your Knowledge

1. Find an article in a current newspaper that talks about an issue that affects another part of the world. Discuss whether or not the United States is involved. If the United States is involved, discuss how and include how it might affect things within the United States.
2. Find out about civil rights movements in your community. How do you think they have progressed since 1960?

*A Time of Discontent*

# Houston 1950-1975

Located fifty miles inland from the Gulf of Mexico, Houston has grown from a small ranch town into a large American city. Once green with trees and grass, it has become a mass of concrete, steel, and glass in just a short time. Old buildings stand in the shadows of new high-rise apartments, stores, and offices. The city has grown outward in all directions.

## The Beginning

John and Augustus Allen founded Houston in 1836. They named the new town after Sam Houston, commander of the Texas forces and president of the new Republic of Texas. For a while, the town was the capital of Texas.

Houston, like other towns, had large areas of rich land where cotton could be grown. Nearby forests were good sources for building materials. Narrow marshy channels of water called bayous surrounded Houston, making water transportation possible. Later, when railroads were built, the city was on the main route between New Orleans and the West.

## A Seaport

Realizing a need for better transportation of goods, business people early in the twentieth century started a campaign to collect funds to widen the Buffalo Bayou. This was a fifty-mile channel of marshy land leading to the Gulf of Mexico. Over many years, they gradually gained what they wanted—a deeper waterway. This waterway was called the Houston Ship Channel. Beginning in 1914, large oceangoing vessels could load and unload in Houston.

The Houston Ship Channel has been widened and deepened twice since its opening. Walter Farnsworth was captain of the first oceangoing ship to go through the channel. He looked at it forty years later:

*Over there was a cemetery. . . . They must have moved it to straighten the channel. And see that sugar and molasses plant [factory], that was all red clay. And when we got into port they had to tie up our lines to trees, and took eight days to unload our cargo. It's all a little hard to believe now.*

From Houston, ships carried cargoes of cotton, lumber, and sometimes rice to many countries. With the discovery of oil in fields near the city, petroleum and products made from it became the largest cargo.

*The Houston skyline, looking south, in 1972*

## An Industrial Paradise

Other industries producing metals, electronic equipment, machinery, and foods, moved to Houston at that time. The costs of fuel, raw materials, and transportation were lower there than in many other areas of the country. Wages were also lower, but so was the cost of living. For these reasons, both workers and business leaders moved to Houston in large numbers.

The city and other nearby local governments helped attract industry to the Houston area through favorable tax policies. They also made it easier for people to build in Houston by not having any zoning laws. Anyone could put up buildings, shopping centers, or factories wherever they could buy land. Houston has been the only large American city without zoning laws.

## Space City, U.S.A.

In 1961, Houston was chosen by the National Aeronautics and Space Administration (NASA) to be the site for a new center for the government program for putting astronauts into space. The city was chosen because it had excellent land, air, and sea transportation available. The seaport "provided an excellent means of transporting bulky space vehicles to other NASA locations, especially Cape Canaveral." The modern airport offered all-weather jet service. The warm climate of southeastern Texas permitted year-round work. Many local industries could provide needed supplies, and engineers, scientists, and other skilled workers already lived in the area. There were many universities and research laboratories in the city.

*Mission Operations Control Room of the Spacecraft Center*

President John Kennedy visited the Manned Space Center after construction began in 1962. He said:

[During the next five years] *your city will become the heart of a large scientific and engineering community. . . . [In that time] the National Aeronautics and Space Administration expects to double the number of scientists and engineers in this area. . . .*

His prediction came true. Rice University became the first school in the nation to have a department of Space Science. Many more industries and science firms moved to the city. New jobs were created. NASA workers and others moved into the area.

Houston became known as "Space City, U.S.A."

## Always Growing

But even before that time, constant building had been the chief characteristic of Houston. New people meant more building, and the city was always growing. When the city's population reached one million in the 1950's, Jesse Jones, a millionaire who helped build Houston, commented:

*I always said that someday Houston would be the Chicago of the South and it is. Railroads built this town, the port made it big, cotton and cattle kept it rich, oil boomed it, and now we're the chemical capital of the world. Growing, growing, growing, that's Houston.*

The population of Houston has doubled many times. In 1975, it was the fifth largest city in the nation. Some people believe that Houston will be the largest city on earth by the year 2050.

## A City on Wheels

Reaching out in every direction, Houston has been built as a city of the automobile age. "This is not a city for pedestrians," an economist pointed out in 1966. "It was built for people on wheels." In the 1960's, the people of Houston drove 60 percent more automobiles than those of Baltimore. More than half of the land in downtown Houston was paved for either streets or parking lots.

Public transportation service was poor because 95 percent of the people in Houston used cars. Despite efforts to improve service, city buses carried fewer and fewer passengers as they moved slowly among the many automobiles. A newspaper writer said, "A kingly elephant hemmed in by a flood of . . . mice could feel no more helpless than a bus driver in downtown traffic."

Many attempts have been made to solve Houston's traffic problems. One solution is called "CarShare." Drivers with similar schedules and needs are matched by a computer so they can form car pools. The CarShare system was established on a city-wide basis. Many companies urge their employees to use it.

## A Boon to the City

By 1975, most of the people in Houston could afford to live in attractive modern homes in the many miles of suburban areas. The average Houston family lives in a house with many modern conveniences. But unlike the homes of most middle-income families in the North, those in Houston also have air conditioning.

Air conditioning has greatly improved everyday life in Houston. For much of the year, the weather is uncomfortable, and it is sometimes difficult to work in the heat and humidity. In the 1920's, hotels began to install air-conditioning systems. Gradually, almost all public places had it. By the 1970's, many people in Houston began to drive air-conditioned cars from their air-conditioned homes to air-conditioned places of work. In the evening, they could even go to a baseball game in the air-conditioned Astrodome, Houston's multimillion dollar sports stadium.

## The People of Houston

A large number of the people living in Houston have come from other parts of Texas and the United States. Some have come from other countries. Since so many people of different cultures live in the city, organizations have been formed to help them. One example is the League of United Latin American Citizens (LULAC). It was founded in the 1950's to help Mexican Americans, Latin Americans, and other Spanish-speaking citizens adjust to life in the United States.

The major goal of the LULAC is to help stop discrimination and prejudice against these citizens. This is partly done by helping people find jobs and helping them learn English. The "School of 400" was started to help Spanish-speaking children learn at least four hundred English words.

The LULAC also gives scholarships to students going to college or technical school.

New opportunities began to open up for black people and Mexican-American people in Houston in the 1960's and 1970's. Some Mexican Americans in the 1970's sought better employment. "Why aren't Mexican Americans hired?" a reader complained in the Houston *Post* newspaper about the jobs at one Texas government agency. The head of the agency replied that Mexican Americans with college degrees and work experience had not been taking the qualifying examination. He invited them to do so.

Blacks at that time still worked at less-skilled, lower-paying jobs and lived in the poorest housing in Houston. But the growing awareness of the civil rights movement helped to improve their lives in many ways. Although there were still barriers, some blacks began to advance professionally and politically.

*Barbara Jordan of Houston*

## Taking the Opportunity

The rise of Barbara Jordan to national prominence showed how a black woman could take advantage of new opportunities. Barbara Jordan, born in Houston in 1936, is the daughter of a Baptist minister who also worked as a warehouse clerk. As Jordan went through the segregated schools of Houston, her father expected good grades and wanted her to speak correct English. She did not disappoint him. Jordan was an outstanding student at Texas Southern University and then attended Boston University Law School. Looking back on her childhood, she said:

*When I was growing up, we didn't focus on being poor and black. Segregation was there. It was the way of life, and if you were fortunate and would just drive hard*

*enough, you might be able to break out of it a little bit.*

In 1962, Jordan ran for the Texas House of Representatives and lost. She learned that "It was necessary to be backed by money, power, and influence." She commented:

*I considered abandoning the dream of a political career in Texas and moving to some section of the country where a black woman candidate was less likely to be considered a novelty. I didn't want to do this. I am a Texan; my roots are in Texas. To leave would be a cop-out. So I stayed, and 1966 arrived.*

In 1966, Jordan had gained the needed support and was elected to a seat in the Texas Senate. Barbara Jordan was the first black to be elected to such a seat since 1883.

She was a hardworking member of the state senate and won election to the United States House of Representatives in 1972. Looking back, she said, "I'm glad I stayed in Texas."

## A Good Place to Live

For many of the young people growing up in Houston, there are great advantages. Splendid buildings, the Astrodome, and other recreational facilities in the city, give residents a sense of pride. An even greater pride is seen in the achievements of the scientists and astronauts at the Space Center. There are excellent medical facilities. Patients come from many countries for surgery at the Texas Medical Center and the Texas Heart Institute. The University of Houston and the privately-owned Rice University offer an excellent education—the opportunity to become a doctor, lawyer, engineer, teacher, or just about anything. There is a symphony orchestra, numerous musical and theatrical groups, and an art museum.

Many have watched the people of the city learn how to deal with some of the problems of air pollution, water pollution, and rapid growth. They have seen some solutions to the automobile problems of the city begin to work.

As a rapidly growing city of the space age, Houston has had many problems, but it also offers many advantages. Most young people in Houston think it is a good city in which to grow up, a good city in which to live.

*The city of Houston*

# Challenges
# for America

Aim: to help students recognize that American attitudes, policies, and institutions change and that this is the challenge facing all Americans.

Events of the 1960's and 1970's gave the American people many reasons for both hope and worry. In foreign affairs, the country was able to withdraw from the longest and most costly war in its history. Policy changes by President Nixon promised new relations with other countries and possible world peace.

At home, civil rights movements lost some strength as the federal government gave less attention to new laws or to policies that ended segregation. Many groups tried harder to improve their opportunities for education and jobs. The nation went through its worst political

*The landing of American astronauts on the moon in 1969 was truly "one small step for a man, one giant leap for mankind."*

scandal between 1972 and 1974. It tested the strength of American government and the faith of the American people in their leaders.

In 1976, the United States celebrated its bicentennial birthday. The nation had undergone very great changes in its first two hundred years, and its citizens could expect more changes in the years to come.

# A Giant Leap

In 1969, Americans achieved the goal set for their space program by President Kennedy eight years before. On July 20, astronauts Neil Armstrong and Edwin Aldrin landed on the surface of the moon while astronaut Michael Collins circled around it in the command ship. Armstrong became the first human to step foot on the moon. As he did so, Armstrong told millions of people watching the event on television back on the earth that it was "one small step for a man, one giant leap for mankind." The United States made five more moon landings by the end of 1972. World scientists will spend years studying the samples and information brought back to earth from these trips to outer space.

In 1961, President Kennedy had established a national goal to land an American on the moon by 1971. See p. 479.

# Nixon and Vietnam

Candidate Richard Nixon had told the American people that he would gain peace in Vietnam. As President, Nixon announced a policy to do that. He called it Vietnamization. Under this policy, the United States would continue to give aid to South Vietnam, but American soldiers would be slowly withdrawn from the fighting. The South Vietnamese would take over the fighting alone. Peace talks between the sides fighting in Vietnam had begun also. President Nixon insisted on the release of all American prisoners of war before any agreement could be made.

In 1969, the first groups of American soldiers came home. In 1970, however, American troops joined with the South Vietnamese to invade neighboring Cambodia. The North Vietnamese were using Cambodia to bring soldiers and supplies into South Vietnam. President Nixon said that he wanted to destroy the North Vietnamese bases in Cambodia to prevent attacks while American soldiers were being withdrawn. Protesting citizens and members of Congress charged that Nixon

The Communists used the Ho Chi Minh trail in Laos to bring troops and supplies from the North to the South through Cambodia. Doing this, they avoided contact with American and South Vietnamese troops operating in South Vietnam.

*Challenges for America*

# Walk on the Moon

On July 20, 1969, American astronauts became the first people to ever land on the moon. Their mission was called Apollo 11. Two years later, David Scott and James Irwin landed on the moon, the fourth team of astronauts to do so. Scott, the commander of the Apollo 15 mission, later expressed his thoughts about his experience.

*Sixty feet above the moon, the blast of our single rocket churns up . . . lunar dust that seems to engulf us. . . . With an abrupt jar, our lunar module, or LM, strikes the surface and shudders to rest. . . .*

*When we descend the ladder of the LM and step onto the moon's surface, Jim and I feel a . . . sense of freedom. For five days we have been crammed into the tight confines of the spacecraft that brought us here. Now, all at once, we regain the luxury of movement. . . .*

*As we advance, we are surrounded by stillness. No wind blows. No sound echoes. Only shadows move. Within the space suit, I hear the reassuring purr of the miniaturized machines that supply vital oxygen and shield me from the blistering 150 [degree] surface heat of lunar morning.*

*. . . Without the familiar measuring sticks of our . . . planet—trees, telephone poles, clouds, and haze—we cannot determine whether an object stands close at hand or at a considerable distance, or whether it is large or small. . . . gradually the moon becomes a friendlier place. A thought occurs to me: Would human beings born on the moon be able to find their way among the trees and clouds of earth?*

*. . . We feel a sense of pride in the accomplishments of our program, yet we cannot escape a sense of deep concern for the fate of our planet and [its people].*

*This concern has led us to add certain items to the equipment we are leaving on the moon. . . .*

*. . . A plaque of aluminum affixed to the deserted LM [shows] the two hemispheres of our planet; upon it are engraved the name of our spacecraft, the date of our mission, and a [list] of the crew. From these data, the equipment, and even the [size] of our footprints, intelligent beings will readily [discover] what kind of creatures we were and whence we came.*

*In a little hollow in the moon dust we place a . . . figurine of a [person] in a space suit and beside it another metal plaque bearing the names of the 14 . . . Russians and Americans . . . who have given their lives so that [people] may range [through space]. . . .*

*Occasionally, while strolling on a crisp autumn night . . . I look up at the moon. . . . I do not see a hostile, empty world. I see the radiant body where [we have] taken [our] first steps into a frontier that will never end.*

was trying to step up American action in the war as President Johnson had done. Nixon answered that Vietnamization would continue.

In 1973, the United States, South Vietnam, North Vietnam, and the Vietcong signed an armistice agreement in Paris, France. The United States agreed to withdraw all of its remaining troops. Elections were to be held to determine the government of South Vietnam. Over fifty thousand Americans had been killed and 300,000 wounded.

# The Middle East

The area of northeastern Africa and western Asia is called the Middle East. Because of its location, the Middle East has long been important to trade, and its lands are rich in oil. Much of the area was controlled by England and France until after World War II. Weakened by the war, both countries gave up most of their power there. As newly independent countries were formed, the United States and the Soviet Union took great interest in the Middle East. Both countries needed the oil of the Middle East trade, and the Soviet Union hoped to gain a naval base on the Mediterranean Sea. Both countries had also immediately recognized the Jewish state of Israel when it was formed on part of the land of Palestine in 1948. Arab and Muslim people made up most of the population of Palestine, and they fought the Jews over this land for many years. The Jews successfully defended their new state and took more land in these wars.

Arabs and Israelis fought wars in 1948, 1956, 1967, and 1973.

The Soviet Union recognized Israel but supplied the Arab nations with military weapons. The American government supplied Israel with weapons but tried to keep friendly relations with the Arab nations also. A serious war between the Arabs and Israelis took place in 1973. American leaders feared that fighting in the Middle East might lead to a major war between the United States and the Soviet Union. Secretary of State Henry Kissinger helped to arrange a cease fire, or halt in the shooting, and President Nixon visited the leaders of several Arab nations shortly after that. He wanted to keep a working relationship with these countries.

# New Policies

The United States also sought to improve relations with China and the Soviet Union. These two countries were fighting a cold war with each other and were willing to ease tensions with the United States. Soviet and Chinese forces had clashed in a border dispute in 1969. China had also developed nuclear weapons of its own and was testing long-range missiles. Their forms of Communist government were not alike, and Soviet leaders worried about China's growing power.

Nixon and Kissinger worked out a policy toward the Soviet Union called "detente," which is a French word that means to relax tensions. They began talks with the Soviet Union leaders in 1969 to lower the number of nuclear weapons that each country would make. An agreement about that was signed in 1972 when Nixon became the first United States President to visit Moscow. Earlier that year, he had also become the first President to visit Peking, the capital city of Communist China.

The American President was welcomed in Peking, partly because the United States had changed its policy toward the admission of Communist China to the United Nations after more than twenty years. The United States had recognized only the Nationalist Chinese government until 1971. That year, Communist China was given a seat in the United Nations. The Nationalist representatives, having lost their seat, returned to Taiwan.

*With the changing attitude of America toward Communist China, Nixon became the first President to visit its capital, Peking.*

# The New Federalism

The increasing costs of the Vietnam War had stirred inflation in the United States, and prices of homes, food, clothes, and other goods rose higher each year. President Nixon and his advisers believed that they could lower prices if the government spent less money in some areas and made less money available for others to spend. One of the steps taken to do this was raising the cost of borrowing money. As more people stopped borrowing and buying, businesses began to cut back their production of goods. Unemployment increased. Prices, however, continued to rise.

President Nixon had stated his view that there should be little government regulation of the economy. In 1971, he changed his stand and received authority from Congress to begin wage, price, and rent controls. These controls slowed the rate of inflation but did not encourage new business or lower the number of people without jobs.

In 1972, Congress passed the State and Local Fiscal Assistance Act to begin a revenue, or tax money, sharing plan that Nixon had suggested three years earlier. Under it, the federal government would give back part of its revenue to the states, counties, and cities. There would be few rules about how the money should be spent. The federal government had given money to local governments before, but it was only to be spent on certain things like building highways or low-cost housing.

Many members of Congress agreed with federal revenue sharing. They felt that local governments knew more about their citizens' needs than did officials in Washington. Others were against revenue sharing. Some mayors of large cities said that their governments would receive less money than under the old federal programs. Many people, including most black leaders, feared that the money would not be used to help all the people equally without more federal rules. The 1972 revenue sharing act set aside more than thirty billion dollars to be given out over a five-year period. State governments received one third of the money, and local governments received the rest.

The "New Federalism" was a term used to describe President Nixon's attempt to reverse the federal-state-local government relationship. He said that he wanted to lessen the power of the federal government and return more decision making to local levels.

# School Desegregation

Many leaders of minority groups withdrew support from Nixon because of his policies on government spending and revenue sharing. They also charged that Nixon and Attorney General John Mitchell

Segregation in the South had been referred to as *de jure*, or "by the law," while Northern segregation was considered *de facto*, or "in actuality."

were not doing enough to carry out the 1955 Supreme Court order to desegregate public schools. Early work in desegregation had begun in the South because schools there were clearly segregated by law. During the late 1960's and early 1970's, however, more people began to call for an end to segregation of schools in the North where the reasons were not so clear. There were many more separate neighborhoods of white or black people in the North. School boundary lines were usually drawn up to keep schools within the neighborhood boundaries. Most white children went to their neighborhood school which meant that they attended classes only with other white children. The same was true for black students.

Civil rights leaders and groups like the NAACP and the Congressional Black Caucus favored busing students from one neighborhood to another if necessary to end segregation. But busing was not accepted by many black and white people as the best way to desegregate the schools. Some parents refused to let their children go to school outside their own neighborhoods. Parents also worried about the safety of their children if violence was used to stop busing. School leaders often complained that their school systems could not afford the cost of busing for purposes of desegregation. President Nixon asked Congress to pass a law against busing, but Congress did not provide one. By the middle of the 1970's, federal courts had increased their orders to use busing when this appeared to be the only way to bring about the desegregation of schools.

# Women's Rights

Women made up more than half the country's population by the 1960's, and more women's groups became active in working for better economic opportunities and legal equality. There had been a sharp increase in the number of women working outside their homes after World War II. By 1970, more than 40 percent of all jobs were held by women. Most women faced discrimination in the kinds of jobs they could find and in the amount of money they were paid. In the middle 1970's, most women worked as secretaries, teachers, sales clerks, nurses, house cleaners, hairdressers, cashiers, and typists. They earned only 60 percent as much money as men and were generally paid less even for doing the same jobs as men. Very few women had opportunities to move into higher level jobs in most companies. Women like Katharine

These are the same "traditional" occupations for women.

# The United States of America

WASH.
- Olympia
- Salem
OREGON

MONTANA
- Helena

IDAHO
- Boise

NORTH DAKOTA
- Bismarck

MINNESOTA
St. Paul

MICHIGAN

N.H.
Concord
VT.
Montpelier
ME.
Augusta

NEVADA
- Carson City
Sacramento
San Francisco
CALIFORNIA
Los Angeles

WYOMING
- Cheyenne

SOUTH DAKOTA
- Pierre

WISC.
- Madison

Lansing
Detroit

N.Y.
Albany
CONN.
Boston
MASS.
Plymouth
Providence
R.I.
Hartford

SALT LAKE CITY
UTAH

NEBRASKA
- Lincoln

IOWA
- Des Moines

Chicago
IND.
Muncie
Springfield
ILL.

OHIO
Columbus
Indianapolis

P.A.
Harrisburg
N.J.
Philadelphia
Trenton
New York
Dover
DEL.
Annapolis

COLORADO
- Denver

Topeka
Abilene

Jefferson City

KANSAS

MISSOURI

KENTUCKY
Frankfort

W. VA.
Charleston
MD.
VA.
Richmond
Washington, D.C.
(Secota)

ARIZONA
- Phoenix
Santa Fe

NEW MEXICO

Oklahoma City
OKLAHOMA

ARKANSAS
Little Rock

TENNESSEE
Nashville

N.C.
Raleigh

Columbia
S.C.

TEXAS
- Austin
Houston

MISS.
Jackson

LA.
Baton Rouge
New Orleans

ALA.
Montgomery

GEORGIA
Atlanta

FLORIDA
Tallahassee

ALASKA
- Juneau

HAWAII
Honolulu

Graham, chairperson of the board of directors of the Washington Post Company, Barbara Walters, news personality, and Chien-Shiung Wu, a professor of physics at Columbia University, were some of the exceptions. Very few women were accepted in schools for training as doctors, lawyers, and other professional roles.

Groups like the National Organization for Women (NOW), started in 1966, worked to end discrimination against women in education and jobs. They spent many of their early years in trying to make more women aware of the difficulties they faced. Women, like men, were very accustomed to thinking of only certain roles as being acceptable for women. Women's groups worked to see that laws like the Civil Rights Act of 1964 and the Equal Employment Opportunity Act of 1972 were carried out. Through the Equal Employment Opportunity Commission, they took cases to court to force employers and unions to obey the laws.

The National Women's Political Caucus was formed in 1971 to help women get elected to political offices. Women in this group felt

Title VII of the Civil Rights Act of 1964 forbids discrimination by employers or unions.

*By the 1970's, women in America had the right to vote, but they still had to work for their rights to equal opportunities in education and the working world.*

that many men were not aware of certain issues important to women. These included programs like the one offered by Representative Barbara Jordan of Texas to include homemakers in the Social Security plan. The issue of building more child-care centers was also very important to some women who worked outside the home to support their families.

Congress proposed the Equal Rights Amendment to the Constitution in 1972. This act states that equality of rights under the law cannot be denied any citizen on account of sex. Supporters of the act say that equal rights for women must be clearly guaranteed in the Constitution. Those who are against the amendment say that there are enough laws to guarantee women's rights and that the amendment is not needed. There are other arguments offered by both men and women against the amendment. Some feel that it could make it necessary for women to serve in combat roles in the armed services or that it would weaken American family life because women would lose their customary right to be supported by husbands. To become law, the amendment would have to be ratified by thirty-eight states no later than 1979.

# The Election of 1972

In 1972, President Nixon ran for reelection against Senator George McGovern of South Dakota, the Democratic candidate. McGovern promised an immediate end to the Vietnam War, less spending for military purposes, and more spending for the poor. Many people thought that he would do well with strong support from young voters. The Twenty-sixth Amendment, lowering the voting age from twenty-one to eighteen years, had been ratified in 1971. Nixon did little campaigning but scored a huge victory. He won the electoral votes of every state except Massachusetts and 61 percent of the popular vote.

# Watergate

In 1973, the American people learned of a political scandal that involved the President and members of his staff. In June of 1972, five people had been arrested while breaking into the Democratic party headquarters office in Washington, D.C. The office was located in the

Watergate office building, and the scandal that followed was called Watergate. While investigating the break-in, federal officials learned that the people arrested worked for members of the committee to re-elect President Nixon in 1972. At their trial, some of the people pleaded guilty, and the others were found guilty by the jury. They were sentenced to prison.

Watergate burglars were gathering information about Democratic campaign plans, candidates, and finances.

The *Washington Post* led other newspapers in printing a series of articles that charged members of the President's staff with wrongdoing. The charges included planning the break-in, as well as other illegal activities against Democratic party candidates for the presidential nomination. Both the Senate and the House of Representatives set up committees to investigate the charges. In July of 1973, the Senate committee began to hold public hearings that were seen across the nation on television. Millions of Americans became familiar with Senators Sam Ervin, Daniel Inouye, Howard Baker, and others as they questioned witnesses hour after hour. Presidential aide John Dean told the committee that President Nixon knew of the break-in himself shortly after it happened. Nixon had not reported the crime, so he was guilty of an illegal act if Dean's charges were true. The committee further learned of a tape recording system used in the White House for all talks in which the President took part. Committee members believed that the tapes might prove whether or not the President had known of the Watergate break-in and had used his power to cover it up.

The President maintained that it was his "executive privilege" to control any documents concerning business conducted by his office. He said this was necessary to maintain separation of powers between the three branches of government as provided in the Constitution.

President Nixon denied any knowledge of the break-in. But he refused to turn any tapes over to the special prosecutor, Archibald Cox, who had been appointed in May of 1973 to head the Department of Justice's investigation of Watergate charges. When Cox insisted on getting the tapes, the President had him fired. The public was outraged. A new special prosecutor, Leon Jaworski, was appointed later with the promise that he could take the President to court to obtain the tapes if necessary.

# The Vice-Presidents

During the time of the Watergate tapes issue, the American people received another blow to their faith in government leaders. Vice-President Spiro Agnew resigned from office in October, 1973. Federal officials were investigating charges against Agnew of accepting bribes while he was governor of Maryland and later as Vice-President.

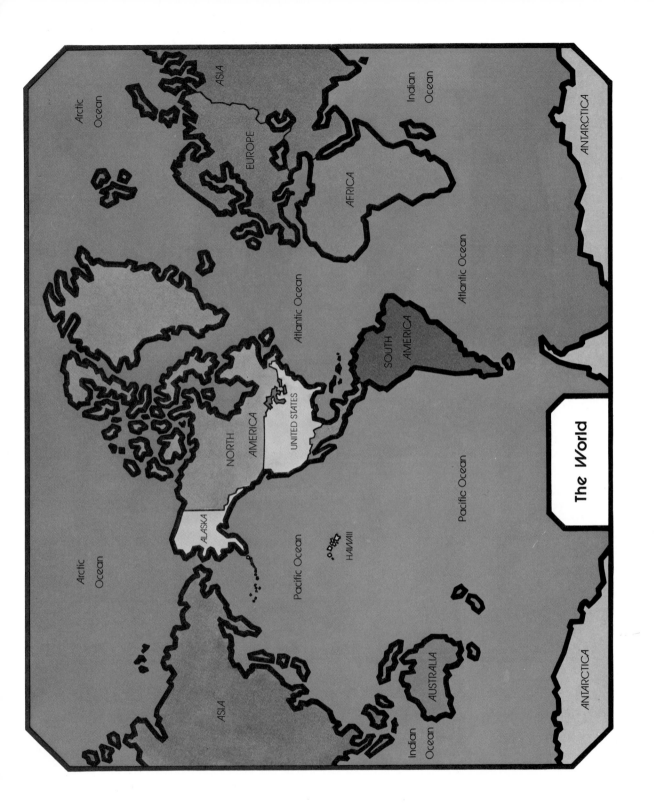

The World

At a later trial on charges of cheating on his income tax, Agnew was fined ten thousand dollars and put on three-years probation.

To fill the office of Vice-President, President Nixon appointed Republican Representative Gerald Ford of Michigan. After hearings, Congress approved the appointment. Ford was the first person to become Vice-President under the Twenty-fifth Amendment which had been adopted in 1967. It set up rules for filling the office of President or Vice-President if either person is unable to carry out duties.

# Impeachment

In March of 1974, presidential aides H. R. Haldeman and John Ehrlichman, Attorney General John Mitchell, and several others were charged with covering up the Watergate break-in and lying about it to government officials. At a later trial, they were found guilty and sentenced to prison.

*When Gerald Ford became President, one of his most difficult tasks was to renew the faith of Americans in their government.*

In April, the President turned over written copies of some of the White House tapes and said that they proved his innocence. To many readers, they seemed to prove many of the charges against him. In July, the Judiciary Committee of the House of Representatives held six days of televised hearings. During this time, they debated and then approved three articles of a bill of impeachment against the President—for blocking justice, misusing power, and refusing to supply the committee with ordered information. On the evening of August 8, 1974, Nixon appeared on national radio and television and announced that he would resign as President. On August 9, Gerald Ford became the thirty-eighth President of the United States.

Nixon was the first American President to resign from office, and Ford was the first President who had not been elected to either the presidency or vice-presidency.

# A Difficult Time

President Ford took office at a time when most Americans were very upset by the scandal of Watergate and seemed to have lost faith in many federal government leaders. President Ford was respected for long years of service in Congress and reminded the American people that: "Our long national nightmare is over. Our Constitution works. Our great Republic is a government of laws and not of men."

President Ford said that he felt it was best for the nation to put the scandal of Watergate behind them as soon as possible. Although Nixon had resigned, he was still open to court charges. Within a month of taking office, President Ford gave an official pardon to Nixon for any crimes that he might have committed. Nixon would never have to stand trial to prove whether or not he had been involved in the Watergate cover-up.

A person may not be pardoned after being impeached. Reference the Constitution, Art. II, Sec. 2.

The pardon hurt the popularity of both President Ford and the Republican party. In the Congressional elections of 1974, Democrats won many seats from the Republicans. Throughout his term of office, Ford could not develop his own program for the nation without the help of Democrats in Congress. He had only a little more success than President Nixon in controlling inflation. The high price of imported oil had added to an energy crisis in America.

After the Arab-Israeli War of 1973, Arab nations with large oil resources had stopped selling oil to nations friendly to Israel. When they lifted this embargo in 1975, the new price of oil was four times higher than in 1973. Ford asked Americans to make special efforts to save on fuel. He asked Congress to pass laws to help Americans find new sources of energy.

Ford carried on Nixon's policy of detente with the Soviet Union. Late in 1974, he met with Soviet leader Leonid Brezhnev at Vladivostok, Russia. There, they signed another agreement to limit the making of nuclear weapons which cut some of the high costs of the arms race. In 1975, the United States and the Soviet Union also cooperated in a space mission to successfully join two spaceships in flight. Soviet cosmonauts and American astronauts visited each other's countries before and after the mission.

Congress was interested in cutting costs in other areas of government spending. It refused to vote for new funds to aid South Vietnam. In 1975, two years after American soldiers had been withdrawn, the Communists defeated the South Vietnamese and gained control of the whole country. More than a million Vietnamese had died in the many years of fighting, and large areas of the countryside had been destroyed. In September of 1977, Communist Vietnam took its place in the United Nations.

# *Birthday Parties*

On July 4, 1976, the United States celebrated its two hundredth birthday. Most communities enjoyed the celebrations all year long with special programs and activities. On Independence Day itself, there were plays, speeches, parades, and fireworks throughout the country. For many citizens, it was also a time to look again at the ideas for which the people of America had declared their independence in 1776. It was clear that ways of living in America had changed greatly in the last two hundred years.

In the 1770's, most Americans earned their livings by farming. Two centuries later, most Americans lived in cities and earned their livings in factory or business work. In 1970, only 5 percent of all the Americans who worked were farmers. They, however, produced enough food to meet the needs of the people of the United States and to export large amounts to other countries of the world.

In the 1970's, large corporations controlled much of the country's economy. Of the total money received by companies and corporations in the United States, over 90 percent of it was controlled by less than one fifth of those companies and corporations. The improvements that helped bring continued growth in the economy and in the size of the

*Countries around the world sent "tall ships" to the United States during the bicentennial in 1976. Many American boaters also joined the celebration in New York's harbor.*

companies also brought problems. Farmers used chemicals to increase the size of and shorten the time needed to grow many crops. Mining companies used giant machinery to dig more ore and coal. People began to worry more about the effects on the environment—the air, soil, and water.

Americans in the 1970's demanded protection for the environment. Mining companies were required to put soil back when they had stripped it away. Factories had to clean up chemical wastes before returning water to rivers and lakes. The federal and state governments began to make laws against the use of certain chemicals found to be harmful to humans and animals. This protection of the environment and of people's health had a price. The cost to businesses for cleaning up or preventing damage was passed on to their customers in higher prices for products. People began to question how much they were willing to pay for environmental protection.

# Immigration Changes

With the exception of the American Indians, the United States is a nation of immigrants. Throughout most of its history, the country's largest number of immigrants had come from Europe. Laws to control immigration had greatly reduced the number of new immigrants in the twentieth century. Healthy economies in European countries also lowered immigration from there. More people entered the United States from countries in the Western Hemisphere and Asia. Filipinos are the largest Asian immigrant group in America, although they are not yet the largest group of Asian Americans. Following the Vietnam War, the United States welcomed over 100,000 Vietnamese who were fleeing from the Communists. Many Mexicans continue to come to the United States as immigrants. Many of them also enter the country illegally to work in unskilled jobs. Puerto Ricans, who are citizens of the United States, came to the country in large numbers in the 1950's, but in the 1970's, more returned to Puerto Rico than entered the mainland of the United States.

# Indian Issues

Maria Martinez is a resident of San Ildefonso Pueblo in New Mexico. She and her husband Julian rediscovered the old Pueblo methods of making pottery. Their business success greatly aided the economy of the Pueblo people and helped to renew interest in American Indian crafts.

Some American Indian groups try to keep their traditional ways while living in American society. People like Maria Martinez have been able to improve their living standards by selling products of their crafts and arts. Many Americans have come to appreciate the history and culture of some Indian groups through these works. But even in the 1970's, most American Indians are the poorest and least educated of all Americans. Those Indians who left their reservations to work in cities had difficulty finding jobs. Although life on the Indian reservation is very poor, it continues to be the center of Indian life. More than 50 percent of all American Indians leave it to work outside at some time in their lives. Only 20 percent of those remain away.

In the 1950's, federal government policy was to make Indians enter fully into American society by ending government recognition and support of the reservation. One such reservation belonged to the Menominee Indians of Wisconsin. The land which had been set aside for them by treaty and federal law became a county in Wisconsin through the new policy. The Menominee tried to hold the land by forming a corporation, but their sawmill and lumber business did not make enough profit to pay the taxes due. In 1973, the Menominee finally won a court case that returned the land to a reservation. The new reservation was smaller, however, than the land they had formerly held.

Land continues to be the major issue of most Indian movements formed since World War II. Many large land claims are still before the Indian Claims Commission which was set up in 1947. Some groups also bring cases to protect their fishing and hunting rights from people outside the reservations. Companies continue to try to gain large holdings of natural gas, oil, coal, and uranium on Indian lands. In 1976, twenty-two Indian groups formed a council to improve their bargaining power over the use of the land. They intend to use the money from leasing the land to help their people gain better education and better living conditions.

# Rights for Handicapped People

Many Americans suffer from some sort of physical or mental problem like blindness, deafness, or mental retardation. In the 1970's, some handicapped people began to press for their rights to better opportunities in school, work, and other areas of life. They felt that other Americans expected them to be unable to do many things instead of giving them the chance to prove that perhaps they could.

In 1973, Congress passed the Rehabilitation Act which makes it illegal to discriminate against people just because they are handicapped. Local governments and groups have also begun to work toward removing barriers for handicapped people. Some areas have passed laws requiring all public buildings and pathways to be accessible to people using wheelchairs by providing ramps near stairs where needed. Many groups have joined the movement to hire more handicapped people so that they have a better chance to take care of themselves.

# The Election of 1976

President Ford ran for election in 1976 against Democrat Jimmy Carter, former governor of Georgia. Carter won the very close election. He had stated that his administration would meet the problems of the

# Patsy Mink

Patsy Takemoto Mink is the best-known woman in Hawaiian politics since Liliuokalani, the last queen of Hawaii. Mink served six terms in Congress and became an Assistant Secretary of State in 1977. She was born in a small village on the island of Maui in 1927. Her parents were of Japanese background. During World War II when Japanese Americans on the West Coast were put in relocation centers, those in Hawaii remained undisturbed. Mink was president of the Maui High School student body during the war. She later went to the University of Hawaii and the University of Chicago Law School. After graduation, she started her own law practice in Hawaii.

Mink entered politics by winning an election to the Hawaiian House of Representatives. She was later elected to the Hawaiian Senate. There she presented a bill giving women equal pay for equal work. Mink was first elected to Congress in 1964. She said, "What I can bring to Congress is an Hawaiian background of tolerance and equality that can contribute a great deal to better understanding between races."

As a member of Congress, Mink was active in seeking legislation to provide federal aid to education and the handicapped. She also wanted to improve the living conditions of people in the Western Pacific. Mink failed to win a seat in the United States Senate in 1976. In 1977, President Carter made her Assistant Secretary of State for Oceanic and International Environmental and Scientific Affairs.

nation with a better organized group of workers. One of his main goals would be to reduce the size of the federal government. He believed that fewer departments could perform the work at lower costs to American taxpayers.

One of the first big problems to face President Carter was the continuing energy crisis. To meet this problem quickly, Carter wanted Congress to pass laws that would make some forms of energy more expensive. People would have to cut down on their use of such things as gasoline. Carter's plans did not pass in Congress or please many citizens. Automobile makers argued that such ideas as putting an extra tax on large cars would hurt their sales badly. Workers in the industry worried about losing their jobs if sales dropped very much. Many Americans did not favor adding taxes to the cost of gasoline. In one of the worst winters in the country's recorded history, however, most Americans did respond to the President's request for lower temperatures in homes, schools, churches, and places of business.

As President, Carter spoke out in favor of the human rights of people all over the world. In Africa, the United States became more involved in pressing the white-controlled governments of South Africa and Rhodesia to include the people of their black majority populations. The President's stand on human rights angered the Soviet Union. The Russians were strongly criticized for their treatment of Jews and people who disagreed with the government. The Soviets called off an arms meeting with Americans, using the President's stand as their reason. Carter continued to support human rights and made

*Jimmy Carter was elected President in 1976. He urged people to find new ways to save natural resources and energy at home, and he worked to promote human rights for people all over the world.*

special efforts to include minority groups and women in his administration. In 1977, he issued a presidential order that government departments should work harder to end discrimination in hiring and promoting women in jobs.

The nation's economy had slowed down, and the periods of great expansion seemed far away. American farmers were still able to grow more than enough food for the American people, but the country's raw materials were becoming scarcer. There were many important decisions to be made in the coming years. In his inaugural address, President Carter had offered Americans this challenge:

> We have learned that "more" is not necessarily "better," that even our great nation has its recognized limits, and that we can neither answer all questions nor solve all problems. ...So together, in a spirit of individual sacrifice for the common good, we must simply do our best.

# Chapter 25 in Perspective See Teacher's Manual, page 135T.

## Identify

| | | |
|---|---|---|
| Neil Armstrong | Chien-Shiung Wu | Leonid Brezhnev |
| Henry Kissinger | Gerald Ford | Jimmy Carter |
| Katharine Graham | | |

## Explain

| | | |
|---|---|---|
| Vietnamization | detente | Equal Rights Amendment |
| Middle East | revenue sharing | Indian Claims Commission |

## Check Your Memory of the Facts

1. How did relations of the United States with China and Russia improve under President Nixon?
2. What legislation was passed by Congress to support the rights of women?

3. What events and questions were part of the Watergate scandal?
4. What agreement did President Ford make with the Russians at Vladivostok?
5. What information shows a contrast in American life from 1770 to 1970?
6. What demands did Americans make about the environment? What were some results of these demands?
7. What laws have been passed to protect the rights of handicapped people?

## Check Your Understanding of the Ideas

1. Why is it important to keep good relations with Middle East countries?
2. What actions did the government take under President Nixon to control inflation?
3. What was a major change in civil rights action in the 1970's?
4. What was the outcome of the Watergate scandal?
5. What kinds of problems faced the Carter administration when he took office?

## Expand Your Knowledge

1. Write a report on what you consider to be the most important changes in the history of the United States.
2. Identify major changes that you believe might take place in the United States in the next fifty years. Explain why you think these changes might occur and whether or not the country will be better because of them.

# Study Aids

# The Declaration of Independence

In Congress, July 4, 1776
The Unanimous Declaration of the Thirteen
United States of America

[These annotations, or notes, explain the Declaration of Independence in today's language.]

When it becomes necessary for people to separate themselves from others and become independent, they should give their reasons for doing so.

It should be clear to everyone that God has given certain rights to all people including the right to life, to liberty, and to seek happiness. To keep these rights, people set up governments based on powers agreed to by the people. When a government works against the interests of the people, they have the right to change or replace that government. It is wise not to change governments which have lasted a long time for small reasons. And experience shows that people will put up with much suffering, rather than to change things. But continued abuses and attempts by the government to take away rights and to completely control people create a situation which the people have a right and a duty to change. This is the case that now forces the colonies to change their system of government. The King of Great Britain has caused injuries to, and taken away the rights of, the colonies. To prove this, here is a list of the facts—

When in the course of human events, it becomes necessary for one people to dissolve the political bands which have connected them with another, and to assume among the powers of the earth, the separate and equal station to which the laws of nature and of nature's God entitle them, a decent respect to the opinions of mankind requires that they should declare the causes which impel them to the separation.

We hold these truths to be self-evident, that all men are created equal, that they are endowed by their Creator with certain unalienable rights, that among these are life, liberty, and the pursuit of happiness. That to secure these rights, governments are instituted among men, deriving their just powers from the consent of the governed; that whenever any form of government becomes destructive of these ends, it is the right of the people to alter or to abolish it, and to institute new government, laying its foundation on such principles, and organizing its powers in such form, as to them shall seem most likely to effect their safety and happiness. Prudence, indeed, will dictate that governments long established should not be changed for light and transient causes; and accordingly all experience hath shown, that mankind are more disposed to suffer, while evils are sufferable, than to right themselves by abolishing the forms to which they are accustomed. But when a long train of abuses and usurpations, pursuing invariably the same object, evinces a design to reduce them under absolute despotism, it is their right, it is their duty, to throw off such government, and to provide new guards for their future security. Such has been the patient sufferance of these colonies; and such is now the necessity which constrains them to alter their former systems of government. The history of the present King of Great Britain is a history of repeated injuries and usurpations, all having in direct object the establishment of an absolute tyranny over these states. To prove this, let facts be submitted to a candid world.

He has refused his assent to laws, the most wholesome and necessary for the public good.

He has forbidden his governors to pass laws of immediate and pressing importance, unless suspended in their operation till his assent should be obtained; and when so suspended, he has utterly neglected to attend to them.

He has refused to pass other laws for the accommodation of large districts of people, unless those people would relinquish the right of representation in the legislature, a right inestimable to them and formidable to tyrants only.

He has called together legislative bodies at places unusual, uncomfortable, and distant from the depository of their public records, for the sole purpose of fatiguing them into compliance with his measures.

He has dissolved representative houses repeatedly, for opposing with manly firmness his invasions on the rights of the people.

He has refused for a long time, after such dissolutions, to cause others to be elected; whereby the legislative powers, incapable of annihilation, have returned to the people at large for their exercise; the state remaining in the meantime exposed to all the dangers of invasion from without and convulsions within.

He has endeavored to prevent the population of these states; for that purpose obstructing the laws for naturalization of foreigners, refusing to pass others to encourage their migrations hither, and raising the conditions of new appropriations of lands.

He has obstructed the administration of justice, by refusing his assent to laws for establishing judiciary powers.

He has made judges dependent on his will alone, for the tenure of their offices, and the amount and payment of their salaries.

The King has refused to approve laws for the good of the people.

He has forbidden the governors to pass laws without his approval, but he has failed to take action on laws presented to him.

He has refused to pass laws for the good of large numbers of people unless they agree to give up their right to have representatives in the legislature.

He has called meetings of the representatives at places far away in order to make them tired so they would agree to his wishes.

He has ended the meeting of legislatures for opposing his attempts to take away the rights of the people.

He has then refused to let new representatives be elected. Meanwhile, the colonies are left without leadership, order, or protection.

He has tried to keep the colonies from growing by not allowing immigrants to become citizens or by not passing laws to encourage people to move to the colonies. He has made it harder for people to get new land.

He has gotten in the way of justice by refusing to agree to laws to set up courts.

He controls judges by deciding how long they will be in office and how much pay they will receive.

He has set up new offices and sent out more officials to bother the people.

He has kept an army here in time of peace without the agreement of our legislatures.

He has tried to make the authority of the military higher than that of our government.

He has joined with others to control us with laws against our rights as citizens. He has given his agreement to these acts—

For housing and feeding a large army among us;

For protecting the army from punishment even if they murder someone in these states;

For cutting off trade with other parts of the world;

For making us pay taxes without our agreement;

For taking away the right to a trial by jury;

For taking us overseas to be tried for pretended crimes;

For taking away the English laws in a nearby country [Canada], setting up a government of his own will there, and making it larger so as to slowly take over the colonies;

For taking away our charters and laws and changing the powers of our government;

For stopping our legislatures and declaring that he could make laws for us in all cases.

He has given up his right to govern here by saying that we were out of his protection and by waging war against us.

He has stolen from our ships, invaded our coasts, burned our towns, and destroyed the lives of our people.

He is sending large numbers of hired foreign soldiers to complete these works of death and destruction.

He has erected a multitude of new offices, and sent hither swarms of officers to harass our people, and eat out their substance.

He has kept among us, in times of peace, standing armies without the consent of our legislatures.

He has affected to render the military independent of and superior to the civil power.

He has combined with others to subject us to a jurisdiction foreign to our constitution, and unacknowledged by our laws; giving his assent to their acts of pretended legislation:

For quartering large bodies of armed troops among us;

For protecting them, by a mock trial, from punishment for any murders which they should commit on the inhabitants of these states;

For cutting off our trade with all parts of the world;

For imposing taxes on us without our consent;

For depriving us, in many cases, of the benefits of trial by jury;

For transporting us beyond seas to be tried for pretended offenses;

For abolishing the free system of English laws in a neighboring province, establishing therein an arbitrary government, and enlarging its boundaries so as to render it at once an example and fit instrument for introducing the same absolute rule into these colonies;

For taking away our charters, abolishing our most valuable laws, and altering fundamentally the forms of our governments;

For suspending our own legislatures, and declaring themselves invested with power to legislate for us in all cases whatsoever.

He has abdicated government here, by declaring us out of his protection and waging war against us.

He has plundered our seas, ravaged our coasts, burned our towns, and destroyed the lives of our people.

He is at this time transporting large armies of foreign mercenaries to complete the works of death, desolation, and tyranny, already begun with circumstances of cruelty and perfidy scarcely paralleled in the most barbarous ages, and totally unworthy the head of a civilized nation.

He has constrained our fellow citizens taken captive on the high seas to bear arms against their country, to become the executioners of their friends and brethren, or to fall themselves by their hands.

He has captured citizens at sea and forced them to fight against their fellow citizens.

He has excited domestic insurrections among us, and has endeavored to bring on the inhabitants of our frontiers, the merciless Indian savages, whose known rule of warfare is an undistinguished destruction of all ages, sexes, and conditions.

He has gotten us to fight among ourselves and has encouraged the Indians to attack us.

In every stage of these oppressions we have petitioned for redress in the most humble terms: our repeated petitions have been answered only by repeated injury. A prince, whose character is thus marked by every act which may define a tyrant, is unfit to be the ruler of a free people.

We have asked in the most proper way to have these things changed only to meet more injuries. Such a person is unfit to be the ruler of a free people.

Nor have we been wanting in our attentions to our British brethren. We have warned them from time to time of attempts by their legislature to extend an unwarrantable jurisdiction over us. We have reminded them of the circumstances of our emigration and settlement here. We have appealed to their native justice and magnanimity, and we have conjured them by the ties of our common kindred to disavow these usurpations, which would inevitably interrupt our connections and correspondence. They too have been deaf to the voice of justice and consanguinity. We must, therefore, acquiesce in the necessity which denounces our separation, and hold them, as we hold the rest of mankind, enemies in war, in peace friends.

We have warned the British people of the attempts by their legislature to rule us unjustly. We have reminded them that we have the same ancestors as they, but they too have ignored us. We must therefore accept our separation and regard them as we do others — enemies in war, friends in peace.

We, therefore, the representatives of the United States of America, in General Congress, assembled, appealing to the Supreme Judge of the world for the rectitude of our intentions, do, in the name and by authority of the good people of these colonies, solemnly publish and declare, that these united colonies are, and of right ought to be, free and independent states; that they are absolved from all allegiance to the British Crown, and that all political connection between them and the State of Great Britain is and ought to be

Therefore, as representatives of the United States of America, we declare the colonies to be free and independent states. We no longer feel any loyalty to England or to the King. We take for ourselves all the powers that free and independent states have. We believe that what we do is right and that God will judge and protect us. In support of these beliefs, we pledge to each other our lives, our fortunes, and our sacred honor.

totally dissolved; and that as free and independent states, they have full power to levy war, conclude peace, contract alliances, establish commerce, and to do all other acts and things which independent states may of right do. And for the support of this declaration, with a firm reliance on the protection of Divine Providence, we mutually pledge to each other our lives, our fortunes, and our sacred honor.

*John Hancock,* **President**

**New Hampshire**
*Josiah Bartlett*
*William Whipple*
*Matthew Thornton*

**Massachusetts**
*Samuel Adams*
*John Adams*
*Robert Treat Paine*
*Elbridge Gerry*

**New York**
*William Floyd*
*Philip Livingston*
*Francis Lewis*
*Lewis Morris*

**New Jersey**
*Richard Stockton*
*John Witherspoon*

*Francis Hopkinson*
*John Hart*
*Abraham Clark*

**Pennsylvania**
*Robert Morris*
*Benjamin Rush*
*Benjamin Franklin*
*John Morton*
*George Clymer*
*James Smith*
*George Taylor*
*James Wilson*
*George Ross*

**Delaware**
*Caesar Rodney*
*George Read*
*Thomas M'Kean*

**Maryland**
*Samuel Chase*
*William Paca*
*Thomas Stone*
*Charles Carroll*
    *of Carrollton*

**Rhode Island**
*Stephen Hopkins*
*William Ellery*

**Connecticut**
*Roger Sherman*
*Samuel Huntington*
*William Williams*
*Oliver Wolcott*

**Virginia**
*George Wythe*
*Richard Henry Lee*

*Thomas Jefferson*
*Benjamin Harrison*
*Thomas Nelson, Jr.*
*Francis Lightfoot Lee*
*Carter Braxton*

**North Carolina**
*William Hooper*
*Joseph Hewes*
*John Penn*

**South Carolina**
*Edward Rutledge*
*Thomas Heyward, Jr.*
*Thomas Lynch, Jr.*
*Arthur Middleton*

**Georgia**
*Button Gwinnett*
*Lyman Hall*
*George Walton*

# The Constitution of the United States

We the People *of the United States, in order to form a more perfect union, establish justice, insure domestic tranquillity, provide for the common defense, promote the general welfare, and secure the blessings of liberty to ourselves and our posterity, do ordain and establish this* CON-STITUTION *for the United States of America.*

## ARTICLE 1
## [LEGISLATIVE BRANCH]

### Section 1 [Congress]

All legislative powers herein granted shall be vested in a Congress of the United States, which shall consist of a Senate and House of Representatives.

### Section 2 [House of Representatives]

The House of Representatives shall be composed of members chosen every second year by the people of the several states, and the electors in each state shall have the qualifications requisite for electors of the most numerous branch of the state legislature.

No person shall be a representative who shall not have attained to the age of twenty-five years, and been seven years a citizen of the United States, and who shall not, when elected, be an inhabitant of that state in which he shall be chosen.

Representatives and direct taxes shall be apportioned among the several states which may be included within this Union, according to their respective numbers, which shall be determined by adding to the whole number of free persons, including those bound to service for a term of years, and excluding Indians not taxed, three fifths of all other persons. The actual enumeration shall be made within three years after the

[These annotations, or notes, explain the Constitution in today's language. The preamble, or introduction, states the general goals of the Constitution.]

We, the people of the United States, in order to form a more perfect union, to establish justice, to ensure peace at home, to provide for defense of the country, to help the well-being of the people, and to make sure of the blessings of liberty for ourselves and for future citizens, do establish this Constitution of the United States.

Powers to make laws will be given to a Congress. It will be divided into two groups: the House of Representatives and the Senate.

Members of the House will be chosen every two years by the people of the states. Any citizens who are qualified to vote for members of their state's house of representatives (largest branch) may vote for a member of the United States House of Representatives.

No one may serve in the House unless that person is at least twenty-five years of age, has been a citizen for seven years, and lives in the state where elected.

Both the amount of taxes and the number of representatives are to be based upon a state's population. [The part on taxes was changed by Amendment 16.] A state's population is determined by adding the number of free persons, plus indentured servants, but not Indians who are not taxed. All other persons (slaves) count as three fifths of a person. [The three-fifths reference to slaves was canceled by Amendments 13 and 14.]

529

A census is to be taken every ten years to decide the number of federal representatives each state shall have. States are allowed one representative for every thirty thousand people, but each state will have at least one representative. [Congress passed a law in 1929 that limited the size of the House to 435 members so that it would not become so large, as the country's population increased, that it could not get any work done.]

The governor of a state shall call for a special election to replace a representative who can no longer serve out a term.

Only the House may impeach, or charge, federal officials with not carrying out their duties.

The Senate will be made up of two members from every state who will serve for six years a term. Each senator will have one vote in the Senate. When they first meet, they will be divided into three groups. The terms of office of the first group will end after two years, the second group after four years, and the third group after six years. Every two years thereafter, one third of the senators will have to run for reelection as their terms of office end. The governor of a state may appoint someone to replace a senator who can no longer serve out a term. [Amendment 17 changed the part saying that senators must be elected by state legislatures.]

No one may serve as senator unless that person is at least thirty years of age, has been a citizen for nine years, and lives in the state where elected.

first meeting of the Congress of the United States, and within every subsequent term of ten years, in such manner as they shall by law direct. The number of representatives shall not exceed one for every thirty thousand, but each state shall have at least one representative; and until such enumeration shall be made, the State of New Hampshire shall be entitled to choose three; Massachusetts, eight; Rhode Island and Providence Plantations, one; Connecticut, five; New York, six; New Jersey, four; Pennsylvania, eight; Delaware, one; Maryland, six; Virginia, ten; North Carolina, five; South Carolina, five; and Georgia, three.

When vacancies happen in the representation from any state, the executive authority thereof shall issue writs of election to fill such vacancies.

The House of Representatives shall choose their Speaker and other officers; and shall have the sole power of impeachment.

## Section 3 [Senate]

The Senate of the United States shall be composed of two senators from each state, chosen by the legislature thereof, for six years; and each senator shall have one vote.

Immediately after they shall be assembled in consequence of the first election, they shall be divided as equally as may be into three classes. The seats of the senators of the first class shall be vacated at the expiration of the second year, of the second class at the expiration of the fourth year, of the third class at the expiration of the sixth year, so that one third may be chosen every second year, and if vacancies happen by resignation, or otherwise, during the recess of the legislature of any state, the executive thereof may make temporary appointments until the next meeting of the legislature, which shall then fill such vacancies.

No person shall be a senator who shall not have attained to the age of thirty years, and been nine years a citizen of the United States, and who shall not, when elected, be an inhabitant of that state for which he shall be chosen.

The Vice-President of the United States shall be President of the Senate, but shall have no vote, unless they be equally divided.

The Senate shall choose their other officers, and also a President *pro tempore*, in the absence of the Vice-President, or when he shall exercise the office of President of the United States.

The Senate shall have the sole power to try all impeachments. When sitting for that purpose, they shall be on oath or affirmation. When the President of the United States is tried, the Chief Justice shall preside; and no person shall be convicted without the concurrence of two thirds of the members present.

Judgment in cases of impeachment shall not extend further than to removal from office, and disqualification to hold and enjoy any office of honor, trust, or profit under the United States; but the party convicted shall nevertheless be liable and subject to indictment, trial, judgment, and punishment, according to law.

The Vice-President of the United States will be the President of the Senate but will have no vote unless there is a tie vote. The Senate will choose a temporary President for the Senate to serve when the Vice-President is absent or becomes the President of the United States.

Only the Senate may try persons impeached by the House. A two-thirds vote is necessary to find them guilty. The Chief Justice of the Supreme Court shall be the judge in an impeachment trial of the President.

The Senate may only remove a person from office who is impeached and found guilty. Regular courts may still try the person for any crimes committed.

## Section 4 [Both Houses]

The times, places, and manner of holding elections for senators and representatives shall be prescribed in each state by the legislature thereof; but the Congress may at any time by law make or alter such regulations, except as to the places of choosing senators.

The Congress shall assemble at least once in every year, and such meeting shall be on the first Monday in December, unless they shall by law appoint a different day.

The legislature of each state is to decide when, how, and where the members of the Senate and the House are to be chosen. Congress may later change the rules except the one about where.

Congress will meet at least once a year. [The opening date of Congress was changed by Amendment 20.]

## Section 5 [The Houses Separately]

Each house shall be the judge of the elections, returns, and qualifications of its own members, and a majority of each shall constitute a quorum to do business; but a smaller number may adjourn from day to day, and may be authorized to compel the attendance of absent members, in such manner, and under such penalties, as each house may provide.

Each group in Congress will judge its own elections, the counting of votes, and the qualifications of its members. More than half of the members must be present for either group to do any official business. A smaller number may meet and postpone an official meeting until later. Each group may make rules and penalties to make members attend meetings.

Each group may make rules about how to hold meetings and how to punish members for misconduct. They may remove a member from Congress with a two-thirds vote.

Each house shall keep a journal, or record, of its business and publish it from time to time. Business which the members think should be kept secret does not have to be published. The voting record of each member may be kept in the journal if one fifth of the members present vote to do it.

Neither group may adjourn, or end its meeting, for more than three days during a session of Congress, nor meet in any place other than where they have been meeting, without the agreement of the other group.

The members of Congress shall be paid an amount determined by law from the Treasury of the United States. Except in cases of treason, serious crime, or breaking the peace, members cannot be arrested during sessions of Congress or while going to or from them.

No members of the Senate or the House may be appointed to other government offices during their terms. No person holding any other office in the government of the United States may be at the same time a member of Congress. [A member of Congress appointed to another government job, such as the President's Cabinet, would have to quit serving in Congress.]

All bills for raising money through taxes must begin in the House of Representatives. The Senate may propose changes in the bills or agree to them as with any other bill.

Every bill, which must be approved by both the House and the Senate, must be presented to

Each house may determine the rules of its proceedings, punish its members for disorderly behavior, and, with the concurrence of two thirds, expel a member.

Each house shall keep a journal of its proceedings, and from time to time publish the same, excepting such parts as may in their judgment require secrecy; and the yeas and nays of the members of either house on any question shall, at the desire of one fifth of those present, be entered on the journal.

Neither house, during the session of Congress, shall, without the consent of the other, adjourn for more than three days, nor to any other place than that in which the two houses shall be sitting.

## Section 6 [Privileges and Restrictions of Members]

The senators and representatives shall receive a compensation for their services, to be ascertained by law, and paid out of the Treasury of the United States. They shall in all cases, except treason, felony, and breach of the peace, be privileged from arrest during their attendance at the session of their respective houses, and in going to and returning from the same; and for any speech or debate in either house, they shall not be questioned in any other place.

No senator or representative shall, during the time for which he was elected, be appointed to any civil office under the authority of the United States, which shall have been created, or the emoluments whereof shall have been increased, during such time; and no person holding any office under the United States shall be a member of either house during his continuance in office.

## Section 7 [Method of Passing Laws]

All bills for raising revenue shall originate in the House of Representatives; but the Senate may propose or concur with amendments as on other bills.

Every bill which shall have passed the House of Representatives and the Senate shall, before it become a law, be presented to the President of the United States; if he approve he shall sign it, but if not he shall return it, with his objections, to that house in which it shall have originated, who shall enter the objections at large on their journal, and proceed to reconsider it. If after such reconsideration two thirds of that house shall agree to pass the bill, it shall be sent, together with the objections, to the other house, by which it shall likewise be reconsidered, and if approved by two thirds of that house, it shall become a law. But in all such cases the votes of both houses shall be determined by yeas and nays, and the names of the persons voting for and against the bill shall be entered on the journal of each house respectively. If any bill shall not be returned by the President within ten days (Sundays excepted) after it shall have been presented to him, the same shall be a law, in like manner as if he had signed it, unless the Congress by their adjournment prevent its return, in which case it shall not be a law.

Every order, resolution, or vote to which the concurrence of the Senate and House of Representatives may be necessary (except on a question of adjournment) shall be presented to the President of the United States; and before the same shall take effect, shall be approved by him, or being disapproved by him, shall be repassed by two thirds of the Senate and House of Representatives, according to the rules and limitations prescribed in the case of a bill.

the President before it becomes law. If the President approves the bill, he will sign it. If he does not approve it, he will send it back to the group who started it, along with his objections to it. That group must then write the President's objections in its journal and begin to reconsider the bill. If two thirds of the members vote to pass the bill, it will be sent to the other group. If the other group reconsiders and two thirds of its members vote for the bill, it will become law. The names of all members and how they voted [yes or no] will be written in the journal. If the President does not return a bill within ten days, it will become law. If Congress adjourns so that the President cannot return a bill in time, it will not become law.

Every order, resolution, or vote which requires the agreement of the House and Senate, must be presented to the President of the United States. Before such order, resolution, or vote can take effect, it must be approved by the President. If it is not approved, it must be passed by two thirds of the members of the Senate and House according to the same rules that apply to bills.

## Section 8 [Powers Given to Congress]

The Congress shall have power:

To lay and collect taxes, duties, imposts, and excises, to pay the debts and provide for the common defense and general welfare of the United States; but all duties, imposts, and excises shall be uniform throughout the United States;

To borrow money on the credit of the United States;

To regulate commerce with foreign nations, and among the several states, and with the Indian tribes;

Congress shall have the power:

To make laws for charging and collecting taxes, including taxes for imports and goods made within the country, in order to pay for the defense of the country and to provide services for the people. The rate of taxes must be the same throughout the United States.

To borrow money in the name of and to be repaid by the United States.

To make rules for trade with other nations, among the states, and with groups of Indians.

To make rules so that persons who are not citizens can become citizens of the United States. Congress will also have the power to make rules so that a company which cannot pay its debts (bankruptcy) may sell its property to do so.

To coin money and to set its value, to set the value of foreign coins, and to set up a system for weighing and measuring things.

To make rules for the punishment of people who illegally coin the money of the United States.

To establish post offices and the roads needed to connect them.

To promote the progress of science and useful arts by not allowing others to copy the works of authors and inventors for a limited time.

To set up other federal courts which are lower, or have less authority, than the Supreme Court.

To decide on laws for piracy and serious crimes done aboard ships at sea and to decide punishments for them. It will also have the power to make laws for the punishment of crimes against international law (laws agreed to by several nations).

To declare war, permit citizens to build and arm ships for war, and make rules concerning the capture of prisoners on land and at sea.

To raise and pay for an army, but no money for that purpose will be given for longer than two years.

To begin and keep up a navy.

To make rules for the military forces.

To decide on the way to call up the militia (state armies of private citizens) to enforce the laws, stop rebellions, and protect the country from invasion.

To organize, arm, and make rules for the militia which may serve the federal government, but the states will choose the officers and train the troops according to the rules set up by Congress.

To establish a uniform rule of naturalization, and uniform laws on the subject of bankruptcies throughout the United States;

To coin money, regulate the value thereof, and of foreign coin, and fix the standard of weights and measures;

To provide for the punishment of counterfeiting the securities and current coin of the United States;

To establish post offices and post roads;

To promote the progress of science and useful arts, by securing for limited times to authors and inventors the exclusive right to their respective writings and discoveries;

To constitute tribunals inferior to the Supreme Court;

To define and punish piracies and felonies committed on the high seas, and offenses against the law of nations;

To declare war, grant letters of marque and reprisal, and make rules concerning captures on land and water;

To raise and support armies, but no appropriation of money to that use shall be for a longer term than two years;

To provide and maintain a navy;

To make rules for the government and regulation of the land and naval forces;

To provide for calling forth the militia to execute the laws of the Union, suppress insurrections, and repel invasions;

To provide for organizing, arming, and disciplining the militia, and for governing such part of them as may be employed in the service of the United States, reserving to the states respectively the appointment of the officers, and the authority of training the militia according to the discipline prescribed by Congress;

To exercise exclusive legislation in all cases whatsoever over such district (not exceeding ten miles square) as may, by cession of particular states, and the acceptance of Congress, become the seat of the government of the United States, and to exercise like authority over all places purchased by the consent of the legislature of the state in which the same shall be, for the erection of forts, magazines, arsenals, dock-yards, and other needful buildings;—and

To control any land to be used for the capital of the United States as well as land bought for forts, places to store weapons and ammunition, dock-yards, and other needed buildings. These lands will be bought only with the approval of the states where they are located.

To make all laws which shall be necessary and proper for carrying into execution the foregoing powers, and all other powers vested by this Constitution in the government of the United States, or in any department or officer thereof.

Congress shall have the power to make any other laws which might be necessary to carry out the powers listed here for itself and for any department or officer of the federal government.

## Section 9 [Powers Forbidden to the United States]

The migration or importation of such persons as any of the states now existing shall think proper to admit, shall not be prohibited by the Congress prior to the year one thousand eight hundred and eight, but a tax or duty may be imposed on such importation, not exceeding ten dollars for each person.

Until 1808, Congress cannot stop the states from bringing into the country any persons which they wish. Congress may put a tax on these persons, but not more than ten dollars each. [This was put into the Constitution to prevent Congress from passing laws to stop the slave trade. In 1808, Congress did stop the importing of slaves.]

The privilege of the writ of habeas corpus shall not be suspended, unless when in cases of rebellion or invasion the public safety may require it.

The privilege of habeas corpus cannot be stopped by the government unless in cases of rebellion or invasion. [A writ of habeas corpus is an order for a person held by law officers to have a hearing in a court and be charged with a specific crime or be released. This is to prevent persons from being held for no reason.]

No bill of attainder or ex post facto law shall be passed.

Neither a bill of attainder nor an ex post facto law may be passed by the government. [A bill of attainder is a law passed by a legislature to sentence and punish one particular person for a crime. This bypasses the courts and allows a legislature to act as judge and jury. An ex post facto law makes an action illegal which was done before the law against it was made.]

No capitation, or other direct, tax shall be laid, unless in proportion to the census or enumeration herein before directed to be taken.

No direct tax shall be charged unless it is based upon the number of people in each state. [For instance, if one state had 10 percent of the population of the country, it would have to pay 10 percent of any tax. This was changed by Amendment 16.]

No tax or duty shall be laid on articles exported from any state.

Federal rules for trade will not favor one state over another. Ships entering or leaving one state will not be forced to pay a tax on entering or leaving any other state.

No money will be taken from the Treasury without laws being made for it. A regular statement of money received and money spent must be published from time to time.

No title of nobility (such as king, prince, or duke) shall be given to anyone by the United States. Also, no official of the government may accept any present, reward, favor, or title from any king, prince, or country without the permission of Congress.

No individual state may make a treaty or alliance, allow citizens to arm ships for war, coin money, or give bills of credit. It may not pass laws to allow people to pay debts with anything but gold or silver coins. States may not pass any bill of attainder, ex post facto law, or law which will interfere with people making contracts with one another. States may not grant titles of nobility. [These powers are forbidden to the states because some are powers of Congress only. Others are forbidden to any level of government.]

No state may charge any tax on imports and exports without the consent of Congress except to cover the cost of inspecting cargo. Any profit from such taxes will go to the Treasury of the United States. Such tax laws may be changed by an act of Congress.

No state may charge a tax based on the weight of the cargo carried by a ship. States may not keep troops or warships in times of peace or make any agreement with another state or another country. They may not make war unless they are actually invaded or in such danger that they cannot delay protecting themselves.

No preference shall be given by any regulation of commerce or revenue to the ports of one state over those of another; nor shall vessels bound to, or from, one state, be obliged to enter, clear, or pay duties in another.

No money shall be drawn from the treasury, but in consequence of appropriations made by law; and a regular statement and account of the receipts and expenditures of all public money shall be published from time to time.

No title of nobility shall be granted by the United States: And no person holding any office of profit or trust under them, shall, without the consent of the Congress, accept of any present, emolument, office, or title, of any kind whatever, from any king, prince, or foreign state.

## Section 10 [Powers Forbidden to the States]

No state shall enter into any treaty, alliance, or confederation; grant letters of marque and reprisal; coin money; emit bills of credit; make any thing but gold and silver coin a tender in payment of debts; pass any bill of attainder, ex post facto law, or law impairing the obligation of contracts, or grant any title of nobility.

No state shall, without the consent of the Congress, lay any imposts or duties on imports or exports, except what may be absolutely necessary for executing its inspection laws; and the net produce of all duties and imposts, laid by any state on imports or exports, shall be for the use of the treasury of the United States; and all such laws shall be subject to the revision and control of the Congress.

No state shall, without the consent of Congress, lay any duty of tonnage, keep troops, or ships of war in time of peace, enter into any agreement or compact with another state, or with a foreign power, or engage in war, unless actually invaded, or in such imminent danger as will not admit of delay.

# ARTICLE 2
# [EXECUTIVE BRANCH]

## Section 1 [President and Vice-President]

The executive power shall be vested in a President of the United States of America. He shall hold his office during the term of four years, and, together with the Vice-President, chosen for the same term, be elected, as follows:

Each state shall appoint, in such manner as the legislature thereof may direct, a number of electors, equal to the whole number of senators and representatives to which the state may be entitled in the Congress: but no senator or representative, or person holding an office of trust or profit under the United States, shall be appointed an elector.

The electors shall meet in their respective states, and vote by ballot for two persons, of whom one at least shall not be an inhabitant of the same state with themselves. And they shall make a list of all the persons voted for, and of the number of votes for each; which list they shall sign and certify, and transmit sealed to the seat of the government of the United States, directed to the President of the Senate. The President of the Senate shall, in the presence of the Senate and House of Representatives, open all the certificates, and the votes shall then be counted. The person having the greatest number of votes shall be the President, if such number be a majority of the whole number of electors appointed; and if there be more than one who have such majority, and have an equal number of votes, then the House of Representatives shall immediately choose by ballot one of them for President; and if no person have a majority, then from the five highest on the list the said house shall in like manner choose the President. But in choosing the President, the votes shall be taken by states, the representation from each state having one vote; a quorum for this purpose shall consist of a member or members from two thirds of the states, and a majority of all the states shall be

[Congress makes the laws, and it is the duty of the executive branch to see that they are carried out.] The executive power shall be given to the President of the United States. He shall hold office for a term of four years, as will the Vice-President. They will be chosen in the following way:

Each state shall appoint a number of electors equal to the total number of senators and representatives they have in Congress. Rules for appointing the electors will be made by each state legislature. No senator or representative or anyone holding an office in the federal government may be an elector.

The electors will meet and vote for two people. One of the people for whom they vote must live in another state from their own. They will make a list showing the votes cast for each person to be sent to the President of the Senate. The President of the Senate will count the votes in front of Congress. The person receiving the most electors' votes over a majority will be President. If two people have the same number of votes, the House of Representatives will choose one of them for President. If no one receives a majority, then the House must choose the President from the top five vote-getters. Members of the House from two thirds of the states are needed to carry out this business with each state having one vote. A candidate must win a majority of the states' votes to be President. The person with the second highest number of votes will be Vice-President. The Senate will choose the Vice-President in case of a tie vote. [This was replaced by Amendment 12.]

Congress will decide when the electors will be chosen and also when the electors will cast their votes for President and Vice-President. This time will be the same throughout the country.

No person except a citizen born in the United States or a person who was a citizen when the Constitution was adopted may become President. A person must be at least thirty-five years of age and have been a resident of the United States for fourteen years to become President.

In case of the death or removal of the President from office, or if the President cannot carry out duties, the Vice-President will become President. Congress may make laws to decide what will happen if both the President and Vice-President are removed from office or cannot carry out duties. Any officer who replaces the President or Vice-President will carry out those duties until such time as that person can again do them or until a new President is elected.

The President will receive payment for serving which will not be increased or decreased during the term of office. The President cannot receive any other payment, reward, or favor during the term from either the United States or any of the states.

[The President must take the oath of office.]

The President is the commander in chief (highest officer) of the armed forces and also the

necessary to a choice. In every case, after the choice of the President, the person having the greatest number of votes of the electors shall be the Vice-President. But if there should remain two or more who have equal votes, the Senate shall choose from them by ballot the Vice-President.

The Congress may determine the time of choosing the electors, and the day on which they shall give their votes; which day shall be the same throughout the United States.

No person except a natural-born citizen, or a citizen of the United States, at the time of the adoption of this Constitution, shall be eligible to the office of President; neither shall any person be eligible to that office who shall not have attained to the age of thirty-five years, and been fourteen years a resident within the United States.

In case of the removal of the President from office, or of his death, resignation, or inability to discharge the powers and duties of the said office, the same shall devolve on the Vice-President, and the Congress may by law provide for the case of removal, death, resignation, or inability, both of the President and Vice-President, declaring what officer shall then act as President, and such officer shall act accordingly, until the disability be removed, or a President shall be elected.

The President shall, at stated times, receive for his services a compensation, which shall neither be increased nor diminished during the period for which he shall have been elected, and he shall not receive within that period any other emolument from the United States, or any of them.

Before he enter on the execution of his office, he shall take the following oath or affirmation:—"I do solemnly swear (or affirm) that I will faithfully execute the office of President of the United States, and will, to the best of my ability, preserve, protect, and defend the Constitution of the United States."

## Section 2 [Powers of the President]

The President shall be commander in chief of the army and navy of the United States, and of the militia of the several states, when called into the actual service of the United States; he may require the opinion, in writing, of the principal officer in each of the executive departments, upon any subject relating to the duties of their respective offices, and he shall have power to grant reprieves and pardons for offenses against the United States, except in cases of impeachment.

He shall have power, by and with the advice and consent of the Senate, to make treaties, provided two thirds of the senators present concur; and he shall nominate, and by and with the advice and consent of the Senate, shall appoint ambassadors, other public ministers and consuls, judges of the Supreme Court, and all other officers of the United States, whose appointments are not herein otherwise provided for, and which shall be established by law; but the Congress may by law vest the appointment of such inferior officers, as they think proper, in the President alone, in the courts of law, or in the heads of departments.

The President shall have power to fill up all vacancies that may happen during the recess of the Senate, by granting commissions which shall expire at the end of their next session.

## Section 3 [Duties of the President]

He shall from time to time give to the Congress information of the state of the Union, and recommend to their consideration such measures as he shall judge necessary and expedient; he may, on extraordinary occasions, convene both houses, or either of them, and in case of disagreement between them with respect to the time of adjournment, he may adjourn them to such time as he shall think proper; he shall receive ambassadors and other public ministers; he shall take care that the laws be faithfully executed, and shall commission all the officers of the United States.

## Section 4 [Impeachment]

The President, Vice-President and all civil officers of the United States, shall be removed

militia when it is called to service by the federal government. He may require the heads of the departments in the federal government to give advice or opinions in making decisions. The President will have the power to delay punishment or give a pardon for crimes against the United States. The President may not give pardons in the case of an impeachment.

The President shall have the power to make treaties with other countries. Two thirds of the senators present must approve any treaties made. The President shall also appoint ambassadors and other officers to represent the United States in other nations. Justices of the Supreme Court, and all other officials who are not provided for in the Constitution, shall be appointed by the President with the approval of the Senate. Congress may pass laws allowing certain other officials to be appointed by the President, by the courts, or by the heads of federal departments without the approval of Congress.

If there is an open office or position during the time when the Senate is in recess, or not working, the President shall have the power to appoint someone to the job. That person will serve until the end of the Senate's next session.

The President shall tell Congress about conditions within the country from time to time. [This is traditionally called the State of the Union and is made in a speech and sent in writing to Congress by the President.] The President may recommend bills to Congress. The President may call Congress or either house to do business, or can decide the time to adjourn if Congress cannot decide. The President shall also receive ambassadors and officials from other countries, faithfully carry out the laws, and shall give authority and duty to the officers of the United States.

The President, Vice-President, and officers other than military officers shall be removed from office if found guilty of treason, bribery, high or very serious crimes, or misdemeanors which are less serious crimes.

[The power to make judgments is the duty of the courts.] This judicial power of the United States is given to one Supreme Court. Congress may set up lower courts as needed. Judges of the courts will hold their office for as long as their behavior remains proper. They will be paid for their services and the amount of pay may not be lowered while they serve.

The judicial power includes all cases about law and rights under the Constitution, other laws and treaties of the United States. It also includes all cases involving ambassadors and other officials representing the United States, and cases involving questions of trading and shipping on the seas. The power will include cases by or against the United States, and cases between two states, between a state and a citizen of another state, between citizens of different states, between citizens of the same state who claim land given to them under the law of another state, and between a state or its citizens and a foreign country and its citizens. [The right of a citizen to file a lawsuit against a state was changed by Amendment 11.]

Cases involving ambassadors and other representatives of the United States to foreign countries, or those involving one of the states, must be handled only by the Supreme Court. The Supreme Court may review all other cases according to laws set up by Congress.

from office on impeachment for, and conviction of, treason, bribery, or other high crimes and misdemeanors.

# ARTICLE 3
# [JUDICIAL BRANCH]

## Section 1 [United States Courts]

The judicial power of the United States shall be vested in one Supreme Court, and in such inferior courts as the Congress may from time to time ordain and establish. The judges, both of the Supreme and inferior courts, shall hold their offices during good behavior, and shall, at stated times, receive for their services, a compensation, which shall not be diminished during their continuance in office.

## Section 2 [Authority of United States Courts]

The judicial power shall extend to all cases, in law and equity, arising under this Constitution, the laws of the United States, and treaties made, or which shall be made, under their authority;—to all cases affecting ambassadors, other public ministers, and consuls;—to all cases of admiralty and maritime jurisdiction;—to controversies to which the United States shall be a party;—to controversies between two or more states;—between a state and citizens of another state;—between citizens of different states;—between citizens of the same state claiming lands under grants of different states; and between a state, or the citizens thereof, and foreign states, citizens or subjects.

In all cases affecting ambassadors, other public ministers and consuls, and those in which a state shall be party, the Supreme Court shall have original jurisdiction. In all other cases before mentioned, the Supreme Court shall have appellate jurisdiction, both as to law and fact, with such exceptions, and under such regulations as the Congress shall make.

The trial of all crimes, except in cases of impeachment, shall be by jury; and such trial shall be held in the state where the said crimes shall have been committed; but when not committed within any state, the trial shall be at such place or places as the Congress may by law have directed.

Except in cases of impeachment, all trials of crimes shall be by jury, and the trial must be held in the same state where the crime took place. If a crime did not take place in any state, the place of the trial will be decided by laws passed by Congress.

## Section 3 [Treason]

Treason against the United States shall consist only in levying war against them, or in adhering to their enemies, giving them aid and comfort. No person shall be convicted of treason unless on the testimony of two witnesses to the same overt act, or on confession in open court.

Treason against the United States shall be limited to mean making war against the country or helping its enemies. No person shall be found guilty of treason unless two people say in court that they actually saw the person do something. [Traditionally, enemies has meant only those governments against which the United States had declared war.]

The Congress shall have power to declare the punishment of treason, but no attainder of treason shall work corruption of blood, or forfeiture except during the life of the person attainted.

Congress has the power to decide the punishment for treason but may not punish a person's family or relatives.

# ARTICLE 4
# [RELATIONS OF THE STATES TO EACH OTHER]

## Section 1 [Official Acts]

Full faith and credit shall be given in each state to the public acts, records, and judicial proceedings of every other state. And the Congress may by general laws prescribe the manner in which such acts, records, and proceedings shall be proved, and the effect thereof.

States must honor the laws, records, and court decisions of other states. Congress may make laws to decide how the laws, records, and court decisions of one state may affect another and what changes have to be made.

## Section 2 [Privileges of Citizens]

The citizens of each state shall be entitled to all privileges and immunities of citizens in the several states.

A person charged in any state with treason, felony, or other crime, who shall flee from justice, and be found in another state shall, on demand of the executive authority of the state from

The citizens of each state shall have the same rights and protections as the citizens of any state which they may visit.

A person who is charged with a crime and then goes to another state shall be returned to the state where the crime took place on the demand of the governor of that state.

No person who is lawfully held for the purpose of working in one state may escape to another state but must be returned upon request of the person for whom the work is being done. [This law applied to runaway slaves and was changed by Amendment 13.]

New states may be admitted to the Union by Congress. No state may be divided to make other states nor can two states be joined to make one without the agreement of the state's legislature and Congress.

Congress shall have the power to control all territories and property of the United States. Nothing in the Constitution is meant to harm the claims of either the United States or the states. [Since land west of the original thirteen states was claimed by several states, this last sentence was added to say that the issue had not yet been decided.]

The United States shall make sure that every state has a republican, or representative, form of government. The United States shall also protect every state from invasion and from violence within that state when asked to do so by either the legislature or the governor if the legislature is in recess.

Amendments, or changes, to the Constitution may be offered by two thirds of the members of both groups of Congress or a convention requested by two thirds of the legislatures of the states. Such changes shall be considered equal to all other parts of the Constitution when ratified by the legislatures in three fourths of the states or by special conventions in three fourths of the states. Congress shall decide which method of ratification to use. No amendment made before 1808

which he fled, be delivered up, to be removed to the state having jurisdiction of the crime.

No person held to service or labor in one state, under the laws thereof, escaping into another, shall, in consequence of any law or regulation therein, be discharged from such service or labor, but shall be delivered up on claim of the party to whom such service or labor may be due.

## Section 3 [New States and Territories]

New states may be admitted by the Congress into this Union; but no new state shall be formed or erected within the jurisdiction of any other state; nor any state be formed by the junction of two or more states, or parts of states, without the consent of the legislatures of the states concerned as well as of the Congress.

The Congress shall have power to dispose of and make all needful rules and regulations respecting the territory or other property belonging to the United States; and nothing in this Constitution shall be so construed as to prejudice any claims of the United States, or of any particular state.

## Section 4 [Protection of the States]

The United States shall guarantee to every state in this Union a republican form of government, and shall protect each of them against invasion; and on application of the legislature, or of the executive (when the legislature cannot be convened) against domestic violence.

# ARTICLE 5 [AMENDMENTS]

The Congress, whenever two thirds of both houses shall deem it necessary, shall propose amendments to this Constitution, or, on the application of the legislatures of two thirds of the several states, shall call a convention for proposing amendments, which, in either case, shall be valid to all intents and purposes, as part of this Constitution, when ratified by the legislatures of three fourths of the several states, or by conventions in three fourths thereof, as the one or the other mode of ratification may be proposed by the Congress; provided that no amendment which may be made prior to the year one thousand eight hundred and eight shall in any manner affect the first and fourth clauses in the ninth section of the first article; and that no state, without its consent, shall be deprived of its equal suffrage in the Senate.

may affect the first and fourth parts of the ninth section of Article One. No state, without its agreement, shall lose its equal vote in the Senate. [The first part mentioned forbids the United States to stop the slave trade. The fourth part says that taxes must be based upon a state's population. Both of these have since been changed.]

# ARTICLE 6 [GENERAL PROVISIONS]

All debts contracted and engagements entered into, before the adoption of this Constitution, shall be as valid against the United States under this Constitution, as under the Confederation.

The debts and other agreements made under the Articles of Confederation will be honored by the United States under the Constitution.

This Constitution, and the laws of the United States which shall be made in pursuance thereof; and all treaties made, or which shall be made, under the authority of the United States, shall be the supreme law of the land; and the judges in every state shall be bound thereby, anything in the Constitution or laws of any state to the contrary notwithstanding.

The Constitution and the laws and treaties made under it are the highest laws of the land. Judges in every state will be bound by them over any state laws or constitutions.

The senators and representatives before mentioned, and the members of the several state legislatures, and all executive and judicial officers, both of the United States and of the several states, shall be bound by oath or affirmation to support this Constitution; but no religious test shall ever be required as a qualification to any office or public trust under the United States.

Senators and representatives, members of state legislatures, and all state and federal executive and judicial officers must take an oath to support the Constitution. Religion may never be used as a requirement to hold any government office.

# ARTICLE 7 [RATIFICATION OF THE CONSTITUTION]

The ratification of the conventions of nine states shall be sufficient for the establishment of this Constitution between the states so ratifying the same.

Nine state conventions must ratify this Constitution before it goes into effect among those states.

Done in convention by the unanimous consent of the states present the seventeenth day of September in the year of our Lord one thousand seven hundred and eighty-seven, and of the independence of the United States of America the twelfth. In witness whereof we have hereunto subscribed our names.

*George Washington*, **President and Deputy from Virginia**

**New Hampshire**
*John Langdon*
*Nicholas Gilman*

**Massachusetts**
*Nathaniel Gorham*
*Rufus King*

**Connecticut**
*William Samuel*
  *Johnson*
*Roger Sherman*

**New York**
*Alexander Hamilton*

**New Jersey**
*William Livingston*
*David Brearley*
*William Paterson*
*Jonathan Dayton*

**Pennsylvania**
*Benjamin Franklin*
*Thomas Mifflin*
*Robert Morris*
*George Clymer*
*Thomas Fitzsimons*
*Jared Ingersoll*
*James Wilson*
*Gouverneur Morris*

**Delaware**
*George Read*
*Gunning Bedford, Jr.*
*John Dickinson*
*Richard Bassett*
*Jacob Broom*

**Maryland**
*James M'Henry*
*Daniel of St. Thomas*
  *Jenifer*
*Daniel Carroll*

**Virginia**
*John Blair*
*James Madison, Jr.*

**North Carolina**
*William Blount*
*Richard Dobbs*
  *Spaight*
*Hugh Williamson*

**South Carolina**
*John Rutledge*
*Charles C. Pinckney*
*Charles Pinckney*
*Pierce Butler*

**Georgia**
*William Few*
*Abraham Baldwin*

**Attest: *William Jackson*,**
  **Secretary**

[The first ten amendments are called the Bill of Rights. They were proposed at the first meeting of Congress to better protect the rights of the people. They were all ratified by December, 1791.]

# [AMENDMENTS]

Congress cannot make laws about setting up a religion or to limit the freedom of worship. It cannot make laws to limit freedom of the press, or the freedom for people to gather peaceably together, or their right to petition the government about problems.

## Amendment 1
Congress shall make no law respecting an establishment of religion, or prohibiting the free exercise thereof; or abridging the freedom of speech, or of the press; or the right of the people peaceably to assemble, and to petition the government for a redress of grievances.

## Amendment 2

A well-regulated militia being necessary to the security of a free state, the right of the people to keep and bear arms shall not be infringed.

Because a militia is necessary for the safety of a state, people shall have the right to keep and carry arms.

## Amendment 3

No soldier shall, in time of peace, be quartered in any house, without the consent of the owner, nor in time of war, but in a manner to be prescribed by law.

No soldier shall, in time of peace, be kept in a person's home without that person's permission. No soldier shall be kept in a person's home in time of war except in a manner provided by law.

## Amendment 4

The right of the people to be secure in their persons, houses, papers, and effects, against unreasonable searches and seizures, shall not be violated, and no warrants shall issue, but upon probable cause, supported by oath or affirmation, and particularly describing the place to be searched, and the persons or things to be seized.

The government's right to search or take people's houses, papers, or other property is limited. A legal order stating what is being sought is needed before any search or seizure can take place.

## Amendment 5

No person shall be held to answer for a capital, or otherwise infamous crime, unless on a presentment or indictment of a grand jury, except in cases arising in the land or naval forces, or in the militia, when in actual service in time of war or public danger; nor shall any person be subject for the same offense to be twice put in jeopardy of life or limb; nor shall be compelled in any criminal case to be a witness against himself, nor to be deprived of life, liberty, or property, without due process of law; nor shall private property be taken for public use, without just compensation.

No person may be brought to trial for a serious crime without first being charged with a crime by a grand jury. This does not apply to people in the armed forces or the militia during war or time of public danger. No person may be tried for the same crime twice. People may not be forced to testify against themselves. No person may have life, liberty, or property taken without going through the system of courts established by law. Property belonging to private citizens may not be taken for public use without fair payment.

## Amendment 6

In all criminal prosecutions, the accused shall enjoy the right to a speedy and public trial, by an impartial jury of the state and district wherein the crime shall have been committed, which district shall have been previously ascertained by law, and to be informed of the nature and cause of the accusation; to be confronted with the witnesses against him; to have compulsory process for obtaining witnesses in his favor, and to have the assistance of counsel for his defense.

Trials shall be held as quickly as possible and be open to the public. Courts shall use juries which favor neither side, and trials shall be held in the area where the crime took place. Persons being tried shall be told of the charges against them and shall be able to question those who give evidence against them. They may call others to witness in their defense and have the services of a lawyer.

In a dispute involving common law where the value in question is more than twenty dollars, a jury trial is required. No fact considered by that jury may be retried by any court of the United States except by the same common law rules. [Common law is a set of rules and laws, often unwritten, based on customs brought to the United States from England. They usually apply to disputes between two people or groups of people. They were developed over centuries by English judges and were used over and over again by later generations. Much of American written law is also based on common law. The colonists wished to see these customs continued in the Constitution.]

An unreasonable amount of bail shall not be required, nor shall unreasonable fines be charged to people who commit crimes. People may not be given cruel or unusual punishments (such as torture). [Bail is money that a person may pay to the court in order to be released while awaiting trial. The money is returned when the person appears for trial.]

The listing of certain rights in the Constitution does not mean that these are the only rights of the people.

Any powers not given to the United States by the Constitution are left to the states, and any not forbidden to the states are left to the people.

[Adopted in 1798, this amendment changed the powers given to federal courts by Article Three of the Constitution.] The federal courts do not have the power to hear cases brought against a state by citizens of another state or another country.

## Amendment 7

In suits at common law, where the value in controversy shall exceed twenty dollars, the right of trial by jury shall be preserved, and no fact tried by a jury shall be otherwise re-examined in any court of the United States than according to the rules of common law.

## Amendment 8

Excessive bail shall not be required, nor excessive fines imposed, nor cruel and unusual punishments inflicted.

## Amendment 9

The enumeration in the Constitution of certain rights shall not be construed to deny or disparage others retained by the people.

## Amendment 10

The powers not delegated to the United States by the Constitution, nor prohibited by it to the states, are reserved to the states respectively, or to the people.

## Amendment 11

The judicial power of the United States shall not be construed to extend to any suit in law or equity, commenced or prosecuted against one of the United States by citizens of another state, or by citizens or subjects of any foreign state.

# Amendment 12

The electors shall meet in their respective states and vote by ballot for President and Vice-President, one of whom, at least, shall not be an inhabitant of the same state with themselves; they shall name in their ballots the person voted for as President, and in distinct ballots the person voted for as Vice-President, and they shall make distinct lists of all persons voted for as President, and of all persons voted for as Vice-President, and of the number of votes for each, which lists they shall sign and certify, and transmit sealed to the seat of the government of the United States, directed to the President of the Senate;—the President of the Senate shall, in the presence of the Senate and House of Representatives, open all the certificates and the votes shall then be counted;—the person having the greatest number of votes for President, shall be the President, if such number be a majority of the whole number of electors appointed; and if no person have such majority, then from the persons having the highest numbers not exceeding three on the list of those voted for as President, the House of Representatives shall choose immediately, by ballot, the President. But in choosing the President, the votes shall be taken by states, the representation from each state having one vote; a quorum for this purpose shall consist of a member or members from two thirds of the states, and a majority of all the states shall be necessary to a choice. And if the House of Representatives shall not choose a President whenever the right of choice shall devolve upon them, before the fourth day of March next following, then the Vice-President shall act as President, as in the case of the death or other constitutional disability of the President.—The person having the greatest number of votes as Vice-President, shall be the Vice-President, if such number be a majority of the whole number of electors appointed, and if no person have a majority, then from the two highest numbers on the list, the Senate shall choose the Vice-President; a quorum for the purpose shall consist of two thirds of the whole number of senators, and a majority of the whole number shall be necessary to a choice. But no person constitutionally

[Adopted in 1804, this amendment changed Article Two of the Constitution by providing for separate votes for President and Vice-President.] The electors will meet and vote for President and Vice-President. One of the people for whom they vote must be from a state other than their own. They shall vote for one person for President and another person for Vice-President. A separate list of the votes for President and for Vice-President will be sent to the President of the Senate. The President of the Senate will count the votes in front of Congress. The person having the most votes for President shall be President if that person receives a majority of the votes. If no one receives a majority, the House of Representatives shall choose the President from among the three top vote-getters. The votes shall be taken by state with each state having one vote. Two thirds of the members of the House must be present to do this, and a candidate must win a majority of votes to become President. If the House of Representatives does not make a choice by the fourth day of March, then the person already serving as Vice-President shall act as President. The candidate having the largest number of votes as Vice-President shall be Vice-President if that person receives a majority of the votes. If no one receives a majority, then the Senate shall choose the Vice-President from among the two top vote-getters. Two thirds of the senators must be present to do this and a candidate must win a majority of votes to become President. A person who cannot meet the requirements for President may not be Vice-President.

ineligible to the office of President shall be eligible to that of Vice-President of the United States.

## Amendment 13

*Section 1.* Neither slavery nor involuntary servitude, except as a punishment for crime whereof the party shall have been duly convicted, shall exist within the United States, or any place subject to their jurisdiction.

*Section 2.* Congress shall have power to enforce this article by appropriate legislation.

[Adopted in 1865.] Slavery, or any other forced labor, is forbidden except as a punishment for crime. In the case of punishment for a crime, the person must be convicted through a court of law. This law applies to all of the United States and any place governed by its rules or laws. Congress has the power to pass other laws in order to enforce this one.

## Amendment 14

*Section 1.* All persons born or naturalized in the United States, and subject to the jurisdiction thereof, are citizens of the United States and of the state wherein they reside. No state shall make or enforce any law which shall abridge the privileges or immunities of citizens of the United States; nor shall any state deprive any person of life, liberty, or property, without due process of law, nor deny to any person within its jurisdiction the equal protection of the laws.

*Section 2.* Representatives shall be apportioned among the several states according to their respective numbers, counting the whole number of persons in each state, excluding Indians not taxed. But when the right to vote at any election for the choice of electors for President and Vice-President of the United States, representatives in Congress, the executive or judicial officers of a state, or the members of the legislature thereof, is denied to any of the male inhabitants of such state, being twenty-one years of age, and citizens of the United States, or in any way abridged, except for participation in rebellion, or other crime, the basis of representation therein shall be reduced in the proportion which the number of such male citizens shall bear to the whole number of male citizens twenty-one years of age in such state.

*Section 3.* No person shall be a senator or representative in Congress, or elector of President

[Adopted in 1868. Naturalization is the method provided by law through which people born outside the country may become citizens.] All persons born or naturalized in the United States and under its laws are citizens of both the United States and the state where they live. No state shall make or enforce any law which takes away the rights and protections of its citizens. No state may take away any person's life, liberty, or property without going through the courts, nor deny any person equal protection of the law.

The number of representatives to the House shall be determined by the number of people in each state, except Indians who do not pay taxes. When any state denies the right to vote in an election for President, Vice-President, Congress, or officers of a state to any male citizen twenty-one years of age or older, then that state may lose some of its representatives. Citizens may lose the right to vote for taking part in a rebellion or other crime against the United States.

No person may hold any federal or state office who took an oath of office and later took part or Vice-President, or hold any office, civil or military, under the United States, or under any state, who, having previously taken an oath, as a member of Congress, or as an officer of the United States, or as a member of any state legislature, or as an executive or judicial officer of any state, to support the Constitution of the United States, shall have engaged in insurrection or rebellion against the same, or given aid or comfort to the enemies thereof. But Congress may by a vote of two thirds of each house, remove such disability.

*Section 4.* The validity of the public debt of the United States, authorized by law, including debts incurred for payment of pensions and bounties for services in suppressing insurrection or rebellion, shall not be questioned. But neither the United States nor any state shall assume or pay any debt or obligation incurred in aid of insurrection or rebellion against the United States, or any claim for the loss or emancipation of any slave; but all such debts, obligations, and claims shall be held illegal and void.

*Section 5.* The Congress shall have power to enforce, by appropriate legislation, the provisions of this article.

in a rebellion or gave aid to the enemies of the United States. However, Congress may allow such a person to again hold office by a two-thirds vote of each group.

The debts of the United States, including those for paying the cost of fighting a rebellion, will be honored. Neither the United States nor any state is allowed to honor any of the debts which came about as a result of helping a rebellion against the United States, nor to pay for the loss of slaves. All such debts and claims are illegal and ended.

Congress has the power to pass other laws to enforce this one.

# Amendment 15

*Section 1.* The right of citizens of the United States to vote shall not be denied or abridged by the United States or by any state on account of race, color, or previous condition of servitude.

*Section 2.* The Congress shall have power to enforce this article by appropriate legislation.

[Adopted in 1870.] The right of citizens to vote shall not be denied or limited by either the United States or any of the states because of race, color, or from having been in forced labor (a slave).

Congress has the power to pass other laws to enforce this one.

# Amendment 16

The Congress shall have power to lay and collect taxes on incomes, from whatever source derived, without apportionment among the several states, and without regard to any census or enumeration.

[Adopted in 1913, this amendment changed Article One, Section Nine, of the Constitution.] Congress shall have the power to collect income taxes from any source without dividing the amount of the tax according to the population of the states.

# Amendment 17

The Senate of the United States shall be composed of two senators from each state,

[Adopted in 1913, this amendment changed Article One, Section Three, of the Constitution to allow senators to be chosen by a direct vote of the people.] The Senate of the United States shall be made up of two senators from each state elected by the people. Each senator shall have one vote in the Senate. The electors (voters) in each state must meet the same requirements for voting as those who vote for the largest branch of their state legislature.

When a Senate seat is open, the governor of a state will call for an election to fill that seat. The legislature of any state may allow the governor to appoint someone to fill the seat until the people elect someone.

This amendment does not affect any senator who was elected or was serving before it became a part of the Constitution.

[Adopted in 1919, this amendment was later repealed, or removed, from the Constitution by Amendment 21.] One year after this amendment is adopted, the sale, manufacture, or shipment into or out of the United States of intoxicating liquor for drinking is forbidden.

Both Congress and the states shall have the power to enforce this law.

This amendment must be approved by the legislatures of the states as provided in the Constitution within seven years to become law.

[Adopted in 1920.] The right of citizens of the United States to vote shall not be denied or limited by either the United States or any state because of a person's sex.

Congress has the power to pass other laws to enforce this one.

elected by the people thereof, for six years; and each senator shall have one vote. The electors in each state shall have the qualifications requisite for electors of the most numerous branch of the state legislatures.

When vacancies happen in the representation of any state in the Senate, the executive authority of such state shall issue writs of election to fill such vacancies: Provided, that the legislature of any state may empower the executive thereof to make temporary appointments until the people fill the vacancies by election as the legislature may direct.

This amendment shall not be so construed as to affect the election or term of any senator chosen before it becomes valid as part of the Constitution.

## Amendment 18

*Section 1.* After one year from the ratification of this article the manufacture, sale, or transportation of intoxicating liquors within, the importation thereof into, or the exportation thereof from the United States and all territory subject to the jurisdiction thereof for beverage purposes is hereby prohibited.

*Section 2.* The Congress and the several states shall have concurrent power to enforce this article by appropriate legislation.

*Section 3.* This article shall be inoperative unless it shall have been ratified as an amendment to the Constitution by the legislatures of the several states, as provided in the Constitution, within seven years from the date of the submission hereof to the states by the Congress.

## Amendment 19

*Section 1.* The right of citizens of the United States to vote shall not be denied or abridged by the United States or by any state on account of sex.

*Section 2.* Congress shall have power to enforce this article by appropriate legislation.

# Amendment 20

*Section 1.* The terms of the President and Vice-President shall end at noon on the 20th day of January, and the terms of senators and representatives at noon on the 3rd day of January, of the years in which such terms would have ended if this article had not been ratified; and the terms of their successors shall then begin.

*Section 2.* The Congress shall assemble at least once in every year, and such meeting shall begin at noon on the 3rd day of January, unless they shall by law appoint a different day.

*Section 3.* If, at the time fixed for the beginning of the term of the President, the President-elect shall have died, the Vice-President-elect shall become President. If a President shall not have been chosen before the time fixed for the beginning of his term, or if the President-elect shall have failed to qualify, then the Vice-President-elect shall act as President until a President shall have qualified; and the Congress may by law provide for the case wherein neither a President-elect nor a Vice-President-elect shall have qualified, declaring who shall then act as President, or the manner in which one who is to act shall be selected, and such person shall act accordingly until a President or Vice-President shall have qualified.

*Section 4.* The Congress may by law provide for the case of the death of any of the persons from whom the House of Representatives may choose a President whenever the right of choice shall have devolved upon them, and for the case of the death of any of the persons from whom the Senate may choose a Vice-President whenever the right of choice shall have devolved upon them.

*Section 5.* Sections 1 and 2 shall take effect on the 15th day of October following the ratification of this article.

[Adopted in 1933. Before this amendment was adopted, a newly elected Congress did not meet until thirteen months after the election. Meanwhile, the old Congress was making laws for the country with some members who had not been reelected (called lame ducks).] The terms of President and Vice-President shall end on January 20, and the terms of the senators and representatives shall end on January 3 of the same year in which their terms would have ended if this law had not been passed. The terms of the people elected in their place shall begin on the same day.

Congress shall meet at least once a year, beginning on January 3, unless they decide on another day.

If the person elected to be President dies before taking office, then the person elected to be Vice-President becomes President. If no one has been chosen to be President by the time set for the term to begin, or if the person chosen does not meet the requirements to be President, then the Vice-President shall act as President until a person elected to be President meets the requirements. Congress may make laws for a case in which neither the person elected to be President, nor the person elected to be Vice-President, meet the requirements. Congress will decide who will act as President as well as how the person will be chosen. That person will serve until a President is elected.

Congress may make laws to decide what will happen when the House of Representatives must choose the President and one of the candidates dies, or when the Senate must choose the Vice-President and one of the candidates dies.

This amendment becomes law only if it is approved by the legislatures of three fourths of the states within seven years.

[Adopted in 1933.] Amendment 18 is canceled.

The shipment of intoxicating liquor into any state, territory, or possession of the United States is forbidden if it is against the laws of the local area.

This amendment becomes law only if it is approved by conventions in the states as provided in the Constitution.

[Adopted in 1951.] No person may be elected to the office of President more than twice. If a person serves more than two years of another person's term as President, then that person may be elected only once. This amendment does not apply in any way to the person holding the office of President at the time it goes into effect.

This amendment becomes law only if it is approved by the legislatures of three fourths of the states within seven years.

## Section 6

*Section 6.* This article shall be inoperative unless it shall have been ratified as an amendment to the Constitution by the legislatures of three fourths of the several states within seven years from the date of its submission.

## Amendment 21

*Section 1.* The eighteenth article of amendment to the Constitution of the United States is hereby repealed.

*Section 2.* The transportation or importation into any state, territory, or possession of the United States for delivery or use therein of intoxicating liquors, in violation of the laws thereof, is hereby prohibited.

*Section 3.* This article shall be inoperative unless it shall have been ratified as an amendment to the Constitution by conventions in the several states, as provided in the Constitution, within seven years from the date of the submission hereof to the states by the Congress.

## Amendment 22

*Section 1.* No person shall be elected to the office of the President more than twice, and no person who has held the office of President, or acted as President, for more than two years of a term to which some other person was elected President shall be elected to the office of the President more than once. But this article shall not apply to any person holding the office of President when this article was proposed by the Congress, and shall not prevent any person who may be holding the office of President, or acting as President, during the term within which this article becomes operative from holding the office of President or acting as President during the remainder of such term.

*Section 2.* This article shall be inoperative unless it shall have been ratified as an amendment to the Constitution by the legislatures of three fourths of the several states within seven years from the date of its submission to the states by the Congress.

## Amendment 23

*Section 1.* The District constituting the seat of government of the United States shall appoint in such manner as the Congress may direct:

A number of electors of President and Vice-President equal to the whole number of senators and representatives in Congress to which the District would be entitled if it were a state, but in no event more than the least populous state; they shall be in addition to those appointed by the states, but they shall be considered, for the purposes of the election of President and Vice-President, to be electors appointed by a state; and they shall meet in the District and perform such duties as provided by the twelfth article of amendment.

*Section 2.* The Congress shall have power to enforce this article by appropriate legislation.

[Adopted in 1961. The District of Columbia is not a state and has no representatives in Congress. This amendment allows the people living there to vote for President and Vice-President.] Congress will decide how the District, which is the seat of the United States government, shall appoint:

As many electors for President and Vice-President as it would receive if it were a state. However, the District may not receive any more electors than the state with the fewest people. They shall act the same as electors from any other state according to the method established by Amendment 12.

Congress has the power to pass other laws to enforce this one.

## Amendment 24

*Section 1.* The right of citizens of the United States to vote in any primary or other election for President or Vice-President, for electors for President or Vice-President, or for senator or representative in Congress, shall not be denied or abridged by the United States or any state by reason of failure to pay any poll tax or other tax.

*Section 2.* The Congress shall have power to enforce this article by appropriate legislation.

[Adopted in 1964. A poll tax is money which a person may be made to pay before voting.] The right of citizens to vote in any election for President, Vice-President, or for senators or representatives in Congress cannot be denied or limited because that person did not pay a poll tax or other kind of tax.

Congress has the power to pass other laws to enforce this one.

## Amendment 25

*Section 1.* In case of the removal of the President from office or his death or resignation, the Vice-President shall become President.

[Adopted in 1967. Eight times in American history, a Vice-President has taken over the office of President, leaving the office of the Vice-President empty. This amendment lists ways to deal with that problem.] In case the President is removed from office, resigns, or dies, the Vice-President shall become President.

Whenever the office of Vice-President is empty, the President shall choose someone to fill the position, with the approval of a majority of both groups in Congress.

When the President states in writing to the President *pro tempore* (the person who is President of the Senate in place of the Vice-President) and to the Speaker of the House of Representatives that the duties and powers of the President can no longer be carried out, the Vice-President shall act as President. The Vice-President shall do so until the President states again in writing that he or she can again carry out the duties of the office.

The Vice-President and more than half of the Cabinet, or another group chosen by Congress, may state in writing to the heads of both groups in Congress that the President is no longer able to carry out the duties of the office. Then the Vice-President shall serve as Acting President until the President states in writing that he or she can again perform the duties of the office. If a President writes that the duties of the office can be done, and the Vice-President and a majority of the Cabinet or other group appointed by Congress disagree, then the Congress must decide by a two-thirds vote if the President can take over the duties or if the Vice-President shall continue to do them.

*Section 2.* Whenever there is a vacancy in the office of the Vice-President, the President shall nominate a Vice-President who shall take the office upon confirmation by a majority vote of both houses of Congress.

*Section 3.* Whenever the President transmits to the President pro tempore of the Senate and the Speaker of the House of Representatives his written declaration that he is unable to discharge the powers and duties of his office, and until he transmits to them a written declaration to the contrary, such powers and duties shall be discharged by the Vice-President as Acting President.

*Section 4.* Whenever the Vice-President and a majority of either the principal officers of the executive departments, or of such other body as Congress may by law provide, transmit to the President pro tempore of the Senate and the Speaker of the House of Representatives their written declaration that the President is unable to discharge the powers and duties of his office, the Vice-President shall immediately assume the powers and duties of the office of Acting President.

Thereafter, when the President transmits to the President pro tempore of the Senate and the Speaker of the House of Representatives his written declaration that no inability exists, he shall resume the powers and duties of his office unless the Vice-President and a majority of either the principal officers of the executive departments, or of such other body as Congress may by law provide, transmit within four days to the President pro tempore of the Senate and the Speaker of the House of Representatives their written declaration that the President is unable to discharge the powers and duties of his office. Thereupon Congress shall decide the issue, assembling within 48 hours for that purpose if not in session. If the Congress, within 21 days after receipt of the latter written declaration, or, if Congress is not in session, within 21 days after Congress is required to assemble, determines by two thirds vote of both houses that the President is unable to discharge the powers and duties of his office, the

Vice-President shall continue to discharge the same as Acting President; otherwise, the President shall resume the powers and duties of his office.

## Amendment 26

*Section 1.* The right of citizens of the United States, who are eighteen years of age or older, to vote shall not be denied or abridged by the United States or by any state on account of age.

*Section 2.* The Congress shall have power to enforce this article by appropriate legislation.

[Adopted in 1971. The voting age in most states had been twenty-one years before this amendment was adopted.] The right of citizens of the United States who are eighteen years of age or older to vote shall not be denied nor limited because of age.

Congress has the power to pass other laws to enforce this one.

# Presidents and Vice-Presidents

| No. | Name | Born | Died | Yrs. in Office | Party | State* | Vice-Pres. | State |
|---|---|---|---|---|---|---|---|---|
| 1 | George Washington | 1732 | 1799 | 1789- | None | Va. | John Adams | Mass. |
|  | George Washington | 1732 | 1799 | -1797 | None | Va. | John Adams | Mass. |
| 2 | John Adams | 1735 | 1826 | 1797-1801 | Federalist | Mass. | Thomas Jefferson | Va. |
| 3 | Thomas Jefferson | 1743 | 1826 | 1801- | Republican† | Va. | Aaron Burr | N.Y. |
|  | Thomas Jefferson | 1743 | 1826 | -1809 | Republican | Va. | George Clinton | N.Y. |
| 4 | James Madison | 1751 | 1836 | 1809- | Republican | Va. | George Clinton | N.Y. |
|  | James Madison | 1751 | 1836 | -1817 | Republican | Va. | Elbridge Gerry | Mass. |
| 5 | James Monroe | 1758 | 1831 | 1817- | Republican | Va. | Daniel D. Tompkins | N.Y. |
|  | James Monroe | 1758 | 1831 | -1825 | Republican | Va. | Daniel D. Tompkins | N.Y. |
| 6 | John Quincy Adams | 1767 | 1848 | 1825-29 | Nat.-Rep. | Mass. | John C. Calhoun | S.C. |
| 7 | Andrew Jackson | 1767 | 1845 | 1829- | Democratic | Tenn. | John C. Calhoun | S.C. |
|  | Andrew Jackson | 1767 | 1845 | -1837 | Democratic | Tenn. | Martin Van Buren | N.Y. |
| 8 | Martin Van Buren | 1782 | 1862 | 1837-41 | Democratic | N.Y. | Richard M. Johnson | Ky. |
| 9 | William H. Harrison | 1773 | 1841 | 1841 | Whig | Ohio | John Tyler | Va. |
| 10 | John Tyler | 1790 | 1862 | 1841-45 | Whig | Va. | | |
| 11 | James K. Polk | 1795 | 1849 | 1845-49 | Democratic | Tenn. | George M. Dallas | Pa. |
| 12 | Zachary Taylor | 1784 | 1850 | 1849-50 | Whig | La. | Millard Fillmore | N.Y. |
| 13 | Millard Fillmore | 1800 | 1874 | 1850-53 | Whig | N.Y. | | |
| 14 | Franklin Pierce | 1804 | 1869 | 1853-57 | Democratic | N.H. | William R. King | Al. |
| 15 | James Buchanan | 1791 | 1868 | 1857-61 | Democratic | Pa. | John C. Breckinridge | Ky. |
| 16 | Abraham Lincoln | 1809 | 1865 | 1861- | Republican | Ill. | Hannibal Hamlin | Me. |
|  | Abraham Lincoln | 1809 | 1865 | -1865 | Republican | Ill. | Andrew Johnson | Tenn. |
| 17 | Andrew Johnson | 1808 | 1875 | 1865-69 | Democratic | Tenn. | | |
| 18 | Ulysses S. Grant | 1822 | 1885 | 1869- | Republican | Ill. | Schuyler Colfax | Ind. |
|  | Ulysses S. Grant | 1822 | 1885 | -1877 | Republican | Ill. | Henry Wilson | Mass. |
| 19 | Rutherford B. Hayes | 1822 | 1893 | 1877-81 | Republican | Ohio | William A. Wheeler | N.Y. |
| 20 | James A. Garfield | 1831 | 1881 | 1881 | Republican | Ohio | Chester A. Arthur | N.Y. |
| 21 | Chester A. Arthur | 1830 | 1886 | 1881-85 | Republican | N.Y. | | |
| 22 | Grover Cleveland | 1837 | 1908 | 1885-89 | Democratic | N.Y. | Thomas A. Hendricks | Ind. |
| 23 | Benjamin Harrison | 1833 | 1901 | 1889-93 | Republican | Ind. | Levi P. Morton | N.Y. |
| 24 | Grover Cleveland | 1837 | 1908 | 1893-97 | Democratic | N.Y. | Adlai E. Stevenson | Ill. |
| 25 | William McKinley | 1843 | 1901 | 1897- | Republican | Ohio | Garret A. Hobart | N.J. |
|  | William McKinley | 1843 | 1901 | -1901 | Republican | Ohio | Theodore Roosevelt | N.Y. |
| 26 | Theodore Roosevelt | 1858 | 1919 | 1901- | Republican | N.Y. | | |
|  | Theodore Roosevelt | 1858 | 1919 | -1909 | Republican | N.Y. | Charles W. Fairbanks | Ind. |
| 27 | William H. Taft | 1857 | 1930 | 1909-13 | Republican | Ohio | James S. Sherman | N.Y. |
| 28 | Woodrow Wilson | 1856 | 1924 | 1913- | Democratic | N.J. | Thomas R. Marshall | Ind. |
|  | Woodrow Wilson | 1856 | 1924 | -1921 | Democratic | N.J. | Thomas R. Marshall | Ind. |
| 29 | Warren G. Harding | 1865 | 1923 | 1921-23 | Republican | Ohio | Calvin Coolidge | Mass. |
| 30 | Calvin Coolidge | 1872 | 1933 | 1923- | Republican | Mass. | | |
|  | Calvin Coolidge | 1872 | 1933 | -1929 | Republican | Mass. | Charles G. Dawes | Ill. |
| 31 | Herbert Hoover | 1874 | 1964 | 1929-33 | Republican | Cal. | Charles Curtis | Kan. |
| 32 | Franklin D. Roosevelt | 1882 | 1945 | 1933- | Democratic | N.Y. | John N. Garner | Texas |
|  | Franklin D. Roosevelt | 1882 | 1945 | | Democratic | N.Y. | John N. Garner | Texas |
|  | Franklin D. Roosevelt | 1882 | 1945 | | Democratic | N.Y. | Henry A. Wallace | Iowa |
|  | Franklin D. Roosevelt | 1882 | 1945 | -1945 | Democratic | N.Y. | Harry S. Truman | Mo. |

| | | | | | | | | |
|---|---|---|---|---|---|---|---|---|
| 33 | Harry S. Truman | 1884 | 1972 | 1945- | Democratic | Mo. | | |
| | Harry S. Truman | 1884 | 1972 | -1953 | Democratic | Mo. | Alben W. Barkley | Ky. |
| 34 | Dwight D. Eisenhower | 1890 | 1969 | 1953- | Republican | N.Y. | Richard M. Nixon | Cal. |
| | Dwight D. Eisenhower | 1890 | 1969 | -1961 | Republican | Pa. | Richard M. Nixon | Cal. |
| 35 | John F. Kennedy | 1917 | 1963 | 1961-63 | Democratic | Mass. | Lyndon B. Johnson | Texas |
| 36 | Lyndon B. Johnson | 1908 | 1973 | 1963- | Democratic | Texas | | |
| | Lyndon B. Johnson | 1908 | 1973 | -1969 | Democratic | Texas | Hubert H. Humphrey | Minn. |
| 37 | Richard M. Nixon | 1913 | | 1969- | Republican | N.Y. | Spiro T. Agnew | Md. |
| | Richard M. Nixon | 1913 | | -1974 | Republican | N.Y. | Gerald R. Ford | Mich. |
| 38 | Gerald R. Ford | 1913 | | 1974-77 | Republican | Mich. | Nelson A. Rockefeller | N.Y. |
| 39 | James E. Carter, Jr. | 1924 | | 1977- | Democratic | Ga. | Walter F. Mondale | Minn. |

\* States are those where candidate was living at election time.

† Sometimes called Democratic-Republicans. This is not the same party as the Republican party established in 1854.

# Important Dates

13,000 BC (approx.)    First people entered New World

100 BC–500 AD (approx.)    Mound burial culture in Ohio Valley

1200 (approx.)    Mississippian Indian culture

1492    Columbus' first trip to New World

1500's    Africans brought to the New World; Spanish conquests in New World

1538    Black guide, Estevanico, explored Southwest

1541    Coronado explored Southwest

1565    St. Augustine founded by Spanish

1600's    Plains Indians adapted to horse

1605    Nova Scotia founded by French

1607    Jamestown founded by English

1619    Virginia House of Burgesses elected

1620    Pilgrims founded Plymouth colony; Mayflower Compact made

1623    First colonies founded in New Jersey and Maine

1624    Dutch founded Albany and New Amsterdam

1630    Massachusetts Bay Colony founded

1634    First settlement in Maryland

1636    Williams founded Rhode Island; Connecticut colony founded

1638    Hutchinson settled in R.I.; first New Hampshire towns founded

1650    Bradstreet published poems

1663    Charter granted for Carolina colonies

1664    Dutch colonies taken over by English

1681    Penn founded Pennsylvania colony

1682    LaSalle explored Mississippi River

1702    Royal colony of New Jersey formed

1704    Delaware separated from Pennsylvania

1718    French established New Orleans

1733    Georgia colony founded

1754    French and Indian War began

1763    Proclamation of 1763

1765    Stamp Act passed; Stamp Act Congress met

1767    Townshend Acts passed

1769    Spain founded California colony

1770    Boston Massacre

1773    Boston Tea Party

1774    First Continental Congress

1775    Battles of Lexington and Concord; first antislavery society founded

1776    Spain founded Yerba Buena colony; Paine wrote *Common Sense*; Declaration of Independence

1781    American victory at Yorktown; Articles of Confederation adopted

1783    Treaty of Paris ended Revolution

1786    Shays' Rebellion

1787    Constitutional Convention held; Northwest Ordinance passed; Del., Pa., N.J. ratified Constitution

1788    Ga., Conn., Mass., Md., S.C., N.H., Va., N.Y. ratified Constitution

1789    George Washington elected first President; Judiciary Act established courts; N.C. ratified Constitution

1790    Samuel Slater built mill; R.I. ratified Constitution

1791    Vermont admitted to Union; Bill of Rights adopted

1792    Kentucky admitted to Union

1793    Eli Whitney invented cotton gin

1794    Whiskey Rebellion

1796    John Adams elected President; Tennessee admitted to Union

1798    Alien and Sedition Acts passed; Virginia and Kentucky Resolutions passed; Eleventh Amendment adopted

1800    Thomas Jefferson elected President; Capital moved to Washington, D.C.

1801    John Marshall appointed Chief Justice

1803    Louisiana Purchase; Ohio admitted to Union; *Marbury v. Madison* decided

1804    Twelfth Amendment adopted

1807    Robert Fulton built successful steamboat; Embargo Act passed against Britain

1808    James Madison elected President

1811    Tecumseh formed Indian confederation; National Road begun; Battle of Tippecanoe

1812    War of 1812 began; Louisiana admitted to Union

1813    Battle of Lake Erie; Tecumseh killed at Battle of Thames

1814    Capital burned by British troops; National Anthem written by Key; Treaty of Ghent ended war; Battle of New Orleans

1816    James Monroe elected President;

Seminole War; Indiana admitted to Union

1817 Miss. admitted to Union

1818 Illinois admitted to Union

1819 Alabama admitted to Union; Spain gave Florida to the U.S.

1820's–1830's Canal building

1820 Missouri Compromise passed; Maine admitted to Union

1821 Mexico won independence from Spain; Emma Hart Willard opened Female Seminary; Missouri admitted to Union

1823 Monroe Doctrine

1824 J. Q. Adams elected President

1825 Mexico opened Texas to American settlers

1828 Andrew Jackson elected President; Baltimore and Ohio Railroad begun; Webster introduced dictionary and speller

1830's Indian removals began; Osceola led war against U.S.

1830 Webster-Hayne debates in Congress

1831 Nat Turner led slave revolt; McCormick introduced mechanical reaper

1832 Nullification crisis

1833 American Antislavery Society founded

1836 Texas declared independence from Mexico; Arkansas admitted to Union; Martin Van Buren elected President

1837 Michigan admitted to Union

1838 Trail of Tears began; Battle of Wolf Creek

1840's Sojourner Truth began her antislavery activities

1840 William Henry Harrison elected President; Indian groups made peace near Bent's Fort; Battle of Plum Creek; President Harrison died; John Tyler became President

1841 Frederick Douglass began his antislavery lectures

1843 Americans organized Oregon territory

1844 James K. Polk elected President; Samuel Morse sent telegraph message

1845 Term Manifest Destiny coined; Florida and Texas admitted to Union

1846 California declared independence; Mexican War began; Elias Howe invented sewing machine; Iowa admitted to Union

1847 Mormons founded Salt Lake City

1848 Women's rights convention held; Treaty of Guadalupe Hidalgo signed; gold discovered in California; Zachary Taylor elected President; Wisconsin admitted to Union

1850 Harriet Tubman, Underground Railroad helped slaves to escape; President Taylor died; Millard Fillmore became President; Compromise of 1850 passed; Fugitive Slave Act passed; California admitted to Union

1852 Harriet Beecher Stowe's *Uncle Tom's Cabin* published; Franklin Pierce elected President

1853 Gadsden Purchase; Perry opened trade with Japan

1854 Kansas-Nebraska Act passed; Republican party organized

1856 James Buchanan elected President

1857 Dred Scott decision made

1858 Lincoln-Douglas debates held; Minnesota admitted to Union

1859 First successful oil well drilled; John Brown raided Harpers Ferry; Oregon admitted to Union

1860 Abraham Lincoln elected President; South Carolina seceded

1861 Kansas admitted to Union; Confederate States of America organized; Fort Sumter, beginning of Civil War

1862 Morrill Act passed

1862–1864 Charlotte Forten; Port Royal Experiment

1863 Emancipation Proclamation; Battle of Gettysburg; West Virginia admitted to Union

1864 Nevada admitted to Union

1865 Lee surrendered at Appomattox; President Lincoln assassinated; Andrew Johnson became President; Thirteenth Amendment adopted; Freedmen's Bureau established

1865–1866 Black Codes passed in the South

1865–1870's Sharecropping developed

1866 Civil Rights Act of 1866 passed; Ku Klux Klan organized; Kelly-Bessemer steel process developed

1867 Radical Reconstruction began; Standard Oil Company organized; Alaska bought from Russia; Grange organized; Nebraska admitted to Union

1868 Fourteenth Amendment adopted; President Johnson impeached; Senate voted against conviction; U. S. Grant elected President; Republic of Puerto Rico declared

1869 Transcontinental Railroad completed; Wyoming granted voting rights to women; Knights of Labor organized

1870 Hiram Revels became first black senator; Fifteenth Amendment adopted; last seceded states returned to Union

1872 Crédit Mobilier scandal; Montgomery Ward began catalog sales

1876 Battle of the Little Bighorn; Bell showed telephone at Philadelphia; Rutherford Hayes elected President; Colorado admitted to Union

1877 Nationwide railroad strike; war against Chief Joseph and Nez Percé

1879 F. W. Woolworth opened five-and-ten store

1880–1890 Immigration totaled five million

1880 James Garfield elected President

1881 President Garfield assassinated; Chester Arthur became President

1882 Clara Barton organized American Red Cross; first restrictive immigration law passed; Chinese Exclusion Act passed

| | | | | | |
|---|---|---|---|---|---|
| 1883 | Pendleton Act passed | 1912 | Children's Bureau established; N.M., Arizona admitted to Union; Woodrow Wilson elected President | 1933 | Twentieth Amendment adopted; Twenty-first Amendment adopted |
| 1884 | Grover Cleveland elected President | | | 1934 | Indian Reorganization Act passed |
| 1886 | Haymarket Square riot; American Federation of Labor founded | 1913 | Federal Reserve Act passed; Sixteenth Amendment adopted; Seventeenth Amendment adopted | 1935 | CIO formed; Wagner Act passed; Social Security Act passed; Neutrality Act passed |
| 1887 | Dawes Act passed; Interstate Commerce Act passed | 1914 | World War I began; Panama Canal opened; Clayton Antitrust Act passed | 1936 | Mary McLeod Bethune became Director of Negro Affairs in Nat. Youth Administration |
| 1888 | Benjamin Harrison elected President | | | | |
| 1889 | Jane Addams established Hull House; N.D., S.D., Montana, Wash. admitted to Union | 1915 | Ku Klux Klan reorganized | 1940 | President Roosevelt elected third time |
| | | 1916 | Villa raided U.S. border; Pershing led troops to Mexico | 1941 | Lend-Lease Act passed; Atlantic Charter made; Japanese attacked Pearl Harbor; Japanese Americans interned |
| 1890's | Blacks excluded from voting in South | 1917 | Puerto Ricans made U.S. citizens; U.S. entered World War I; immigration law of 1917 passed | | |
| 1890 | Sherman Antitrust Act passed; Idaho, Wyoming admitted to Union | | | 1942 | Invasion of Africa; Battles of Midway and Guadalcanal |
| | | 1918 | President Wilson's Fourteen Points announced; Eighteenth Amendment adopted; armistice ended World War I | 1943 | Chinese made eligible for citizenship; invasions of Sicily and Italy |
| 1891 | Queen Liliuokalani became Hawaiian ruler | | | | |
| 1892 | Populist party formed; Grover Cleveland elected President | 1919 | Nationwide steel strike; Eighteenth Amendment adopted | 1944 | Invasion of France |
| 1895 | Booker T. Washington's Atlanta speech | 1919–1920 | Red Scare | 1945 | Battles of Iwo Jima and Okinawa; surrender of Germany; Yalta Conference held; President Roosevelt died; Harry Truman became President; atom bomb dropped; surrender of Japan; United Nations founded |
| | | 1920's | Garveyism; Harlem Renaissance | | |
| 1896 | *Plessy v. Ferguson* decided; Utah admitted to Union; William McKinley elected President | 1920 | Nineteenth Amendment adopted; two stations began radio broadcasts; Warren Harding elected President | | |
| 1898 | Hawaii annexed to the U.S.; Spanish-American War began; Puerto Rico and Guam given to U.S.; Philippines bought by U.S. | 1921 | American Foundation for the Blind founded; Order of the Sons of America founded; immigration quota act passed | 1946 | Philippines became independent |
| | | | | 1947 | Taft-Hartley Act passed |
| | | | | 1948 | European Recovery Act passed; Berlin crisis |
| 1899 | Filipino revolt against U.S.; Open Door Policy | 1923 | President Harding died; Calvin Coolidge became President | 1949 | NATO formed |
| 1900's | Black migration to North | | | 1950's | Indian reservation termination policy began; Puerto Rican immigration to U.S. |
| 1900–1910 | Nine million immigrants; large Mexican immigration to U.S. | 1924 | Japanese excluded from immigration; Indian citizenship act passed | | |
| 1901 | City commission government began; President McKinley assassinated; Theodore Roosevelt became President | | | 1950 | Korean War began |
| | | 1927 | Lindbergh flew across the Atlantic; first talking movie made | 1950–1954 | McCarthy years |
| | | 1928 | Herbert Hoover elected President | 1951 | Twenty-second Amendment adopted |
| 1903 | DuBois' *Souls of Black Folk* published | 1929 | Stock market crash | 1952 | Puerto Rico became commonwealth; McCarran-Walter Immigration Act passed; Japanese made eligible for citizenship; Dwight Eisenhower elected President |
| | | 1929–1940 | Depression | | |
| 1905 | Niagara Movement founded | 1930–1940 | Mexicans, Mexican Americans deported | | |
| 1907 | Gentlemen's Agreement made; Oklahoma admitted to Union | | | | |
| 1908 | City manager government began; William Taft elected President | 1932 | Franklin Roosevelt elected President; Frances Perkins chosen Secretary of Labor; Good Neighbor Policy | 1953 | End of Korean War |
| | | | | 1953–1958 | Refugee relief acts passed |
| 1909 | NAACP founded | | | 1954 | *Brown v. Board of Education* decided |
| 1911 | National Urban League founded | 1933–1936 | New Deal | | |

| 1955 | Rosa Parks' arrest led to Montgomery bus boycott; AFL-CIO merged |
|------|---|
| 1957 | Civil Rights Act of 1957 passed; Soviet Union launched Sputnik |
| 1958 | National Defense Education Act passed; first U.S. satellite launched |
| 1959 | Alaska and Hawaii admitted to Union |
| 1960's | Sit-ins staged throughout the South |
| 1960 | Civil Rights Act of 1960 passed; John Kennedy elected President |
| 1961 | Peace Corps established; Twenty-third Amendment adopted |
| 1962 | John Glenn orbited the earth; Cuban missile crisis |
| 1963 | Nuclear Test Ban Treaty signed; March on Washington held; President Kennedy assassinated; Lyndon Johnson became President; Americans entered Vietnam combat |

| 1964 | Twenty-fourth Amendment adopted; Economic Opportunity Act passed; Civil Rights Act of 1964 passed; Gulf of Tonkin Resolution passed; riot by blacks in Harlem |
|------|---|
| 1965 | Voting Rights Act of 1965 passed; Immigration and Nationality Act passed; Elementary and Secondary Education Act passed; Medicare and Medicaid established; riot by blacks in Watts; César Chávez led farm workers' strike |
| 1966 | National Organization for Women founded |
| 1967 | Twenty-fifth Amendment adopted |
| 1968 | Treaty halting spread of nuclear weapons signed; Martin Luther King, Jr., assassinated; Robert Kennedy assassinated; Richard Nixon elected President |
| 1969 | First Americans withdrawn from Vietnam; American astronauts are first to land on moon |
| 1971 | National Women's Political |

| | Caucus founded; Twenty-sixth Amendment adopted |
|------|---|
| 1972–1974 | Watergate scandal |
| 1972 | Revenue sharing act passed; Equal Employment Opportunity Act passed; President Nixon visited Peking and Moscow; nuclear arms limitation treaty signed |
| 1973 | Vietnam armistice agreement signed; Vice-President Agnew resigned; Gerald Ford appointed Vice-President; Rehabilitation Act passed |
| 1973–1975 | Arab oil embargo |
| 1974 | President Nixon resigned; Gerald Ford became President; nuclear weapons test treaty signed |
| 1975 | Joint space mission by U.S. and Soviet Union |
| 1976 | America's bicentennial celebrated; Jimmy Carter elected President |
| 1977 | Andrew Young, first black appointed U.S. ambassador to UN |

# Glossary

## A

**abolitionist** one who believed in and worked toward the ending of slavery.

**alien** a person who is not a citizen of the country in which he or she lives.

**alliance** a union between countries for a specific purpose.

**allies** people or countries who are members of an alliance.

**amendment** a change in, or addition to, the Constitution.

**American Independent party** a political party organized in 1968 to support George Wallace of Alabama for President.

**amnesty** a general pardon granted by the government or head of state of a country to members of a group who have broken national law.

**anarchism** the belief that organized government is unnecessary and should be abolished.

**ancestor** a relative of a past generation, such as one's great-great-grandmother.

**annexation** adding new land to a territory run by the same government.

**apprentice** a person who is bound by a legal agreement to serve another in order to learn a skill or trade.

**armistice** an agreement to end fighting.

**arms race** the competition between various nations, most importantly the United States, Russia, and China, to build better military weapons.

**artisan** a worker who is trained in a particular skill or craft.

**assassinate** to murder; usually used in the case of a political or government leader.

## B

**balance of power** a situation in which no one group or nation is strong enough to overpower another group or nation.

**bill** a suggested or proposed law that has been presented to a lawmaking body.

**bill of rights** a list of the basic rights and privileges of individuals to be protected by their government; used especially for the first ten amendments to the United States Constitution.

**Black Codes** laws passed by many southern states after the Civil War which limited most opportunities and rights of blacks.

**blockade** closing off an area to prevent certain things from going in or coming out.

**board of directors** a group of individuals chosen by the stockholders of a corporation to select its management and make its policies and decisions.

**bond** a certificate bearing a written promise to repay with interest an amount of money borrowed, at some specific date.

**boycott** a refusal to buy or use certain products as a means of protest.

## C

**Cabinet** the heads of the departments of government who serve as advisers to the President.

**capitalism** an economic system based on private ownership of property.

**carpetbaggers** northerners who packed all their possessions in carpetbags and went to the South after the Civil War, usually for the purpose of gaining money through political power.

**caucus** a meeting of members of a political party or group to make plans or select candidates.

**cease-fire** in war, a temporary agreement to halt the fighting.

**chain stores** two or more of the same type of store owned and managed by the same company.

**charter**  the basic plan for an organization or government.

**charter colony**  one of three types of American colonial government. It operated under a charter that was agreed to by the colony and the king. It was run by a legislature which was elected by the colonists and a governor who was selected by the legislature.

**checks and balances**  a system written into the Constitution, which allows each branch of government to check on, or balance, the power of every other branch.

**civil government**  government established by the citizens, instead of by the church or the military.

**civil rights**  rights that protect individuals from discrimination by government or by other individuals, organizations, or groups.

**civil service**  the jobs of most persons employed by government who are not in the military services.

**cold war**  the conflict of ideas and actions between nations that does not result in military battles.

**colony**  a settlement made by a group of people who go to another land to live and work but who continue to be citizens of their own country.

**commerce**  trade, or the buying and selling of goods and services.

**commission**  a group of persons responsible for performing a particular duty.

**commonwealth**  an area under self-government with control of local affairs but which is part of another country.

**communes**  small communities whose members live together on jointly owned property and share the work necessary to keep the community going.

**communism**  an economic system based on ownership of all property by society as a whole.

**compact**  an agreement between two or more people or groups.

**competition**  in economics, refers to the attempt by sellers to outsell all other sellers of similar goods or services either by offering lower prices or by offering a better deal.

**compromise**  an agreement where each side gives up part of what it wants.

**concentration camps**  prison camps. The Nazis used them in Germany to imprison persons whom they disliked, mostly Jews and Communists.

**confederation**  a union of independent states where most of the powers of government are kept by the states.

**constitution**  the basic rules and framework of government.

**consumers**  people who buy and use goods and services.

**convoy system**  a system in which warships travel along with supply ships to protect them from attack.

**corollary**  a statement or policy which adds to, or follows up, an earlier statement or policy.

**corporation**  a form of business organization that acts by law as a single person even though it may be owned by any number of persons called stockholders.

**credit**  a financial system where those who have money lend it to those who can use it. The money is expected to be repaid with a profit to the lender.

**culture**  the behavior and way of life of a particular group of people.

**currency**  the money in use at a particular time.

**customs**  in economics, a term meaning taxes on goods from a foreign country.

# D

**debtor**  a person who owes something to another.

**declaration**  a public statement.

**delegate**  a representative; someone sent to vote in place of others.

**democracy**  a form of government that is run by the people living under it. Decisions are made either directly by the people or indirectly by their elected representatives.

**demonstration**  a public display of feelings by a group toward a policy, a cause, or a person.

**deport**  to force a person to leave a country.

**depression** an extremely slow period in business activity causing prices to drop, business and banks to fail, and people to lose their jobs.

**descendants** persons related to a family or group in the past.

**detente** a French term meaning to relax tension; used by the Nixon administration to describe the policy of the United States toward the Soviet Union.

**dictator** a leader who rules with total power without asking the approval of others.

**discrimination** different and usually unfair treatment of a person or group because of race, religion, national origin, or sex.

**displaced person** a person who has been forced to leave his or her home or country because of personal or political reasons.

**distribution** in economics, a term meaning the giving out or selling of goods and services.

**dividend** a share of a company's profits paid to its stockholders.

**domino theory** an idea that all nations bordering a country which falls under Communist control will also soon fall.

**draft** the selection of people to serve in the military.

**duty** a tax on imports.

## E

**economic growth** growth in a nation's production of goods and services.

**economy** all of the things which make up or influence the making, selling, and buying of goods and services.

**electoral votes** the votes cast by electors in the Electoral College, the process through which a United States President and Vice-President are elected.

**electors** persons chosen by the voters to vote for President and Vice-President. Each state has as many electors as it has members in both houses of Congress.

**emancipation** to set persons free, such as freeing slaves.

**embargo** a law or government order that limits trade.

**environment** the total of all the physical, social, and cultural conditions which influence the life of a person or group. It sometimes refers only to the physical environment—the air, land, and water.

**ethnic group** a group of persons of the same national origin, race, or culture.

**exclusion** to keep someone or something out.

**executive** a person or group who controls or directs an organization and is responsible for carrying out policies.

**export** to send goods out of the country for sale.

## F

**factory** a building or group of buildings where goods are manufactured.

**Fascist party** a political party in Italy under Mussolini from the 1920's to the 1940's.

**federal** having to do with the central government in a system where states are joined under one central control but keep some governing powers.

**Federalist party** the political party of those early Americans who favored the new Constitution and wanted a strong federal government.

**Federal Reserve System** a system of twelve Federal Reserve banks which do business only with other banks. Member banks must keep a certain amount of funds in reserve at their district Federal Reserve bank.

**foreign policy** a nation's general plan for dealing with other nations.

**forty-niners** people who went to California in 1849 to look for gold.

**Free Soil party** a political party formed by antislavery people during the campaign for the 1848 presidential election.

**frontier** a new area to explore or develop.

## G

**goods** material things which satisfy the wants and needs of people.

**gross national product** the value of all the goods and services produced in a country.

**guerrilla warfare** warfare by parttime citizen-soldiers, called guerrillas, who carry out bombings and ambushes and then return to their homes or hideouts.

## H

**hemisphere** half of the earth's surface.

**historian** a student and writer of history.

**holding company** a company that owns or holds enough stock in other companies to control them.

## I

**ICBM** a missile that can be launched from one place and travel to nearly any target on earth.

**immigrant** a person who comes into a country to live.

**impeach** to charge a person with a crime while that person is holding a government office.

**imperialism** a policy where one nation gains control of another either through directly taking over the land or by controlling the government or economy of another country.

**import** to bring in goods from other countries to sell.

**income** any money people receive from working, from the use of their property, or from lending their money.

**income tax** tax on the income of individuals or companies.

**indentured servant** a person bound by contract to work for another for a certain amount of time.

**industry** the making and selling of goods; also refers to all of the business activity of a country or to all the companies making the same product, such as the steel industry.

**inflation** a continuing general rise in prices.

**initiative** the right of voters to propose laws or constitutional amendments by petition without going through the legislature; compare to *referendum*.

**injunction** a special court order that requires a person or group to do or not to do something.

**interest** in economics, the amount charged for borrowed money.

**interstate** between two or more states, such as trade or highways.

**isolationism** the idea and practice of staying out of the affairs of other nations.

## J

**joint stock company** a company formed by a group of people for the purpose of selling stock to raise money for a business venture.

**judicial review** the power to judge whether or not a law is constitutional.

**judiciary** the branch of government responsible for the court system.

## K

**Know-Nothing party** a political party, also known as the American party, formed in the 1850's by people who opposed the large number of immigrants entering the United States.

## L

**labor force** everyone over the minimum legal working age who has a job or is actively looking for one.

**labor union** an organization of workers that bargains with employers for better wages, benefits, and working conditions for its members.

**laissez-faire** a French term meaning let the people do as they please. In economics, it means that the government does not regulate business.

**land grant** a gift of land by a government to an individual or company.

**legislative power** the authority to make laws.

**legislature** the group of people given the power to make laws.

**lobby** an attempt to influence legislation and government policy.

**loyalists** American colonists who remained loyal to England during the time of the Revolution.

**lunar module** a space vehicle that carries an astronaut or equipment from a command vehicle to the surface of the moon and back.

# M

**Manifest Destiny** the idea that it was the certain fate of the United States to stretch its boundaries from the Atlantic Ocean to the Pacific Ocean.

**mass production** the manufacture of goods in large quantities, usually by machines.

**Medicaid** a program paid for jointly by the federal and state governments to help families with low incomes pay for medical care.

**Medicare** a federal government program that gives aid to older people for medical bills.

**mercantilism** an economic system to increase a country's wealth by increasing its manufacturing and exports, by taxing imports, and by establishing colonies to provide raw materials and new market places for exports. Colonies exist only for the profit of the founding country.

**merit system** a system where people compete for government jobs and promotions through testing.

**militia** a group of citizens with military training who can be called on in emergency situations. The National Guard is a militia.

**minimum wage** the lowest wage allowed by law to be paid for certain types of jobs.

**minority group** a part of a population that differs from the majority of the population in religious, racial, or national background.

**monarchy** a form of government with a leader who rules for life and gains title through family ties.

**monopoly** a situation in which a company or group controls the making and distribution of a product to the degree that it can control the price of the product.

**moving assembly line** in factories, a moving belt which carries a product from one worker to another until all parts are in place.

# N

**nationalism** a feeling of pride in the nation as a whole and loyalty to its goals.

**naturalization** the admittance of a person to citizenship by a country.

**Nazi party** the name given to the National Socialist German Workers party led by Hitler from 1933 to 1945.

**negotiate** to discuss in order to reach an agreement or work out terms.

**neutral** taking no side in an argument or war.

**nuclear weapons** atomic and hydrogen explosives.

**nullification** the idea that a state may cancel a federal law within its own borders.

# O

**open shop** a factory or other place of work where employees do not have to join a labor union to be hired or to keep a job.

**ordinances** rules or laws.

# P

**pacifism** the policy of being against war as a way of settling disputes.

**pact** an agreement between groups or nations.

**parallel** one of the imaginary lines circling the earth to mark degrees of latitude.

**Parliament** the legislative body of government in England.

**partnership** an association of two or more persons who own or operate a business.

**patent** a government grant giving only one person or company the right to make or sell a new invention for a certain number of years.

**patriotism** love and loyalty for one's country.

**patriots** those who love their country and strongly support its authority and interests.

**pension** a guaranteed retirement income.

**petition** a formal request, often a written document, to a government asking for solutions to certain problems or expressing support or opposition to something.

**platform** a statement of the goals of a political party for a particular election campaign.

**political boss** a state or local political leader who runs a political machine.

**political machine** a successful state or local political organization usually run by a boss or a small group of party members.

**political party** people with similar ideas and outlook who are organized to win elections and operate government.

**politics** the art or science concerned with winning elections and controlling government and governmental policies.

**poll tax** a tax paid to vote at election places.

**polls** a place where votes are taken in an election.

**popular sovereignty** an idea that a government receives its authority from the people. Before the Civil War, it was used to allow the settlers in each new area to decide by voting whether or not slavery would be allowed in their territory.

**Populists** members of the National People's party, formed in 1892. Most were farmers and laborers who wanted the coinage of silver, an income tax, and the election of United States senators by popular vote.

**Preamble** the introduction to the Constitution that explains its purpose.

**prejudice** an attitude or opinion about a person, group, or race, which is not based on sound reasoning.

**primary source** an eyewitness or firsthand report of an event.

**prime minister** in some countries, the head of a cabinet who directs the administration of government, as in Great Britain.

**private enterprise** an economic system in which individuals may establish businesses and conduct their economic affairs with little government direction.

**proclamation** an official public announcement.

**production** the making of goods and services.

**profit** the income left after payment of all expenses.

**Progressives** the name given to the reformers of the early twentieth century who believed their ideas would lead to progress.

**prohibition** the forbidding by law of the manufacture, shipping, and selling of alcoholic beverages.

**proprietary colony** one of three types of American colonial government. These colonies operated under a charter that was granted by the proprietor, a person who had been given a land grant by the king.

**protective tariff** a tax on imported goods. This tax protects goods made at home by making imported goods more expensive.

**proviso** a special condition added to a law or a contract.

**public (national) debt** the total amount of money owed by the federal government.

## Q

**quota** an amount assigned to a group for certain purposes, such as immigration.

## R

**radical** extreme or sudden changes from the usual; a person who favors extreme changes in beliefs, habits, or institutions.

**Radical Republicans** a group of Republicans after the Civil War who wanted to make major political changes.

**ratify** to give formal approval to a law.

**rationing** setting the amounts that an individual or organization can buy or have to use.

**raw material** something that can be finished into a product for sale or use.

**rebate** a return of part of a payment.

**recall** a procedure of some states that allows voters to remove an elected official from office before his or her term is up.

**Reconstruction** the period from about 1865 to 1876 in which the United States was recovering from the Civil War.

**referendum** the right of voters to have a law that has been passed by the legislature placed on the ballot for popular vote; compare to *initiative*.

**reform** to improve; also a policy or law aimed at improving government or society.

**regulate** to control by rules or laws.

**relocation centers** camps in the United States where Japanese and Japanese Americans were forced to live during World War II.

**repeal** to cancel or do away with a rule or law.

**representative government** a system of government in which the people elect representatives to act for them in making and enforcing laws and decisions.

**republic** a form of government in which the people elect representatives to act for them but final authority rests with the people.

**reservation** a piece of land set aside, as for the use of American Indians.

**resolution** a formal statement of opinion or position.

**revenue sharing** tax money given by the federal government to states or cities.

**revolution** the overthrow of a government.

**royal colony** one of three types of American colonial government. These colonies elected their own lower house, but the upper house and governor were appointed by the king.

**rural** of or relating to the country and surrounding areas as opposed to the city.

## S

**scalawags** southern whites who supported the Republican party after the Civil War.

**secede** to withdraw from an organization or group.

**sectionalism** taking pride in a particular part of a country and feeling loyalty for its goals.

**sedition** writings or actions that cause or could cause rebellion against a government.

**segregation** a separation or setting apart, especially of blacks and whites.

**self-government** government controlled by the people living under it rather than by an outside power or authority.

**settlement house** places established in the late nineteenth and early twentieth centuries in many large American cities as meeting centers or places of education for the poor, immigrants, minorities, and other groups.

**sharecropping** a system in which people farm land they do not own in return for a share of the crop.

**shareholder** one who holds or owns a share of a company.

**siege** a continuing attack, usually where one army surrounds an area held by another army.

**sit-in** a protest in which demonstrators sit in or occupy a place in order to draw attention to their cause.

**socialism** an economic system in which certain important sections of the economy (such as transportation) are owned and controlled by the government. The government also makes overall plans for the economy.

**social security** a program of government aid for older, disabled, and unemployed citizens.

**society** a community, nation, or group of people with common interests and traditions.

**sociologist** a person who studies and records the way people live and work together in groups.

**space race** the unofficial contest between the United States and the Soviet Union to be first in space accomplishments.

**speculation** buying stock or land only for the purpose of selling it for a profit when the price goes up.

**spoils system** the system of rewarding friends and political supporters with government jobs.

**standard of living** the amount of goods and services used by a nation or the individuals in that nation.

**stock** a certificate of ownership of part of a corporation.

**stockholders** the owners of the shares of stock in a corporation.

**stock market** a place where shares of stocks are bought and sold.

**strike** a refusal by workers of a company to work until that company's management accepts their demands or offers an acceptable compromise.

**strikebreaker** someone hired to replace a striking worker.

**suffrage** the right to vote.

## T

**tariff** a tax on imported goods.

**tax** money charged by government to pay for the expenses of public services.

**technology** the scientific knowledge used in the production of goods and services.

**temperance** limiting actions, thoughts, or feelings; usually refers to the drinking of alcoholic beverages.

**tenement house** an apartment house, generally lacking in sanitation, comfort, and safety.

**trust** an organization of several companies which are run as one company.

**tyranny** unjust or cruel use of power.

## U

**Underground Railroad** a system for helping runaway slaves reach Canada and the free states in the North. Slaves were guided by "conductors" generally at night from "station" to "station" (usually the homes of abolitionists).

**urban** of or relating to a city or town, as opposed to the country.

## V

**veto** a refusal by one branch of a government or organization to approve an action by another branch.

**Vietcong** the Vietnamese Communist party which carried on guerrilla war in South Vietnam.

**vigilantes** a group of citizens who take the enforcement of law and order into their own hands.

## W

**welfare** a common name for public assistance in which money and other benefits are given to people on the basis of need.

**Whig party** a political party formed in 1824 by people who were against Andrew Jackson. The party lasted until 1852.

## Y

**yellow-dog contract** an agreement made by a worker with a company before being hired that he or she will not join any labor union.

## Z

**zoning laws** laws which limit the use of land within certain areas. Some land may only be used for homes, some for business, and some only for factories.

# Index

National Broadcasting Company (NBC), 393
National Defense Education Act, 472
National Farm Worker's Association, 485
National Forest Reservation Act, 351
National Grange of the Patrons of Husbandry, 312-315
National Housing Act, 460
National Industrial Recovery Act (NIRA), 416, 421
nationalism, 154-156, 162, 233
Nationalist Chinese, 462, 504
National Labor Relations Board (NLRB), 416-417
National Labor Union, 315
National League, 344
National Organization for Women (NOW), 508
national parks, 351
National People's party, 327-331
National Recovery Administration (NRA), 416, 420-422
National-Republicans, 172, 174
National Road, 158-159
National Urban League, 347
National Women's Political Caucus, 508-509
National Youth Administration, 415
natural resources, 293-295, 351
Nauset, 62
Navaho Indians, 191
Navigation Acts of 1660's, 88
Navy, United States, 149, 152, 201, 250, 334, 337-338
    after World War II, 480, 487
    during World War I, 370, 373, 381-382
    Filipinos, 402
    World War II, 433-436, 442
Nazi party, 431-436, 439-441, 444-445
Nebraska, 238, 314
    Bellevue, 322
    Omaha, 297, 327
*Negro World*, 398
Netherlands, 32, 95, 462
neutrality, United States, 129
Neutrality Act of 1935, 432-433
Nevada, 193, 203, 248, 300, 322
Neve, Felep de, 448
Nevins, Allan, 9

New Amsterdam, 52, 70, 261
New Bedford, Massachusetts, 296
new colonial policy, 91-92
New Deal, 413-422, 458
    Agricultural Adjustment Administration (AAA), 413-414, 421-422
    Civilian Conservation Corps (CCC), 417
    National Labor Relations Board (NLRB), 416-417
    National Recovery Administration (NRA), 416, 420, 422
    Social Security, 417, 422
    Works Progress Administration (WPA), 416-417
New England, 4, 13, 43-50, 56-62, 66, 73-74, 89, 102
*New England Girlhood, A*, 215
Newfoundland, 39
New France, 32, 34
New Frontier, 477-478, 481-483, 486
New Guinea, 442
New Hampshire, 5, 49, 484
New Harmony, Indiana, 184
New Haven, Connecticut, 49, 66
New Jersey, 52, 196, 213, 243, 254, 322
    during colonization, 52
    Jersey City, 265
    Menlo Park, 293
    Princeton, 444
Newlands Reclamation Act of 1902, 351
New Mexico, 7, 30, 191-193, 198, 201-203, 233-236, 238, 350, 374, 485
    Alamogordo, 443
    Bat Cave, 7
    Santa Fe, 192-193, 201, 234
New Orleans, Louisiana, 34, 131, 136, 153-154, 164-169, 185, 216-217, 252, 294
    Battle of, 153
    Congo Square, 166
    French Market, 167-168
    French Quarter, 166
Newport, Indiana, 237
New York, 158, 160, 164, 182-183, 203, 208, 231-235, 280, 283, 354, 416
    after World War II, 459, 474, 478, 484

Albany, 52
    during colonization, 52, 67, 70, 87-88
    during Revolutionary War, 94-95, 102
    Manhattan Island, 52
    New Amsterdam, 52
    New York City (see New York City, New York)
    Rochester, 232
    Saratoga, 102
    Troy, 181
New York Central Railroad, 298
New York City, New York, 102, 122, 158, 231-232, 299, 304, 308, 311, 319, 326, 336, 346, 405
    Bronx, 70, 478
    Central Park, 261, 265
    draft riot, 264
    during Civil War, 261-266
    during colonization, 52, 75-76
    during Progressive Era, 345-348
    during Revolutionary War, 102
    education, 263-264
    Factory Investigating Commission, 346
    Fifth Avenue, 261, 265
    Harlem, 394, 488
    Henry Street Settlement, 347
    Manhattan, 261
    Triangle Shirtwaist fire, 346
    Wall Street, 265
New York Stock Exchange, 410
Nez Percé Indians, 200, 302
Niagara Falls, Canada, 357
Niagara Movement, 357
Nicaragua, 372
Nichols, Thomas, 213
Nineteenth Amendment, 396
Nixon, Richard, 477, 492, 500-506, 509-514
Noble Order of the Knights of Labor, 315-318
Normandy, 440-441
North American Air Defense Command (NORAD), 471
North Atlantic Treaty, 462
North Atlantic Treaty Organization (NATO), 462, 471
North Carolina, 248, 258, 329

# Acknowledgments

Thanks are due to the following authors and publishers for the material quoted on the pages indicated: **p. 3**: Bailey, Philip James. *Festus*. Boston: Benjamin B. Mussey & Co., 1850. **p. 3**: *The Liberator*, Vol. I, No. 7, page 1, February 12, 1831, Boston, Massachusetts. **p. 6**: *The Writings and Speeches of Daniel Webster*. Vol. IV. Boston: Little, Brown, & Company, 1903. **p. 6**: Heckewelder, John. *Account of the History, Manners, and Customs of the Indian Nations, Who Once Inhabited Pennsylvania and the Neighboring States*. Philadelphia: American Philosophical Society, 1819. **pp. 8, 87**: Crèvecoeur, J. Hector St. John. *Letters from an American Farmer*. New York: Albert & Charles Boni, 1904. **pp. 8–9**: Bancroft, George. *History of the United States of America*. Vol. II. New York: D. Appleton and Company, 1891. **p. 9**: Nevins, Allan. *The Emergence of Modern America 1865–1878*. New York: The Macmillan Company, 1927. **pp. 16–21**: Lorant, Stefan (ed.). *The New World*. New York: Duell, Sloan & Pearce, 1946. Reprinted by permission. **p. 24**: Major, R. H. (trans. and ed.). *Select Letters of Christopher Columbus*. London: The Hakluyt Society, 1870. **p. 37**: Johnson, Chapman and Marston. *Eastward Ho*. Ed. Felix E. Schelling. Boston: D. C. Heath and Company, 1903. **p. 45**: *The Mayflower Compact*. As quoted in Commager, Henry Steele. *Documents of American History*. New York: Appleton-Century-Crofts, 1973. **pp. 56–59, 61, 62**: Bradford, William. *Of Plymouth Plantation 1620–1647*. Ed. Samuel Eliot Morison. New York: Alfred A. Knopf, Inc., 1952. Reprinted by permission. **pp. 59, 61**: Pory, John, Altham, Emmanuel, and De Rasieres, Isaack. *Three Visitors to Early Plymouth*. Ed. Sydney V. James, Jr. Plimoth Plantation, Inc., 1963. Reprinted by permission. **p. 60**: Morison, Samuel Eliot. *The Story of the "Old Colony" of New Plymouth*. New York: Alfred A. Knopf, Inc., 1956. Reprinted by permission. **pp. 67–68**: Mittelberger, Gottlieb. *Journey to Pennsylvania*. Ed. and trans. Oscar Handlin and John Clive. Cambridge, Massachusetts: The Belknap Press of Harvard University Press, 1960. **p. 69**: Edwards, Paul (abr. and ed.). *Equiano's Travels*. New York: Frederick A. Praeger, 1967. **p. 71**: Ellis, John Harvard (ed.). *The Works of Anne Bradstreet*. Gloucester, Massachusetts: Peter Smith, 1867. **p. 73**: Dwight, Timothy, *Travels in New England and New York*. Ed. Barbara Miller Solomon. Vol. II. Cambridge, Massachusetts: The Belknap Press of Harvard University Press, 1969. **p. 80**: Birket, James. *Some Cursory Remarks*. New Haven: Yale University Press, 1916. **pp. 81–82, 83, 83–84, 84–85**: *The Life and Letters of Benjamin Franklin*. Eau Claire, Wisconsin: E. M. Hale & Company. Reprinted by permission. **p. 82**: Bridenbaugh, Carl and Jessica. *Rebels and Gentlemen*. New York: Oxford University Press, 1942. **p. 82**: Van Doren, Carl. *Benjamin Franklin*. New York: The Viking Press, 1938. **p. 96**: Longfellow, Henry W. *Paul Revere's Ride*. Portland, Maine: L. H. Nelson Company, 1905. **p. 97**: O'Brien, Harriet E. (comp.). *Paul Revere's Own Story*. Privately printed by Perry Walton, 1929. **p. 99**: Fast, Howard. *The Selected Work of Tom Paine*. New York: The Modern Library, 1943. **p. 106**: Butterfield, L. H. (ed.). *Adams Family Correspondence*. Vol. I. Cambridge, Massachusetts: The Belknap Press of Harvard University Press, 1963. **p. 116**: *The Papers of James Madison*. Vol. II. Washington, D. C.: Langtree & O'Sullivan, 1840. **p. 116**: Schrag, Peter. *The Ratification of the Constitution and the Bill of Rights*. Boston: D. C. Heath and Company, 1964. **p. 143**: Mitchell, Stewart (ed.). *New Letters of Abigail Adams*. Boston: Houghton Mifflin Company, 1947. **pp. 143–144**: Beston, Henry. *American Memory*. New York: Farrar & Rinehart, 1937. **pp. 144–145, 146**: Smith, Mrs. Samuel Harrison. *The First Forty Years of Washington Society*. Ed. Gaillord Hunt. New York: Charles Scribner's Sons, 1906. **p. 145**: Young, James Sterling. *The Washington Community 1800–1828*. New York: Columbia University Press, 1966. **p. 155**: Cobbett, William. *The Emigrant's Guide*. London: Mills, Jowett, and Mills, 1829. **pp. 164–165**: Hall, A. Oakey. *The Manhattaner in New Orleans*. New York: J. S. Redfield, 1850. **p. 166**: *The Complete Poetry and Prose of Walt Whitman*. New York: Pellegrini & Cudahy, 1948. **pp. 167–169**: Ripley, Eliza. *Social Life in Old New Orleans*. New York: D. Appleton and Company, 1912. **p. 171**: Tocqueville, Alexis de. *Democracy in America*. Ed. Phillips Bradley. Vol. I. New York: Alfred A. Knopf, Inc., 1945. **p. 175**: Kappler, Charles J. (comp. and ed.). *Indian Affairs. Laws and Treaties*. Vol. II. Washington, D. C.: Government Printing Office, 1904. **p. 175**: Curtis, B. R. *Reports of the Decisions of the Supreme Court of the United States*. Vol. X. Boston: Little, Brown and Company, 1855. **p. 177**: Armstrong, Virginia Irving (comp.). *I Have Spoken*. Chicago: The Swallow Press Inc., 1971. **p. 196**: Richardson, James D. *A Compilation of the Messages and Papers of the Presidents*. Vol. IV. Washington, D.C.: Government Printing Office, 1897. **p. 196**: Blair & Rives (eds.). *Appendix to the Congressional Globe*. Washington, D. C.: Printed at the Globe Office, 1844. **pp. 207–208, 209–210**: Soulé, Frank, Gihon, John H., and Nisbet, James. *The Annals of San Francisco*. New York: D. Appleton & Company, 1854. **p. 208**: Camp, William Martin. *San Francisco Port of Gold*. Garden City, New York: Doubleday, 1947. **p. 209**: Barry, T. A. and Patten, B. A. *Men and Memories*. San Francisco: A. L. Bancroft & Company, 1873. **p. 213**: Nichols, Thomas Low. *Forty Years of American Life*. New York: Stackpole Sons, Publishers, 1937. **p. 215**: Larcom, Lucy. *A New England Girlhood*. Boston: Houghton Mifflin and Company, 1889. **p. 220**: Northup, Solomon. *Twelve Years a Slave*. Eds. Sue Eaken and Joseph Logsdon. Baton Rouge, Louisiana: Louisiana State University Press, 1968. **p. 224**: Quincy, Josiah. "Travel Journal (June 1801)" *Massachusetts Historical Society Proceedings*, (May 1888), p. 124. **p. 235**: *Narrative of the Life of Frederick Douglass*. Boston, 1845. **pp. 254, 255**: Epler, Percy H. *The Life of Clara Barton*. New York: The Macmillan Company, 1915. **pp. 261, 263–264**: Dicey, Edward. "Three Weeks in New York." *Macmillan's Magazine*, (April 1862), pp. 454, 458, 461–463. **p. 262**: Russell, William Howard. *My Diary North and South*. Vol. II. London: Bradbury and Evans, 1863. **p. 264**: Burn, James D. *Three Years Among the Working-Classes*. London:

Smith, Elder and Co., 1865. **p. 265:** Nevins, Allan and Thomas, Milton Halsey (eds.). *The Diary of George Templeton Strong.* New York: The Macmillan Company, 1952. **p. 265:** Skinner, John E. Hilary. "After the Storm." As quoted in Still, Bayard. *Mirror for Gotham.* Washington Square: New York University Press, 1956. **p. 267:** Garrett, Franklin M. *Atlanta and Environs.* Vol. I. Athens, Georgia: University of Georgia Press, 1954. **p. 268:** Coulter, E. Merton. *Georgia, A Short History.* Chapel Hill: The University of North Carolina Press, 1947. **p. 268:** From the *Macon Daily Telegraph and Confederate,* December 12, 1864. As quoted in Garrett, Franklin M. *Atlanta and Environs.* Vol. I. Athens, Georgia: University of Georgia Press, 1954. **p. 268:** Massey, Kate. "A Picture of Atlanta in the Late Sixties." *The Atlanta Historical Bulletin,* 1940-41. **pp. 268-269:** From a letter on file at the Atlanta Historical Society. As quoted in Garrett, Franklin M. *Atlanta and Environs.* Vol. I. Athens, Georgia: University of Georgia Press, 1954. **p. 269:** Thompson, C. Mildred. *Reconstruction in Georgia.* New York, 1915. As quoted in Garrett, Franklin M. *Atlanta and Environs.* Vol. I. Athens, Georgia: University of Georgia Press, 1954. **p. 270:** From the *Daily Intelligencer,* September 13, 1865. As quoted in Garrett, Franklin M. *Atlanta and Environs.* Vol. I. Athens, Georgia: University of Georgia Press, 1954. **p. 270:** Adapted from Hughes, Langston, Meltzer, Milton, and Lincoln, C. Eric. *A Pictorial History of Blackamericans.* New York: Crown Publishers, 1963. **p. 273:** Billington, Ray Allen (ed.). *The Journal of Charlotte Forten.* London: Collier-Macmillan Ltd., 1953. **p. 276:** From *The Americans at Home* by David Macrae. Published in 1952 by E. P. Dutton, and reprinted with their permission. **p. 291:** Somers, Robert. *The Southern States Since the War.* New York: Macmillan and Co., 1871. **p. 291:** Straker, Augustus. *The New South Investigated.* As quoted in Fleming, Walter L. *Documentary History of Reconstruction.* Vol. II. Cleveland: The Arthur H. Clark Company, 1907. **p. 291:** Smith, E. A. *Report on Cotton Production of the State of Alabama.* As quoted in Fleming, Walter L. *Documentary History of Reconstruction.* Vol. II. Cleveland: The Arthur H. Clark Company, 1907. **pp. 304, 305-306:** McCoy, Joseph G. *Historic Sketches of the Cattle Trade of the West and Southwest.* Kansas City: Ramsey, Millett & Hudson, 1874. **p. 306:** Hunter, J. Marvin (comp. and ed.). *The Trail Drivers of Texas.* Vol. II. Published by George W. Saunders, 1923. **pp. 306-307:** Beston, Henry. *American Memory.* New York: Farrar & Rinehart, Inc., 1937. **pp. 307-308:** Wilder, D. W. *The Annals of Kansas.* Topeka, Kansas: T. Dwight Thacher, Kansas Publishing House, 1886. **p. 308:** Cushman, George L. "Abilene, First of the Kansas Cow Towns." *The Kansas Historical Quarterly,* Vol. IX, August 1940. **pp. 308, 309:** Jameson, Henry B. *Heroes by the Dozen.* Abilene, Kansas: Shadinger-Wilson Printers, Inc., 1961. **p. 309:** From the Abilene *Chronicle,* February 8, 1872. As quoted in Dykstra, Robert R. *The Cattle Towns.* New York: Alfred A. Knopf, Inc., 1968. **p. 309:** As quoted in Dykstra, Robert R. *The Cattle Towns.* New York: Alfred A. Knopf, Inc., 1968. **p. 316:** *Autobiography of Mother Jones.* 1925. **p. 332:** Washington, Booker T. *The Story of My Life and Work.* Toronto: J. L.

Nichols & Company, 1901. **p. 339:** Olcott, Charles S. *The Life of William McKinley.* Vol. II. Boston: Houghton Mifflin Company, 1916. **p. 346:** Stein, Leon. *The Triangle Fire.* Philadelphia: J. B. Lippincott Company, 1962. **p. 360:** As quoted in Kogan, Herman, and Wendt, Lloyd. *Chicago: A Pictorial History.* New York: Bonanza Books, 1958. **pp. 361-362:** *Reminiscences of Chicago During the Great Fire.* Chicago: R. R. Donnelley & Sons Company, 1915. **pp. 363-364:** *Transactions of the Illinois State Historical Society for the Year 1906.* Springfield: Illinois State Journal Co., 1906. **p. 364:** *Transactions of the Illinois State Historical Society for the Year 1920.* Springfield, 1920. **pp. 364-365:** Addams, Jane. *Twenty Years at Hull-House.* New York: The Macmillan Company, 1910. **p. 383:** Gibbs, Philip. *People of Destiny.* New York: Harper & Brothers Publishers, 1920. **p. 383:** Bonn, M. J. "America Turns Away From Europe." *The Living Age,* Eighth Series, Vol. XVII, April, May, June, 1920. **p. 386:** Glazier, Captain Willard. *Peculiarities of American Cities.* Philadelphia: Hubbard Brothers, Publishers, 1883. **p. 386:** Stark, George W. *Detroit at the Century's Turn.* Detroit: Wayne University Press, 1951. **p. 388:** Olson, Sidney. *Young Henry Ford.* Detroit: Wayne State University Press, 1963. **pp. 389-390:** Ford, Henry. *My Life and Work.* Garden City, New York: Doubleday, Page & Company, 1922. **p. 391:** Parkins, Almon Ernest. *The Historical Geography of Detroit.* Lansing: Michigan Historical Commission, 1918. **pp. 404-405:** U. S. Bureau of the Census, *Historical Statistics of the United States, Colonial Times to 1957,* Washington, D.C. **p. 415:** Holt, Rackham. *Mary McLeod Bethune.* Garden City, New York: Doubleday & Company, Inc., 1964. **pp. 424, 425, 426, 427:** Excerpted by permission of Harcourt Brace Jovanovich, Inc. from *Middletown* by Robert S. and Helen M. Lynd, copyright, 1929, by Harcourt Brace Jovanovich, Inc.; copyright, 1957, by Robert S. and Helen M. Lynd. **pp. 428, 429:** Excerpted by permission of Harcourt Brace Jovanovich, Inc., from *Middletown in Transition* by Robert S. and Helen Merrell Lynd, copyright, 1937, by Harcourt Brace Jovanovich, Inc.; copyright, 1965, by Robert S. and Helen M. Lynd. **p. 440:** Eisenhower, Dwight D. *Crusade in Europe.* Garden City, New York. Doubleday & Company, Inc., 1948. **pp. 448, 450, 452:** *Los Angeles, A Guide to the City and its Environs.* Comp. Workers of the Writers' Program of the Work Projects Administration in Southern California. New York: Hastings House, Publishers, 1941. **p. 452:** Rosten, Leo C. *Hollywood.* New York: Harcourt, Brace and Company, 1941. **p. 474:** Floherty, John J. *Television Story.* Philadelphia: J. B. Lippincott Company, 1957. **p. 484:** As quoted in *Martin Luther King, Jr.* Ed. Flip Schulke. New York: W. W. Norton & Company, Inc., 1976. **pp. 494, 496-497:** "Greater Houston: Its First Million People—and Why." *Newsweek,* July 5, 1954, p. 39. **p. 496:** Oates, Stephen B. *Visions of Glory.* Norman, Oklahoma: University of Oklahoma Press, 1970. **p. 498:** *Newsweek,* July 4, 1976, p. 70. **p. 498:** Jordan, Barbara. "How I Got There." *Atlantic Monthly,* March 1975. **p. 502:** Scott, David R. "What Is It Like to Walk on the Moon?" *National Geographic,* September 1973. Reprinted by permission.

2 3 4 5 6 7 8 9 10 11 12 13 14 15 — 85 84 83 82 81 80 79 78